Leg over Leg

Volumes Three and Four

Letter from the General Editor

The Library of Arabic Literature series offers Arabic editions and English translations of significant works of Arabic literature, with an emphasis on the seventh to nineteenth centuries. The Library of Arabic Literature thus includes texts from the pre-Islamic era to the cusp of the modern period, and encompasses a wide range of genres, including poetry, poetics, fiction, religion, philosophy, law, science, history, and historiography.

Books in the series are edited and translated by internationally recognized scholars and are published in parallel-text format with Arabic and English on facing pages, and are also made available as English-only paperbacks.

The Library encourages scholars to produce authoritative, though not necessarily critical, Arabic editions, accompanied by modern, lucid English translations. Its ultimate goal is to introduce the rich, largely untapped Arabic literary heritage to both a general audience of readers as well as to scholars and students.

The Library of Arabic Literature is supported by a grant from the New York University Abu Dhabi Institute and is published by NYU Press.

Philip F. Kennedy
General Editor, Library of Arabic Literature

About this Paperback

This paperback edition differs in a few respects from its dual-language hardcover predecessor. Because of the compact trim size the pagination has changed, but paragraph numbering has been retained to facilitate cross-referencing with the hardcover. Material that referred to the Arabic edition has been updated to reflect the English-only format, and other material has been corrected and updated where appropriate. For information about the Arabic edition on which this English translation is based and about how the LAL Arabic text was established, readers are referred to the hardcover.

Leg over Leg

Volumes Three and Four

BY

Aḥmad Fāris al-Shidyāq

TRANSLATED BY
Humphrey Davies

VOLUME EDITOR
Michael Cooperson

NEW YORK UNIVERSITY PRESS
New York and London

NEW YORK UNIVERSITY PRESS
New York and London

Library of Congress Cataloging-in-Publication Data
Shidyaq, Ahmad Faris, 1804?-1887.
Leg over leg or The turtle in the tree concerning the Fariyaq : what manner of creature might he be / by Faris al-Shidyaq ; edited and translated by Humphrey Davies.
volume cm — (Library of Arabic literature)
Includes bibliographical references and index.
ISBN 978-1-4798-0072-8 (vols. 1-2 : ppk : alk. paper) — ISBN 978-1-4798-1329-2 (vols. 3–4 : ppk : alk. paper) — ISBN 978-1-4798-3288-0 (ebook) — ISBN 978-1-4798-8881-8 (ebook)
1. Shidyaq, Ahmad Faris, 1804?-1887. 2. Shidyaq, Ahmad Faris, 1804?-1887—Travel—Middle East. 3. Arabic language—Lexicography. 4. Middle East—Description and travel. I. Davies, Humphrey T. (Humphrey Taman) translator, editor. II. Shidyaq, Ahmad Faris, 1804?-1887. Saq 'ala al-saq. III. Shidyaq, Ahmad Faris, 1804?-1887. Saq 'ala al-saq. English. IV. Title. V. Title: Turtle in the tree.
PJ7862.H48S213 2015
892.7'8503—dc23 2015021915

New York University Press books are printed on acid-free paper, and their binding materials are chosen for strength and durability.

Series design and composition by Nicole Hayward
Typeset in Adobe Text

Manufactured in the United States of America
10 9 8 7 6 5 4 3 2 1

Contents

Leg over Leg

or

The Turtle in the Tree

concerning

The Fāriyāq

What Manner of Creature Might He Be

otherwise entitled

Days, Months, and Years

spent in

Critical Examination

of

The Arabs

and

Their Non-Arab Peers

by

The Humble Dependent on His Lord the Provider

Fāris ibn Yūsuf al-Shidyāq

The writings of Zayd and Hind these days speak more to the common taste
　Than any pair of weighty tomes.
More profitable and useful than the teachings of two scholars
　Are what a yoke of oxen from the threshings combs.

Contents of the Book

Book Four

Book Three

Chapter 1

Firing Up a Furnace

Are they not enough, the troubles to which men are subject by way of misery and *care*, effort and *wear*, toil and *disease*, hardship and *dis-ease*, of deprivation and *lucklessness*, despair and *unhappiness*? Men are carried to nausea and craving, born in pain and suffering, nursed to their mothers' *detriment*, weaned to their *imperilment*. They crawl only to *stumble*, climb only to *tumble*, walk only to *lag*, labor only to *flag*, find themselves *unemployed* only by hunger's pangs to be *destroyed*. They languish and grow weak when they go *without*, suffer indigestion when they eat and grow *stout*. When they thirst, they *lose weight*, and when they drink, become sick as poisoned birds, gulp air, and *nauseate*. Lying awake at night, they waste away, worried and *fraught*, and sleeping, their allotted share of hours goes by and gains them *naught*. Old and feeble, they're a burden to *kith and kin*, yet, should they die before their time, they cause them such grief as may *do them in*. 3.1.1

In the midst of all this, they must strive to obtain the means to earn their daily *bread*, while tormented by the need to make a show of dress and *thread*. The bachelor's desperate to find a woman to call his *own*, the family man preoccupied with spouse and care of children, be they young or *grown*. When they fall ill, he does so too and when they *mourn*, he mourns and grieves in *turn*. Woe to him should his wife be overly *fertile*, but so too should she be barren and 3.1.2

sterile, for then he sees other married men surrounded by bonny *faces* and children with pleasing *graces* and says to himself, "Verily, in sons lies all this world's *pleasure*, and I am as one who dies (and what a fate!) leaving no *successor*!"

3.1.3 How often by the fall of a single fingernail is the whole body *defeated*, how often by the extraction of a single molar is most, if not all, of its power to endure *depleted*—not to mention the sicknesses that defy all doctors' *skills*, the chronic *ills*, the passage of time and the passing of the *years*, the succession of sorrows and shifts of fortune that this worn-out, debilitated body *bears*, for in winter it is exposed to wind, nasal congestion, sputum, and the damp chills, to incontinence and miasmatic *airs*; in summer, to cholera, fever, and headache, bloating, and stagnant *weirs*; in spring, to the imperious *demands* of the rising blood and its evil *commands*; in autumn, to the stirring of the black bile, the wind's *bane* and its piercing of the *bone*.

3.1.4 In addition, some are born afflicted with (among the various defects and diseases)

jana',	"bending of the upper back over the chest"
or *fasa'*,	"prominence of the chest and bulging of the abdomen"
or *faṭa'*,	"concavity of the back and convexity of the chest"
or *ḥadab*,	"too well-known to require definition" [hunching of the back]
or *ḥusbah*,	"the whitening of a man's skin as a result of a certain disease, followed by the corruption of his hair, after which his skin turns white and red"
or *ḥaṣbah*,	"pustules that break out on the body"
or *shabb*,	"a disease, too well-known to require definition" [?]
or *ḍabūb*,	"a disease of the lip"
or *ṭanab*,	"length in the legs combined with laxness, or in the back"

or *ʿakab,*	"thickness of the lip or chin"
or a *ghaḍbah,*	"a fleshy lump on the upper eyelid (as an inborn defect)" 3.1.5
or *ghiḍāb,*	"a certain disease, or smallpox"
or *ghalab,*	"thickness of the neck"
or *qalab,*	"extroversion of the lip"
or *qulāb,*	"disease of the heart"
or *quwabāʾ,*	"those things that appear on the body and break out on it"
or *kanab,*	"a thickening that covers the leg and hand"
or *kawab,*	"thinness of the neck and largeness of the head"
or *nāqibah,*	"a malady that affects a person as a result of extended intercourse"
or *jawath,*	"largeness of the belly in its upper part, or flaccidity of the same in its lower"
or *khawath,*	"flaccidity of the belly"
or *ḍamaj,*	"a pestilence that affects a person"; it also means "the aroused state of a passive sodomite" 3.1.6
or *ʿināj,*	"pain in the backbone"
or *faḥaj,*	"pointing toward one another of the foreparts of the feet in walking with splaying out of the heels; *fajaj* and *fakhaj* are worse forms of the same"
or *lakhaj,*	"the worst form of bleariness of the eye"
or *majaj,*	"flaccidity of the corners of the mouth"
or *jalaḥ,*	"the retreat of the hair from the sides of the head"
or *ṣafaḥ,*	"excessive width of the forehead"
or *naṭaf,*	"a disease against which people are cauterized"
or *farkaḥah,*	"wide spacing of the buttocks"
or *faṭaḥ,*	"breadth of head and tip of the nose"

3.1.7	or *falaḥ*,	“a split in the lower lip”
	or *qādiḥ*,	“erosion of the teeth”
	or *qalaḥ*,	“yellowing of the teeth”
	or *kasaḥ*,	“a chronic disease of the hands and legs”
	or *lajaḥ*,	“fleshy swelling around the eye”
	or *maraḥ*,	“extreme watering and deterioration of the eye”
	or *masaḥ*,	“chafing of the inside of the knee due to coarseness of clothing or the rubbing against one another of the thighs; synonym *mashaḥ*”
	or *wadhaḥ*,	“chafing on the inside of the thighs”
	or *bazakh*,	“concavity of the chest and convexity of the back”
3.1.8	or *zullakhah*,	“a pain that affects the back”
	or *fatakh*,	“flaccidity of the joints, or broadness and length of the hand and foot”
	or *nuffākh*,	“the eruption of a swelling as the result of the occurrence of a disease”
	or *jarad*,	“hairlessness”
	or *darad*,	“toothlessness”
	or *riddah*,	“recession of the chin”
	or *suwād*,	“a disease resulting from drinking water”
	or *qawad*,	“elongation of the neck and back”
	or *kubād*,	“pain in the liver”
	or *lahd*,	“a disease in people’s legs and thighs”
3.1.9	or *adar*,	“the *ādir* [active participle], or the *ma’dūr* [passive participle], is he whose peritoneum bursts, causing his gut to fall into his scrotum . . . ; the verb is *adira*”
	or *bajar*,	“protuberance of the navel and broadness of the belly”
	or *bakhar*,	“foulness in the mouth”
	or *bāsūr*,	“too well-known to require definition, plural *bawāsīr*” [“piles”]

or *ḥathar*,	"pustules; *ḥathirat al-ʿayn* means 'red pimples appeared on its lids'"	
or *ḥadrah*,	"an ulcer that appears on the white of the eyelid"	
or *ḥuṣr* or *ḥaṣar*,	"*ḥuṣr* is constipation of the bowels; *ḥaṣar* is dejection, or miserliness, or stammering"	
or *ḥafar*,	"scaling at the roots of the teeth"	
or *ḥumrah*,	"swellings of the bubonic type"	
or *muḥanjar*,	"a disease of the belly"	
or *ukhayḍir*,	"a disease of the eye"	3.1.10
or *dhahar*,	"blackening of the teeth; synonym *tadhyīr*"	
or *zaḥīr*,	"looseness of the bowels"	
or *zaʿar*,	"scantiness and thinness of the hair"	
or *zawar*,	"twisting of the throat; the *azwar* is one who suffers from this . . . and one who looks from the outer corners of his eyes"	
or *shatar*,	"the inversion and cracking of the eyelids, upper and lower, or flaccidity of the lower"	
or *ṣaʿar*,	"smallness of the head"	
or *ṣafar*,	"a disease of the belly that makes the face turn yellow"	
or *ẓafar*,	"a disease of the eye"	
or *ẓahar*,	"a disease of the back"	
or *ʿawar*,	"too well-known to require definition" ["being one-eyed"]	3.1.11
or *taqṭīr*,	"non-retention of the urine"	
or *qaṣar*,	"stiffness of the neck"	
or *maʿar*,	"lack of hair"	
or *nāsūr*,	"a malady of the inner corners of the eyes, or a malady in the environs of the posterior, or a malady of the gums"	
or *kuzāz*,	"a disease caused by extreme cold"	
or *sulās*,	"dementia"	
or *fuqās*,	"a disease of the joints"	

	or *faṭas*,	“the nose’s being squashed on the face”
	or *qaʿas*,	“convexity of the chest and concavity of the back; antonym of *ḥadab* (‘hunchbacked-ness’)”
3.1.12	or *qafas*,	“largeness of stool”
	or *qanʿasah*,	“extreme shortness of the neck, as in one with a hunchback”
	or *kasas*,	“shortness or smallness of the teeth, or their adhering to the gingiva”
	or *niqris*,	“swelling and pain in the joints of the ankles and toes”
	or *hawas*,	“a touch of insanity”
	or *ḥamash*,	“thinness of the legs”
	or *khafash*,	“smallness of the eyes and weakness of vision (as an inborn defect), or deterioration, without pain, in the eyelids, or having night but not day vision”
	or *dawash*,	“dimness of vision and smallness of the eye”
	or *ramash*,	“redness of the eyelids accompanied by a flow of liquid”
	or *ṭarash*,	“the mildest form of deafness”
3.1.13	or *ṭushāsh*,	“a malady like nasal congestion”
	or *ʿuṭāsh*,	“a disease whose victim cannot quench his thirst”
	or *ʿamash*,	“weakness of vision accompanied by constant tearing”
	or *madash*,	“flaccidity of the sinew of the hand, or its having little flesh and being thin”
	or *namash*,	“white and black spots and blotches on the skin that contrast with the color of the latter”
	or *bakhaṣ*,	“flesh forming a lump above or below the eyes in the shape of a swelling; *tabakhkhuṣ* is inversion of the eyelids”

or *baraṣ*,	“too well-known to require definition” [“leprosy”]	
or *taʿaṣ*,	“leg muscle pain caused by walking”	
or *ḥāṣṣah*,	“a disease that causes the hair to fall out”	
or *ḥawaṣ*,	“constriction in the outer corners of the eyes or in one of them”	
or *khawaṣ*,	“sinking of the eyes [into the skull]”	3.1.14
or *khayaṣ*,	“smallness of one eye [compared to the other]”	
or *ramaṣ*,	“foul white matter that collects in the inner corner of the eye”	
or *shawṣah*,	“pain in the belly, or flatulence that affects the ribs, or swelling in the diaphragm”	
or *ghamaṣ*,	“dripping *ramaṣ* [q.v.]”	
or *qabaṣ*,	“a pain that afflicts the liver as a result of eating dates on an empty stomach, or largeness of the crown of the head”	
or *qirmāṣ*,	“shortness of the cheeks”	
or *qafaṣ*,	“acidity in the stomach from drinking water after eating dates, or burning in the throat”	
or *laḥaṣ*,	“abundant wrinkling on the upper side of the eyelid”	
or *lakhaṣ*,	“fleshiness of the upper eyelid”	
or *laṣaṣ*,	“closeness of the shoulders, or the teeth”	3.1.15
or *māṣṣah*,	“a disease that affects young boys and consists of hairs on the edges of the vertebrae,” etc.	
or *maʿaṣ*,	“a twisting in the sinew of the leg”	
or *maghaṣ*,	“too well-known to require definition” [“stomachache”]	
or *waqaṣ*,	“shortness of the neck”	
or *ḥaraḍ*,	“morbidity of the stomach, body, judgment, and mind”	
or *haraḍ*,	“dry mange that breaks out on the body as the result of hot weather”	

	or *khubāṭ*,	“a disease resembling insanity”
	or *adhwaṭiyyah*,	“one who is *adhwaṭ* has a small chin”
	or *asaṭṭiyyah*,	“one who is *asaṭṭ* has long legs”
3.1.16	or *saraṭān*,	“a bilious swelling that starts the size of an almond or smaller; when it grows larger, red or green veins appear on it that resemble the legs of a crab; there is no hope of its being cured and it is treated only to stop it from getting worse”
	or *ḍaraṭ*,	“sparseness of the beard and thinness of the eyebrow”
	or *ḍawaṭ*,	“crookedness of the mouth”
	or *ṭaraṭ*,	“sparseness of the hair of the eyes, the eyebrows, and the eyelashes”
	or *qaṭaṭ*,	“shortness and tightness of the hair”
	or *maraṭ*,	“sparseness of the hair”
	or *maʿaṭ*,	“lack of hair”
	or *jaḥẓ*,	“protuberance or largeness of the eyeball”
	or *bathaʿ*,	“the appearance of blood on the lips, or the inversion of the lip on laughing”
	or *jalaʿ*,	“non-contiguity of the lips”
3.1.17	or *khalaʿ*,	“twisting of the hamstring”
	or *rasaʿ*,	“morbidity of the eyelids”
	or *ramaʿ*,	“yellowing of a woman’s face as the result of a disease that affects her clitoris”
	or *zalaʿ*,	“cracking on the exterior of the foot, as also *salaʿ*”
	or *zamaʿ*,	“superfluity of digits”
	or *ṣudāʿ*,	“pain in the head”
	or *ṣalaʿ*,	“recession of the hair of the front of the head”
	or *taṣawwuʿ*,	“patchiness of the hair”
	or *qaraʿ*,	“too well-known to require definition” [baldness caused by ringworm]
	or *qafaʿ*,	“bending of the toes back toward the foot”

or *qulāʿ*,	"a disease of the mouth"	3.1.18
or *qamaʿ*,	"morbidity of the inner corners of the eye, or an inflammation [of the same], or a pustule that breaks out at the roots of the eyelashes"	
or *kataʿ*,	"the turning of the fingers toward the palm"	
or *kathaʿ*,	"inflammation of the lip and its becoming so full of blood that it almost inverts"	
or *kalaʿ*,	"cracking and dirtiness of the feet"	
or *kawaʿ*,	"proximity of the wrists to the shoulders"	
or *lakhaʿ*,	"flaccidity of the body"	
or *laṭaʿ*,	"whiteness on the inside of the lip," etc.	
or *wakaʿ*,	"proximity of the large toe to the second toe"	
or *hanaʿ*,	"stooping of the body"	
or *bathagh*,	"the appearance of blood on the body"	3.1.19
or *dhalagh*,	"the inversion of the lip"	
or *fadagh*,	"twisting of the foot"	
or *fawagh*,	"largeness of the mouth"	
or *wabagh*,	"scurf of the head"	
or *janf*,	"depression and sucking in of one side of the breast, the other being straight"	
or *ḥashafah*,	"an ulcer that breaks out in a person's throat"	
or *ḥanaf*,	"crookedness of the leg"	
or *khanaf*,	"the sucking in of one of the two sides of the chest or back"	
or *sa'af*,	"cracking and frowsiness of the area around the nails"	
or *saʿfah*,	"ulcers that break out on a child's head and face"	3.1.20
or *sha'fah*,	"an ulcer that breaks out on the bottom of the foot and that goes away if cauterized but which, if cut, causes its victim to die"	
or *shanaf*,	"inversion of the upper lip from above"	
or *ṭarfah*,	"a red blood spot that occurs in the eye as the result of a blow or some other cause"	

	or *ghaḍaf,*	"flaccidity of the ear"
	or *ghaṭaf,*	"abundance of eyebrow hair"
	or *kutāf,*	"pain in the shoulder"
	or *kalaf,*	"something that covers the face and resembles sesame seeds . . . and a dull redness that covers the face"
	or *araqān,*	"a pest that affects crops and humans; synonym *yaraqān*"
	or *bakhaq,*	"the ugliest form of one-eyedness"
3.1.21	or *bahaq,*	"a fine whiteness on the surface of the skin," etc.
	or *ḥawlaq,*	"a pain in a person's throat"
	or *ḥamāq,*	"smallpox and similar diseases"
	or *khunāq,*	"a disease that is accompanied by an inability of the breath to reach the lungs"
	or *rawaq,*	"projection of the upper incisors over the lower"
	or *sulāq,*	"pustules that break out at the roots of the tongue, or flaking at the roots of the teeth and thickness of the eyelids"
	or *shadaq,*	"capaciousness of the jawbone"
	or *shamaq,*	"the mirth of insanity"
	or *ghamaqah,*	"a disease that affects the backbone"
	or *fataq,*	"a sickness of the peritoneum"
3.1.22	or *fawaq,*	"a distortion of the mouth or the vagina"
	or *lasaq,*	"the sticking of the lung to the side as a result of thirst"
	or *mashaq,*	"injury done by one fleshy mass to another"
	or *wadaq,*	"red spots that break out in the eye and suffuse it with redness, or a piece of flesh that grows there, or a sickness in it that leads to the decay of the ear"
	or *sakak,*	"a defect of the ear"
	or *sāhik,*	"itchiness of the eye"

or *shākkah*,	“a swelling of the throat”	
or *shawkah*,	“a disease too well-known to require definition [‘plague’], or a redness that covers the body”	
or *farak*,	“flaccidity of the base of the ear”	
or *fakak*,	“the unknitting of the shoulder blade as a result of flaccidity”	
or *alal*,	“shortness of the teeth and their turning inward toward the palate; synonym *yalal*”	3.1.23
or *badal*,	“a pain in the *ba’dalah* (the flesh between the armpit and the breast), or a pain of the joints and hands”	
or *buwāl*,	“a disease that causes an increase in urine”	
or *tha‘al*,	“the overlying of one another by the teeth”	
or *thalal*,	“loss of teeth”	
or *ḥadhal*,	“redness of the eye, or an ulceration of the eye with tearing”	
or *ḥiql*,	“a disease of the belly”	
or *ḥalal*,	“flaccidity and pain in the tendon”	
or *ḥawal*,	“too well-known to require definition” [“squint”]	
or *khabal*,	“morbidity of the limbs, or hemiplegia”	
or *khazal*,	“a fracture in the back”	3.1.24
or *khumāl*,	“a disease of the joints”	
or *daḥal*,	“largeness of belly”	
or *dakhal*,	“any morbid condition, mental or physical, that may affect you”	
or *sabal*,	“a film over the eye resulting from the inflation of its exterior veins”	
or *saghal*,	“one who is *saghil* has a small body with mean limbs, or is one whose limbs are disordered, or one whose physical constitution and nutrition are poor, or one who is wrinkled and emaciated; the verb *saghila* applies to all the preceding”	

	or *sulāl,*	"too well-known to require definition; synonym *sill*" ["tuberculosis"]
	or *sawlah,*	"flaccidity of the belly and other parts"
	or *ṣaḥal,*	hoarseness
	or *ḍaʿal,*	"weakness of the body resulting from too-close consanguinity"
3.1.25	or *ṭaḥal,*	"a disease of the spleen"
	or *ṭulāṭilah,*	"falling of the uvula so that neither food nor drink easily passes through it"
	or *ʿafal,*	"something that breaks out in women resembling the scrotal hernia [in men]"
	or *ʿaqal,*	"knock-kneedness"
	or *ʿaqābīl,*	"an eruption on the lip following a fever"
	or *ghamal,*	"the festering of a wound as a result of its being tied too tightly"
	or *qabal,*	"the turning of one of the two pupils toward the other"
	or *namlah,*	"a pustule that erupts on the body as a result of inflammation and chafing and which quickly destroys the flesh where it is and then takes hold in another place"
	or *uṭām,*	"retention of the urine and feces due to a disease"
	or *ḥujām,*	"a disease of the eye"
3.1.26	or *judhām,*	"too well-known to require definition" ["leprosy"]
	or *khasham,*	"change in the smell of the nose due to a disease"
	or *raḥam,*	"pain in the womb"
	or *saram,*	"pain in the buttocks"
	or *ḍajam,*	"crookedness of the mouth, jawbone, lip, chin, and neck"
	or *ʿasam,*	"stiffening of the wrist or ankle joint resulting in distortion of the hand or foot"

or *ghamam*, “the spreading of hair in such a way as to narrow the brow and the nape”

or *faqam*, “advancement of the upper incisors so that they do not meet the lower”

or *qaʿam*, “a distortion and raising of the buttocks”

or *kazam*, “shortness of the nose”

or *kasham*, “inferiority of physique or of pedigree” 3.1.27

or *mūm*, “the most extreme form of smallpox”

or *baṭan*, “belly disease”

or *thafan*, “a disease of the *thafinah*, which, in a human, is the knee, or the place where the shank and the thigh meet”

or *danan*, “bowing of the back, walking with short steps, and lowering the chest and neck”

or *zaman*, “an affliction [of the body]; synonym *ḍaman* [chronic or crippling sickness]”

or *tasawwun*, “flaccidity of the belly”

or *qaʿan*, “repugnant shortness of the nose”

or *āhah* or *māhah*, “*āhah* is measles and *māhah* is smallpox”

or *jalah*, “recession of the hair from the fore part of the head”

or *shawah*, “both longness and shortness of the neck (one word with two opposite meanings)” 3.1.28

or *fawah*, “capaciousness of the mouth”

or *qarah*, “*qarah* [jaundice] is to the body what *qalaḥ* [yellowing] is to the teeth”

or *qamah*, “lack of appetite for food; synonym *qaham*”

or *marah*, “festering of the eye as a result of failing to apply collyrium”

or *balah*, “lack of native wit”

or *talah*, “confusion, or *walah*,” which means “losing one’s mind as a result of sorrow”

or *dalah*, “losing one’s mind as a result of worry and so forth”

or *bazā'*,	"a bending of the back at the buttocks, or projection of the middle of the back over the anus"
or *jaḥw*,	"capaciousness and flaccidity of the skin"
3.1.29 or *jalā*,	"[a form of hair loss] short of baldness"
or *jawā*,	"a disease of the chest"
or *ḥaṣāh*,	"hardening of the urine in the bladder until it turns into something like stones"
or *ḥaqwah*,	"pain in the belly from eating meat"
or *khadhā*,	"flaccidity and floppiness of the ear"
or *rathyah*,	"a pain of the joints, hands, and feet, or a swelling in the legs, or one's not being able to turn as a result of old age or pain"
or *sharā*,	"small red itchy pimples"
or *shaghā*,	"variation in the manner of growth of the teeth, some being long, some short, some pointing in, some pointing out"
or *ḍawā*,	"meagerness of the body, or paucity of the body, either as an inborn trait or as a result of emaciation"
or *ṭanā*,	"[the verb] *ṭanā* means 'his spleen and his lungs stuck to his ribs on the left side'"
3.1.30 or *faghā*,	"a distortion of the mouth"
or *qaʿā*,	"the projection of the tip of the nose followed by its turning up toward the bridge"
or *qaṭā*,	"a disease of the buttocks"
or *laqwah*,	"a disease of the face"
or *lawā*,	"a pain in the stomach, or a crookedness in the back"

not to mention other blemishes, such as being a dwarf or a runt, or undernourished, potbellied, and thin-necked, or a beanpole or a midget or squat and fat or short and ugly, or diseases for which no name as yet is known and which it is impossible to enumerate in their entirety since they are too many to be contained within these twenty-eight letters.[1] The most trying and harmful of them all are erotomania and erectile dysfunction, to which last our contemporaries have added venereal disease, for which our noble language has no word.[2]

Again I say, "Is it not enough for men that their lives are *short* and spent mostly in lengthy *thought*, their lot hard, each in enough care, struggle, and grief *drowned* to suffice him and still leave a balance to go *round*? The seeker after knowledge, to elucidate issues and clarify matters of debate must burn the midnight *oil*, to scrape the barest living the craftsman must bend over his work all day in resentful *toil*. The emir is preoccupied with laying down the law and maintaining his *domination*, the president frets over his *administration*. The king lives in *dread* lest his ministers conspire to administer to him a potion that will leave him *dead*, the ministers *quaver* lest he find fault with them and withdraw his *favor*. The merchant goes early to the shop he *hires*, worried that his goods will find no *buyers*. The physician fears people living more sensible lives and dispensing with his *skills*, leaving his drugs to go rancid and the liquids in his bottles to go stagnant, while corrupted become his powders, electuaries, dry doses, and *pills*. The judge prays that no young lady come before him to snare him with her *looks* or disconcert him with matters not found in his *books*, entrapping him in *floss* till, as to her affairs, he's at a *loss*. The ship's captain's on guard lest a storm *arise*, the general against the outbreak of war's fire, whose fuel is *lives*—saying, on seeing that his sultan's thinking is *quirky*, his mood *murky*, 'God protect me from time's upsets and make this quirkiness a passing *spell*, gone before the supper *bell*, for in the face of my king and commander I see designs for the clash of titans and the lineaments of *battle*, while I have a companionate wife and children, property, and *cattle*! God make the foreigners hold their tongues and cease their *slander*, cast terror of him into their hearts and wipe from his breast aught that may make him rage or rouse his *dander*!' The ploughman is afraid of too much *rain* and the *hurricane*, the educator that men will turn from a thirst for knowledge 3.1.31

to one for ignorance, the educated that later writers will say something *biting* and of the consequences of *writing* (writing, that is, a book that will suck *dry* what remains of patience's limited *supply* and keep him from any *distraction* or *attraction*), the singer and player of instruments that prices will become *inflated* or the hearts of the rich *desolated*, the playboy that men will be guided to become more *serious*, the poet that he'll find the object of his panegyrics as impervious as rock or his beloved unresponsive and *imperious*, the author like me of lunatics (meaning he's on his guard against them, not that he's one of them),[3] who may bar his *path*, burning his book and tearing his hide to pieces in their *wrath*, the husband of the decampment of his *wife* and of his daughter's staying a spinster for *life* (as are they, in turn, of his stinginess with his *pelf* and denial of access to his *wealth*), the priest of the philosophers' *books*, and the philosophers of the priest's threats, fulminations, and thunderous *looks*. Thus, in sum, everyone with a trade fears lest its benefits be *diverted*, each prays God his affairs go right even if his friend's must be *perverted*, for scarce any of the aforementioned can his own interests *fulfill* without another, of necessity, faring *ill* (as Abū l-Ṭayyib al-Mutanabbī put it, 'The setbacks of some are for others opportunities'), despite which each claims he has a right to what he asks for, that he deserves to be granted his *prayers*, and that the proof of his claim lies in the sayings of the Glorious and Almighty Truth, that most truthful of *sayers*."

3.1.32 And yet again I say, no matter at what length I have already spoken, "Is it not enough for man—fear of a death that may take him *unawares* while peaceably engaged upon his *affairs*, or grieve him through loss of a dear one *deceased*, be he of his kin, his offspring, or his brethren, or a boon companion, or even a *beast* (for some are as fond of horses, birds, cats, and dogs as they are of family and friends), or terror lest one of them should break his neck by falling off the back of one of his *nags*, or his house catch fire, his heirlooms and prized possessions be burned to ashes and he reduced to *rags*, or fall into a torrent and be swept to God knows where, or the earth swallow him up, or the ceiling collapse upon him from above, or a missive reach him from a distance of two hundred leagues, to disquieten him, cost him his sleep, maybe even make him weep blood, or that a robber come and steal the goods upon which his livelihood depends, or lest he lose all that's in his purse or waistband while on the road, or a stick pierce his eye and he lose its use, or one of his muscles become paralyzed and thenceforth be of no worth, or he eat something harmful and be killed by it, or he drink a poisoned potion and his guts and limbs collapse because of it, or he behold a comely woman and be kept awake by her beauty so that he gets up the next morning beside himself and love-sick, complaining to the doctor of his *disease* and to the poet of his passion, for the latter will neither his hunger *appease* nor grant him his *desire* nor will the former bring him any good or provide him with a *cure*, or behold an ugly one who strikes such terror into his *heart* as makes all appetite *depart*, or lest the dogs bark at him and rip his *clothes*, so that his tackle's laid bare or his blood *flows*, or he be sitting one day on a *seat* and from down below be heard a *tweet*, so that his name becomes mud among his brethren and *band*, the people of his village and his *land* (in which case they may name him in derision 'the farter,'[4] 'the snarter,' 'the varter,' 'the browner,' 'the bottom burper,' 'the queefer,' 'the queeber,' 'the poofer,' 'the pooter,' 'the butt trumpeter'), or the nightmare fall upon him one night, so that the blood stops flowing to his heart and he perishes before morning?"

In truth, all this has not been enough to stop some men from 3.1.33
rushing to outfit against others the battalions of guesswork and *supposition* and unleash against them the squadrons of surmise and *suspicion*. Thus one such company would attack another waving the lances of *defamation*, wielding the swords of *imprecation*, thrusting with spearheads of dispute that find their mark and pierce right *through*, firing arrows of debate that transfix and are ever *true*. One said, "Verily, the degrees of Heaven are one hundred and five!" while another, "Verily, they are one hundred and four, *no more*!" Then yet another declared, "You both lied and deserve to have your

tongues *excised*, your eyes put out, your testes *pulverized*! They are one hundred and six *for sure*!" At this another arose who said, "Verily, the degrees of Hell are six hundred, six and *sixty*!" to which someone else responded, "Verily they are six hundred, five and *fifty*!" while a third declared, "You both *lie* and true belief *defy*, have *erred* and the shackling of your hands and feet *incurred*, in addition to the plucking of both your cephalic and your *pubic hair*! They are seven hundred and sixty-seven, *I declare*!" Then another stood up to say, "Verily, the length of Satan's horn is three hundred, five-and-fifty *cubits*!" and another responded, "Untruth clear and falsehood outrageous! It is, on the contrary, three hundred and fifty-six!" (to which a third added, "And a *few bits*!"). Now another said, "And it is made of iron, as witnessed by how heavily it weighs on people and *torments them*!" to which another answered, "Verily, it is made of gold, as evidenced by how it distracts and *tempts them*!" To this another, however, responded, "Nay, it's made of squash, because it grows and then gets *shorter*, swells and then gets smaller, contracts after having got *tauter*!"

3.1.34 Another now arose, stood atop a tall ladder and said in a loud *tone*, "Verily, you are possessed, good people, of a little piece of skin that must be cut off, using a whetted piece (neither too large nor too small) of *stone*!" to which another replied, "Nay, using a sharp knife, neither too long nor too *short*!" to which a third one made *retort*, "You're both fools! That bit of skin to us is *dear*, to our hearts *near*, and is not with either stone or knife to be made *shorter* or scratched by aught else, be it even of silver, for it is connected to the jugulars and tied to the *aorta*. Anyone who cuts it is guilty of *infidelity* and deserves to burn in Hell for all *eternity*!" Someone else declared, "Nay, to cut it off is a duty, for it is nothing but a mere appendage!" to which the first objected, maintaining that it should not be cut off and saying, "Verily, we see that nothing else is cut off, so why make cutting its peculiar privilege?" to which the other answered, "On the contrary, mustaches are trimmed and nails clipped!" The other said, "But then they grow back while that does not!" The first now declared, "My conclusive proof that cutting it is obligatory is its uselessness to its owner!" to which the other replied, "God has created nothing in vain and to no purpose!" "On the contrary," said the other, "he created you to no purpose!", to which the second responded, "Not at all, it's you who were created in vain!" Each party then mustered its cavalry and its *footmen*, and the two armies clashed, using weapons and *acumen*, and what with blades chopping, arrows shooting, hands bashing, tongues wagging, and pens *decrying*, heads were scattered, blood flowed and limbs sent *flying*, the inviolable was violated and honor *debased*, wealth looted and lands reduced to *waste*, while grudges were borne in men's *breasts*, ill will both patent and hidden stored up in their *chests*, horses were saddled and warriors *armed*, roads became impassable and the earth was *harmed*, men awaited their chance for *retaliation*, and the nights were filled with *vituperation*.

Good people, think of those who have passed on to the eternal 3.1.35
domains and of how they are now but mortal *remains*, when there were among them men whose *name*, during their lives, was uttered with blessings but now is spoken of with *blame*, men who once were to their people as lamps brightly *burning* but now are become nothing but smoke and dust *swirling*, men who would eat till their bellies *extended* and eyes *distended*, whose tongues *wagged* and lips *sagged* and are now become the food of worms (though certain insects find them noxious). Good people, you whose masses are in a coma while the rest are in a *daze*, flee self-conceit! Beware the chilly rigors of the *grave*! Hasten to perform some good work that may bring you closer to your *God*, and be reconciled before you quit this earthly *sod*! Would you die your hearts by hatred against your opponent *chilled*, your mouths with curses against those who disagree with your assertions *filled*? Has not the Truth instructed you, "Be, O mortals, brothers on this earth, for you are of one father and one mother and all of you shall surely die!"[5] Be your faces brown, red, yellow, black, or white, all of you are mortal, your lives all are soon *erased*, all see, feel, hear, smell, and *taste*. Why is it that the

prepuced among you the unprepuced loathes, the ironlike the squashy *hates*? Will you not be with each other as *mates*? Have I not made myself manifest to you in the sun's rising and setting and the stars' appearing and *disappearing*, in the fire's dying and *flaring*, in the wind's dropping and *blowing*, in the waters' welling and *slowing*, in Destiny's reverses and *perversities*, its cares and *adversities*, in the blackness of hair and its *whitening*, in the aging of the body and its *lightening*, in the ages and how they follow in *procession*, in the years and their *succession*, in the advance of nations and their *recession*, in the thickets when they *blossom* and the meadows when they *bloom*, in the trees when they leaf and *fall*, in the birds when they twitter and *call*, in the tongue when it *pronounces* and the pen when it writes with sweeping *flounces*? There is, I swear, among the ravening beasts and rapacious birds less enmity and *hate*, less grudge-bearing and *spite*, than there is among you.

3.1.36 Remember the day your preacher climbed the pulpit with frowns and *scowls*, issued threats and uttered *disavowals*, accused your adversaries of error and misbelief, urged you to *fight* and incited you to defend the *right*, then prayed and sought God's *clemency*, asked His guidance and proclaimed that you'd surely achieve *ascendancy*—that day you raided your neighbors and violated all that your brothers held sacred, sundered suckling child from *mother*, woman from *lover*, fathers from the offspring they'd *sired* and all they owned and had *acquired*! Remember the day your leader mustered his lieutenants and urged family and friends to betray his liege lord (and what a betrayal!), all because he differed with him over assessments and *estimations*, interpretations and *considerations*, conclusions and *explanations*! Remember the day you marked yourselves with the tokens of holy *struggle*, saying, "This is God's *battle*! This is a war for the Lord of *Creation*! This is the day to gain reward and from torment attain *salvation*—so overwhelm the enemy by land and sea and by this pious act win God's *approbation*"! Remember the day you argued over what foods to eat and what drinks to drink, what water to use to wash the *dead*, on what kind of bedding to lay your *head*, what clothes to wear, how a certain phrase might best be *said*, how to arrange table, chair, and *bed*? Were you placed in this world only to *quarrel*? Were you commanded to fight and *squabble*? How come the doctors of mathematics, geometry, and astronomy don't differ over their *proofs*, or if they do, don't set the world to the torch to assert their *truths*, while you set fire to it at every chance you *find*, with every fancy that comes to *mind*? You'd do better to agree on a single view, as have *they*, and to the needs of God's flock attention *pay*, than to drive them into such a *strait* and in such sticky matters *implicate*, to guide them to the straightest path to *follow* than muddle them in such a murky *wallow*. Leave them to strive for their daily *fare* and don't ask them to grasp what's over your head and *theirs*. And you too, work two hours with your hands for every hour you do with your darting tongues, and agree beforehand that, when preferences *differ*, you'll be friendly and submissive to one *another*. Have you forgotten what it says in that Book of Psalms that you canter through and *cantillate*, that you so *adulate*, and to which you have for so long *adhered*: "Behold, how good and how pleasant it is for brethren to dwell together in unity! It is like the precious ointment upon the head, that ran down upon the beard, even Aaron's *beard*"?[6]

Verily I say unto you, "Do not forbid what God has made lawful 3.1.37
unto you by way of *good things*, and do not seek officiously to uncover other men's *sins*! Do not sell the goods stored up for you in *Paradise* by being on earth men of idleness and *lies*! For a Market-man to marry a Bag-woman is no *shame* and if a Bag-man marries a Market-woman there's no *blame*, for differences regarding the Unknown are matters of *surmise* and should pose no obstacle to the carrying off of such a *prize*,[7] whose value is by the unschooled as *appreciated* as it is by the *educated*. Are you not aware that 'wombs' (*arḥām*) from 'mercy' (*raḥmah*) are *derived*, that they were designed that men might, through marriage, be *allied*, and that the word to 'ties of kinship' is *applied*,[8] for brotherhood and harmony were *created*, to mutual affection *dedicated*, and for the seizing of fortune's offerings

designated? Why then do you hold yourselves from such things at a *distance*, withdrawing and showing *resistance*? Why do you all in the ocean of doubt and suspicion *wade*, why make commerce from surmise and therein *trade*? God will never listen to the prayer of you *Orientals* unless it first be approved by the *Occidentals*,[9] nor will you be to the next world *admitted* unless your conduct in this world to this model you have *fitted*. Let then now the towheaded man shake hands with the *black*, the round-headed-with-bonnet with the cone-headed-with-*cap*. Let each of you harbor toward his brother pure and loving *intentions* and fulfill toward him his *obligations*. Then, since your disagreements with regard to Creation will have *ceased*, you'll not differ as to the Creator, for He is Lord of all that's west and *east*. It is His desire that the Orientals among you, should they travel to the *west*, should be welcomed by its people and taken to their *breast*." Accept this advice and listen to what comes *next* by way of choice phrases and witty topoi in the *text* of this coming chapter which I have named ☞

Chapter 2

Love and Marriage

I mentioned at the end of Book Two that God first afflicted the Fāriyāq with many diseases and more books, then rescued him from them all, and that, believing himself pardoned, he felt great relief and devoted himself to song. Now I must relate how that episode *turned out* and all that this sinful pursuit *brought about*. To get down to detail, the house that contained the Bag-men was next door to the house of a merchant who had a daughter[10] who loved music, diversion, and the raptures of art, reserving a specially soft spot for singing. Every time she heard the Fāriyāq singing or playing in his room, she'd climb to the roof of her house and listen attentively until he was done, then go back down to her chamber. When the Fāriyāq discovered that she was making the climb for him—for it was not to be imagined that anyone else could have been exhibited to her[11]—his soul fell ardently in love with her and felt for her the promptings of desire. 3.2.1

At the same time, however, he was by nature so averse to the idea of marriage that he considered married men the least happy of people, for all that can be seen, in general, of the married state is its trials and tribulations. If ever he was told, "So-and-so has married," he'd be overcome by pity and would mourn for him as for one swept away by a mighty torrent or afflicted by some other terrible calamity. At that moment, then, the two elements of love and caution 3.2.2

waged war within him, the latter in the end coming to outweigh the former in the scale. He therefore decided that it was a better idea simply to look than to make any sign indicating that he was head over heels in love.

3.2.3 The two of them continued in this fashion for a while, he behaving more shyly than the loon, which dives the moment it senses danger, until that day when he saw her wipe her eyes with a handkerchief (whether from the heat of the sun or for some other reason) and convinced himself in the depths of his soul that she was wiping away tears of yearning for him. At this his breast burst the gussets of *resignation* and emotion drove him to abandon *circumspection*. To himself he said, "Would any but I confront the tears of a weeping woman by turning away? And behind those tears can there be anything but love? How can they not melt me, when my heart's no *rock*, I no knave of low-mannered *stock*? I know that the greatest pleasures in life *depend* on finding a boon companion and sympathetic *friend*. I am a stranger, in need of one to cheer me when I long *for home*, a comrade when I'm all *alone*. Who better to cheer one than a *wife*, and what benefit lies in bachelorhood once God has provided one with food and the other needs of *life*?"

3.2.4 By such speedy calculations, he reconciled himself to bearing the burdens of love from wherever it might come and this opened the door before the two of them to signing back and forth with a hand placed now upon the heart, next upon the cheek, a finger yoked to another, beseeching arms extended with a gulp and a sigh, pursed lips, a nodding head, and other such things to which love's novices resort (old hands in contrast being satisfied with nothing less than the "twisting of the side-tresses"[12] specified by the master, Imru' al-Qays). The era of the sign lasted for many long days, without speech, but when the hands and other limbs could no longer translate what was in the heart, especially in view of the distance between them, they came up with a stratagem by which they might meet in a certain place, so that the lover might behold his beloved.

When he saw her close up, he found her to be a woman big of bosom and bottom, the credit for this going to the inventor of Egyptian dress, for had she been wearing Frankish clothes, he would never have known if the things on her chest were dyed wool, cotton bolls, cotton cardings, teased wool, papyrus cotton, wool waste, silk, or breasts,(1) or whether what was behind her was a bustle or flesh and fat. These two characteristics—by which I mean bigness of bosom and bigness of bottom—are the best one can want from a woman, for the first assures the appeal of the forward dimension, the second that of the rearward. I might add that it is reported that Our Master Sulaymān, peace be upon him, said in praise of bigness of bosom (Proverbs, chapter 5), "Let her breasts satisfy thee at all times."[13] Someone might object that, should the two bodies be gathered together in one place, the presence of colored wool, etc., would not—given the presence of hands and possibility of their giving the body a good squeeze here and there as one would when testing a ram for fatness(2)—prevent the investigation of the status of the abovementioned characteristics. The response would be that such a situation is generally prohibited in the lands of the East, especially on the first occasion; the rest of the world has no such prohibition, which is why the use of bustles has spread, which no one can deny. 3.2.5

(1) *ʿihn* is "wool, or wool that has been colored by dyeing"; *birs* is "cotton, or something resembling it, or papyrus cotton"; *khurfuʿ* is "carded cotton"; *ʿuṭm* is "teased wool"; *baylam* is "papyrus cotton" and "sugarcane cotton"; *qishbir* is "the worst cotton, or cotton waste"; *nawdal* means "breast."

(2) *jatt* is "feeling a ram, to know what part of it is fat and what lean."

Now, given that we were previously presented, in Book One,[14] with a description, in the Frankish style, of a donkey, there can be no harm in presenting here too a description in the same style of a man on the verge of marriage. Thus we declare: it is a time that seduces him with thoughts of the joys of being *wed* and makes him drool as he anticipates the pleasures of the *bed*. No thoughts of future troubles cross his mind—all he can *surmise*, the most his mind *devise*, is "My state is not like that of my friends and neighbors 3.2.6

who married and were disappointed in their *hopes*. They didn't give marriage its due, didn't cling with confidence to its *ropes*, for some wedded when unequal to its demands, either for want of *magnanimity* or of *liquidity*, or because of a disparity between them and their wives in age or, in their instrument, some *debility*, or were prone to come at the rim, before entering the *hole*, or rejected by their wives, or reduced to a constant tizzy by the husband's *role*,(1) or because their emir had exiled them from their *houses*, or because their mothers constantly spied on their *spouses*, or because of quarrels with their neighbors over where to water their *cattle*, or because their imams regarded their wives as *chattel*.[15] For all these reasons, squabbles would break out between man and *wife* and they'd go for long periods in a state of *strife*, shifts would be ripped from in front and from the *rear*,[16] heads and pubes plucked of their *hair*, uproar would never *stop*, skins would be scratched with fingernails, and the scented herbs upon the beds would go to *rot*.

(1) "The *muṣlif* is one 'whose wife finds no favor with him' and also a man 'who is in low spirits and whose wealth has decreased.' The *mushafshif* is 'one who suffers from trembling and confusion out of jealousy and worry over his wives.'

3.2.7 "I, though, am free, praise God, from any such *flaw*. Nothing need come between me and my wife, no man will jostle me for her affections, she won't find me a *bore*. My happiness will be hers, my wishes and hers the *same*. I am neither toothless nor foul of breath nor hunchbacked nor *lame*. I have two hands with which to *work*, two legs that, to earn their living, will not *shirk*, and if in my body there's any *distemper*, it's covered by my excellence of *temper*. I will object to none of her cooking, her clothes, or her manner of *reposing*, for she'll sleep next to me and adopt what suits us both by way of *clothing*. What then should stop me from taking a *mate*, one possessed of each such happy *trait*, even should people, hearing that my spouse is full of *affection*, that with me her honor enjoys full *protection* and her face no visitor *sees*, envy me such abundant *ease*? Every choking *sorrow* will then seem easy to *swallow*, and it's no secret what pleasure lies in giving the envious the *finger*—a pleasure over which no connoisseur will hesitate to *linger*. Not to mention the delight found by the psyche in the companionate *gender*, whose nearness to the heart comfort, and in times of stress an outlet, doth *render*. One who endures his toil by day only by night to sleep alone and who no bedmate to breathe into his nostrils or warm his blood from in front and behind *owns* is meet to be counted among the dead and thrown among the *bones*. In addition, I shall by her saliva to the need for drink be made *immune*, by the smell of her hair to the need for musk and other *perfume*, for they say that the smell of a woman from the roots of the hair (be those in the body's cracks and crevices or on the head) may be *inhaled* and by it all the senses are *derailed*. Likewise, the heat of her body will suffice as fuel to keep me *warm*, the sight of her serve as antimony and *balm*, meaning that I shall save at least one silver coin a *day*, half of which for a daily morning visit to the bathhouse I'll *pay*, leaving me the other half to live on, which is riches *indeed* and will suffice for any *need*.

"As to what people say about 'women's wiles' and how they ride 3.2.8
their husbands so hard they're left beyond the reach of *consolation*, in most cases this isn't true—and no rule's without exceptions to its general *application*. I may be the first to expose this *qualification* and fashion, in praise of marriage for bachelors, such a *commendation*, and how could this not be so, when I'm a master of chaste language and *eloquence*, a man of craft and *intelligence*? Thus none of her cunning ways will *defy me* and none of her attempts at concealment *get by me*. I shall oppose her and *remonstrate*, and that my superiority to her compels her to obey and comply I shall *demonstrate*. One day I'll tell her, 'This is a day on which the married desist and active lovers to celibacy *keep*' to which she'll reply, 'I shall be the first to desist and the last to *sleep*.' Should I tell her, 'It's not attractive for a respectable married woman to put her charms on *display*,' she'll tell me, 'Or flirt and *play*,' and if I tell her, 'A wife her husband once a week has a right to *expect*,' she'll tell me, 'While remaining chaste and worthy of *respect*.' If I tell her, 'Jewelry's no requirement for a *wedding*,' she'll tell me, 'and nor is brocade, that most evil *cladding*.' Taken as a whole, my life with her will be easy, my state happy, my

good fortune extensive, my food *wholesome*, my drink healthy, my clothes clean, my bed comfy, my possessions well guarded, my house no longer *lonesome*. Good cheer will be there, my every effort *blessed*, my status one of note, my endeavors guaranteed *success*. Hie ye then to marriage with a jolly girl who's full of *coquetry*, whose looks provide a cure for *bankruptcy*, and to bed whom is to ride the road to *victory*!" End.

3.2.9 I further declare that it is a fact, deeply rooted in our sticky human clay, that when a man sets his heart on getting married, God endears his spouse to him however she be and makes him believe she's the best of people, morally and physically. And that's not all: the man may well believe that he's been elevated above his peers and distinguished among his brethren to the point that he dismisses as trivial what previously he saw as important and imagines that he has become a new person, for whom the face of the earth ought, by rights, to be remade. It follows that the Fāriyāq no longer found contentment in the old familiar songs and poetry; instead, he substituted for them other, new ones of his own composition. In the process, he composed two poems[17] in which he attempted to invent a strange new style, with the result that they turned out quite titter-making, as you shall see—and had he had the ability to invent a new form of speech to express his passion and rejuvenation, he would have done so.

3.2.10 Thus, should he lay eyes on a married man, he'd call out to him and sing as follows:

On the racetrack of marriage, I'm the front-runner
While you're the also-ran last-placer.
My shaft soon will take the prize
While your luckless stick's a failure.[18]

Or, should he see a bachelor, he'd tell him:

Bachelors, the creed of the single man
I have renounced, so do as I have done.
There is no wealth but marriage, so have at it, friends:
Enrich yourselves and gain what I have won.

And one day, infatuated with the idea of creating something strange and new, he became obsessed with the idea of composing a collection of poetry that would consist entirely of single verses.[19] He wrote four and then gave up. They were:

Like a month is an hour of separation from you, but a year
In your company passes like an hour.

I spend the long night gazing at the stars enamored—
My contemplation being of heavenly bodies that are rounded.

My heart beats unbidden whene'er the east wind rises,
And the bright moon recalls to me your countenance.

Would I might know how long a heart that melts as it endures
Can suffer from separation in its many modes.

It would be officious of us to say here that he used to tell his fiancée, "You are the delight of my eyes, and I believe you to be the best of humankind. We are the envy of others and with you I have no need of riches. When close to you, I'm *glad*, when far, I'm *sad*. We shall always be as we are now. Your beauty distracts the *unwed* and I'm jealous of the breeze that ruffles the jet black tresses on your *head*. We are two bodies with one soul or two souls with one body. Each day you'll find in me a lover *new* and all the time I'll find fresh charms in *you*. We shall be the paragon of spouses and of lovers," and so on in the usual vein adopted by such as he.

Another thing he said was that the best days of a person's life are those immediately preceding and following marriage. I note: according to the Franks these number a month, which they call "the moon of honey (*'asal*)" and which follows the wedding. According 3.2.11

to us Arabs, however, they number two, are called "the two moons of intercourse (*'asl*)," and last till the hive has been filled, every bee has reverted to being a hornet, and everything has gone back to the way it was. I note further that love is something planted in our human clay the day we're placed in the cradle and that lasts till the day we're laid on the bier. The human must inevitably therefore feel love for some person or other, some object or other, some abstraction or other, and the more his love grows in the area of one of these loci, the further it declines in another. At the same time, one of these loci may become a stimulus to his adding love for another. An example would be a person who devotes himself to poetry, singing, or painting and whose devotion to these things becomes a spur to his loving a beautiful person. One who devotes himself to scholarship or fighting or honor or the exercise of power must inevitably lose some of his desire for women; indeed, he may be too busy to think about them at all. One who devotes himself to purebred horses and fine weapons may find that this devotion is an incitement to love of another or not, as the case may be. Some count among this last kind the *sarābātiyyah*, who are the latrine cleaners, but others exclude them from it on the grounds that they practice a profession that people are forced to undertake to make a living, not a pastime that people undertake because it suits them to do so.[20]

3.2.12 The preceding are three states deriving from three different stimuli. There are a further three states with respect to paucity, abundance, and their midpoint. The first is one of parity and consists of the lover loving his beloved as he loves himself; thus he never indulges himself in anything or pleasures himself with anything unless the one he loves is there to share that pleasure with him. This is how men are before and just after they get married, and it is not inconsistent with good sense and judgment. The second is the excessive, which is to say the one that goes beyond parity and consists of the lover loving his beloved more, as it were, than himself; it is characteristic of fathers and mothers in their love for their children and of certain lovers. The father will sacrifice his own life for that of his offspring and deny himself pleasures and treats so as to use them to give them pleasure: if he finds himself incapable of eating or of enjoying marital relations while his son enjoys both, this makes him happy. At the same time, however, he is not devoid of good sense and judgment. The lover may prefer the object of his affections to himself but unlike the parent behaves in a disordered way, doing things that are inappropriate to their place and time. The third is the ordinary situation and consists of a person loving his beloved but loving himself more; this is the commonest.

There are also three locational states, namely proximity, distance, 3.2.13
and their midpoint, and these have different impacts depending on the differences among people's dispositions. One whose love is true will love to the same extent whether he be near or far; indeed, separation may urge him on to greater longing and passion. No one has described this situation better than the one who said

> Methinks the beloved a sun that separation
> Refuses to take as "oryx doe."[21] Rather, it makes it burn yet hotter.

The free-grazing male, on the other hand, the one with a roving eye, never puts one leg forward without holding the other back.

There are a further three states that are temporal. These are 3.2.14
childhood, youth, and maturity. The affection of the child is that most quickly given and the most tenacious, that of the youth the hottest and strongest, and that of the mature person the most firmly grounded and longest lasting. The mature person also values his beloved's good qualities and advantages more highly and his love for that person is both more bitter and more sweet. The bitterness comes from his knowing that he is exposing himself to the reproach and censure of the reproachful and censorious among the young and inexperienced, as well as to his own anxiety that his beloved may grow bored with him. Thus his heart ever *burns*, his mind to his beloved ever *turns*. The sweetness comes from his greater awareness of his beloved's worth, as noted above, and from his love being

as a result permanent and strong, for he believes with all his heart that he is pursuing what will bring him happiness and his due portion of good fortune.

3.2.15 Love has likewise three states with respect to means or the lack thereof—by which I have in mind material comfort, hardship, and their midpoint. The affection of the man of comfortable means is the coolest and most fickle, for his wealth allows him to change beloveds and shift from state to state. Let respectable women beware this type of man lest he spread scandal among them, unless they have no fear for their secrets and their honor, for the rich man has as little against giving away secrets as he has against piling up money, and to him everything is to his coin *subservient*, to his greed *obedient*. The affection of the poor man, in contrast, is the most excessive, deviant, and agonized, for his poverty, being an obstacle to his removal of the impediments that stand between him and his beloved, leads him in no time to despair, insanity, or suicide. The love of the man of middling means is the most balanced and healthy.

3.2.16 There are three more states of love, namely abjection, pride, and equality. Abjection usually is the state of the suitor, pride that of the one to whom suit is made. One of the most amazing kinds of affection is love mixed with hatred. An example would be a man who loves a woman who loves another man, and therefore refuses his advances. His fervor then urges him to pursue union with her as a form of vengeance against her. If he is successful in this, his love overcomes his hatred for her; if he isn't, it doesn't, and he remains in this state until some consolation distracts him from her. Generally speaking, the lover doesn't forget his beloved when the latter treats him with aversion and denial but only on winning another who resembles the first physically and temperamentally (though how rarely that happens!).

3.2.17 As to the incitements to love, these include a single sighting that touches a sensitive chord in the seer's heart, after which he is pervaded by the same feelings conducive to ardor and longing that long association would create. In such cases, in my opinion, the lover must previously have pictured in his mind certain characteristics and specifics of comeliness and fallen in love with these; then, when he sees them as he had pictured them, realized in a particular body, his heart and mind cleave to it and he is like one who finds something he had lost and was looking for. Love may also come about as a result of hearing about someone for such a long time that, little by little, the hearer becomes so familiar with that person that he becomes devoted to them. The commonest causes of love, however, are looking and association.

Know too that many people have fallen in love with beautiful pictures, of males or females, and not for any lewd or immoral reason but simply because by so doing they found their souls were set at rest and their minds afire, being strengthened in this by the tradition that runs "He who loves, keeps silent, is chaste, and dies, dies a martyr." In such a situation, the suitor is pleased with the slightest thing his beloved may give him: a kiss, to his mind, is a victory, a triumph, a prize of war. As al-Sharīf al-Raḍī says: 3.2.18

> Ask my bed of me and of her, for we
> Are content with what our beds may tell of us.

(If I were given a free hand with this verse, I'd change it to "of her and of me.")[22] And Ibn al-Fāriḍ, may God have mercy on his soul, says:

> How oft he spent the night at the mercy of my hand, when we were joined in love!
> Within his doubled mantle godliness resides—we are innocent of all pollution.

This kind of passion is called "platonic love" by the Franks, in reference to Plato the philosopher; it does not exist among them in reality, being merely a term they use. Among us it is known as "ʿUdhrī love," after ʿUdhrah, a tribe in Yemen, and not after the *ʿadhrah* of the slave girl, meaning her virginity and intact state as well as something else that comes from her.[23] It is related of Majnūn Laylā that Laylā came to him one day and started talking to him, but he said, “Away with you! I am too busy with my love for you.” And al-Mutanabbī says in the same vein,

I was distracted from returning your greeting
And the source of my distraction was yourself.

3.2.19 The woman most worthy of love and esteem is she who adds culture and beauty of expression and voice to beauty of appearance, and the most fortunate of persons is “a lover who’s got a lover who loves him,” as it says in an Egyptian *mawāliyā*. In such a state, he will be emboldened to undertake the toughest of tasks and mightiest of endeavors and, his thoughts being ever preoccupied with his beloved’s charms, will perform them as though they were nothing. In such a state, were he to shoulder a rock, or even a mighty mountain, he’d fondly suppose he was lifting his beloved’s slippers or, to be more precise, his legs. Moreover, despite all the moments of misery, disappointment, deprivation, and, above all, the torments of jealousy that accompany love, there is nothing good about the life of the fancy-free. Love stimulates manliness, pride, gallantry, and generosity. It inspires the one in love with refined ideas and nice notions. It imbues him with godly morals and makes him want to do something great for which his name will be remembered and that will bring him praise, especially from his beloved. Rarely have I met a person in love who was cold and *crude*, foolish and given to *hebetude*, or base and *rude*.

3.2.20 A certain abstemious person (who must, I think, have been a premature ejaculator) once said, “If the only thing—all considerations of continence and godliness aside—to prevent one from falling in love with a woman were the necessity of doing so, it would be enough, for when a person knows he is compelled and obligated to love something, he naturally finds it irksome and eschews it. It follows,” he went on, “that love of a woman is contrary to nature, though this is only if the man is perspicacious, self-respecting, and high-minded. The rabble, by contrast, have no self-respect and fall in love with women haphazardly, at the drop of a skullcap." I say, "These are the words of one who has never tasted love, or was loathed by his wife. Had he ever heard a woman say to him, 'Bear, my darling, this load of firewood on your head' or 'Bump along, my sweetheart, on your backside like a little boy,' he'd obey her in both bearing and bumping.(1)"

(1) *zaḥanqaf* ("bumping along") is "moving over the ground on one's backside."

3.2.21 It is also the case that lovers follow different schools in love. Some love a woman who is all artifice, affectation, and vanity, while others do not find these things pleasing, preferring natural beauty and that their beloved should have a degree of naïveté and simplemindedness. This is what al-Mutanabbī was alluding to when he said:

In the city, beauty's an import, freshened up for the market.
In the desert there's a beauty that needs no importing.

An example of the first kind is the man who is offered a certain dish when he has no appetite, so it has to be spiced up and faked. An example of the second is the man who suffers from diochism[24] or metafaucalophagy,(2) so that the absence of spicing and herbs cannot stop him from guzzling, tidbitting, and lapping until he's licked the bottom of the bowl clean after first polishing off its contents. As far as the desire of certain people for naïveté and simplemindedness is concerned, it is based on the fact that the lover is always demanding things that he needs from his beloved and if the latter is possessed of cunning and intelligence, he will fear she may find this irksome and refuse him.

(2) the *sīfannah* is "a bird in Egypt that eats all the leaves of any tree it alights on"; one who is *sarṭam* is "wide in the throat and swallows quickly."

3.2.22 Another kind of lover is the one who loves a woman more if she is proud, a spitfire, difficult to handle, so that conciliating her calls for energy and effort. Most of those who undertake such a task have no other occupation than love and divert themselves with it wherever they find it. Another is the man who loves a woman who possesses the traits of nobility, self-command, and dignity; this is the way of men of ambition and capacity. Any man who sees a woman of humble station who resembles one nobly born and falls in love with her simply because of the resemblance belongs to this category, and the members of this school are called "comparators." It is more common among women, for a woman can scarcely see a man without saying, "he looks like one of the emirs of the olden days," or today's days, or the coming days. Another is the man who falls in love with the woman who is abject, meek, and affectionate; this is the way of those who are kind and sensitive. Another is the man who falls in love with the woman whose countenance bears signs of grief, depression, and worry; this is the way of the tenderhearted and those easily moved by music. Another is the man who falls in love with the woman who is full of joy, unrestrained, and fun-loving; this is the disposition of those who are sad and wretched, for to look at a woman of that type dispels *care* and brings light where once reigned distress and *despair*. Another is the man who falls in love with the woman who is full of mirth and frivolity, flightiness, chatter, and hilarity; this is the way of fools and the ignorant. Another is the man who falls in love with a woman for her culture, understanding, eloquence, readiness of tongue, and quickness of wit; this is the course of scholars and litterateurs. Another is the man who falls in love with women who have lots of trinkets and dress elegantly, who are full of coquetry and affectation; this is the road of those given to extravagance and excess. Another is the man who falls in love with the wanton, shameless, brazen woman; this is the case with depraved lechers. Another is the man who falls in love with the inconstant, sensual, nymphomaniacal, unclean woman; this is the disposition of the man to whom whoring has done its worst. Another is the man who falls in love with the chaste virgin who refuses to let any man have his way with her, in the hope of corrupting her and then boasting of it among his peers; if, subsequently, she gives in to him, he grows tired of her or wishes she hadn't. Such men, in my opinion, are more evil than those who make love to nymphomaniacs. And another is the man who loves the coming together of all these different traits in his beloved, as appropriate.

So much for the moral dimension. As for the physical, the thin man falls for the fat woman and vice versa, the brown-skinned loves the white and vice versa, the tall loves the short and vice versa, and the smooth-skinned loves the hirsute and vice versa. As far as women are concerned, the man they love most is the bull-necked horseman, dashing and daring.

Riches and poverty have no bearing on the matter. A rich man 3.2.23
is as likely to become infatuated with a poor woman as he is with a rich one. Indeed, a rich miser prefers to fall in love with a poor woman because he believes he can make her happy with only a little money. Also, as a rule, people prefer to fall in love with members of strange races so as to find out about the exotic things they imagine are peculiar to them, unless an ignorance of their language makes this impossible; when this is the case, the scope for the imagination is cramped. It is also true that men like women's gentleness and sprightliness, especially in bed, while women like men for their young sappiness and tall, youthful strappiness. No woman can look at a man of such a description and not say in her heart, "There's everything I need! There are riches enough for me!" The ancient Arabs recognized this fact when they derived *ṭawl* ("might") from *ṭūl* ("height"). At the same time, however, women, for the most part, glean their pleasure from every crop and sip from its sources both sweet and sour. Such women are like the bee that gathers its nectar from the flower though the latter is on a dung heap. As to jealousy, it is an inborn trait natural to every human, providing he has good taste: a man is jealous of his material possessions being violated by another; how much more so will he be then in the case of his supposedly inviolable wife? The claim that the Franks feel no jealousy with regard to their women has no truth to it whatsoever. A Frank has been known to kill his wife and himself together on learning that she has been unfaithful. True, they give them so much free rein in many matters that Orientals might regard them as pimping them, but this contains at the same time its own protection against betrayal, for it is a given among them that should a man forbid his

wife to leave the house or keep company with other men, he will prod her into taking a second lover, which he would not if he were to consent to her indulging in such pleasures outside the home.

3.2.24 When it came out that the two honey-seekers[25] (the Fāriyāq and the girl) were meeting in contravention of accepted custom, her mother felt the serpent's tooth of filial ingratitude and consulted some of her friends on the matter. These told her, "We cannot agree to such a marriage because he is a Bag-man, while you belong to the most august house among the Market-men, and never the twain shall meet." She responded, "He isn't of Bag-man stock, but rather an interloper among them." "It makes no difference," they said, "for the stench of the bag is upon him and fills our nostrils," and they gave her dire warnings against him, even though in the preceding chapter I had issued warnings to them and their like against such meddling. When the girl learned what they had said, the spirit of rebellion rose within her and she declared, "Such differences are no concern of women. They are the concern of those who would use them as a path to a career and high status. The goal of marriage is the mutual satisfaction and agreement of a man and a woman. If you refuse this marriage, I warn you I shall have nothing more to do with Market-men." At this, her mother thought it best to take her away from that place in the hope that distance would make her forget. All the tempests of love then arose in both honey-gatherer and honey-giver, in keeping with the words of Abū Nuwās, "Reproach me not, for reproach is a spur."[26] When the mother saw that no amount of haranguing would keep the girl from the hive, no hatchet work hinder her extracting honey,(1) she went back to her house, summoned the Fāriyāq, and said to him, "I have discovered that the Market-men are opposed to having you as an in-law, so if your mind's set on marrying my daughter, you must become a Market-man, if only for a day." "That's fine," said the Fāriyāq, and with that understanding he became a Market-man for the day of his wedding, and both she and the girl were happy.

(1) *jazr* means "the extraction of honey from its cell."

At night, the instruments were brought, the cups sent around, and a good time was had by all, the Fāriyāq applying himself so devotedly to ensuring the regular passage of the cup and to praising the players with repeated calls of "Ah!" and "Ay!" and "Ooh!" that both his hand and tongue tired and, seeing that the company was determined to spend the entire night till morning drinking, he stole out and climbed to the roof to take a rest, it being a moonlit summer night. When he was slow to return, the others thought he must have slipped the knot, so they began searching for him as one searches for a woman with large *breasts*, or one who so hates her husband she'd curse him with her last *breaths*. When they found him, and realized that he had different things in mind than they did, they left him and his bride alone in a room and made to depart—but "No!" said the mother. "Will you not wait to see the bloody proof(1) with your own eyes?" The reason for this is that it is the general custom among Egyptians for a man to marry a woman without first keeping her company or finding out about her character; he just gives her a single look as she hands him a cup of coffee or a glass of sherbet in the presence of her mother. If she pleases him, he asks for her hand from her relatives; if not, he stops visiting them. Some of them marry without having ever seen their wives. This happens when a man sends his mother, or an elderly female relative or acquaintance, or a priest to her and these describe her to him according to their own taste and experience. Usually the girl's mother bribes the priest to give a good description of her daughter and so make the man want to marry her. Some will marry a woman who resides in some distant town, writing to one of his acquaintances in that area to ask him to send him a description in a letter, after which he asks God for guidance and inserts his head into the noose. Despite this, such couples live happy lives. In the Levant, the city people do as the Egyptians, but the people of the Mountain have a different custom. There the man can see the woman and find out about her character. This being 3.2.25

(1) *al-baṣīrah* ("the bloody proof") is "a quantity of blood used to track a game animal, or the blood of a virgin [when displayed on a sheet following her defloration by her husband]."

the case, and because the Fāriyāq had contravened the custom of Egypt by meeting with the girl on numerous occasions both in the presence and absence of her mother, the mother wanted to distance her from any shame by displaying the sign of her virginity, so that report of her daughter's innocence might be broadcast throughout the land.

3.2.26 Most people have nothing better to do than talk, and a band of these, once they had brought the bride and groom together, gathered behind the door, one or another of them keeping up a chant of "Open the door, bolt-holder!" The Fāriyāq thought that the person doing this wanted to come in to them and teach him how the thing should be done, so he opened the door to him, at which the other told him, "That's not the door I had in mind. I meant 'the door of relief.'" The Fāriyāq went back to his bride, but heard another saying, "Enter the dome, enterer!" and another, "Widen the wound, lancer!" and someone else, "Quench the thirsty one, quencher!" and another, "Away with the down, wool-carder!" and someone else, "Empty the bucket, water-drawer!", "Tread on fast, slippery-foot!", "Fill the milk-skin, skin-filler!", "Swizzle the swizzle stick in the kohl-pot, swizzler!", "Dive into the deep sea, diver!", "Crack the egg, egg-cracker!", "Polish the toothpick, polisher!", "Climb atop the wall, warrior!" and "Break in the filly, horseman!", and they kept this up until he had got it all the way in and handed her mother the bloody proof. At this their faces broke into smiles of joy and delight, hands clapped in pleasure and happy *expectation*, tongues proclaimed her innocence, and they ended it all with *congratulation*. Then they left, like raiders returning laden with *riches*, while the mother, at this manifest victory,[27] grew another six *inches*.

3.2.27 The Two Titter-Making Poems[28]

I was not the first lover among mankind
To pursue the object of his passion from both in front and behind,

Or to think, one day, that tears would be his helper and intercessor
Or, on another, to make a weeping man laugh,
Or to be felled by love, chattering and salivating,
Putting on airs, approaching, retiring,
Jumping, flirting, and courting,
Wrinkling his nose in disgust, snapping his fingers, making popping noises with his finger in his cheek,
Chanting, singing, and whistling,
Fluting, drumming, and piping,
Now yawning and stretching,
Now sticking out his chest or creeping close to the ground.
Should such a one be confronted with a well-guided opinion, he
Ambles and delays its implementation
For passion outwits one's wits and turns the lover from right judgment
Leaving him to lose his mind and caper madly.
I used to be amazed when they said, "A jinni-possessed poet"[29] and think it was a lie
Till I met my two little friends[30]—
Who then turned out to be fashioned of clay.
Beauty has been created as a paradise for the crazed lover's eye 3.2.28
And for his heart a fire that makes him burn yet fiercer.
Small wonder then that the face of him who loves
Should turn red and suffer its passion as though flayed.
Would that man, one day, might be rendered capable of dispensing
With women as something to be sold or bought!
Would that beauty in them were like salt
In the food pots that makes one vomit if there is too much!
Nay more—would that they had been created the ugliest thing to be seen
That we might not wander love-smitten, confused, not knowing which to choose!

tazabbub ("chattering and salivating") means "talking too much" (synonym *tazbīb*) and *tazabbaba famuhu* means "the saliva collected in the sides of his mouth"; *takassus* means "affectedness."

Would that the perky-breasted ones were droopy-dugged! How excellent then in appearance
(We crying, "Oh no! What horror"!) would the long-uddered be!
Would that this slim one were as squat as a box
And this big-buttocked one had no tush at all, that we might find delight in sleep!
Would that these huge eyes were narrow and the well-strung
Pearls in her mouth had turned yellow!
Would that each plump shank were
A prickly artichoke stem, or thinner yet and more shrunken!
Would that a shining forehead with, above it,
Hair like night had never struck, like an unsheathed sword, any tyro who rushed into peril!

a *dirdiḥah* is "a woman whose height and breadth are equal"; a *dahsā'* is a woman who is large-buttocked; a *falḥasah* is "a woman . . . with small buttocks."

3.2.29 Would that any length of neck might appear to our eyes
Short, and something abominable!
By beauty itself I swear, ugliness is comelier in a countenance
Since what is seen of it does not make the eye weep!
For what reason are our minds and hearts
Preoccupied with the love of plump and easygoing maidens above all else,
And why have they, before all others, been blessed
With every precious thing and every proud adornment?
By what right have they set themselves above men in their insolence
When they are beneath them, whether on their fronts or their backs,
And how long must the bull camels be patient,
When the doings of these beauties exceed all bounds, confusing the steadfast?
They came out of us, yet send us out of our minds
When they go in or out—how foolish would be any who disputes that!
And why should redress not be demanded of one
Whose glance has split the heart of the love-sick in twain?

And why is it permitted to sip the saliva from
The mouth of the sweet-mouthed, dry-cunted woman, when it makes you drunk
And wherefore should the woman comely of body and color glory in a sword blow
To the head that, morning and evening, lays passion bare?
Ask her, "Does the oven burn hot as it should 3.2.30
Each month, or is it late some months?"[31]
Where are the high deeds and noble acts? Where is he who
Will bring pride to mankind through his glory and show his strength?
The name of the pretty, smooth, young girl, should it be mentioned to him, takes command of him
Willingly or unwillingly, though he could defeat an army,
And though she belch poisonous fumes for an hour in his face,
He will say, "I am intoxicated with ambergris!"
The grown man may fall in love and then be sent mad by
Wind from the lovely one that permeates his nostrils.
Had He-of-the-Two-Horns[32] gone along with her wiles,
He would have found a third horn added to the other two.
Were it not for women, you would not see any man accused of sin
Or declared a fool, a lecher, a rake,
Or a bankrupt, nor would any be paraded on a donkey or accused of impotence
Or of being a wittol or be taken around on a donkey with bells on or be held up to blame
Or be love-sick or love-crazed or love-wasted
Or beaten to a pulp, or found fault with or made a spectacle of.
Skulls would not be seen scattered in the tumult 3.2.31
Neath the shoes of the horses as they strike fire from the helmets

tajbīh [verbal noun of *mujabbaban*, "paraded on a donkey"] means "painting the faces of the two adulterers red and mounting them on a camel or a donkey, each facing in the opposite direction, though, by analogy, they ought to be facing each other, since the word is derived from *tajbīh* [in the sense of 'brow-to-brow']"; *kashkhān* means "wittol" and *kashkhanahu* means "he said to him, 'You wittol!'"

Nor would nation-states crumble because of them—states that disported themselves
And then were visited by destruction by night and found themselves by morn beneath the sod.
The histories of nations long gone addressed me,
So I repeat the words of those who before me have written:
"Dear Lord, women charmed our minds;
Change then their charms into despised ugliness
Or make a film descend upon our eyes
Or, if not, then blind those who can see
Or grab us by our forelocks or castrate us or geld us
Or emasculate us (with amniotic fluid, naturally, to be more appropriate)."

3.2.32 THE SECOND

To whom should I complain, when my heart today
Is mine own enemy?
To whom should I complain, when my mind today
Is outwitted by my desires
And my eye has delivered my soul to perdition
And my own soul it is that brings me ill?
My reproachers are those who once,
Even when I was absent, were my friends.
My troubles are from my failure to reach
The full-bottomed ones among them.
Hopes never realized
Have destroyed all other hopes.
He[33] watched the fire of love flare up
To burn and sear
But what do I care for my loins,
That the fire should engulf them, or my cauls?
He says, "Death from intercourse
Though I live a life of destitution,

Is more pleasing to me than living
One day without penetration.
A life with one's semen trapped in one's loins is a gloomy one
And the murk may be cleared only by the exhausting of one's sperm."
No advice given him is of any effect 3.2.33
Even when accompanied by a pledge of safety.
Is there any who can judge between us
To read an official ruling?
His absences and his summonses of me
In my mornings and my evenings,
His anger and his beatings,
Are to humiliate and repel me.
Things have gone too far and now
I have no one to doctor me and my ills.
Thus my subjection to pain never ceases
Because of his fondness for doing me injury.
So do not let my satires, my eulogies,
And my praises distract you:
My head is at the beck and call
Of one who calls on me to relapse into my desires.
There is no hope for a spineless reprobate,
A slave to seduction.
If my neck is snapped by him, 3.2.34
Do not remonstrate, my friends, at my twitching like a slaughtered animal,
And if my head is broken by him,
Do not weep at the shedding of my blood.
If my teeth are crushed by him,
Do not pretend not to see the bruising on my lip.
If my eye is poked out by him,
Do not turn a blind eye to the fact that I have been blinded.
Providence of old has acted
To mislead me and make me miserable

For had it wished it could have kept me
Sound, and how well it could have done so!
Had it wished, it could have blinded me
To a fat-thighed, long-legged woman.
Let this passion distress me
And give me hope of being cured,
And let this love consume me
And do not care about my imminent perdition,
For these are my bones and this my skin,
This my nature and my condition.
3.2.35 None will come between me
And a desire that is in my guts
But one who is coarse and inquisitive,
Ignoble, evil, and a scandalmonger.
If I force you to listen to my complaints against the beloved,
Number me among the sheep
And do not spare my collar,
My robe, or my limbs,
For the dullard is he who
Hears someone reproach his beloved and turns away without remonstration,
While the noble man is he who
Voices a complaint after first saying something conciliatory.

3.2.36 The Songs

O Moon, you have no like
In your enchanting beauty
So have mercy on a lovelorn youth
Whose mind's confused.
Torment me as you will—
Only indifference do I fear.
My sufferings have lasted too long,
While you have forgotten about me.

You Yūsuf of beauty
  (May you be spared the prison!)[34]
You have demolished the foundations
  Of my hopes with sadness.
Who is it who has made it attractive to you
  To repel any who love you?
This suitor's eye is weeping,
  His body worn out.
For how long this avoidance,
  This fending off, this deprivation?
Beauty without charity
  Is like irrigation by mirage.
Your passionate lover 3.2.37
  Is bereaved of your acceptance.
Would that I might have an understanding of what
  My censurers accuse me of.
Sleeplessness has wasted my body
  And passion has been hard on me.
I have no goal, no goal at all
  But you, you precious one,
You enchanter of lovers
  With looks and glances.
Blessed be the Creator,
  The guardian of your beauty.
I would give my money, my soul, and
  My family as ransom for you.
Your acceptance is dearer to me than
  Living a long life.

Another 3.2.38

My eye sees none like you,
  Rashā,[35] so have mercy on the one you have slain!
All that is desired is your greeting,
  And then, should you wish, your favor.

Everything about you's charming—
  My liver's wounded by it.
My eye, faithful unto death, offers itself at your tomb as ransom—
  And the love that's in it is true.
You, O Moon, are toying with me,
  While I am seared by your avoidance.
Any who's once tasted your love
  Will never again taste sleep by night.
O Rashā, who brushes me off out of coquetry
  (All the answer I got was, "No no!"),
Speak to your slave
  And respect the Almighty!
I give you my enslavement and abjection
  And my insane love, the origin of my going astray.
Would that another might want you,
  That he might be eaten away by avoidance like me.
3.2.39 I have grown tired of your abandonment—
  Would that I might of my longing!
I ever keep my pledge to you
  But you pay no heed to yours to me.
If there is to be union, tell me when.
  In you alone I put my trust.
I ask God that you may live long
  And that is my dearest wish.
O King of All Beauty,
  The slave offers up a request—
Call him one day your serving boy,
  If you should ever chance to think of him.
Long have I stood waiting at your door—
  A glance from you is all I ask.
He who one day sees your figure,
  Is lost thenceforth in love and grows thin.
My full moon is indeed a gazelle,
  What captivates me in him is his coquetry.

O you who reprove me, reproach me not!
Verily, love is sanctioned by religion.

ANOTHER 3.2.40

A tryst would be my physician,
O you who've captured my heart,
And love has been my fate,
From the day I became intoxicated.
In my grief's A complaint,
should you take pity.
O twin of the graceful tree trunk,
Why all this scorn?
O Yūsuf of Beauty,
Love is hard.
You lisp coquettishly when you speak.
You're a wonder to behold.
Should you inquire of my state,
Even your reproach would be of help,
But if you continue to toy with me,
That will be of no benefit as a cure.
From bearing your rejections
I have become as I am now.
From the postponement of your promises,
My body has been worn out.
My tears are my witness,
As is my preoccupation.
There is no escape
From the rule of love.
My abuser took pity on me
When he visited me on my sickbed
And my keening rose high
From what had oppressed me.

Your morning-bright face
Led me further astray.
You most beautiful of the charmers,
Grant me a meeting!
Command what you will,
You'll find me obedient.
You'll find me his willing ransom,
So far as I am able.
My passion has been set ablaze
By your amazing looks.
My body has been emaciated
By your saying no.
Any who have experienced what I have,
Will know my story.
My only portion of you
Is promises.
Enough of this rejection,
O source of my choking agony!
By you alone
Am I afflicted.

3.2.41 Another

O lazy-lidded one, what came over you
To give the cold shoulder to a lover of your beauty?
O ben tree trunk, what made you turn
From one besotted who hopes for union with you?
Torture as you wish, my gazelle,
Except with coldness (that thing that makes the reprovers gloat).
May the Good Lord make my mind happy one day through union with you!
May the Good Lord make your mind happy as long as you live!
Why give me the cold shoulder, when I have done you no wrong,
And my heart from your love has never turned?

By Him who has granted you everything you want,
Let me kiss, if but once, the hem of your robe!
I have no more stamina to bear your rejection
And this longing of mine has lost patience with you.
I have no desire for any but you
And will my eye ever behold your like?
You deprived my eye of sleep by night
And I said, "I am content, hoping that he will be too."
I wonder, is your rejection of me imposed upon you?
But who, O Rashā, can have given you a ruling to kill me?
I implore you (and may God obtain for me my solace!)
Be a companion to me, O hoped-for one!
What you can see of my thinness is enough,
May the Lord of the Throne protect you from such a thing!

ANOTHER 3.2.42

O Moon, tell me,
This abandonment of me,
Were you seduced into it,
Or is it your own wish?
Grant me a tryst,
O ben tree branch!
You'll be rewarded for it
Or for the intention at least.
All that is hoped for
Is to see you one day
For love has reached
A state of tribulation.
Fear no reprover
Among those who have misled you.
They are but commanders
To injury.

Grant me joy,
May God grant you the same,
You with the
Flirtatious eyelids!
I shall be made well,
May you be ever well,
For I suffer pains
In the innermost recesses of my soul.
You have risen above all mankind
By virtue of what you possess
Of tresses
Like a princess's.
He desires,
That slave whom you've taken prisoner
With your coquetry,
A close proximity.
For how much longer this temporizing
Without a lover's union?
It is not what's desired,
This way of behaving.
These acts,
O You of the Mole,
O You Who Command Passion,
Are death for me.
You are the one desired
Among all mankind.
There is none who is your equal
Among humanity.
Where is Su'ād[36]
Among the beauteous?
You are an angel
Or a houri.

Another

3.2.43

Come hither, Moon!
You are my desire.
All have garnered acceptance
From you except for me.
O you who bewitched me
With your coyness as you strut,
And distressed me
As you passed with glance askance,
Your blooming countenance
Has filled me with longing
And my love has led me
To the point of death.
Whene'er I encounter you
Turning from me
I feel my love growing
But my body turns sick.
O dark-lipped one,
Till when will you show no consent?
Reward one who loves you
On whom you have imposed this emaciation.
Glory to Him
Who gave you this beauty unequaled!
(How many an ardent lover has he enchanted
Who has been brought low by his love!)
You are the beauteous,
And the longing in my heart increases,
Grief has weakened us
To the bone.
I have paid the cost
For this passion with the dire blows of love
That you might grant me my request,
But how unlikely is that fulfillment!

Will not some friend,
One who will see that I gain the rights
That love has decreed,
Help me attain my desire?
O Moon, do not
Listen to the reprover's words
But observe loyalty.
Let it be enough that my ardor kills me!
You exceed all people
In beauty, so exceed them too in granting boons.
Bestow wine From thy mouth,
O you whose fruits are sweet!

3.2.44 Another

If love's ways confuse you,
Don't open to it your door.
Don't fill your days with it,
Lest it impose on you grief and care.
I came to passion without dissimulation
And drank of its cups one after another.
What I tasted of its bitter aloes
Induced me to taste no other flavor.
Passion has a point at which it starts
But you will not find its end.
It makes the suitor taste sleeplessness
And wears through the skin and the bone.
O you who have branded my heart
With the fiery mark of this coquetry and pride,
If you will not hear out my reproach,
To whom can I complain of my disease?
It has made an end of me, what I experience
Of longing that burns.
My soul and body have been given to ransom you
So be, for once, to me a peacemaker.

You have gone to excess in cold-shouldering me 3.2.45
And put love in charge of my affair.
And now, by God, I know not
If it be magic or a dream
That you might cure a sick man
Who seeks his well-being from you
And put out the fires of love.
So say, "Be extinguished!" and take whatever you wish.
The one whom you've made heartsick, O love,
Is patient now and has no heart
And tears are poured out for you
So that their water may be irrigated with your mouth.

Another 3.2.46

My bird! None other!
I cannot do without him for an hour.
O people of goodwill,
Please scare off him who would scare it.
My tears pour forth
And the fire of my longing cannot be hidden.
I have a heart
That makes obeisance to love.
I am the one mad with love,
Going all day without the love of the well-proportioned,
My night spent in waking,
My eyes not closing for an hour.
I complain of my devotion
But you add only more rejection.
Take pity on a slave
Whose pains you have made diverse!
I have no patience
And how can I have patience, O moon,
When this coldness
Has hurt my greedy soul?

Rejection has gone too far
And nothing cures burning love
Like forgetting
But my soul is near to death.
Separation has shown me
The varieties of grief and demise
And my passion for the beauteous one
Is above my capacity to bear.
Continued rejection
Has reduced the wasted lover to indignity
And grace of form
Creates in him his desires.

3.2.47 Another

Did my tribulation not continue,
You'd not be hearing my complaint
And he'd not know my weeping place—
He who abuses me in love.
You have multiplied your rejections of me,
You who fail to keep your promises to me.
You have not observed your pledges to me
And have not asked me how I fare.
You turned from me in pride
When to grant me union would have been proper.
I have quite run out of patience
From the excess of what has struck me.
You loaded me with heavy burdens
And were happy to think no more about me.
Tell me "Yes!" or "No no!"
For prevarication has worn me out.
You of unique beauty,
You full moon, make me well!
You have given my censurers reasons to gloat.
Have not my sufferings been enough?

Glory to Him who created 3.2.48
  This most marvelous visage
And placed beauty in its entirety
  In your bewitching eye.
Love is an abasement
  That makes bodies grow thin.
No one would choose it
  Did he not suffer from it.
My lord, O my lord!
  O object of my desire!
Take unto you none but me
  And do not forget me for another!

Chapter 3

Contagion

3.3.1 It has been stated previously, in the first *maqāmah*,[37] that the contagion of evil spreads more widely than that of good and that one man with mange may infect a whole city while a healthy man will infect none of his neighbors, and the same is true of disorders of the brain and the heart. The proof of this, as they claim, is that the brains of teachers of small children go soft and their judgment turns foolish because they spend too much time in their company and mix with them too much. The same goes for those who spend too much time mixing with women—their hearts grow soft and their natures effeminate and they are stripped of that audacity and courage that mark the more exasperated among us.

3.3.2 I know many of my race who have lived among the Franks but have become no more refined in nature as a result of that contact, or it was their vices that they picked up, not their virtues. One such will not rise from the board without first wiping the plate he's been eating from so clean that it needs no washing, or enter an assembly, without bowing to one of its sides and letting rip a fart, as loud as any donkey's, that echoes round the chamber, which he will then try to atone for by saying "*Scusi*!" (meaning "Excuse me!"). Another will wear those special Frankish shoes and walk in them all over your special Arab cushions, or will wear his hair loose like a woman's and the moment he takes his seat in the assembly pull off his hat and sit there sending the scurf flying over your lap. Another, if he finds himself in an assembly among his brethren, acquaintances, and others and notices two men of letters engaged in a contest or telling curious anecdotes, will start whistling, but a mongrel, off-key whistle that is neither honest-to-goodness Frankish—given that he won't have lived among those people long enough to master that noble art—nor authentic Arab. Another, on sitting down, will stretch out his legs, thrusting the soles of his feet toward the face of the person sitting with him.[38] Another will come to pay you a visit and glance every little while at his watch to show that he's an extremely busy man with lots of things to attend to, despite which he'll stay with you until he sees you nodding off or sees you've gone and gotten your pillow and said, "May your sick friend get well!" as al-Akhfash did to those who visited him when he was ill.

At the same time, there's no denying that the Franks have numerous good qualities. <u>One</u> is that they consider it shameful to borrow furniture, pots and pans, books, and other things. <u>Another</u> is that if a friend visits one of them and sees that he's busy, he turns on his heel and goes back where he came from and doesn't sit and wait for him to finish what he's working on; indeed, even if he finds that he's free, he spends as little time sitting with him as possible, and if he sees notebooks or papers on the table, doesn't snatch them up so as to read them and discover their contents. <u>Another</u> is that if one of them who has a visitor has a sick child or his wife has just given birth or has fallen ill, he won't leave the patient and sit with his visitor to exchange pointless courtesies and gossip. <u>Another</u> is that a Frank won't marry a woman unless he has first seen her and kept her company and that they kiss women's hands and the faces of their daughters and see no disgrace or disrespect in that. Also, no meal-scrounger,(1) sponger who attaches himself to invited guests, or guest who invites other guests exists among them and none of them says to his friend, "Lend me your handkerchief so I can blow my nose in it" or "Lend me your clyster syringe so I can give myself an enema." 3.3.3

(1) [An *awshan* is] "A man who goes to a man, sits with him, and eats his food."

Another is how easygoing they are on authors and how ready they are to put up with their ignorance and mistakes and attribute them to absent-mindedness or exoticism. They do not, for example, find fault with someone if he says, *Fulān shamma l-narjisa wa-ḥabaq* ("So-and-so smelled narcissi and farted") or *ḥabaqa wa-shamma l-narjis* ("He farted and smelled narcissi") or *shamma fa-ḥabaq* ("He smelled and farted") or . . . *thumma ḥabaq* (". . . and then farted"),[39] though our authors would not allow this.

3.3.4 An acquaintance of mine from the Syrian lands once wrote a book in English about conditions there and the ways of their people. After first describing a wedding he had attended in Damascus, he stated that they had concluded the celebrations with a song he could still remember word for word and which he had kindly decided to translate into the aforementioned language. In fact, it was a funeral lament for a woman, of which I recall two verses, as follows:[40]

By God, O grave, have her charms been quite expunged,
  Her verdant features all undone?
O grave, you are no garden or celestial sphere,
  So how can flower and moon in you be gathered as one?

Despite this, the English put his account down to exoticism and none of them held him to account by asking, "How can the people of Damascus, who are described as being of sound taste and upright nature, conclude their nuptials with laments that make one weep?" Had he, however, given this version of his in Arabic and had it reached the ears of Arabic speakers, they would have convened two assemblies, one for the common people and another for the elite.[41]

3.3.5 At the one for the common people, someone would have said, "My my, a lament at the end of a wedding, brother? Listen, everyone, and wonder at what a clever transmitter of poetry[42] he is!" The next would have said, "Yes, indeed! A lament instead of a song! Did you ever hear such a thing, good people?" Then someone else would have said, "Heavens to Betsy! Couldn't the simpleton find anything better than a lament to put at the end of the wedding?"

and another, "I find myself quite gobsmacked! Could anything be sillier than the wedding guests finishing off their party with a lament and not seeing any ill omen in that?" and a third, "God bless this transmitter's pointy little head! Is he a fool or a madman to tell such lies to those people and fill his book with stuff and nonsense?" and yet another, "Good Lord! I swear this is the strangest thing I ever heard—people using lamentation in place of singing, weeping in place of laughter, and smacks to the back of the neck[43] in place of handshakes." Then, though, someone else would say, "But the ones who read his book must have been asses or lunatics! Wasn't there anyone among them to tell him (if he was a Christian), 'Khawājā!' or (if he was a Muslim, or passing himself off as one), 'Effendi! The people of your country follow omens and are quick to see evil portents. It's not possible they'd use a lament at a wedding,'" and another, "Glory be! He's a donkey and he's made a fool of other donkeys. Brother, let's forget about him," and another, "Amazing! We'd love to know the whole story. Was he serious or joking?" To this another would respond, "How could he have been joking? What he'd printed as a book was going to be sold in shops, with a picture of him on it holding a sword with tassels and buttons," and another, "Which leads us to ask, 'How could the English swallow everything vomited down their throats by a stranger holding a sword with tassels and buttons?'" and another, "I suspect that all Franks believe cock-and-bull stories," and another, "Brother, that's another story entirely! What all this business comes down to is a bit of foolishness from the transmitter and a bit of stupidity from his listeners"—and so on and so forth by way of criticism and faultfinding.

In the elite assembly, however, the matter would have taken a 3.3.6
more portentous and dangerous turn. They would have looked at it from the perspective of the scholarly fatwa and the jurisprudential responsum. The most important man of letters at the gathering would have been asked to issue a ruling with the words, "What says the leader of the *literati* and crown of the *illuminati* of an author who has claimed that the people of Syria employ laments to conclude

their nuptials? Should such a man be considered a credible witness, or not?" Responsum: "In our opinion, such a man shouldn't be considered a credible witness regarding the tail of a *hinny*, even if every copy of his book were sold among the Franks for a golden *guinea*." Another Form of Request for a Ruling: "What says the compilers' *resource* and authors' *recourse* of a man who claims that he heard with his own two ears a lament being sung at the conclusion of a wedding in Noble Syria? Are his words to be believed and is his book to be licensed for perusal or not?" Responsum: "He is not to be believed nor is anything he may have seen with his two eyes, by day or by *night*, nor may aught he has heard with his two ears, be they long as a donkey's, be considered *right*." Another Request for a Ruling: "What says he whose words banish *delusion* and bring clarity to *confusion* of a writer who has put into a book he has written numerous accounts that he claims are his own(1) and stories of bastard origins that he claims are authentic, and asserts, in everything he's written, that the people of Syria chant laments at the conclusion of their nuptials? Should his entire book be judged on the basis of this lie, or not?" Responsum: "Anyone who lies about a matter as well-known as this is likely to lie about everything else, so it would be more appropriate to judge his whole book on the basis of that one lie."

(1) *hadhāhidh* [from which the author derives the adjective *hadhāhidhiyyah* ("[accounts] that he claims to be his own")] are men who say of everyone they see that he belongs to them, or is one of their servants.

3.3.7 Another Request for a Ruling: "What says the critic most *eminent*, of people of good sense the *referent*, of a man who has written a book in which he states that he knows many emirs and ministers, judges and *scholars*, and says they are his friends and intimates, in-laws and *brothers*, and then states somewhere in the same book that he attended a wedding in Protected Damascus that was adorned with *flowers* and sweet-smelling *bowers*, songstresses and songsters, and that the last thing they sang there was a lament for a woman? Supposing this to be a lie, should the fact that he is acquainted with ministers argue for our believing him on other matters?" Responsum: "He is truthful in neither that nor other matters, and his acquaintance with emirs cannot be allowed to argue on his behalf for anything, as witness the verses that state

No claim of acquaintance with notable or prince
Can save the mendacious transmitter."

Another Request for a Ruling: "What says he over whose words no other words can claim *superiority* and without whom no matter can be settled with *authority* of a man of aspect *refined* and pantaloons that are big both in front and *behind* who has written a book in which he included what he saw and heard in his own land, including his statement that he's seen a bride being promenaded while a lament for a woman was chanted before her? Does his refinement of aspect provide a basis for the acceptance of his report?" Responsum: "Reporting has nothing to do with refinement of aspect and his clothing cannot be taken as a basis for information on either the dead or the living, as witness the verse that states: 3.3.8

Not his finery, nor even his drawers, when he opes his mouth or pens a line,
Can save the mendacious transmitter."

Another Request for a Ruling: "What says the reference of all *humanity*, may the All-Knowing King treat him with *magnanimity*, of a man believed and credited on every important matter by those of non-Arab *race*, a man who delights the eyes of their women as they gaze at the whiskers on his *face*, his pantaloons and *gewgaws*, his frowns and gaping smiles, his floppiness and *hee-haws*, who then clasps them in his *claws* and makes them through passion and love his *cat's-paws*, a man who's written a book about his (which is to say, our) country in which he has put all that may beguile the said women and *please*, allure them and their instincts *tease*, among said things being that he witnessed a noble nuptial and party well-*attended*, adorned with brilliant lights, glowing faces, tasty dishes, wholesome drinks, and plants sweet-*scented*, and that, just as they set off to take the bride to her groom in *procession* and faces lit with 3.3.9

anticipation at the impending opening of her *lock*, suddenly there appeared chanteurs and chanteuses, singers and songstresses the bride's way to *block*, on their faces the lineaments of mourning *austere*, and launched into a long lament, for a woman who'd been dead for many a *year*? Should his description be allowed to pass the *test* and should his clasping of the non-Arabs to his *breast*, his lusting after them like a bitch in *heat*, his partisanship of them and throwing of himself in sworn alliance at their *feet*, his *anterior* and his *posterior*,[44] be allowed to put in a good word for him?" Responsum: "No credence can be given his words when they're *fake*, even if he has as many non-Arab cronies as he has hairs on his *nape*, as witness the verse that states

> No partisans among the non-Arabs, who know not what drivel he spouts,
> Can save the mendacious transmitter."

All this is despite the fact that the author's words contain nothing so injurious to his countrymen that it calls for any to take sides against him, for the worst that can be said of him is that he attributed to them an inappropriate act. Such, however, is their custom in fault-finding and scarce an author escapes their attentions.

3.3.10 If, on the other hand, the writer of the book in question were to tell the English that the men in his country wore palm fiber and fronds while the women adorned themselves with bits of earthenware and potsherds, could speak with their mouths closed, see with their eyes shut, and hear with their ears stopped, that they slept for an hour in the middle of the morning, half an hour at noon, an hour and a quarter in the afternoon, one and three quarter hours in the evening, and two hours and forty minutes at night, they would accept it from him as an example of exoticism.

3.3.11 To this category (that is, of a person's adopting the blameworthy rather than the praiseworthy characteristics of his fellows) belonged the display of the "bloody proof," meaning the evidence of virginity mentioned above, for it is a contagion that has spread to the Christians of the Levant from the Jews, following the precepts stated in their books. Despite this, the latter race has many virtues for which it has been known from time immemorial until now. Among these is their knowledge of how to amass money and gems and their practice of such refined and gentle professions as money changing, coin testing, moneylending, and the dyeing of old clothes to look like new. Another is that they love one another so much that the stranger among them who belongs to their race never has to ask for alms from anyone else and never needs fear indigence or that he will end up eating roots so long as he is in their care, or that he will have to become a flatterer and prostitute his honor to outsiders. On the contrary, he finds a warm welcome in any land in which he may take up residence and in which his people are to be found. Among their virtues too is that they have come up with a language[45] that they use to express anything that may cross their minds in the realm of daily affairs, and that there is no difference between a Jew from the furthest west and another from the further east[46] in morals, conditions, customs, or opinion.

In this they differ from the Christians, for if an oriental Christian goes to a land of the occidental Christians, the first greeting he'll meet with from them after they set eyes on him will be, "He's a Jew"or "a Turk." Furthermore, if he needs a place to stay or some food from them, they'll hand him over to the head of the police station, who will hold him in a place without light or air until the judge can decide what to do with him—as happened this year to the emir of al-Quffah,[47] who came from Dayr al-Qamar to Paris: though well provided for and visiting their country simply for the pleasure of observing them, he was cheated by some, tricked by others, robbed by a third set, and lost the shirt off his back at cards to a fourth, so that he returned to his country plucked and flayed. 3.3.12

How, in this case,[48] did the Christians of the east come to abandon all these good qualities that characterize the Jews, only to acquire from them the one trait that brings with it only grief and envy? Is it acceptable for the rich man of any sect to take his gold 3.3.13

coins in his hands and toy with them before the eyes of the homeless pauper when the latter doesn't own a fingernail clipping? Or for the well-fed to wave his bowl of pottage in the face of the man ravaged by hunger? If you say that this display is natural and for the most part the only people who see it are already married, so no envy is involved, I reply that if the custom were natural, we'd find that all nations practice it, but in fact the Franks to whom we have been referring, who are the most knowledgeable and informed as to the natural sciences, do not. On the contrary, they condemn those who do so and say that "testing for *virginity* leads largely to *sterility*."(1)[49] I'd also point out that as soon as one of their bridegrooms feels that slackly tied knot around his neck, he takes his bride to a place where they can be alone and none of God's creatures can see him, to avoid any cause for *jealousy* (of which perturbation and sorrow are ever the *legacy*) for they do not see why one man's pleasure should be a cause of unhappiness in others. I say "slackly tied" because among them the knot of marriage may be undone with the greatest of ease.

(1) *ʿuqr* [in the first sense] is "the exploration of a woman to see if she be a virgin or not."

3.3.14 As for your statement that the mark, being seen only by married men, provides no occasion for envy, this is what someone would say who seeks to deceive, equivocate, or outwit or who (please don't be offended) has neither penetration[50] nor experience. All scholars—the pauper and the starveling, the beggar and the down-at-heel, the naked and the tatterdemalion, the jailed and the shackled, the accused and the condemned—agree that the married man has a more envious eye than the bachelor. The reason is that everyone thinks that anyone who practices the same calling as he must be better-off than he is and can think only of the other's greater fortune, ignoring any hardships he may suffer. Given too that the night of the consummation of a marriage is a brilliant affair however dark, it has to be an occasion for the inspiration of envy in the breast of any who has lived through the same experience, while distracting him from the remembrance of what comes after. As the proverb says, "If you want to know what to expect, ask one who has had the experience."

With this in mind, I beg the gracious pardon of your most honorable eminence, our grandest guarantor of what is right, our prized High Priest, for what I wish to ask you (by way of enquiry, not criticism), to wit: "How can you know, O you of penetration, that this 'bloody proof' with which the handkerchief is stained and which is raised like a flag to announce the girl's virginity is in fact a sign of virginity? Is it not possible that, on the night the wedding was consummated, the baker's oven flared up, the heated pot boiled over,[51] or that this had happened previously and some spots had remained and it was with these that the handkerchief was embellished, or that the man, if it was he who had already plucked that rose, had cut the throat of a sparrow or cut one of his fingers, or that the girl had kept a little blood in one of those caskets of theirs? Were you to reply that in the latter case the man would discover this by virtue of his greater experience, I would say, 'By my life and that of your father, this is not a time of keeping his wits about him and rational *thought* but of being knocked off his rocker and becoming *distraught*, especially if there's a group behind the door insisting and *clamoring*, urging him on and *yammering*! Answer me that! I await your *reply*, bring it you to me from far or from *nigh*.'" 3.3.15

Chapter 4

Analepsis

3.4.1 It is the custom of my fellow writers sometimes to go back and leap over a period of time and connect an event that happened before it to an event that happened after it. This is called analepsis (*tawriyah*), that is, "taking backward" (*warāʾ*). They may also start by mentioning everything about the protagonist from his first whisperings into his beloved's ear until his reappearance as a married man. In the course of this, the author will relate such long and tedious matters as how his face paled and his pulse raced when he met her, how he was reduced to a tizzy and felt ill while he waited for her answer, how he sent her an old woman or a missive, how he met with her at such and such a time and place, and how she changed color when he spoke to her of the bed, of drawing her close, of embracing, of leg over leg, of kissing, of kissing tongue to tongue, of intercourse, and the like.

3.4.2 Sometimes the same writers make rude insinuations about the mother and father too, often stating plainly that the mother is content for her daughter to be a source of discord among those who lay eyes on her and allows her free rein to flirt with a passel of men so she can share some of them with her. Likewise, that the father, given that his mind is in his wife's lap, not in his own head, is powerless to prevent such goings-on and that the servants all connive with the wife against the husband—the females because they seek to imitate their mistress's way of doing things and the males because they want her. All in all, they turn the house of the girl being courted into an alehouse, a brothel, a den of iniquity, and a spawning ground for every sort of corruption, trickery, and wile. Each of these fellow authors of mine comes up with a device off the top of his head and then attributes its invention to someone else.

The leap backwards is acceptable, in my opinion, if the author finds himself faced with a block to composition; afterwards, he can return to what he was about. But leading the man to his bride's bed and then shutting the book on the couple without peeping through the crack in the door to find out how they fared next I cannot accept; I have to know what happened to them after the wedding. Many women who were reckoned females before assuming that noble station turn into men, just as men turn into women. I have therefore decided to follow the Fāriyāq more closely after his marriage than I did before it, for talk of two invites more admiration than talk of just one. Chasing after low matters, digging up dirt, and pursuing trivial affairs are not, however, my way. Allow me then, my dear sir, and permit me, my dear madam, to make use of "the leap" and say, 3.4.3

During the time when the Fāriyāq was caught in the noose of love but before he got married, one of the Bag-men had invited him to the Island of the Foul of Breath[52]—meaning that island whose inhabitants speak a mephitic tongue—to take over the post of dream interpreter[53] at a wage higher than that which he received from the Bag-man in Cairo. He determined to undertake the voyage and informed his fiancée of this a while before the wedding. She said, "So be it. A husband has the right to take his wife with him wherever he wills, and every spot on earth should be for her, in his company, a home and a homeland." Then he informed her mother of the same and she agreed. 3.4.4

When the day appointed for the wedding arrived and the knot had been tied, the Fāriyāq said to his wife, "Now we must make ready for the voyage, for the Bag-man's dreams are multiplying in his head and he's afraid they'll get away from him before they can be 3.4.5

interpreted." She replied, "Are you really serious? Is it the custom for women to travel immediately following their marriage, exposing themselves to barrenness and danger? Are we not exempted, here in Cairo, from the need to be strangers and voyagers? How am I to leave my brothers and my parents and go to a land in which I have no friends or intimates?" "I haven't presented you with a surprise, or told you anything different from what I told you before," he replied. "I didn't know about marriage then," she answered, "what I know now. People likened it to the smelling salts the physician gives a sleeper or a drunk to make him wake. Now I realize that women were not created for travel but travel for them." "I promised the man that I would go to him," he said, "so I must fulfill my promise. The proverb says that a man is tied by his tongue,[54] not his horn. Moreover, this Bag-man of ours will be traveling with us along with his wife, so you're just like her." She said, "I am not like the Bag-man's wife, for I am newly inducted and in the limbo between virginity and marriage, and I have yet to grow tired of land that I should go to sea." When her mother heard this, she insisted that she travel, so she said, "Let me then consult a doctor and find out if travel by sea is injurious to the newly wedded woman or not."

3.4.6 A doctor was brought who, when he heard what she had to say, laughed and said, "You eastern Christians make pledges to churches in the hope that the patron saint will grant you pregnancy or a cure from some illness. Here we make pledges to the sea, for when our women despair of getting pregnant, they make for the back of that Friend of God[55] and beseech his blessing. Some of them return pregnant with a single child and some bear twins, especially if the ship's captain has a soft spot for women and can provide them with the food they desire" (at which the Fāriyāq said to himself, "God grant that the captain of our ship be ill-humored, ill-tempered, ill-affected, ill-natured, ill-disposed, and irascible!"). When his wife heard what the doctor had to say, her fears abated and she took to the idea of travel, so they got together their provisions and made the journey to Alexandria.

To travel from Būlāq by bark is one of the greatest pleasures a person can enjoy. The Nile is calm and the captain of the bark stops in front of each village to take on supplies of chickens, fresh fruit, milk, eggs, and other things, not to mention that the water of the Nile is sweet and good for the health. Thus the passenger on such a bark spends the whole day happily eating and taking pleasure at the sight of the greenness of the countryside and the fertility of the villages. He may even hope that the journey will be prolonged, despite being engaged on an important mission. On this occasion, then, the Fāriyāq took full advantage of this opportunity and assiduously devoted himself to "the two sweetest things,"[56] forgetting about Cairo and its pleasures, its luxuries and its baths, its eye diseases and its pestilences, its books and their shaykhs, its saddlebags and their Arabic-murdering owners, its offices and their drainpipes, the tambour and its strings, the donkey and its flight, the doctor and his obscenity, the miracle man and his insanity, the prince and his smell, and the plague and its evil effects, and he continued in that fashion till he reached Alexandria fed and watered, having taken on supplies sufficient to the needs of his looming idleness at sea. He had triumphed and succeeded—and with what triumph and what success![57] 3.4.7

Chapter 5

Travel, and the Correction of a Common Misconception

3.5.1 The Bag-man who was the Fāriyāq's traveling companion had sent a letter from Cairo to some acquaintances of his in Alexandria asking them to prepare lodging for them, and after reaching that city they spent some time there awaiting the arrival of the "fire-ship"[58] that went to the island, all eating at one table and discussing baggish business, the forthcoming voyage, and so on. Now the Fāriyāq's wife was familiar with nothing but her parents' house and spoke of nothing but things that had happened between her and her mother, or her mother and the maid, or the last and the other two, and if she were telling the story of how, for example, the maid had gone to the market to buy something, she would divide each sentence from the next with a long laugh, so that it would take as much time for her to tell the tale as it had taken the maid to go to the market and back.

3.5.2 The reason for this was that the girls of Cairo and Damascus know no company but that of servants and members of their family, and their mothers explain to them nothing of the affairs of the world for fear that the scales will fall from their eyes and that they will work out what it is that is going to be required of them. As a result, the sum total of what they know comes exclusively from the maids, and these believe that they are bound to do very well for themselves if they give the girls news of things they like and are attracted to. Thus if one of them sees, for example, a comely young man, she goes directly to the girl and tells her, "Today, my lady, I saw a handsome, charming young man who's just the thing for you, and when he saw me, he stopped and looked at me hard as though he wanted to speak to me, and I think he's found out that you're my mistress, so the next time I see him, I'll speak to him" and similar stuff that will make the girl her ally should the mother ever be angry with her.

Now it is no secret that if girls do not know how to read and write or hold their own in conversation, or the conventions of the polite gathering, the dining table, and so on, they will inevitably compensate for that ignorance by acquiring a knowledge of stratagems and wiles so that they can deploy these to get what they want. If girls were to busy themselves with the study of a certain art or in reading useful books, it would divert them from dreaming up tricks. If, on the other hand, they have nothing to do but keep to the house, where no one is to be found except the maid, they will single-mindedly focus their thoughts and desires on how to use her as a tool and a support, for she has greater credibility in their eyes than do their mothers. 3.5.3

In my humble opinion, then, it would be better to keep girls busy with a beneficial art or science, either theoretical or practical. Do you not see that it is in the nature of the female to love the male just as it is in the nature of the male to love the female? It follows that girls' ignorance of the world is no obstacle to their finding out about men and studying their ways. Indeed, such ignorance may result in girls becoming infatuated with them and submitting to them without regard for the consequences. Were they, on the other hand, to be raised so as to acquire good qualities and the knowledge appropriate to them, they would, under such circumstances, obtain whatever knowledge of men they might through observation and reflection. 3.5.4

And there is another point, too, to wit: that if women discover for themselves that they are men's equals in understanding and knowledge, they will use this knowledge as a shield against them and deploy it to make themselves unassailable when men treat them 3.5.5

without due respect. Indeed, men themselves will recognize their worth and refrain from overstepping the bounds of decent behavior with them. For instance, if a young man meets with a girl in private and the youth is well-read and informed while the girl knows only how to talk about clothes and makeup and going on picnics, the young man will quickly violate the canon of good manners, because he will believe she has been placed in this world simply to give him what he wants of her. Were he, on the other hand, to see that she has opinions that are *intelligent* and can make points that are *pertinent*, ideas that are *apposite* and an understanding of matters both distant and *proximate*, can hold her own in conversation and come up with a ready answer, has objections to raise and arguments with which to dispute, he will hold her in awe and respect her. What I am saying here does not contradict what I said in "Angering Women Who Dart Sideways Looks, and Claws like Hooks";[59] it all comes down to the means by which knowledge is imparted. The whole point of this digression was to say that, even though the Fāriyāq's wife had picked up little information about men and women, she showed, by standing up to her mother when the social good of marriage clashed with the social evil of the Fāriyāq's baggishness, that she could strike down any *argument* and silence any *combatant*. In other ways, however, she remained ignorant.

3.5.6 One day, for example, when the Fāriyāq was at table, the Bag-man informed him that the "fire-ship" had arrived and urged him to get ready to leave. Hearing mention of the "fire-ship," the Fāriyāq's wife asked, "What's that?" to which the Bag-man replied that it was a ship made with planks and nails but moved by the power of steam, generated by fire. "And where's the fire?" she asked. "In a furnace on board," he replied. "Goodness gracious!" she said, "How can I travel in a ship with a furnace and expose myself to fire? Isn't the voyage from here to the island going to be in a bark like our voyage from Būlāq?" "A bark won't do for the open sea," he replied. "As far as I'm concerned," she then said, "I'm not going. Let those go who want to get burned." The Bag-man and his wife pleaded with her but she was adamant. When the time came to sleep, she lay down in the bed and turned her face to the wall.

And this is the purpose of this chapter—to alert people to the fact that this is one of those customs whose practice people misunderstand, since there is nothing in the backside to indicate anger. On the contrary, the locus of the latter is the front side. If a woman faces her husband when she lies down and scowls at his face, wrinkles her brow, sticks her nose in the air, blocks her nostrils, and closes her eyes so that she cannot smell his smell or see his ugly countenance, or covers both mouth and nostrils with her hands, her sleeve, or a handkerchief, that is a sign of anger, but when she turns her backside to him, there is nothing to indicate that. Were you to tell me that if she faced him she still might faint at his breath because the foul smell would inevitably penetrate her nostrils even if they were blocked, from which it follows that she has no alternative but to turn her backside to him, I would reply that in that case it would be better for her to lie flat on her stomach, thus avoiding unpleasantness altogether. 3.5.7

To proceed: the backside is one of those things that people have gone to great lengths to exalt, magnify, and aggrandize both materially and immaterially. On the material side, they use padding, wadding, stuffing, packing, pillows, cushions, supports, bolsters, and bustles to lure the hearts of onlookers and fascinate the minds of suitors. How, one must ask, can one and the same thing be used as a means to contentment and ire at one and the same time? It is a blatant contradiction. On the immaterial side, scholars, litterateurs, and our masters the poets never stop singing its praises and competing in descriptions of its breadth and capacity, one of them going so far as to say 3.5.8

Who has seen the like of my beloved?
She's like a full moon should it appear.
Her waist comes in today,
A day later her rear.

while ʿAmr ibn Kulthūm spoke of

> A rump that the door's too narrow to admit,
> And a waist that's driven me insane!

Here one must point out that the poet describes the waist simply as a cause of his madness and any implication that it is slender is based on the fact that it drives people insane, since it, like the rump, is not actually visible. The same implicit understanding should preferably be applied to all parts of the body, since had he said "a rump that has driven me insane," it would be self-evident that it fills the door with some left over. I would also very much like to know whether the *al-*[60] preceding the word *bāb* ("door") is generic or referential[61] and whether Imam al-Zawzanī[62] devoted any attention to the elucidation of this matter.

3.5.9 One of the things that most exercises a woman's mind and keeps her from sleeping at night is how, through exaltation of that high and elevated place, she may charm any who see her. She may even be so taken up with it that she's distracted from paying attention to her face and the rest of her body and leave them unadorned. Though her face grow gaunt and the plumpness of her body dissipate with sickness or old age, thus reducing her dependence on her charms, she will still depend on and maintain that, since it is, for her, the capital she uses to attract and arouse desire. There isn't a woman who doesn't wish she had an eye in the back of her head so that she could keep it under perpetual observation and maintenance. She may think nothing of standing for an hour, walking for two, or dancing for three but will not sit down for an instant for fear lest it be roughened or squashed, and should she, when walking or dancing, look over her shoulder, it is to draw attention to what lies behind it. Her voluptuous gait and the swinging of her hips are the most entangling snare in which a man's heart may find itself caught and she walks that way because she knows that the Divine Wisdom has designed things, from before the beginning of time, so that the greatest quantity of flesh and fat (in terms of the rest of the body, not of butchers' shops) should be in that spot, thus making it an attraction for kings and sultans, emirs and judges, imams and priests, as well as rabbis, mages, sages, scholars, rhetoricians, preachers, men of letters, poets, apothecaries, pharmacists, players of musical instruments, and everyone else—not so that they can make kabobs of its flesh or cooking grease of its fat or light lamps with it or use its skin to make a tabla,(1) but as a means to delight their eyes and bring joy to their hearts (for a man's eye, despite its small size,[63] is never satisfied, even when filled with something a thousand times larger and broader than itself) and as a sign to them that all their wisdom in this world, all their refinement and pride and glory, though they be higher than cloud-scraping peaks or lofty mountains, are still lower than the foothills of that place.

(1) The *kūbah* ("tabla") is "a small, waisted drum"; it may be what the common people call a *darabukkah*.

The woman well knows, too, that should you, for example, seat 3.5.10 one of the aforementioned great and good before a public convenience(2) that has been placed on a gilded dais over which you have previously raised a silver-coated, decorated, embellished, engraved, and ornamented dome draped with silk and brocade and wreathed with flowers and sweet-smelling herbs, he would scorn to stay there half an hour, whereas he would never scorn to stay next to that lofty structure night and day, without interruption, head bare, hair disheveled, feet naked, mouth open, tongue lolling, spittle dribbling, eyes staring, tail between legs, arms extended, neck twisted, ears pricked, and generally in the vilest shape one can imagine for a person of standing. Things would reach such a point that, should he hear a peep from that place, he'd think the sultan must have sent him an orchestra to congratulate him on such a terrific triumph and comprehensive conquest and imagine that the lute would never have acquired the most plangent sound of all instruments had it not been fashioned in the likeness of a half of that place, and that had it been formed from both halves together it would be heard to speak Arabic complete with grammatical

(2) *manāṣiʿ* are "places in which people seclude themselves to urinate or defecate."

endings; likewise, that the dome takes its shape from it and from it ambergris derives its smell, that the Arabs were so enamored of it that they added the letters of its name to six-letter verbs, which indicate a request for an action or that a thing is considered to possess a certain quality,[64] that all the breadth of a man's chest and all the width of his back are worth nothing compared to the breadth of that thing, that when big-buttocked women press eminent princes with their requests, the princes are brought low, that that posterior sack, whether it be "bearing," as some poets would have it,[65] or "borne," as in reality it is, is no more of a burden to the one who lifts it than a purseful of gold, that it is the hottest of all the parts of the body in the winter, when it needs no heating, and the coolest in the summer, that being the first part of the body to touch the ground on sitting, it is always smoother than the cheeks and the sides of the neck below the ears, which is why the ʿUdhrī kisser finds more pleasure in kissing it than he does in kissing the chin, nose, eye, or forehead, that in common parlance people give it the names of kings and *sultans*, men of power and eminence, and leading *imams*, and that for some (forgive me, Lord!) the Most Beauteous Names[66] are as nothing before it, albeit their daily magnificat is to chant, "O Lord, glorious be thy name!"

3.5.11 Well too she knows that many a beast is more intelligent than any human or enjoys a happier state by virtue of instinct, for the male among the dumb beasts is aroused by two lumps of flesh on his female, even though they encompass both front and back,[67] only at a known season, while that animal that has been endowed with the power of speech is in a permanent state of arousal over them, frothing and foaming, groaning and moaning, bellowing and whinnying, glugging and gurgling, roaring, driveling, screaming, and drooling, and sometimes going insane as well, for no better reason than a delusion on his part that, being butts, they will help him to pierce the bull's-eye with his arrow from the front, or what would be the point of all this insanity? Indeed, she knows too that that spot, despite its being located in the lower confines of the body, is vertically aligned with the head, implying that its low placement in no way detracts from its worth or dignity. Even were it to be imagined that it was placed at the level of the feet, it would retain that status and be regarded with exactly the same respect. Some women think it better to bare it than to bare their mouths, for the former is less likely to do harm than the latter, since to this day no one is known to have been killed by anything escaping unexpectedly from the backside whereas slips of the tongue that have resulted in deaths are too numerous to be counted. Based on this, they make a point of going out on windy days, which, in their view, are holy holidays. Some of them think that the backside is worthy of being hung with jewelry, made up, and painted, whether openly or under wraps. As a certain connoisseur of backsides has said,

O you who ask what part's prettiest
In a girl who's cute and plump,
Our master has passed this down to us:
"One half of all beauty is found in the rump."

The reason for this is that it comes in so many shapes and sizes. Thus, if you consider the shape of the underside of the single buttock(1) it will look to you like a cone, while if you think of it as being twinned with its partner it will look to you like a semicircle, or a crescent. However, if you trace it from the tip of the coccyx to the opposite end of one side of the continuous crack, you will observe what is level, or flat, and should you do the same from the same place to a less distant point, you will find yourself presented with a dome and a curve, and if you consider it when the person is lying on their stomach, you will find yourself confronted with what is concave,[68] and so it continues. No other part of the body has so many shapes. I declare: how exciting are the lines of that celebrated man of letters Shaykh Nāṣīf al-Yāzijī, that go 3.5.12

(1) N.b. After writing this book, I saw in Ibn Khālawayh the Grammarian's work *Laysa* that the two buttocks together may be referred to as *al-ṣawmaʿatān* ("the monk's cells") or *al-ṣawfaqatān* (?),[69] a usage overlooked by the author of the *Qāmūs*.

And her buttocks heaved like waves, leaving the lover
To drown where the billows clash!

3.5.13 In addition, it would seem from the presence in this magnificent language of ours of the word *mirfad*,[70] as well as from the statement by the author of the *Qāmūs* that "the *mukhaddam* is the cord of the drawers at the lowest part of a woman's leg," that the garments of the Arab women of ancient times were like those of the women of Syria now, though perhaps these garments were peculiar to the women of the cities—although on the other hand al-Mutanabbī's words "I abstain from what is in the drawers" suggest that they were in general use, based on the fact that it was desert girls that he was wooing, as indicated by his words, quoted above, "*In the desert* there's a beauty that needs no importing." In the *Qāmūs* the author says, "*Al-dubr* and *al-dubur* are 'the opposite of *al-qubl*' and mean 'the afterpart or back part of anything'... or the anus, or the back."

3.5.14 I would add that the names of the letters making up this word have their own meanings and, no matter how you switch them around, they'll give you a new meaning each time.[71] Similarly, if you combine each two letters of the word, they add up, according to their numerical values,[72] to even numbers, in allusion to the paired nature of the two sides, while again the two "*u*"s imply ponderousness and gravity[73]—the entry on this word in the *Qāmūs* is one of the richest in that work. Whether the coining of the word occurred posterior to that of *mu'akhkhar* ("posterior") or anterior to that, and whether it is derived from the idiom "I came to you *at the end of the month* (*dubura l-shahr*)" or vice versa,[74] are open questions; what is clear is that the abstract and the figurative derive from the concrete, leaving for debate the question of its derivation from "the afterpart of anything."[75] In the Qur'ān one finds "they [would certainly] turn their backs."[76] Metropolitan Atanāsiyūs al-Tutūnjī, in *Al-Ḥakākah fī l-rakākah*, denies this.[77] Know too that the Arabs compiled some ninety terms for the backside, divided among names, nicknames, and epithets. Some of these appeared above in "Raising a Storm."[78]

Epithets include Umm Suwayd, Umm al-ʿIzm, and Umm Khinnawr,[79] and had they not held it in the same esteem as they did lions, swords, and wine in terms of doughtiness, fatal impact, and ability to intoxicate, they would not have coined epithets to describe it.[80]

Irrelevant here is what that Bedouin said of the cat: "God damn the animal! Lots of names and a low price." We would claim that the low price of that animal (a function of its large numbers) does not reflect poorly on its value or virtues and that the multiplicity of its names is simply a matter of piling like on like in order to achieve some resemblance to a possessor of Umm Suwayd,[81] from the perspective that the cat is a highly fertile animal and it is in its nature to play and fight, though this often results in scratching and bleeding, or gashing and sudden death, or gnashing of teeth and blinding. Also, it is so good at surviving accidents and injury that it is said to have seven lives. There is no height too high for it to ascend and no abyss too deep for it to descend. If it smells food that it likes, it will climb the highest wall and insert itself into the narrowest space to carry it off. If a hand passes over it, it sticks up its tail and produces a snoring and a susurration that express the pleasure it derives from being touched. Also natural to it are cleanliness and its way of eating secretly and shyly, or as though frightened. 3.5.15

If you refuse—as has been your wont from the start of this book—to leave anything uncontested you say, "How is it, if the giving of names depends on the respect accorded to or the usefulness of the thing named, that there are so many words for disasters and old women and so few for the sun and the moon?" I will respond, "The large number of words for old women is related to the fact that they were once young girls, or that they may be used as a means to get hold of one.[82] As far as disasters are concerned, it's because they create fear, and respect may result from fear as it may from tender affection. The sun and the moon do have a large number of names, but these are not well-known among us. This is not the first unfair accusation that people have leveled against the language, as I have demonstrated in another book."[83] 3.5.16

3.5.17 Here is the full list—to which I have devoted considerable research—of names and characteristics that have been invented to describe a woman possessed of a "Mother of a Little Black Thing": *al-athīnah* ("the luxuriantly growing"), *al-khabandāh* ("the fat and full"), *al-rājiḥ* and *al-rajāḥ* ("the weighed down"), *al-radāḥ* ("the heavy-thighed"), *al-dulaḥah* ("the fattily fleshed"), *al-habyar* ("the one whose buttocks are so fat that she runs out of breath when she walks"), *al-shawtarah* ("the big-buttocked"), *al-ʿajizah* ("the large-buttocked"), *al-ʿajzāʾ* ("the mightily buttocked"), *al-muʿajjazah* ("the huge-buttocked"), *al-dahās* and *al-dahsāʾ* ("the mightily buttocked"), *al-bawṣāʾ* ("the mightily buttocked"), *al-laffāʾ* ("the huge-thighed"), *al-rakrākah* ("the mightily thighed and buttocked"), *al-zakzākah* ("the large-buttocked"), *al-wakwākah* ("the mightily buttocked"), *al-ḍibrik* ("the massively thighed"), *al-ḍunʾak* ("the firm-fleshed and tendonous"), *al-ʿaḍannak* ("the huge-thighed, the meeting point of whose thighs has become constricted due to her plumpness"), *al-warkāʾ* and *al-warkānah* ("the large-rumped"), *al-thaqāl* ("the well-rumped"), *al-jazlah* ("the massively buttocked"), *al-sajlāʾ* ("the massively uddered"),[84] *al-mikfāl* (the well rumped), *al-hirkawlah* ("possessed of haunches that quiver"), *al-muʾakkimah* ("the massively posteriored"), and *al-alyā* and *al-alyānah* ("the large-buttocked"). Curiously, the author of the *Qāmūs* mentions *astah* and *sutāhī* ("a man who has, or is seeking, a large backside") but fails to vouchsafe us their feminine forms, so I note them here, with his permission. Further examples are: *nufuj al-ḥaqībah* ("huge-haunched and -buttocked"), *dhāt al-ahdāf* ("she of the shooting butts"), *dhāt al-taʾkīm* ("she of the thick buttocks"), *dhāt al-raḍrāḍ* ("she of the quaking buttocks"), all with reference to "women with big buttocks" (*niswah bilākh*); *balkhāʾ* is also used,[85] even though al-Fīrūzābādī mentions it only in the sense of "stupid."

3.5.18 The above are in addition to words that give direct expression to this joy and happiness, such as[86]

jaʿbāʾ,	"huge and large"	
jalanbāʾ,	"fat"; synonyms *khunḍubah, khaḍʿabah, kabkābah, ḥawthāʾ, waʿthah*	
khidabbah,	"huge"	
dikhdibah,	"firm"	
sarhabah,	"immense"	
ṭubākhiyyah,	"fleshy"	
lubākhiyyah,	"well fleshed"; synonym *diʿkāyah*	
mubarnadah,	"well fleshed"; similarly, *hudkūrah*	
thaʾdah	sturdily built and "well fleshed"	
thahmad,	"fat and large"	
rajrājah,	a woman whose flesh quivers upon her	3.5.19
ḍamʿaj,	"a perfect, huge woman"	
baydaḥ,	"corpulent"; synonym *baldaḥ*	
daḥūḥ,	"large"	
dumluḥah,	"huge and full-bodied"	
ṣaldaḥah,	"broad"	
baydakhah,	"full-bodied"	
murmūrah,	"with skin that is smooth and flesh that quivers"	
dakhūṣ,	"full of fat"	
raḍrāḍah,	"having flesh that quivers upon her"	
biliz,	"huge or light"	3.5.20
daḥmalah,	"huge and full-bodied"	
dumaḥilah,	"fat and comely of physique"	
rabilah,	"massively thighed"	
qiṣāf,	"huge"	
muzannarah,	"tall and large-bodied"	
mulaʿʿaẓah,	"well built, tall, and fat"	
haykalah,	"huge"	
ḍunʾakah,	"firm-fleshed and tendonous"	
kināz,	"with much flesh, and solid"	
munizzah,	"hard and tight"	3.5.21
mulazzazah,	"well knit and vigorous"	

khanḍarif,	"huge and fleshy with large breasts"
qahbalis,	"huge"
shakhīṣah,	"immense"
dayyāṣah,	"well fleshed and short"
ʿānik,	"fat"
ʿabīlah,	"massive"
maʾlah,	"fat and huge"
warihah,	one says "the woman became *warihah*" meaning "her body fat increased"
khaẓiyah baẓiyah,	"fat and plump"

and others too many to cite. Does "His Honor Our Lord the Most Excellent" judge or "Our Venerated" emir have half as many names and sobriquets? This ends our demonstration of the misconception regarding the practice of this custom.[87]

3.5.22 Now I declare: the next morning, once the aforementioned business of the backside-turning had taken its course, the Fāriyāq beseeched her to travel, supported in this by the Bag-man and his wife, all of them promising her she would see marvels on the island that would make her forget the unpleasantness of separation from her loved ones. With God's help and His intervention for a happy outcome, she agreed, and they set off on the "fire-ship." The Almighty also was kind enough to harden the heart of the captain against her: every time he heard her moan with pain he would get angry, mutter to himself, and damn the eyes of women and their traveling. Among the servants, however, there was a comely young man who tried to take his place, though he failed to do so because of the shortness of the distance, which was on the order of five days (enough, on land, to seduce five girls, ten grown women, and fifteen widows). Then they reached the island's quarantine, where they stayed for thirty days, after which they entered the town, each family taking lodgings appropriate to its situation.

Chapter 6

A Banquet and Various Kinds of Hot Sauce

The Fāriyāq and his wife now set about exploring the streets of the city,[88] dressed in the costume of the people of Egypt. He was wearing wide drawers, whose bottoms wrapped themselves around him in front and in back as he walked. She had enveloped herself in a white woolen hooded cloak so as to cover her sleeves, which otherwise would have swept the ground. The passersby and shopkeepers were amazed by them and didn't know whether his wife was a woman or not, some asking, "Is it a man or a woman?", some following along behind them, some touching their clothes and staring into their faces and saying, "We never saw the like of this day—something that's neither a man nor a woman!" One of the more intelligent English *faqīh*s, whose name was Steven,[89] happened to run across them; having looked hard at their faces and worked out that the Fāriyāq was a man and the Fāriyāqiyyah a woman, he went up to them and said, "You, Man, and you, Woman, will you have lunch at my house next Sunday?" "How very kind of you!" they replied. "My house," he said, "is in Across the Sea,[90] at such and such a place. Come in the morning before lunch." 3.6.1

On Sunday, they took a skiff and set off for his house, where they found him about to go out, for it seems he wanted to bring a few of his acquaintances to gawp at his guests. Apparently he then got drunk on the road or at his friends' house and he never came back. 3.6.2

When he saw them, he told them, "I have to go and see to some business but here's my wife and these are my daughters, so make yourselves at home with them till I come back and then we can all have lunch together." "By all means!" they said. Then they sat down with his wife. In the sitting room was a young Englishman who was whispering sweet nothings into the ear of one of the daughters of the English *faraḍī* and holding her hand. Then he started kissing her in front of her mother and the visitors. The Fāriyāq's face turned yellow, his wife's turned red, and the mother beamed. "How," said the Fāriyāqiyyah to her husband, "can this young man kiss the girl and not be embarrassed by our presence?" He replied, "Kissing isn't considered shameful by the Franks. Among them, a visitor is obliged, when he enters the house of a friend, to kiss the man's wife and all his daughters, especially if it's a holiday; this is despite the fact that 'to kiss' is sometimes used by them to mean what follows. Such, though, is their custom." "But," she asked, "isn't he embarrassed by us, given that we are strangers?" "If a thing is permitted," he replied, "it is permitted before kinsman and stranger alike. Or it may be that the man thinks we are ignorant of this practice in our country."

3.6.3 "Who could be so ignorant as to believe that?" she asked. "Kissing among us is always accompanied by panting, sighing, sucking, smelling, and closing of the eyes. But this fellow seems to me to be doing no more than delivering a light puff of breath, devoid of any feeling, as one might if one had no regard for the matter at hand." "I find in the Qāmūs," he said, "that *mukāfaḥah, mulāghafah, muthāghamah, lathm, faghm, ka'm*, and *taqbīl* all mean a man's kissing a woman on the mouth, or doing so while simultaneously chewing on it." She said, "It makes no difference! The Arabs have set the standard for both orientation and osculation,[91] for to kiss the brow, as the Franks do, is meaningless. But why is the kissing of parts other than the mouth and the cheek devoid of the pleasure that the kisser experiences at those two spots?" "Because," he replied, "one who is thirsty cannot quench his thirst by planting his mouth at the top of the water pitcher or on its side." "Speaking of thirst," she then said, "why do the poets describe saliva sometimes as sweet and sometimes as thirst-quenching, which is a contradiction?" "Perhaps," he replied, "that should be considered one of the mysteries of poetry or one of the intricate issues involving women." "And speaking of mysteries and intricate issues," she said, "can the lover find pleasure in drinking salivary secretions from any part other than the mouth?" "Quite possibly, where some of the Arabs are concerned," he answered, "but the Franks object to doing so even from the mouth. Indeed, the only name they know for such things is 'spittle.'"

"Speaking of the different names for things," she said, "what 3.6.4
would one call this mother who is comfortable watching her daughter in such a state? Would one call her a procuress?" "'Procuring' may be used properly only of a man, if he procures for his womenfolk," he replied. "In fact," she replied, "it happens more often with mothers than with fathers, for mothers fill with happiness when they watch a man pay suit to one of their girls, because when a mother sees a suitor paying court to her daughter she imagines that whatever beauty he finds in the girl he must find in the mother, seeing that she's the original, and that he can hardly love the branch without feeling affection for its root."

They continued their conversation at length until it was noon, 3.6.5
when one of the *faraḍī*'s daughters came in, a piece of bread and a chunk of cheese in her hand, and started eating where she stood. Then she turned around and brought another and did the same. The aforementioned *faqīh* had seven daughters and a number of boys. When it was two o'clock, the mother said to the guests, "You must be feeling hungry, for it is past noon and my husband is late." "Let us wait," they said, "until he comes." At five, the dinner bell was rung to gather the scattered children of the house, as is the custom with English parents. An hour passed, the bell was rung again, and the hours continued to pass until it was eleven o'clock, during which time the mother would visit the kitchen and the girls whisper to one

another in secret as though the same downfall had befallen them as befell the Barāmikah.[92] The Fāriyāq told his wife, "If we don't leave now, we won't find a skiff or anywhere suitable to spend the night in this 'Across.'" So they got up, said good night to the mistress of the house, boarded a skiff, and at midnight re-entered the town, where they ate in a restaurant, having a dinner that was also a lunch.

3.6.6 A few days later, the Fāriyāq's wife said to him, "I have seen strange things in this town." "What were they?" he asked. "I see that no hair sprouts on the faces of the men here, and that they have no shame." "Explain!" he said. She said, "I haven't seen a beard or a mustache on the face of a single one. Are all of them then beardless?" "What you do not know," he said, "is that they shave their faces every day with a razor." "Why?" she asked. "To please their women," he replied, "for they like a smooth, clean cheek." "On the contrary," she said. "A woman derives her pleasure in a man from all the things that point to his manliness, and a profusion of hair on the face of a man is the equivalent of its absence on the face of a woman." "And what," he asked, "did you mean by saying that they have no shame? Did one of them ask something indecent of you?" "That has yet to happen," she replied, "but I note that they wear their drawers so tight that their private parts are on display at the back." "And that," he responded, "is something that should please women, according to your statement." "Indeed," she replied, "such a costume is more pleasing to the eye than that worn by the Arabs. It shows off the thighs, the calves, the stomach, and the buttocks. However, going too far in such tightness is an offense to decency for those who are not accustomed to it, albeit at the same time handsomer and more captivating. But be that as it may, what is going on with those priests? I see that they go to even greater excess than the common people with those short breeches of theirs, which is inappropriate to their station. Even uglier is their shaving of their mustaches, though the mustache is an adornment to the face of a young man just as the beard is to that of an older man. What has seduced them into adopting this custom, when they don't marry and don't have to please their womenfolk? I swear, were one of them to go to Egypt, the people would think he was one of those effeminates called *khawals*[93] who pluck the hair from their faces and remove it from their bodies in imitation of women, and may God bring disgrace to any man who behaves effeminately!" To which he added, "And every woman who behaves masculinely!" "Indeed," said she, "and any person who practices evil customs! Observe how custom here has made the shaving of the hair a mark of bounty and perfection when, to us, it is a sign of deficiency and corruption."

"You're right," he said, "but I'd like to ask you about something, 3.6.7
now that the conversation has come around to what men want from women and women from men. Since you've started to develop an understanding of these differences, tell me by the roof (for it was his custom, whenever he asked her about something important, to make her swear by the roof to which she had climbed before they got married) and tell me true, is the pleasure a woman gets when she looks at a man's body equal to a man's when he looks at a woman's?" "They're the same," she said, "or perhaps the former is the greater." The Fāriyāq went on,[94] "Then I said, 'How can that be when there is no softness or smoothness to a man's body while a woman is distinguished by numerous charms that are absent in a man, such as softness of skin, fineness of digit, shapeliness of finger and fingertip (these being likened to the *ʿiswaddah*,(1) to *asārīʿ*, to the *ʿudhfūṭ*, and to the *ʿanam* tree), the quality called *dasʿ*, softness of the *kaʿs*, the *dakhīṣ*, and the *rawājib*, and the way the flesh covers the *rawāhish*

(1) "'The *ʿiswaddah*: "a small white creature to which virgins' fingers are likened"; *asārīʿ*: "white worms with red heads that live in the sand in a valley known as al-Ẓaby; singular *usrūʿ*'"; the *ʿudhfūṭ*: "a smooth white creature to which girls' digits are likened"; the *ʿanam*: "a tree of the Hejaz that has a red fruit to which stained fingers are likened"; *dasʿ*: "the hiding of the sinew by flesh"; the *kaʿs*: "the bones of the phalanges or the bones of the finger joints"; the *dakhīṣ*: "the flesh of the inside of the hand"; the *rawājib*: "the joints of the roots of the digits, or their backs"; the *rawāhish*: "the veins of the visible part of the hand"; *ʿursh*: "the top of the foot between the prominent bones and the digits"; *ʿasīb*: "the top of the foot; also the coccyx"; *mafāhir*: "the flesh of the chest"; *ʿaṭaf*: "length of eyelash"; *ḥārr*: "nose hair"; *rayash*: "ear hair"; *ghafar*: "neck and nape hair"; *surbah*: "the hair from the middle of the chest to the belly"; *daʾḍ*: "fatness and fullness and the absence of any blemish on the skin."[95]

so that a dimple appears on each knuckle; or softness of hand, smallness and suppleness of foot, fullness of wrist and heel and flatness of instep, smoothness of *ʿursh* and of *ʿasīb*, strength of arm and comely largeness of calf, massiveness of calf muscle and roundedness of kneecap, hugeness of haunch, posterior, thigh, backside, and belly; or narrowness of waist, grace of shoulder, declivity of flank, and glossiness of clavicle, breast, and *mafāhir*; or as length of neck, *ʿaṭaf*, broadness of brow and length of hair; or sweetness of voice and odor, absence of *ḥārr*, *rayash*, *ghafar*, and *surbah* and of hair on her mons veneris, her vagina, or her anus; or her ears being small, or cutesy-comely and tiny, or ornamented, or well-defined and pointy and pricked (and what a feast for the eye they are when the upper parts are hung with earrings!)?

3.6.8 "'Greater than all of this and more wonderful, however, is the protuberance of her two breasts and their perkiness,[96] their prominence and their pertness, their bulginess and their curviness, their roundness and their compactness, their firmness and their constrictedness, their massiveness and their glossiness, their creaminess and their smoothness, their convexity and their poutiness, their gibbosity and their slipperiness, their incrassation and their turgidness, their slickness and their sturdiness, their rotundity and their ampleness, their orbicularity and their curvaceousness, their resplendence and their fairness, their lustrousness and their silkiness, their curvature and their satininess, their bulbosity and their thrustingness, their tumescence and their sleekness, their heaviness and their bounciness, their globosity and their whiteness, their incandescence and their tremulousness, their fullness and their fatness, their solidity and their pearliness, their albescence and their sphericalness, their jerkiness and their crammed-togetherness, their curvity and their tightness, their suavity and their distendedness, their cleftness and their bustiness. They are known, among other things, as "the weights" because they can be weighed, either in the hand or in the mind. They are likened to pomegranates and to euphorbia fruit and their nipples are likened to *saʿdān* prickles.[97]

Now, it is also the case that. . . .' 'Stop now,' she said, 'for you have gone to excessive lengths in your description while failing to mention the best part of what they signify.' 'Pray tell!' said I. She continued, 'If you had cited a word that referred to gobbling on them or rubbing up against them, it would have served better than many of those adjectives.' 'That's not my fault,' I said. 'I failed to find any such pearl in the *Qāmūs*.'

3.6.9 "Then I went on, 'That's one thing, and another thing I'd like to ask you is why everyone finds it agreeable for a female to have a certain amount of soft hair or down on her face and particularly on her lip, while the hairless, the beardless, and the smooth-faced male are hated by God and man alike?' 'As for the first,' she said, 'it's because the woman, knowing that nothing in the world can take the place of a man for her, is inspired with longing for one by the slightest thing. Even if, after uttering in front of a woman the words *aʿūdhu bi-llāhi mina l-shayṭān* ("I seek refuge with God from the Devil"), for example, you start to say *ra* . . . , she will immediately start fantasizing about a man and straightaway blanch or blush, depending on the direction in which her thoughts have taken her.[98] The same will happen if you begin to pronounce *ra* . . . following the words *bi-smi llāh* ("In the name of God").' 'God bless you for a refined and honest woman!' said I. 'If such is your nature and its inborn disposition while still unformed, what will they be like when they mature?'

3.6.10 "Then she said, 'Concerning the good attributes to be found in the woman and not the man (according to your statement and that of the poets who write amatory verses to, and the painters who revel in the depiction of, the former), their absence in the man is no obstacle to his being loved. A woman knows that nothing but a man can bring her joy, so his presence in any shape or form inspires longing in her, as you mentioned earlier. Do you not observe that the women of the lands of the blacks love their menfolk more than women do their husbands in our and other countries? It's like the situation of a man who has lots of books containing different stories and anecdotes as compared to another who has only one to read.

You will notice that the man with many books will move from one to another and reach the last without anything having stuck in his mind and thereafter find the idea of rereading them distasteful. The man with only one book, on the other hand, knowing that he will find nothing else to read when he gets to the end of that, will not move on from a page he is reading until he has pondered it well, mulled over its meanings, committed it to memory, learned from it, scrutinized it, thought about it, absorbed it, weighed it, examined it, conned it, picked at it, finecombed it, and meditated upon it. I came up with this simile of the books because I've noticed how taken you are with reading, but I have lots of other examples too.

3.6.11 "'To proceed: a man has numerous charms that women do not. These include the breadth of his chest and of the pelt that's upon it, the height of his shoulders and capacity of his breast, the straightness of his legs and the thickness of his arms and the number of muscles in them, the massiveness of his hands and the fact of his being strong and hard,[99] stalwart and hearty, stalward and husky, stalworthy and strapping, stalworth, stout, and sturdy, stark and lusty, stith, stour, staunch and shredded, robustious, robustuous, rumbustious, robustic, wrast, mettlesome, doughty, puissant, potent, rugged, hale, flush, ripped, buff, diesel, beast, built, cut, jacked, yoked out, fine-looking, and loud-voiced.(1) All these attributes we women consider to be among men's charms, and he has other, intangible, good qualities too, such as when he climbs the pulpit, for example, to preach, or rides a fine horse, or bears arms—and how fine a figure a man cuts when he walks along, his sword grazing the ground!'

(1) A list of further synonyms for these words may be found at the end of the chapter.

3.6.12 "Then she said, 'If only I knew how to read and write, I'd write more books about men and women than did that shaykh whose name you once mentioned but which I've forgotten because he's dead on all the sciences put together.' 'That would be Imam al-Suyūṭī, God have mercy on his soul,' I said. 'Right,' she said, 'more than al-Suyūṭī and all the other suits too,' to which I responded, 'And all the sots as well.'[100] 'However,' she continued, 'it's all the fault of those who left me without an education. The Arabs claim that a knowledge of reading will corrupt women and that as soon as a woman is able to stick one character next to another, she'll spell out a letter to her lover. In fact, though, if left to her own devices, she will have in her shyness and sense of decency a minder stricter than any father or husband. If, on the other hand, she's penned in and cooped up, she'll keep trying to squirm out of and get away from the restrictions imposed upon her. It will be with her as it is with water, which becomes purer and more appetizing the faster it gushes and runs, or with a fast-walking person, who feels the air to be colder the faster he walks.' 'I swear they did the right thing!' I thought to myself. 'If she'd learned how to read and write, not one line of my poetry would have been left without her splitting it into hemistichs and inserting between them others of her own or building new stanzas based on what I've already written,[101] so as to twist it to her purposes. May God direct what she already knows to useful *ends*, and spare me the evil that any increase therein *attends*!'"

Postscript[102] on synonyms for "strong and vigorous" or "hard and tough," and other words of similar meaning: *ʿutʿut, kunbuth, kunduth, mikalth, milyath, maghith, ʿuḍāfij, ʿafḍaj, ʿullaj, hamarraj, ṣalawḍaḥ, ṣalanqaḥ, ṣamaḥmaḥ, ṣamaydaḥ, kirdiḥ, kaldiḥ, daḥūḥ, mujlandā, jalʿad, jalmad, ṣalkhad, ṣimqid, ḍahyad, ʿirbadd, ʿaṣlad, aqwad, dhifirr, dhimirr, dhaymurī, zibirr, zimirr, ṣamʿarī, ḍabīr, ḍibaṭr, ḍabaghṭarā, ʿayzār, ʿashanzar, qabaʿtharā, qunāṣir, kumātir, tiyazz, julabiz, julāfiz, khuzākhiz, turāmiz, dakhz, ḍubāriz, ʿaḍamazz, ʿilkiz, ʿalankaz, fiyazz, qilizz, kilizz, mulazzaz, ḥumāris, dakhnas, durāhis, dalahmas, mutashammis, ʿatras, ʿakandas, ʿamarras, qalammas, qunāʿis, hakallas, hamallas, furāfiṣ, kiyaṣṣ, mutakhammiṭ, ḍabanṭā, ḍifaṭṭ, ʿamallaṭ, muʿallaṭ, ḍalīʿ, ṣaniq, damakmak, ṣamakīk, ṣamallak, ʿabannak, ʿarik, janaʿdal, ḥuwwal, ʿarandal, ʿunthul, kamtal, kunbul, kanahdal, nabtal, buhṣum, dilaẓm, mirjam, ḍirghāmah, ʿardam, fayyim, qirshamm, hayzam, hayṣam.*

Chapter 7

That Stinging Sensation You Feel When You Get Hot Sauce up Your Nose

3.7.1 Our previous comments on the Fāriyāq, made at a time when he was single, were an intrusion; how much more so would they be now, when he's a husband? I think it better, therefore, to leave him now, in his married state (for this conversation of theirs took place at night, and there's no call for us to spoil the rest of it for them), until they awake and he goes to his Oneiromancer's Chamber, meaning the place appointed for him to interpret dreams. Your Eminence may likewise be ready, after suffering the stinging sensation induced by all that hot sauce, to go to bed. Rest a while, then, and if you dream tonight, tell your dream to the Fāriyāq, for he is now considered to be one of the world's great dream interpreters.

Chapter 8

Dreams

Behold the Fāriyāq, seated on a chair, in front of him a table bearing a large number of books, among them, for all the scraps of paper they contained, not a scrap of food,[103] in his fingers a long pen, and in his hands a pot containing ink as black as tar. He has started interpreting dreams seen by the head of the Chamber[104] in his sleep. 3.8.1

The First Dream. The aforementioned hag-ridden person beheld himself traveling to India, where he met upon the road a mare, getting on in years and with no saddle upon her. When the mare saw him, she approached him and stopped, whinnying. He went some steps beyond her and lo, she ran after him. Catching up with him, she stopped again, causing him to say to himself, "There is some mystery behind this mare. I shall take hold of her forelock that I may see what her matter may be." As soon as he laid his hand upon her, she lowered her head, as if to say, "Mount, and fear not the lack of a saddle!" so he mounted her, for he was fatigued with walking, and proceeded for a short distance. Suddenly, he found himself at a saddler's shop, so he got down from the mare and bought her a saddle. Then he remounted and proceeded down a thickly forested ravine and a branch trapped his head and prevented him from going further. He tried to move forward but could not and he did not want, for pity, to force the mare forward with his spurs, so he stopped and thought about all that had befallen him, wondering greatly. At that 3.8.2

moment, he happened to scratch his head, and lo, it had sprouted six horns, two in front (one on each temple), two in back, and two in the middle, and the branch in question was caught in them all. He managed to cut the branch off the tree, but it remained caught in the horns. He then proceeded in this state and all who saw him wondered at him and said, "Look at the six horns on the head of that man!" but he paid them no attention.

3.8.3 Eventually, he entered a dark and narrow place overlooked by rocks and boulders and four of the horns smashed against one of the rocks and broke and fell off, leaving him with only the two in front. One of these, however, now leaned toward the other, touching it, so that they rubbed and knocked against each other, and every time they knocked against one another they made a mighty sound, and people came from afar to behold him and gaze at him. Finding himself helpless before them and seeing that the crowd was preventing him from proceeding, he resolved to turn back, but the mare refused to let him do so and started bucking and bounding forward, and the more he kicked her with his leg to make her turn, the more she bucked and moved ahead. Wondering, he looked at her and lo, her color was no longer what it once had been, so he said to himself, "Maybe this is not the animal that I first mounted," and he got down to take a look at her teeth. When he tried to put his hand in her mouth, she reared up and knocked him over, giving him such a powerful wallop that he fainted. When the mare beheld him cast down and prostrate on the ground, she seemed to take pity on him and commenced to breathe into his nostrils and lick the place where the horns had broken off until he revived somewhat and started moaning and bellowing out prayers to God to rescue him from his plight. The mare indicated to him with her head that he should mount so that they might return by the road by which they had come and, gathering all his strength, he arose and mounted. When he reached the same thickly forested place, those same broken horns grew back and became as they had been, and he kept touching them with his hand as he proceeded.

When evening came, he alighted at an inn so as to spend the night there and ordered the innkeeper to take care of his mount and to bring both her and him dinner. When he awoke the next morning, he found that the saddle had been stolen and said to the innkeeper, "You lost my mare's saddle while it was in your keeping and I cannot easily ride her without it." "On the contrary," said the other, "your claim is false, for when you came, you were riding it bareback," and a quarrel broke out between them and they seized the front of each other's robes. When the man realized that he would receive no benefit from this, he decided to make the best of a bad job and go back and he went to the mare and mounted her and kept moving until the evening, when he found another inn on his road so he stayed the night there. When morning came, and he wanted to mount, he could not find the bridle, and things took their course with him and this innkeeper as they had with the other. Then he spent a third night in another place and in the morning he found that his mare had lost its tail, and so it continued: every night he spent in an inn, he lost another of the mare's limbs, so that he reached his city on foot, the mare having disappeared entirely. As for the horns, four vanished with the mare and the two in front remained. 3.8.4

The Interpretation 3.8.5

When this horny dream was thrown at the Fāriyāq, he set about playing with his mustache, as was his custom, rubbing his forehead, and pinching the place between his eyes, until he was guided to an understanding of its meaning, at which he wrote in the margin the following:

This is the interpretation offered by the humble slave named the Fāriyāq to the honorable and most excellent gentleman Flummox son of Lummox of the dream that he saw in his sleep. The mare stands for a woman. The walking and the fatigue stand for bachelorhood. The saddle stands for the woman's good manners and the bridle for her honor. The thickly forested place stands for the feasts, banquets, and visits that the married man is obliged against his 3.8.6

will to become involved in and into which he has to stick his head and that of his wife. The branch stands for certain of the invitees who get their claws into the wife. The horns stand for the married state existing between the man and the woman and their sprouting and their disappearance stand for the changing of that state and its return to how it was before. His staying at the inns stands for his traveling with his wife and the vanishing of the mare stands for his losing her. The rest of the dream is self-explanatory[105]—though God knows best.

3.8.7 After the master of the Chamber had taken the interpretation and examined it for a while, he returned to the Fāriyāq in haste, signs of anger on his face, and said, "Your interpretation is wrong on many points. Firstly, you express yourself briefly, in contrast to the custom of oneiromancers. Secondly, the mare cannot stand for a woman because among us the woman cannot be less than, which is to say under, the man; on the contrary, she is higher than he. Your interpretation has to be made in our terms, not those of your people. Thirdly, the bridle cannot stand for a woman's honor because the bridle is placed in the mouth and a woman's honor lies elsewhere. Now, though, you must set that aside and start on the interpretation of the second dream. Exert yourself, then, in writing and *expatiation*; haply you may hit the mark and gain heavenly *compensation*."

Chapter 9

The Second Dream

The master of the Oneiromancer's Chamber—may God prolong his *days*, exalt his standing among the hag-ridden and give it a *raise*—beheld in a dream one day that he had conceived the desire to write a sermon and read it out to the congregation on a feast day, so he took pen and paper and wrote a single letter and lo, he heard his wife calling to him from her room to help her put on her stockings, so he left his writing and hastened to her. After he had helped her to put on her stockings and returned, he saw that a second letter had been added to the first in an ink that was not his. "Who, I wonder," he said to himself, "entered my room and penned this letter, which fits what I wanted to say?" Then he took up the pen and wrote another letter and lo, he heard his wife calling to him to fasten the strap of her sandal, so he went to her and did what she asked of him and returned and found another letter had been added to the first three, thus completing the word. At this, his wonder grew. Then he took up his pen and wrote a whole word and lo, he heard his wife calling him once more to comb her *kuʿkubbah*,[106] which seems to mean (though only God knows for sure) the front part of her hair, so he went to her and combed it gently and smoothly and then went back and found that a whole word had been added to his word, complementing it. Then he took up his pen and wrote two words and lo, he heard his wife calling him to put up the hair at the back of her neck, 3.9.1

so he left his notebook and went, and when he returned he found two whole words. Once a line had completed itself, his wife called to him to tie on her bustle. When he returned, he found another whole line. He continued until, when he had finished a page, his wife called to him once more, and when he came back he found a second whole page, and when he had filled a quire, he found another quire, and so it continued until the whole notebook was full.

3.9.2 His wife having now completed the donning of her finery and her toilet, he carried the notebook to her and told her what had happened to him. She was overjoyed beyond description and told him, "All that was thanks to the service you did me and your help to me in getting dressed. You must continue, my dear, and be regular about so doing." The next day, he did as he had done the day before in terms of both writing and serving and it happened to him exactly as it had the first day, and both grew happier still. When it was the day of the feast, he climbed up to the pulpit and read out the first notebook, so astonishing his audience with his eloquence, the felicity of his wording, and the niceness of his choice of tropes that, when he was finished, the people set to congratulating him and saying to him, "Never have our ears been struck by words as eloquent as yours." "That," he told them, "is by the grace of the sandal strap," but they didn't understand. Then he returned to his house, happily uttering hallelujahs, and told his wife what had happened. "My advice to you, my dear," she said, "is to devote your efforts to serving and to writing, so that when you have fifty notebooks, we can make our way with them to some distant lands and read them there, for in this country you can only read a sermon on a feast day and the feasts here are few, and it would be a shame for these magnificent notebooks to go unread." "I was thinking the same thing myself," he said.

3.9.3 Then they prepared themselves to travel to certain Eastern lands, taking with them the notebooks, which filled precious teakwood chests on which they had spent a huge sum. When they reached those shores, they rented a spacious house overlooking verdant gardens and he sent a crier to cry through the markets, "Attend, good folk, the sermon of Master Flummox son of Lummox on such and such a day at such and such a time, that he may expose your ears to such elegant tropes as you have never heard before!" People then crowded in to hear him, drove after drove. When they had settled down in the gathering place, he ascended a staircase that had been set up for him there and opened up the first notebook that his own congregation had found so admirable and lo, it was erased, and contained nothing but the letters he had written with his own hand. He tried to link them up to extract from them some sort of meaning but could not do so, so he came down from the pulpit in embarrassment, and it was in that state that he woke from his sleep.

The Interpretation 3.9.4

This is the interpretation offered by the God-needy slave the Fāriyāq to Master Flummox son of Lummox: "The letters, words, lines, pages, quires, and volumes that you imagined had been added to your words and that your congregation admired will not work in countries other than your own because of their tie to the tying of the bustle and the sandal strap—though God knows best."

When these words reached the person in question, he burst in 3.9.5 upon the Fāriyāq, stamping the ground with his foot and sticking his nose in the air, and said, "This interpretation is more incorrect than the first and the expression is even more succinct. One can barely understand what you are saying, and if the interpretation of dreams is to be as mysterious and murky as the dreams themselves, there is no call to employ oneiromancers and put people to the trouble of reading the incomprehensible." The Fāriyāq responded, "This is how it is done in our country, which is the fountainhead of dreams and the font of dream interpretation, for your heads derived this feature from our heads and ours only, and were it not for us, you wouldn't have been capable of dreaming a single dream all your life long." At this, the man appeared to come to his senses and he calmed down. Then he said, "You have one dream left now and here it is."

Chapter 10

The Third Dream

3.10.1 The master of the Oneiromancer's Chamber—may God prolong his tenure as spokesman for all *hag-ridden dreamers* and realize his dreams along with those of other *high achievers*—saw one day in a dream that a tall staircase consisting of a hundred steps had been set up for him so that he could climb it and preach to the congregation from the top. After he'd shaved his beard and mustache and donned his stair-climbing clothes, he dispatched someone to gather the faithful in an appointed place and all had been informed as to this in advance and gone there before him, while he tarried a while waiting for his wife to get out of bed so that he might wipe her nose[107] and embrace her before setting off. Having done so, he took his notebook under his arm and took off at a run in the direction of that mighty assembly, looking neither right nor left.

3.10.2 When he reached the place and saw that the staircase was set up and the people gathered around it, he was beside himself with joy and said to himself, "This is an opportunity such as Fate has granted to no other. Today I shall send these folk back to their homes with hearts like mine and morals like mine. Should I never perform another good deed, it will be enough and my future reward will have been entered in God's records." Then his thoughts took him to *extremes* and he grew drunk with happy *dreams* and he approached the staircase in a state of distraction and almost before he had reached it took a flying stride onto its first step, omitting to first extend greetings to any of those present.

He opened his sermon with the words, "Praise be to God, who commanded the erection of this staircase and found it pleasing to serve as His throne . . . ," on hearing which invocation one of those standing said to the person behind him in disavowal, "It seems to me that our preacher today is out of his mind, and I have no desire to hear more from him" and he turned and left. The preacher now climbed the second step and said, ". . . and has brought the people to this blessed assembly, each spreading his ears like a cloth to catch his words . . . ," causing another of the bystanders who heard his words to say, "This clause is worse than the first: it doesn't matter to me if the staircase is a throne or a bier, but it makes me angry to think of my ears being spread out like a cloth!" and he turned and went. The preacher, however, went on pronouncing another lame sentence of the same sort with each new step he climbed and with each another bystander withdrew, which he failed to notice, being too taken up with the joy that distracted him, and by the time he reached the hundredth step everyone had abandoned him. 3.10.3

Once he had settled himself upon it, he turned his head to right and left and saw no one, so he said to himself, "I composed my sermon and brought the people here for it. Now I see that they have turned their backs but the sermon is still with me. Let me then read it out aloud in this noble place that is elevated above the defilements and filth of the earth. Even if they do not hear it, God and His angels will, for it is said, 'The further a person is from Earth, the closer he is to Heaven,' and I see no place more proper for sermons than this. Perhaps some passerby will catch some word of what I say and it will bring about the salvation of his soul and those of his family and his neighbors. A single word from a single mouth may make the difference between death and life, and it would be shameful if I were to return to my wife and tell her that the sermon remained unread." Then he mopped his brow, cleared his throat, and adjusted his clothes, having first placed the sermon on the Scriptures and 3.10.4

knelt and briefly prayed, calling on God to inspire someone to pass that way and hear him. Then he arose, full of vigor and happiness, and said, "Listen, beloved brethren, and hearken well to what I tell you!"

3.10.5 Now it happened that a certain misguided poet was passing by at the time and when he heard him say that and saw that he had no one to listen to him, he stopped and said, "Who can have put this madman at the top of this staircase and where are his brethren whom he is addressing? Or could it be that he is speaking with the jinn in the air? Verily, there is something wondrous here!" Then he shouted to him, "Come down, man, and do not expose yourself to scorn and derision, for not one of God's slaves is listening to you!" The preacher, however, paid him no attention because he was gazing toward Heaven. The man therefore decided that he must be touched in the head and wanted to get him down by any means possible and set about cutting the pegs and ropes securing the staircase and before he knew it, the staircase had disintegrated and fallen down and the preacher and his notebook had fallen down with it onto the head of the man, which is to say onto the head of the poet, and both were smashed and broken into little pieces.

3.10.6 The Interpretation

"A preacher shouldn't be a chatterbox and if our long-winded master persists in his chatter, he will not escape a fall that will break his neck—though God knows best." This interpretation was more hurtful and vexing to the man than those that preceded it because of its abstention from prolixity and its brevity of expression.

3.10.7 A few days later, the master brought him a piece of paper bearing the following: I dreamed that one of my friends gave me a cauliflower of the sort that grows on Jordan's plain. I had it for dinner, went to sleep, and dreamed that I smashed the walls of a city in the air that resembled the city of Jericho in the sturdiness and impregnability of its fortifications. The Fāriyāq wrote next to it

If a glutton eats cauliflow'r for dinner,
From the siege-tower of his anus he'll pelt the air with balls of clay,
Only for those to be recast as bullets
Once the holes in his nose have become clogged with the spray.

The man showed this to his wife, who said, "The man seems now to have become acclimatized to this country: I note that he has begun to hit the target and that that vehemence in deed and word that he previously displayed has left him. I, now, shall myself try him out concerning a dream I saw last night." Then she took a piece of paper and wrote on it, "Madame Ditzia, wife of Flummox son of Lummox, dreamed that she held a polished, glossy lock with many keyholes in her hand while in her husband's was a rusty key with a single hole." Beneath this the Fāriyāq wrote 3.10.8

Husband and wife tend alike
To passion and depravity
But while the key of the first is all worn out
The latter's still good as a cavity.

When she'd inspected the contents, she told her husband, "The same had occurred to me before he came up with this interpretation. How close he now is to accuracy! Take him this additional sheet of paper." So the man handed it over to the Fāriyāq, who found written on it, "Madame Ditzia dreamed that she wrote on her husband's brow a figure 2 and when he saw himself in the mirror he tried to wipe off the two strokes[108] but she was too fast for him and grabbed his hand and he managed to wipe off only one, though the other was no longer clearly readable." Below this the Fāriyāq wrote 3.10.9

It's a husband's religious duty to pleasure his wife once each night
While a supererogatory act on top is often considered polite.
Should he swap, though, *rafḍ* for *farḍ*,
You can be sure she'll swap *ʿirḍ* for *ʿarḍ*.[109]

3.10.10 She admired the lines greatly and handed her husband a further sheet on which she had written, "Madame Ditzia, wife of Flummox son of Lummox, dreamed that with her right eye she saw black as white and with her left eye white as black." Beneath this the Fāriyāq wrote

How hard it is to please a wife,
  Especially once she's laid eyes on an eloquent preacher!
Thenceforth she'll think your every beauty a blemish
  And his every blemish a comely feature.

3.10.11 The wife found these lines witty and told her husband, "I find that he interprets the short dreams of women very well. Dream me now a short dream, my dear, and write it on a sheet of paper and I'll give it to him to see whether he proceeds in the same fashion with you." The next day, then, she brought the Fāriyāq a sheet of paper with the words "The dreamer saw in his sleep something elongated, which then seemed to the dreamer to turn into something rounded, and then again into something elongated, and then again into something rounded, and so on." Beneath this the Fāriyāq wrote

I once thought the world like the vulva
  For both are shifting in shape.
I said, when they claimed it's more like the anus
  In its circularity,[110] "Each doth the other ape."

3.10.12 When he showed these lines to his wife, she laughed and said, "I see that he only minds his manners with me and that he has a fine nose for the understanding of women's affairs; he must be a true lady's man. However, why not try him with a further dream and then we can decide what to do with him?" So the following morning, the master brought him a further sheet, on which was written, "I dreamed that a hand drew a figure 3 on my temple and then vanished. I put my hand to my temple to rub it off and it erased the two teeth, so that what was left formed a crooked figure 1."[111] Beneath this the Fāriyāq wrote

My wife tasks me with three but I can't take
More than one tumble—a weakness in "it," not in me.
My heart and eye, like her vagina, ne'er tire,
But that thing will just never agree.

The man took the response and hurried off with it to his wife. After perusing it, she laughed and said, "With you, he just gets crazier and more impudent. You should leave him alone for a while now and get down to some tumbles." So they set to, and the Fāriyāq took a few days off.

Chapter 11

Physicking the Foul of Breath

3.11.1 Now it had reached the ears of the island's ruler that the Fāriyāq had arrived there to interpret dreams and that he was a great expert in that art. He had also heard that he had a talent for treating those with bad breath. One day, therefore, he sent a chamberlain to him to tell him, "The ruler has summoned you to come to him today on a matter of importance, so you must attend him." At the appointed hour, the Fāriyāq made his way to the ruler, apprehensive lest he might have dreamed some grand sovereign dream that would be difficult for him to interpret, for great men dream only great dreams—they know nothing of cauliflower cannonballs, worn-out keys, "tumbles," and other such low stuff as befits only vagabonds.

3.11.2 When he reached the ruler's council chamber, the ruler said to him, "The news of your arrival on this island to stay with the Bag-man, of how he bothered you with his endless dreams, and of how, not content with that, he taught his wife to dream like him has reached me. So how would you feel now about taking on a task that will reduce his dreams and increase your purse?" "What might that be, my lord?" he asked. The ruler replied, "On this island there is a people with breath so foul that no one can bear to get close enough to them to understand them when they open their mouths.[112] I hear that you know how to cure them. Would you be interested, then, in treating them and in earning yourself a goodly reward from us for doing so?" "It is for you to decide, my lord," he replied. "I am, however, the priest of the Oneiromancer's Chamber." "I shall send someone to the Bag-man now," said the ruler, "to inform him of this, so don't worry about him doing you any mischief." "May God reward you well!" said the Fāriyāq. "You are indeed deserving of God's good fortune and bounty." Then he left his presence, and without retreating backwards, for Frankish rulers do not rebuke a man if they see his nape, his back, or for that matter his belly; in fact, the bellies of those people are more conspicuous than their backs.

When he got home, he told his wife what had happened. **3.11.3**
She, who had just started learning how to read and write, said, "What a blessed day—I saw in a jeweler's shop a rope of precious stones that seemed to me to bear letters that might have been *p-r-o-f-i-t-f-r-o-m-t-h-e-f-o-u-l-o-f-b-r-e-a-t-h*. Can any meaning be extracted from them?" "The meaning that may be extracted," said the Fāriyāq, "is that I'm supposed to buy the necklace for you from the money I earn from the foul-of-breath job." "Quite right," said she, "for I used to hear my mother telling my father that if a man spends the 'cap' of whatever wealth he accrues on jewelry and clothes for his wife, God will reward him the 'tail' (meaning the 'tail' of his wealth, not of his wife)."[113] "And what," he asked, "would be the benefit of this expenditure if the benefit were to extend to only one of the two parties?" "The greater beauty of his wife!" she replied. "Speaking for myself," he said, "I'm content with your present, natural beauty, so for whom this increase?" "It will make you love me even more," she said, "and drive others to envy you and wish I were theirs." "God protect us from the evil of such increase!" he thought. "But I shall have to buy the rope: better that than untie the knot"[114] and he made her a promise to do so, which she accepted, praise God, touching her neck. A month later, when he received his salary, he fulfilled his promise, causing her to say, "It may come from the money from the foul of breath, but it's better than ambergris. God has provided us with a most just division: take

the earnings from the hag-ridden and give me those from the foul of breath—I declare myself satisfied before God with them (*bihim*)." "Don't say '*bihim*,'" he told her, "say '*bihā*.' '*Bihim*' would refer to the foul of breath."[115] The Fāriyāq continued: "At this point, she started muttering words of which I could make out only the last: '. . . and what's wrong with *them*?!' so I answered her, 'And what an ugly old matron you are!' at which she turned to the door but could see no one, so asked me, 'What patron?'"[116]

3.11.4 The Fāriyāq continued to hold the two abovementioned jobs, as oneiromancer and physician, long enough for him to take care of his wife's needs and buy luxurious furnishings and good-quality pots and pans, and he began inviting people over and holding banquets for them. Now the ruler had a custom of inviting all the more distinguished persons in his service, on the eve of a certain feast, to dance in his presence, the men with the women, and the Fāriyāq and his wife were among those invited. When his wife saw the men dancing with their arms around the women's waists, she asked her husband, "Are those women the wives of those men?" "Some are and some aren't," he replied. "Then how can they put their arms around their waists?" she asked. "Such is the custom of the people here and in all the lands of the Franks," he answered. "And after the waist-holding?" she asked. "What happens then?" "I don't know," he said, "but when the party breaks up, everyone goes to his own home." "As God is my witness," she said, "no man puts his arm around a woman's waist without next putting his belly on her belly!" "Don't think badly of them. It's just a custom they've adopted," he said. "I grant you," she responded, "that it may be a custom, and a fine one at that, but what of the feelings of the woman when a beautiful man touches her and puts his arm around her waist?" The Fāriyāq went on, "I told her, 'I don't know. I'm a man, not a woman.' 'I do know,' said she. 'God placed the waist in the middle to be a focus for both the higher and the lower sensations. That is why when women dance, or are pinched anywhere on their bodies, they bend from the waist.' Then she heaved a deep sigh and said, 'Would that my parents had taught me to *dance*, for I see nothing to bring a woman a contemptuous *glance*.' I said, 'If you'd "opened" the *ṣād* with each hemistich, it would have made a perfect line of verse,'[117] to which she replied, 'How dare you! How can you say such a thing[118] in a gathering such as this?' I replied, 'To the house *get thee*! I've seen and heard enough tonight to quite *suffice me*!' but she said, 'I have to watch the dancing to the end!'" "So," said the Fāriyāq, "we stayed until morning, when I took her away, she saying as she walked along, 'Women dancing with men! Men dancing with women! Dancin' girlies, dancin' boys! Dancin' boys 'n dancin' girls!', which made me say, 'Dah-da-dah-dah dah-da-dah! Dah-da-dah-da dah-da-dah!'[119] She went on, 'Men and women, boys and girls! How . . . when . . . where . . . ?!'"

A few days later, the Fāriyāq was brought a difficult dream about a monster with horns, lots of tails, and marks and spots all over its skin, the master of the Oneiromancer's Chamber demanding to know his interpretation of each horn and the secret of every spot. Finding it beyond his powers to give a succinct account of its meaning, he went home feeling miserable and angry. "What ails you?" asked his wife. "Worry and dudgeon!" he replied. "And what is their cause?" she asked. "Whenever I work my way clear of one pitfall, I find myself up to my knees in another that's even worse," he said. "First I had to eulogize the prince in ways that I didn't want,[120] then I became the companion of madmen,[121] then an oneiromancer, and then a physician for the foul of breath, and all these were contrary to my own desires. What an awful way to live, and how straitened the world appears to me! Is there in life no broader prospect than this?" 3.11.5

"Cheer up, sir!" said she. "Everyone in the world has a portion of sorrow and worry coming to him. Even a woman is not free of worries. Every day it is her habit to pluck her eyebrows, put kohl on her eyes, rouge her cheeks, practice walking in a ladylike fashion, and look in the mirror a hundred times to make sure no hair is out of place. Then she talks to herself in the mirror, laughs, tries out a smile, whispers, winks, turns her neck and shoulders, heaves deep sighs, and so on, to find out how these actions may look on 3.11.6

her to others' eyes." The Fāriyāq went on, "I told her, 'Is this the time for jest? I tell you the monster has tails, horns, and marks that aren't susceptible to interpretation at *all* and you talk to me about winking, smiling, and putting on *kohl*?' to which she replied, 'A monster like that doesn't come to you every day, but a woman's worries are a terrible trial to her every single morning and evening. Our living apart from our families is itself cause enough for worry and sorrow.' I said, 'You should be delighted here, where you enjoy the freedom to go out on your own and see and be seen by people in a way you never previously experienced in the land of the face veil and the wrap.'

3.11.7 "'The only thing that vexes me,' she said, 'is that I cannot tell the people of Egypt—meaning the Christians there, whether Copts or Levantines—the things they don't yet know about what may be expected of a marriage, since they reckon that the Almighty created the woman simply as a source of gratification for the man—in his bed, in waiting on him, and in keeping house for him. You'll find that the expression on the face of one of their menfolk stays the same whether he has come home and is face-to-face with his wife or he is away from her, and that when he sits down, he keeps his distance from her, full of suspicions and regrets. When he looks at her, all he looks at is her hair, to see whether it's tidy or not, and he won't tidy it for her in public if the wind or something of the sort has mussed it. He spends no time with her and doesn't take her by the arm when they walk together. Indeed, he rarely walks with her, unless she goes to see her parents, when he is then very much on guard lest any man talk to her on the road or set eyes on her and she return pregnant (with a single child should he merely have seen her and twins if he actually talked to her). When she brings him his dinner, he eats in gloomy silence, as though the food he's eating were poisoned. He may also ask her to wash his feet before he goes to sleep or to massage them until sleep comes and will blink, open and close his eyes, yawn, stretch, and then fall asleep without a cuddle or a kiss, and whenever it's the feast of some sex-starved monk,[122] he holds himself aloof from her. He obliges her to address him in the presence of others with, "Yes, my lord" and "Thank you, my lord" when that "lord" may be a slinking wolf, or supremely stupid, while she is sensible and bright; despite which, she has no choice but to treat him as her lord and master and if she sees him commit some folly, she can do nothing to bring him to his senses, for it is a matter of settled fact to idiots and simpletons that for them to go against the wishes of their wives is a praiseworthy act of obedience to God. Even if he flew head over heels and landed headfirst on the ground, he'd direct his blame and reproof at his wife.'"

The Fāriyāq continued, "I told her, 'According to al-Nakhaʿī, obedience to women is a sign of the Last Hour,' to which she replied, 'Methinks I saw the Franks gathered, or being gathered, as for the Last Hour that other night!' Then she went on to say, 'And more horrid than all of that is that when a man in our country reaches a certain age, he feels no embarrassment at wedding a girl of not yet half his years, and when she takes up residence with him, he immediately sets about raising her, nourishing her in the hope of profiting from her and breeding from her womb, and he treats her with hypocrisy and soft soap. He may be a lecherous wretch and convince her that he's a righteous and God-fearing man who has nothing to do with diversions or music or keeping company with wiseacres. It never crosses his mind that the difference in age between him and his wife is one of the main reasons that she hates him. On the contrary, he believes that simply because he is the active partner and she the passive that's enough to give him precedence and superiority over her.' I responded, 'Claims of precedence based on who plays the active role seem to me invalid, for *mufāqamah*, *mubāḍaʿah*, *muwāqaʿah*, and similar forms[123] all point to the fact that the act is a collaboration between two and any precedence should go to the initiator.' She responded, 'Initiation is no more the assigned role of one than of the other, so whoever starts is in the right, and that means that neither has precedence over his or her partner. Moreover, how often, just because of this delusion, will a 3.11.8

man leave his wife alone in the house and spend the night with one of his friends, where he takes wine with him until he's drunk and the little common sense he has vanishes and the only way he can get home is borne between two men, as though at a funeral! Plus, it makes no difference to him whether his wife is pregnant or not and you'll find that he talks to her when she is in that state exactly as he did before. He may burst in on her with an animalistic cry and give her a shock, or say to her, "Boo!" or "Ta-daa!" or "Gotcha!" or "Watch it!" or "Shush!" or "Whoa!" or "Woa!" or glue himself to her like birdlime or chrysocolla, or crush her with his body, or stick himself against her, or fail to perform, or fall uselessly on her like a dead weight.

3.11.9 "'The furthest extent of his kindness to and pity for her is to buy her a slave girl or employ a maid. In so doing, however, he does not intend only to lighten her work. His purpose is to make the slave girl or the maid her warden so that she can't betray him with regard to his honor (I don't say, "with regard to his wealth" because he never leaves the house without first locking his money chests). Despite this, such a slave girl will inevitably collude with her mistress against him, even if the mistress curses and insults her in his presence, for it doesn't matter to her whether her mistress loves one man, or two, or ten. All she cares about is eating and drinking well while in her house. Thus, if any "slip," as it is called, on her mistress's part becomes known to her, she tells her mistress so and is emboldened to ask her for whatever she wants. In fact, she wants her mistress to take as many lovers as she can because she hopes for gifts and handouts from them, and it's a known fact that the more lovers there are the more gifts there will be.

3.11.10 "'To resume: it is in the nature of women at all times and in all places to be attracted toward considerations of love and occasions of passion and believe that everyone else has abandoned themselves to these and thinks of nothing else. Thus the slave girl who is in the household of a "respectable" mistress (assuming such a thing exists) will quickly anger her to the point that she urges her husband to sell the girl, after which it will be her fate to serve some other woman who isn't so "respectable." Not to mention that men are simpletons. Yes, simpletons! As for their vaunting their generosity in buying jewelry for their wives during the springtimes of their good fortune, it all ends up as part of their own wealth in the end because they're quick to strip them of it during the autumns of their hard times and bankruptcy. What woman can accept that she should stay at home like a mare saddled and ready for riding while at the same time being deprived of social intercourse?'"

The Fāriyāq continued, "I said, 'Never have you spoken better! Now the signs of your natural brilliance begin to shine, may God preserve you and conserve you!' to which she replied, 'What's "conserve you" mean?' 'Nothing at all,' I replied.[124] 'But to me,' she said, 'it's a sign of the benefits of doubling up.' I said, 'You seem to be saying that it's like pairing one word to another so that they give off an aroma of marriage.' 'Indeed!' she answered. 'Marriage is a pleasure, even where words are concerned.' I said, 'But I still have an objection to something you said, namely your suggestion in the course of this eloquent sermon of yours, which has benefited me more than any of those by the master of the Oneiromancer's Chamber, that I tidy your hair and your clothes in public, or that I ought to do so, which is unthinkable.' 'You haven't done so yet,' she said, 'but you soon will, God willing, for I believe you esteem women and wouldn't scant them in their rights, and I am one of that mortal company.'" 3.11.11

Chapter 12

A Voyage and a Conversation

3.12.1 The following day, the Fāriyāq went to the Chamber apprehensive about having to interpret the monster dream, but the master came to tell him, "The idea has sprung to my mind of making a trip to the Syrian lands for a change of air: the air of that clime is good and dreams dreamed there are true and easy to interpret. I see that you, like me, are weakened in your powers, thin of body. Prepare yourself then for the journey. May God smooth the path and we return in good health!" So the Fāriyāq requested the ruler's permission to undertake the journey, and the latter, out of his kindness and generosity, granted that.

3.12.2 Then he went to his wife to bid her farewell and said, "My charge to you, my wife, is to remember, before all else, the roof. Let it be an incentive to you to keep your troth and your affection, and likewise, after I *depart*, to take good care of my son, in leaving whom in your keeping I leave my *heart*. Should any profligate bring you news of me, confirm it for yourself. In other words, should any of those who envy me for having you tell you, 'Your husband died at sea and was eaten by a whale and nothing remains of him in the world of the living but his name,' pay him no attention till you receive a letter from me that you can rely on." "But how will you write to me if the news is true?" she asked. "I told her," continued the Fāriyāq, "'the master of the Chamber will write to you. But anyway, I hope to arrive safely and enjoy the sight of my family and yours and to pass on to them your greetings.' 'Won't you set me a date by which you must have sent the letter?' she replied. 'Two months,' I said. She said, 'That's as long as all eternity! What woman can wait two months?' I said, 'We shall be traveling by sailing ship. The doctor has told the master that it is more suitable than a steamship, because the latter smells of coal, which is bad for those with chest problems.' 'I shall do as you think best,' she said, 'but be careful you don't recover and fall in love with someone else,' to which I replied, 'I'll be careful only of the second, not the first!' to which she said, 'Nay, it's me you'd better be careful of!' 'I only meant' I said, 'that I'd be careful not to fall in love.' 'Right!' she said. 'Be on guard against it, because it'll only make you worse!' I said, 'The lands to which we are going provide less cause for worry in that respect than this island,' to which she responded, 'Men and women are the same in all countries, especially now that you'll be wearing the garb of the stranger and that women everywhere go into ecstasies over exotic men, just as men do over exotic women.' I said, 'I understand what you mean, but don't forget that a respectable woman can walk between two armies and emerge as she entered.' 'Indeed,' she responded. 'She goes in a woman and comes out a woman.' 'Where did the respectable woman go?' I asked. 'You appear to have struck her off the list.' 'She was in the preadamic period,' she answered. 'And what's "the preadamic period"?' I asked. 'The age when mankind had yet to be created,' she replied. 'Where did you learn that odd word?' I asked her. 'I heard you use it once,' she said, 'so I learned it by heart, which is proof of that same infatuation with the exotic.'

"Then she was silent for a while, thinking, after which she burst 3.12.3
into laughter. 'What are you laughing at?' I asked her. 'Is it "preadamic"?' 'No,' she answered. 'I just thought of a story about a woman whose husband left her to go on a voyage, and I laughed.' 'And what story is that?' I asked. She replied, 'A woman was married to a man about whom she sometimes harbored doubts, but she wasn't sure what about him made her suspicious. Now he happened

to leave her to go on a voyage. She was sad to see him go but angry with him too, so sometimes she'd call on God to bless him and at others to curse him, telling herself, "If he's innocent, the blessings will reach him and if not, the curses will!"' 'And do you intend to do as she did?' I asked her. 'God forbid I should call on God!' she exclaimed. 'Tell me "call on God to do what" exactly, to make the meaning clear,' I said. 'To curse you,' she said. I responded, 'I can see there's no getting around you! *Je t'adore!*' At this she turned to the door and said, 'There's no one there.'[125] I said, 'Don't bother me, I beg you, with talk of patrons[126] and who's at the door: I'm about to set off on a journey.' 'Go,' she said, 'in God's good keeping, and harbor no doubts. There's a time for joking and a time for being serious, and a woman's honor belongs to the latter.' I replied, 'That too contains an insinuation, as though you were saying it isn't something to be brought to the forefront.' Said she, 'Put your mind at rest. Whether it belong to the former or the latter, you will find me as you left me, God willing.'"

3.12.4 He went on, "Then I bade her farewell, my tears bathing her neck, and she wept too to see me go, for it was the first time I had left her. It was part of her nature that when she wept, her face took on an arousing look and appealingly comely expression—and women are as attractive as can be when they cry (though these words shouldn't be taken as an incitement to beat them: paralyzed be the hands of any who touches them in anger!)." Then he continued, "At the sight of her tears, mine increased too and at that moment I truly felt the agony of parting. We set sail and no sooner had the land disappeared from sight than pangs of desire rose in my breast and everything she'd said passed through my mind, tinged with misgivings and forebodings." He added, "And stay-at-homes who never leave their houses and the scent of whose wives never leaves their nostrils know nothing of the pain of *separation*, after nights of hugging and love's *consummation*, especially when it happens for the first time. It behooves me therefore to picture to the mind of our stay-at-home, ever nostril-fed friend something of the pain that separation brings the lover, so that perhaps his heart then may soften and he may pray that all those far from their loved ones may soon be at one with them, reunited. I therefore declare as follows:

"Separation—be it for a longer or shorter period, be its ending in sight or far off—consists of the detachment of one of two would-be lovers and his deprival of the joys of the company of his friend. His agony may be sharper than that of death, for separation from the dead is accompanied by regret and sorrow while separation from the living is accompanied by both of these plus jealousy, and, though comparable to the despair caused by separation from the dead, is yet more distressing. (The foregoing refers to married couples who are in love; when they hate one another, neither case brings either regret or sorrow.) Furthermore, if the departed lover, on leaving his beloved, finds in some other country an easy life, replete with delicious food to eat, a delightfully heady nightlife to enjoy and songs to listen to, wonderful novelties and gracious, sparkling, eye-catching faces to behold, the first thing he'll think of will be his distant beloved and he'll say to himself, 'How I wish that he[127] were with me now to share with me in this luxury! This day, I think, he must be bereft of all such things; nay, his heart may well be enveloped in a veil of grief and mourning. How can I sport and play while he grieves? How can I find food appetizing, drink refreshing, when he, at this very moment, may be too lonely and depressed to have any appetite for them?' and so on and so forth by way of gloomy *cogitations* and sorrowful *speculations*. 3.12.5

"If, however, the lover experiences toil and trouble after his departure, he'll say, 'Alas! Alack! Too bad! *Dear me*! Oh woe! *Oh gee*! Now I live a life that's *dour*, I'm lonely and my heart is *sore*. I agreed with my friend that we'd be partners for better or for worse, through thick and through thin, but now, I think, he lives cushioned and *cosseted*, lodged in luxury's lap, petted and *posseted*, on an even keel and relieved of all *loads*, riding on the flat on the straightest of *roads*, partying by night with crafty *sophisticates*, hanging out by day with clever *profligates*. I can see him (meaning her)[128] now, smiling 3.12.6

a smile of consent and admiration at someone who, having praised her charms and beauty, is telling her, "I wish you would obtain an amulet, to protect you from envious eyes! If it were up to me, I would allow no one to look upon this radiant, effulgent face, for there would be nothing strange if someone afflicted with an ugly wife were to gulp back tears over you, for the envious eye is a reality, and your beauty is unique." What could her response to him possibly be other than to tell him, "How excellent your eyes, for they see things as they are! My husband's, on the other hand, are covered with a film and he belongs to that evil school of thought that says, 'If the eye becomes familiar with something, no matter how outstanding its beauty, the soul desires it less,' or, as the common people say, 'What the hand holds, the soul renounces.' Yet I fear that if you look at me too much and grow too close to me, you'll quickly join his school and see me as something other than what I am now."

3.12.7 "'To this he will reply, "I seek refuge with God! Such is the talk of the ignorant. Those such as I (and how few we are!) who are honest in their love ever take as their example the words of Abū Nuwās, to wit,

Her face appears more lovely to you
The more you gaze upon it.

"'"As God—and His favored angels, prophets, and honored messengers—is my witness (and what better witness than He!), should you live with me your whole life long, my eye will never find any more comely than you!" Then she'll say to him, "Men are ever thus: they flatter a woman so that they may seduce her and traduce her. One time they say to her, 'Blessed be the Creator!' another, 'I would give my life for the shy gazelle!' and a third, 'Happy is he to whom you belong!' or 'Fortunate the one who sees your phantom in his sleep!' Sometimes they look at her, their eyes brimming with tears, sometimes they sigh and sob—and all this so that they may have their way with her once or twice, after which they set her *aside* and bruit her secret far and *wide*. That's why we're on our guard when you're *about*, for we know you all, inside *out*." To this he'll respond,

"God forbid! God forfend! God forgive you! My way's not that of the hypocritical *flatterer*, my nature not that of the *adulterer*. On the contrary, my tongue is inadequate to express the love for you that my heart *enfolds* and mind *holds*. Would that I knew a language by which I could express how excessive are my passion and my longing for you! Could you but see my conscience, you would believe me and know that I am like no other man and that my devotion is above all others. Keep company with me for but a little longer, even without consummation, so you may be sure of the truth of my words." To which she will reply, in full cry now and molars ground to a powder, "And what good would that do? A woman is not a star whose rising and setting are to be observed, nor a flash of lightning to be watched to see whether it will bring rain or is only an empty promise, nor is she a riddle to be solved or guessed at. She doesn't care whether she is more beautiful than other women. All she cares about is being the most desirable and attractive to men, and attractiveness depends less on physical beauty than on excellence of personal traits, quickness of wit, humor, ability to entertain, sensuality, coquetry, brilliance of smile, slyness of glance, hesitancy, seductiveness of eye, delicacy of walk, and willowiness." Says he, "How true! Glory to Him who has gathered all these praiseworthy traits together in your own unique self! Everything about you is desirable and everything in me desires." She then tells him, her face now beaming with pride and admiration, "They say the lover's pulse races. Let me feel yours, to know whether what you say is true," at which he tells her, "Yes, yes! Take my hand and feel the pulse, and place your other hand upon my heart!" which she does. Next he says, "Let me do with you as you have done with me, so that the truth may be clear to each of us." On hearing him say, "Let me *do* with you," she is sent into a tizzy, blushes, and her pulse consequently races. Then she quiets down and extends to him her hand and he takes hold of it with one of his, places the other on her heart, moves it upward a little, eyelids reddening and tongue lolling, heaves a long sigh, and says,

God bless you for a red euphorbia berry that my hand has cupped
And whose holder is as one who holds the terrestrial sphere!
For its calyx I'd give the pupil of my eye as ransom
Along with all the goods and chattels I hold dear!

3.12.8 "'She (all tickled up) then says, "But the veins in which one's blood pulses are not only in one's hand and one's heart; they are in all one's members, which means that we ought to feel every member we have to find out which of us is the more charged, the more shaken, the more disturbed, the more pulsating, the more simmering, the more throbbing, the more constricted, and the more bursting at the veins, since it is incorrect to pass judgment on anything without first subjecting it to thorough investigation and examination." And he (ecstatic by now with passion and joy) says, "What truly truly truly excellent words you have spoken! At the same time, though, given that a person, while unaware of his own condition, may find it natural to notice in another what he does not in himself, this examination ought to be reciprocal, or in other words . . ." and here she interrupts him, saying, "I take your meaning, which is self-evident and calls for no explanation, and is just what I was going to say myself. So give me your hand and take mine"—and so it continues until their hands have roamed all over, groping and grasping, swiping and wiping, searching and seeking, poking and stroking, squeezing and teasing, clasping and parting, slapping and tickling, rooting and rummaging, delving and digging, rubbing and pinching. She (throbbing as never before) now says, "Come closer! Come closer! What you said has, for both cases, proven to be true" and he says to her, "May your wishes be granted and your efforts aided! How often have I raised my arms in prayer that I might hear this call *reanimating*, this tune *intoxicating* . . . !"

3.12.9 "'Was it on this,' bursts in the lover, 'we agreed when we parted? Was it for this you encouraged me to travel when you said one night, "It seems to me, good man, you are a little tired. Should you travel to a land where the air is good, your former vigor would return to you and we to our earlier happy state"? Was that just a trick of yours to make me leave so you could have a clear field in which to strut as you please and practice the science of measuring pulses and the motions of the limbs? Don't I have a pulse, like everybody else, on which you could learn this noble science, or would you claim it has grown so weak it will no longer serve to learn on—when, if it is indeed weak, it is so because of you, and when I know that, prior to our wedding night, it throbbed, shook, and wagged? Do lovers thus act when far *apart*, is this how each betrays his *counterpart*? Does God condone for you a life of *luxury* while I know hard times and *misery*? Wantonly you feel men's pulses while my brow is covered in *sweat*; indeed, with an onset of feverish chills I *fret*. Were they not enough, my sufferings with you at home, when I'd leave in the morning to toil and return worn *out*, you'd vent all your worries upon me, and all your reproaches at me you'd *spout*? To keep you in comfort I wore myself to a *sliver*, I went without sleep because you were soon to *deliver*.(1) I tired myself out that you might *eat*, worked hard that you might enjoy a life that was *sweet*, went cold that you might be *warm*, worried that you might be *calm*, kept vigil that you might sleep a portion of the *night*, grew thin that your belly with food might grow *tight*. Now it's clear which of us is *faithful*, which a hypocrite and *ungrateful*. Back then I'd tell you honesty's a rarer thing in women than in the *male*, for men are always preoccupied, their situation *frail*. They're distracted from pleasure, for work and toil they *must*, and good sense and brains turn them from *lust*. Women have no worries but how to excite longing and stir dissension among *men*, with no regard for where or *when*. You'd reply, "Not so. In fact women are more respectable and *modest*, less greedy and *dishonest*, more given by nature to *chastity*, further by inborn temper from *hypocrisy*." If, then, fate should ever reunite us and we talk at large of *loyalty*, of affection and *sincerity*, I'll give you arguments against which you cannot *prevail* and demonstrate how far superior is a man to any who wear the *veil*—those treacherous

(1) *ajaḥḥat al-mar'ah* ("the woman approached term") means "she conceived and came close to her time and her belly grew large."

treasonists, those fibbing *fabulists*. And if you hold fast to denial and disdain, the cudgel will be there to make sure you're *whomped*, as will the hand, to slaps and punches ever *prompt*, and if you grab my forelock or the front of my *gown*, and broadcast my shame all over *town*, I'll hang you like a crucifix from a *nail*, or throttle you till you *wail*.(1)' When these thoughts waylay him, his anger stirs him to a frenzy, and he wishes he could fly home in a cloud of *dust*, his joy being turned to grief, his mind *nonplussed*.

(1) One says *dha'aṭa*, of which the verbal noun [as here] is *dha'ṭ*, [and also] *za'aṭa*, *ẓa'aṭa*, *daghata*, *dha'ata*, *dha'ata*, *za'ata*, *zarata*, and *sa'ata*, all meaning "he throttled."

"Despite which," went on the Fāriyāq, "sorrow is, in principle, beneficial. It prevents random but seductive hopes and desires
3.12.10 from driving out insight and good sense. This calms the mind and prevents it from mooning about at the water holes of the *inconceivable*, and things settle down to a point at which the soul can wean itself from the *unachievable*. I allude to this in the following verses of mine:

Many a sorrow has saved the heart from silliness
As rust conserves a pot whose metal's thinning.
All one to me are love's raptures, so quickly passed,
Come they at its end or its beginning."

He continued, "The clearest and most creative thoughts are those that occur during one of three states: the first is at the onset of sorrow, the second in bed just before falling asleep, and the third in the latrine. The last involves the breakdown of concentrated matters exhaled by the bowels and the intestines and this breakdown and exhalation taking place in the lower part has the effect of breaking down, at the same time and place, whatever may have coagulated in the higher folds of the brain. Some of this matter then departs in a downward direction while some of the images formed by the brain rise, like steam rising from the earth to thicken into a raincloud.

3.12.11 "From the preceding you will have worked out that more benefits result from sorrow than from joy, because joy, which consists of a proliferation of fancies and dispersal of thoughts, incites to lightheadedness, distractedness, and the scattered distribution of thoughts among the fancies of the soul and its disparate desires. Sorrow, on the other hand, consists of their ingathering and collection, which is why most scholars have been impoverished tramps and few of those who have excelled at intellectual pursuits have been rich or comfortably off, unless some kind of asceticism and abstemiousness, accompanied by sorrow, happens to have taken root in their constitutions." He went on, "The best ideas that have occurred to me have been occasioned by unhappy *presentiments* and grief-inspired *sentiments*, due either to the loneliness of *separation* or to disappointment and *deprivation*, or to envy of some knowledge or skill—but of money or wealth, never, unless it were for a good deed, such as the construction of schools or the charitable support of some needy person. I am truly amazed at all those monks, not one of whom, for all the loneliness and deprivation that they experience, has ever shone as a scholar or left behind him any legacy. If I were a monk, I'd fill the monastery with verse and prose and write fifty *maqāmah*s on lentils alone. I wish I knew how it is possible for any man alone in his cell, with the rich, fragrant, dark green forests, tranquil sea, and ships in full sail below him, the towering, snowcapped mountains to his right and left, the cloudless empyrean above him, and the villages and houses before him, to spend his whole day winking and blinking,(1) yawning, stretching, and limbering up his stomach without writing a word of prose or poetry, especially given that the beauty of the women of these lands has the capacity to induce serenity and peace of mind. If all these magnificent scenes do not inspire those ascetics to write a book, what else can? Moreover, many prisoners while in dire straits have written exquisite works of which residents of vast palaces are incapable. As for ʿAbd Allāh ibn al-Muʿtazz,[129] of whom it is said that he would look at the pots and pans in his house and use them to make similes, I can say only that not every slave is an ʿAbd Allāh.[130] Thus we observe that nowadays, as people's wealth increases, their wit decreases.

(1) *arḍaka ʿaynayh* ("he blinked his eyes") means "he opened and closed them."

3.12.12 "In sum, the loneliness of separation incites the heart to come up with finely tuned tropes, and the same is true of rejection, abandonment, avoidance, shilly-shallying, reproach, scornful looks, coquetry, aloofness, and prideful behavior on the part of the beloved. The intention, however, is not to seduce the beloved into abandoning his lover as a way to make the latter write poetry, or into deliberately going away as a way of inciting him to describe the longing and agony that he feels, for the best such descriptions are the ones that fate brings, not those we chase after. I now hereby declare my innocence before lovers and married couples alike and say: should any separation imposed by loneliness, or loneliness imposed by separation, or any rejection, coldness, or stubborn *dissension*, any argument or *contention*, any hair *clasping* or *grasping*,(1) or any wrestling involving tripping, flipping, head drops, pinning the other to the mat, catching-as-catch-can, takedowns, catching the other off guard or doing the same using a shorter word, trick moves, grappling, wrist gripping, hand grasping, headlocks, or leg falls befall you, no rebuke or blame accrues to me." Here ended the Fāriyāq's words (and how well he spoke them!).

(1) *taqāfasā bi-shuʿūrihimā* ("they clasped each other by their hair"); *faqasa fulānan* means "he pulled so-and-so downward by his hair", from which [the verb of reciprocity] *tafāqasā*.

3.12.13 On the other hand, he omitted to say that when sad he was impatient and infirm, much given to suspicions and misgivings, barely able to plot or plan, inconstant in his views, and incapable of keeping his thoughts to himself. Thus, almost before the island's shoreline had had time to disappear, he started complaining about women and how they loved to play when their husbands were away. When they heard him, the Bag-man and his wife said to him, "What are you complaining about? You don't need to worry about interpreting the monster[131] for as long as the voyage lasts, and when I reach your homeland, God willing, I shall dream only straightforward dreams." "It's not of the monster or of devils that I complain," he replied, "it's of the human race, because today I heard such and such and suspected such and such and I may return to find such and such, or not find such and such, or not return and not find at all." When the Bagman's wife heard him say this she said to him, all the fiends of Hell pouring from her nostrils, "Have you become so lightheaded as to cast suspicion on married women?" "Mild and moderate men have suspected as much about them before me," he responded. "No such propensity exists among us Franks," she replied. "My husband here would never harbor a doubt about me"—to which the Fāriyāq responded that the master was so preoccupied with his dreams there was no room left in his head for anything else: "Does not your learned Byron say, 'How treacherous the wife, when her husband's away?'" She replied, "He's a poet, and the words of poets are not to be taken into account when judging women, unless they be erotic verses or love poetry."

Suddenly, while they were thus engaged, the wind stirred up the waves, the ship shook and was violently convulsed, and everyone kept to his room for four days until none of the passengers could tell whether he was coming or going, and after a voyage of twelve days they reached the city of Beirut, hungry, *tired*, haggard, and near *expired*, with the Hag-ridden One waiting for the first chance in a long time for dreams to descend. On their entering the place, the first words in the lame dialect of its natives to assail their ears were those of the public crier to the effect that the people of the Mountain had thrown off the yoke of obedience to the viceroy of Egypt and taken up arms against him,[132] throwing the city's inhabitants into tumult and unrest, while the giddiness of sea and *separation* still had the Fāriyāq's head in a state of *perturbation*. He set off upwards in the direction of the Mountain to see his family but on the outskirts of the city ran into an encampment of native soldiers, one of whom terrified the Fāriyāq by firing his rifle, sending half his heart flying from his breast, though adding nothing thereby to that of the terrifier[133] (but some people enjoy putting themselves in harm's way even if they gain nothing from doing so). Then God took pity on him and rescued him from that company, and he reached his family's home. When news of his arrival reached the inhabitants of 3.12.14

the village, they came to greet him in twos and threes and fours, and he looked at them and marveled at how old-fashioned their ways now seemed to him. The women, for instance, would come and sit on the ground in front of him, some squatting on their heels, some with their legs drawn up beneath them, some cross-legged, some with their legs spread wide, some staying at home,[134] some on their shanks with their knees open, some placing their buttocks on the ground and resting their weight on their calves, some with their legs drawn up and wrapped in their garment, or resting their weight on their toes with their buttocks pressed against their heels, or with their weight distributed evenly over their thighs, or rubbing their bottoms on the ground, or as though ready to leap up, or sitting on their anuses like apes, while at the same time hiking up their shifts so that the cracks of their vaginas showed through their bloomers, which is a custom they've become used to and in which they see no shame; most also display their breasts, be those rounded and perky or long and pendulous or huge and sagging.

3.12.15 That day he was deluged with questions. One woman would ask him, "Fāriyāq, how come you're so *desiccated*?" and another would say, "And how come you're so *emaciated*?" and another, "What happened to your ugly mug to make it so *unanimated*?" and another, "And to your face that your looks are so *devastated*?" and another "And to your teeth that they've became so *ensaffronated*?" and another, "And to your brow that it's become so pitted and *excavated*?" and another, "And to the tip of your nose that it's become so *incrassated*?" and another, "And to your forehead that its become so *striated*?" and another, "And to your skin that it's become so *armor-plated*?" and another, "And to your lip that it's become so *ulcerated*?" and another, "And to your neck that it's become so *suppurated*?" and another, "And to your eye that its lids have become so heavy-*weighted*?" and another, "And to your upright figure that it's become so *corrugated*?" and another, "And to your hairs that they've become so *bifurcated*?" and another, "And to your backside that it's become so *exiguated*?" and another, "And to your chin that it's gotten so *depilated*?" and another, "And to your accent that it's become so *granulated*?" The Fāriyāq continued, "I felt I was being jinxed by all these rhymes and thought, 'All that's left after their enumeration of all these words ending in *-ated* is for them to say, "And to your what's-it, that it got so *penetrated*?"!'"

Then one of the women said, "Huh! And here's another trifle that got added to you" and another, "Humph! And here's something else that's been subtracted" and they started turning him around and inspecting him like a buyer turning goods over before buying, all saying to one tune, "Fāriyāq! Fāriyāq! Where are the fun times we had with your *tambour*? Where are your verses on hair ribbons and the *ṭanṭūr*?[135] Have you forgotten the day that ... or the night when ... ?" He went on, "I was happy with their good company and the freedom of their minds from any sin, this being the way the women of our country were created. They have no objection to being touched by a man or approaching them close, or to the meeting of knees, if not of pubes. Despite this, their questions to me were many and they stayed with me for a long time when I was in need of rest and to be alone. In any case, though, it is enjoyable to sit with women, especially if one has just spent twelve days at sea without seeing any, and if they pluck out one's beard and mustache with their questions after all that time, no harm is done." 3.12.16

He continued, "Even stranger, I would observe the emirs sitting on rush mats and lying down on them and going to sleep, all together on a single mat, and at times making do with eggs, rice, and milk in place of squabs, chickens, or hens and going without wine, fruit, or nuts. Their feet were visible, for when they sat down on a mat they'd take their footwear off and put it close to them, keeping it in sight. Also, one of their servants might be observed standing at (meaning next to, not on top of) the head of one of them with a spoon in his belt and another with a silver drinking cup in the front of his robe, as a sign of how rich their emir was and how he belonged to that class of people that did not want for things to spoon or drink. Such an emir would sit there with his head bowed—no book to read, no 3.12.17

companion to keep him company, no musical instrument to entertain him—and spend hours of the day thus occupied; indeed he might spend a whole day, or days, and never set eyes on a woman, till his eyes went blurry, his thoughts darkened, he got cross, and his stomach shriveled.

3.12.18 "What a contrast with the salons of the Franks, which are adorned with cushions of precious stuffs and spread with luxurious carpets that are trod by footwear and over which lovely women come and go! A slim-bellied lass may do them the honor of a step, a delicate maiden that of a skip, a radiant girl that of a twirl, a big-bosomed woman that of a shake, a big-buttocked one that of a tumble. Who then can put up with a state such as theirs? O emir of the gathering, member of the *elite* and thrower of the palm-branch javelin[136] at the sons of men from the back of your horses *fleet*, tell your servant, the carrier of the cup, to remove your footwear from before you! Or better still, put it on and come with me to the lands of the Franks, there to see their emirs with their arms around the waists of their wives and children, proceeding with them to the parks, gardens, and other places of diversion, sport, and enjoyment. No guilt adheres to their wives if they smile or turn their heads or look people in the face or walk languidly or move their eyes here and there or run hither and thither or walk with their legs not close together or walk awkwardly or walk in a comely fashion or take long strides or fall down, nor to their children if they leap and have fun. Even if these emirs spend a sleepless night, they do so on comfortably made-up beds with their comfortably upholstered wives. Would that I knew why you do not add, to the number of these manservants, boy servants, lackeys and flunkeys, pageboys, domestics, valets and maids, assistants, majordomos and retainers who surround you, three players of stringed instruments to scour from your mind, every day in the late afternoon or during dinner, the rust of worry caused by your loneliness and isolation.

3.12.19 "Permit me likewise to entreat you to allow your neighbors to come and share with you in your enjoyment, that they may pray for the continued success of your *governance*, the continuation of your *permanence*, the immortalization of your *felicity*, and the sublimity of your upward *mobility*, and to ask you, why not set aside a day each year as a holiday to celebrate your birthday or that of your lady wife or your children, God protect them, as a day of joy and happiness for you and all who pertain to you on which you might hold a banquet and invite to it both commons and elite? Where's the good in your throwing the palm-branch javelin and injuring your wretched enslaved page's shoulder, or his molar, leaving him unable to eat? At it you will forget even the best, truest, most accurate, and deadliest of throws. At it you will be safe from anyone telling you, 'Boo! Boo!'—quite the opposite: they'll tell you, 'Bravo! Bravo!'—not to mention from the pain caused by the throwing of the javelin to your sweet-smelling, high-class armpit.

"And what benefit is there in your page standing before you 3.12.20
with a spoon in his belt or a tray on his head or a trencher and wine pitcher on his chest or a glass and a wooden cup in his hand or a table on his shoulder or an earthenware pot around his neck when you don't eat with your lady wife and her children or take your son and put him on your knee, or carry him on your back, or bow your head so he can jump on top of it or place him in your lap or hug him, or carry him on your hip, or embrace him, or turn your cheek to him so he can kiss you, or let him play with your mustache or bite your finger or your nose so he can laugh a little (and I a lot), or feed him with your hand so he may feel that you are his benefactor, or eat something he has been chewing on, or mount him on a donkey foal and let him ride it, or sing to him at night so he may go to sleep to the sound of your voice and wake in the morning singing you a song more enchanting than that of the phoenix or of Maʿbad[137] or Abū l-Baddāḥ or Siwāṭ or al-ʿAthʿath or Khalīlān or ʿAmr ibn Bānah or al-Zunnām or Mamdūd ibn ʿAbd al-Wāsiṭ al-Rabbānī or Zalzal or ʿIrfān or al-Jarādatān or Ibnat ʿAfzar or Sallāmah or Shamūl or Ibn Jāmiʿ al-Sahmī or Dubays or Raqīq or Ibn Muḥraz or al-Mashdūd or Hāshim ibn Sulaymān or Daḥmān al-Ashqar or Ṭuways or Ibn

Shurayḥ or al-Dalāl ibn ʿAbd al-Naʿīm or Ibn Ṭunbūr al-Yamanī or Ḥakam al-Wādī or Ibrāhīm al-Mawṣilī or more heartrending than

3.12.21 the *runum* or the voice of any *duʿbub gharīḍ*,	*runum* are "celebrated women singers"; *gharīḍ* means "a celebrated male singer" and *duʿbub* means the same
or *tubaʾbiʾ* him or speak lovingly to him,	*baʾbaʾahu* means "he told him, 'I would give my father as your ransom!'"
or speak endearments to him or *tubāghim* him,	*bāghamahu* means "he spoke to him in a caressing voice."
or *tunādigh* him or *tarʾam* him,	*nādaghahu* means "he flirted with him" and *raʾimat al-nāqah waladahā* means "[the she-camel] displayed affection for her child, and she stayed close by it."
or *tunaghghir* him or *tarkhum* him,	*naghghara l-ṣabī* means "he tickled him," synonym *naghghazahu*; *rakhamat al-marʾatu waladahā* means "[the woman] played with [her child]."
or watch over him or *turaʿʿim* him,	*raʿʿamahu* means "he wiped away his *ruʿām*," meaning "his nasal mucus"; however, the author of the *Qāmūs* prescribes "[the nasal mucus of] a woman" as the object of the verb; in fact, the obvious way to understand his phrasing is "he wiped away the nasal mucus of a *ruʿmūm* (meaning 'a smooth-skinned woman')." Whatever the case, we beg pardon for them both.
or *turzim* to his *razamah*,	*arzamat al-nāqah* means "the she-camel lowed to her child," while the *razamah* is the sound made by a child
or *tatajannath* at him,	*tajannatha ʿalayh* means "he displayed affection for him and showed him love," as well as "he wrapped the thing up to hide it."

or *tuqarrim* him or *tusammit* him,	*taqrīm* means "teaching (*taʿlīm*) how to eat and" *tasmīt* means "uttering a prayer for one who sneezes."(1)	(1) There is something unclear to me in the definition of *taqrīm*: it may well be that *taʿlīm* is used here in the sense of *ʿalāmah* ("marking"), in which case *akl* ("eating") would mean *ṭaʿām* ("food")[138] and the sense would be the same as that in his entry (root *r-s-m*) "*rasm*: a piece of wood with writing carved into it used to stamp food" and (root *r-sh-m*) which is too well-known to require definition ["to write"]: "*rashama l-ṭaʿām*: he stamped it"; if not, it is in its correct place.
or *tufdī* him or *tuṣhī* him,	*afdā* means "to dance" one's son and *aṣhā* means "to anoint him with clarified butter and put him in the sun."	
or *tudassim* his *nūnah*,	The *nūnah* is the dimple in the chin of a small child, synonym *faḥṣah*, and *tadsīm* is blackening the latter "so that the 'eye' may not afflict him."	3.12.22
or perform *bajbajah* on him,	*bajbajah* is "something one does when speaking endearments to a child."	
or *ḥawfazā*,	*ḥawfazā* is "flinging a child onto one's feet in order to lift him."	
or tell him, "*ḥalqatan*,"	They tell a child when it belches, "*ḥalqatan*," meaning "May your head be shaved (*ḥuliqa*) time and time again (*ḥalqatan baʿda ḥalqah*)."	
or *baḥbāḥi*,	*baḥbāḥi* is "a word that gives notice that something has run out or has ceased to exist."	
or *maḥmāḥi*,	*maḥmāḥi* is the same as *baḥbāḥi*; further synonyms *ḥamḥāmi* and *hamhāmi*.	
or *kikh kikh*,	Said "on reproving a child for taking something in its hand."	
or be worried by his *danaʿ*,	"The child experienced *danaʿ*" means that "It became exhausted, then hungry, then yearned for food, then	

	became greedy, then was brought low, and then became abject and avaricious.”
or by his *qaqqah,*	“The sound made by a child, or made by a child when frightened.”
or heed his *ba’ba’ah* or his *babbah,*	*ba’ba’ah* referring to a child means “he said *bābā* (‘papa’)” and *babbah* is “onomatopoeic for the sound he makes.”
3.12.23 or his *taghtaghah* or his , *thaghthaghah*	*taghtaghah* is “onomatopoeic for the sound of laughter” and *thaghthaghah* is “a child’s biting before its central milk teeth have grown in.”
or his *ta’ta’ah* or his *da’da’ah,*	*ta’ta’ah* is onomatopoeic[139] and also means “the way of walking of a child” and *da’da’ah* is “onomatopoeic for the sound of rocking a child in the crib.”
or his *da‘ba‘ah* or his *ḥatārish,*	*da‘ba‘ah* is “onomatopoeic for the sound made by a child suckling” and the *ḥatārish* of a child are its “movements.”
or his *idrām,*	The *idrām* of a child is “the moving of its teeth to make way for others.”
or his *faṣīṣ* or his *intidāgh,*	One says “the child *faṣṣa,*” verbal noun *faṣīṣ,* when it “cries feebly,” and that it *intadagha* when it “laughs to itself.”
or give a thought to his *mi‘qād,*	The *mi‘qād* is “a string bearing beads hung around a child’s neck.”
or his *qirzaḥlah,*	“beads worn by children”
or his *darrājah,*	The *darrājah* is “the carriage used by a child to take its first steps.”
or his *ḥiqāb,*	The *ḥiqāb* is “something tied around a child”s loins to repel the eye.”
or his *ṣumtah*?	The *ṣumtah* is “any food or other thing given to a child to pacify it”; synonym *suktah.*

"By the fealty I owe you and the liberties you allow me, my lord, will you not put him one day on your knee or let him ride on your back? Likewise, there would be no harm in your letting him play with the children of those who have been adorned with the honor of your service, for he is still young and knows nothing of these distinctions. And there would be no harm either in your spending that same evening among your esteemed womenfolk, along with those men of your village, and their wives, who know how to comport themselves politely in the presence of women, for I observe that the mistress is oppressed by her lonely state, which you have no books or entertainments to relieve. There can be no doubt that you would both benefit from spending some time in social intercourse with your subjects. The poor man's brain is not so much narrower or smaller than that of the emir that it cannot hold cogent opinions that may be lacking from that of the other, even if the latter's turban be larger and his head thicker at the back. How can you ask that the mistress and her daughters have good sense and understanding if they are to live hidden away in your ever-flourishing house? And how can you consent to their being—pardon my presumption!—ignorant and stupid? 3.12.24

"And you, my lords (rulers, shaykhs, grandees, metropolitans), try just once to bring your families and wives together with the families of your neighbors (though metropolitans have no wives because of their vows of celibacy) and to overcome the differences of sect between you, for to do so is more likely to bring you good fortune and happiness. What is the world if not women? What is the world if not children? Know, God have mercy on you, that mixing with women will not undermine the dignity of your position. Know, God guide you, that difference of views over religion does not preclude familiarity and friendship. Know, God set you to rights, that greater pleasure is to be found in your carrying your child on your back and wrapping his sweet legs around your neck than in increasing the length of your gown, widening your sleeves, and winding your turban or than in having servants standing by with their hands 3.12.25

on their hearts. Know, God increase your understanding, that the reason the Arabs gave names to the actions of small children was that they wanted you to notice those children and pay attention to them—to the degree that they coined for their excrement two strange words that have no like in terms of structure in the entire language,[140] namely *ṣaṣaṣ* and *qaqaq*. Know, God grant you success, that the *mister*, the *monsieur*, the *Herr*, and the *signor* enjoy greater peace of mind and better material conditions than you." Know, God grant you victory, that the Fāriyāq has now returned to Beirut and that his biographer, your undeserving slave, is contemplating the composition of a *maqāmah* that will please bachelor and married among you alike.

(Footnote: I think those lords and masters of ours alluded to above failed to hear my advice and that as a result my words to them have gone with the wind.)

(Notice: I have gone on at some length in this chapter that is about to bid you farewell so as to match the one on marriage.)

Chapter 13

A *Maqāmah* to Make One Stand

Faid al-Hāwif ibn Hifām in lifping tones,[141] "By the Recoiler I was seduced" (I seek refuge with God from such an introduction!) "—that Recoiler who whispers in men's *ears* every dark thought and all that feeds their *fears*—into thinking I'd married a woman cunning and *deceitful*, loudmouthed and *lustful*, shrewish and *frigid*, censorious and *rigid*, one moment vanished without *trace*, the next in your *face*, a woman *lewd* and *rude*, answering questions never *asked*, throwing down the gauntlet with none to take to *task*, proposing things to which no coin could *aspire*, and casting me into perils ringed about with *fire*. Thus at times my way was one of *restraint*, at others of *complaint*—at which she'd grow yet more wicked and more of a *prig* (though for my reproaches she cared not a *fig*). I then said to myself, 'By God, either it's the cold shoulder and making her think I've no interest in her *snatch*, or I roam the earth to see if I can find her *match*.' I chose the second view, having first sought protection through Qur'anic *recitation*, and left my house despondent and downcast, full of misogynistic *exasperation*. 3.13.1

"Before I'd gone too far upon the *road*, a flock of them suddenly past me *strode*, each strutting in a garment woven *tight* and jewelry that shone *bright*, their antique perfume wafting to horizons *infinite*. Among them I beheld the slim-waisted and the plump, the handsome, radiant sisters to the houris of the *Garden*, curers, through 3.13.2

their blandishments, of those whose members never *harden*. With them my soul hankered to have *union*, by their beauty my mind was driven to *confusion*, and, forgetting the humiliations I'd suffered at home, *exclaimed*, 'Would that you were mine (should wishing be of any use)!' and then *declaimed*

I see sweetness in the women walking by
  Though I wonder, do they in their harems still beguile?
In my hussy wife, however, be she walking or standing still,
  I find naught but hatred, aversion, and cause for bile.
With my eye I see her as she is—
  Could she, even to a blind man (which I am not), be less than vile?

3.13.3 "One, with a neck like that of a *deer*, eyebrow like the crescent moon should it *appear*, now addressed me and said, 'Don't take it so hard: you're not alone among *men*. My husband has written, with his *pen*,

I ponder the base nature of my wife
  And hate all members of the feminine gender,
But then recall not all of them are she,
  And toward all of them feel equally tender.'

"Then another, her brow with morning's light all *wreathed*, her glances as like to draw blood as a sword *unsheathed*, turned to me and said, 'Hear how my husband has *descried me*, and be not one of those who *vilify me*:

My wife tries her hand at every art
  Fearing no embarrassment or sophisticate's rebuff.
Though she be mistaken on every issue,
  One mistake she never makes is to cry "Enough!"'

3.13.4 "Then another—her sweat in beads like *pearls*, dark as night her *curls*—came up to me and said, 'Listen to what my husband has *composed* and see what if any likeness may be *supposed*:

More than anything, my wife wants me as a slave
A pathetic creature at her beck and call.
Should she though hanker for what can't be got,
I have to play Creator and meet her needs in full.'

"Then another—shimmying with pride and *coquetry*, her smile revealing teeth of unequalled *symmetry*—approached and said, 'Here's what my partner recited to me our first *night*, and has since proclaimed, with persistent sorrow for his *plight*:

My wife, by nature's gift, has twice my share
Of lips and mouths and fauces.
How can I be meant to satisfy her then,
When she keeps crying, "Give me more, please! Give me more, please!"?
Some member of mine will have to be doubled.
If not, watch for the commission of farces!'

"Then the fifth—shier than a deer in its covert out of *sight*—came toward me and said, 'Let me *recite* what my old man said, on the sixth *night*, to wit: 3.13.5

If others say, "'Wife' is a form that's used,"[142]
I'll say "spouse" without feminine declension.
I find nothing of the feminine in her deportment—
Nay, 'gainst stallions in battle, there'd be no contention!'

"Next the sixth came forward with smiling face and friendly *mien* and said, 'Let me pass on, on my husband's say-so (though he's an inveterate liar), these verses *twain*:

My wife watches over me in sickness and in health,
By day and by night, from afar and from nearby.
It's gotten so that when, dreaming, I hug the phantom of the one I love,
By the doorstep I see her watchful eye.'

3.13.6 “Up walked the seventh, with ample booty *armed* and countenance *charmed*, and declared, ‘My libelous husband along the same lines has *said*, with audacity unprecedented by husband toward the spouse who shares his *bed*:

> My wife’s so jealous of me that,
> If she sees me sick, she too falls ill.
> She never sees me with a given condition
> But she takes a chance on it as well.’

“Then the eighth appeared before me, wantonly *strutting*, one well equipped to please her husband in his *rutting*, and said, ‘I heard my husband singing these verses after going two weeks with head bowed looking at the ground, like one who, having first lost an *eye*, is then given the news that he’s about to *die*:

> My wife would love it dearly
> If I had two things quite off-putting—
> A what’s-it like a donkey’s when it’s pissing
> And a horn like a bull’s when it’s butting.’

3.13.7 “At this the ninth did me *invite*—lips parting, revealing pearls of shining *white*—saying, ‘Similar are what my offsprings’ father of me has *said*—words that to many in this and other lands he’s *fed*:

> Should any, scholar or ignoramus, come to see me,
> My wife accosts him and puts him to the test.
> Then, should she find he’s an expert lover, she declares,
> “All the sciences are gathered in this man’s breast!”’

“The tenth—of well-formed figure and roving eye—now blocked my *path*, saying, ‘More terrible still is what my husband recites, on the highway and before the *hearth*:

> Should a youth of good morals some day come to see me,
> My wife will corrupt him and he’ll depart a profligate,

Or if he's a doting debauchee already, she'll feed him
And hover over him, jealous and infatuate.'

"Then the *eleventh*—willowy and of well-formed *presence*—called to me and said, 'My husband—who's the suspicious *kind*—accuses me wildly of every thought to cross his *mind*, saying: 3.13.8

My wife sees men, then hides from their sight
But this owes nothing to any love of what is right.
In fact she fears a cardiac syncopation
Resulting from excessive desire for copulation.'

"Then the twelfth—short and stout, plump and *hot*—leaned toward me and said: 'Barrenness and infertility to the likes of my raving husband, since he has cast on women a wholesale *blot*! He says:

Chastity in women's no natural trait
But an occasion that to corruption doth persuade.
Like when you pull one tooth to save another
And your regret for the one you lost is plainly displayed!'[143]

"So I said, 'No question, I must go to where these poets *congregate* and make of each an *associate*. Who knows, perhaps I'll acquire from them *good sense*, discover some guidance in their *vehemence*, for their words are very *wise* and from seeking them out some clarity may well *arise*.' Now it was their custom to hide *away*, each *day*, and from after the afternoon prayer till the evening prayer was *called*, swap tales of this *world*, and how it *turned*, especially where women were *concerned*. I therefore enquired as to their *congregation* and was directed to their *destination*, and there I found them all together, a bench by the sea their *seat*, under an awning set up to protect them from the *heat*. Having approached their *meeting* and offered them my *greeting*, I asked, 'Will you agree to let one sit with you who feels toward you the ties of *affection* and has been led by your words to seek you out in hope of *direction*?' 'To the new arrival,' they replied, 'we extend a *welcome*, even if he be no longtime *companion*!' 3.13.9

3.13.10 "No sooner had I settled in my *chair* than one burst out, addressing those assembled *there*, 'I must finish what I began, its essence and import *reveal*. As I was saying, for what was this universe created if not women's *weal*? Is there a man who hasn't been the victim of their *guile*, not suffered to attain their love, not by their impossible demands been put to *trial*? They are the ones who enjoy the good things of life and its luxuries, its pleasures and its *flavor*, who its jewelry and gems, curios and curiosities, get to *savor*. They present us with ideas both practical and quite out of the *equation*, and task us with things that can lead to *decapitation*. For each limb they have a specific *trinket*; sometimes they acquire two or three and still there's room for more, though you wouldn't *think it*.'

3.13.11 "Then he bared his *teeth*, smiled, and continued with his *speech*: 'And on each member of ours are wounds that they've inflicted, never to be *cured*, bite marks to which we'll ne'er become *inured*. Master and man alike are, by their love, *prostrated*, rich man and vagabond, in their need for them, *conflated*. They cast men into perilous *places*, confused situations and constricted *spaces* so that they may provide their womenfolk with a sufficiency of food and *copulation*[144] and award them the opportunities presented by *separation*—for they sail seas, brave deserts, expose themselves to blade of sword and summer's *heat*, winter's cold and terror from the *elite*, enemy assault and the breaking of their noses by heavy *packs*, agonies of thirst and famine, toil and fatigue that break their *backs*, the humoring of the *watchful* and competition with the *reproachful*, to shame a closing of the *eyes* and final submission to an early *demise*; and each time a husband returns, he finds the lock on his honor *smashed*, his secret affairs in every corner *splashed*, and sees in his place rivals for her favors and *customers*, intimates and *cuckolders*.

3.13.12 "'Often he returns, neck broken, shank snapped, jaw *dislocate*, eyes bloodshot, money gone—a parlous *state*—and the first thing out of her mouth, before any greeting's made, is, "What present have you *bought*, and how many a gift and geegaw have you *brought*?" Even if you clothe her in a robe befitting *Būrān*,[145] put her up in the palace of *Ghumdān*,[146] feed her the most exquisite *foods*, offer her nectar from the hands of lovely lads and serenade her with *ouds*, take her for picnics to the flowery meadows of *Paradise*, carry her on your shoulders and do for her everything that's *nice*, you'll never find her *satisfied* or willing to ensure that you too are *gratified*. And woe to you should you approach fifty and lose your capacity to *provide*, or white hairs show in your sideburns when you're forty, or an illness afflict you at any *tide*; then she'll act as bold as any boy or brazen *lad* and proposition any man, willing or not, who may be *had*. She'll leave you in bed exhausted and, seated by the *window*, signal from it to any who may obey her *pronto*, indicating, "From Fate this occasion *snatch*; there's no *catch*, since he's in bed, unconscious and *unaware* and can't see who's with me *here*." Then she'll tell him, "Make your will, you, for your end is *near*, visitors and bed alike are fed up that you're still *there*, neither doctors nor friends any longer *care*." And—as you well know, married man—it's well within her power a trick on him to *play* and take, should she desire, a new lover each *day*; she'll find him behind the door all ready and waiting, ever *energetic*, always returning, a lover *frenetic*, her hook to get him a wink of the eye, her desire from him a milky *burst* to extinguish her raging *thirst*. Men are not so *made*, for they're ever busy at their *trade*, as though their worries had them roped and trussed with *cord*, or they're fearful of spending money they can't *afford*, or of *deflation* or premature *ejaculation*. How then can it be said that men and women have, for the bearing of life's burdens, equal *responsibility*, in withstanding its injustices equal *accountability*? Can any among you resolve my *perplexity*?'

"At this the one who'd attacked women without distinction[147] 3.13.13
confronted him and said, 'Here's your answer, delivered at *speed*, so pay it *heed*, and with the truth be *agreed*. I didn't attack women for being better off than us and less subject to *bane*, or more likely to enjoy pleasures and delights *obtain*, but rather for creating dissension and leading us *astray*, for causing torment and making us *pay*. What I said of them then, I said while *jealous*; what I say now I

say in a spirit of good sense and inquiry *zealous*. A woman, so long as she, a maid, in her parents' house is *hidden*, to emerge *forbidden*, has not one *friend*, not one intimate with whom to *unbend*. All the while though, her brother sports and *frolics*, capers and *rollicks*, travels and sees the world, makes friends with whomever he *pleases* and keeps company with whomever he *chooses*; and the more he gets to *laugh*, the happier and more joyful his father on his *behalf*.

3.13.14 "'Then, when she *weds*, she can do nothing her husband *forbids*; now it's he who has her at his beck and *call* and whatever she does, he's responsible for *all*. She can scarce leave her house without his *permission* and does nothing without first confirming his lack of *prohibition*. If he tells her, "You have my consent," he does it as though graciously bestowing on her the inheritance left him by his *sire*, and if he says, "You do not," she returns pitiful as a saint, burning with chagrin like a *fire*. In addition, for fear of his brutality she has to mollify his *mood*, take care of his bag and baggage, cook each day whatever he proposes by way of *food*, make new any old things of his he may throw her way, look after his bed and bedding, provide for his wants, and raise his *brood*. How many a night she spends coddling them while they fill the place with their *squawking*, *squalling*, and *bawling*, for it is she who *cleans them* and *weans them*,[148] *handles them* and *dandles them*, *cuddles them* and *swaddles them*, *jiggles them* and *juggles them*, *dresses them* and *caresses them*, *pats them* and *pets them*, *wipes them* and *gripes them*,

warms them and *tulbi'* them,	*alba'a* means "to feed on *liba'*," which are beestings
tuda'di' them and *tuhdi'* them,	*da'da'ah* means "moving and quieting," and *ihdā'* means "quieting"
tuzaqziq them and *tubāghim* them,	*zaqzaqah* means "making dance" (synonym *zahzaqah*), and *mubāghamah* has been mentioned above.[149]

turabbit them and *tuhamhim* them,	*tarbīt* means "lightly striking the child's side with one's hand to make it sleep," and *hamhamah* means "a woman's sending a child to sleep with her voice"
tuhadhid them and *tura‘‘im* them	"*hadhada* the child" means "he moved it to send it to sleep," and *tar‘īm* has been mentioned above[150]
jests with them or sports with them, hums to them, or *tuqārib* them,	*qāraba* means "he spoke quietly to it with pleasant words"
tuhaddin or *taṣrab* them,	*haddana* means "he gave the child what it wanted" and *ṣarb* is "tying a child's belly so that it gets fat"
tadghar them or *tuḍabbib* them,	*daghr* means "a woman's lifting a child's uvula with her finger" and "*ḍabbaba* the child" means "he fed the child with *ḍabībah* ('a mash made for a child in a small butterskin')"
trains them and *tudharrib* them,	*tadhrīb* means "a woman's holding a child up so that it may do its business"
tuqarrim them and *tujawrib* them,	*taqrīm* has been mentioned earlier[151] and *jawraba* means "he dressed him in his socks"
sits them down and *tunassis* them,	"*nassasa* the child" means "he said *is is* to make it urinate or defecate"; I say that it ought, by analogy, to be *ayyasa*
protects them with charms and *tunajjis* them,	*tanjīs* was mentioned above in Book One, Chapter 16[152]
swaddles them and *tarsa‘* them,	"*rasa‘a* the child" means "he tied beads on its arm or leg to ward off the eye"

prinks them and *primps them*.

"'These are the facts, and were pregnancy the only agony a 3.13.15
woman has to face in life, it would be enough—either for the burdens she must face *thereafter* (if it's her husband who's the *father*)

and which none but another of her sex could *bear*, or, if he is not, for the scandal in which she must surely *share* (we may assume she'll feel no sense of *guilt*, for scholars have said that when a woman gives birth to a child by someone other than her spouse it's painless, followed merely by a certain *wilt*); not to mention that, in addition to all that's gone *before*, God tests women with trying conditions and perils *galore*. These include lactation though not pregnant,[153] postpartum *pain*, retention of milk in the breast following birth (requiring a female neighbor to suck on it a couple of times to make it *drain*),[154] drying up of her milk and clotting of the colostrum in the udder, plus shriveling of the child in the *womb*, postpartum prolapse, and miscarriage and casting of the child before or after *term*, as well as childbed (that limbo between death and life), when for an undetermined period she's *confined*, and any *ʿiddah*, when her freedom is restricted for a number of days that has been *defined*,[155] and the menses that each month *afflict her* and often with shortness of breath *constrict her*—for they bring her pains in the back if *late* and cramp her chest and destroy her patience when too little or too *great*—plus, during pregnancy, cravings, morning sickness, and yearning for many things whose absence she cannot *face*, even when bitter to the *taste*, this leaving her unruly and *unbiddable*, furious and *hysterical*, debilitated and subject to *ennui*—along with other ills and conditions of which men are *free*. Any who views the matter with good sense and *fairly* will never argue to the *contrary*.'"

3.13.16 Al-Hāwif resumed, "At this, his opponent seemed to run out of steam, *deflate*, *equivocate*, and finally fear a *mutiny*. So another stood up and said, 'We've heard enough, good folk, for now. Let's leave the final determination to our return and further *scrutiny*,' and they went their ways, the evidence *defective*, the attempt to untie the knot having proved *ineffective*. To myself I said, 'I still may come across one from whom the final word on this matter I can *prise*, thus sparing myself further inquiry and *surmise*, for it seems to me that the speakers were like two horses in a *race*, each rider jockeying with knowledge and rhetoric for *place*. Each, though, I think, spoke according to what his mood *suggested* and not—as should those who report and relate—by ensuring that the truth was fully *tested*.' Then the Fāriyāq appeared, jogging through a certain *market*, depositing what food appealed to his eye and took his fancy in a *basket*, which I seized, crying, *exultant*, 'My *consultant*! My *consultant*!' To this he replied, 'Hunger *terrible*, miserable and *horrible*! No advice should be built on it, or proof, or double-witnessed *attestation*, and it's the judge himself who's hungriest for a *collation*, the one most owed a drop of something *wet*, or, if you prefer, a *coquette*.' 'That's precisely the area in which guidance is *sought*,' I said, 'and fear not for the safety of what's in the basket or of what you've *bought*.' 'What's the *beef*?' he asked. 'What's the cause of *grief*? Did you wade into a discussion of women with those who've taken that as their field of *battle*, wearing yourself, along with them, to a *frazzle*?' 'Indeed I did!' I said. 'Not for nothing did Qaṣīr cut off his *nose*,[156] nor was it by fate's decree alone that the boon companion abandoned the one to whom he'd been so *close*.'[157] Then I told him what had befallen me at home with the women as well as among the *bards* and said, 'Give me the answer by doubt *unmarred*.' He hung his head for a while, then said, 'Here it is, to the best of my ability, for hunger has made me to effort *averse* and left me no clear and truth-telling thoughts for *verse*:

Each spouse is the other's like with regard to pleasures 3.13.17
Each on a par in terms of what they need to live.
"Stand, woman!" and "Sit, woman!" are like "Hand over, sir, hand over!"
And "Do as I say, woman!"'s the same as "Give me, sir, give!"
The male in his youth to folly's more prone
Or in it more daring than the maid,
For she's by many an ill
Over and above the menses (and what an ill that is!) waylaid.
Then, when it's said, "He's older, now, dried up,"
The turn is hers, until a certain age she attains—

Sixty years at most—after which she abstains from all excesses.
  Thereafter, both can be considered mere remains.
True, the male is tormented among men
  By a weakness of his, at this point, in carrying out the deed,
But for her among the greatest of fears—
  The ones that make her choke as though dying—to which she pays heed
Is that her lover be as old as she
  When what she desires is a youthful lover's clasp.
Each has a measure of weakness
  That remains unchanged to their last gasp.'

"Then he ran off with his basket, nibbling at its *sides* and wreaking havoc on its meager *supplies*."

3.13.18 Continued al-Hāwif, "Truly, he hit the nail on the *head*, and I realized there was no self-interest in what he *said*, so I inclined to be reconciled with my *wife*, to rein in my rashness and curb our *strife*, and I went *home* where, finding her wearing her fingers for me to the *bone*, I threw myself into her arms as one who's been too long *away* and told her all that the two poets and the Fāriyāq had had to *say*, to which she responded, 'God reward him on my *behalf* and protect him in his exile from all dangers that may cross his *path*!' Then we continued in mutual *accommodation*, pledging each other to maintain our *association*."

Chapter 14

Raveningly Ravenously Famished

When the Bag-man found that living in Beirut was good for neither his body nor his mind,[158] he decided to leave it and set off for the Mountain, for he had gotten it into his head that he'd like to live in a Greek Orthodox monastery. He therefore proceeded with his wife and the Fāriyāq and they put up in a village below said monastery[159] for a few days. Now certain local beauties used to keep the Fāriyāq company there and share his meals, and when one of these learned that he was going up the following day to the monastery, she burst into tears, seemingly thinking he'd decided to take monastic vows. It occurred to him that she was at odds in this with women's ways, for women love monks more than they do common folk, since the seduction of a contemplative ascetic calls for a more than usually persuasive deployment of desire and deviousness, which is something that appeals to women, or vice versa;[160] afterward, when they find said ascetic to be obedient to them, they return to their former ways so that they can try out every kind of love and let not one escape them. 3.14.1

In short, the Fāriyāq was wept over enough at his departure this second time in his life to be counted among the ranks of those who have been loved, and he went the following day to the monastery, where he took a cell without lock or key, thus joining the company of Shitter Bāy,[161] whose doors cannot be closed (which, I declare, 3.14.2

is a strange way to build). This monastery was a place where all the people of the surrounding villages gathered, depositing their belongings there for fear that the Egyptian soldiers might attack them, the monastery being a safe sanctuary. When they arrived, they would go into any cell without exception, including that of the Fāriyāq, and if they found papers on his bed containing the interpretation of a dream or anything else, they'd snatch them up and read them. Some would understand enough for their tongues to turn, some enough for their heads to turn, some enough for their whole bodies to turn—meaning they'd turn their backs on him and leave—and some enough for their hands to turn, in which case they'd raise them so as to fall with a thud on writer and writings alike. Some would scoff at them and say, "They're just nonsensical dreams" and others would say, "They are inappropriate to a time of war" and he found no one among them who approved. Among these uninvited male visitors were uninvited female visitors, among them those whom it was an obligation to greet with "Hello!", "Well met!", and "Welcome!", others for whom just one of those would do, others who were worth two greetings in quick succession, and yet others who weren't worth even one.

3.14.3 All of this, taking the rough with the smooth, was bearable. What could not be borne was the hunger, which was caused by the closing of the highways. At the same time, the Fāriyāq had just emerged from the sufferings of the sea voyage, which had imposed on him a fast of successive days, and he could not do without something to snack on. This led him to go to the village and call out, "Any woman who has a chicken to sell should sell it to me!" to which one of them would answer, "You see that hen roaming with the others in the field? I want to sell it. If you want it, run after it and grab it with your hands," so he'd run after the chickens and jump over walls with them, and if he was lucky enough to break the leg of one or to tire it out, he'd pounce on it. As he ran after the hen, his thoughts would run alongside him, and he'd say to himself, "Here I am running after a hen. Is my wife, on the island, running after a rooster?" With all this running, I have to stop and point out that I mentioned earlier that the Fāriyāq was full of rashness, impetuosity, and apprehension. It was his nature, when away from his family, to keep contrasting his state with theirs, either sequentially or non-sequentially. An example of the first would be his saying, "Here I am running after a hen. Is my wife running after a rooster?" or his saying, for example, when dressed, "Is she at this moment naked?" or when standing, "Is she now flat on her back?" and so on and so forth. An example of the second would be "I am now running after a hen. Is a rooster running after her?"

The bread at the monastery and in the villages at that time was adulterated with darnel[162] and when the Fāriyāq ate it, he'd imagine he was still in the ship, at the mercy of sea monsters, and this would be confirmed for him by the entry of one of the monks into his cell while he was in that state. When he had reached the end of his tether, he composed some verses and sent them to the head of another monastery, thinking he might have some surplus supplies. They went as follows: 3.14.4

Would that I knew what use is eloquence
    On an empty stomach, or clarity of expression, or all the kinds of
        brilliant style:
When there's naught to eat
    They sear the throat and tongue like bile.
I'll give you a thousand metaphors for a single loaf
    And, compared to a lettuce, Taftāzān's[163] of paltry value.
Arabists, get lost!
    "Zayd struck ʿAmr"[164] will ne'er set bread on table.
Where oh where are the kebabs, the rice and
    Cracked wheat, the bowls of them spilling, so full they are, the
        cloth upon?
The days of stew are done and come is the turn of hunger,
    Whose dwelling place is Lebanon.
What ignominy! We dispatch gold coins
    But no one for them strives.

There is no selling and buying in a land
Where the staff of life is nowhere to be found, whilst darnel thrives.
I spent so long in the monastery 'twas as though
I were a monk the others could not stand,
For they saw about me books and pens
Of the sort their metropolitan has banned.
I'm hungry for gay company but live alone.
No woman, nor any man, e'er sees me—
My life's so bad that, were I shown it in a dream,
Bad grammar would never thenceforth make me moan.

The head of the monastery sent him some loaves that contained no darnel, along with these lines:

Your verses have reached me, dear Farqiyān,
But our role in this life is to be celibate.
We have no food of the sort you crave
And no wine or women to celebrate.

3.14.5 The Fāriyāq bustled off to see him and upbraid him for changing his name. In the monastery he caught sight of a woman connected to some emir, who had come to the monastery seeking refuge from the soldiers. When he saw the head, he told him, "My Lord, the bread may make up for the metrical faults in your verses, but why did you change my name?" Then he mentioned the lady he'd seen and said, "And you said too that monks don't have women, but I've just seen a lovely lady, filling her clothes with fat and flesh." Replied the other, "I changed your name for the sake of the rhyme, which is permitted to poets, and when I say 'We don't have women' I mean we have no wives. We don't deny, though, that the wives of others visit us sometimes for the blessings we bestow." "Which of you could bestow such blessings?"[165] asked the Fāriyāq. The man didn't understand but the lady got it and invited him to the usual water pipe. He stayed with her for a while, which further helped to make up for the changing of his name, and returned to his cell content.

There he found that a branch from the first dream[166] had remained caught in the head of the master of the Oneiromancer's Chamber and made him even more demented. Thus, on hearing the sound of drums from the soldiers' tents or seeing the glint of their weapons, he'd say, "Do you not hear Satan's drum which one of the monks is *drubbing*? Do you not see Satan's horns and the sparks that fly from them, the women against them *rubbing*?" His wife paid no attention to his shouting or to the soldiers' camping near the monastery, for love of "the Branch" had left room in her heart for nothing else. Then the Almighty vouched safe that the situation should improve and the soldiers left the country, the roads and highways became safe, and the master of the Chamber calmed down and decided to go to the city of Damascus, passing by Baalbek to see its wondrous castle, and they hired themselves horses and mules and resolved to travel.

Chapter 15

The Journey from the Monastery

3.15.1 The Fāriyāq and the Branch each mounted a mule, and the mistress and her husband each a mare, and a company of travelers joined them and they set off, making for Damascus. Somewhere along the road, the Fāriyāq's mule took fright at some passing surmise that occurred to it, bolted with him, and then threw him, and he landed with his thigh on a rock so that when he stood up he limped like a hyena. The master of the Chamber was saddened, being worried that the work of oneiromancy might be delayed, while the man's wife gloated since she regarded him as a spy, watching her and her Branch, and thus it is that what makes a man sad may make a woman glad; and here you must add to your extensive store of information the following, namely, that there is no kind of travel more wearisome than riding those obdurate mules. They have neither saddles nor bridles nor stirrups, and the imbeciles who rent them out provide ropes connected by rough metal chains in the place of a bridle. The rider holds this chain in his hand. If the mule bolts, the hand holding the chain will be too weak to check it, and usually when one mule bolts, they all do.

3.15.2 Next the Branch's mule took fright; he was thrown half off its back, his foot caught in a rope, and he hung there, his head bumping along the ground. At this, the mistress lost whatever fortitude she may have had regarding him, while no one could stop the mule.

The mistress's eye appeared to be going in one direction and her heart in another, while parts of her grew larger and parts smaller, parts went dry and parts stood on end, parts went wet and parts fell apart, parts got goose bumps and parts bristled, parts wagged and parts shook, parts darted like the tongue of a snake and parts waggled the same way, parts darted their heads forwards and backwards like an angry snake and parts bulged and parts got dirtied, and she started to fidget and twist, toss and turn, and for the first time in her life the wish entered her head that she might be a man so that she could protect him. Finally, God alleviated their plight and the mule stopped, and the Branch righted himself and they proceeded until they reached Baalbek, the Fāriyāq being at death's door. There he went and took shelter in the shade of a tree, where the breeze made him nod off and he slept, awaking exhausted.

Then they remounted and continued until they made Damascus, 3.15.3
the Fāriyāq being unwell the whole way, and he rented a room in a caravanserai and stayed there for days, unable to go out. When he had largely recovered, he made his way to his wife's family's house and informed them of what had happened, and they were delighted to see him. Then the fever took him once more. Then he revived and wanted to go to the bathhouse to bathe, but when he returned, it returned too. One day he happened to have gone down to the latrine when he fainted and fell down and his head went into the hole of the latrine and he started shouting, "My head's in the hole! There's a hole in my head!" and the people came running and found him in that state, and some laughed at him and some felt sorry. Then he got a little better and it seemed to him and his companion[167] that they should leave—but before he departs that noble city I must crush him and press him hard till he gives us a description of the charms of its women, that being the only thing he's fit for, for any talk of the peculiarities of its plants, its minerals, its air, the number of its inhabitants, or its political affairs would be beyond him.

He declared: "I entered the city of Damascus with a fever that had 3.15.4
accompanied me from Baalbek, and I had barely recovered by the

time I left the place. I can, therefore, give only a poor description of its women. If you accept this, I say, 'When I entered the city, I put up at a caravanserai called Khān Fāris, and the owner assigned an old woman to serve me. I observed, from her gentle treatment and caco-euphonious speech (meaning the way she mixed soft words with harsh), that old women play a large role there in women's dealings, by which I mean that they enter people's houses on the excuse that they will sell the women clothes to wear and come out having undertaken to strip them totally bare, for they are the closest means to hand and the trustiest method for bringing lover and beloved together. At first sight, it seemed to me that the Muslim women were better looking than the Christian ones, just as the Muslim men were more handsome and more chaste in speech, as they are in all the lands of Islam. The women's color is generally white flushed with red and most are tall and have fine figures. On the other hand, the white wrap that they wear when they leave their houses is not as appealing to the eye as the *ḥabar* of the women of Egypt.[168] Both conceal the charms of the figure, and it may be that they wear these deliberately to spare men their seductiveness, in which case they are to be thanked. But for what then this flirtatiousness and peering about, and what is this shaking of the buttocks as they walk and this voluptuousness of stride? Does not the heart have eyes to see what lies beneath the wrap? Does an overcast of clouds, without which the eye would be unable to gaze upon the sun, conceal the same? The clothes they wear indoors are as attractive and captivating as can be.'" The Fāriyāq continued, "When I was sick with fever, after I had left the caravanserai and breathed in the scent of the Christian women who came to visit me, they too appeared to me so entertaining and well-spoken, and had such pleasant traits and were so eloquent,[169] that I came to believe that my cure lay in such things, and had I not feared being called a miser for dispensing with the services of the doctor and, especially, had I not been obsessed with the idea that while in Damascus I might join my father who had died there, I wouldn't have needed the attentions of any physician. While, from my pillow, I was stealing glances at these women, I noticed on their breasts something that heaved and reared as they breathed.

"I also observed some Muslim notables who would visit the master of the house and talk with him at their ease—men of considerable dignity and gravitas—and I don't know what persuaded Metropolitan Jirmānūs Farḥāt to say, in his collected poems, 3.15.5

Meseems, then, I'm Aleppo, by nature refined,
While your nature, in its coarseness, is Damascus.

"The same imbecile would probably say, 'Your Aleppine's a dandy and your Damascene's a dog,' despite the fact that the Damascenes are more refined by nature than the Aleppines, of purer morals, freer of tongue, hand, and demeanor, more openhanded and generous. The proof of this is that because the Prophet once honored Damascus with the impress of his foot, and because it is the resting place of a number of his Companions and has become a place from which people set off for the Kaaba and has remained, from that time on, a staging post for pilgrims, the Christians who are there occupy spacious houses and capacious dwellings within its walls, unlike the Christians of Aleppo, who are allowed to live only outside the city and enter it only to buy and sell. Furthermore, God has preserved the area of Damascus from the earthquakes that occur frequently in Aleppo as well as from that unpleasant pimpliness that so often disfigures the faces of those affected by it and that is caused by its water. Did the metropolitan perhaps mean to say that it is the Christians of Aleppo, uniquely, who are more refined? Or could it be that he thought it acceptable for us to deprive people of their just deserts to make a rhyme for prose or an assonance? On that principle, one might call a Catholicos garrulous, a prelate a pitchy distillate, a priest a greedy beast, a monk a drunk,[170] a Market-man a charlatan, or a Bag-man a reticule-man. As far as language is concerned, there is, I swear, no comparison between the chaste speech of the Damascenes and the lame language of the Aleppines, for Aleppo, bordering as it does the lands of the Turks, has been infiltrated by many foreign words from the latter's speech. Thus they say *anjaq bi-yikfī* ('it's barely enough'), articulating the *j* in *anjaq* as though it were the Turkish *jīm*,[171] *yitqallanu* meaning 'he uses it,'[172] *khōsh khuy*,[173] and so on, and all this on top of their strange-sounding dialect and the foreign-tinged accent with which they pronounce Arabic words."

3.15.6 The Fāriyāq and his companion then traveled to Beirut and from there to Jaffa, where the deputy to the British consul (who was *not* the skilled and sagacious Khawājā Asʿad al-Khayyāṭ)[174] invited them and the ship's captain to join him in taking the drink made of water and sugar known as sherbet (which is a word that has gained fame among Frankish authors too, though they use it in their books only and not in their houses). They went with him and he served each with a cup appropriate to his body size. When the party was over, they set sail for Alexandria and from there to the island, where they were housed in its quarantine quarters. The Fāriyāq sent to his wife to inform her of his arrival and invite her to join him in his isolation, but she said, "I like neither isolation nor idleness." Afterwards she complied, and the Fāriyāq, regaling himself after the ardors of travel, breathed in the scent of a woman.

Chapter 16

Ecstasy

It's the smell of Umm Dafār, in which all that walks or flies or plows the seas is as one, and it is made plain in the title. Can you smell it?[175] 3.16.1

Chapter 17

An Incitement to Nudity

3.17.1 The two of them[176] then entered the town and the Fāriyāq went back to interpreting dreams and physicking the foul of breath. After a short while, a Persian, of whom it was said that he had been a Muslim and become a Christian and that he was a master poet well-known among the scholars of Persia, came to visit the master of the Chamber. The latter therefore took the Fāriyāq to welcome him in the quarantine quarters. He turned out to be a short, squat, round, bearded little fellow, and when he entered the town, he put up at the Chamber. Now the master decided, right at the outset, that he should shave off his beard. The barber was brought and set his razor to work but when he got to the poet's mustache, the latter covered it with his hands. The master approached him with a book in his hand from which he drew proofs for the necessity of shaving mustaches and they discussed and argued until the master agreed to limit the sacrifice to half.

3.17.2 On another of those ill-omened days, the Fāriyāq went to the Chamber and there found that the master had stripped himself of every stitch of his clothing and set to roaming around the house in that state and inciting people to follow his example, saying, "Dear People, clothes were made to cover the pudenda but he who is pure and innocent of all sin has nothing of which to be ashamed. When Adam was in Paradise, in a state of sinlessness and innocence, he had no need of clothes." When he went to his wife to persuade her to undress, she told him, "Women are without sin only at night, so they have to be covered by day." The Persian saw him in this state and asked the Fāriyāq, "What has made our friend change his black clothes today and put on red ones?" The Fāriyāq replied, "He's a soldier of the Bag and soldiers here wear uniforms."

The derangement of both husband and Persian increased and became so entrenched that the wife feared they might find themselves together in some tricky situation and get into an argument and a fight. She therefore requested that the Fāriyāq take the Persian into his home. In the midst of all this, the Branch had now caught up with her, coming from the Syrian lands, bringing with him the delirious promise of delicious fruit and a sturdy trunk.[177] She therefore put him up in her house, treating him like an honored guest and trying constantly to have the Chamber to herself with him, even at the cost of her husband's continued derangement and her own loss of her family. The Branch thus stayed there in the lap of *luxury*, while she stayed with him, her hands fuller than those of Dhāt al-Niḥyayn,[178] in the utmost *ecstasy*, and her husband continued to incite people to *nudity*, claiming it as a sign of innocence and *purity*. 3.17.3

The Persian stayed with the Fāriyāq, who accepted him only because of his meekness, weakness, and general taciturnity. Then, one night, after seeing lovely ladies visiting the Fāriyāq's wife, his tongue was untied and he said things that indicated that it was not by divine guidance that he had become a Christian but that he had been compelled by poverty and hunger. The man went to bed that night with his heart afire with passion and during the night he left his room and set off for that of the Fāriyāqiyyah. Her husband noticed what was going on and set upon him with a rope, and the other was unable to defend himself. In the morning, the Fāriyāq consulted his wife on the matter. She said, "I think this Persian has gone insane because he isn't married, and the same applies to all other madmen. Didn't you see how, when he saw the girls at our house yesterday, 3.17.4

his face lit up and he started talking?" The Fāriyāq said, "I replied, 'I don't believe you're right this time, for our friend the Bag-man went mad *after* he got married.' 'But,' she responded, 'the balance of his mind had been disturbed before that by the dreams, and when he got married he failed to give marriage its due, so marriage got its own back at him, and others should take him as a warning.' I said, 'How did you come to know that?' and she replied, 'Married men shouldn't be inquisitive and stick their noses into things that don't concern them.' I said, 'That would be in restraint of men's daily business.' 'There'd be no restraint,' she said, 'because I wouldn't prevent them from going about their work, just from idle *conversation* and an obsession with dream *interpretation*. Plumbing the science of the supernatural requires more effort than succumbing to compliance with the super-stupid. If it were up to me, I'd treat all madmen with women, through women, and against women.' 'Do all the "particles of attraction"[179] belong to women?' I asked. 'Indeed,' she replied. 'All attraction is to be found in women.' 'But you omitted "particles,"' I said. 'On the contrary,' she answered. 'They're still there.'[180]

3.17.5 "'Enough banter,' I said. 'Give me a ruling on this madman.' 'Take him back,' she said, 'to the Chamber. I hate the idea of his staying with us for long because I'm afraid that if I get pregnant, the child will come out like him.' 'By what means,' I asked, 'would madness be able to get into a fetus?' 'Aren't children born white and bonny,' she enquired, 'when their fathers are hideous? If the mother's eye didn't have some special influence during her pregnant cravings, it wouldn't be so.' 'That's a view,' I said, 'that will lead to unbelief and absurdity. Unbelief because you are claiming that women are participants in the creation of mankind and absurdity because if women had some special influence over that, sons would either all look like their fathers or all be bonny.' 'Responding to your accusation of unbelief,' she returned, 'it is unquestionable that God, Mighty and Majestic, has created this feature in women, and He is the prime mover, meaning that the esurient power placed in her by the All-Capable Creator has an impact on the child's environment. Responding to that of absurdity, the last thing women ever want their children to look like is their fathers, and any son you see who looks to you like his father is likely to be her eldest.' 'May God produce many more like you!' I said. 'You must have done your theology[181] in the school of "the Hairy One"!'[182] 'You're right,' she said. 'We're talking here about hairy ones, not shaven or plucked ones.' 'The potty one!' I cried. 'Tell me what to do with the potty one and enough of your potty tongue! You've almost driven me mad as well with your seminary[183] talk!' 'And since when,' she answered, 'did you hate semen? It's all you care about. As for the madman, it must be as I said. Take him off to the Chamber and leave him there without telling anyone.'"

The Fāriyāq continued, "So I took him off and put him in one of 3.17.6
the rooms there and locked the door on him. When he got hungry, he kept trying the door to see if he could get out and the servant heard him and let him out. The wife of the master of the Chamber managed to send him back to where he came from and she decided to take her husband back to her own country. Another man from his country came to deputize for him where oneiromantic matters were concerned but didn't stay long, for reasons that will be explained.[184] Before revealing these, however, we must close this chapter with the verses composed by the Fāriyāq when the master of the Chamber was inciting people to take off their clothes. They go as follows:[185]

You want us, then, friend, to go crazy 3.17.7
And take our clothes off today
And not sleep tonight when it gets dark
Or harbor suspicions about women
And not see when Ḥannā[186] comes
And, if he doesn't, say, 'He must be sick, depleted'![187]
And if some lecher[188] comes to us and his joints go weak,[189]
We're to mount him on horses, so he be not distressed

And make the wife a shield for him,
To protect him from any tormentor who may hurt him[190]
And not care if we see that a horn
Has appeared on our temples, dinging and donging—
For you have seen that the mind exhausts the body
And denies the free man what he hopes for
And none will attain good fortune in serenity
Unless he display what he has concealed.
3.17.8 Shush, you old man who has grown long in the tooth!
What have you to do with the whickering doe, the snickering buck?[191]
You get into difficulties and you suffer
And do not care should you find yourself feeble.
What did you meet with from a preacher who went mad—
And from one who goes around here—and who wept?[192]
You appeared before us in an ill-omened month that crushed
The loving couple[193] so we said, 'Verily,
No abode we have stayed in with you
Has been without some evil upset that occurred.
Every one among us who has dependents complains of you.
You have brought a specimen of every misfortune—
Madmen who have exposed their willies,[194]
One afflicted with fever who suffers from a lingering disease,
And a sickly invalid who moans[195]
Till even his enemy would mourn for him and feel sorrow.
Enough! Slow down! You have ignited sorrow in us
And burdened the city with a worry that has preoccupied it utterly.
Be off, God guide you, and depart from us
Before you cut off our supplies of flour
And dry up the water and drive away good fortune
From a town that previously was secure,
And choose some other place to hole up in
Where you can take refuge, in comfort and quiet.

It won't matter if you are sold short there 3.17.9
    And repulsed as harshly as an orphan or if you are flung aside
Or if you came prattling and boasting vaingloriously
    And thinking that all that's ugly in you is comely
So that you will never see your like
    Or an enemy who harbors a secret grudge against you,
Just as here you did injury to a crabbed little man[196]
    Whose molars and then his other teeth turned a rusty color
        because of you.
Were he able, he would make you a guest in prison
    Where you would be a pawn to disasters.
His devil[197] has accused you of a crime:
    He says he's grown old from your tobacco.
You have put in the house of prayer an oven
    Whose smoke has gone everywhere and blinded the heedless.'
A company said, 'His spittle has turned smelly
    And his mistakes in Arabic amount to an injury to us,
So let him seek a friend in some other abode than there
    And it matters not to us if he is generous or miserly
Or if he weeps at his misfortune or sings
    Or calls sincere blessings on us or curses us
Or roars with hunger and humiliation and wails
    Or says, "We have become [nothing] after we were
        [something]!"'
You never loved us, conceited one,
    And never spoke to us in Arabic and never pleased us,
So may God not reward you with good fortune on our behalf!"

Chapter 18

A Drain

3.18.1 When the Fāriyāq was left with no more dreams to interpret, he was charged with the translation of a book[198] on behalf of the Committee[199] in the land of the English, so he translated it for them into this language of ours, according to its proper rules. It so happened that at the same time Metropolitan Atanāsiyūs al-Tutūnjī the Aleppine, author of *Al-Ḥakākah fī l-rakākah* (*The Leavings Pile concerning Lame Style*), traveled to the same country on some pot-scraping business and got to know the aforesaid Committee, whom he proceeded to inform that the Fāriyāq's language was utterly corrupt because of his failure to observe the conditions that he had laid down for translators and Arabizers in the abovementioned book. He also told them that the Christians[200] loved disorderly, disarranged discourse, that he had been raised in this craft since many a year, that he had trained many others at the school of ʿAyn Tirāz and elsewhere,[201]

And that the books of the church have their own method
Which differs from that of the rest of mankind and is at variance with it,
And that there is blessing in the lame phrase
And good fortune for a people whose shame is conspicuous

And that the richness of their solecisms in speaking is to them
Like a song sung to a rhythm and the common factor is obvious[202]
And that the use of al-Mawlā[203] in reference to God is an abomination
And that all should be on guard against saying *wallawu l-adbāra*[204]
And that *tukāh* is to be found as the plural of *muttaki'*[205]
And that *maṣūn* is rare compared to *muṣān*[206]
That *sha'b* is more common than *qawm*[207]
And great sins lie in saying *malak* and not *malāk*[208]
And that *'abīd*, when preceding "God,"
Is more proper than *'ibād*,[209] and that is a judgment no one can deny
And that the plural of *'adhāb* is of the pattern of *rakākāt*,[210]
And that *sā'ir* is not a synonym of *bāqī*[211]
And one shouldn't say *wā'iẓīhā* but *mū'iẓīnahā*[212]
And that any who says *addaw* rather than *waddaw*[213] is a renegade
And from *radda* say, if you wish, that the active participle may be formed as
muridd;[214] so say the Christians of the latter days.
And as to *yaẓharu*, cancel it and take *yabānu*[215] as its equivalent
And *ṣirnā banīnan bi-tadhakhkhur*[216] is common
And likewise "a *maṣaff* gathered glorifying God"[217]
And that a *wāw* immediately follows *ka-mā* used as a conjunction[218]
And that *idh* must take the jussive[219]
And that the use of the relative adjective *alladhī* after the dual is an impeccable tradition[220]
As is writing imperative *–ī* with the weak verb,[221]
As told him by that modern, the priest of Choueir,[222]
And that retention of the *nūn* of *-ūna* following *kay*
And *an*[223] is widespread—so Zākhir insists.

And that after *yuʿṭā* to put the subject supplying the agent in the accusative is
A necessity,[224] just as the omission of *fa-* in the conditional clause is common,

and asked the aforementioned Committee to entrust the Arabization of the abovementioned book to him, so that it might find acceptance among the Christians, which if they didn't, it wouldn't. When they saw that he had a beard and, especially, that he was adorned with the charisma of a metropolitan—a metropolitan being of necessity to them a man of learning and merit—they believed that he must be possessed of merit and learning and handed the work over to him. For this reason, specifically, the Chamber closed and all that remained to the Fāriyāq was his salary from his job of treating the foul of breath.

3.18.2 Here it must be noted that no people in the world accord more importance to titles than the English. If someone visits them from a foreign country bearing the title Emir, or Shaykh, or Metropolitan, he receives their utmost consideration, especially if he speaks French. The title of metropolitan is one that in their eyes relieves its possessor of the need for any further recommendation or reference, since they translate the word by the equivalent in their terms, which is archbishop, and any who reaches that rank among them has an income of four thousand golden guineas. Where beard length is concerned, this is no indicator among the Arabs of understanding or distinction, as is clear from the story of al-Ma'mūn and the jurisprudent ʿAllawayh.[225] Arabs and non-Arabs, however, differ in their ways.

3.18.3 When the Fāriyāq's vacation from treating the foul of breath—the three months of summer each year—arrived, he resolved that he would travel to Tunis and embarked on a ship whose captain was one of those natives of the island who are between the Market-men and the Bag-men, and sometimes between the latter and the philosophers.[226] After a voyage of twelve days, each one full of peril and suffering, they reached Ḥalq al-Wād. During the voyage, some of the sailors had claimed that it was taking so unusually long simply because the captain had, contrary to the custom of all other ship's masters, set sail on a Friday—something they never do, either out of respect for that day or because they view it as ill-omened.[227] The Fāriyāq, however, knew the real reason, which was his own inborn ability to hex, just as he knew that the goal of any voyage he might undertake, be it near or far, could not be reached in anything less than twelve days. However, he kept this from them.

Declared the Fāriyāq, "As for the city, its markets are cramped and its shops small. Its air and its food and drink are, however, good and it has a great variety of fruits. Its inhabitants are kindhearted and generous and they honor guests and love strangers. It has many singers and instrumentalists, most of them Jews, whose women are fat and white and have large, dark eyes. This is despite the Christians' claim that God cursed and transfigured the Jews following their crucifixion of Our Lord Jesus, peace be upon him, stripping them of all inner and outer beauty. I think though that if the priests were to catch sight of one of their statuesque, plump, heavy-haunched women, they would call the propagator of this point of view a heretic and confute him; only those among them who spend all their time with Christian women and see no others could make this claim, it being a known fact that the appetite favors what is to hand and *present* over what is missing and *absent*. Or perhaps they mean that this transfiguration befell only the men and spared the women—a point on which they should be interrogated. Moreover, many of these untransfigured women are by no means without willowiness and grace, and it is a habit of theirs to walk with their faces unveiled and their calves exposed." 3.18.4

When it was almost time for the Fāriyāq to leave the city, one of his local acquaintances told him, "Were you to write a eulogy of its ruler *august*, you would find him the most generous of those who give and *entrust*, of all people the one most content to be generous and do favors." He responded, "I have made my mind up now to leave and I can no longer change it." Then he returned to the 3.18.5

island, there being among the other passengers two Austrians, one of whom was a rich merchant's son, the other the son of an officer in the army of the Pope. The latter had borrowed one of those thin phosphoric matches from the Fāriyāq; this he returned after two days.[228]

3.18.6 When the Fāriyāq had settled once more at home, it occurred to him to compose an ode in praise of the abovementioned most honored lord, so he wrote a long ode mentioning all the beauties of that land that he now missed (albeit without allusion to those of its Jewesses). To his surprise, in only a few days the abovementioned lord had sent him a gift of diamonds such as kings might begrudge their closest companions, and with it a letter from his companion *august* and vizier most *just*, Treasurer Muṣṭafā Pasha, of which the following is the text:

> To the well-beloved (whose affairs will, we may hope, be ever protected by *affection*, his talents, seat of his action and tongue, by *perfection*), that man of letters *skilled*, with fullest measure of all arts *filled*, of most excellent morals and winner, on rhetoric's racetrack, of the victor's *mark*, the distinguished *Fāriyāq* (may his talents remain forever bright as a *spark*, his rhetoric like stars in nighttime's *dark*)! To proceed: His Excellency, Guardian of Our Blessings, Lord, and Master, Counselor[229] Aḥmad Pasha Bāy,[230] Emir of Tunis's Autonomous *Province* (may it remain forever protected by his *presence*!) is in receipt of an ode, a specimen of your literary *oeuvre* (may it as an adornment to your verses *serve*, cast further light upon your *exaltation*, and assure the permanence of your *reputation*!). And how excellent its author, creator, and elaborator doth to us *appear*, for he has mastered rhetoric's every reach, both far and *near*, and it has submitted itself and its keys to his *care*. Our Master (may God aid him!) deems your missive worthy of his high *consideration* and praises your eloquence and literary *articulation*, and has dispatched to you from his elevated presence a casket, that you may keep the memory of his affection to *hand*, as of his territories

> and *land*. Accept it, then, as a token of his favor and the least his duty owes you, and may God keep you in the eye of His *solicitude* and drape you in the covering of His *plenitude*! Written by the Poor-in-His-Almighty-Lord Muṣṭafā, Treasurer of the Tunisian State, on the twenty-fourth day of the sacred month of Dhū l-Ḥijjah, 1257.[231]

While these events were unfolding, Metropolitan al-Tutūnjī arrived on the island. Informed of his coming and unaware of the lies that the metropolitan had told about him to the English, the Fāriyāq went to greet him and invite him to a feast that he had prepared in his honor, and the metropolitan took up residence in a house where he busied himself with the translation of that very book to which he'd contested the Fāriyāq's right. From time to time, the Fāriyāq would pass by and see him without picking up from him a sense that anything was amiss. After a few days, a dust-laden,[232] twisting, grit-bearing, shifting, raging, piercing, unflagging, blasting, blighting, track-obliterating, ground-hugging, veering, swirling, whirling, hot, scorching, blistering, howling, lightening, gusting, rain-bearing, buffeting harmattan of a wind arose, followed fast on its heels by odors overpowering,[233] rotten, rank, putrefying, putrid, puent, fetid, fecal, feculent, stinking, reeky, reechy, rancid, rancidous, noisome, cacodorous, maleolent, mephitic, flatulent, flatuous, armpit-redolent, smegmatic, nidorous, hircine, plebeo-sudoral, latrinal, urinal, annulo-vermicular, oleaginous, nose-wrinkling, catamitic, tannic, and oro-dyslalic, mixed with Himyaritic hapax legomena, mispronunciations, lispings, misspeakings, schwa-ations,[234] sibillations,[235] and shibillations;[236] and lo and behold, the aforementioned metropolitan, in attempting to translate the book in question into Arabic, was found to have fallen headfirst down a widemouthed well and, given that he was as ignorant of how to clean out the mud[237] as he was of the language, these foul smells inevitably carried to the Fāriyāq's house, for the director of the printing press was a friend of his and had asked him to correct the typographical errors 3.18.7

in it, without reference to the mistakes of translation. The Fāriyāq then discovered the reason for the metropolitan's arrival and all his tricks and he bagged a few revolting puffs of those smells, sent them to the aforementioned Committee, and awaited their response.

3.18.8 A while later, it happened that the August Master Sāmī Pasha the *Grand* (celebrated for praiseworthy qualities throughout the *land*) arrived on the island. As the Fāriyāq had a special place in the latter's heart, he went to congratulate him on his safe arrival and the person in question tasked him to stay with him for the period of seclusion in quarantine, and the Fāriyāq informed his wife of this. She told him, "How many times do I have to tell you there's nothing good to be had from reclusion?"[238] He replied, "There's no harm in it if one's with an emir, for then the honor of the name is enough." "The name can never take the place of the deed," she answered. "I responded," continued the Fāriyāq, "by saying, 'On the contrary, lots of people have accepted the one for the other.' 'Will he be with one of his wives?'[239] she asked. 'I don't know,' I answered. 'If the name were enough,' she said, 'a woman could just write "emir" somewhere on her body.'[240] 'I'll make up for the time that's lost,' I said, and she said, 'Or else set about compensating me right now!' 'How fast women are!' I said and she, 'And how they prefer taking it slow!' I said, 'I used to wish God had created me a woman, or turned me into a woman, but now I don't, as women don't have the patience of men, and to live in this world one needs patience.' She said, 'If women weren't more patient than men, they wouldn't outlive them on this earth, despite the pains they suffer in pregnancy and childbirth.'

3.18.9 "I said, 'That's not the reason. The reason is that the righteous, in contrast to the unrighteous, do not live long on this earth.' 'Do you mean to tell me,' she said, 'that righteous men exist, when there is no evil of which they are not the originators? Do females corrupt females the way males do males? Who is it that corrupts women if not men? And who is it who falls head over heels for them, seeks their company, wheedles their way into their hearts, woos them, and seduces them with promises of money, affection, and fidelity, if not they? And then, when one of them has gained the confidence of one of us and wins her heart, he goes and tells everyone. He may get drunk with some acquaintances, or pretend to do so, and then make himself out to be a hero in front of them by revealing things that should be hidden and violating what should be inviolate. You men, I declare, put all your trust in the strength and might that God has made yours and believe as a result that you are better than women in all things. If honor lay in strength, elephants would be better than humans. True, we enjoy seeing a man who's tall, youthful, and strong, but it is inappropriate for him, given that he is so, to come to his poor, weak wife and treat her frivolously,[241] bad-temperedly, dementedly, ill-humoredly, tetchily, coarsely, boorishly, nonchalantly, cholericly, roughly, rudely, truculently, peevishly, pettishly, petulantly, frappishly, froppishly, protervously, severely, and angrily, or with beady looks, harping and bellowing, or with huffing, or with insults, vituperation, tirades and diatribes, or with abuse of her rights and with infidelity, or by knocking her to the ground—and then go to another woman and delude her into thinking that he's her captive, her prisoner, her retainer, her slave, her bondsman, her serf, her servant, her thrall, her chattel, who is abjectly enamored of her, sick from his passion, demolished by his ardor, laid low by his thirst for her, slain by his desire for her, and a martyr to his love for her, and that God Almighty has placed him in this world simply to make her happy.'"

The Fāriyāq continued, "I told her, 'While the man may be at fault in this, the woman is not innocent either, for believing him and allowing herself to be led by him.' She said, 'She believes him because her heart is pure, her feelings uncorrupted. The honest person doesn't doubt the words of others and the noble man is easily deceived. If people were to hear that a married woman had fallen in love with someone other than her husband, they would view her with the greatest disapproval and regard the matter with the greatest disgust. Drums would be beaten, heads nodded, books written, 3.18.10

and there would be no one left in town who did not have some tale, or lie, to tell about her. If, however, they were to hear that a man had fallen in love with someone other than his wife, they'd put what he'd done down to sickness and make excuses for him, accusing his wife of withholding her favors or of being no good in bed and wetting it, or of defecating while being fucked or of keeping him out of her bed, or of whinnying through her nostrils or of being *ghabūq* [?][242] or of spraying water during intercourse and making a noise with her vulva, or of having a hernia and making a sound with her vagina, or of having a hole too small to admit the penis and being given to farting, or of being insatiable in intercourse and having a mons veneris that both squeaks and passes wind, or of snorting like a madwoman during intercourse and having lopsided breasts, or of having no flesh on her thighs and a bottomless tunnel, or of having smelly foreparts and a loose vagina, or of leaving her anus half washed and stinking and having privates on which no hair grows, or of having breasts that do not develop and never having a period, or of coming as soon as a man plays with her and having a tiny "thing," or of menstruating through her anus, or of having a vaginal fistula and being unable to hold her water, or of not menstruating, or of having no flesh on her thighs, or of not having been circumcised and having a wide space between her anus and her vagina, or of having a flabby vagina, or of having thighs so tightly pressed together there is no gap between them, or of having sweaty foreparts and body, or a cold vagina, or long pubic creases and a soft wide vulva, or a large wide vagina, or of suffering from leucorrhoea, or a vaginal hernia, or a slanted slit, or of being wide-woofed, or straddle-thighed, or quick to conceive, or of being given to miscarrying, or not having periods, or having never-ending periods, or of putting kohl on one eye only and wearing her shift inside out, or of having a mutilated nose, or foreparts that produce much fluid, or buttocks that are skewed and raised, or of not conceiving for years even though she is not barren, or having a rectum and vagina that form a single passage, or of having a long clitoris, or wide sexual organs, or of being one who, having the vagina and rectum as a single passage, loses control of her bowels during intercourse, or of having thighs that rub against one another, or of other flaws, while seeing nothing revolting in what he had done, even though a woman has more reasons to go astray than a man.'

"'Pray state them so that I may avoid them,' I said. She said, 'The first is the husband's failure to provide his wife with her full rights, meaning her marital rights for the sake of which she abandoned her father and mother, her family, her home, her country, and, not infrequently, her religion.' 'Dear God,' I said, 'I beseech Your indulgence and forgiveness! What next?' 'Others are his neglect of her affairs and lack of interest in anything that might bring her ease, give her pleasure, or raise her spirits, or in entertaining her, distracting her, giving her enough to drink, adorning her, warming her, perfuming her, consoling her, strengthening her, taking her for walks, taking her to lunch, encouraging her, lastingly delighting her, gladdening her, or preserving her.' 'Indeed,' I said, 'and in making her strip, drip, secrete, spot, undress, caress, and reveal!' 'Indeed,' said she, 'all that and more, seeing that she's the prisoner of his house throughout the day, serving him and looking out for his affairs, while he roams the town from place to place and moves from market to market, and then, when he finally comes home, falls to the ground like one in a swoon and says that overwork has exhausted him and exhaustion overworked him and that this occurred to him and the other befell him, though it was he who exposed himself to the first and chased after the second. Other reasons are the softness of the woman's heart and the compassion that the Almighty Creator has made one of her innate traits, such that she is incapable of meeting a man's love for her with anything but affection or his flattery of her with anything but interest and encouragement, to say nothing of the common origin and formal similarity of the words *raḥim* ("womb") and *raḥmah* ("mercy").' 3.18.11

"I said, 'Even more amazing than the etymology that you have adduced in evidence is the conformity of the meanings of *kays* 3.18.12

("cleverness")—in the *Qāmūs*, its author says, "*Kays* is the opposite of *ḥumq* ('stupidity') and denotes 'sexual intercourse, an intelligent man skilled at his work,[243] generosity, the mind, and victory achieved through cunning'"—or between *sirr* ("secret" or "heart") and *surūr* ("joy"), or *basṭ* ("delectation") and *sharḥ* ("gladness"),[244] or *buḍʿ* ("vulva") and *biḍāʿah* ("commodity"), or *shuʿūr* ("sensation, feeling") and *mushāʿarah* ("sleeping together within a single garment"), or *lamj* ("nibbling" or "sexual intercourse") and *qamṭ* ("tasting" or "sexual intercourse"), or, especially, between Abū Idrās ("the vagina") and Abū Idrīs ("the penis"), may their concordance long remain, in form as in meaning!' At this, she laughed out loud and said, 'God honor our language, which brings together sense and shape!', to which I responded, 'though on occasion this may require the offensive or the inappropriate, as in the case of *arra*, which means both "to have intercourse with" and "to expel one's excrement," or *jannaḥa*, which means both "to piss" and "to screw (one's slave girl)," or *maʿaṭa*, which means "to have intercourse with," "to pluck one's hair," and "to fart," or *jalakha*, which means "to have intercourse with," "to flay (someone's belly)," and "to chop (a chunk of flesh off someone with one's sword)," or *matakha*, which means "to have intercourse with" and "to expel (one's excrement)," or *malakha*, which means "to have intercourse with," "to drag something in one's grip or one's teeth," and "to waver pointlessly," or *malaqa*, which means "to have intercourse with" or "to strike with a stick," or *jaẓẓa*, which means "to have intercourse with," "to chase away," "to throw to the ground," and "to oppress (someone, with a surfeit)," or *khajja*, which means "to have intercourse with" and "to expel (one's excrement)," or *lakhaba*, which means "to have intercourse with" and "to slap (a male)," or *matara*, which means "to have intercourse with" and "to expel (one's excrement)," or *jalada*, which means "to have intercourse with" and "to beat (a male) with a whip and injure his skin," or *ʿaṣada*, which means "to have intercourse with," "to twist," and "to force (a male) to do something," or *ḍafana*, which means "to have intercourse with" and "to expel (one's excrement)," or *maḥana*, which means "to have intercourse with" and "to strike," or *mashana*, which means "to have intercourse with" and "to scratch," or *aswā*, which means "to fornicate," "to dishonor," and "to insert (the penis, into a woman)," and likewise *ḥasha'a* ("to have intercourse with" or "to whip"), *haṭa'a* ("to have intercourse with" or "to defecate"), *ḥala'a* ("to have intercourse with" or "to strike [with a sword]"), *khaja'a* ("to have intercourse with" or "to strike [with a stick]"), *raṭa'a* ("to have intercourse with" or "to expel [one's excrement]"), *zaka'a* ("to have intercourse with [one's young slave girl]" or "to strike"), or *lata'a* ("to have intercourse with" or "to shoot"), plus innumerable others.' She replied, 'Every other difficulty pales into insignificance next to such things,[245] and "he who gathers honey must bear the stinging of the bees." In addition, I gather your drift to be that such verbs are too many to count in our noble language and that most senses have numerous words, which scholars call, as you once told me, "assy-nonymous."'[246] 'I didn't say assy-nonymous,' I responded. 'I said "synonymous," and I told you that this act alone has more than two hundred words pertaining to it, for every word that denotes pushing, pricking, pressing, or inserting denotes it too.' She said, 'And can you cite me a single term that pertains to abstention from women, out of chastity and God-fearingness?' I said, 'No such term has come my way, or I would have memorized it, for I dote on every term that has to do with them. It seems the Arabs were unaware of any such thing, though *tabattala* and *bakuma* each denote it in one of their senses.' 'That counts for little,' she replied.

"Then she resumed her earlier theme, saying, 'A further reason, 3.18.13
and one to be found in most women in abundance, is that, when a woman feels that her husband has turned from her or is indifferent to or distant with her, even though she still loves him, offers herself to him, and is docile toward and intimate with him, fecund with advice and with children, affectionate toward him, eager to

please him with obedience and attire, obliging, kindly, companionate, cheerful with him, intimate with him, lighthearted, quick to slip out of her drawers, full of levity, responsive to his requests for coupling, yielding, retentive of the semen in her womb, submissive as the hen to the cock, attentive to her husband's needs while making love, gripping his member tight with her slit, not to say head over heels in love with him and perfectly willing to entertain any request he might make for anal intercourse, she will turn her attention to someone else, to incite his jealousy and make him love her as he did before. Some imbeciles only recognize their wives' worth when they see other men loving them. In such cases, her love for another becomes the cure that restores his love for her, and this we call *daghdaghah* or *zaghzaghah* ("tickling") or *saghsaghah* ("working to and fro like a loose tooth").

3.18.14 "'As far as men's faults are concerned, I swear they are more than women's, though if their only fault was premature ejaculation that would be enough. Whether dissolution of the marriage is permitted or forbidden in such a case is a matter of debate. The Christians forbid it, even though they claim that the purpose of marriage is, specifically, procreation and the preservation of mankind, while the natural scientists and philosophers require it on precisely the same grounds, as well as out of consideration for the woman's marital rights regarding her husband, which are a natural thing both necessary and unavoidable. Thus the marriage remains a matter for the two partners to decide: if they wish, they may remain as they are, or if not, they may separate, which is better—and I swear that any woman who consents to reside with her husband without consummation of her conjugal rights deserves to have a day set aside to celebrate her at the beginning of each year. Does not your mentor, the author of the *Qāmūs*, whose words you quote whenever some topic concerning women comes up, say, "*Rajul* ('man'): too well-known to require definition; also, one who has frequent intercourse"? If, then, the husband isn't a man, why should he keep in his possession a woman whom he does not provide with her rights? Is it lawful for a man to own a riding animal if he cannot feed it?' (I seek refuge with God from this comparison!) 'Or for a man to own land if he doesn't plow it, or sow it, or water it? Is it not, in such a case, the duty of the legitimate ruler to purchase it from him and put someone in charge of it who will maintain it and exploit it? And if procreation and the preservation of mankind are the joint responsibility of the man and the woman—with, indeed, the preponderance of their basic elements being specific to her and dependent upon her—why should not divorce also be their joint responsibility, when occasion requires? Divorce for no cause is, in my opinion, wanton and shameless.

"'Uglier still is the fact that the Christian leadership permits the separation of the husband and wife in such cases but does not allow them to remarry, even though the man's disorder is inveterate and it is not to be expected that it will be cured during the period of his separation from his wife. Where is the wisdom in that, and what harm is there in her marrying someone else who can cause her to bear boy and girl children? If one of her boys should turn out to be lazier or lamer in his use of Arabic than most, he can always become a monk or a metropolitan, and should any of her girls turn out to be particularly fond of confusions, delusions, and dreams, she can become a nun. What's more, it is told in the Old Testament that the Almighty Creator said, "Multiply and fill the earth"[247] (ignoring the exaggeration, for if the earth were to fill with people it would necessarily be ruined, not made prosperous) and Saint Paul says that "a woman saves herself by raising righteous children."[248] Is the suspension of husband and wife from remarriage an application of what these two authorities have laid down? Look at the people of this island and you'll find that most of the men are separated from their wives and living in sin, and their priests insist that this is more proper than legal marriage even though the priests know nothing about conjugal rights because they aren't married. Would it be right to choose an army's leaders from those who are not skilled at the art of war and combat?' 3.18.15

3.18.16 "'How clever you are!' I said. 'But where did you acquire all this knowledge, given that, when we first came to this island, you couldn't tell a beardless boy from a man who'd shaved off his beard?' 'Many a spark has lit a furnace,' she replied. 'I always knew in myself that it wouldn't be long before I became an expert in such things because of all the conflict and quarreling, complaining and contradicting that I saw and heard concerning married couples, and especially now that I've seen a country and people other than my own and have had experience of new customs and strange situations. That spark that was lodged in my mind beneath the dung heap of loneliness and isolation burst into flame the moment the gusts of changing circumstance and varied affairs veered across it, especially on the unforgettable night of the ball. From that time on, it's been on my mind to dictate to you a book on the rights of men and women, and you must make a start on it.'

3.18.17 "'I shall do so,' I said, 'God willing, but the emir is expecting me to go to him in the quarantine quarters tomorrow, and I shall have to go to see him before writing down the book.' 'I'm feeling a little better now,' she said, 'after what I told you, so go to him, and I just hope that the same fit doesn't take me again when you're not here, for if it does I shall have to call on God for help and *inspiration*, seek refuge with Him and say, "From God we are come and He is our final *destination*."'" Then the Fāriyāq went to the aforementioned emir and, after spending the period of his quarantine with him, traveled with him to Italy. Then he returned to the island, surrounded by tokens of the emir's *hospitality* and *liberality*.

Chapter 19

Assorted Wonders

Wonders! Marvels! Prodigies! Miracles! Sensations! Astonishments! Things to gawp at, things to learn from! Things stupendous! Things incredible! Things beyond understanding! Things beyond imagining! The fantastic, the extraordinary, the bewildering, the outlandish, the awesome, the amazing! Bewilderments and puzzlements! Descriptions beggared! Beliefs staggered! Holy mackerel and holy cow! Verily, men delude themselves. 3.19.1

This bitty-buttocked,[249] thin-thighed, shrivel-shanked, barely boobed, ant-armed mistress of mine uses pads, stuffing, and balls of yarn to puff out her shift at her breasts so as to make people think she's big-busted and well-endowed, but from where, my lady, are you supposed to have acquired this ample form, this appetizing flesh, when we can see that your arms are like writing-reeds or prickly artichoke stems, your neck like a stick, your hands like combs, your face like the cake of soap a fuller uses to wash the clothes of army blacksmiths and camel drivers, donkey drivers, and camp followers, your rib cage like a chicken coop, and your shoulders honed and boney, thinned and flattened, delineated and desiccated, weedy and woggly? How could Nature have made such a mistake as to fatten you at those two noble spots and turn a blind eye to the rest? 3.19.2

This short,[250] little, teeny, tiny, diminutive, itty-bitty, shrimpy, stunted, stubby, runty, scrunty, strunty, squaddy, knurly, squabby, 3.19.3

hodmandod, miniature, minuscule, micromorphic, dwarfish, pygmy, puny, pint-sized, homuncular, hop-o'-my-thumb, gnomish, nanoid, fubsical, sesquipedalian chit of a mistress of mine leaps and bounds, stretches her neck out and holds her head straight, sticks her neck out with head held high, walks like an ostrich, or an estrich, cranes and strams, peers toward things, frisks, prances, rushes like a stream of melting snow—and thinks the onlookers aren't measuring her inch by inch with their eyes, aren't groping her span by span and cubit by cubit in their minds, and aren't thinking over what bed would suit her best.

3.19.4 This black,[251] sable, ebony, pitchy, inky, tar-bedaubed, raven-like, charcoal-tinted, swarthy, smutty, dusky, sooty, melanic, melanous, melanotic, melanoid, melanistic mistress of mine paints her face with Indian yellow, saffron, ceruse, rouge, and lipstick and then makes a sour face at men and looks at them askance, bestowing on them from on high glances of coquetry and pride. Should any try to see any other part of her body, she turns on them the part that's painted and rouge-*caked*, embellished and *faked*, and makes that the intercessor for the rest of her limbs, causing them to believe that the parts of her that are covered are of a whiter white than the part that's exposed and that her color by night is more fluorescent than by day, especially if seen in *seclusion*, when it increases in beauty and *profusion*. She may tell a long tale of how, when she got up in the morning, she had no time to set herself to rights, that she dressed in a hurry and left, she has no idea how.

3.19.5 This old,[252] aged, elderly, decrepit, withered, shrunken, wizened, wrinkly, crabbed, shriveled, long-in–the-tooth, infirm, weak, debilitated, moth-eaten, doddery, tottery, grandevous, gerontic, badgerly, veterascent, senescent, doting, hoary, feeble, ravaged, wasting, superannuated mistress of mine, who kicks up the dirt as she waddles along bowlegged like a geriatric,(1) affects, for all that, girlishness, maidenly ways, and childishness, cinching her robe tight around her waist and smiling if a young man come to visit her in her den.

(1) The words for old women are too many to count.

This beautiful, plump and handsome, graceful, juicy and comely, bonny and bright, lovely (both inwardly and outwardly) and delicate, smooth and black-eyed, virginal, chaste, and big-buttocked, sweet-breathed and pearly-toothed, soft-voiced and small-nosed, silken-breasted, glabrously ribbed, prettily smiling, melodiously speaking mistress of mine, who intoxicates with her coquettish *shilly-shallying*, enchants with her *dallying*, captivates the heart of him who never in his life felt desire before, robbing him of his senses and leaving him *disturbed*, enslaving him and rendering him *perturbed*, even though he be on his guard against her and call upon his good sense and *endurance*, his self-discipline and *conscience*—this mistress of mine you will observe walking with her head averted and eyes lowered from *bashfulness*, too shy indeed to step out and display her *lusciousness*, and showing not a sign of flirtatiousness, bedizenment, or *finery*, or walking with a provocative gait, or dressing *flashily*, or wearing brocade, or being prideful, or rocking and rolling from side to side as she walks, or being *coquettish*, or shaking and swaying, or plucking her eyebrows, or taking wide steps like an *ostrich*, or her beauty *flaunting*, or reveling in the first flush of her youth or empty *vaunting*, even though, should she enter the presence of the king, he'd rise to bid her *welcome*, handing over to her, to honor her, both scepter and *baton*, and reciting 3.19.6

I hereby ransom you from any fealty to us,
　To honor which the very caliph's throne its head should dip.
Take my crown, but give me in return the lightest kiss
　From the edges of your mouth, or tiniest sip!

or should she enter the presence of the august confidant of the *emir*, his honored *vizier*, he'd be too taken aback with admiration and esteem to go on with his *mission*, would toss her his ring in *submission*, and recite

To you I cede judgment in all things
　Over the highest-ranking emir or vizier

For what is *dustūr*[253] if not *dussa tawrun*[254] to you?
How then can you refuse this career?

3.19.7 and, should she enter one of the chief judge's *sessions*, he'd bestow on her treasure, pearls, and all his *possessions*, and recite

She has an advantage over me in love—
Two parts to which the male can lay no claim.[255]
Thus I am owed two things, which I demand
Of her—and both this and that my lust enflame,

and, should she drop in on a physician treating a man for impotence, he'd prescribe him a rub with the cartilage of her nose-*end* or a sniff of her neck-*bend*, and recite

As fat of skink and theriac for all ills
Is your mouth's saliva, and for the limp lover too,
So that when he's squeezed of every drop of spittle,
You may feed him sips of wine—and what a wine!—in lieu,

3.19.8 and should she pay a visit to an astrologer, he'd throw down his astrolabe in surprise and *stupefaction*, babbling and *distraction*, and recite

We can see naught but your beauty, bright as forenoon,
For that it is which fills with light the pitch dark night.
Your sphere-like breasts confuse the gazer when at the stars he stares,
So you now must take his charts and set them right,

or to a philosopher, he and his wisdom alike would go for *naught*, he'd find he'd no good sense left to stop him feeling *fraught*, and he'd recite

When two bodies rub together, sparks fly—
So say followers of the philosophers' creed

> But this is false for if mine rubbed yours,
> > Water would flow and I would bleed,

or an engineer, his shapes she'd *muddle* and his mind *befuddle*, and he'd recite 3.19.9

> Would that your breast-work might be ransomed
> > By every cube, convexity, and concavity in sight!
>
> Would that that crescent shape you have inside you
> > Might be firmly seated on my own upright!

or a logician, he'd violate *analogy*, flail in *ambiguity*, and recite

> Would that her legs might straddle my neck—
> > How fine that would be as both subject and predicate!
>
> I have become her conclusion, though I'd rather be her premise,
> > Since every pleasure therein is promised!

or a grammarian, he'd lose all sense of active and *passive*, decide that knowledge of such things was simply *invasive*, and recite 3.19.10

> Gently, lady! I come not to you in a state of sin[256]
> > Nor have I committed offenses worth the name.
>
> I washed my hands of the grammarians, I swear,
> > When "precedence of the masculine" they made their claim[257]

or a prosodist, she'd break his heart into *feet*, so that with "crawling"[258] and "propping"[259] he'd find himself *replete*, and recite

> You've won me, O you of ev'ry charm possessed,
> > And left my heart with passion dizzee.
>
> By night I watch the stars that in you rise and set and—let me say it—
> > I want pussy, I want pussy, I want pussee![260]

or a poet, he'd hang out his tongue as he drooled with *delight*, then lick his lips and smack them, bite upon his index finger to check his excitement, and *recite* 3.19.11

Many an ardent lover's grown haughty from overweening pride and
self-esteem,
But your "shame" inspires me to worship and to passion
insane.[261]
If my paronomasia brings me closer to you and makes me more
your like,
I'll praise my punning and rhyme only in that vein.

3.19.12 Indeed, were she to stroke your neck and mine, dear reader, such stroking would both render them unneedful of anti-goiter medicine and strike from them all growths,[262] lumps, bumps, protuberances and swellings, pimples, pustules, papules and glands, knots, nodes, nodules, nodulosities, and nodulations, abscesses, ulcers, blisters, blebs, bullas, blains, boils, and sores, furuncles, carbuncles, tetters, tubercles, and buboes, moles, nevuses, and strawberry marks, puckerings, calluses, and callosities, pockmarks and pits, blackheads and whiteheads, yellowing of the teeth, bruises and contusions, goiters and wattles, stiffness and pain, bullneckedness and ewe-neckedness, bending, twisting, kinkiness, cricks, and crookedness, swellings and pain of the throat, quinsy, diphtheria, laryngitis, tracheitis, scars, cicatrices, and scarifications, weeping wounds, open wounds, festering wounds, suppurations, bite marks, hickeys, welts, scratches, scabs, sloughs, cariosities, and necrosities.

3.19.13 And this man-mannered, ill-natured,[263] shrewish, base, disobedient, worthless, shamelessly staring, irascible, wayward, two-timing, unblushing, exhibitionistic, immodest, sharp-tongued, unneighborly, loudmouthed, wanton, whorish, chambering, nocturnally mobile, promiscuous, trampy, brassy, brazen-faced, interfering, spoiled, ugly, languorous, loose, depraved, insatiable, predatory, lustful, estrous, philandering, incontinent, begging, in-heat, backside-presenting, rug-spotting, swollen-vulvaed, termagant, vixenish, foulmouthed, lewd, obscene, bawdy, clamorous, nymphomaniacal, slave-chasing, lecherous, licentious, lascivious slut of a mistress of mine, whom every male in town who sees her strutting through its markets, streets, alleys, lanes, and cul-de-sacs believes to be inviting him, with her eyes and her every limb, to look lively and apply himself to intercourse,[264] to cock a leg, to snatch a kiss, to become erect, to copulate, to bed, to swive, to screw, to thrum, to wimble, to ejaculate (inside and outside), to have coitus (interruptus and non-), to meng, to frig, to frot, to hug, to mount, to hump, to pump, to jigger, to jagger, to jangle, on all fours, with her on her back or her front, with her legs splayed or closed, from the side or at an angle, during menstruation or not and with or without deep penetration, as well as to "wham-bam!" and "schlup-flup!" and "jiggy-jiggy!" and "hokey-pokey!," sits in the chambers of the dame of gossips and never stops accusing her neighbors of looking out the window, laughing, dressing, perfuming themselves, putting on their jewelry, and then going out and walking around affectedly.

But have you forgotten, my mistress, the day you told your teacher,[265] "Everyone who falls in love blanches at the mention of the beloved" and he answered you, "It isn't always so" and you got on your high horse and insisted on your claim and he did the same and insisted on denying it, and you told him, to convince him, "If you were to mention to me the name of . . ." and then blanched and fell silent and he asked you, the horn hatching from his head with a rending sound, "The name of whom?" and you laughed and said, "I don't know!"? Or the windy day[266] when he took you out to raise your spirits and you set off (he, in his naïveté, being none the wiser) having exposed half your chest and buffed to a shine your décolletage, the skin of your chest, and the aureoles around your nipples, and when he turned to look at you and found you in this state, you said it was the wind that had done it? Or the day when he was walking with you and you said, marveling at love's dominion, "I'd give my life for the one I love!" and when he asked you, you said, "You, of course! You're the one." Or the day when you sent your servingman, or on which you dispatched your serving girl,[267] or the morning you wrote a slip of paper inviting the one who desired you, or the forenoon you were so late, or the evening you put on perfume, or 3.19.14

the time you made excuses, or the occasion you claimed you were having your period, or the night you raved and talked in your sleep, or the moment you raved and muttered and mumbled or put on your finery and dolled yourself up or tied a piece of string around your finger[268] or made a sour face and submitted or said it was wrong—right up until you'd taken it all the way to the hilt? Weren't all these sins as bad as your neighbor's looking out of her window?

3.19.15 In the meantime, this Metropolitan Atanāsiyūs al-Tutūnjī had become a translator and an Arabizer, a writer and a pen-pusher, though he hadn't the balls for the job and he didn't care if in translating into Arabic he made a balls-up. He also believed that no trade was more difficult than another and toiled and moiled,[269] strained and heaved, warsled and wrestled, struggled and sprattled, carked and swinked, taved and teveled, bungled and botched, bumbled and stumbled, fumbled and floundered, muddled and marred, fudged and faked, foxed and jouked, pretended and presumed, dissembled and dissimulated, bragged and boasted, stammered and stuttered, twisted and turned, and ducked and weaved, while being "more conceited than a woman with a tattoo on her backside."(1)

(1) A *muttashimah* is "a woman who has tattooed her backside so that it may be more comely for her" and one says proverbially that someone is "more conceited than a woman with a tattoo on her backside."

3.19.16 Is there in the universe no glass,[270] no mirror, no looking glass, no seeing glass, no pier glass, no pocket glass, no tire-glass, no swing-glass, no peeper, no psyche, no speculum, no reflector in which these mistresses of mine may gaze at their faces and see how they look? Is there in the East no Sībawayhi to deliver a slap to the back of that man's neck? Is there in the West no Ibn Mālik to cry, "Enough!", no Akhfash to leap to the defense of this language and crush the head of that gecko? How can a person think himself a scholar when he has been schooled in nothing, or a man of letters when he is barely literate, or a jurisprudent when he has no prudence? Granted, he cannot see his ignorance in the mirror as he does his face, but are not books the mirror of the mind? When he read the books of the scholars and failed to understand them, he should have realized the limits of his learning, but Metropolitan Atanāsiyūs al-Tutūnjī, metropolitan of Syrian Tripoli[271] (albeit resident in every land but that) has never opened a work of scholarship in his life. His reading in grammar[272] never went beyond the chapter on "the doer and the done," his reading in metaphor beyond the figure of "stripping,"[273] his reading in jurisprudence beyond the chapter on defilements, in prosody beyond "the movable peg,"[274] in eloquent style beyond "having the buttock echo the breast."[275] This is the sum total of what he learned and bragged about at the school of ʿAyn Tirāz when he was head monitor there.

As to the reasons behind his flight from there to Rome, from Rome to Malta, from Malta to Paris, from Paris to London, from London to Malta, and then, this year, to London from some cities in Austria where he'd been roaming around with his beggar's sack over his shoulder, and behind how he was exposed and disgraced there in the newspapers to the point that he was forbidden to practice any longer that profession that had suited him so well for so many years, how he eked out a living during the London season by putting together a troupe of female and male singers from the house of Ashiq Bāsh in Aleppo, how he conned them, in his greed for profit, into going to the season, how he went into it with them and their partners in the first place on an "expenditures and equipment" basis and then took back the money he'd given them and forced them to give him a share of the profits without participating with them in the pains, this being the return for his conning them, and how his ugly scheming became the reason for the two leaders of this troupe sustaining a huge loss, all this there is no space to detail in this work. 3.19.17

Here someone may say, "You, Mr. Author, have reproached people for deluding themselves but it seems to me that in this chapter you too have made a fool of yourself, for you have introduced into it discourse inappropriate to women, surpassing that of even Ibn Abī ʿAtīq and Ibn Ḥajjāj." In response I would declare: "Two things drove me to do that. One was to show off the beauties of our noble language and the second that I wanted to awaken a desire in 3.19.18

those readers who cover the walls of their houses with pipe stems[276] to buy a book in that language. Dear *reader*, then, and dear *listener*, dear shame-faced *abstainer*[277] and dear *blind-eye turner*,[278] tell the troublemaker among you, 'To the bitter, nothing is sweet.'"

3.19.19 To proceed: I now throw myself at the feet of that sexually voracious mistress of mine, that beetle-bodied mistress of mine, that flat-breasted, small-buttocked mistress of mine, and that soot-bedaubed mistress of mine and ask them all to excuse the tyranny of the pen, for I shan't be able to sleep tonight if they are angry.

Chapter 20

A Metropolitan Theft

When the Fāriyāq returned from his time with the aforementioned emir, he informed his wife of the latter's kindnesses to him and that he had promised him a good post in Cairo. "I'll go ahead, then," she said, "while you wait for him here. I miss my parents greatly, so let me go to them." "So be it," said he, and when the time for her departure drew close, he set about bidding her farewell, saying, "Remember, wife, that on this island you have a husband who cares for you and a lover who will not forget you," to which she replied, "O that I might have such a one!" The Fāriyāq resumed, "I asked her, 'Whom do you mean by "such a one"?' 'You, of course!' she responded. 'On the contrary, the more obvious interpretation is someone else,' I said. 'Must facts always depend on your readings, you Arabs?' she responded. 'Is it still your way to go scratching up any secrets that may be in a woman's *breast,* breaking open any thoughts that, egg-like, in her head may *nest,* reviling her on the basis of gossip and *delusion,* dealing with her on a basis of conjecture and gnawing *suspicion,* behaving toward her according to misgiving and unsupported claims, without, for each story, *confirmation,* as well as practicing *defamation,* subjection to ungrounded *accusation,* false report and *condemnation,* instead of turning a blind eye and winking at *transgression,* overlooking error and granting tender *consideration,* being discreet and observing one's marital *obligation,* 3.20.1

kissing and *flirtation*, hugging and *copulation*?(1) Were the Almighty to call his servants to account for their thoughtless words as severely as you do,[279] there'd be nobody left on the face of this earth.'

(1) *dathth* means "reviling someone on the basis of reports"; *qasm* means "that some notion finds a place in your heart, and then you think that it may be true, and then that suspicion becomes stronger until it becomes a truth"; *raḍkh* means "a report that you hear and of which you are not sure"; *tadhaqqaha lahu* means "he accused someone of a crime, charging him with something of which he was not guilty"; *waghm* and *laghm* mean the same and also "to report something on less than certain evidence"; *rasīs* means "a report that turned out to be untrue"; *ʿams* means "to make out that you know nothing of the matter at hand when you do," synonym *jalhazah*; *ʿasm* means "to bring the eyelids together until they touch"; *wazm* means "to pay off a debt"; *jamsh* means "to flirt and play"; *faghm* means "kissing" and *daʿm* means what follows.

3.20.2 "I responded, 'Most of these misunderstandings are generated by our language, which is so wide that it allows every expression to bear numerous possible meanings.' She replied, 'I would rather it were tight!' 'That,' I responded, 'goes with the other!'[280] to which she responded, 'And the other goes into this!' 'And on top of it,' I said. 'And underneath it,' she retorted. 'Better not to say anything then.' 'Not while going to it,' I said. 'You men,' she said, 'all snort, groan, and talk dirty like women when you're having sex.' 'How come you know that?' I asked. 'Back to delusion and suspicion!' she said. 'Better,' said I, 'we return to saying our goodbyes.' 'Indeed!' she responded. 'I shall travel, leaving behind no man I shall miss.' 'Am I,' I asked, 'one of the unmissed?' 'You're not "a man,"' she said. I said, 'That too is an ambiguous statement. Am I not a man?' 'In one of the two meanings,'[281] she said. 'Do I still owe you one?' I asked. 'More than one,' she replied. I said, 'Do you have the accounts for that in your ledger?' 'I do,' she replied. 'The way you poets drool over poetry deceived us into thinking you were both sayers and doers, but it turns out that the only thing you do well is describe.' 'And who are the good doers?' I enquired. 'Those who are no good at description,' she replied. 'So where does literature get to have its say?' I asked. 'In scholars' sitting rooms, not women's dressing rooms,' she replied.

"'What you've just said could lead to the dismemberment of our relationship,' I said. 'And your saying that could lead to the dehydration of your member,'[282] she countered. 'How then can we part?' I asked. 'If you wish,' she said, 'you can make good on your arrears now. If not, leave it till you come to Cairo.' 'How,' I asked, 'can I make good in hours or days on *arrears* that have been outstanding for *years*? I'd hate to be taken before my time with a balance still to pay.' 'If you weren't afraid to meet your *obligation*, why should it occur to you to fear early *obliteration*?' she asked. I replied, 'You have made one who had forgotten remember, and for long now I had reckoned all people to be like me.' She said, 'And you have made one who remembered forget, because I have seen none as ill-used as I.' I said, 'Remember the rooftop and forgive!' She said, 'There can be no forgiveness without mention of top[pling].' 'I meant the old kind of top[pling],'[283] I said. 'And I want the new,' she said. I said, 'There's a proverb that says, "Blessing lies in what's old."' She said, 'There's another that says, "Pleasure lies in everything that's new."' 3.20.3

"'How can we part,' I said, 'when there's *ḍighn* in your heart?' 'And what better than *ḍighn*?' she replied. 'If it's in the sense of "yearning,"' I said.[284] 'Indeed!' she replied. 'It's one of the strange words that I've learned from you, like *ʿIqyawn*,[285] *fiṭaḥl*,[286] and *ḥabrah*.'[287] 'Maybe what appealed to you about *ʿIqyawn* was its closeness to *ʿiqyān* ("gold"), about *fiṭaḥl* its closeness to *faḥl* ("stud bull"), and about *ḥabrah* its closeness to *ḥibarah* ("a kind of wrap").'[288] 'Tooth decay and wraps don't go together,' she responded. 'They can,' I retorted, 'for they say that *niʿmah* ("luxury, comfort") comes from *nuʿūmah* ("softness").' She replied,[289] 'And they also say that *tasdīd* ("the plugging of holes") is from *sadād* ("proper behavior").' I replied, 'No command prohibiting that has come down.' She said, 'It's by analogy with its opposite.' I said, 'That's seed cast on salty land' and she said, 'And that's cleared land left unplowed.' I said, 3.20.4

'We were talking about seed' and she said, 'Food doesn't nourish while it's still on the palate and drink doesn't quench till it's passed down the throat.'" Following this duel of wits, they bade each other farewell and he saw her onto the steamer and then returned to his house gloomy and downcast, for often she had guided him to the right way and shown him the path to the correct opinion.

3.20.5 Before a few days had passed, the metropolitan's stinks spread once more, this time more harmfully than the first, so he sent another portion to the aforementioned Committee[290] and wrote to them saying, "If you don't put a stop to the pollution of the air here by this stink, everyone with a nostril will complain about you." When his letter reached them and they submitted it to the scholars in their country, they found that what he said was correct and deemed it proper to stop up the metropolitan's pores to prevent them from exuding any more of this malignancy. They also decided to bring the Fāriyāq over to them to retranslate the book in question. In addition, the Fāriyāq had written a book on the state of the island's inhabitants[291] in which he reproached them for certain customs and religious and secular practices that set them apart from the Christians of his own country. Examples included dunking church bells in baptismal water and giving them the names of saints, taking the figurines and statues from the churches for an outing during the day and lighting candles in front of them, and so forth. The said book also reviled a Muslim whom the metropolitan used to visit. The metropolitan happened to pay the Fāriyāq a visit and saw the book on an occasional table and recognized its author's handwriting. The man pretended not to notice until the Fāriyāq had left the room, then took the book and cut out of it the pages containing mention of those customs. These he then sent to the head of the infirmary for the foul of breath,[292] having written on them in Italian, "Look, dear sir, and see whether or not the writer of these lines is worthy to be under your directorship." The head, however, given his ignorance of what the pages contained, compounded by his lack of authority to dismiss an employee of the state, was obliged to return them to their author.

By the time the pages were returned to the Fāriyāq, the metropolitan had fled the island and the air had become free of his stink, and had he stayed longer, he would have been punished for the theft in a manner appropriate to such as him. At the same time, the Fāriyāq was invited to travel so as to carry out the mission in question, meaning the translation of the book, and he sent a letter to his wife telling her what had been decided and instructing her to return, since he wanted to remain in England after finishing the book. However, it is customary in the lands of the Franks to draw the language teachers at their universities from their own race only, even if they were ignorant. When the Fāriyāqiyyah returned, the Fāriyāq made ready for the journey. Observe him then putting his copies of the *Qāmūs* and al-Ashmūnī into his trunk, and observe me, rushing off to see to an urgent need. Allow me then a little time to rest. 3.20.6

END OF BOOK THREE

Book Four

Chapter 1

Unleashing a Sea

Only one who has traveled the seas and experienced the misery of their tempests and swells can properly appreciate the ease of life on land. Whenever, then, my dear landlubber of a reader, you feel a need for clean water, tender meat, fresh fruit, succulent greens, or soft bread, you must bear in mind that your seafaring brethren are deprived of all such things, that their vessel never stops moving beneath their feet, tossing them, turning them, and throwing them up and down, that before every mouthful of food they swallow they must first choke, and that before lying down to sleep they must first suffer a bellyache. 4.1.1

Likewise, when food of just one kind is placed before you, think only of that and know well that others too are dining at this hour, and perhaps on something more meager still. If you do so, you will find solace and distraction. If, however, you lift your eyes to the palaces of kings and princes and the mansions of ministers and wonder what they are eating and drinking, you will certainly tire and torment yourself to no avail. Do you really imagine that the aged wine drunk by the prince is more delicious than the water you are drinking, so long as you are informed as to the affairs of this world and the next and are proficient in the management of some business of yours that provides for yourself and your family, so long as your wife sits before you or on your right or left while your small child sits on 4.1.2

your knee, singing to you one moment, passing you with his sweet hand anything you may have asked your wife to give you the next, and so long as on your departure, they accompany you to the door and on your arrival, take you upstairs and seat you on the best cushion in the house?

4.1.3 As for you, my dear rich gentleman, you would do better to leave your prosperous city to see with your own eyes what you cannot see in your own country and hear with your own ears what you cannot hear there, to experience how other people live and their customs and ways, to discover their morals and modes of thought and how they govern themselves. After that, you may compare the good things in their land with the bad things in ours. And when you enter their country and are ignorant of their language, don't insist on learning the dirty words from them first or delight in words for the sake of the things they denote, for every language in the universe has fair and foul given that language expresses the actions, deeds, and thoughts of men, which encompass, as all will agree, both the praiseworthy and the blameworthy. I hold you in too high esteem to imagine that you will be like those travelers who learn of other people's languages only the names of certain parts of the body and other despicable terms. On the contrary, when you arrive safe and sound in a country you must, before anything else, make for the schools, printing presses, libraries, hospitals, and lecture rooms (by which I mean those places where scholars speak on every art and science; some of these are equipped only for public addresses while others contain every instrument and device required for the science in question).

4.1.4 And when you return, by God's grace, to your own town, exert yourself to write a book about your travels and publicize it among your countrymen so that they may benefit—but without any intention to make money from the sale of it. Would that you might partner too with some of your fellow rich in establishing a printing press on which to print further books that may be useful to men, women, and children and to each category of person so that they may learn what their rights and duties are, whether those books be written originally in Arabic or translated into it. Be careful, though, that in copying from the non-Arabs, you do not confuse the fair with the foul, the sound with the defective. Great cities are as full of vices as they are of virtues.

True, among those people there are some who will refuse to see anyone when they are at table and, if compelled to do so, will not invite him to taste any of what is before them. Others, though, will invite you to their mansions in the countryside, where you may stay for a week, or two weeks, with everyone at your beck and call. True, some will begrudge a response to your greeting, and if you enter the house of one such who is your friend and his salon is full of friends of his who do not already know you, not one of them will bestir himself to stand and greet you or pay you the slightest attention or even turn toward you. On the other hand, there are those who, once they have gotten to know you, will be as solicitous of your welfare when you are absent as they are when you are present, and if you confide a secret to them, will keep it as long as they live. True, there are those who will call you names as soon as they set eyes on your mustaches, beard, or turban and will tug on the skirt of your robe from behind, but there are also those who have a passionate desire to become acquainted with strangers, are happy to be in their company and to do good to them, and think it a duty to aid and protect them. True, there are those who will mock you when they see you making mistakes in their language, but there are also those who will be intent on teaching it to you without charge, either themselves or via their wives or daughters, and on lending you books and other things that may be of use to you and guide you to whatever may serve your interests and success. 4.1.5

True, there are those who will reckon that you have turned up in their country to compete with them for their livelihoods and therefore scowl in your face and look at you askance, but there are also those who will regard you as a guest in their country to be honored, respected, and defended so that you depart without harboring 4.1.6

the slightest hard feeling against their countrymen. True, there are those who will use you as forced labor, to translate for them or teach them, and never say, "Thank you, translator!" or "Thank you, teacher!" but there are also those who will regard it as sinful to speak to you without sending you payment for opening your mouth and closing your lips. True, there are those who, if they are compelled to invite you to eat with them and then notice you coughing, blowing your nose, or flaring your nostrils, will tell their wives, "He must be sick; you don't have to give him a lot of food" so that you rise from the table starving while they make a great show of you among their guests, claiming that in the year so-and-so and month so-and-so, on such and such a day, they held a great banquet for you, treating that night as though it marked the start of some new historical era. On the other hand, there are also those who, on discovering that you are staying in some village in their country where there is no trade and nothing to be obtained by way of green vegetables or fruit, will send you, from their own gardens and orchards, enough to stop your mouth against any complaint. Thus it was with Mr. Drummond,[293] when the Fāriyāq found himself fated to reside in one such village and his complaints were carried on the wind to people's ears.

4.1.7 How I wish the presence in your home of a hundred books did not count as less of a witness to good fortune than that of a hundred tobacco pipes or a hundred water pipes, even though the cost of a hundred books is less than that of three pieces of amber![294] Isn't the presence of a printing press in your country more important than all these cashmere shawls, sables, precious vessels, and expensive pieces of jewelry? If a person looks at a piece of jewelry, he derives no benefit from it either for his body or his brain; his pleasure in it lasts no longer than the month in which he bought it, and after a few months have passed it's no more to him than scrap metal, the only pleasure to be derived from it being that of selling it. A book, on the other hand, grows more valuable with each passing year, and its benefits multiply. Are not your readings in history, geography, and the literatures of the world an adornment to you among your brethren and acquaintances that surpasses gemstones? If you teach your family and dependents a portion of such things and, from books of medicine, of the principles necessary for the preservation of their health, will you not win reward from God and protection from many an injury that might befall them as a result of their ignorance?

If you say, "We have no books in Arabic suitable for women," 4.1.8
I reply, "Supposing you are right, do not the Franks have books written by refined and virtuous men specially for women and children? Why do you buy fabrics and furnishings from the Franks and not knowledge, wisdom, or literature? Then again, no matter what lengths you may go to in order to shield your wife from seeing the world, you will never be able to hide it from her heart. A woman, wherever and however she be, is this world's daughter and its mother, sister, and co-wife. Do not say to me, 'A book won't set an evil woman to rights but will make her yet more wicked, and if she's righteous, she doesn't need one,' for I will reply that a woman was a girl before she became a woman and a man was once a boy. No one can deny that educating the young is like carving on rock and that if you raise your offspring with knowledge, general education, virtue, and praiseworthy qualities, they will grow up as you have raised them and you will have performed the duty that God has imposed upon you of making them into decent people, in which case you will leave them (after a long life, God willing) with a clear conscience and a mind at ease and serene."

The only argument left to you is to say, "My father gave me no 4.1.9
education, just as my grandfather gave my father none, and I have followed in their footsteps," but I tell you, the world in your late grandfather's and father's day was not as it is now. In their day, there were no steamboats or railway *tracks* to bring close far-off *tracts* and create new *pacts*, to connect the *disconnected*, and make accessible what was *once protected*. Then, one didn't have to learn many languages. It could be said of anyone who knew a few words of Turkish—Welcome, my lord! How nice to see you, my lord!—that he'd make

a fine interpreter at the imperial court, and of any who could write a hand worse than the hand with which I have penned this book (not the one you're actually reading now, for whose typeface I take no responsibility)[295] that he was a skilled calligrapher who would make a fine secretary to a king's council. Not now!

4.1.10 When our friend the Fāriyāq made his decision to leave the island for England, someone told him, "You are going to a land over which the sun never rises"; another, ". . . to a land where no wheat or green vegetables grow and the only foods to be had are meat and turnips";[296] another, "I fear that you may lose your lungs there for lack of air"; another, "or your intestines for lack of food"; and another, "or your chest or some other part of your body." When he got there, though, he found that the sun was the sun, the air air, water water, men men, and women women, that the land was populated and the cities well inhabited, the earth plowed and pleasing to the eye, well signposted and marked, resplendent with woods, mighty trees, and forests, green with meadows, proud in its *fields,* succulent in the green vegetables its soil *yields*; had he listened to those people, he would have missed seeing all of that. Thus, if you're afraid that you would hanker for the pleasures of the water pipe or of having your legs massaged before going to sleep, know that the marvels you will see there will make you forget all such luxuries and distract you from everything to which, in your noble position in society, you have become accustomed.

4.1.11 How can you allow yourself to leave this world without ever having seen it when you have the means to do so? Abū l-Ṭayyib al-Mutanabbī has said

And no failing have I seen among men
To equal the falling short of those who have means.

How can you limit yourself to knowing a quarter of a language[297] and not yearn to know what others think? Under their hats may be ideas and thoughts that have never occurred to what's under your tarbush—so much so that, did you but comprehend them, you'd wish you could have been their thinker's contemporary, had the honor of his acquaintance, and held a splendid feast for him, decorated with sheaves of rice and wheat. How can you have reached the thirtieth year of your life without composing something of benefit to the people of your country? All I see before you are ledgers of sale and purchase, pages of outgoings and incomings, and letters full of corrupt phrases and lame expressions over which you pore morning and evening.

If, on the other hand, your intention in traveling is simply to be able to boast and say, for example, during some gathering when your noble friends and mighty peers are visiting, "I saw such and such a city and beheld its wide clean streets, spacious homes, fine ships, magnificent markets, beautiful horses, wonderful women, and hosts of soldiers, and ate such and such there on the first day and drank such and such on the second, after which we went to a place of entertainment and from there to a lady who entertains and I spent the night with her on a soft bed, and in front of the bed there was a large mirror as long and wide as the bed itself, so I could see myself in it just as I was in the bed, and then I got up in the morning and a bonny maid brought us breakfast (liquid or otherwise) and then I went back to my lodgings and found so-and-so waiting for me, the time being then eleven o'clock, or about an hour before noon, and we set off together for the park known as the Royal Park and while we were walking there, looking at the towering trees and ornamental flowers, I suddenly caught sight of the girl I'd spent the night with walking with a man who was paying court to her and when she saw me, she smiled and said hello, and her greeting didn't seem to upset the man, for he doffed his hat to me, and I was very much surprised at his lack of jealousy, as, had the girl been mine, I'd have hidden her from the light," then it all amounts to nothing but what's called in chaste Arabic *hadhar* ("prating"), *hurā'* ("prattling"), *haft* ("nonsense"), *harj* ("confusion"), *halj* ("making incredible claims"), *saqaṭ* ("false reporting"), *haysh* ("talking too much"), *watagh* ("mindless verbiage"), *khaṭal* ("excessive nonsense"), *ikhlā'* 4.1.12

("vacancy"), *lakhā* ("much ado about nothing"), *ṭafānīn* ("idle talk"), *hadhayān* ("senseless jabber"), *thartharah* ("chattering"), *farfarah* ("chittering"), *ḥadhramah* ("loquacity"), *habramah* ("garrulousness"), *hathramah* ("garrulity"), *khazrabah* ("rambling"), *khaṭlabah* ("ranting"), *ghaydharah* ("raving"), *shamrajah* ("blathering"), *nafrajah* ("blethering"), *hamrajah* ("blabbering"), *thaghthaghah* ("gabbling"), *faqfaqah* ("burbling"), *laqlaqah* ("clattering"), *waqwaqah* ("barking"), and *hatmanah* ("bombast")—and in the ordinary speech of the common people, since it's of no use to anyone, *fashār* ("bragging") and *ʿalk* ("yakkety-yak").

4.1.13 It would be different were you to tell them that if a handsome young man there attends a gathering where there are women, he doesn't wink at one of them or flash his costly ring about foolishly in her face as he talks or make false boast of his conquests.(1) He doesn't tell her that he visits women of unblemished reputation with and without the permission of their husbands and eats and drinks in their homes, then stays alone with them in their bedchambers and returns home in good cheer, and that many a time he has put his hand into his pocket and found there a purse full of gold coins or a draft drawn on a moneylender, or that when he walks through the markets, the girls crowd the casements, windows, apertures, peepholes, and skylights to catch sight of him, some making signs to him with their hands or their heads, others making sheep's eyes and putting their hands on their hearts, one throwing him a flower and another a posy of stocks or a scrap of paper bearing a verse. He doesn't say in their presence "My drawstring came undone" or "I've got jock itch because my package is so big" or scratch his anus or weigh his "yardarm" in his hand, or stretch, loll, sprawl, extend his body, lie at full length, elongate himself, protract himself, lounge, drape himself, lie flat on his face, extend his arms to their full length, spread himself out, or flop vacantly around. On the contrary, he speaks to them politely and

(1) One says of a man that he *tabaẓrama* ["flashed his ring about foolishly"] "if he is stupid and is wearing a signet ring and he talks and waves it about in people's faces" and that he *ibtahara* ["made false boast of his conquests"] if he "makes false claims and says 'I committed adultery' when he did not."

respectfully, averting his gaze and lowering his voice, and he asks the eldest among them what news, stories, and edifying anecdotes have come her way that day, or he mentions that he has commenced that very day the composition of a beneficial book that will make comprehensive mention of the antiquities left by the ancients and their histories, and then puts some literary puzzle to the youngest of them to keep her entertained. Such things ensure that he is honored on his arrival and praised on his departure.

It would be different too if you were to tell them that the rich merchant there doesn't wear diamond or emerald rings or adorn himself with gold chains or collect rare furniture, vessels, and carpets but spends his wealth instead on charity, assistance to the hard-pressed, and provision for widows and orphans, on building schools and hospitals, mending roads, and cleaning the city and clearing it of refuse and filth, as well as on educating his children in literature, science, and the virtues, as a result of which you find that from the age of twelve they can talk to you of matters that one of ours would not be able to talk to you about were he twelve plus twenty years of age. And it would be different too if you were to be so good as to mention that any person among them of a middling condition has a case of valuable books on every art and science and that there isn't a house that doesn't have a folder full of newspapers; that any man among them is better informed as to the conditions of foreign countries than are those countries' own inhabitants; that most of their peasants can read and write and peruse the daily newspapers and are aware of the rights and obligations that govern the relationships between owner and owned, ruler and ruled, man and wife; that some of their printed newspapers run to fourteen million copies a year, that the sum paid to the state treasury for the printing of their licenses comes to more than fifty thousand lira, and that if a single issue of such a newspaper were translated into Arabic, it would come to two hundred pages; and that when a head of family there sits down to table in the morning with his wife and children, he kisses each, asks after his health, and provides him with profitable 4.1.14

pieces of advice and caution to guide him through the coming day and they talk to him and are full of delight and joy, viewing his presence among them as a comfort, never disobeying his orders or thinking his demands upon them a burden yet acknowledging their status as his children and honoring him as children should a father.

4.1.15 It is with this and its like that you, God set you to rights, should be beguiling the ears of your noble friends in the hope that they may bestir themselves to build a school, translate a book, or send their children to a country where they can learn praiseworthy manners and noble traits. But beware, my dear sir, before anything else, of taking over from some of them their ignoble qualities, such as frivolity, impetuosity, stinginess, depravity, and arrogance, or showing the soles of your feet to someone sitting with you, for, as I pointed out to you above, countries with many virtues also have many vices and everyone has some fault, or indeed faults. Each of us, however, must seriously strive to follow the path of perfection and to refine his morals and his inner senses by making the best use of everything that appears to his outer senses. Likewise, given that one experiences sensual pleasure through the front of the body rather than its rear, every rational animal that possesses a body should determine to move in a forward direction in pursuit of knowledge, understanding, and praiseworthy qualities till he can go no farther. I would also wish that even one of our countrymen might pass on to his brethren and acquaintances some virtue or memorable deed taken from those people in the same way that news or accounts of events are passed on, and I wish that all kinds of diamonds, emeralds, rubies, jasper, mother-of-pearl, pearls, gold, amber, and crystal (and monk's hoods too, since they're considered to belong to the category of jewels and treasures) might be turned into books, upper schools, elementary schools, and printing presses.

Chapter 2

A Farewell

When the time for the Fāriyāq to travel was close, and as soon as he had put his copies of the *Qāmūs* and al-Ashmūnī into his trunk, he set about bidding his wife farewell.[298] He said, "Just think, wife—we've lived together a goodly span of time." "That's all I think of," she replied. The Fāriyāq resumed his narrative. "I asked her, 'Hatefully or gratefully?' and she replied, 'Half the latter and half the former.'[299] 'Application of *naḥt* brings us back to the first,'[300] I said, to which she responded, 'or the first brings us back to another meaning of *naḥt*.'[301] 'Which first did you have in mind?' I asked.[302] 'You have no business interpreting my intentions,' she responded. I replied, 'I'd be content if you'd just explain to me what you did mean,' and to this she responded, 'If you think you can belong to both me and others, then it's "hatefully," if not, it's "gratefully."' 4.2.1

"'You forbade me before to deal with you on the basis of suspicion,'[303] I said, 'but now you're the sinner in that regard.' 'On the contrary,' she replied, 'I'm the one sinned against.'[304] I asked her, 'Does the word "no" have no place in your mouth?'[305] She said, 'It used to be pronounced "yes."'[306] I said, 'A no from a woman is a boon,'[307] to which she replied, 'And a yes means pleasure.' I asked, 'Have you made the latter your habit?' to which she replied, 'Indeed—and become habituated to the rewards.' I said, 'That's not fitting for a woman with children,' to which she countered, 'If a 4.2.2

woman doesn't fit properly, she'll never give birth.'[308] I said, 'It's the same Matter,' to which she responded, 'If the Matter isn't "copious and inseparable," it must necessarily take different Forms.'[309] I said, 'And how can it remain inseparable if the Forms are different?' 'The individual nature of the Forms is not a problem,' she replied, 'for one may stand for all. What we are discussing here is how to define "quantity."' 'And what are the terms of the argument?' I asked. She said, 'That in seriousness is humor and in humor seriousness.'

4.2.3 "'What would you think,' I asked her, 'if I got someone to deputize for me in that matter while I'm away?' She laughed and said, 'According to my taste or yours?' 'To yours, naturally,' I replied. She said, 'No man would agree to such a thing unless he was devoid of jealousy, and a man can be devoid of jealousy only if he hates his wife and is enamored of someone else, so you must be enamored of someone else.' I said, 'I am neither enamored nor inconstant, but when a man is deeply in love with his wife he hopes to please her in everything, though we must not overlook the fact that jealousy is not always, as people would have it, a product of love: some women's jealousy regarding their husbands comes from hatred of them and a desire to hurt them. An example would be if a woman were to prevent her husband from going out to a park, a place of entertainment, or a bathhouse along with a number of other married men; she knows that they cannot meet up with women in such places and she only does this to exercise control over him and to stop him from talking about women with his friends and enjoying himself in ways that can do her no harm. It's the same if she forbids him to look out of his window at a street or a garden frequented by many women, and the same judgment applies to a man if he behaves the same way with his wife. People call such things "jealousy" but in reality they are a form of hatred, or it may be that hatred begins where jealousy leaves off, just as excessive laughter is the first stage of tears. However that may be, a man cannot truly love his wife if he doesn't allow her to enjoy herself in the way she wants and with whom she wants.' 'Does anyone in the world behave that way?' she asked. 'Indeed,' I responded. 'Many behave so in countries not far from us.' 'Good for them,' she replied, 'but what about their women? Do they behave the same way with their husbands?' 'They have to,' I answered, 'to keep things in balance.' 'Personally,' she said, 'I wouldn't put up with such evenhandedness. As far as I'm concerned, a tilt is better.' 'That's my opinion too, in certain circumstances,' I said. 'And where the circumstances of certain people are concerned,' she riposted.[310]

"'Let's get back to traveling,' I said. 'I leave today.' 'Indeed,' she said, '—for the lands of the white-skinned beauties.' 'Do you talk of men or women?' I enquired. 'I talk of one sex,' she replied, 'but what worries me is the other.' 'And why should that sex be a concern,' I asked, 'when it's you women who, in any circumstances, are the ones pursued, which is why they call a beautiful woman a *ghāniyah*?;[311] as the author of the *Qāmūs* says, "the *ghāniyah* is a woman who is pursued and does not herself need to pursue."' She said, 'Excellent words, but earlier he says, "*ʿawānī*[312] is a word for women, because they are mistreated and no one takes their side," though the dot on the one ought to put in a good word for the other.'[313] 'Love of "dotting,"' I said, 'is an ancient habit among you women.'[314] 'As "scripting" is among men,'[315] she retorted, 'but be that as it may; our being desired is the root of our worries, for the woman who is desired is by definition a woman whose honor is valued and guarded. Woe betide her then if she betrays her guardian and woe betide her if she denies the one who desires her, for then she will spend the night worrying over having denied him and over his disappointment and the fact that she has become a cause of his sleeplessness, anguish, and sorrow, and the woman who chases men ends up unchased.'[316] I said, 'Men's morals are not all the same where that's concerned,' to which she returned, 'I mean the men who desire, and fall in love with the ones they desire, not those fornicating omnivorous fickle-hearted ones whose custom is to take a nibble here and a nibble there and move from one object of desire to another, taking only what is of use to them without caring about 4.2.4

what may be of use to others. How few, though, are the former! Is there a single man who can maintain an affection and not deviate from it every day? I swear, were women to desire men as much as men desire women, you wouldn't find a single man unbewitched.'

4.2.5 "'Is there a single woman who can maintain affection and not deviate from it each day a thousand times?' I asked her. 'All books bear witness to the trustworthiness of men and the treachery of women.' 'Weren't the ones who wrote those books men?' she countered. 'They're the ones who made up those stories.' 'But only after investigation and experience,' I answered. 'If you go to the arbitrator alone, you win,' she said. 'Quite the reverse,' I said. 'They have provided testimonies. The words of Our Master Sulaymān, who said, "I have found one righteous man among a thousand but I have not found a single righteous woman" may serve as sufficient proof and evidence.' 'Even if Our Master Sulaymān was granted wisdom given to none other,' she said, 'his excessive indulgence in women rendered him incapable of distinguishing the righteous among them from the unrighteous. Have you not observed how the musk-seller's sense of smell weakens from length of exposure to its strong odor until he can no longer distinguish any more delicate scent? As far as providing the testimony of men against women without providing that of women against men is concerned, it is patent injustice and high-handedness.'

4.2.6 "'Indeed,' I said, 'evenhandedness in such citations would be preferable but, glory be, you women level every possible charge against men and then fall over one another to make a fuss over them!' She responded, 'Were it not that society works to make them *martyrs*, women wouldn't allow such ideas anywhere near their *medulla oblongarters*.'"[317] "I laughed," continued the Fāriyāq, "and said, 'What kind of a plural is that?' to which she replied, 'I made it by analogy.' 'Are the original word and that formed by analogy to it equal?' I asked. 'There's no difference,' she replied. 'On the contrary,' I said, 'they're entirely different, because lexicon cannot be derived by analogy. If it could, there'd be no conformity between male and female or between female and male,[318] or between the masculinization of the true feminine[319] and the feminization of words that have no equivalent.'[320] 'Another example of men's high-handedness and confusion of the issue!' she said. 'They are virtually incapable of dealing with anything straightforwardly.' 'And there you go again!' I retorted.

"She said, 'I swear I don't know what to do about men' and I said, 'And I swear I don't know what to do about women, but let's get back to saying farewell. I give you my word that I will never be unfaithful to you.' 'On the contrary, you will ever be unfaithful to me,' she said. I said, 'What reason do you have to be suspicious of me?' She replied, 'I observe that men who are in a country where they're unknown perform the worst abominations. Just look at how the foreigners who come to this island give themselves over to whoring and depravity. The moment one of them sets foot on land, he asks where the brothel is, especially the Syrians,[321] and amongst them especially the Christians, and amongst those especially the ones who have acquired a little knowledge of the ways of the Franks and their languages; they come off the ships like hornets, plunging their stingers here, there, and everywhere.' 'Perhaps they were like that in their home countries,' I said. 'They don't have the means to behave abominably there,' she returned. 'Or perhaps they're corrupt by nature,' I said. 'You're right,' she said. 'They have a latent disposition to corruption and the moment they smell the Frankish air, it comes to life, which is why you will find that they always drool as they talk of the lands of the Franks and their customs and conditions. If you were to ask one of them about their food, though, he'd say he didn't like it, or about their music, that it didn't move him, or about their nobility, that they didn't invite him to their banquets, or about their bathhouses, that they didn't appeal to him, or about their weather, that it hadn't suited him, or about their water, that he'd found it hard to swallow. The sole reason for their constant praise of those lands and for their lauding of the good things in them is abomination. 4.2.7

4.2.8 "'And you—who can guarantee me that your nature is not corrupt, when every day I hear you muttering about women with quivering flesh, women with firm and swelling flesh, women with fleshy flesh, women with masses of plump flesh, women with pretty white flesh, and tall, full-fleshed women with long necks, all of them phrases that would, I swear, make the Baptist salivate and excite a hermit?' I said, 'They're just words,' to which she replied, 'Every war begins with words.' 'Would you have me abandon this craft and its *obsession*, this all-consuming *profession*?' I asked. 'So long as you don't visualize, while describing, a specific person, I have no objection,' she answered. I responded, 'If I don't visualize a person, my mind will remain a blank.' 'In that case,' she said, 'it's a sin.' 'And how,' I asked, 'may I expiate it?' 'By visualizing only me and no one else,' she replied. 'But you,' I responded, 'are devoid of some of the characteristics that have to be mentioned,' to which she responded, 'If a man truly loves his wife, he will find in her everything that is fair and see in each hair of hers a beautiful woman. By the same token, if he loves some other woman, he will, for her sake, love her country, its weather, its water, and the language, customs, and manners of its people.' 'Aren't women the same,' I asked, 'when they love a man?' 'They're worse,' she answered, 'because they have larger reserves of love and passion.' 'And why is that?' I asked. 'Because,' she said, 'men spend time on things that do not concern them. Thus you'll find this one seeking position, that one power, and a third delving into religions and all that is obscure, be it profane or divine. Women pay no attention to any of that.' 'Would that you might busy yourself with the same concerns as men!' I said. 'Would that I had,' she rejoined, 'two hearts to devote to these concerns of ours.'[322] 'Do you, then,' I asked, 'see in me everything that is good, as you claim?' 'I hold you in high regard,' she said. 'In that case,' said I, 'let's get back to saying good-bye—or maybe not: let us, in fact, get back to the matter at hand, for I'd like to settle it before I depart; otherwise, it will preoccupy me throughout my journey and may spoil my work for those I go to serve. If that happens, I shall pin the blame on you and on women in general.'

"'You should know,' she said, 'that women are aware without having to be told that they are the adornment of this universe, and similarly that everything in it was created to be an adornment for women, not men; not because men are innately in no need of such adornment or because women are in need of it in order to look and sound attractive to the eyes of the beholder and the ears of the listener, but because men are not suited to it. Adornment is something one takes, receives, and assimilates and which then becomes an embellishment—modes more appropriate to women than to men. Based on this—which is to say, on the fact that everything in the universe was created for women, in part by design and in part through preference and predilection[323]—one of her beliefs is that the male sex too was created for her, albeit not in the sense that she should be wife to all men, for that would be an impossibility, from two perspectives. One is that no woman could survive such a thing, for the concubine of that certain Jew mentioned in Judges, chapter 19[324] could not survive the men of a single village (Gibeah), few though they were, for a single night; on the contrary, she died the next morning and her master believed she was asleep; the story is mentioned there as a caution to women. The other is that, if women's right to the exclusive possession and arbitrary disposal of men is admitted, then their right to everything else must be admitted too—though only in the sense that they're qualified to keep company with all men and be acquainted with what they are up to. Thus they may entertain from one a word of flattery, from another a word of praise, from some other courtship, from yet another conversation, and so on, none of which need stand in the way of her feeling love and affection for her husband. Nay, on the contrary . . .'" 4.2.9

The Fāriyāq continued, "At this I said, 'Go straight to the end of this "nay-on-the-contrary"—as far as I can see it's just the preface to another example of the cunning ways of women and the introduction to another of their wiles.' She laughed and said, 'Likely your 4.2.10

misgivings about women make you say so. Nevertheless, I'm afraid that fear and trembling will overtake you as you try to understand it and you'll find yourself unable to leave on time, or will suppose that that's how I conduct myself where you are concerned. God forbid! Never have I betrayed you, with friend or with foe. Everything I know I have learned from other women, for women hide nothing from one another where love and the ways of men are concerned.' 'Be brief, then,' said I, 'for I'm disquieted and *frightened*, and my perspiration level's *heightened*.'

4.2.11 "'Know then,' she said, 'that there are two reasons why some women feel no qualms about making love to men other than their husbands. The first is their failure to get from the latter their established due, for men accustom them at the beginning to what they are incapable of giving them at the end, and it's no secret that there are, among women,[325] the nymphomaniac, who "devours everything," the sworn virgin, who "abstains completely from intercourse,"[326] the two-timer, who "takes two lovers," the prick teaser, who "incites without making herself available," and the bluestocking, who "loves the conversation of men but does not fornicate" (which is the way I am) . . .'" The Fāriyāq continued, saying, "'Thank God for that!' said I, and she said, '. . . and the ball-breaker, "who flirts with you but doesn't avail you of herself."

4.2.12 "'The second reason is her desire to find out what men are about and to put them all, sturdy and weak alike, to the test, simply in order to know, so that nothing about them may escape her. There are those too who suppose, given women's firmly established belief that men have no interest in anything but flirting with and sweet-talking women, that their husbands will betray them at the first opportunity. Thinking so, any time she finds a means of leaving the strait and narrow, she hurries to seize it, imagining that she is taking revenge preemptively, which is to say before the time otherwise allotted for it—despite which women never lose their love for their husbands. On the contrary, any such straying may be conducive to an increase in love for them on their part.'

"'May God not send me a love that springs from nymphomania or infidelity!' I said. 'How, though, can this promiscuity be conducive to an increase in love[327] when the woman, once she has sampled the thrusting prick, the strong prick, the hard prick, and the huge, mighty-headed prick, will never thereafter be able to limit herself to her husband, given that he can never escape the particular attribute with which he was created? And the man likewise, having once sampled women who are sweet-mouthed and dry-cunted, narrow-quimmed, high-twatted, tight-tunneled, and bulgy-beavered will find his wife ever after diminished.' She laughed and said, 'Were these attributes essential in order for a woman to be a woman and their diminution a defect, they wouldn't be found only in a small number of individuals, for most women are not like that. The reason why affection increases, as women claim, with promiscuity is that the husband, given his long familiarity with and lascivious interest in his wife, and the fact that the touching of one of them by the other no longer produces in the body of either the toucher or the touched any shaking, trembling, or tendency to faint, is able to keep going longer, penetrate more deeply, and maintain a harder erection than the stranger. The two last characteristic abilities[328] will elude the latter, either because of his voracity and discombobulation, or because the woman keeps going back to him after short breaks for more, or because what is forbidden is not always as appealing as what is permitted. 4.2.13

"'The pleasure she gets from him derives largely from her conceptualization[329] (meaning her conceptualization of him as other than her husband) just as her boredom with her husband derives largely from her conceptualization of him as something familiar. This aside, it is a fact that licit pleasure is more powerful. Conceptualization, however, is almost as important as performance. The proof of this is that if a man believes that a woman other than his wife is going to spend the night with him and then his own wife does so without his knowing, as happened with Our Master Yaʿqūb,[330] peace be upon him, he'll find that his wife, that night, possesses all 4.2.14

the characteristics that he conceives of as being possessed by other women, and the same is true for a woman. Based then on what has been said above about the woman believing that every kind of beauty, adornment, and delight in the universe is most appropriately hers, she will conceptualize, and preoccupy herself with, the attributes of beauty as though they were a universal absolute. Should there, therefore, be a particular example close by, she will deal with it as she would with the universal, to the degree that her thoughts will often go on beyond any one man in his particularity, two or three men pulling them this way and that until she is reduced to a tizzy in her attempts to decide between the beguiling and the yet more beguiling, which amounts in reality to her being surrounded on all sides by sensual pleasure, like someone who wants to drink from three water pitchers and puts them all to his mouth at the same time.' 'Your words,' I said, 'put one in mind of the lines of the poet that go

If my heart's distracted by the young ladies
My eye beholds, and whose beauty's divided, a little to each,
I mount in my fancy a face that attracts me
On a body that suits it and then feel the itch.

"'Earlier, however, you forbade me to visualize any particular woman when celebrating women's bodies in verse and said it was a sin, so wouldn't you agree that what you're suggesting is sinful too?' 'The former,' she replied, 'is sinful because it constitutes a pointless and excessive use of language. Words of dalliance have, in fact, no value and are worthless however used.

4.2.15 "'As far as the act, on the other hand, is concerned, women view it as determining the comeliness of their children and this explains why you will find a child with a nose like Zayd's, a mouth like 'Amr's, and eyes like Bakr's;[331] this is also a riposte to those who claim that it is in the wife's interest for her husband to see lots of other women because on his return his libido will have been increased by his contact with them.[332] It is different, however, when the woman goes out, for her libido is contained within her. Those idiots who claim that what a man visualizes has an effect on the shaping of the fetus in the womb should look at no women whatsoever other than their wives, lest their offspring turn out to be all females, or at least hermaphrodites, the reason being the discrepancy in the different ways in which the father and the mother visualize.[333] Indeed, a woman who exchanges her husband for another in thought and visualization should be nothing less than all men's object of praise and her husband should think of none but her.' I said, 'The necessary implication of your words is that women who are shielded from seeing the generality of men will find no pleasure in one particular man.' She replied, 'As for the woman who sees the generality of men, that is so. However, it is not so in the case of the woman who sees none at all, for water, no matter how hot, puts out fire.' 'That is true,' I said, 'and so it is if read backward, meaning that fire, no matter how cool, heats water.' 'It *is* true,' she replied, 'if read backward, but frontward is better.'[334]

"'Into how many divisions may pleasure be divided?' I asked. 4.2.16
'Into five,' she responded. 'The first is visualization of it before its occurrence. The second is discussion of it before the same. The third is its actual realization accompanied by these two essential elements. The fourth is the visualization of it after the act. The fifth is discussion of it afterward. Whether the pleasure of visualizing it is greater before it takes place or afterward is a matter of debate. Some believe the first is greater because when it hasn't yet happened one's thoughts about it roam more widely, delve more deeply, and do not stop at any limit. Others claim that the actual occurrence provides one's thoughts with a known shape and a specific form as a benchmark against which to measure any replay or repetition. Similarly, there is disagreement over the times of its visualization, as also of its discussion, though the crucial point is the clearness of the visualization and the foulness of the tongue. The best time for it is the summer in women's opinion and the winter in men's. As to the number of times, some people are Unitarians, some Dualists,

and some Trinitarians.' 'And some,' I said, 'Muʿtazilites and some Muʿaṭṭilites.'[335] 'The last,' she said, 'are without redeeming qualities and are unworthy to be counted among mankind.'[336]

4.2.17 "'What are we to think of men who marry two, or three, wives?' I asked. 'It's against nature,' she replied. 'How can that be,' I asked, 'when it was the custom of the prophets?' 'Is this a discussion about religion,' she responded, 'or about natural phenomena? Do you not observe that those animals, such as the rooster and the sparrow for example, that have been granted the capacity to live with a multiplicity of females have also been granted the capacity to satisfy them all? The others live with only one and are satisfied with her. Given that a man cannot satisfy three, he is not qualified to possess them. To return to the matter in hand—why is a *woman* forbidden to marry three men?' I replied, 'A multiplicity of women for a single man results in the multiplicity of offspring on which the world depends in order to thrive. This wouldn't apply in the case of a multiplicity of men for a single woman, though I have read in some book that such a custom continues to be observed among certain savages.' 'Gently, gently!' she said. 'Are they really the savages while you're the civilized and sagacious ones? As for your claim concerning the multiplication of offspring when there's a multiplicity of wives, are the inhabitants of the earth now so few? Is not its surface already too confined to hold them? Do not its innards groan under their weight and is not its skin ripped open? What motive is there then for this increase other than hubris and greed?'

4.2.18 "'You've reverted to heaping blame on men, so let us revert to saying farewell. I shall depart from you today and leave my heart in your keeping, so that if anyone visits you I shall sense his presence.' 'How will you sense anything when your heart's not with you?' she asked, 'for people say it is the heart alone that has the capacity to feel and *perceive*, be joyous and *grieve*.' 'My sense of feeling,' I said, 'is in my head.'[337] 'Where in your head?' she asked. 'At the tip-top of my head,' I answered. 'Naturally!' she responded. 'There is sympathy between things that resemble one another. But where will you leave it?' 'On the doorstep,' I replied, 'so that no one may set foot on the latter.' 'And what if he jump over it?' she enquired. 'In the bed, then,' I said. 'And what if he's in some other bed?' she went on. 'In you, then,' I said. 'That,' she responded, 'is the best place for it. I promise that I will abide by the love and affection that we have shared from the time of "the roof" till now. The moment, however, that I sense and feel, from here, that you've switched your *roofing* feelings for a *roving* eye, I'll match every deed of yours with one of mine, and "the initiator is the more unjust."' I said, 'You're much given to suspicion and very jealous; what's to make sure that anything you sense isn't generated by suspicion?' 'On the contrary,' she said, 'any suspicions I may have are more likely to be the result of what I sense.' I said, 'We've come full circle,' to which she replied, 'Try then to break it.'[338] 'It is a duty,' I said, 'and must be performed,' to which she replied, 'And it is a performance that must be demanded as a duty.' 'Will it seal our covenant?' I asked. 'If such contracts can ever be sealed,' she replied. 'I reject such a characterization,'[339] I said. 'I wish,' she said, 'that someone would tell me what such a characterization means.' I said, 'Was the contract over the condition?'[340] and she replied, 'And was the condition without a contract?'[341] I said, 'We're as mad as that lunatic,'[342] to which she responded, 'But for madness we would never have married.' I said, 'That is true of most people.' 'Many a person's off his *head*,' was her response to this, at which 'Praise be to God, Lord of the Worlds,' I *said*."

Chapter 3

Assorted Pleas for Mercy

4.3.1 Those who are by nature mendacious and given to slander, or who know nothing about women, will be suspicious of this farewell and attribute it to the embroidering and hyperbole of a poet. But who can gainsay one who has made it her habit, practice, custom, convention, utmost goal,[343] wont, way, fashion, and observance to riposte, jest, banter, chaff, rally, sally, and respond with alacrity? Often, indeed, two or three of his friends would gather with the Fāriyāq and take on a topic on which she would rise to their challenge, keep pace with them, oppose them, and out-argue them. No speaker, however persuasive, should she oppose him, could find his tongue, and any master of rhetoric, should she enter the lists against him, would tremble, learning by experience that a woman's answer is faster than a man's and that one who has dedicated himself to scholarship may be slower to answer than one who has not, for the former will only venture to answer after cogitation and deliberation.

4.3.2 That said, the utterances that I have reported above from this woman so persuasive (despite her having read not a word in the art of rhetoric) fall far short of the original, for I was incapable, in reporting her words, of reporting likewise the gestures she made along with them and of picturing for the reader eyes that flirt and eyebrows that hint, a nose *aquiver* and lips that *shiver*, cheeks that flush, a neck that twists and a hand that gestures, breathing that rises and falls, and a voice that dips low and soars high, to which may be added the wiping of the eyeball to indicate incipient tears, a succession of sighs to symbolize sadness and joy, a display of foolishness to give notice of regret, a movement from side to side to announce grief and pain, and other things of that sort that lent power and rhetorical force to her words. This is the second time you've made me regret my ignorance of the craft of photography, the first being in Book One, chapter 14, when fair women in all their diverse beauty were discussed, and I may yet feel the same regret a third time.

Here I have to stand up straight and request permission from the powers that be to declare that it is the custom of all governors and kings, with the exception of the king of the English, to invite no one to enter or exit their lands who has not first paid to their ministries or their agents known as consuls a sum of money in keeping with the fertility or barrenness of their possessions. They do this on the pretext that if a traveler spends one or two hours in their country he is bound to see their spacious palaces and ever-victorious armies or their thoroughbred horses and luxurious vessels, thus putting him on a par with one who enters some place of entertainment, which no one would do without paying a fee. 4.3.3

If anyone objects, saying, "In a place of entertainment we hear the voices of the singers, male and female, and the sounds of the musical instruments, see the decorative lights and varied decorations, the shining faces of the lovely ladies and their dazzling displays, laugh with them when they laugh, are transported when they dance, and fall in love with them when they flirt, but we see none of these things when we view one of your cities; indeed, as soon as we enter them we are fleeced by your merchants, meaning that what we gain from our coming in is but little compared to what they gain in terms of their incomings," they will tell you, "Your arrival in our country may coincide with a musical performance by our soldiers, and that can be in lieu of any transports you may experience in that place of entertainment. As far as women are concerned we give you permission to enjoy any of them that takes your fancy and run 4.3.4

after any of them you wish, so long as you have ready cash. It's not right, however, for you to liken our cities, graced as they are with our presence, to some place of entertainment, especially as the payment of these fees is an ancient custom followed by our ancestors (God bless the sod!) that has been practiced for so many years and eons that it can no longer be changed. If the king commands something, that thing becomes custom and law, as witness the words of the psalmodist when he says, 'The king's heart is in the hand of the Lord,'[344] meaning that whenever the king thinks of something the hand of God renders his judgment infallible with regard to it. This is how the divines in our country explain this verse and the reward of any who disagrees is crucifixion.

4.3.5 "But to return to our argument: if the king starts changing customs and exchanging conventions, this may lead to him too being changed. His situation is comparable to that of the rooster that searches for a grain of wheat on the ground and in so doing stirs up the dust till it covers his head (though this is an unworthy comparison). Better then that everything stay as it is. And again, it makes no difference whether the one bound for our country is rich or poor, pious and righteous, a thief and a libertine, a man or a woman—all are obliged to hand over the fee and put up with the fleecing . . ." "But my lord and master, I am a woman in straitened circumstances obliged to pass through your happy city because my poor dear hubby came to your royal country to conduct some business and the Almighty determined that he should meet his end there, so I left young children I have writhing with hunger in our little cottage and came to see my poor dead hubby (since he can't see me), not to mention that I'm considered one of those good-looking women who deserve to be looked after and well treated by those in positions such as yours. Why then should I be obliged to bear the fee, not to mention the costs of travel and the loss of my hubby, who was a support to me?" "Return, woman, to whence you came! This is no time for pleas for mercy, for the rules set down in the ledgers of kings admit of no change or modification and no exceptions can be made . . .”

“And I too, my master, am a poor little fellow whom fate has bombarded with its calamities for reasons known only to God and I have made my way to your country hoping to obtain some minor post that will satisfy my needs. I am no seducer or sower of dissent nor am I one who pokes his nose into the policies of kings and their governance. All that I wish for is to make a living, though I do know something that the inhabitants of your ever-prosperous land do not and my presence here may be of benefit to your happy realm. Should a sublime decree be issued that I be examined and tested as to my claims, you would provide me with a house, to say nothing of issuing the permit for me to enter without a fee . . .” “You there, policeman, watchman, guard, nabber, grunter, rozzer, runner, cop, slop, constable, catchpole, cozzpot, woodentop, nabman, beagle, derrick, nubbing-cove—put that man in prison! He’s surely a spy come to spy out our land. Search him. No doubt you’ll find papers on him that’ll tell us what he’s up to.” 4.3.6

“And I too, my lord and master, am a poor young laddie. I have come to see my father because he has told me that, on his way home, he entered your country, where the clement climate afflicted him with a malady that prevents him from moving. When my mother, who is also sick from the grief and care that have consumed her as a result of his long absence, learned of his illness, she sent me to him, in the hope that I might serve him and nurse him and his spirits then revive at the sight of me and recover, for when a sick father sees his son the latter takes the place of medicine.” “We’re not children’s nannies and our country’s no schoolhouse that they should come and go without paying a fee. Get on with you and show you’re a man by paying it right away . . .” 4.3.7

“And I too—O my shield and my refuge, my succor and my resort, my haven and my shelter, my support and my prop, my foundation and my stay, my strength and my security—am a poet and man of 4.3.8

letters who wrote a poem in praise of a certain emir, for which he granted me a hundred gold coins. With half of these I bought provisions for my family, with a quarter I covered what I needed to clothe them, and I have a quarter left. Having heard of the merits of your magnificent, splendid, fertile kingdom and of the treasures and curiosities that it contains, to be found in no other country, I desired to let my eyes roam and my mind saunter in the midst of this luxury for a few days. Who knows? Maybe on seeing it, brilliant tropes that no one has beaten me to will come to my mind and from them I shall fashion, before anything else, a brilliant eulogy in praise of your elevated *position* and gracious *condition,* broadcast praise of you in every *clime,* at every *time,* skillfully describe your noble qualities in books . . ." "How many a dilettantish and doleful poet we have in our country! How many are their writings and how little their income! Either you pay the fee, or you turn around and go home, or we consign you to the madhouse."

4.3.9 Rarely, though, does the puissant, magnificent master honor the ears of the wretched pleader with the like of such negative responses, for mere negativity from the great is a boon. Usually it comes with humiliation and a slap to the back of the neck, a punch on the snout, the pulverizing of a tooth, the slitting open of a belly, the slicing off of a leg, or the snapping of a back. For this reason, the Fāriyāq, being one of those who couldn't spare any of his limbs, when he resolved to travel, requested five consuls to honor his passport with their stamps. The consuls of Naples, Leghorn, and another city in the Papal States, as well as the consuls of Genoa and France stamped it, because the steamer passes by the ports of each of those cities and docks in them for a few hours. The city of Naples is famous for its numerous carriages, ships, gardens, and forests, Leghorn for the sweetness of its air and the height of its buildings, and the same holds true for the city of Genoa. The Fāriyāq said, "In my opinion, the last is better than the other two. The papal city is as disagreeable as can be, since it has none of the glamour of sovereignty or royalty and there is nothing in it to please the eye."

When the Fāriyāq reached Marseilles, his trunk was taken to the customs office and he was shown by signs that he was to follow it. The customs officers asked him to open it so that they could search through it, but he thought they wanted to look through his notebooks so that they could know what was in them and said, "I haven't written satires on your sultan or your metropolitan, so why would you look through my notebooks?" but none of them understood him and he understood none of them. When they were done, they gestured to him to close the trunk and he breathed a sigh of relief. Then one of them started feeling his side with his hands, so that the Fāriyāq imagined that he was "rubbing" him,[345] in the sense of seeking blessing from him, because he'd found his notebooks in their strange hand. Afterwards, however, he learned that they were searching him to see if he was carrying any tobacco or intoxicating spirits. 4.3.10

Next he traveled from Marseilles to Paris, where he and his trunk were likewise searched at its customs house. The customs officers of the latter city seemed to believe that their colleagues in the former had gone to sleep while on night duty and the devil had urinated in their ears and as a result their eyes had been made too blurry to see what was in the trunk, or that they'd taken a bribe, like other civil servants. He stayed in Paris three days, in the house occupied by the embassy of the Sublime State,[346] where he enjoyed the privilege of kissing the hands of the August Ministers and Honored Marshals Rashīd Pasha and Sāmī Pasha. Then he left Paris for London; these two mighty cities will be described later. From London he went to a village in peasant country, where he hung up his hat and where I too shall now call a halt. 4.3.11

Chapter 4

The Rules for Retelling

4.4.1 In all his life, the Fāriyāq never spent a more unpleasant and arduous time than he did in that village,[347] for the villages of England are altogether without places in which to be entertained, to meet, to enjoy oneself, or to have fun; enjoyment and fun are to be had only in the large cities. In addition, such food and drink as are sold in them are no cause for celebration, for anyone who has a chicken or anything special sends it to one of the nearby towns. Anyone who wishes to cut himself off from the world or feels a calling to be a monk should hie himself to them. As for their women, some of them will cure a loss of appetite or even bestow a raging lust, but the outsider is denied access to them. Every cloven hoof stays close to her bull and the only loose, free-ranging beasts are the old ones.

4.4.2 After two months in these calamitous conditions, he moved to the city of Cambridge, wellspring of the clergy and of the science of theology, since most English clergymen go there or to Oxford to learn divinity and apologetics. These two cities are also home to all other students, in all their diversity of class and standing. The celebrated philosopher Newton was the brilliant son of one of the Cambridge colleges. There the Fāriyāq rented, as is the custom, two sets of rooms in a house, where he stayed, translating the rest of the book referred to earlier.[348] In the same house there was a full-breasted girl with wide black eyes, which is how most of the maids there are. Every night the Fāriyāq would see her going up to the room of one of the lodgers. Then, after a time not longer than it takes to say "Good evening!" he would hear her produce a kineto-penetrative gasp. The mistress of the house used to see her coming down from the man's room at ten or so at night but had no interest in her ascents and descents. In the morning, when the girl came to make the Fāriyāq's bed, he would stare at her and observe her closely but could see no sign to indicate that she was the gasper. He therefore assumed that it was a delusion born of his fervent desire for penetration. Then night would come and the gasp would be there again, and so would his certainty. With morning the staring would be repeated as would the pretence of virtue, and the doubt would be there and so would the confusion, and so on and so forth. Things got so bad that the Fāriyāq's mind almost became unhinged and started to spoil the translation, which he had long feared might fall victim to shortcomings and mistakes due to some issue related to women.

Here I have to squat down on my haunches and declare: "This 4.4.3
feline characteristic (i.e., the ability to take one's food without being noticed), though its presence may be observed in women in general, is especially pronounced among English women. Such a woman, if distinguished by those features ascribed to the sexually voracious woman in the *ḥadanbadā* chapter,[349] will put on a show during the day of God-fearingness, piety, reticence, and distaste and look at her devotee as though she had no idea who he was, deluding any who are watching her into thinking she is virtuous and has nothing to do with men. She may have memorized religious sayings and devout narrations to fling at people, making them venerate her and believe her to be righteous, and when you enter her home you may find on the table copies of the Old Testament and the Gospels and other books on worship and self-abnegation (the visible edges of whose pages she will sometimes dirty to give the false impression that she studies them frequently) and a man may not be allowed to utter in her presence the name of any of his members. As a result,

the pleasure of such women, according to the rule pronounced by the Fāriyāqiyyah, will be incomplete, because it will lack the element of discussion.[350]

4.4.4 "And we have it on her authority too that any talk of pleasure must be congruent with the reality. If it involves a man of high status at night, it must be discussed with a woman of high status at night, if someone of low status in the morning, it must be discussed with a woman of low status in the morning, and so on and so forth for all the various other times and persons—unless there is reason to fear that the opportunity will be lost: in other words, if it happened at night, for example, but cannot be discussed that same night, it is permissible to discuss it at dawn or in the morning, or if it involves a man of high status but none of his kind is available, it is permissible to discuss it with a man of low status; the pleasure derived from talking about it will not be spoiled thereby. If by any chance she cannot find anyone from any of these categories, she can discuss it with herself. She may do this by inserting her head into an empty water jar, well, pit, vault, or anything of the sort that produces an echo, and speaking with clear and eloquent tongue of everything that happened to her; the responding echo can take the place of an intimate interlocutor. If, on the other hand, the memory is kept in her breast, chestiness and diphtheria are to be feared.

4.4.5 "It is also a rule in her view that the retelling be congruent with the act. Thus, for the pressings, an accentuation of the voice,[351] for the jabs, a catch in the airflow, for the movements, a vocalic motion, for the moments of inertia, an inert letter, for the prolongations, a prolongation of the *a*, for the rushed bits, a gabbling of the recitation, for the softenings of the voice, an apocopation, and for the languorous moments, a slowing of pace. Also, that special attention be given to the doubling of the letter *dhāl*,[352] if the retelling is done in this noble language of ours, and that there be a flirtatious flash to the eyes, floods of saliva, and a moistness to the tongue, and that the hands sketch what the words describe. This being established, you will have gathered that the trait mentioned as present in

Englishwomen is an infraction of the rules of pleasure, and it may be said that the pleasure they take in visualization is so strong because it takes the place of two other pleasures, or that they put their heads inside a cask or the like.

"And on the authority of the Fāriyāq, we have it that the beauty that is in women, in all its disparate forms, has ways of speaking, calling out, inviting, pointing, and signaling. For example, there is the type that says to the one who gazes upon it, 'I'm not interested in little sticks' and the type that says, 'Seize your opportunity now!' or 'Tarrying has its disadvantages' or 'You won't find me wearied by large numbers' or 'Let not the shy-eyed one deceive you!' or 'Come hither!' or 'O who will bring him to me right now?' or 'I see none who can satisfy me' or 'The best way to mend a slit is to sew it up'[353] or 'Where oh where is the one who can satisfy me?' or 'Where is Ibn Alghaz?'[354] or 'Where is a member of the Banū Adhlagh?'[355] or 'Before me the hard man is humbled' or 'After all that effort, who can find fault with you?' or 'No conscious effort is entirely wasted' or 'Feed and thou shalt be satisfied' or 'To taste is to know' or 'To touch is to praise' or 'The early bird catches the worm' or 'If at first you don't succeed . . .'[356] or 'Always count twice'[357] or 'Keep in touch with others and others will keep in touch with you.' There is also the type that looks at you as though to say, 'Use cunning' or 'Make your visits discreet' or 'Watch out for the neighbors' or 'Slow and steady wins the race' or 'Come early as the crow.'"[358] 4.4.6

The beauty of Englishwomen is of the sort that falls under the heading of "Where is Ibn Alghaz?" "Where oh where is the one who can satisfy me?" and "Before me the hard man is humbled." You see them turning disdainfully to one side,[359] shying, flying, starting, bolting, flinching, fleeing, proudly turning, racing, baulking, jibbing, bounding, leaping, escaping, like a mirage dissipating, while running full tilt, head high, nose in air, chest out, back straight, and even though the divine creative power has uniquely blessed them with buttocks ample and copious (or so it is reported), yet they apply bustles to these, using the latter to make the former large 4.4.7

enough to stop any who lies in wait in his tracks, as though dumbfounded by a head-on encounter, after which he cannot stop his knees from knocking together in wonder and awe at such aggrandizement, his teeth from smoking, his tongue from lolling, his uvula from wagging, his neck from twisting, his jugulars from swelling, and his eyelids from reddening, or himself from being overcome by lust and assaulting her, and the said person is taken by an agitation,[360] a trepidation, a commotion, a flutteration, a trembling, a shaking, a quaking, a shuddering, a shivering, a quavering, a rocking, a jolting, a jarring, a jerking, a bobbling, a wobbling, a fainting, a giddiness, a dizziness, a light-headedness, a twitching, a tottering, a teetering, a staggering, a faltering, a languorous folding, a stiffening of the joints, a chattering of the teeth, and a rattling of the jaw, and the four humors set him ablaze, each mix[361] demanding its own bustle. Ideas and misgivings bombard him, hopes and fears pull him this way and that, choking passions make him splutter, he trembles with lustful emotions, and he doubles over with yearning and desire, in accordance with the words of the poet

I knew you as one celebrated for your generosity,
And the throbbings of longing and hope swept me to you

and he remains so confused and at a loss, speechless and flabbergasted, perplexed and bewildered, astonished and amazed that, when he returns safely to his house, he believes everything that pops up before him there is a bustle, or that thing that lends the bustle its bulk.

4.4.8 Whenever the Fāriyāq left the house and beheld these well-endowed mounds, he would return to his refuge with a thousand poetical images crowding his head. A poem he recited in honor of one such enchantress went as follows:

Wonder of wonders! Let every man, "Wonder of wonders!"
Exclaim, of those who love with women to tussle,

"Not a mound's to be seen
In this place that isn't a bustle!
No indeed! And not a dip
That isn't accompanied by its own little hump—
No indeed again!—and not a euphorbia fruit[362] to be bought
That isn't a high-breasted woman's pink bump.
Longing makes me boldly approach each big-bottomed waddler
Who invites the celibate to play,
Yet fear of impotence induced by too much lust
Keeps me away.
What must people say of him who
Roars from a bursting milk skin that absence of opportunity plugs,
Or how can the stomach of an Arab
Be too weak to drink deep from those great jugs?
O for a spigot that I might fill the cup
From my counter-levered love pail!
O for a bustle like one of those domes
Of which I might myself at night avail!
O for a palpation of one of those
Bummikins in my home!
This, I swear, is the way of those starved
Of sex and this same practice is my own."

Chapter 5

The Superiority of Women

4.5.1 Just as the women of this country are distinguished by this characteristic, so its men are distinguished by that of kindness to the stranger, once they have been introduced to him. Before he's been introduced, however, if he greets one of them, the response will be a sidelong glance or a brisk nod of the head. Thus it was that one of their students of Arabic, having learned of the presence of the Fāriyāq and having been informed as to his noble pedigree and plentiful property, came to visit him and invited him to go with him to his house, which was some distance from Cambridge, and to stay there as an honored guest. The Fāriyāq accepted the invitation because the inhabitants of the city, despite the large number of schools and places of learning there, were exceptionally unwelcoming to the stranger, especially if he differed from them in dress; they made so much fun of his red cap, for example, that he often hid in his room and would leave it only at night.

4.5.2 On this topic, he wrote

Cast by the tempest on Cambridge's shore,
Lest I be seen and mocked by the rabble, I kept to my house.
Then, when night had driven me mad,
I'd go out in safety, like a flittermouse.

Similarly, since the dogs too would sniff at his fur coat and follow him around, he wrote of them

I've got a fur coat that the dogs all come to sniff at
    But when I repel them not one retires.
They snarl as they rip into my skin and the coat's—
    You'd think I'd had it made from the skins of their sires.

And because the people of the house where he was staying would take a share of his food and not allow him access to their persons, he wrote about them

In Cambridge I've got dependents undisclosed
    Who partake of my food when there's no one there to watch—
All I know of my lady guest is that her name is So-and-so
    And all I know of the man is that his name is Such and such.

Likewise, because he couldn't find a way to be alone with one of those "domes," he wrote of them

What's the use of a comfy mattress
    If there's no sex to be had on it for all its softness?
What use a nightdress without a cunny
    Or a nice bit of quim if you can't find a cubby?
What use is life with no snatch in your bed?
    No matter how long you live, you're better off dead.

They took the railway together and arrived at the house at night, and no sooner had the Fāriyāq entered the room that had been prepared for him than he decorated it with the following: 4.5.3

What an excellent thing is the railway! How many a bottom
    On its seats spreads wide, while breasts there quiver galore!
If that alone were all it did for us—never mind its forward
        dashing—
    One couldn't think to ask for more.

atw ["forward dashing"] is "directness of motion, and speed."

Then when he got up the following morning, it came to him how far still his new abode was from home but he said, "I seek refuge with God!" and "We are God's and to God we return!" and put a brave face on it, because such complaints do not find a sympathetic ear among those people—so much so that a few days after his complaining of how long he'd been separated from his wife, his friend told him, "The other day you spoke extravagantly. You said, 'I long for my wife!' but it would have been more proper to say 'for my children.'" "What," the Fāriyāq asked him, "is wrong with a man speaking of his wife as he might of his children? Without the wife, there wouldn't be any children! Nay more: without women there would be nothing in this world, neither religion nor anything else." "Hush, hush!" said his friend. "You go too far."

4.5.4 "Listen to what I say!" said the Fāriyāq. "Were it not for Pharaoh's daughter, Moses would not have been saved from drowning and were it not for Moses, there would be no Old Testament. Were it not for a woman, Joshua would not have been able to enter the Promised Land and take possession of it.[363] Were it not for a woman, Abraham would not have found favor with the King of Egypt and obtained from him gifts and presents, thus preparing the way for the descent of the Jews into Egypt after him.[364] Were it not for a woman, David would not have been saved from the hand of Saul when he decided in his breast to kill him, which was achieved by his placing an image in his bed,[365] and were it not for David, there would be no psalms. Nay more, were it not for a woman, meaning the wife of Nabal,[366] David would not have prevailed over his enemies. Were it not for Bathsheba's stratagem against David,[367] Solomon would not have made his son king and the temple of God would not have been built in Jerusalem. Were it not for a woman, Jesus would not have been born and the news of his resurrection would not have been broadcast. Were it not for a woman, the Anglican sect would not be doing as well as it is today.[368] Furthermore, your painters depict angels in the form of women and your poets never cease writing poems to women, without which no poet would ever shine."

"As far as I can see," said the other, "you are merely lusting after a woman—a trait, it seems, that is common to all Arabs." "Indeed," he replied, "I am their epitome and pattern, and every man who utters the *ḍād* has a weakness for the *ḍaʿd*."[369] The man hung his head for a moment, then said, "You may be wiser than those who deviate toward the *mīm*,[370] for I have heard that there are many *mīm*-ists, who abandon the broad highway in favor of ignoble back alleys, which is the ugliest thing imaginable. Uglier still, though, is the fact that certain Arab authors have composed books on the subject and deceitfully sought to present arguments that the *mīm*-ist craft is the better." "That is so," said the Fāriyāq. "Among them is a book I came across in the Cambridge library on which I found written in English the title *A Book on the Laws of Marriage*, the one who bought it seemingly having failed to grasp its contents. One of the most scurrilous arguments made in support of such things is the words of a certain poet who said 4.5.5

I make no final decision between buggery and mainstream
fornication—
I merely follow the words of those who've written,
'Gratification all lies in the dirtier of the two neighbors,
So choose, if you can, the more beshitten.'

"The reason why the likes of these woman-shy authors wrote such books is either their impotence, for women will have nothing to do with anyone who is so afflicted, or their stinginess, because women are more expensive to maintain, or their lack of the means to attract them, or some other defect. Those of sound makeup, however, never leave the straight path in the first place."

The Fāriyāq stayed at his friend's house for a while, during which he was invited to splendid banquets in the homes of certain notables. It is customary at their banquets for the women to sit at the table with their arms and breasts exposed, so that the observer can see the flesh of their chests, their bosoms, their breasts, and their cleavages, and if he stretches his neck and cranes his head and is good 4.5.6

at holding his head steady, he can see the dark ring around their nipples (ah, what a dream!). It's one of those customs that is to be praised from one perspective and condemned from another, in that this exposure is a general rule for both young and old; indeed, the old women of the Franks, and especially the English, uncover themselves more and put on more youthful airs than do the young girls. Then the invitations became fewer and the Fāriyāq's disquiet grew stronger, since no one who had looked on his countenance once wanted to look on it a second time, and he decided it was better to return to Cambridge. When he arrived there, he found that that the "domes" had grown by some three inches, this being due either to his having been so long away from them or because the more bitter cold required that.[371]

4.5.7 Here an edifying observation must be made, to wit, that given that Cambridge and Oxford are, as previously mentioned, celebrated as schools of learning, and given that most of the students are rich and that each city has something in the region of two thousand of them, the pretty girls from the surrounding peasant villages return time after time to the markets of these two cities to find buyers for their youth and beauty. As a result, you will see in these cities examples of exquisite beauty and dazzling good looks such as you will not find in any other. But "for everything that falls there's something to pick it up,"[372] as they say, which is why our shaykhs the students would look at every addition to the town's population as might a she-cat being robbed of her kittens. Consequently, the Fāriyāq left these tomcats and their females behind—a decision whose correctness was confirmed in his view when he came across the proverb that says, "When you enter the land of al-Ḥuṣayb, run!"[373]—and stayed in London for close to a month.

A Description of London, or Londra,[374] according to the Fāriyāq 4.5.8

See the proud and capricious lady in her *duds*, strutting before the manly *studs*! With a furious stare she gives them a *zap*, dragging behind her her skirts and her *wrap*. As I say in a poem of mine

Coquettishly she set off, dragging her train,
Causing the suffering lover yet more pain.

Among them she finds no *match* and mocks them with her smiles—they're not up to *scratch*. Be mindful, fair lady, that among them is to be found the strongest and the ablest, the manliest and the wealthiest, the speediest and the toughest, the strongest and at stripping the quickest, the best at felling and the pressingest, the proddingest and the pokiest, the lippiest and labia-lovingest, the sticky-outy-est and the largest thingy-est, who, when he hugs, *moans*, when he smells, snorts and when aroused, *groans*; who if winked at, responds in a flash and, the moment he sees a drum, plays on his pipe; who on seeing a woman with body *lavish* is quick to *ravish*.

Be mindful that among them is an Arab who with passion *yearns*, 4.5.9
with thirst and torment *burns*, one quick to make love and quick to *lay*, to devour with kisses and engage in *play*, energetic in bed and *nimble*, ever ready to hunt the *thimble*. With what can we flatter you, when haughtily you turn aside your *eyes*, with what entice you, when you treat our words as *lies*? Are you not *aware* that not only do we seek your kindnesses but also that of your kind we've known our *share*? How many a headstrong woman we've been able to *pacify*! How many a willful woman we've known how to *gratify*! How many a disdainful one have we bent to our *will*! To how many a love-hungry one have we given her *fill*! How many a bolter have we given reason to *pause*! To how many a love-sick complainer have we given *cause*! How many a *prude* have we, to their satisfaction, *screwed*! How many an obdurate woman has sung our praises while homeward *bound*, returning later for a second *round*! Let not your stately stature seduce you into being *stiff*, your wide eyes into

staying *aloof*, your swanlike neck into churlish *demurral*, into denying your fate that auburn *curl*, your gap-teeth into a refusal of men's *due*, into contempt for lucre your cheeks' rosy *hue*, your swelling breasts into pride and *vanity*, your firmness of skin into voracity and *avidity*, the curves of your *hips*[375] into a pursing of *lips*! Let not firmness of calf tempt you to haughtiness in the form of an expression of half-hearted *disdain* for a peek-sneaker or love-sick *swain*—an expression that closes said calves *tight* and wraps itself around them to keep them out of *sight*, or envelops them despite their plumpness and spares their down from any shearing or *peeling*, any shaving or plucking, or from touching the *ceiling*! Let not what sticks out *behind* make you to proper respect be *blind*, or what lifts your bosom's *sheeting* into refusing salutation or *greeting*!

4.5.10 We have enough shandy and champagne every thirsty drinker to *inebriate*, every veiled lady to *intoxicate*, enough meat from the *grill* every empty belly to *fill*, enough *coin* to blow the knots of every lady's waist wrapper from off her *groin* and undo them utterly and moisten them mightily—and with moistening comes munificence, with undoing, dresses.[376] By Him who conferred on you a *charm* that all who hear and see you must *disarm*, think kindly of your suitors and give them fewer angry looks and such *disdain*, for each yearns your lover to be and each at your harsh words has moaned *in pain*!

4.5.11 To proceed: I'm talking about just one time, though if you find the encounter *agreeable*, you can make it *habitual*. In any case, you're free to do as you please, and if you don't—how many and long are this city's roads, how many those who make their way *there*, how many a spacious shop it contains, how many a *square*, how many an open space and *lake*, garden and wood, pathway and *park*! How splendid are its places of entertainment and its pleasure *grounds*! What a stream of carriages it has and how its traffic *abounds*! How vast its churches and well-attended its *councils*! How prosperous its dwellings and stately its *vessels*! Run about in it wherever you *wish*: all men strive in pursuit of *bliss*.

Chapter 6

A Discussion

When the Fāriyāq had finished his work in that city so crammed with beautiful women, he went to Paris, where he stayed for three days, which wasn't enough to allow him to write a description of it. We therefore decline to provide one at this point, for a proper description should be comprehensive. From there he went on to Marseilles and then to the island, where God, of His all-encompassing bounty, granted him the boon of beholding his wife in the very house in which he'd left her, though he'd expected to find that she'd flown off with a phoenix or the chimera, and he re-consummated his marriage with her for this the sixth time (the second time having been after he arrived back from the Syrian lands, the third after his return from Tunis, the fourth after he emerged from quarantine quarters with the Honorable Sāmī Pasha, and the fifth after her return from Egypt). 4.6.1

Then he recited 4.6.2

He who'd like to keep wanting his wife
 Should take many a woman to bed.
Then let him leave her for a little while—
 And he'll find her like a newlywed

to which she responded, "But the wife won't find a new groom in her husband when he comes back!" The Fāriyāq continued, "I told her, 'That's because she's the contrary of men in everything.' 'Right,' she said, 'and if it weren't for that contrariness, there'd be no harmony.' 'How,' I asked, 'can harmony come from contrariness?' 'Just as woman is created contrary to man physically,' she replied, 'so she is contrary to him in disposition, and each of these contrarieties is an inducement to him to feel affection for her and take good care of her. Do you not observe how, when a wife does everything that her husband wants, she is like a tool in his hands, and he neither pays attention to nor approaches her because he believes her to be dependent on the movement of his hand, eye, or tongue, a mere adjunct to the movement of his hand on that tool? The opposite is true if all he meets with from her is contrariness and refusal to compromise; then, he clings to and humors her.' 'This,' I said, 'is not what people are used to thinking.' 'Not at all,' she responded, 'it's what women have been used to thinking all along. It's why you'll find that they're all tricked out with this trait.'[377]

4.6.3 "'But,' I said, 'if disagreement multiplies and goes too long without *settlement*, the upshot will be mutual cutting of relations and *disgruntlement*.' 'A woman's eyes,' she declared, 'are always trained, or ought to be trained, on the loci of cutting and connection. Otherwise, one of these will gain supremacy over the other and the situation I have described will come about.'[378] 'I disagree,' I said. 'Constancy of connection leads to constancy of concord,' to which she replied, 'Not at all. It's an inducement to discontent and restlessness, for that is how people are by nature.' 'What discontent can there be,' I asked, 'in connection with the beloved?' 'Discontent,' she replied, 'is the dominant emotion of humans in all things because of their desire to exchange good situations for worse.' 'Did you then,' I asked her, 'grow discontented with your present situation?' 'I did,' she replied, 'and then I found a way around being discontented.' 'How, then,' I asked, 'do you account for the fact that everyone says, "O delight of my eye!"?'[379] 'The fact is,' she replied, 'that the eye finds delight in one thing only until another comes along and presents itself as something novel.' 'And what of the heart?' I asked. 'It is as fickle and as partial as the eye,' she replied. 'And what of the blind?' I asked. 'Their insights,' she replied, 'are keener than those of people who have eyes that see.' 'And whose hearts,' I asked, 'are the most fickle?' 'Those who think most,' she answered. 'Dumb beasts are steadier and more patient than people because they don't think.'

"'So bad comes of good?' I said. 'Indeed,' she replied, 'just as good comes of bad.' 'What good,' I asked, 'comes of sickness?' 'Relief for mind, blood, and thought from the pain of love and lust,' she replied. 'And what good,' I asked, 'comes of poverty?' 'Abstention from the gluttony and intemperance that lead to perdition,' she said, 'for more people die of too much food and drink than of too little.' 'And what good,' I asked, 'comes of marriage to an ugly woman?' 'Prevention of your neighbor from visiting your house,[380] and abstention of your emir from following your every move, though she will not lack for a suitor of her own type (some evils, however, are lesser than others).' 'What good comes of ugly children?' 'If they discover their situation on their own,' she said, 'they will give up play in favor of study and strive to improve their inner makeup and so compensate for their outer.' 'What good comes of a person's upper parts graying before his lower, when the hair on the lower sprouts before the hair on the upper?'[381] 'It makes him realize that an animal's absolute nature is more powerful than its contingent nature, which is why the first part of him to turn grey is his head, which is the seat of the rational faculty, while the place where he feels the most powerful pleasure is the lower,' she replied. 'And what does it lead to?' I asked. 'A reduction in the capacity to think,' she replied. 'And what is the point of his needing an ounce of meat to fill his face, and finding it's turned into a pound on his buttocks?' 'That,' she said, 'belongs to the first category.'[382] 'You seem to be saying,' I said, 'that men were created to serve the needs of women.' 'Quite so,' she responded, 'just as women were to serve the needs of men.' 4.6.4

"'And what good,' I asked, 'comes of the crumbling of the teeth?' 'Slow eating,' she replied, 'so that the food is well digested.' 'And what good,' I asked, 'comes of the dimming of the eyes?' 'Inability 4.6.5

to see the ladies at night,' she replied, 'for that is when they are at their most delightful and captivating.' 'And what good comes,' I asked, 'of being lame?' 'Relief,' she replied, 'from running after quickly tripping women who bowl along like a ball.' 'What good comes,' I asked, 'of a stuffed-up nose?' 'Indifference to sweet-smelling women,' she replied. 'Of deafness?' I asked. 'To smart-talking girls,' she replied. 'And of ignorance?' I asked. 'Abundance of health for the body and rest for the mind,' she replied, 'for the ignorant man gives no thought to minute and tiresome matters. When he sleeps, his slumber makes him happy and when he eats something, it does him good—unlike your habit of muttering day and night, so that all I hear from you is your voice as on it *drones*, counting off rhymes and speaking of trenches and *firestones*,[383] campsites *half-erased* and concealed women in camel litters *raised*; and when you sit down to eat, you bring your book with you and for every plate you consume a page, then eat a morsel and read a paragraph, or drink, belch, and recite a line. That is why . . .' 'I gather from this excellent sufficiency that I stand accused of insufficiency, but much reading leads to much visualizing, which gives rise to much desire,' I said. 'But much desire,' she answered, 'gives rise to a state of semi-erection and premature *ejaculation*, when what's called for is piercing *procrastination*, and how often has the presence of the first required a search for the second! But enough of piercing-places and plunging-places. How did you find London?'

4.6.6 "I replied, 'I found the women there outnumbered the men and were better-looking.' 'If a woman were to go there,' she said, 'she'd find the opposite. The English women on this island are not beautiful, and the men have all the looks.' 'These,' I said, 'are the cream of the country, chosen by the state for their good looks, so that they may scare the enemy in battle.' 'Not so,' she said, 'it's the other way around. The beautiful man can never scare, even if he's an enemy. It's only the ugly that are scary. Do you not observe that they speak of a man being *bāsil* or *mutabassil* when they mean "courageous," even though in origin they mean "of unpleasant appearance"?'[384] I responded, 'And they also say *rāʿahu*, meaning both "he delighted him" and "he scared him."' 'The meaning's the same,' she responded. 'It is taken from *rūʿ*, meaning "heart," for the sight of beauty falls on the heart, and indeed all the other organs of the body, like a bolt from above.' Then 'And how did you find its shops and markets?' she went on. 'The shops,' I replied, 'were full of silk-wool, silk, and amazing trinkets.' 'Are the people inside them like the things inside them?' she asked. 'There are beautiful, white women,' I replied. 'I ask you about one thing and you tell me about another!' she responded. 'I knew you had a wandering eye, so I will never ask you again about the people, I will simply consult my own eye. This is one of your traits, you men: you see no comeliness in your own sex.' 'And it's just like your trait, O women, of not seeing any beauty in your own. We go together.' 'How can we go together when there's a gap between us?' she asked. 'All good things come to those who wait,' I said. 'And every good thing should make love,'[385] she answered. 'I cannot accept such a "universal" statement,'[386] I replied—'You should say "*some* good things,"' to which she countered, 'If some goes down easily, the whole will not be choked on.' Then she said, 'Tell me about the markets,' to which I replied, 'They are high-ceilinged, wide, spacious, clean, and so well-lit that it's impossible for a man to be on his own with a woman under any circumstances. So bright are they they even light up the fog at night.' 'Then they belong to the category of the Harmful Public Service,' she said. 'Ah, if only I might have the good fortune to see the attractions of that cosmopolis just once before I die!' 'Don't despair!' I said. 'I hope we shall all[387] be able to go there together in a while.' 'God grant our wish!' she replied."

Then evening came and each spent the night drunk on such thoughts of London as accorded with his personal wishes and the next morning she got out of bed and said, "I saw London in a dream, and its men outnumbered its women and its streets were wide and full, as you said, of lights (though it would be possible for a woman to be on her own in them with a man and I think you only alleged 4.6.7

what you did so that I wouldn't harbor any suspicions about you, and I will never believe you again if I find out for sure that you were deceitful in the first telling)." Then again, after a long discussion, they went to bed the next night with the name of London on their lips and in the morning she said, "I dreamed that I bought a dress of red red red brocade from one of its best shops." "You're still mad about that color," he said, "but the people of London don't like it, either for silk or for humans." "Why is that?" she asked. "Because red in people comes from too much blood, and too much blood implies too much eating and drinking and is a sign of greed and gluttony. What they like is dull white, a color beloved of the Arabs too, for the greatest of their poets has said,[388]

> Like the first egg of the ostrich—its white mingled with yellow—
> Nurtured on water pure, unsullied by many paddlers."

She said, "If we're talking about men's dislike of that color, it's due to their fear that women will lord it over them in the color red, which indicates strength, energy, liveliness, headstrongness, and love of intercourse. This deludes them into thinking that they are incapable of satisfying them. If, however, it's women's dislike of it that we're talking about (should they in fact ever express such an opinion), it must be simply equivocation and deception, for humans love the color red by nature, as one may observe in children; not to mention that blood, which is the essence of life, is red." The Fāriyāq continued, "Then I said, 'But the quintessence and best part of blood is of that color[389] that the people of London crave.' 'So that's the reason!'[390] she said. '"Now the truth has come to light"[391] and is made plain. As far as I'm concerned, I'll never abandon my position, and "one man's meat is another's poison."'

4.6.8 "I said, 'I wish I were red red red that you might love me, even if I were dumb dumb dumb.' 'And what good would love do you if you were dumb?' she asked. 'Any good would redound to *my* benefit, from your leaving me alone with "the red."'[392] 'Are you claiming,' I asked, 'that scholarship in men prevents women from carrying out what they have in mind to do, while stupidity makes it possible for them?' 'Certainly not,' she replied. 'In fact, a woman may get more out of stupidity, for the stupid husband stays close to his wife and never stops staring at her, while the scholar stares at his notebooks. Be that as it may, I know of nothing more idiotic than the man who keeps his wife on a tight leash and sticks close to her, for the more a man angers his wife and annoys her by staying next to her and never leaving the house, the more she will persist in her excesses, for nothing can keep her from doing what she wants to except her own sense of decency and her modesty.

"'The stupidest and most ridiculous of men is the one who, if **4.6.9**
he harbors doubts that his wife may have taken a liking to a certain person, tells her, to arouse dislike for him in her, "So-and-so is without honor, irresponsible, a lecher who doesn't care what he says or does. If he attends a gathering of litterateurs, the first thing to come out of his mouth will be, 'I made a pass at (such and such a woman) and beguiled her and charmed her, and she became my mistress and I became her lover'"—as though he (meaning the husband) were warning her against yielding to his advances and scared she might make a scandal of herself in front of everyone; or the one who tells her, "So-and-so is God-fearing and pious. He is as scared of flirting with women as he is of vipers"—as though he were telling her, "If you declare your love to him, he will repulse you, drive you away, and make a scandal of you." Men have got it fixed in their minds that any matter, whether to do with this world or the next, can mar a woman's honor and violate her sanctity, but in fact nothing tickles her imagination so much as hearing it said of a man that he is so excessively far gone in some way or other that he can do her no harm. In such a case, she will go out of her way to make a conquest of him so that she can dissuade him from whatever he is up to in favor of herself and redirect his excesses into love for her.'" The Fāriyāq went on, "And I said, 'Quite right. Great indeed is women's guile.'"[393]

Chapter 7

Compare and Contrast

4.7.1 Humankind, as the Fāriyāqiyyah said, has a predisposition toward discontent and ennui, and no sooner does it gain the object of its desire than a desire for other objects takes over. Likewise, given that the married man is a fixture around the house and hears nothing from his wife but "Fetch!" "Buy!" "Renew!" and "Repair!" he dearly wishes he might be a bachelor again, even if it means being a monk in a cell. Then, if he leaves the latter and sees men walking side by side with women, whether wedded wives or lady loves, he becomes fed up with his cell, and the longing to have a wife with him and to walk with her like those others (even if their promenading is leading them at that very moment to trial and litigation before His Honor the Judge)[394] rises within him. In such cases, the husband who never leaves his nest ought constantly to imagine to himself that he is a stranger in a distant land living with people who dupe him, cheat him, and inflame his senses with their bustles, or that his wife has left him to go to people who will compete to fill her *glass* and lay her down on an ostrich-feather *palliasse,* or who, should they flirt with her, will find she tells them "*Yes!*" and, on making love to her, find that she to them will *acquiesce*. If he does this, the chant of "Fetch!" and "Buy!" will seem less unbearable. Here is a table, composed on the authority of the Fāriyāq, in which he sets out the conditions under which the married man says,

"Would that I had no wife!" and	"Would that I had a wife!"	4.7.2
When she picks out a red or yellow dress, dresses to make herself look *fine*, smoothes her skin and makes it *shine*, makes herself look easy to *get*, puts on perfume and plays the *coquette*, and tells him, "Off with us to where the people gather, to the crowded places and the crush, to the night spots and the dance floors!"	When he goes alone to where the people get together, to the crowded places and crammed places, to the night spots and dance floors and sees the women there all wearing red or yellow dresses, dressed up to look fine, etc.	
When he goes out with her after she's plumped out her chest and adjusted her bustle and then she never stops sticking out her bottom, swinging her hips, strutting, swaying from side to side, and bending her neck and head.	When he strikes out alone and sees women who have plumped out their chests, adjusted their bustles and then set off sticking out their bottoms, swinging their hips, etc.	
When he's walking with her and she sees a drop of water on the road and hikes up her dress, exposing her calves so that everyone can see the mud on them.	When he walks alone and sees the women who have hiked up their dresses, exposing their calves, on seeing a drop of water on the road, etc.	
When he sets out with her on a windy day and she deliberately lets her dress reveal glimpses of her breast and her backside.	When he sets out alone on a windy day and sees the women who deliberately let their dresses reveal glimpses of their breasts, etc.	

When she makes a habit of dropping her handkerchief or tying her sandal strap, so that she has to bend over and show off her backside.

When he sets out alone and sees the women bending over to fasten the straps on their sandals or picking up their handkerchiefs, thus showing off their backsides.

4.7.3 When she puts something in her mouth and chews on it as she walks, making her young male admirers think that she's mouthing a kiss at them, or when she winks at one of them and arches an eyebrow or rolls her eyes.

When he observes women chewing something as they walk and thinks they're mouthing kisses at him and then they start winking, arching their eyebrows, rolling their eyes, skipping, hopping, and springing.

When she happens on a male acquaintance of hers in the street and keeps on rebuking him for not having come to see her for so long, then takes hold of his hand and gives him a big wink.

When he sees a woman rebuking a man for not having come to see her for so long and then taking his hand and giving him such a big wink that the winker blushes and the winked-at blanches, or vice versa.

When she encounters a woman in the street who is wearing an expensive brocade and she starts asking her about the price and who sells it.

When he encounters two women one of whom is stroking the other while the one stroked points to some place with her delicate hand.

When she happens on some man in the street and makes a sign to him as though to say, "Follow us!" and he walks along on her right side and she turns her face from

When he finds a man between two women or a woman between two men, for in the first case, the man is seeking to "mix the rough with the smooth"[395] while in the her husband and makes most of her conversation with the chump.

second the men are confident of getting enough, for "food for two will satisfy three."[396]

When they return to the house and she plainly states, or hints, that they should buy the brocade and he doesn't have enough money to pay for it.

When he returns to the house and sees that he has plenty of money but there's no one to wear brocade or sit at his side.

When she tells him at table (to make him choke), "How handsome is (such and such a young man) who walked along with us and how amusing and kind and full of *savor*, how full of youth and sap and *ardor*!"

When he sits down to eat alone 4.7.4
and sets to thinking, saying to himself, "How beautiful is (such and such a woman) whom I saw walking with (such and such a man) and how amusing she is and full of *savor* and how full of youth and *ardor*!"

When he goes to bed that night and he's tired and has a headache and dozes off for a while and then feels her moving against his side and he performs his marital duty with gritted teeth.

When he goes to bed and he's relaxed and full of beans and then feels himself moving and puts out his hand and it comes up against the wall, or a nail, or a peg, and comes away covered with blood.

When he lives in a certain house and his closest neighbor is a beautiful youth who keeps dropping by in the name of good-neighborliness.

When he lives in a certain house and his neighbor is a beautiful girl and he cannot use good-neighborliness as a way to get to her.

When he falls ill and is stuck in bed whining and *moaning* while she's stuck to the window wolf-whistling and *groaning*.

When he sees his neighbor sick in bed whining and *moaning* while his wife's at the neighbor's side *groaning* and *bemoaning*.

When summer comes and he feels listless and lifeless, unsexed and unmanned, and his sinews go slack and he'd prefer to sleep alone.

When winter comes and he feels shaken and stirred, distended and agitated, and his sinews throb and he'd prefer to spend the night with someone puffing in his face.

4.7.5 When a journey looms that is unavoidable and on which he cannot take his wife.

When his neighbor goes off on a journey and leaves his wife now appearing, now retreating, now blatting, now bleating.

When he's away from his wife or she's away from him and she writes him things that make him jealous, lay snares for him, and leave him a broken man.

When some man's away from his wife or she's away from him, and she writes him things that help him endure, comfort him, and give him hope.[397]

When he reads in books that all women are unfaithful and their brains are in their vaginas.

When he hears of some woman that she has never betrayed her husband and has returned, out of love for him, the gifts of many suitors.

When he finds he has too many children to feed and can't provide for his family and his wife's no longer beautiful enough to be of any use to him.

When he sees a beautiful woman walking with a small child of hers who's cute and bright and he falls down and she pulls him up again and he cries a little, so that his cheeks turn red.

When he comes home from work and his wife meets him with scolding and bad temper, bickering, bellowing, and bawling.

When he sees his neighbor's returned from work and hears him and his wife billing and cooing, whispering and rustling, talking in low, sweet voices, and, finally, talking dirty.

When he's been out of the house and returns only to find his bed in a mess and his wife's hair disheveled even though she had tidied both before he left.

When he returns to his house 4.7.6
having pulled off some triumph only to find his bedding neatly folded and no one to fill it with a nice warm body, and then comes across a lock of hair among his things.

When he sees her sharing confidences with the manservant or maid, enjoying their company, becoming familiar with them, and doing them favors.

When he sees a woman not sharing confidences with her manservant or maid or smiling at them or never spending time on her own with either of them.

When he sees her pausing as she walks whenever a handsome man passes, claiming her shoe is too tight or something of the sort.

When he sees a woman walking with her husband, her eyes fixed on him and paying as little mind to any who passes by as if they didn't exist.

When she lies down in such a fashion that anyone who is higher or lower than she can see her, and a woman is never more desirable than when she lies down on her side!

When he sees a woman who has been required to lie down but refuses to do so out of modesty and decorum, whether in the presence or absence of her husband.

When she's full of love and attachment for a particular set of people and can't stop talking about them.

When a woman has no special inclination or liking for anyone and thinks she needs no one but her husband.

4.7.7 When he leaves his house and then returns and doesn't find his wife, or knocks on the door and she doesn't open it right away.

When he sees that whenever his neighbor returns to his house he finds his wife about her work and barely has time to knock on the door before it is opened to him.

When she hears musical instruments and starts swaying and undulating and saying, "Ah! Ooh! Aiee!"

When he hears a woman saying, after hearing musical instruments, that her little boy's voice is sweeter.

When she talks and laughs with the young men at such length that in the end she gives a belly laugh, her eyes being at that moment flirtatious, her cheeks flushed.

When he sees a woman talking with each of those present according to his standing and doesn't hear any belly laughs from her and her face is neither flushed nor pale.

When she writes on her shift letters that mean nothing to him or he sees the traces of bites or devouring kisses on her lips or cheeks.

When he hears that a woman has written the letters of her husband's name on her shift and there is no trace of anything to be seen on her lips or cheeks.

When he hears her saying men's names while she's dreaming or when she pretends to dream just

When he hears that his neighbor devours his wife's lips and lies with her under her shift, so she

so as to be able to mention things that would please him or give him satisfaction.	neither dreams of him nor he of her.[398]	
When he sees that she hates her children and pays more attention to her finery and toilette than she does to them or to the housekeeping.	When he sees a woman who loves her children and carries them about and lets nothing distract her from them or her house.	4.7.8
When she sits at the window sewing something and looks up after every stitch she makes and her work turns out poorly and she's obliged to unpick it and repair it.	When he sees a woman sewing something for her husband or her children without interspersing the stitches with looks and sighs, and her work turns out well-done from the first moment.	
When she puts the cooking pot on the fire to cook something and then starts singing and gets so caught up in the song that she forgets about the pot and the cooking and it burns.	When he sees a woman put the cooking pot on the fire and allow nothing to distract her from it, and the food turns out tasty, stimulating of the appetites, and conducive to intercourse and sleep.	
When she wants to be in the places where lots of men go, such as a hotel or an inn or the like.	When she stays away from meeting places and has no desire to enter crowds lest some man pinch her or wink at her.	

	When she states or hints to her husband that she likes, for example, tall, well-fleshed men and he isn't one of them.	When the wife says in front of her husband or anyone else that she doesn't like tall men, because her husband is short.
4.7.9	When she rebukes her husband for being characterized neither by insatiability nor continence.	When the wife holds herself aloof from her husband out of modesty when having her period and complains of both her husband's insatiability and his continence.
	When he turns up at his house at lunch or dinnertime tired and hungry and finds nothing to eat because his wife has been too busy mending her clothes and trying on her dresses to prepare lunch and too busy getting dressed and sitting at the window to see and be seen by the passersby to prepare dinner.	When he turns up at his house at lunch or dinnertime and finds everything his heart could desire on the table and eats and drinks and feels well content, then looks out of his window and sees the woman next door putting on her dresses and looking over her shoulder to see if they're a nice snug fit.
	And so on and so forth.	And so on and so forth.

Chapter 8

A Voyage Festinate and Language Incomprehensibly and Inscrutably Intricate

The Fāriyāq continued to treat the foul of breath but was at his wits' end, for the treatment did no good. He tried, therefore, to wiggle his way out of this trade, and all the more so as he was by nature given to boredom and disquiet. During this period, it so happened that the August Master, Aḥmad Pasha, Honored Bāy of the Autonomous Province of Tunis, made a trip to France and distributed vast sums of money, that were everywhere spoken of, to the poor of Marseilles and Paris. Then he returned to his seat. It therefore occurred to the Fāriyāq to write him a congratulatory ode, which he did, sending it by hand with someone to deliver to His Excellency. Before only a few days had passed the captain of a warship knocked on his door. When he had come in and settled himself, he told the Fāriyāq, "Your ode has reached Our Most Noble Master and he has commanded me to bring you to him in my ship." 4.8.1

When the Fāriyāq heard this, he took it as an omen that he was soon to be freed from his trade and declared, "I swear I thought the days had left no market where poetry might find a buyer, but if God wishes good fortune for His slave not even poetry can get in the way of it. Rictulate, dear risible Fāriyāqiyyah, and vociferate (though not in *alarm*)! Today not even she-wolves could do me *harm*! Dunk yourself in every ounce of unguent you *possess*; dab it and daub it, and take silk brocade for your *dress*! On such a day as this, our 4.8.2

copulatorium must be redolent of *musk*—even its limpest occupant must experience *lust*! The giddy-pate, on such a day, must run *amok* and enjoy his *luck*! On such a day as this, the swooning prude[399] faints with *pleasure*, the stud that shies from service gives full *measure*, the wide-wooed woofer and back-passage bleeder[400] bear *twins*, the single-barreled bawd,[401] followed quickly by the termagant, throw pups despite their *sins*! Up with you, woman, and from today play the mooning she-camel that lives its false calf to *lick*, for I see curly shavings on the fire *stick*!"[402] The captain, to whom these words sounded like a foreign tongue, asked, "What language is this that you speak? I swear I didn't understand a word of what you said! Is this the tongue you'll carry in your head to Tunis? Are these the words with which you will address our master and the great men of his realm?" "No," replied the Fāriyāq. "It's just a private language we've agreed on between ourselves and use only rarely." The captain then said, "You must get ready to travel, and you may bring your family with you if you like, for our lord is the most generous of men and such a thing could never upset him." So the Fāriyāq and his family got ready, embarked on the ship, and after a twelve-day voyage (the wind, as usual, being contrary), reached Ḥalq al-Wād, where the aforementioned master commanded that they be put up at the admiral's house.

4.8.3 Here we must draw attention to the propensity for generosity with which the Almighty has distinguished the Arabs to the exclusion of all other races, for the invitation of the previously mentioned master was not intended for everyone who trod the boards of the Fāriyāq's house: on the contrary, it was peculiar to him alone. However, when news of the arrival of his eulogizer, with family, reached his ears, he was not upset and did not say, "What an ill-mannered guest you are and how deserving of a slap on the face for coming to us and bringing others with you!" Likewise, he didn't say to his captain, "You disobeyed protocol and the orders of your monarch, so we shall strip from your shoulders the epaulettes of your rank that you be a warning to those who take heed!" On the contrary, the captain continued to bear the honor of his epaulettes while the Fāriyāq continued to enjoy his services and was lodged in the most generous style in the admiral's house and supplied with ample goods and plentiful good things. If a Frankish notable invited someone and that person went and brought with him anyone but his own self, the notable would confront him when they met; in fact, he wouldn't even meet with him at all. Indeed, when their womenfolk used to invite the Fāriyāqiyyah, they would tell her, "The invitation is for you only," meaning that she was not to bring her maid and her child with her.

I'd be intrigued to know which of their kings ever sent a warship so that he might bring a poet into his presence and shower him with money and costly gifts. I swear that all anyone who writes eulogies to their kings ever gets by way of reward is patronizing treatment and ridicule. Even though no people are more punctilious in insisting that others thank them and praise them, they turn their noses up at a poet who, in hopes of gaining their favor, eulogizes them.[403] For whom, then, is all that money that they store away? Against what disaster do they set it aside, when they are already well-clothed and *fed*, well-watered and *banqueted*? Are they afraid they'll be laid low by a surfeit of children or by poverty, or do they believe that a gift to a poet is an extravagance? 4.8.4

This fact—that generosity is a trait peculiar to the Arabs—explains why no truly glorious and distinguished poets equal to theirs have emerged in any other nation at any place or time, reckoning from the Days of Barbarism to the end of the caliphs and the Arab empire. The Greeks boast of a single poet, namely Homer (*Ὅμηρος*), the Romans of Virgil, the Italians of Tasso, the Austrians of Schiller,[404] the French of Racine and Molière, and the English of Shakespeare, Milton, and Byron, while the number of Arab poets who surpass all of these is too large to count. Indeed, over one period during the days of the caliphs there may have been more than two hundred poets, all of them brilliant and outstanding, the reason being that "purses," as they say, "open throats." Moreover, 4.8.5

there is no comparison between the poetry of the Arabs and theirs: they do not observe the rules for rhyme-consonants and rhymes[405] and do not have poems with a single rhyme or stylistically exquisite embellishments, despite the large number of metrical infractions with which their verse is stuffed. In fact, their poetry is less demanding than our rhymed prose, and not one of the poets of the Franks would have been good enough to be a boon companion to his king: the highest degree of good fortune and favor any of them may reach is to be licensed to recite some of their verses in certain theaters.[406] And again, what shame would attach to the august person of the king from taking a poet as the companion of his potations and conversations? Or is one to suppose that the poets of the Franks are so numerous that the king couldn't make up his mind which to choose? Tell me, what are they, compared to his auspicious treasury? How many prose writers are there now in England, how many poets in France?

4.8.6 And here I must draw attention to a further point: rarely does a poet, Arab or otherwise, come to prominence who pleases all. Some poets like eloquent and ringing words more than innovation in meaning while some concern themselves with meaning more than with words. Some search for the refined word and the harmonious expression, others for amatory or other effect. All these traits are unlikely to consort together in a single poet, just as not everybody's predilections are likely to be in concert regarding them. Any connoisseur of women who is an oryx bull, rubbery and blubbery, a silver-tongued sweet-talker, a lady's man, one who delights in their company, their fervent supporter, their friend and companion, their follower, their soul mate, their constant visitor, who dies to talk with them, a beaver-boring beetle,(1) bruising their bungholes wherever they go, sniffing around wherever they pee, will have no interest in derring-do and snicker-snee. He will believe that the words of Imru' al-Qays that go[407]

(1) The *ḥurqūṣ* ["beaver-boring beetle"] is "a small creature like a flea with a stinger like that of a hornet, or a tick that clings to people, or something smaller than a beetle that bores through waterskins and enters the vaginas of young women."

Whenever he whimpered behind her, she turned to him
With half her body, her other half unshifted under me

are better than those of ʿAntarah that go[408]

So I thrust him with my lance, then I came on top of him
With a trenchant Indian blade of shining steel.

Likewise, anyone who is uninterested in or indifferent to women, or unwilling to have relations with them even though he is able, or who is of no use to and without any predisposition toward them, or is a confirmed bachelor, or is scruffy and takes no interest in his appearance, or wears no perfume and doesn't adorn himself, or smells foul, or breaks wind disgustingly, or is of no value generally, with no pressing desire for the delicate, fine-looking, white-skinned, plump, full-bodied woman or the short, curvaceous, tightly-knit woman (God save us from such things!) will divert his attention to poems of asceticism and sage advice. End.

Next, the Fāriyaq moved to the city, where he became acquainted 4.8.7
with a group of persons of virtue and culture, some of whom invited him to their banquets while others assured him of every luxury. There he had the honor of kissing the hand of the August Master,[409] from whom he received copious gifts. The minister of state enquired of him whether he knew French, to which he replied, "No, my lord, I have not bothered to learn it, for as soon as I started learning English I found myself forgetting an equivalent amount of my own language. Fate has decreed that my head shall hold only a predetermined amount of knowledge and that when that expands in one direction, it shrinks in another."

When he informed his wife of this, she said to him, "Haven't I 4.8.8
told you more than once to have done with writing love poems to women and to learn that useful language? You would not, however, abandon your obsession. What need have you of love poetry when you have someone to take care of your every conjugal *need*?" Said the Fāriyāq, "And I replied, 'True enough, and a wanton strutter

indeed.' 'What good to you,' she went on, 'are descriptions of beauties as being "dark of pupil, white of eye," when you will never get from them what you want? Do you not have a watchful warden looking over your shoulder, in the shape of my good self?' 'By God, I do!' I replied. 'Every time I find myself alone with a woman in my dreams, I see you right behind her. In fact, I've often seen you ripping her dress and pulling out her hair, then taking up residence in her place and sending her off empty-handed.' 'Thank the Lord,' she said, 'that you're as scared of me asleep as you are awake!' 'It had occurred to me,' I replied, 'to move from writing love poems about women to satirizing them, in the hope of moving into a better situation.' 'Do as you please,' she replied, 'though you must take care not to include me along with the rest—but stop, stop! Don't speak of women in either your erotic or your scurrilous verses, for as soon as you mention their name your head turns and the old Adam throbs within you. No, and again no!'

4.8.9 "I said, 'But in my eulogy of Our Lord the Emir,[410] I mentioned a woman's name.' Eyes flashing with rage, she enquired, 'And who was this blankety-blank woman?' 'It's an Arabic name,' I replied. 'Ah!' she said, 'One of those ancient delusions of yours![411] If it had been a foreign name, I would have gotten up this second and burned that poem collection of yours that is more harmful to me than a co-wife, because you spend half your nights at work on it.' 'But that half,' I said, 'doesn't stop you from getting the whole thing.' 'But I have a right to the whole thing,' she replied, 'plus two more of the same.' 'You're right,' I said. 'Women were created for the night and only for the night.' 'I grant you the first,' she replied, 'but not the second, for women were created for the daylight too.' 'I agree,' I said, 'and for each hour of it, and a man has nothing to concern him in this life but his wife.' 'You ought to say "to interest him,"' she replied. 'Every interest is also a concern,' I countered. 'That is the case with men,' she responded, 'because of their failings, but women are not like that.' 'That,' I said, 'is because of the levity of their minds and the gravity of their appetites, for sensual pleasure blinds them to both this world and the next.' 'Not so,' she replied. 'They combine the three[412] in one place and time, whereas whenever you devote yourself to one, you forget the other. This is one of the characteristics that the Almighty Creator has bestowed on us and not on you. Do you not observe that when a woman listens, for example, to a handsome preacher calling on people to turn from the things of this world, she thrills to his words, falls in love with his good looks, and weeps in a paroxysm of renunciation?'

"'I wish,' I said, 'that women would preach from the pulpits as 4.8.10
men do.' 'Were they to do so,' she replied, 'they would make them weep blood. But how unlikely it is that that will ever happen, for men, in their selfishness, have taken full control of all affairs, both mundane and spiritual, and all ranks of dignity and honor, and have forbidden women to share in them with them. How joyful and prosperous the universe would be if women were to take control of these positions! And, just as the word *dunyā* ("world") is feminine in gender, as are the words for heaven, earth, paradise, life, spirit, soul, prophecy, prophetic mission, happiness, grace, joy, renown, comfort, ease of life, splendor, greatness, eloquence, chasteness of speech, rhetoric, tolerance, courage, virtue, manliness, truth, the community of believers, the law of God, national territory, sovereign power, leadership, presidency, government, authority, intendancy, syndicship, chieftainship, monitorship, princedom, caliphate, ministry, kingdom, sultanate, and, most especially, affection, pleasure, and sexual desire, how appropriate it would be for that world to be overseen by women!' 'You forgot chastity and inviolability,' I said. 'They never occurred to me or I would have mentioned them,' she replied.

"'Anyway,' I said, '"intercourse" is masculine.' 'And what would 4.8.11
you know about intercourse?' she said. 'Not to mention,' I said, '*hakhakah*.'[413] 'And what is *hakhakah*?' she asked. 'It's a reduplicative formed from *hakka hakka*,[414] meaning "jiggy-jiggy," meaning "sheeka-beeka," meaning "bonky-bonky."' 'It's better than the ones that preceded it,'[415] she said. I said, 'So say, "At last!" Otherwise

it'll lead to corruption[416] and *disbelief*.' 'That would be no fault of women, for in them lies *relief*.' 'Yes indeed,' I said, 'relief (*faraj*)—and if they look well, they'll see that *farj* ("vagina") resembles *faraj*,' to which she said, 'As it does *araj* ("the sudden blazing of a scent")' and I, 'And *maraj* ("chaos"),' and she, 'And women have the better right to the boy with *baraj* ("comeliness of face"),' and I, 'And to him who performs *nayraj* (i.e., who "screws"),' and she, 'And when you combine the two, you get *balaj* ("joy"),' and I, 'And the one who comes back with a second strike after the first has cried, "Quarter!" is *aflaj* ("the more victorious"),' and she, 'And has the tongue that is the more *alhaj* ("silver").'" Then they decided to return and the aforementioned *lord* had them sent back on steamer-*board*.

Chapter 9

Form and Shapes

After the Fāriyāq returned home, an acquaintance came and asked him why he was leaving, so he took him aside and said, his eye trained on the door to his wife's room, that the Jewesses of Tunis were still beautiful and that their race hadn't yet been turned into monkeys, as the Christians pretend—that only applied to the men. From behind the door his wife said, "I heard what you said. You're wrong—it's the women who were turned into monkeys," to which he replied, "Since you heard our private conversation and none of my secrets are hidden from you, come and join us, so that we may continue this pleasant discourse." 4.9.1

"You're quite right," she declared, "not the softest whisper escapes my ears, nor the tiniest speck my eyes" and she came out into the middle of the parlor and said, "What I like about the dress of the Tunisian men is that their pantaloons are short, which makes their calves visible." The Fāriyāq continued, "Then I said, 'You're wrong. The dress of the women is more pleasing and alluring; the men's calves may be covered by socks, not to mention that their pantaloons cover their midriffs and adjacent parts. The calves of the women, on the other hand, are in plain sight and nothing hides their posteriors. You will see a woman walking during the hot weather and everything that's rounded and domed, concave and coned, well-turned and tumescent may be seen through her mantle.' She 4.9.2

responded, 'I wish women's clothes could take the shape of their bodies.' I said, 'That would be an abomination, from two perspectives: if the woman wearing them were big-buttocked, big-breasted, and big-thighed, she'd be a source of strife among the people and keep God's servants from their work, but if she were as wide as she was tall, or ugly, she'd be a plague upon people and force them to take refuge in their houses lest she bring them bad luck.'

4.9.3 "'Tell me why,' she said, 'the men in this country dress in form-fitting garments and no one reproaches them and there's nothing forbidden about looking at them. Does this mean that everything men do is to be swallowed with ease and everything women do choked on? I swear this dress is better than that worn by men in our country: there you find men who wear pantaloons and walk with their legs held far apart like ewes waiting to be milked, and sometimes these pantaloons get wrapped around them, in front or in back, and prevent them from walking, to say nothing of running. Let us suppose, for example, that a man wearing such pantaloons were at his place of work and someone came and told him, "A bonny, strapping young man came to visit you today at your house, and when he didn't find you, he stayed to wait for you and he's still there, right now, and your wife gave him a warm welcome and made him feel right at home, and it was she who insisted he stay and ordered the maid to be sick, or to pretend to be sick, so that you wouldn't have any misgivings, because if she'd sent her to you and they'd been left alone together, you'd have been suspicious and thought that his visit to her must have been prearranged and that she, and not a longing to see your ugly face, was the object of the visit," and other things to make the blood boil and the eyelids swell. Under circumstances such as these, how can he rush home with the thing between his thighs knocking him this way and that?'

4.9.4 "Then she laughed and went on, 'Indeed, and you'll see a man walking along wearing a *jubbah* with its skirts sweeping the ground so that everything on it that's polluting and filthy sticks to them, and when he reaches his house, he fills it with a bad smell, enough of which clings to his wife to make one avert one's eye from her even if she be a sweet-scented woman, for, as they say, "bad smells drive out good." Furthermore, out of one *jubbah* many of those things the Franks wear down to their waists[417] may be made and a man who wears one is left with no shape or style, for it hides his whole figure and neither his midriff nor any other part of him may be seen. God would not have created humans in the form that they have unless He had wanted it to be visible the way it is.' I replied, 'I have seen the Franks in their own countries in summer and in winter and, behold, they cover their buttocks with those tight *jubbah*s of theirs and do not walk around outside with their backsides showing the way the shameless folk on this island do.' 'And what of their bellies and thighs?' she asked. 'Exposed,' I said. 'So that makes up for the other,' she said, 'but when both are covered, it's horrible. I swear, people have yet, to this day, to arrive at a good-looking form of dress that goes with the shape of the body, is suitable for work, and has some style. I don't like that hat they wear and it's ill-suited to the face, whether on a woman or a man, because it looks like nothing so much as a bin,[418] basket, caddy, swad, punnet, molly, scuttle, trug, frail, haskie, peck, prog, pancheon, bag, barge, sack, barrel, box, bran-tub, wash-tub, poke, cawl, pandan, vat, piss-pot, chamber-pot, jam-jar, firkin, cask, hamper, pannier, satchel, gunny-bag, leather bottle, leathern pottle, tun, or platter, and all those turbans are even uglier.

"'And those cloaks that the women of Egypt wear have nothing attractive about them, as well as being expensive. Uglier than all the foregoing is that waistband that the men tie around themselves, for it fills up the midriff and the chest and prevents food from being digested. Uglier still is the tape with which they tie their pantaloons below the knee, because it stops the blood from running properly through the legs. The only good thing about the dress of Frankish women is that it is adapted to the bustle. I have spent many a night puzzling over this and trying to invent attire that looks good and is alluring, graceful, elegant, dignified, and as in harmony with the 4.9.5

shape of the body as possible, and so far God has failed to inspire me. Maybe it'll come to me soon, and I'll be awarded a place among the creative minds of the age.'

4.9.6 "'In all this creativity of yours,' I asked, 'do you never give a thought to economy?' 'Never,' she replied, 'because money is never better spent than on a woman.' 'Quite the contrary,' I said. 'It is never better spent than on a closet such as this,' and I indicated the bookcase. 'Can you hug a book at night,' she answered, 'and sleep with it under a single blanket?' 'When a man sleeps with his wife under a blanket at night,' I responded, 'she isn't bedecked with garments and ornaments. Quite the contrary, she's naked among some groups, and wears a single shift or is wrapped in a single sheet or blanket among others, thus fulfilling the promise of the verses that go

One dresses his best for most of the day
    So that at night of a damsel he may take advantage.
Then, when they're settled in bed, his ass may be seen,
    Bare as a billy goat's under its little appendage.'

4.9.7 "'You're wrong,' she said. 'A woman who decks herself out and wears her adornments is alluring by day and arousing for her husband by night.' 'Indeed,' I said, 'and for her neighbor too.' 'Say rather,' she responded, '"and for herself too."' 'I didn't grasp that final scintillating point,' I said. 'Does a woman feel a desire to make love when she sees her own adornments?' 'Without a doubt,' she replied. 'For adornment is a form (and what a form!) of pulchritude and everything pulchritudinous puts her in mind of a handsome man. Even if she sees a perfect horse, or a precious object, or any of the adornments of earth or sky, the first thing to enter her mind will be a male distinguished by beauty.' 'Pulchritude, then,' I said, 'is the visualization of something absolute rather than something specific?' 'If it's the thing most attractive to the eye, then it'll be the thing most readily seized on by the mind,' she replied. 'Otherwise, any old thing would do.' 'And if we were to suppose that the husband was present and assuming that he was not without at least a touch of beauty, would the thought of him cross her mind?' I asked. 'If he could be accommodated within the terms of intercourse and copulation, he might cross it, though not in terms of his specific attributes but as an example of the attributes of the absolute.'[419]

"'I have already noted that point,' I said, 'and understood its true meaning. But let me ask you a question, purely heuristically and with no ulterior motive or parti pris: should not a wife put her husband before all others in terms of recall and visualization, given that he has a right to certain prerogatives and privileges, and in view of the fact that he is her shaykh and father, her lawful mate and conjugal benefactor, her bedmate,[420] her playmate, her copemate, her messmate, her tentmate, her roommate, her classmate, her pewmate, her bunkmate, her waymate, her cupmate, her tablemate, her couchmate, her watchmate, her clubmate, her intimate?' 'Indeed,' she replied, 'as well as being her watcher, her insulter, her disturber, her pursuer, her angerer, her attacker, her pesterer, her pouncer, her scrutinizer, her opposer, her clutcher, her jostler, her name-caller, her needler, her hair puller, her tress-tugger, not to mention the one who spies on her, stalks her, raises the alarm against her, beats the clapper-board[421] to raise the hue and cry against her, tells tales on her, and is her nightmare, not to mention her guard and whistle-blower.' 4.9.8

"I went on, 'Our master, the author of the *Qāmūs*, says, "A woman's *dall* or *dalāl* ('coquettishness') with her husband is when she shows boldness toward him in terms of flirtatiousness and dressing up, as though she were quarreling with him when there is no quarrel."[422] He says too, "*taba''alat* means 'the woman obeyed her *ba'l* ("husband")' or 'she put on her finery for him,'" and elsewhere "*taqayya'at* means 'she displayed herself to her husband and threw herself upon him' (End)." This goes to show that her husband and none other should be the object of every action a woman takes.' She replied, 'Your friend's[423] linking of these actions exclusively to marriage can be only his personal interpretation, or he was following the lead of some particularly jealous and jaundiced philologists. It is 4.9.9

men's habit to claim that women were created only to please, entertain, and flatter their husbands, and they have created the language in such a way as to serve their exercise of tyrannical power over and violence against women. This is despite the fact that language is a female,[424] and had women created it (which would have been more proper, given that all generation and creation must be female in nature), they would have created words denoting men who think only of their wives, and how men should avert their glances from all but these, sicken when they sicken, groan when they groan, dress them and divest them of their clothes, comb their hair and obtain some sweepings from it to gaze on if they are ever away from her, and spend everything they have to keep them happy, as well as denoting men who think their wives are the best of women, whose love for their wives increases the more they contemplate other women or who close their eyes whenever another woman appears before them or faint or fall flat on their faces or are taken by dizzy spells or acute diarrhea, and men who get hold of her picture and put it everywhere on their walls, in their books, and among their possessions, with her shown sometimes standing, sometimes lying down, sometimes stretched out on her back, and sometimes flat out on her front.

4.9.10 "'Anyway, we have left the language to you and you can do with it as you like, so why can't you leave us our thoughts and ideas, which are neither voweled nor unvoweled?[425] And as to your claim to prerogatives and privilege, let me tell you, as one who feels no need to mumble at you out of hypocrisy or prudishness, that the man has no prerogative over the woman in anything whatsoever, for there is no prerogative belonging to the man the like of which does not also belong to the woman. As to men's wardship of their wives, I have to draw your attention here to a nice point with which few have engaged, namely that two individuals may be involved in a commercial partnership, for example, or an invitation, or a marriage, with one of the two believing privately that he is doing his partner a favor, while the other, to whom the favor supposedly has been done, inwardly believes and outwardly proclaims that he is hard done by. An example of a marriage of this sort would be if the girl has been in love, before marriage, with a young man but has been unable to marry him, so she marries someone else, from whom she witnesses deeds and habits that she finds unacceptable, and then she happens to think of the other, whom she failed to marry, and says to herself, "He was perhaps innocent of such conduct, and if I'd married him, I'd now be living the happiest of lives," while at the same time her husband believes that he has done her a great favor in marrying her after she'd failed to marry her first beloved. Men and women must pay close attention to the conditions surrounding a marriage before they insert their heads into its noose. A man should not marry a woman who was in love with another man before him and a woman should not marry a man who avoided marriage out of fear of expenses and impoverishment, or who was in love with another woman when a bachelor.

"'An example of a commercial partnership of this sort would be 4.9.11
if one of the two partners is the one who advances the capital out of his own pocket and puts the burden of responsibility for managing things on his comrade's shoulders; each of them then believes that he is doing the other a favor. An example of an invitation of this sort would be if someone invites you to lunch in the afternoon while it is your custom to take lunch at noon, or he offers food you find unpalatable (for the belief that what he finds agreeable must be agreeable to others is an entrenched part of everyone's nature) or a tiny piece of meat, or a mere crust of bread, or the smallest sip of something to drink, unaware that the stomach of a person invited to a feast grows larger at the house of the host and his guts more capacious, or if he invites you to his house and the latter is so far from the city that you are obliged to hire a boat at a cost equivalent to him to that of two lunches and two dinners, or if you are at the house, for example, of some Frankish notable engaged in some business of his, and he is aware that you have gone for a number of hours without eating and he orders his servant to bring you a morsel consisting of

bread and of that smegma-like cheese of theirs, at which moment you are hungry enough to eat his brains. Which of you, in cases such as these, is the doer of the favor and which the one to whom the favor is done?

4.9.12 "'Or it might be that someone is in the service of the emir and the master believes that his servant is indebted to him because he takes his money while the servant believes that his master is indebted to him because he is taking from him his youth and his health, or that someone visits a friend of his to spend the evening in idle chatter while the one visited is suffering from worry and anxiety, so both the visitor and the one visited think that he is the one who is conferring a benefit on his companion—and the same, by analogy, is true of the teacher and the taught, the eulogizer and the eulogized, the singer and the one sung to.

4.9.13 "'It follows that a man shouldn't think he is doing his wife a favor just because he is feeding and clothing her. The rights of women are too many to list.' 'I have taken that in,' I said, 'lock, stock, and barrel. But tell me, what sort of men do women love most?' 'If I tell you,' she replied, 'you'll kick up a row.' 'Speak,' I said, 'and don't worry! Conversation's carpet has been unrolled and will not be rolled back up until we reach its end.' 'At the End of Days,[426] then!' she replied. 'So, you must know that the perky-breasted young female loves adolescent boys and juveniles, on condition that they're good-looking. The young woman loves young men, the same condition pertaining, and may become intimate with an older man in the belief that he will be kinder and more loving. This, however, is not to be called love because it has its origin in self-interest, it being a condition of love that it be devoid of any advantage-seeking—though, sad to say, any lover, should continued lack of access to his beloved and absence of any good from him become a reality, will grow tired of him and may even come to hate him; thus "love," in my opinion, is synonymous with "benefit." The young woman who has moved beyond the age of marriage loves both the two previously mentioned sorts and those who are a little older, the same condition pertaining, and the middle-aged woman loves all three plus the older man, the same condition pertaining. The old woman loves the lot.'

"'What do you think of mustaches?' I asked. 'They are an adornment to the mouth in the same way that eyebrows are to the eyes,' she said. 'And beards?' I asked. 'Old men's embellishments,' she said. 'Side-whiskers?' I asked. 'Squeal! An adornment for the looker and the looked-upon alike,' she answered. 'What element of beauty do they possess,' I asked, 'especially when the mustaches have been shaved off?' 'They are,' she said, 'what calyxes are to a flower, leaves to a bough, a velvet edging to a robe, a hedge to a garden, a halo to the moon!'" 4.9.14

While they were talking, someone knocked on the door. He opened it and there stood a man with a letter from the aforementioned committee containing an invitation asking both the Fāriyāq and his family to come to them. When he acquainted his wife with this, she almost took flight out of joy and pleasure and said, "How blessed a morning is today's, how full of promise its sun!" Then she went over to the trunk and packed everything needed for the journey except the *Qāmūs*. "Not so fast!" said the Fāriyāq. "There is still much to be done before our departure." She crouched then, like one waiting to pounce, and said, "Tell me what, all at one go, so that I can take care of the greater part myself!" "Calm down and be patient," he said. "Your recent statements have put my mind in a spin—pray God the translation of the book isn't spoiled as a result!" Then she left him and busied herself with her own affairs, and I too shall leave him to his obsessing over side-whiskers, for I am not obliged to participate with him in that. 4.9.15

Chapter 10

A Passage and an Explanation

4.10.1 Among the baggage needed for this journey was, over and above the *Qāmūs*, the following precondition: that if the Fāriyāq were to absent himself from the island for two years, he would, on his return, be reappointed to his original position. He therefore wrote a petition to the ruler and settled down to await the answer. After a few days, the answer arrived accepting the condition. Everything was, he found, prepared for their departure, for his wife had neglected nothing in the interval, and all that was needed was for their passport to be honored by the consul's stamp and for the final stamping fee to be paid. It remained unstamped, however, by the consul of Leghorn. When, therefore, they reached that port and the Fāriyāq wanted to enter the country, the head of the customs authority prevented him. The Fāriyāq told him, "I will give you here what I should have given the consul on the island." "No," said the man. "Here you must give twice as much." The Fāriyāq refused and decided to return to the ship but a man with a skiff caught sight of him and his wife and when informed of their situation told them, "I'll get you into the country for half of what that thief of a customs officer demanded from you." They got into his skiff and he took them by a secret route till they were inside the country. Then they returned to the ship, which took them on to Genoa and then Marseilles, from which they departed for Paris.

There the Fāriyāq met Monsieur de Lamartine, the famous poet of the French language, and they stayed for a few days, which considerably trimmed their purse. (Tip: in France, don't stay at a hotel for the English, and in the latter's country, don't stay in a hotel for the former.) Then they departed for London, of which they had dreamed.

When the Fāriyāqiyyah beheld the city with its marvelous curios and exotic, desirable *delights*, resplendent shops and splendid *lights*, she said, "My oh my! My dreams fell short of the waking reality! What a wonderful place in which to *live*, and how nice it would be if we never had to *leave*! Albeit I note among its women something strange and new." The Fāriyāq resumed: "I said, 'Thank God you started with the women, for that augurs well for the book that they want me to translate! But to what novelty do you refer?' 'I have heard you declare, on the authority of some leading figure, that "women's brains are in their vaginas" but I observe that the brains of the women of this microcosm of the world are in their backsides.' 'Explain,' I said. 'I didn't catch your drift.' 4.10.2

"She said, 'If a woman throws herself, recklessly, between the contradictory witnesses of craft and nature, i.e., if she makes, through craft, a great *amount* out of something which, in the form in which God bestowed it, was of little *account*, and provokes people to have the *vapors* (the benefit here going all to the *neighbors*) or, to put it differently, were she to say, using the wordless language of her body, "I own a source of wind like a *twister* that sorts ill with the tight-*fister*, a drum inside which there's a pipe for every piper to *finger*, a whistle that whistles in both satiety and *hunger*, a deep-bottomed *tun* in need, when it brims, of a *bung*, a cup that for a cover *begs*, a hole just right for *pegs*, a deep cave or narrow but spreading *ravine* fit to protect a fleeing sultan (he'd never be *seen!*), a dome with a mighty *frieze* and nests for both birds and *bees*, a refuge for the lair-less in the form of a *burrow*, a shameless, ever-ready, water-holding rock *furrow*, a hollow pecked out in the dirt where eggs may be laid in one big *spurt*, a puling purseful of *dung* kept closed with a 4.10.3

thong, a dip like that for the dripping in a mound of crumbled bread and *meats* that foully fumes (especially when intercourse is foregone in the days before a *feast*), a waterskin with a tied-up *spout* whose string, if undone, will bring destruction *about*, a milkskin which, if it suffer a *prick*, will turn the air *thick* (and oh how thick!), a bellows at whose puffing sparks rise *high*, a scorching wind which, when it blows in the summer, makes men shout, 'Fly! *Fly!*'"; i.e., if she is born and finds no coeval with whom to *consort* and therefore obtains one and puts it behind her to lend her *support*; i.e., if she makes it her sole custom to turn what's flat into *humps* and what's squashed into *bumps*; i.e., if she takes those who look at her for fools and signals to them, "I have a *fellow* on which you may sit, or a *pillow*"; i.e., if she winks at them as though to say, "Beneath where sprouts the desert rose[427] on the desert *floor*, there lies the precious *ore*"; i.e., if she stuffs her backside with cushions, then sets off, gazing at it, admiring it, flaunting it, showing it off, coveting it, feeling good about it, and using it to allure, then finds another woman who outdoes her in this regard, and then this other in turn finds another who beats her too in terms of stuffing, it would be more proper to say that their brains are in their backsides.' (Thus the gist of what she said, though for 'desert rose' she said 'pumpkin,' for 'coeval with whom to consort' she said 'back-hugger,' and for 'backside' she said 'booty.' 'I.e.' is as per the original.)

4.10.4 "I replied, 'It's a custom with them, and you shouldn't quarrel with custom. Our women too have many customs that are disliked in this country, such as painting the eyelids with antimony, penciling in eyebrows, coloring, dyeing, tingeing, staining, striping, dotting, plain-staining, or staining with designs the hands, hair, or fingertips with henna or sometimes with saffron, tattooing, depilation, shaving the face or the head with a razor, removing facial hair using a thread,[428] plucking out or uprooting the hair, shaving the head, removing the pubic hair, using medicaments to narrow the vulva or using a bung made of perfumed rags for the same purpose or the same using a different verb, douching, cleaning the anus after defecation with water or a stone, cosseting slave girls to make them salable and fattening them up, braiding the hair and intertwining the braids with ribbons, and paring and rounding the fingernails, or the exposing of the breast and wiggling of the hips by those who have been pinched or palpated, had their nipples brushed by someone's hand or gently tweaked or pawed. To these you may add payment of compensation for rape, the "pelvic egg,"[429] circumcision of girls, intercourse with young girls, and other such things.'

"I had barely reached the end of this brief speech before she flew into a rage and bristled her feathers ready for a fight, saying, 'Your words have sealed your *doom*, your meddling exposed you for what you are, to me and to everyone in this *room*. How do you know that they should not moan and sigh if winked at, or pirouette if pinched, or use the scented rag or the raisin pits if the well's so wide it swallows everything in gulps, or is too deep to fill and gurgles and glups, or if it's large and flabby and groans like a large door swinging open—tight tunnels being preferred by frequent fuckers—unless you yourself have had experience of them in this regard?' 'It's a widely bruited matter,' I replied, 'thoroughly documented, much noted, celebrated, often alluded to, famous—a scandal hidden from none. It's as though one were to say, "The sky's above us," or "The ground's beneath us," such things not being considered speech by the grammarians.[430] Are you going to get angry over something that can't even be called speech?' 'I don't care,' she said, 'about the speech, my anger is at the deeds. With me you're all talk, with others all do. This isn't how married men are supposed to be. It is not with this that the respectable wife is *tasked*. It's amazing—you feel no shame in asking, while I feel ashamed at being *asked*! Would that there were a judge to decide between a man and his wife, so that everyone might know which of the two is the oppressor and which the oppressed!' 'Say rather,' I responded, '"Would that there were a woman to judge!" for a male judge, by virtue of his being, thank God, a male, will find for the man over the woman.' 'Quite the contrary!' she said. 'The male judge will always find the woman 4.10.5

to be in the right over the man, especially if she breaks down before him and blubbers, and so will all men, unless it's their own wives.' 'Hats off to you, as a woman expert in the affairs of men, and a man expert in the ways of women! I belong to the school of His Honor, for if I was ever present at a dispute between a man and a woman and saw the man to have a clean-plucked beard and a pocket with a hole in it,[431] I'd decide the woman was innocent, especially if she burst into tears, in which case I'd be ready to die for her. But hold on! Don't raise your hackles or *growl*, or stand tall the better to hurl abuse, strike out, make ready for a fight, or *scowl*! These days I can do no more than look; where dying for women's concerned, it's out of my hands.

4.10.6 "'Tell me, though, what is this inborn trait of yours, you women, that lets you weep and laugh at the drop of a hat and for any reason? We men weep only for you and laugh only because of you and for your sake.' 'The reason,' she said, 'is that women are finer by nature, nobler by *creation*, nicer in understanding, more refined of *imagination*, softer of heart and more tender, faster to hear and see and more *kind*, quicker to be moved and more penetrating of *mind*, lighter of touch, deriving from both this world and the next more *pleasure*, more eager to learn, bolder to fall in love, greedier to snatch up every precious *treasure*...'—'Stop! Stop!' I said—'... more serene of *thought*,' she said—'and more ready for conjugal *sport*,' I responded—'... more effective at getting her *way*'—'and at saying *nay*'—'as a friend more *loyal*'—'and more willing the wheels of gossip to *oil*'—'... readier to hand out charitable *grants*'—'and do the horizontal *dance*'—'... more *trustful*'—'and more *lustful*'—'... more likely to provide the needy with a *treat*'—'and more often in *heat*'—'... longer of *love*'—'and of clitoral *glove*'—'... more steadfast in *passion*'—'and in swallowing and *coition*'—'... more agreeable a *scold*'—'and to raise a leg more *bold*'—'... more inventive at finding acceptable ways to pass on thoughtful *tips*'—'and to lick the leftovers off your *lips*'—'... with a voice more *melodious*'—'and a beaver less *commodious*'—'... quicker to *empathize*'—'and to let your legs *rise*'—'. . . sweeter of *discourse*'—'and in talking dirty during *intercourse*'—'. . . with teeth yet *pearlier*'—'not to mention,' I said, 'your vaginal *hernia*.'

"Then said I, 'Your first discourse, on backsides, was enough to give Job the *hump* and make every wrung, strung, and unhung member *jump*, and now you've started praising the virtues of women, as is your wont, and recounting their charms, and you'll end up by giving away all their secrets. Do you want me to present myself to our friend[432] in a state of insanity or imbecility and have the translation of the book go badly?' 'If you go mad here,' she replied, 'you won't be able to hide away at home as one can in the Levant (for there are more madmen in the houses there than there are in the monasteries).' 'Perhaps that's what seduced you with such tormenting excitement,[433] so desist from this provoking, inflaming *discourse*, by Him who gave you that tongue so *coarse*, and prepare yourself to set off for the one for whom I'll be working.' 'Isn't he in London?' she asked. 'No,' I replied, 'in the countryside.' 'Woe is me! The countryside and peasants?' she cried. 'Who could bear to leave this city to live among savages—for peasants are the same in every country.' 'Afterward,' I told her, 'we shall move to a city thronging with men.'[434] 'Are there men there who don't have women?' she asked. 'There are women,' I answered, 'but they're few in comparison to the men.' 'A few women are a lot,' she said." 4.10.7

The next day they set off. When they were on the train, however, and the guard called out the name of the village for which they were bound,[435] the Fāriyāq was so preoccupied with their earlier duel of wits that he failed to pay attention and they went for a long way before he asked one of the silent passengers about his destination and the man told him, "You missed it." Then he got off, regretting his negligence in having failed to remind the guard, and they reached the village only after walking a long way and becoming very tired. 4.10.8

Note: The railway tracks in England are like the lines on the palm of your hand: via them the traveler can go wherever he wants—up or down, east or west.

Chapter 11

A Translation and Some Advice

4.11.1 They now took up residence in that village and the Fāriyāqiyyah began to learn the language of the people. One day her husband said to her, "I want to give you a piece of advice on a matter related to the learning of that magnificent language." "Out with it!" she replied. "It will be the first piece of advice destined for my ears to have left your mouth." "And my heart too," he said. "Speak!" she said. "It is typical of beginners in the science of foreign languages," he said, "to learn at the very first words relating to the human body, such as sinews, muscles, fleshy parts, and so on." "I already knew that," she responded, "so it doesn't count as advice."

4.11.2 The Fāriyāq resumed, "I said, 'Glory be to God, "Man is a creature of haste"![436] I simply wanted to tell you that anyone who wishes to learn this language should begin with the names of things divine, not earthly. The people put on a show of piety and righteousness. Even their prostitutes, flat on their backs, bellow now a prayer, now an obscenity.' 'So there are prostitutes here?' she asked, anxiously. 'Not at all,' I replied. 'The people of the small villages in this country get married just like everyone else and have no opportunity for debauchery. The point is, I'm telling you that they all put on a show of godliness, so, that being the case, you shouldn't right now be learning the names for the fleshy parts. You'll learn all that soon enough. In fact, I have no doubt you will learn it without an instructor and memorize it without a prompter, through your own inquiries and inspiration, for your quickness of understanding, acuteness of mind, and genius make everything difficult easy to you.' 'I swear,' she responded, 'if such words were advice, wisdom would be the cheapest thing there is. Pray tell me, how old are you?' 'What has this question to do with what I just said?' I asked. 'Which season are we in?' she asked. 'Autumn,' I answered. 'So it's the fault of the time of year,' she said. 'Are you trying to tell me I've reached the autumn of my mind?' I asked. 'If you haven't,' she answered, 'how is one to explain this nonsense you're voiding onto me and calling advice?' 'Do what you like, then,' I said. 'I'm preaching to the wind and talking to the deaf.'"

One morning, after a few days had gone by, she came to the 4.11.3
Fāriyāq and said, "How wonderfully this language falls on the ear and the mind, and how light it is on the tongue! Today I learned by heart a few lines of verse without any difficulty, except that I didn't understand what they mean. Would you be kind enough to explain them to me?"[437] "By all means," he said. "Right now, if you'd like. Show me your lightning so I can give you my rain!" "How full of nonsense you are!" she said. "All I meant was, 'Tell me what they mean.'" The Fāriyāq continued, "'And all I meant was the meaning,' I said, 'for I know very well that you didn't have anything else in mind. But recite to me what you've learned.' So she said

Up up up thou art wanted,
She is weary and tormented,
Do her justice she is hunted
By her husband, she has fainted.

"I said, 'The poet complains here of some woman who has gone too far with him—I don't know who the woman is though—for it's in the same vein as

My silly wife wants me to plug both holes at once,
But as the second opens up the first shuts down.

It's like the ear: if scratched, its twin starts itching
And will continue to do so till you give it its turn.'

4.11.4 "At this, her face flushed with anger and she said, 'That's just lies you're making up. You men are obsessed with "plugging."' 'Just as you women,' I responded, 'are obsessed with "opening."' 'These people don't say such things,' she said, 'and their poetry doesn't contain the sort of obscenities and indecent language that are found in the poetry of the Arabs.' 'Aren't their bodies and ours the same?' I asked. 'We're talking about words here, not bodies,' she replied. 'Where does indecent language come from if not the body?' I asked, 'for wherever the body is found, so will the act, and wherever the act is found, so will talk about it. The celebrated Dean Swift, though only one rank below a bishop, wrote a long essay on the anus. Sterne is a similar case, for he too was a priest but he wrote bawdy stuff. John Cleland wrote a book recounting the doings of a harlot named Fanny Hill in which he outdid in obscenity and bawdiness Ibn Ḥajjāj, Ibn Abī 'Atīq, Ibn Ṣarī' al-Dilā', and the author of *Alf laylah wa-laylah* (*The Thousand and One Nights*). He writes, for instance, speaking of the licentiousness of the people of London, that a coterie of notables there, having set up a brothel, gathered together a number of whores and would perform depraved acts with them in front of the others, taking turns. The first to follow the path of bawdiness was, I believe, the celebrated Frenchman Rabelais, who was also a man of the church.'

4.11.5 "'Didn't you just tell me that they put on a show of godliness and piety?' she asked. 'I did,' I replied, 'and they do, but this show has become second nature to them and the audience knows well what is in the hearts of the performers. I'd like to know: if someone puts on, say, ten garments, to fool people into thinking that he has neither front nor back, is the onlooker really taken in?' 'No,' she said, 'and such people are but whited sepulchers.' 'Indeed,' I responded, 'and that's a species that grows rampant in this soil.' 'Woe to the hypocrites!' said the Fāriyāqiyyah with a sigh. 'How am I to put up with their company when I, like most Levantines, am an open book, both in how I am and what I say? I don't hide what is in my heart from those around me.' 'That won't do!' I said. 'You must be ever reticent and on your guard, and beware too of laughing too much, for these people express their mirth through stifled giggles with mouths covered, tepid titters, sarcastic simpers, lukewarm laughs, sniggers, smirks, snickers, wan smiles, laughing behind their hands, and hidden chortles. If you don't, you'll be counted among the cheap girls who laugh till they're fit to *bust*.' 'How can you tell me to be one of the *unjust*,'[438] she said, 'when you're always complaining of women, even those who are the opposite?' 'Not at all,' I said. 'The idea is that you should master your laughter. One says, *taghat al-jāriyah* ("the slave girl tried and failed to suppress her laughter") . . .' but she interrupted me and said, 'Enough, enough! I don't want to hear any more from you about slave girls or girls next door.'

"'And that's not all,' I said: 'Their way of eating consists of snack- 4.11.6
ing,[439] picking, pecking, nibbling, tasting, testing, and chewing over and over again, while their way of drinking consists of sipping little by little, bit by bit, drop by drop, slowly slowly, listlessly and unenthusiastically. Whenever you say something, you must lower your eyes and your voice and display the utmost possible sedateness[440] and solemnity, equanimity and dignity, pleasantness and wariness, courtesy and good manners, finickiness and fastidiousness, modesty and self-deprecation, caution and apprehension, abstemiousness and affectedness, ingratiation and flattery, quick thinking and wit, reticence and confidentiality, deference and acquiescence, scrupulosity and persnicketiness, canniness and costiveness, squeamishness and priggishness, sheepishness and embarrassment, timidity and bashfulness, mawwormism and sanctimoniousness.'

"'My my!' she said. 'What's this? Could it be that you've brought 4.11.7
me to this country to recast me and fashion me into another woman?' 'I'd rather die!' I said, 'so, at this season of the year, speak pauciloquently, meaning only a little, and in the next increase the amount by twenty percent. Should a man or a woman address you,

you must show the speaker how pleased you are and express your appreciation at the end of each sentence. Likewise, you must assent and consent (meaning, say "Amen, amen! Quite so, quite so!"), agree (meaning, say "Yes, yes!"), show respect (meaning, say "Certainly, certainly!"), concur (meaning, say "Absolutely, absolutely!") and go along (meaning, say "How true, how true!"). Also, you must cook nothing on a Sunday, just eat the leftovers from Saturday cold, as do the Jews, because hot food heats the blood and excites the hot humors and also because Our Master Mūsā stoned a man whom he found gathering firewood on the Sabbath; neither can you make any other kind of movement on a Sunday. Have you got that?' 'I have,' she said. 'And don't draw the curtains back from the windows on that day,' I said, 'in case anyone sees you and that too leads to movement. Have you got that too?' 'I've got it,' she said, 'and grasped it and understood it and assimilated it and absorbed it and digested it and am seized of it and have perceived it. But what is the reason for it, when the same day, among us, is a day of pleasure and *exultation*, exchange of visits and *jubilation*?' 'They behave on that day like the dead,' I said, 'because that is the day on which Our Master 'Īsā rose from the dead. Furthermore, you must not take the name of the Sabbath, meaning Sunday (for the thing named may change with the changing of its name), in vain. Thus you should say for example, "What a noble and sublime Sabbath day that last one was, and when oh when will the next Sabbath come that I may again be alone with my Lord? Would that every day had a Sabbath hour! The Sabbath day is truly mighty and *awe-inspiring*, sublime and *beguiling*. How did people survive when they had no Sabbath? How many Sabbaths are there in a year? How many minutes in their hours, how many seconds in their minutes? How lovely are the Sabbath sun and moon, its predawn dark and *hours*, its heat and cold, its birds and *flowers*!"

4.11.8 "'Should you disapprove of any of their doings, be careful not to say so. Praise what you can of their customs and conditions, their landmarks and sites, their dishes and drinks, their banquets and clothing, the length of the nails of both their men and their women, the size of the latter's bustles and the braiding of their side locks, as of their "frights" of hair (by which I mean where it's drawn together at the backs of their heads), and how they expose their backsides to warm them up.[441] When you see any piece of furniture or the like in their houses, say how well it looks and express your admiration, saying, in astonishment, "Oh how lovely is this! Oh how beautiful is that! Oh how pretty are these! Oh how charming are those! How sweet-smelling are your latrines! How aromatic your drains! How spotless your other household offices! How elegant your sewers! How clean your lintels and doorsteps! How cheerful your underground tubes and tunnels!" This is the expedient that strangers here make use of to gain their affection and win their goodwill; I know many who have used it to their advantage.

"'Next, if we are invited to a banquet at the home of one of their great men, you must take care to eat here before you go, for the guests don't eat their fill in the homes of their hosts but fill themselves up before they eat. And just as it is considered good manners on the part of the host in our country to force his guest to eat and to swear on his head, his beard, and his mustache that his guest must eat a chicken thigh or six meatballs or to stuff the same into his mouth, so, among them, it is considered good manners for the host to keep a watch on every movement of the guest's jaw and hands so as to know whether he's a wolfer or a pouncer and a pecker, and whenever at table a mouth moves, or a hand'—here she interrupted me and said, 'or a waist' to which I responded, 'or a rump, or indeed any part of the body whatsoever'—'you must say to the owner of the moving part, "You are to be thanked for that! You are to be praised! You are to be lauded! You are to be commended! You have done well! You are too kind! You are most gracious!" and other stuff designed to proclaim the lowly status, humility, despicableness, insignificance, abjection, baseness, obsequiousness to and exaltation of the other,(1) and the self-abasement, of or by 4.11.9

(1) "'*haṭrah* is "the obsequiousness of the poor man toward the rich" and *kafr* is the adulation by the Persian of his king.

the guest, in comparison to the elevated status, might, sublimity, grandiosity, nobility, generosity, and pride of the host.

4.11.10 "'Also, never, ever, extend your hand to a bottle of wine or bowl of food to take what you want from them, for to do so would be a violation of the sanctity of the table, the gathering, and the village, nay, of the whole kingdom. You have to wait for the host to be generous enough to urge you to do so, and should he offer you a fragment of meat from a rabbit that was strangled a month ago and has been hanging in the air till it has gone rotten, praise the soil on which such a precious animal and its species was raised, as well as the one who strangled it and the one who cooked it. Should you behold a dignified and venerable old man serving an old woman, do not condemn this, as a certain misogynistic poet did when he said

Many an old woman who looks like a demon
  Gestures to, forbids, and commands
Her old man, who stands before her submissively
  And strives without ceasing to fulfill her demands.
She sits talking nonsense
  And her listeners say, "Enchanting!"
She says, "At home I have a dog and a cat.
  The cat panics if the dog starts snarling.
He watches me as I eat—
  Eyes right if I use my right hand, eyes left if I use the other,
And he sticks to my daughter Liza's lap
  Because she shares with him from her portion what's left over
And once I had—with different colors
  On belly, chest, and back—a pup
And took the greatest care of him
  And gave him milk in a cup.
Then the Dear Queen came to me
  And though my eyes were full of tears she begged him from me—
He would sleep on my thighs
  And lick my armpit when he stretched out his body[442]

And in such and such a year so-and-so brought me a little whelp
  But it died and for only a month did it tarry"
And if she's forgotten the date of that momentous day
  She'll ask every Tom, Dick, and Harry . . .

"'and so on until he gets to 4.11.11

Women have made an art, among other things,
  Of eating things like figs by slicing them in cross section
And they eat, their hands concealed
  In skins,[443] and chew with circumspection,
And the tea emits burbling sounds,
  Like hens cluck-clucking, from their bowels
And she spears[444] on her plate portions
  Of meat the size of parings of fingernails
And champs on them for a while
  So that they will slip down after disintegrating,
And the host's wife says to him, "Take, my dear,
  A morsel from what's before you waiting"
And he thanks her and says, "I owe you so much
  For your generosity and being so clever!"
And she sits and divides up the food for the guests
  And hands it out, sliver by sliver,
And with each sliver you get you must bob
  Your head and say "Thank you!" without protest
And if there are two kinds, she'll tell you, "Take
  Your due of what you find tastiest and choose the one you like
    the best"
As though it weren't allowed to combine the two—
  As though if you did so, you'd be screwing two sisters in a row.'

"Said the Fāriyāqiyyah, 'That's too much to cope with. I'm never going to put anything in my mouth in their homes, even if they're having manna and quails.'

"I said, 'Despite this, they have many qualities *well-known* and virtues to which they may *own*, ones not to be found among the 4.11.12

other Franks. Among these are the honoring of promises and punctuality in both arriving and departing, payment in full of the wages of any who works for them and respect for his privacy (meaning, treating him decently, not sparing his wife their attentions).'[445] 'Don't bother to explain,' she said. 'There's nothing exceptional in that.' 'Another virtue of theirs,' I said, 'is that they say little but do a lot, and are good at dealing with matters with order and *diplomacy*, good sense and *sagacity*. One who comes to their country is not asked whether he has a passport or a permit and it will not worry him if his neighbor is the chief judge or the prime minister or a police officer or a constable; he will not fear that, should he live in a house or enter a place frequented by policemen, they will wear him out with questions and suchlike that may lead to his going to prison or paying a fine, for in their country everyone enjoys the same rights inasmuch as they are all human beings.

4.11.13 "'Moreover, the rabble aside, they love strangers, are compassionate to the poor, and go to the aid of those in need. They honor the eminent and the celebrated and know the value of the scholar. They support the acquisition of the sciences and general knowledge in foreign countries and have societies that have been formed for the putting into practice of all that is useful and beneficial and the eradication of all that is evil and injurious. Many physicians here treat the sick without charge, and that's to say nothing of the hospitals that have been set up in every region and district of their country. If a person stays at one of their hotels, or rents a room in one of their houses, the landlady treats him as a friend, keeps him company, coddles and cossets him, nurses him, and invites him to sit with her of an evening and keep her company without her husband thinking there is anything wrong with that. Should some of her acquaintances visit her at such a time, she introduces them to him and sings his praises. If anyone arrives in their country with a letter of recommendation, the addressee makes a fuss over him and invites him to his home and makes his name known to his brethren and acquaintances, sparing no effort to secure his ease and comfort and providing him with disinterested friendship and advice both in his presence and in his absence. A scrap of paper with a commendation in the commender's hand thus gains him a father, mother, family, and brothers. In sum, then, their virtues balance out their vices, and none is perfect but God alone, the Glorious, the Almighty. None of these good points is to be found among the rest of the Franks because the others are disobliging, insincere, and shifty, with hands that are closed and tongues that are loosened, for they are neither like our friends[446] in their good sense and uprightness nor like us in our bonhomie and generosity.'

"'I've grasped all that,' said the Fāriyāqiyyah, 'so let's get back to explaining the two verses above, on condition that you not make anything up, for I know how you love to go to great lengths when talking.' 'You seem to be implying, as you so often have before,' I said, 'that I'm a talker, not a walker.' 'If you've grown used to hearing it,' she retorted, 'it won't do you any harm. If you haven't, consider it a slip of the tongue.' 'Here's the interpretation of them,' I said, 'without further beating about the bush: 4.11.14

Have at it, quickly, have at it! My needs you know,
So do your best to have your fun!
She is bored and has a husband
Who wants to screw her once you're done.'[447]

"'You said,' she said, 'that the poet was complaining of a woman but look, he's complaining of himself,[448] and the woman's not to be blamed for being annoyed under such circumstances.' 'To the likes of you,' I said, 'should be tossed the keys of linguistic *interpretation*!' 'From which,' she replied, 'may be expected relief after *tribulation*.'"

Chapter 12

Philosophical Reflections

4.12.1 After the Fāriyāqiyyah had stayed a while in the land of the peasants, where there was no solace for the stranger and nothing pleasant but the greenery, her patience wore thin, her heart became oppressed, and she was overcome by ennui and anxiety. One day, she said to her husband, "How strange is this world and its ways, the strangest thing in it being this rational beast that walks upon its surface! How strange that no matter how many nights and days pass over him, his desires delude him, while his hopes beguile and distract him in vain, and no matter how hard he runs to catch up with them, they stay ahead of him and keep the same distance from him as his shadow! Each day he believes that he is smarter than he was the day before and that the next day will be better than this. I used to think, when we were on the island, that the English were the happiest of people and enjoyed the greatest peace of mind. But when we came to their country and lived among them, lo and behold, their peasants turned out to be the most wretched of God's creatures. Look at the inhabitants of the villages around us and scrutinize them well and you will see that they are no different from savages. A peasant of theirs sets off in the morning to toil and travail, then returns to his house in the evening without having seen any other human being and without any having seen him. At night he lies down to sleep and the next day he gets up early to more of the same, and so it continues. He is like a machine that turns at an even pace: it has neither gain nor pleasure in its turning nor rest when it comes to a stop, for when Sunday—the day for joy and recreation in all parts of the world—comes, the only pleasure the peasant may enjoy is to go to church, where he sits for a couple of hours like a booby, yawning for an hour and sleeping for the rest; then he goes home. They have no places of entertainment or spots where they can pass the evening in conversation and good cheer.

"Nor is the life of the better-off in the countryside any better than that of the peasants, because the only dishes they know are roast meat and those turnips[449] that are everywhere. But where, in fact, are the better-off in the villages? The only rich people you see are the priest and the stewards who look after the farms and fields on behalf of their owners. They too are no different from the peasants. Despite this, if you enter the palaces of their kings and make a tour of the markets in their cities and see with your own eyes the amazing products, marvelous works of art, stylish machines, valuable stuffs, luxurious clothes, and well-made vessels that are there, especially in London, you will realize that the ones who manufacture these things are the ones who make the world go round while they themselves are deprived of them, for the daily life of the worker is no different from that of the peasant in that he goes and labors all day and has nothing to look forward to at night other than the closing of his eyes. How can it be that this sort of person creates the adornments of this world, makes it a delight to live in, and creates its prosperity, while they themselves are excluded from it and have but little share in it? 4.12.2

"Meanwhile, the cosseted rich do nothing well and sometimes cannot even express themselves properly. If people—God's creatures on His Earth in all their disparate states and statuses—are like one body with all its different members, noble and lowly, then why does justice not apply among them as it does among the members, given that, if a person eats something or dresses in something, he does so for the good of the body as a whole? Or would the rich claim 4.12.3

that, by being more generous to those good-for-nothing weaklings and relieving them of the distress they suffer from the effort of making a living and their inability to raise their children, they would cause them to neglect their work and leave the land uncultivated, so that it become unworkable and turn to desert and they perish of hunger? If that is the case, why do rulers allocate vast sums and magnificent rewards to those whom they appoint to office and promote in rank without fearing that they will spoil their work with their largesse? In fact, if the poor man is compensated by his ruler or master with his provisions—which are a trifle to the latter—he will perform whatever service or work he has to with enthusiasm. He will pray God grant the latter more good fortune and blessings rather than spend his nights, arms raised to heaven, calling down curses on him because of his certainty that he will never give him his due and that what has been taken from him to make him thin and scrawny has gone to others to make them fat and encourage them in their wantonness and arrogance and in the acquisition of purebred horses, fine carriages, and stacks of furniture such as no man should own. Under such circumstances, the rich man eats his food dipped in the curses of the poor.

4.12.4 "Or do they imagine that the Almighty created the poor just to serve them? I swear, the rich need the poor more than the poor need the rich. Or do they refuse to look down, from their sublime and elevated station, on the humble and the obscure for fear lest something of the latter's misery touch them and do them harm—like one who achieves some lofty height while at his feet lies a vast chasm, which he refuses to bend over and look into lest it make him feel dizzy or nauseous and he fall from his pedestal? Would that I knew whether the rich have ever attempted to make the wretched happy by giving them something of their wealth or reviving them with their aid and then found that they rewarded their kindness with ingratitude, refusal to work, and neglect of their duties before God and nature. Such an idea is simply a delusion that has entered their heads with their wine, the former remaining when the latter departs. Let the rich give the poor the opportunity to taste the sweetness of life and see the world as it really is for just one month out of their lives, or for one day in the year, so that they may die happy and gratified! The rich, rather than fearing that some evildoing may result from the leisure or unemployment of the poor, would do better to fear the evil intentions that they may harbor as a result of their poverty and their hatred of them, for wretchedness is more conducive to evil than happiness. Have you not seen the thousands of girls who run around the markets of London and other prosperous cities in rags? How they crowd around those who come and go hoping to obtain the means to buy food or clothes to make themselves pretty, especially the young ones who are still not fifteen? This, I swear, is no more or less than exploitation of children for sex! How can they blame us for this custom in our countries when it is practiced among us in the form of legitimate marriage and among them in the form of illicit relations? If these girls had sufficient sustenance they would not behave so, because a girl at that age has no desire for a man and no craving for intercourse, especially in cold countries, and many men whose lust for them has brought them great harm would be saved from their wiles and their greedy pursuit of money. Moreover, were the state and the clergy to take it upon themselves to set them up with enough money for them to equip themselves for a legitimate marriage—after first giving them some education and polish—they would bear bonny children and adorn the kingdom with the fruit of their wombs, as it says in the Old Testament.[450] Contrarily, if they continue to practice fornication, they will give birth only to rascals and scoundrels and will be like green saplings that not only do not bear fruit but also ooze a poison that puts an end to the thirst of any who taste it. How many a girl, I swear, has become pregnant the moment she set foot in the arena of whoredom and has then aborted the fetus from fear of poverty! Some of them, for lack of any shelter, give birth on the city's streets during the cold nights of winter or spend the night on a single bed with another girl—a custom widespread in London—for lack of means to acquire a bed and a cubbyhole of her own. Under such circumstances, she may fall victim to some harm from her bedmate.

4.12.5 "True, illegitimate children usually grow up to be mighty men and giants, like Jephthah the Gileadite, upon whom the spirit of the Lord descended and who saved Israel from the children of Ammon,[451] or William the Conqueror, who conquered these lands (meaning England); yet it is more right and proper to heed and advance the common good with thrift and *moderation* than that of the individual with extravagance and *misallocation*.(1) Should not the owner of fine productive lands who leaves them uncultivated and a place for wild animals to wallow be censured and likewise the owner of fruit-bearing trees who leaves them unfenced, unguarded, and prey to the depredations of every passing fruit fancier? True, it cannot be denied that the existence of rich and poor in this world is as unavoidable as the existence of beauty and ugliness; were it not so, the universe would cease to move and men's affairs would come to a standstill, or so the theologians assert.[452] However, we speak here of that poverty that cannot be described as conducive to savagery and wantonness, not of the abject poverty that creates constant worries and sorrows in its sufferer's heart and that leads him in some instances to cut his own throat or in others to drown or hang himself, as has become commonplace in these countries.

(1) *irghāl* ["misallocation"] is "the placing of something in other than its correct place," and is, I swear, a word that deserves to become well-known and much used.

4.12.6 "Is it not a shame upon the men in this land—the land of science, industry, urbanization, and civilization—that they will marry a woman only if she is well-endowed in both senses?[453] Uglier still is the fact that the great men here do not marry for love but out of greed for more money: a man whose income is one hundred guineas a day will want to marry a woman whose income is also precisely one hundred guineas; if it's ninety-nine it won't do. This is why you often see handsome young men married to ugly middle-aged women. Unfortunately, most of the men here are late marriers, meaning that they don't marry until they've reached later middle age. Thus they spend their youth in fornication and their thirties in looking for a woman possessed of position and wealth while the poor but beautiful woman is left on the shelf, and the men feel no shame at having children when they are old—this despite the fact that the raising of children under a wife's care is one of the most important reasons for marriage according to the divines and that conception takes place only once every nine months. What I'm getting at is that the children of raddled middle-aged women will not turn out bonny and healthy like those of beautiful young girls. In addition, when a man who gets married at the age of, say, thirty, to a woman aged eighteen, reaches fifty and his wife still has a roving eye and is randy, he will have his children to keep an eye on her. What use is more money to one whom God through His bounty has already made rich? What difference is there between a person who has a hundred guineas a day and one who has fifty, or twenty? Anyone who isn't satisfied with such an amount will not be satisfied with all the gold in the world. Furthermore, if a woman be rich, trouble is bound to follow on her wealth, because she will resolve to throw banquets, feasts, and parties, to visit and be visited, and to hire servants whose lustiness and blooming good looks appeal to her eye, and the moment she feels an ache or a pain in any of her limbs, she'll make out that she feels ill and conceive a notion to go abroad, or to the country, and there, while her husband is preoccupied with political affairs or economic issues in his town house, she will closet herself with whomever she wishes and disport herself with whomever she likes, her manservant finding in his hand enough gold coins to shut his eyes, close his ears, and seal his lips.

"Do not these rich persons suffer the same diseases and illnesses as the poor? Does not death surprise them while they are engrossed in their pleasures? Do not many of them die childless as a result of their intemperance, their desires, their avarice, their corruption, and the recklessness with which they pursue their lusts? Or, if they be blessed with children, do not these live out their short lives thin and famished with hunger, a misery to themselves and 4.12.7

an inconvenience to their parents? An English writer has said that any vigorous, strong child of their great men or princes one may come across is the result of impregnation by one of their retainers. The children of the peasants, on the other hand, you will find to be bonny and strong, with the appetites of horses, and I swear, if their parents didn't have this reward from the Almighty, namely the sight of their children around them, in lively good health and full of affection, they would be no better than dead.

4.12.8 "How did this world come to be built on immorality? How is it that a thousand, or two thousand, men must suffer here for one man to be happy? And what a man! He may have a heart but no mercy, two hands but no work, a head but no sense or brains. And how did this come about in this country whose justice is the stuff of proverbs? There can be no denying that the peasants of our country are better off than these people. Indeed, even the shopkeepers here are in a miserable state despite their wealth, for one will spend the entire day and part of the night on his feet. I asked one once and said, 'Why don't you sit on a chair, of which you have many?' and he told me, 'Those are for the people who honor us by visiting us in order to buy from us. If I were to sit like them, I would become one of them.' They pass their Sundays benumbed of body and mind, brains and eyes alike in a daze. What a contrast with a shopkeeper at home, who crooks one leg over another for a few hours on his bench, then, towards the end of the afternoon, casts his mantle in a heap behind him, and goes to some pleasure garden, walking proudly. If civilization and knowledge are the cause of these things, then ignorance is bliss.

4.12.9 "Not to mention that the peasants here are not only wretched but also extremely ignorant—though how are they to acquire knowledge when they spend all their time toiling to provide for their families and there are no schools where they live? I used to think that they could all read and write well, but it turns out that they do not even speak their own language well. I read something in a book and hear it from them in a form that contravenes its proper usage, not to mention that most of them have never heard the name of our country or our race. One of them once heard that the king had ordered horses to be sent overseas on ships to make war against his enemy and he said, 'I'm amazed that people can fight on horses at sea'! It seems to me that in their ignorance they believe everyone else in the world to be less than they, or they think that men in other countries sell their womenfolk, or eat them, or that they live on a diet of roots and greens. If they knew the conditions of other nations and the peculiarities of other lands, they would be aware that even if they had many times what we do, their cold, the unwholesomeness of their air, and the darkness of their skies mean that it would profit them little and that the wealth that they have from manufacturing cannot take the place of the natural wealth that we enjoy by way of sweetness of air and water, clearness of air, sweet-scentedness, healthiness, and wholesomeness of soil, tastiness of food and drink, picnicking in the meadows and gardens, eating next to running waters beneath verdant trees, visits to the bathhouses, and evenings spent in pleasant conversation and listening to musical instruments. Those of them who have visited our country and become familiar with our good fortune and comforts know this.

"The wise person, however, is he who knows how to extract **4.12.10**
from every reverse some good and, giving thought to all that has befallen him, how to benefit and find lessons for life. I have now learned, from all the loneliness and hardship that I have met with in their country, how to live in ours, should I return to it safely, and how belly laughing, splitting one's sides, laughing like a horse, laughing for no reason, laughing immoderately, laughing oneself silly, peeing oneself with laughter, chuckling, chortling, checkling, kenching, fleering, cackling, cachinnating, and 'ho-ho!' and 'hee-hee!' and 'ha-ha!' and 'tee-hee!' bring the heart greater relief from worry than unbreakable vessels or unshakable buildings. The best of countries, then, is that to whose airs you've become accustomed and in which you've found someone who is sincere in his love for you—and how can there be sincere love without a baring of secrets

and how can secrets be bared and innermost thoughts declared if the tongue isn't let off its leash to run free in the field of speech? Here people keep everything secret and think that for a person to talk of what he feels, loves, and hates is frivolity and folly. I, though, am like the fox who heard a loud noise coming from a drum that was being beaten by the branches of a tree; when he got to it and went to work on it and tore it open, he found it was empty. No wonder then that I no longer surrender my judgment to my hearing. Or, like one at sea who is thirsty and sees water all around him but cannot use it to quench his thirst, I see that the face of the earth here is green but that nothing of that greenness brings a flush of good cheer[454] when eaten because it has nothing appetizing about it, which is because everything that grows in their country is forced out of the soil by over-manuring. If there were a sodomite here, we should ask him what their greens taste like.

4.12.11 "All this is aside from their habit of mixing up solid with liquid food and their adulteration and corruption of the palatable foods with which the Almighty has blessed them. Given this, it is only to be expected that the bread, which is the main support of our bodies, has no taste, for they leaven it with a vegetal scum and mix it with those potatoes of theirs, and then, following the leavening, they pat it down. What good is it to one to say, 'I was in the land of the Franks' if all he found there was loneliness and adversity? Quite the opposite: recalling it later may cause him to choke in distress. To Cairo! To Damascus! To Tunis this very year! There you will find people to visit you or whom you can visit. There you will find cheerful faces devoid of flattery, and generosity devoid of restraint or artificiality—and any other words for scorn and contumely you've mentioned to me. A person cannot live happily if he cannot talk in his own language. Life is not to be valued according to the length of its nights or the number of its days, by views of green land, or by observing instruments and machines. Rather, its value lies in seizing the convivial moment with those who are *dear*, keeping company with persons of culture of whom one thinks with pleasure whether they be elsewhere or *here* and whose affection's *sincere* whether they're far or *near*. This world's worth lies in exchanging bon *mots*."

The Fāriyāq went on, "And I said, 'And in breathing on your *nose*!'—and she, 'In companionable *carousal*'—'And olfactory *arousal*!'—'In mutual *delectation*'—'And *degustation*!'—'In shared *affection*'—'And lingual *refection*!'—'In having *fun*'—'And letting saliva *run*!'—'In friendship's *charms*'—'And taking you in my *arms*!'—'In granting each other's *wishes*'—'And giving you *kisses*!'—'In kind *consideration*'—'And *osculation*!'—'In talking face-to-*face*'—'And mutual *embrace*!'—'In discussion and *debates*'—'And arms around *waists*!'—'In talking in tones that are *soothing*'—'And lying together in one set of *clothing*!'—'In close *associations*'—'And sleeping together in a single pair of *combinations*!'—'In mutual *stimulation*'—'And *exploration*!'—'In witty *contestations*'—'And conjugal *relations*!'—'In *jesting*'—'And *besting*!'—'In *conversation*'—'And *copulation*!'—'In *banter*'—'And going for a *canter*!'—'In *joking*'—'And *poking*!'—and that concluded our *merrymaking*." 4.12.12

Chapter 13

A *Maqāmah* to Make You Walk

4.13.1 Al-Hāwif ibn Hifām faid in lifping tones,[455] "I'd heard so much about women I almost ended up with *sciatica*, for some say that the life of the married man is better than that of the *bachelor*, one safer in all it *entails* than that of shouldering one's way up to water holes guarded by jealous *males*, or enduring the pangs of thirst and *fire*, or exposing oneself to public disgrace and *ire*; and that, should life's worries coat one's heart with *rust*, a smile from one's spouse revealing pearly teeth in a *line*, a sip of saliva like honey, a voice so sweet it obviates the need for musical instruments or sparkling *wine* will polish off the *dust*. For among the things with which the Almighty has singled out woman by way of *merit*, and virtues that He has seen fit to have her *inherit*, is that no ill temper her sweet voice *resists*, no anxiety or heartsickness with it *coexists*. The moment her lips are *moved*, the heart is *soothed*, and when with flirtatiousness her eyes are *lowered*, whoever's in her presence with pleasures is *showered*, so that he *frolics* and *rollicks*, confines himself to the '*little nest*'[456] and is *refreshed*, *capers* and *caracoles*, stiffens and *comes*, dances like a Negro and bangs on *drums*(1). When she walks through her house in a willowy *fashion*, the fates declare (with *passion*), 'Our lives we'd give for you, you merry coquette!

(1) *ḥanbasha* means "to dance, jump, clap, leap, talk, and laugh"; *maḥsh* is "vehemence of intercourse, or of eating"; *taḥfīsh* means "confining oneself to a small chamber"; *darqala* means "to dance, spread one's legs, and strut" and *darkala* something similar; *baḥshala* means "to dance the dance of the Negroes."

If you'd like us to place your husband on high, like a sun at its highest *position*, so he can keep you in the most pampered *condition*, or you'd like him to stay tonight at your *side*, no stratagem could turn us *aside*. If you'd like us to seduce him with the notion of travel (for a year or *more*) to some place (safe or dangerous) far from this *shore*, all that's needed from you (you being to us the noblest of those who forbid and *command*) is a hiss with your tongue or a sign with your *hand*; a mere wink from your *eye* would make us *comply*.'"

He went on, "Likewise I've heard it said that a husband—God grant him protection from all that's *unchaste*, let him in the greenery of His orchard and the plucking of its apples and pomegranates, and with ever more of His charity and bounty make him *blest*!—can enjoy with his spouse whatever pleasures he likes. If he wants, he can *touch*. If he craves intoxication, that too is not too *much*. If he wishes, he can *fondle* and *trifle*, and if he refuses to be *unserious*, wealth and social standing are at his command *imperious*. Also, that he has in her a fastness *high* (but not *dry*)[457] in which she may his cares *dispel*, from which joy and happiness augur *well*, and a fruitful meadow to which the world beats a *path* with glad tidings on display and offerings fit to make him *laugh*. If some affair of his should go awry, with her skill she'll set it *straight* and with a gesture she'll make it *right*. 4.13.2

"I've heard too that if she flirts with him and throws herself upon his neck, dresses up for him and tosses her *hair*—may God increase him in ease and *opulence* and you in patience and *indulgence*!—he'll think he's gained the world and all that's in it, carried off every pleasure and joy that's *there*, and that he's reached the most elevated of *stations*, that of that most mighty monarch, viceroy to the Creator of *Nations*.[458] Should he at that moment the chief judge, passing on his hinny, *observe*, he'll suppose him one of those employed by him to follow and *serve*, and should he a priest or churchwarden *behold*, the honor of any direct communication he'll *withhold* and send in his stead, to the honored first, a male *flunky*, 4.13.3

to the respected second, a lady *lackey* and tell them, 'For any who can conquer and subdue, I have a noble *commission*, for any who inquires as to my well-being or expresses their thanks, a *position*.' Should any man bark at him, cut him dead, or call him a *name*, he'll come right back at him with rough words and *blame*, and should anyone—perish the thought!—cuff his occiput, deal his nape a *thwack*, or subject his feelings to *attack*, he can run to his wife—God grant her strength!—and she'll relieve him of all grief, give him from every terror *rest*, restore his impregnability with her private parts, his prominence with the promontories on her *chest*, and tell him, 'Fear not his wiles and his *spite*: every show of force can be repelled by an equal display of *might*.' He then returns to his former haughtiness and *pride*, his overweeningness and being *snide*. Even should he see a princeling or king's *vizier*, he'll think himself too fine to treat him as his *peer*—for he's the one in clover and luxuriating in a life of *relaxation*, coddled and gazed at with *adulation*. He eats with such pearly teeth and coral lips before him that he thinks pickles are the best of *fare*, that the most blessed of possessions is a shirt of *hair*, that water that's brackish and *briny* is tastier than the wine at any evening *party*. And oh! should he spend the night with her on a mattress stuffed with wooden *shavings* and touch her downy skin—he'll think them the most luxurious of *stuffings*, for any injury suffered along with her is transformed into bounty and *gain*, into revelry and carousal any *pain*.

4.13.4 "From another, though, I've heard it said that the bachelor's life is the happier, the one in which pleasures are more likely to *bloom*, for the ladies view him as ever roaming free, and think one rutting bleat from him will dispel all *gloom*, given that he has none to tie him up each night in order to *tup* or half the night to keep him *up* lest he forget he's now the sheltered *spouse* of one who wears anklet and *blouse*. For this he's beloved of the girls, a prize to which matrons *aspire*, pointed out by randy widows as an object of *desire*. When he goes home, his hands are free, his cuffs *unsoiled*,[459] there being none to tell him, 'Hand over!' or blame him for what's past, quiz him on things to come, seek to have him in matters vaginal *embroiled*, tell him 'Shoo! Shoo! (*ḥaf ḥaf*!)' at every amorous *clucking* (*qayq*) from some other woman and his every roosterous wing *flapping* (*ḥalj*), tie—and how *tie*!—the piece of skin between his belly and his willy (*najf*) before he bids her *good-bye*, or tell him 'Quaff! To the dregs, the water *quaff* (*nazāfi nazāfi*), or else I'll finish you *off*!'(1) nor any to weep before him in *supplication* when he's powerless to support her, even though to do so be his *obligation*. You'll see him ever with a happy, rolling *gait*, full of joy, throwing himself in women's way and never walking *straight*, *laying* and *splaying*, keeping company with women who're ready to *pup* and feeling them *up*. As says a proverb that's making the rounds like a bad *penny*,[460] 'He who has no wife has *many*.' The result, it is claimed, is that the bachelor's stride is *vaster*, his movement *faster*, his words less *trimming*, his cup more *brimming*, his intonation more *melodious*, his cravings more *imperious*, his thrusts more *pressing*, his delicious wine more *refreshing*, his lance's blade of keener *bite*, his arrow truer in *flight*, his breath more *sugarcoated*, his love more *devoted*, his food tastier and more *plenteous*, his vital juices more fluid and *copious*. They forget that the emptying of his basin into more than one plot is the very cause of the dropping of his water table and *lust*, the weakening of his vigor and *thrust*—and so on and so forth by way of phrases that shouldn't be used to describe whore or honest *matron*, or characterize a man, whether he run or trudge to his *damnation*."

(1) *Qayq* is the sound made by a hen when it demands to be trodden; when you say that a rooster *ḥalaja*, you mean that it spread its wings and went to its female to tread her; *ḥaf ḥaf* is a call made to drive away a cock or chickens; *najf* is making it impossible for a buck to mount, which is done by tying a piece of skin between its belly and its member, this piece of skin being called the *nijāf*; when you say that a man *nazafa* the water of the well, it means "he drained it dry"; *azhafa* means "to revile . . ." or, followed by *'alā*, "to finish off (a wounded man)" or by *bi-l-sharr* "to lure to evil," or by *al-khabar* ("report") "to exaggerate [the report], to lie, or to slander."

4.13.5 Said al-Ḥāwif, "The two schools being thus equally balanced, the two claims in *contention*, I said to myself, 'If only the Fāriyāq were with us today so that to this thorny question he might turn his *attention*, for he cleaves more closely to women than does even *doubt* and better knows their ways than any graybeard or youthful *gadabout*. Of them he's tasted both sweet and *bitter*, and of their love he's been both victim and *benefitter*. Were he present with us now, all this confusion that we've *endured* would straightaway be *cured*.' I went then to one of my friends to apprise him of my *dilemma* and, no sooner had I knocked upon the door than he fell upon me, in his hand a *letter*. 'Good news!' he said, 'Good news! Here's a letter from the Fāriyāq that reached me in yesterday's *mail*, written in verse, down to the smallest *detail*.' I snatched it from his hand and here's what it contained:[461]

4.13.6 "'After salutations, be informed that

A procurer's one who goes
With his bride from one land to another
Where the long-necked lovelies
Swoon to the scent of his money,[462]
One who, on every beauty shaking with fat,
Sharpens the two fangs with which he bites,
And stiffens the slackness of his spine,
His resuscitator from misery.[463]
There too are bull camels,
Aroused to mount his recalcitrant she-camel
And to drink up everything
In his trough or his tumbler,
And sometimes they nickname him "pander,"
The ugliest of his evil vocations.
In the end he returns, no
Physician left to him to treat his incurable treachery.

4.13.7 The wise man is he who consults
One well tried in adversities when bewildered,

Especially in the matter of marriage
 And how to bear its crushing atrocity.
He who is attracted by its deceptive coloration
 And the pleasant taste of its comforts
Let him marry in a small village
 That he may deal as he wishes with the contract
For depravity chokes
 Any who cranes his neck to lick it.
The stranger[464] is more harmful than 4.13.8
 One indifferent to his reputation among his own folk—
Or perhaps it is not so, for in the state of bachelorhood,
 While he is his own master,
Lies protection for his money, his privacy, and his peace of mind.
Again though, the present of him who marries
 Augurs better for him than his past
Since, in his state of bachelorhood,
 He missed having someone to keep him company.
He must, though, avoid
 The harboring of doubts.
Marriage, then, and more marriage! Be not
 Distracted from practicing it again and again
So long as the advantages of starting over at it
 Do not damage the ending of what was good.[465]
One must, however, be alert
 To whatever may turn it into catastrophe.'"

Said al-Hāwif, "Once these lines I'd *scrutinized* and, with a fair degree of certainty, the truths at which they hinted had *surmised*, I said, 'What a paragon! How much insight into women's affairs he *shows*, in verse as much as in *prose*! And how greatly we need from him, concerning these creatures, a *fatwah*, be it delivered in person or in *absentia*! Except, though, where he speaks of marriage, of his own state he nothing *vouches*, as though he thought all else of lesser purport and best consigned to that place where, after passing 4.13.9

through the stomach, the food *debouches*.' Then I departed singing his *praise*, all the more desirous of seeing his *face*."

(Note: because he was fond of the Fāriyāq, al-Hāwif didn't take him to task over some of these lines of his, which are awkwardly expressed. It is not my way, however, to pull the wool over the eyes of the reader, with whom I share an old friendship going back to the beginning of this work. Let him, therefore, take note of that fact.)

Chapter 14

Elegy for a Son

It is ingrained in the nature of every father to love all his offspring, 4.14.1
no matter how many, ugly, or vicious they may be, to think each of them the best of persons, and to envy anyone, other than his own father or son, who is superior to him in praiseworthy qualities and virtues; and when a man grows old and too weak to enjoy the pleasures of this world, it is enough for him to watch his son enjoy them. Likewise, there is no greater pleasure for a married man than to spend the night with his wife on a single bed with, between them, a small child of his who neither keeps him awake with his weeping and crying nor wets him with his little willy. By the same token, nothing pains his heart more than to see that same child sick but unable to give tongue to a complaint so that he may know how to treat him. The physicians themselves are at a loss when it comes to treating small children and rarely find the right cure. It would be better if specialized doctors were to be appointed who could devote themselves to their treatment long-term and that those who excel at it be extolled wherever words are written or printed. It is the father's duty, as soon as he sees that his child has fallen sick, to pay him close attention, observe his condition and any new developments, and write everything down in a book so that he may be able to give the doctor a clear account of it. Doing so may avoid the need for many

a medicine that the doctors will sometimes try out as a way of probing the patient's condition.

4.14.2 Food is one of the most important matters that should engage the parents' concern where their offspring are concerned, for, given the child's lack of awareness of the limits to intake, at which the mature person stops, the most frequent cause of his falling ill is food. It is not a form of tenderness or solicitude for the mother to feed her child whatever he wants; it is better to distract him from it with things such as toys, painted pictures, ornamented devices, and so on—though how pretty the child when he asks his father for something, his cheeks blushing with shyness or timorousness forcing him to lower his gaze, and how lovable he is as he throws his delicate arms around his father's or his mother's neck and says, "I want that to eat"! It is equally bad management to deny him what he wants and make him cry over something that can do no harm. I swear that anyone who pays so little attention to keeping his child content that the child cries and his tears flow for any reason other than his being disciplined has no right to be called a parent! The child has to be trained to take light foods six months after birth, breastfeeding continuing for a short while. Solid food nourishes and strengthens him, not to mention that this preserves his mother's health; indeed, extended breastfeeding of the child will sometimes result in her falling ill and benefit her nothing. This is the method followed by the Franks, who are the people with the most offspring. She should never breastfeed the child if she is choleric, or upset and disturbed, or sick.

4.14.3 Moreover, so long as a man is a bachelor or has never raised a child, he will never feel proper feelings of tenderness for the children of others. Yet more, he will never fully appreciate his own parents who raised him until he became a father and a raiser of children himself. Mothers who breastfeed their children are of necessity more tenderhearted toward them than those who hire wet nurses. Without a doubt, any who have children and read the words of the poet, "And many a mother and child have been torn asunder as are soul and body when they part,"[466] will not be able to prevent themselves from shedding tears of heartfelt agony and sorrow, and the same if they should read stories in which fathers are stricken by the killing of their innocent little children, such as the killing of the children of Midian at Moses's command, as recounted in Chapter 31 of the Book of Numbers,[467] whether the children's parents are believers or unbelievers. As to those who have not been graced with fatherhood, such as a monk or his like, should they address you as "My dear son" or "My child," put no trust in their words or faith in their blessings, because only one who has experienced fatherhood can know the affection that goes with filiation.

The Fāriyāq was one of those whom God had given sons as sweet 4.14.4
to the taste as candy only for him thereafter to sip the bitterness of parental bereavement. He had a child who reached two years of age and was as though cast from the very mold of comeliness and beauty, having arrived lacking nothing of what is needed to bring refreshment to the eye. Despite his young age, he had the look of one capable of distinguishing those who cheer from those who oppress and would make friends with any who treated him kindly, be it but by a gesture. When his father gazed at him, he would straightaway forget every sorrow and concern, though there would quickly descend upon him then a touch of melancholy since he had a foreboding that the child would not last long before Fate's dread eye, and he would decide to himself that he was unworthy to enjoy for long that radiant countenance. He would carry him in his arms by the hour, talking to him tenderly and singing to him, until the child became so comfortable with him that he would no longer want anyone else to carry him or entertain him or to eat on his own.

Things went on this way until God, Lord of Death and Life, 4.14.5
decreed that the child should be taken by a cough in that village of which we have spoken and, given that the smaller villages of England, like those in other countries, are without skilled doctors and it was essential to seek the advice of some doctor, of no matter what kind, his parents consulted a quack there who advised them

to bathe him repeatedly up to the neck in hot water. They followed his advice for some days, the child only growing worse until it eventually reached the point that, when he was put into the water, he would pass out and a heart-shaped blotch as red as blood would appear over his heart. Then the sickness grew worse until the cough settled in his chest and his voice became weak, though at the same time he was overcome by repeated tremors and shakes. He continued to struggle for life for six days and nights, moaning weakly and looking at his parents as though complaining to them of his sufferings. The roses of his cheeks were transformed into jasmine, his eyes, with their startling contrast of black and white, became sunken, and no food or medicine any longer went down his throat without difficulty. While this was going on, the Fāriyāq shed copious tears and prayed fervently to God, saying, "O Lord, turn this torment from my son onto me, if that should please Thee! I have no desire to live without him or strength to watch him in this painful struggle. Let me die before him, though by a single hour, so that I do not see him give up the ghost. Ah, how terrible an hour! But if Your decree must be carried out, let him die now!" It may be that the Fāriyāq was the first father who ever prayed for his son to die, out of pity and tenderness, for the sight of the child dying over a period of six days was too much to bear. After the child died and only sorrow and grief remained in their hearts, they could no longer bear the place where they were living because everything in it reminded them that they had lost him, adding to their distress. They left it therefore and departed suddenly for London, having placed him in a casket; and when they had buried him and had settled in a house, his father recited, in lamentation for his death

4.14.6 You gone, the tears, when I recall you, run
And memory, now that dust conceals you, festers like a wound,
O forsaker of a heart that you have left
Exposed to sorrow's every flame

(Or so I wrongly thought, but, after you, where is my heart?
Naught's in my chest but fire—
A meager diet, hard to bear, that has reduced my body
That even so constrains).
What harm to Fate should it have left you to me
As reality and not mere memory?
You lost, nothing more affrights me or delights,
Not of shadows nor of lights.
All one it is to me if night o'ertake me
Or morning come, now you are gone.
Ah how evil was that night, for no desire did it leave me
To see another dawn!
Six nights till then you had me sleepless kept
And on that last, longing for my bed, of a fifth of myself I was deprived.
O little son, they cannot help me to endure,
Those words of theirs "Death's rule on Man's imposed."[468]
No indeed—now you are gone, no consolation's left to cool my heat: 4.14.7
"This world for permanence can furnish no abode."
How oft did I cradle you before I departed of a morning
Or left at night, to return to the best homecoming!
How many a night was I kept awake by fear, though
My tears and lack of sleep availed you nothing!
How often did I pray for a cure to your disease, beseeching,
Though unavailing were my prayers!
How many a dark night did I embrace you lest sudden mishap should you befall—
Such were my fears—
The beauty of your face transporting me
To some fresh forenoon garden.
No painter mayhap your portrait for me painted, yet
In these my verses you are portrayed; they are your guardian—

Or if a narrow grave-shelf has hid you,
For me the Earth today is the narrowest of spaces,
Or if from me you have been hidden, yet still
Nothing in my troubled thoughts remembrance of your charms displaces.
4.14.8 Ne'er shall I forget you—or should I do so, I shall be dead, for never have I known
A time when upon your memory I did not dwell;
Your elegy I'll declaim so long as I remain, and if I die,
Then let the reader my place fill!
What grief! My capacity for patience thereafter was as little as
My ability to conceive of how to bear my loss.
Many gazed upon me, few helped,
And the gloating of my visitors seared my guts,
Leading me to recite a verse uttered by one who'd tasted
The same bereavement and alienation from neighbors as had I:
"I kept company with my neighbors, he with His Lord—
And how different his neighbors from mine!"
What a disaster! It descended, its weight crushing
My shoulders and announcing the snapping of my spine,
On a night when I parted company with the light of my eyes
Forever and he was of me perforce bereft—
Small wonder that, when the darkness of night had passed
From before my eyes, every star had also left.
I would have hoped that happily
He'd outlive me and reach a ripe old age
And wished I might taste my own end before he did his,
But God's choice and mine were not the same
4.14.9 And 'twas I who laid his head to rest with my own hands, by greater force compelled. Would that
He'd laid my head down in keeping with my hopes!
My eye gazed at him and there was nothing I could do.
O for a look that could have brought about my wishes for delay!

My hand fell short of unhanding from him that which brought about his end;
Verily, incapacity is born of a conviction of inability!
How I grieved for him as his eye complained to me
For he could not himself inform me.
How I grieved for him, laid down upon his bed,
And had I been able, he would have lain on my left arm
But the slightest touch added
To his pain and he would wail at the touch of my hairs
And moan the moan of one who seeks aid, heart throbbing
Like a bird that feels the cold yet passes the night with nowhere to alight,
Till I feared my tears might hurt his body,
When they flowed down over him like falling rain.
What a shudder it was that took him off! It left my
Heart to palpitate and suffer memory's desolation.
Would that recuperation had then cooled my eye, after
It had heated, with a shaking off that contained consolation.
How I grieved for him, as he embraced me in the darkness **4.14.10**
And my sleep, for painful pity, was cut short!
How I grieved for him as my singing lulled him
Though, if I stopped, he craved for more!
How I grieved for him when he took from my hand
And returned what he had taken in his, hoping for more!
How I grieved for him as he gummed my cuff,
Leaving shining pearls and fiery stars!
Ah, what a day, on which death fastened its talons into
Soft clay not made to withstand the hooks of its claws!
What a dire affair! It oppressed me, making death and
Life to me as one until my fated end!
Living was sweet to me when he would wave to me
But now that he has gone is naught but gall.
Neither distance can console me nor length of time
Nor change of days and cities.

My sorrows will never end nor can I die of grief
For thus the Creator's decree with me must take its course.
4.14.11 Nay, nor shall my tears extinguish my burning fire
Though they pour forth like rain,
For any fire but the fire of a parent's loss may be extinguished
And any water but that of tears will douse a fire.
Would that tranquillity of life might one day return
And a child, reared by a father sore beset who'd give his life for him!
I would pay with my life for that of my son, facing
My death as one content, freely choosing.
For his sake I would hide away things that could do no harm
But today I do not hide even that which may do harm.
Death and my aspirations, after him,
Are one and the same in terms of what I prefer
So let the days do with me as they will—
After this calamity no further injuries can come.
Let hopes forsake me—
No aims in life are left to me.
Let he who has tasted a bereavement as devastating as mine
Be incapable today of making me endure patiently
But let him weep with me and bear
The excess of my tears from a tear duct overflowing.
Naught demolishes the underpinnings of patience like a child's loss or
Slices through the back so brutally as its severing sword.
4.14.12 The child dies but once, but
His father dies before him many times.
The wresting from him of his child and his disappearance bring down upon him
Repeated episodes of demise, and what episodes!
How unlikely that any man's experiences of the loss
Of his desires will resemble mine

Or that in the violence of others' grief I might find a model
Or in length of life an end deserving of my pursuit!
A person's care will avail him nothing.
All are headed to an end that's been measured out.
Death is the end of every living thing—in this
The well-off and the poor are all as one.
Those who went before one day with those
Who followed after will be gathered in one crumbling clay.
The death of a child, however, is a day more dread, for he has known
No space in which to run and strive.
The one who knows the sweet taste of life is he whom
Loss of a child has passed by, not he who is possessed of riches.
Loss of wealth is like loss of hair—you
Lose it and then it sprouts anew, time after time.
Let him be happy then whose children live as long as he does
And may his well remain of what may muddy it ever free!
Some catastrophes may be easily swallowed but some
Leave a lump in the throat on which to choke until the end of time.

Chapter 15

Mourning

4.15.1 Since the Fāriyāq had no choice but to live close to that ill-fated village,[469] he left with his wife and went to Cambridge. For a long time, they walked around with eyelids half closed and half open, for extreme grief distracts the heart from the natural appetites, or vice versa. Then the knot of sorrow loosened a little from the eyes, though not from the heart because the eyes do not always obey the latter—and how can they when it has been said, "Two weak things will conquer a stronger"?[470] Each permitted himself first to peer,[471] peek, and peep like a puppy opening its eyes for the first time, then to snatch stolen, furtive glances through narrowed eyes that looked askance, then to watch and observe, then to stare and scrutinize, then to crane the neck, cover one eye the better to see, and to contemplate and meditate. Finally, eyes and hearts made peace and the former began to speak on behalf of the latter, though heartbreak still ruled their depths.

4.15.2 Humans, though, were created "from a drop of mingled fluid,"[472] composed of a number of varied humors, essences, and contingent characteristics, and they will continue as long as time shall last to combine this with that and mix the serious with the humorous, joy with grief. On one occasion, then, you will find a man content with his lot, on another as greedy as Ashʿab,[473] at times joyful, at others miserable, one day rapturous and blithe of heart, on another, or part of it, too despondent to sport or play. He is human in form but a ghoul by nature and this unsteadiness of his is nowhere more visible than in his dealings with women. Thus, if he marries a pretty woman, he says, "Would that I'd married an ugly one and saved myself the attempts of my acquaintances and neighbors to muscle in!" and if he marries an ugly one, he says, "Would that I'd been acute enough to marry a cutie and gain prestige and renown!" If his wife is fair, he says, "Would that she were dark-skinned, for the dark-skinned are livelier and warmer in winter!" and if his wife is dark-skinned, he says, "Would that she were white, for white-skinned women have cooler bodies in summer!" If she is short and generously proportioned, he says, "Would that she were svelte and narrow-waisted, for the narrow-waisted are less expensive to feed!" If he leaves her to go on a journey, he says, "Would that it were she who had traveled!" and vice versa. Only when she is pregnant does he have no desire to be in her place. The same rule applies to too many matters concerning women to count, for even the most seemingly obvious matters relating to them are an unplumbable ocean.

In sum, the heart has many contrasting states and conditions 4.15.3
among which it constantly changes, or which keep it in a constant state of change, and, when all's said and done, its very name—*qalb*—points to what it is.[474] One thing only is an exception to this rule and that is man's unshakable insistence, in every state and under every condition, in every place and at all times, on preferring himself over others. If he leads a dissolute life, he believes that no one is more pious in God's sight than he. If he is crass and crude, he thinks every elegant wit his inferior. If he's a miser, he supposes that every letter he utters is the most generous gift and if he is ugly and mean-spirited, he thinks the blame attaches only to those who view him as such. Likewise, just as a man's eye sees only what is in front of it and not itself, so his mental faculties apprehend all the faults of mankind except his own. Should he travel all the way around the world, he won't find anywhere the good qualities that are to be found in his city or village, and the good qualities of his town fall short of those

of his own house, though none of them are to be found among his family to the same degree as they are in him, from which it may be gathered that he is the best thing in the entire world. If he be a poet, or more accurately a poetaster, the only thing he'll do well is to sing the praises of misers or write love verses to Hind and Daʿd,[475] and if he should see scientists and engineers inventing, for example, devices that make it possible to travel five hundred miles in a single day, he'll reckon that his poetry is more useful and necessary than any of those. If he's a singer or a player of a musical instrument and sees that a neighbor of his is an experienced physician who treats and, God willing, cures five hundred patients each day, he'll believe that his trade is more conducive to health and more beneficial and the thought will never occur to him that a person may exist on this earth for a lengthy period without hearing a song or the playing of an instrument.

4.15.4 When, then, will men learn to know themselves and to distinguish between right and wrong? Not to combine the sorrow buried in the heart with peering and staring? Uglier still than these traits is the fact that everyone imagines that everyone else is doing the same and that he is to be excused because all he is doing is keeping pace with them. Exemplary of such ugliness is the woman who wears mourning dress for a dead relative and over the same period flaunts her bold looks and thinks nothing of talking about males, who finds comfort in looking at colors other than black and finds it as music to her ears when someone tells her, "So-and-so is in love with you, and you should be seated on a dais and telling the ladies-(or more accurately, gentlemen-)in-waiting around you what to do and what not to do, and you should never handle anything with this soft hand of yours and never leave your house on this delicate foot of yours, and you have so many suitors in every place and you will never, at any time, be without people to surround you, serve you, indulge you, and make you forget your sadness" as well as other things that are a violation of the respect owed to both death and the dead.

The Fāriyāq resumed,[476] "In England and elsewhere I have seen many women dressed in mourning garb who were more cheerful, rapturous, blooming, and mirthful than a bride and her mother and I never saw one of them, on laughing, look at her black garments and think to herself that her cackling was out of place. If it is the death of a husband that is involved, however, one inclined to clemency may seek to excuse a woman by saying, for example, 'Maybe her husband used to betray her on dark nights, and her dislike for black simply reflects her memories of his evildoings toward her in the blackness of those nights,' or that the days she spent with him were all as black as night. When it comes to offspring or fathers or others of that sort, no woman who wears mourning while showing off and laughing hard can be excused. Moreover, among the Franks a woman wearing mourning dress is as much in demand among and desired by men as a bride, because the studs among them jostle one another to entertain and distract her, well aware of what lies beneath that black and that this is one of those customs whose practice contradicts its theory. 4.15.5

"It appears that the word *muḥidd* ('woman dressed in mourning') in this noble language of ours derives from the *hadd* ('edge') of the knife and from '*aḥaddahā* or *ḥaddadahā*, meaning "He rubbed it with a stone or a file and it thus became sharp (*ḥaddat, taḥiddu*)."'[477] Thus it is as though the lust of the one looking at a woman who is wearing mourning clothes (*ḥidād*) were sharpened by his seeing upon her the traces of sorrow, melancholy, and dejection, this being the most attractive state a woman can be in. It also helps him that a certain kind of black cloth is called *isbād*, a word that also occurs in the sense of 'shaving of the hair,' which is also called *sabd* (and you know better than I the full sense of that word).[478] The *isbād* is also called a *silāb*, while the *salīb* is a person whose mind has been stolen (*mustalab*). Thus it seems that if a woman *tasallabat*, i.e., puts on mourning and dresses in a *silāb*, she steals (*salabat*) the mind of any who looks on her, for the moment his glance falls upon her, his heart 4.15.6

falls with it and he says to her, or to himself, ‘I would give my life in ransom for yours! I would sell my father and my mother for you! What a wonder you are! God protect you! God grant me a chance to give my life as a ransom for you! If you wish me to be the first to implore you to allow him to wipe this sadness from your breast, I will do so, for I am more able than you to bear adversities. Throw then this piercing pain upon me and be you happy and joyful! I have a large musical instrument[479] and many entertaining stories with which to release you from this care. If you would visit me once, or allow me to visit you, none of these sorrows would ever cross your mind again. You are soft and plump, and I can see how hard this loss is for you; it can be removed then only by something equally hard. Would that you knew how I grieve and suffer for your sake! I am prepared to deny myself every pleasure to see you part your lips and reveal those delicious glistening teeth of yours and display on your cheeks, when you laugh, that dimple that has so often dented the hearts of your suitors. What heart could forbear to melt before such dejection? What eye would not shed tears onto this black wrap? Sufficient reward it would be for me to take your sorrow upon myself, enough for me that I lift from you the rust of this care!’

4.15.7 “The woman wearing the mourning is the same, for she is conscious, as she walks, of what is going on in the mind of the man who feels such pity for her and so says, to him, or to herself, ‘Indeed, I swear I need you to lift from me the loneliness and sadness that I feel today! I spent last night drowning in the ocean of cogitations and perturbations, and you look to me to be qualified to pick quarrels with me, to spend the evenings chatting with me, to keep me company, to take me by surprise, to come to me early of a morning, to come and live near to me, to engage in give-and-take with me, to walk hand in hand with me, to discuss with me, to share secrets with me, to travel with me, to ramble here and there with me, and to vie with me in quoting poetry.[480] Praise, then, to God who today has guided me to you and you to me, and decreed that you be mine—for I am a poor dejected woman and must have someone to dispel my grief and cheer me, until, when I have forgotten my sufferings and some disaster falls upon you, it becomes my duty to provide relief (*ufarriju*) to you, for I possess the very source from which relief (*faraj*) is derived[481] and through me you will obtain joys most *sweet*, pleasures most *complete*. Off with us then to social intercourse and evening *prattle*, to repartee and to doing *battle*!'

"This is what comes of wearing mourning and this is why many 4.15.8
women prefer to wear black garments—being confident that they will have the same effect of attracting any men they may run across as does mourning dress. This is also why the Franks love the color black for clothes and never go beyond it and why priests' and imams' robes are black."

Chapter 16

The Tyrannical Behavior of the English

4.16.1 When the Fāriyāq had finished his work in Cambridge, he went to London intending to return to the island and a shaking fever went with him. One of the kind doctors of that city, however, shook that shaking fever off his back and charged him nothing. Next, the Fāriyāqiyyah came down with palpitations of the heart and tongue, for she had by now become skilled in the language of those people. Then he in turn was afflicted with palpitations of mind and thought, the reason being that, his leave of absence from the island over and the time for him to return nigh, he had decided that if he hadn't at first succeeded, he wouldn't if he tried again.[482] This was because the easy living and comfortable housing conditions that had formerly prevailed there had changed, and this was usual for the Fāriyāq: he never entered a land of plenty that he didn't leave a barren waste, as noted earlier. Also, he had missed out on certain benefits there which he was now denied in view of the length of his absence.

4.16.2 Taking this into account, he made his way to the city of Oxford, taking with him a letter of introduction to one of its notables and scholars, a clergyman. He believed it would be difficult to make contact with him, for the scholars of that city are not like those of Cairo in their graciousness and warmth of welcome; on the contrary, they are ruder than the common people and think no stranger comes to their country without a beggar's bag over his shoulder.

Thus it was that when the Fāriyāq went one evening to see one of these scholars, someone confronted him at the door to the college and said, "Whom do you want?" "So-and-so," he replied. "Where do you live?" asked the other. "In such and such a place," he said. "Do you have money enough to pay the rent?" the man asked. "I'm no metropolitan or monk[483] that you should suppose that I come to you as a beggar," he answered.

After this, when he experienced such difficulty in reaching that honorable and mighty clergyman, and found no one there disposed to be kind—with the exception of a student called William Scoltock[484] and a shopkeeper from whom the Fāriyāq bought a piece of rope to tie his trunk but who refused to take payment for it, imagining, seemingly, that the Fāriyāq had only wanted to purchase it after consulting God by divination as to whether he shouldn't use it to hang himself—he returned to London and opened negotiations on the matter with his wife. She told him that the island was less likely to provide a living than Oxford and that "I have become utterly bored with it. We wasted the flower of our youth there and acquired not a single fruit. What then is the point of going back?" At this, he decided to resign from his government position there and wrote a letter to the governor's private secretary informing him of this. 4.16.3

Then the Fāriyāqiyyah's palpitations grew worse and he decided that it would be better for them to live in Paris, because of the popular idea that the air of Paris was healthier than that of London, that living there was cheaper and opportunities were more abundant, that the Parisians were more welcoming to the stranger than the English and more charitable, that the Arabic language was more useful there and more widely known, and other delusions of the kind that sometimes enter people's heads never again to leave them until the soul does so too. Before, however, the Fāriyāq departs that city, we must repeat to you, in compressed form, a description of the good qualities that it contains and of the injustice meted out to its inhabitants—which is to say its *fair* inhabitants—so that you may 4.16.4

decide whether the Fāriyāq's departure was right or wrong. Let this be too your farewell to the English, for the book is drawing to a close and there is no space left for expatiation since I'm afraid that this last book may come out longer than the first and that that would require my censure, from two perspectives. One is that its readers might say that the author had made the chapters at the beginning short and now was making them long, as though at first he'd been unschooled in writing or he now wanted the saying "mature horses run ever longer heats" to be applied to him.[485] The second is that they might say, "He's come close to joining the ranks of those who drive away their listeners by the length of their readings but remains oblivious and unaware, and we've grown bored with his words and his saying again and again 'this is claimed and so is that' and 'once it was and now it is not.' He has taken the reins of debate between his teeth, argued both sides of the issue, and left us no room to review his arguments or object. The reward for a writer who's a *chatterbox* is to have his book cast into the *tinderbox*."

4.16.5 Said the Fāriyāq, "Picture in your mind that you are living in one of London's residential quarters, with two rows of houses, parallel, face-to-face, façade to façade, twenty houses to a row, a door to each house, a lintel to each door, and in front of each lintel a step or tiled threshold. Then conjure up before your eye, God guide you right, forty girls, each of them smart and perky-breasted, fat and virginal, corpulent and compliant, big-buttocked and buxom with a twitch to her backside and bustle, with saliva sweet and teeth that glisten, clearness of brow, length of back, and evenness of cheek and possessed of loveliness, wit, and fun, plumpness and facial chubbiness, good looks and tubbiness, freshness and beauty, pulchritude and handsomeness, goodliness and comfiness, tenderness of skin and attractiveness, succulence and juiciness, pretty length of face and dewiness, well-roundedness and willowiness, each of them being white and comely, bright-complexioned, beaming, blonde, strawberry blonde, near-strawberry blonde, chestnut, ash-blonde, dirty blonde, dusky blonde, or dusky chestnut blonde, of a healthy whiteness and white prettiness, the white and the black of her eyes clearly defined and as large as oryxes', her pupils blue but as though mixed with red, her whites suffused with black, or her pupils blue but as though streaked with red, or wide and black, swan-necked,[486] her eye sockets wide, her eyes widely spaced, her eyebrows delicate, broad and uncreased of brow, mighty-bodied, fine-bridged, snub-nosed, high-bridged, beautifully black-lipped, or with lips between black and red, or brown-lipped, and each of whom is

ruʿbūba,	"tall and languid, or white, comely, soft, and sweet, or smooth"; this word should have been included in the table in Volume Two but I thought that the scrubbers[487] deserved it more, because its meaning is made real in them	4.16.6
labbah,	"refined"	
with a face that is *muṣfaḥ,*	"even and comely"	
buhṣulah,	"of extreme whiteness"	
rabilah,	"mightily fleshed; *rablah,* also pronounced *rabalah,* is any thick piece of meat . . . and *rabālah* is copiousness of flesh"	
ribaḥlah,	"large, well-formed, and tall"	
raybal,	"smooth and fleshy"	
and has hair that is *rajil,*	"between straightness and curliness"	
[and each of whom is] *rafilah,*	meaning "she drags her train behind her in a comely fashion"	
zawlah,	"light, witty, and intelligent"	
and has an eye that is *sablāʾ,*	"long-lashed"	
and a voice that is *kharīd,*	"soft, with a trace of shyness"	
[and each of whom is] *sibaḥl,*	"large; synonym *sabaḥlal*"	4.16.7
isḥilāniyyah,	"a beautiful, tall, splendid woman"	
ṭaflah,	"soft and smooth"	
ʿablah ʿathilah,	"large and stately"	

ʿayṭal,	"long-necked and with comeliness of body"
ʿuṭbūl,	"a beautiful young woman, full-figured and with a long neck"
ʿayṭabūl,	"tall"
ʿamaythalah,	"slow, because of her largeness and the wobbliness of her flesh, and a woman who drapes her clothes coquettishly"
mukattalah,	"rounded and compact"
hayḍalah,	"huge and tall"
4.16.8 *haykalah,*	"large"
hūlah,	"a woman who stuns with her beauty"
ʿayhal,	"tall; synonyms *ʿayṭabūl, ghilfāq, ʿanshaṭah, ghanaṭnaṭah, ʿalhabah, salhabah*"
ʿandalah,	"huge-breasted and also tall"
ʿarṭawīlah,	"comely in her youth and of figure"
ʿarandalah,	"tall, firm, and strong"
majdūlah,	"slender-boned and compactly built"
khathlah,	"huge-bellied"
hirkīl,	"comely of body, form, and gait; synonym *hirkawlah*"
maʾmūrah,	"comely and compactly formed"
4.16.9 *jarīmah,*	"large-bodied; synonym *jasīmah*"
jammāʾ al-ʿiẓām,	"abundantly fleshed"
ḥamāmah,	"beautiful"
darmāʾ,	"whose elbows and wrists cannot be seen" (because they are covered by flesh)
ruʿmūm,	"smooth"
salimah,	"smooth-limbed"
shughmūm,	"tall and pretty; synonym *shughmūmah*"
ḍikhammah,	"wide, pleasant-looking, smooth"

muṭahhamah,	"fat, outstandingly beautiful, with a round, compact face"
fa'mah,	"a woman whose figure has ripened and whose legs have thickened"
qasīmah,	"beautiful; synonym *wasīmah*" 4.16.10
kathamah,	"plump as a result of drinking or other cause"
mukalthamah,	"having the flesh of the cheeks firm but not coarse and ugly"
kamkāmah,	"short and of compact physique"
wathīmah,	"bulging with flesh"
mūshim,	"with budding breasts"
haḍīm,	"*haḍam* is concavity of the belly and delicacy of the haunch"
bathnah,	"a plump young beauty"
bakhdan,	"smooth"
bādin,	[stout] "too well-known to require definition; synonym *bādinah*"
bahnānah,	"having sweet breath and smell, or tractable in her work and her speaking and full of laughter and good company"
bahkanah,	"a succulent young woman . . . and one says of a big-buttocked woman *tabahkanat fī mishyatihā* ('she walked with a swaying gait')" 4.16.11
juhānah,	"young (of a woman)"
ḥabnā',	"huge-bellied"
possessed of hair that is *ḥajin*,	"flowing and loose"
khalīf,	"a woman who wears her hair loose down her back"
rāqinah,	"attractively colored"
with a face that is *masnūnah*,	"comely and even, or with length to her face and nose"

	mashdūnah,	"a barely pubescent girl"
	possessed of *ʿasan,*	"[possessed of] height, with attractiveness of the hair"
4.16.12	*ʿaknāʾ,*	"one whose belly has developed folds of flesh"
	ghaysānah,	"smooth"
	faynānah,	"having abundant hair"
	qatīn,	"beautiful"
	with feet that are *mulassanah,*	"feet and soles that are *mulassanah* are those that have length and delicacy and are shaped like a tongue [*lisān*]"
	wahnānah,	"languorous on rising"
	barahrahah,	"a smooth, white young woman, or one who quivers with softness and smoothness and with glowing good health"
	possessed of *rahrahah,*	"*rahrahah* is the attractive glow of the complexion and the like, and when you say 'his body'" (though it would be better to say "her body") "*tarahraha,* it means 'it grew white with ease' and *rahrāh* and *ruhrūh* and *rahrah,* said of the body, mean 'white and smooth'"
	fārihah,	"a young, pretty girl"
	wadhāʾ,	"a woman of comely coloring, toward the white"
	muwahwahah,	"one who quivers with fullness of flesh"
	sajwāʾ of glance,	"calm, i.e., tranquil, of glance"
	ʿābiyah,	"comely," from "*ʿabā, yaʿbū,* meaning 'his face beamed with light'"
	and comely of *ʿuryah,*	i.e., "the exposed and naked parts that may be seen, such as the face, the hands, and the feet"

"and each of whom has taken in her delicate hands a scrubbing brush, a cake of soap, and a bucket of hot water and gone down on her rounded knees and set about scrubbing the threshold and doorstep of the house, all the while vibrating,[488] shaking, quivering, quaking, shimmering, quavering, shuddering, shivering, shimmying, wobbling, bobbling, jouncing, bouncing, fluttering, flickering, turning, twisting, jerking, twitching, trembling, jiggling, swinging, swaying, tossing, tumbling, jolting, and scudding, the sight of this perhaps coinciding with the hearing of musical instruments being played in the streets, producing oh what a lovely sight and sound!

"But, O rich men and burghers of London, have you not at your disposal any means to contemplate these humps and bumps without demeaning the dignity of respectable good looks? Do you believe it right that beauty's decency be violated and the hands and knees of these fair ladies blistered to make your doorsteps smooth? How is it that your neighbors the French don't do the same but force their servants only to clean the stairs of the house on the inside? There, the servants put something like pattens or sandals on their feet and scrub what they can, and what they can't they leave to the next time, or the one after that. Nor do we charge our women with acquiring this meaningless skill: we just entrust to them things involving board and bed, meaning eating and sleeping arrangements. Yet despite this, you pretend that you respect women and know their value better than us! What a monstrous thing to say![489] And when it comes to sending them out into the dark nights to roam the alleys and streets and dispatching them to distant lands unaccompanied, it wouldn't be considered among us as showing any kind of respect for them. On the contrary, it would more likely be considered panderation,[490] wittolism, whoremongery, pimpism, poncification, hornism, and cuckolderation. 4.16.13

"I wish I knew how a maidservant's heart feels when her mistress orders her each day to 'Scrub the threshold!' or when her colleague asks her, 'Did you scrub your mistress's threshold today?' For sure, did the word 'threshold' occur among you in the sense of 'woman,' as it does in this noble language of ours,[491] her imagination would likely have raced to that conclusion as soon as she was asked. Your 4.16.14

language, though, is stiff and hard and cannot accommodate interpretation or extrapolation. I can see no reason for this outrageous custom other than (though God alone knows the truth) that one of your great men acquired a white, comely, soft, and sweet maidservant some three hundred and fifty years ago, and his wife was ugly, and, the mistress being jealous of the girl, she told her to scrub the threshold and the doorstep every day to make her look abject in the eyes of her master—as though the heart doesn't fall as easily for a pretty but pitiable girl as it does for one in easy circumstances, or as though the thing that quivers has to have a bustle, or the thing that is rounded a cotton wrapper, or the full plump arm a silk-wool padding, or a fine fat leg a stocking of silk. This vile custom then remained something natural to all your great men up to this day of ours, the day of civilization and kindness to women. You are slaves to customs and tradition. Once you've become used to a certain way of doing things, you are incapable of abandoning it. By way of example, you make your young male servants sprinkle white ashes on their heads[492] till they look like old men on top and your old women expose their chests and arms at dinner parties, though to do so is ill-fitted to times of revelry and good cheer and the sight of their naked chests puts everyone off their food. The complicity of people in the imposition of bad customs thought up by princes and notables is not something special to you. On the contrary, it's widespread among all the other nations of the Franks as well.

CHAPTER 17

A DESCRIPTION OF PARIS

4.17.1 The Fāriyāq arrived in that celebrated city on a foggy night and was too bleary-eyed to be able to see its distinguishing features. Then, in the morning, he set off to roam its streets as though he were unemployed and had all the time in the world. He found them to be full of slipways[493] and slides, snares, decoys and baits,(1) traps, lures, ropes, nooses, lassos, nets, hooks, and hunters' hides. It occurred to him then that the mainstay, working gear, support, and central pole of everything in this capital was the presence of a woman. All the eating houses, drinking houses, shops, warehouses, marts, groceries, godowns, depots, countinghouses, butcheries, showrooms, storehouses, workshops, factories, hostels, hotels, boutiques, corner stores, bathhouses, dosshouses, brasseries, bars, magazines, granaries, restaurants, and watering holes were run by women—and what women!—and there wasn't a stub, a daybook, a tax-book, a list of accounts due, or any calculation involving multiplication (*burjān*)(2), any

(1) A *rāmij* ["decoy"] is "an owl used to lure predatory birds" and a *rāmiq* ["bait"] is the same.

(2) The *Qāmūs* gives the following definition of *burjān*: "calculation by *burjān* is when you say, 'How much does such and such times such and such make (*mā judhā'u kadhā fī kadhā*) and what is the square root of such and such times such and such (*mā jidhru kadhā fī kadhā*)?' In other words, the *judhā'* is the product, the *jidhr* is the square root by which two things are multiplied with one another, and the whole thing is called *burjān* [i.e., 'multiplication']." However, under the letter *yā'*[496] he speaks only of *judā'*, with *dāl*, providing the following definition: "*judā'*, of the pattern of *ghurāb*: the amount produced by multiplication, e.g., the *judā'* of three times three is nine"; likewise, he fails to mention the use of *al-ḍarb* in this sense [i.e., in the sense of "multiplication"] in the entry for *ḍ-r-b*.

jottings sheet, invoice, certificate, product, entry book, accounts ledger, record of charges, deed, abstract, liquid account,[494] or precautionary blank-filling[495] that wasn't handled by a woman. He noted too that the clever man among them placed in his store or workplace a pretty decoy that he could wave at the shoppers and those passing on the street. It made no difference whether the said decoy was a member of his family or a stranger; all that mattered was to slip the noose around their necks.

4.17.2 Furthermore, the women of Paris are distinguished by characteristics shared by no other women among the Franks. For example, they speak with such nasality[497] and huskiness, such a catch in the throat, so thrillingly, so tunefully, with such vibrato and tremolo, such resonance, such bravura, such lyricism, such intonation, inflection, and modulation, such melodiousness, such tunefulness, such musicality, such mellifluousness, such sweetness, such a lilt and a swing, so excitingly and so movingly that the listener is intoxicated and loses all awareness of whether they are undoing his buttons or his vertebrae. Another aspect of their appeal is that they change their costumes every little while and all the other women imitate them in this. Thus should one of them don, for example, a cloak, or wear her clothes skintight, everyone straightaway cleaves to a love of cloaks, while skintight dressing becomes a custom. From them too is taken the curling of the hair,[498] its braiding, plaiting, coiling, cutting, gathering, loosening, parting, combing, currying, twisting, tousling, and rumpling, as well as the grooming of the *kuʿkubbah* and the *muqaddimah*.[499] Another thing is that, from their long frequentation of places where people dance, they think that everywhere they set their feet is a dance hall, and you may observe one of these women walking in the markets and streets swaying and bending, loose-limbed and leggy, and how I wish Our Master, the author of the *Qāmūs*, had known the *polka, mazurka, schottische, quadrille, rigadoon,*[500] *valse*, and other kinds of dance that I might relay the words for them here, to the credit of the walking women of Paris!

A further aspect of their appeal is the sway they hold over the men and the power they have over them in every situation. You'll find the man walking next to the woman in abject submission[501] and when he's alone with her at home, she it is who forbids and *commands*, reigns and *remands*, while he is servile, bowed, *licked*, reined in, *whipped*, checked, humbled, *ill-used*, cringing, domesticated, ill-treated, *abused*. They, on the other hand, never cease to crave special foods even when not pregnant and to demand that everything be in full measure, in full supply, shaken down and running over, abundant, *complete*, full, perfect, *replete*. Even the French language is built upon these female cravings, for in speaking they drop the ends of all the masculine words and pronounce them in the feminine[502]—on which topic the Fāriyāq said, 4.17.3

Among the French, the feminine ending
To listening ears must be conveyed.
This points to their women's desire, by nature,
To make it to the end and obtain satisfaction when getting laid.
Or perhaps it's a sign of their complete consummation
(If, among veil-wearers, claim to any such thing may be made).

Some impotent grammarian of theirs, seemingly annoyed by this, made it a rule of their language that the masculine should take precedence over the feminine.[503] It didn't do him much good, though: a single woman here can take on and get the better of twenty men.

Another thing about them is that an epitome of their beauty is written on their foreheads, in verse and in prose. An example of the verse: 4.17.4

A king of beauty is mightier than any king
Of army, ministers, and lofty throne.
Soldiers follow the ruler at his command
But men follow beauty on their own.

and

Who fights the black-of-pupil, white-of-eye by his weapons must
be betrayed
And the whetting of his sword will avail him naught for all his
pluck,
For the eye is a weapon sharpened on his liver
While the sword's merely sharpened on a rock.

An example of the prose:

That nasal *twang* makes of the impotent a *man*. Strong mammary *development* is the most effective form of *blandishment*. The well-fleshed *thigh* brightens the *eye*. Largeness of *leg* makes a man open his throat and *beg*. Small *feet* make your food *sweet*. How many a one in the market has fallen to the *ground* on catching sight of a calf that was *round*! A display of the *chest* brings, after trouble, *rest*. Nothing's more lovable or pleasant to the *eye* than a little miss, pretty as *pie*. Plump girls encourage *infatuation*; whiteness with a rosy flush can be a cause of *dissension*. There's no *regret* that a wagging behind won't make you *forget*. There's no gloomy *thought* that a buttock-rolling walk can't *thwart*. Nothing's as likely as an attractive *gait* to induce abject love and *humiliate*. *Winking* of *eyes* points the way to *linking* of *thighs*. The bustle-pins of *summer* are sharper than any *saber*. No *flight* after a smile *bright*. After exposure of the *wrist*, none can *resist*. A burst of scent! There's nothing more attractive to the *desirer*. Many a smile has won an *admirer*. The eye spins *webs*, the figure spins *threads*. Good looks make a *splash*, gold coins are *cash*. A golden *guinea* unties many a *pinny*. He who gives presents *galore* wins what he's hoping *for*. Sex is for those endowed with worldly goods and the world is for sex. To know her, *taste her*, the rest's *conjecture*. To the play, to the *play*, there to make your move without *delay*! Pour her a second drink from the *flask*, then for whate'er you desire *ask*.

In sum, the difference between the epitome of the beauty of Frenchwomen and that of Englishwomen is that the first belongs to the class of things that cure using opposites and the second to the class of things that cure using things of the same sort. Thus the first epitome speaks of languorousness,[504] lassitude, lethargy, lounging, lolling, lissomenesss, litheness, indolence, inanimation, drooping, draping, pliancy, pliability, and flexibility, and calls out to their opposites such as stiffness, solidity, turgidity, rigidity, hardness, firmness, unbendingness, unyieldingness, tautness, and tensile strength, while the beauty of the others is an epitome of the same qualities that calls out to their likes. Both in a woman are attractive.

4.17.5 Another thing about them is that they regard imitation in love and dress as shameful. Each of them works hard at her art, so as to become a model for others. As far as dress is concerned, some pad out their busts as much as Englishwomen do their backsides and some make two domes, one in front and one in back, so that when she walks she impedes the progress of both those approaching her from behind and those approaching her from in front. Exposure of the calf to make a show of the fleshiness of the leg and the cleanliness of the stockings are usual among them. As far as love is concerned, some add to the quality of the all-devouring vagina that other quality mentioned by Abū Nuwās in his poem rhyming in the glottal stop.[505] Some prefer to take the head of the man's penis into their mouths or to have their clitorises sucked. Those most avid to oblige them regarding the latter are the old experienced men, and telling these "Go get sucked!" or "Go cunnilinger!" is no insult.[506] Some of them offer a combination of the pleasures of the vagina and the anus, each having its price. Some add to this working the little fellow up and down, as requested by Shaykh Jamāl al-Dīn ibn Nubātah, and this has three prices. Some further add to this working it up and down with the hollows of the feet, making four charges. Some are capable of servicing two men at the same time and inserting themselves between them naked. Some add this to the two abovementioned pleasures *plus* working it up and down with the fingertips *and* the soles of the feet, and this is the most expensive of all. Some of them will act like stud bull camels and mount another woman like them, necks astretch, but this type is in short supply and only to be seen by the well-off. Some of them practice the craft of the shield bearer and bang shield on shield. One of the strangest things is that some old Frenchmen, the decrepitude of whose bodies and the feebleness of whose physical motion have inflamed their thoughts and imaginations, favor over all the aforesaid activities the slurping down of feces; one such will lie down, naked, and call for a woman to sit down on top of him and fill his mouth. Others substitute for this the drinking of the copious stream from its point of emergence, gush after gush, or sucking on the clitoris. Sometimes men meet up with a woman and make her stand in front of them naked; two of them then sit down, one in front of her and the other behind, and another starts pouring wine over her chest and back. The two men set to it, opening their mouths wide and drinking the wine as it passes over the two holes. Lustful rich women use men to bring them any men who look to them well-endowed, especially those from the countryside. These go to them in certain houses, where the women's faces are veiled so that they cannot be known, and the women pay them for that purpose. In general, any kind of depravity that might occur to the mind of the most learned scholar may be seen in Paris in the barest detail and by the naked eye.

4.17.6 You must know that the people of Paris have adopted certain conventions regarding matters of daily life and women that distinguish them from all others. Where daily living is concerned, those that eat in the restaurants that are everywhere agree with the master—or, to be more accurate, the mistress—of the establishment to pay her a set amount each month and eat there a set meal, and she gives such a one tickets that display the number of times and he pays her the price for them, then returns the tickets to her, handing over a ticket for each lunch or dinner. This saves him a quarter of the cost. The same thing applies to baths, theaters, and other places of that sort. Where women are concerned, given that the men who buy and sell have taken good-looking women to manage their affairs, as explained above, the latter, on leaving in the evening after finishing their work, are watched out for by men, who invite them to places where they can eat, have coffee, dance, or play. Each then goes with whomever she likes. When the man has accompanied her to one of these places, he knows that his possession of her is only a matter of time. He will either have his fill of her that very night or make an arrangement with her to repeat the contact twice or three times every week, for example, or to give her a set amount at the end of the month. Any remaining hours she then rents out to others for a certain fee. You'll find that one of them has a number of lovers that she makes love to at different times of the day and night. This does not prevent such women from being addressed as *demoiselle*, which is a word applied to virgins as a sign of respect and means an unmarried lady. Some men spend their time getting to know these girls via the dance halls. The man goes up to a girl and invites her to dance. If he likes her, and she likes him, he invites her to take a drink in a private part of the dance hall and contracts with her for a monthly visit. A man who makes a monthly arrangement with one of them will pay less than half for her what he would if he settled with her separately each time. Women in Paris are permitted to enter any public dance hall without paying a thing, as a way of attracting, by their large numbers, the men. They must, however, dance with them if they ask them to do so, unless they refuse them with an acceptable excuse, such as if the invitee were to say, for instance, "Someone else invited me before you, so I have to dance with him" and so on. Nor is there any objection to a man who has rented a room, furnished or unfurnished, in a house having his mistress visit him in his residence—be she one of the kind to which we have alluded, meaning one of those women whose status is somewhere between that of a respectable woman and a prostitute, or of any other kind—and spend the night with him with the knowledge of the neighbors and residents. Such a man, in the eyes of the people of Paris, has the same status as if he were married, and there is no difference in the eyes of the people of Paris between a married woman who has seven sons and seven daughters whom she raises to fear God and obey the king and some little whore who sells her virtue to every passerby and who spreads her legs to any "that passeth by" on the road, as the Old Testament has it.[507]

4.17.7 There are many other occasions for corruption inside the houses. As all businesses in Paris are run by women and among these women are washerwomen and their female employees who take the inhabitants' clothes, and seamstresses, cleaners, and sales girls for food, drink, and clothing, a man may take one of these as his mistress and she may come to him, daily if he wants, on the excuse that she's going to do some work for him or sell him something—or nightly or monthly or hourly or every now and then; this is prohibited in London. Indeed, sometimes a man will take as his mistress a woman from the same house that he's living in, for the houses in this flourishing city, given that they consist of a number of stories and the smallest of them holds at least twenty souls, men and women, allow a man to keep company with his neighbors. In fact, the married men living in these houses cannot ensure the safety of their wives and daughters because if a man leaves his apartment and his neighbor takes his place there with his wife a hundred times a day, the man will have no way of knowing given that the two residences are so close to one another. This is why the people of Paris are the least jealous of their womenfolk of any people in the world: they were raised to it and they have no alternative.

4.17.8 They cannot raise their children at home with them for fear the neighbors will find them annoying, so they send them to the countryside the first week after they are born and there they are raised in the laps of wet nurses, which is a praiseworthy custom from the perspective that the children grow strong there on the good air. There is another reason, which is that the woman who has a child loses more, in terms of what she would make from her trade, through the raising and upbringing of her child than she would pay to the wet nurse, for the women of Paris personally direct all the trades there and see no shame whatsoever in making money. Buying and selling, they ask for more than the men, and the good-looking ones add something as the price of gazing on their beauty. These people consider the regulation of relationships between men and women in the fashion we have described to be important, well-established, and normal, meaning that there isn't a single house in which liaisons between the men and the women do not occur, the respectability of both the visitor and the visited being maintained, the appointed time being strictly observed so that the person visited is not inconvenienced in his work and any annoyance or disturbance to the neighbors' peace and quiet is avoided.

In Paris you hardly ever see a poor woman or a prostitute wan- 4.17.9
dering around drunk at night as you do in London; it's rare to find a woman out late at night and seldom does one of them do harm to a man who visits or solicits her. And there is another difference between the women of the French and of the English, from the moral rather than the physical perspective. Generally, Englishwomen appear proud, disdainful, and self-important while Frenchwomen appear easygoing and cheerful. On the other hand, Englishwomen do not play the coquette with their men and do not put them to the expense of presents, trinkets, dinner parties, theaters, parks, and outings; a serving of grilled meat and a swig of beer are enough to make them happy. Nor do they have the same avarice and *underhandedness*, wheedling ways and *pryingness*, cunning, deceit, and *deviousness* as the women of Paris; an Englishwoman will either fall in love with a person and be happy with him through thick and thin or cut off relations with him. A Parisienne, though, no matter what show she may put on of being pliable, of voice *melodious*, kindly, and with your inclinations *harmonious*, will, if you keep company with her and she senses that you've become ensnared by her love and caught by the *neck*, take liberties and act the *coquette*, be devious and play hard to *get*. She'll give you to think that just by talking to you she's doing you a *favor*, that keeping her happy and submitting

to her wishes is required *behavior*, that so many are dying for her love and in condition *dire*, wandering like lost souls and about to *expire*, that you end up believing that all your many gifts and presents are of little worth, at which point she accepts what she accepts and "thou art among those thankful to her."[508] If you invite her to *dine*, you must tempt her palate with the finest food and give her to drink of your vintage *wine*, while she deigns to devour what she may and quaff what she will, pretending the while to have no appetite and wrinkling her *nose*, making a show of refusing and striking a *pose*. When she laughs, she thinks no other has a laugh of her *ilk*, and when she walks, thinks she should be treading on brocade or *silk*.

4.17.10 This disdainfulness is a characteristic even of married women, for a married woman in Paris will make her husband pay for her outfits alone what an English husband spends on his entire family. Thus all the effort, concern, and worry of a man in Paris go toward keeping his wife happy, but how unlikely it is that she will be so! How excellent the words of the poet on this matter when he says

A wife's ne'er happy unless by those she loves
  Surrounded; if not, expect feathers to fly!
Yet how can a man agree to protect his dependents
  With both hanger and horn?[509] Good people, do edify!

and

A man's inner state will go all to pot
  If a wife of his as Umm Khārijah's[510] viewed,
And he'll lose all sense of proportion if one day told,
  "She's in so-and-so's house, being screwed."

This is why the proverb current among the French has it that "Paris is heaven for women, purgatory for men, and hell for horses."[511] Relations between men and women being as they are, three quarters of the inhabitants of Paris are fornicators, half the remaining quarter are legally married, and the rest are celibates; I was told this by someone whose word is to be trusted. It's also the case that the

English prostitute knows she is not a respectable woman and she knows everyone else knows it, so they don't bother to respect her and she doesn't demand that they glorify her. The French harlot, on the other hand, thinks that the mere fact that she sells sex qualifies her to be honored and *adulated*, made much of and *appreciated*, because they can't do without her and they make a profit from her.

I have already noted that the French make no distinction between the respectable woman and the harlot and all that remains to be said is that no people are more lascivious then they in their desire for intercourse or more lickerish in their desire for fornication. It is enough to mention that, during the great schism that arose in 1793, they put a naked woman on the altar of a church and bowed down to her. Only imagine, then, dear reader, how the men and women of this city are during the long, cold nights of winter, and how many a place of entertainment and resort becomes packed with them, how many a table is set for them with food and drink, how many a bed shakes, how many a couch creaks, how many a flank is pressed to flank, how many a milk skin gushes, how many a bowstring buzzes! The Fāriyāq recited to me the following description of Paris, of his own composition, and licensed me to transmit it: 4.17.11

The pleasures of Paris, I swear, are as those of Paradise—
  Yes indeedy!—and it holds as many houris too.
Here, though, they're forever being touched,[512]
  And there are forty consorts for each man to woo.

On dancers he said

How fine the sight of them dancing for us
  To the notes of the lute where e'er the cup's displayed!
Should their feet e'er happen to tread upon me,
  Of time's misadventures I'll ne'er feel the weight.

And on a decoy, he said

This Parisienne has a face
  Like the morn—I'm smitten with her, I am.

I'd like to greet her of an evening
And tell her, "Bonjour, madame!"

4.17.12 And another time he said, "And just as the pitiful stranger's chest is relieved of everything that crushes it and his eyes brighten at the sight of all those women scrubbing steps in London in the manner described above, so his eye finds relief at the sight of their like in Paris roaming the streets and the markets with no covering on their heads and no impediment to the sight of their haunches and adjoining parts (in which they differ from the habits of the women of London, who never go out without being well bundled up)." I am of the opinion that these two propensities—namely, to scrub doorsteps and to go out without being tightly bundled—explain why there are so few men with eye disorders in these two happy cities. Rarely does one see among their men any who are squint-eyed,[513] cross-eyed, sunken-eyed, rheumy-eyed, purblind, night-blind, bleary-eyed, sand-blind, red-eyed, or walleyed, or who suffer from astigmia, nystagmus, amblyopia, myopia, presbyopia, esotropia, hyperopia, exotropia, anoopsia, or pinguecula. Every man in our country who suffers from rheum and has the means should make for this land so that his sight may be polished back to brightness by these elegant scenes. Let him bring with him too on this emigration an eminent title (which is to say a title that proclaims his nobility and authority), for the people there think highly of such "skin flaps"[514] and believe a man without one to be of no worth. If he's embarrassed to claim one falsely or make one up, his wealth will obtain him one, because if he's rich and makes it his habit to visit places of entertainment and good cheer, he will soon become acquainted with a band of their great and fortunate men and visit them in their homes. When this happens, they will bestow on him some title of nobility so as to honor him and be themselves honored by him, for no one who is not noble like them can ever visit them. Women, and especially Englishwomen, have an interest in such skin flaps that is too extensive to document in this book.

Chapter 18

A Complaint and Complaints[515]

The Fāriyāq then decided to rent an apartment to live in with his family and they saw a number of places, each of which had its drawbacks. During this process the Fāriyāqiyyah got sore feet from climbing staircases, some of which comprised a hundred and twenty steps or more. In the end, they moved into a place but found that the stove didn't work properly and it was only a few days before she began complaining, saying, "It surprises me how sometimes people are deceived about something and extol it without first making sure they know what condition it's in, and once they've made up their minds about something, it becomes impossible to get them to abandon their delusion. It reaches the point that to change a delusion is more difficult than to change what is known to be true, for when someone knows something to be true he does so because he has determined its truth through scholarship, and scholars by nature always look at the evidence and the counterevidence and never stop searching for what is correct and what is more correct. Delusion, however, enters only the head of the ignoramus, and after it has entered it's almost impossible for it to exit. 4.18.1

"We may cite by way of example the popular delusion that Paris is the most beautiful city in the world, though I've observed here faults I have seen nowhere else. Look at its roads and the blood, filth, and waters of varied colors that flow along them, part green 4.18.2

like pond scum, part yellow like turmeric, and part black like coal! All the unclean wastes of the kitchens and sanitary facilities gather there and the smell of them, especially in summer, is even more harmful than the sight. Have no drains or conduits been made underground for them to pass through into a river or something of the sort as in London? Look at the pavement of these same roads, where the carriages and carts have to pass, and you'll see that its stones have been shaken loose and pushed apart so that when a cart moves over them it seems to be climbing a mountain pass or a flight of steps and it keeps rocking and shaking, the reason being that the cobblestones here are not laid in rows or set snugly next to each other and they grow further apart and looser as the years go by. In London, on the other hand, they're laid flush with one another and upright and the carts move over them quickly without rattling or shaking. Look too at the pathways alongside the roads here, meaning where people walk: how narrow and dirty they are, and what little purpose they serve! In many of the side streets, it's impossible for two to walk side by side along one edge of the street; indeed, they're not to be found at all in many roads or do not go the whole way from the beginning to the end, for you'll find they're obstructed in one place, disintegrating in another. Look at how few lights there are in the marketplaces and at how far apart are the lanterns that stick out of the walls! In most streets, one has to walk more than a hundred and twenty paces between one lantern and the next.

4.18.3 "Look at how small the shops are and how poorly lit, and at the wretchedness and hardscrabble existence of the city's inhabitants! Rarely does one of them have a fire, even though this is the coldest month. Look well at these houses and how high their stories rise and how many steps they have and how dirty and badly arranged are their sanitary facilities and latrines—for in a single house, you may find a number of latrines next to apartments along with a number of outlets for water and sewage, and you may well imagine the disgusting smells that issue from them in the morning! In addition to the fact that these latrines are dirty, squalid, and without water supply, they have no bolts on the inside to prevent anyone from bursting in on a person in his privacy. As a result, someone will often intrude upon another before he has finished his business and he will find himself joined by one whose clothes are beshitten and befouled, or whose shit falls on his heels because he's in such a hurry, or whose turd gets stuck half in and half out, or who can't get it out, or who was interrupted while pissing.(1) I asked about the reason for this and was told that if the landlord was a God-fearing man, he'd be uneasy at the thought of installing bolts lest certain of the male and female residents go in together and barricade themselves inside. Nothing filthier is to be seen than the various finger marks on their walls, as though the French liked to wipe their anuses with their fingers. When they clean these latrines at night, they give off a horrible smell that spreads throughout the quarter, and a person has no choice but to sleep with his nostrils plugged.

(1) "A *bidgh* is 'someone who defecates on his clothes,' synonym *amdar*; to say of a man that he *maṣaʿa* his ordure on his heels means that 'he did so before he could stop himself, by reason of fright or haste'; to say that he *jazama* his ordure means 'he got some of it out and some of it stayed where it was'; to say that he *raṭama* his ordure means 'he retained it'; *azramahu* means 'he interrupted him while he was urinating.'

"In addition, many of these houses—despite the fact that they comprise six or more stories (which, along with the poor paving of streets, produces an undeniably excessive rumbling because of the passing of the carts) and despite the fact that they hold numerous residents (some of whom are lechers, male and female, others doting lovers, male and female)—are unfit for habitation because of their lack of light and air, and it's difficult to find an apartment in them in which one can relax, for one finds either that it's close to the latrine, or that the stove doesn't work properly, or that it has a mouse or a rat, or that one's neighbor is noisy and rude, singing day and night or playing a musical instrument or closeting himself with prostitutes with hurly-burly, loud laughter, and hilarity. Inside the apartment itself, there are things to make you laugh and things to make you cry. The crudeness with which the doors and windows are made, the paving of the floor with brick, and the way that some **4.18.4** of the apartments interconnect with others will make you laugh. Those stoves of theirs that are built in the shape of tombs, the first thing to strike a person when he enters his apartment, will make you cry. As they are, they're better suited to be cells for hermits than sleeping quarters for married couples. Stranger still is the fact that the doors to the buildings are always open and that the doorkeepers carry on trades and crafts in a closet of their own which they stick to, night and day. Some work as tailors and some make or mend shoes and other things, which means that anyone can go up the stairs with nothing to stop him. Rarely does the doorkeeper take note of anyone from his closet because his eyes are glued to his needle or his awl. This is why there are more incitements to sin in Paris than in London. The only fine houses and wide, handsome streets are of recent date. How can Paris have had any fame in the past when its historic houses and age-old streets repel the eye and made the gorge rise? How can this be compared to the broad, well-lit streets of London and its attractive, spacious shops, glazed with the finest and most expensive glass, or its clean, well-proportioned houses?"

4.18.5 Said the Fāriyāq: "I told her, 'Or its scrubbers of doorsteps' to which she replied, 'Or the pleasuring of its scrubbers.' Then she continued, 'Or their elegant apartments or their attractive staircases, ever draped with fine carpets. I swear to God, climbing fifty of their steps is easier on me than climbing ten here. Where too are those shiny, iron-clad, wonderful stoves of theirs that are burnished every morning and the well-glazed windows and transoms? Those kitchens where the gas light burns forever and the hot water is ready and waiting for the residents? And all those charming young maids for whom the mightiest of employers at home would want to work as a manservant or cook?' 'Or taster,' I said. 'Or licker,' she said. 'And where oh where is the beauty of the River Thames and its steamboats that go to the outskirts of London in summer and have music on board? Filled with men, women, and children, they look like meadows adorned with flowers. Where are those gardens they call “squares” of which there are so many in every part of the city and which make anyone living in a room overlooking them feel he has moved to the countryside, though should he take a few steps beyond them he would see crowds of people coming and going? Where are those lights that burn on every street and in every shop, so that if you are at the beginning of the street and you set your eyes on its far end, you wonder at its beauty and radiance and imagine that they must be an array of planets strung on a single string? Only those who haven’t seen London, or who have spent only a few days in it without knowing the language, praise Paris.

“‘And where is the kindly fussing of the landladies and the com- 4.18.6
panionship they show their lodgers, be they foreigners or not? There, if a foreigner takes up residence in a house, he joins the family because all of them, from the mistress of the house to the maid (and what shall teach thee what is “the Maid”?)[516] make a fuss of him, keep him company, serve him, cook for him, buy him what he needs from the market, bring him hot water every morning, light his fire, and polish his shoes. I swear, one who stays with them can learn the English language in no time at all by talking to them. Someone lodging in a house in Paris could die overnight and no one would be any the wiser, for there is an unbridgeable gulf between him and the doorkeeper and in most of the houses here one cannot find a bell to ring to make the doorkeeper come to him.

“‘And how can the shopkeepers of Paris, who, if they had the 4.18.7
means to strip a customer, and especially a foreigner, of his skin wouldn’t hesitate to do so, be compared to those of London, with their straight dealing, their honesty in selling and buying, and their friendliness toward and patience with their customers? They have imitated the London shopkeepers by putting price tags on the goods but what difference does it make? A shopkeeper who puts a price of, say, a hundred francs on something will sell it for eighty. They also put in the fronts of their shops types of goods bearing a certain price, but if you want to buy something of that type, they’ll bring you something of inferior quality and swear that it’s the same

as the sample and keep prattling and chattering and swearing oaths and perjuring themselves till you buy it, out of embarrassment or to avoid a quarrel. Often they even give the buyer forged coin.

4.18.8 "'The purveyors of food and drink in this city are even worse cheats and violators than the rest of its inhabitants, for they display a sleight of hand at weighing that I have seen nowhere else, meaning that someone selling you something that has to be weighed will throw it into the pan of the scales swiftly and carelessly, as though he were furious at seeing your face or at the scales, and the second the pan starts to dip will whip it off and hand it to you, and if you send him your servant or your son, he'll sell him leftovers, showing even greater fury at the scales-pan; and this is over and above their adulteration of foodstuffs and drinks and the way they change prices according to the time of day and the weather. The same sleight of hand is well-known too among those who sell goods by volume and by length.

4.18.9 "'Concerning what they say about places for promenading and having fun in Paris, such as the gardens of the Palais Royal and surroundings, I swear that no one who has seen the gardens at Cremorne, Vauxhall, or Rosherville[517] in the suburbs of London, not to mention the numerous gardens in its various quarters, will thereafter find it in him to speak of any others. True, the gardens of the Palais Royal here are attractive, despite their small size, which is due to their being in the heart of the city, while the former are at a distance from the center; but what is one to say of the heart of this city? How many reprobates, male and female, does that garden bring together each day! It is in essence a meeting place for fornicators, because women frequent it to hunt for men: the woman sits down on a bench next to a man whom she fancies but doesn't know; he will have in his hand a book that he's reading and she will have in hers a handkerchief that she's embroidering or something else of the sort; he reads a word from the book and for each word gives her a look; she likewise sews a stitch and for every stitch throws him an amorous glance, and by the time they get up, they're lovers (even if the next day each of them changes his bench and his affections).

4.18.10 "'As far as beauty is concerned, there is no comparison between that of the women of Paris and that of the women of London. In the first, a woman with lupus[518] and one who might be considered handsome only when there were no others about (*al-khafūt*)(1) would be regarded here as combining every possible beauty of body and disposition since the short supply of beauty here renders it much esteemed, for when something is in short supply, it comes to be regarded highly and people become more intent on it and their competition over it becomes more intense. The most amazing thing to me is that women of outstanding beauty in London go around in rags while in Paris ugly and misshapen women strut about in silk and cashmere. Dance halls in London open every evening and in Paris three nights a week only, and in most streets in London you can hear singing coming from pretty serving-girls, and musical instruments, night and day, without penalty or fine; in Paris, this is rarely to be found. The most one can say in praise of Paris and its claims to precedence is that it contains elegant places to drink alcohol and coffee where men and women sit inside and out, face to face and back to back. Are a few people sitting on chairs enough to make one judge in its favor or for it to have had over the ages the reputation among both elite and commons of being the most beautiful city in the world? How too can the modest decency of the young Englishmen and their good manners with women, whether indoors or on the streets, be compared to those French youths with their bold eyes who glare and stare(2) into women's faces, be they respectable ladies or prostitutes, and who when they see a woman bend over to tie her shoelace, surround her, making an annulus around her anus and a ring around her rectum, especially when they go to the *pissoirs* here and pull out their tent pegs . . .'"[519] The Fāriyāq: "I said, 'Keep on talking and say what you want, just don't stop and stare at the tent

(1) The *khafūt* is "the woman who is considered comely on her own but not among other women."

(2) The *haṣhāṣ* is one with bold eyes and *haṣhaṣahu* means "he made eyes at him."

pegs.' 'You become jealous,' she asked me, 'even when I'm only talking? I only paused out of amazement at a world built upon pegging and being pegged. For sure, were I a king or an emir, I would eat nothing that had been touched by the hands of men.'"

4.18.11 While they were thus engaged in conversation, a man knocked suddenly on the door. The Fāriyāq opened it to him, chagrined at his entering to find them talking of tent pegs. The man spoke and said, "I heard of your arrival and am come to you in the hope that I might be able to study with you some text in Arabic. In return, I'll give you fifteen francs a month." When the Fāriyāqiyyah heard this, she laughed excessively, as was her wont, and said to her husband, "Here's your first evidence of the generosity of these friends of ours over whom the world has made such a hullabaloo!" The Fāriyāq told the man, "I don't want any money from you. Just give me lessons in your language in exchange for lessons in mine." The man agreed. Some days later, one of Paris's learned men came to him and said, "I heard of your arrival, and that you're passionate about poetry. If you were to write a few verses about Paris and speak in them of its charms, it would serve as a recommendation to its people, for people here love praise and flattery, meaning that they love the outsider in their midst to butter them up with praise, just as, if they're outsiders in countries other than their own, they write in praise of the rulers of that country and gain from them respect and status." The Fāriyāq did as he advised and wrote a long poem in praise of Paris and its inhabitants that he named "the Presumptive" since for him to praise them before he got to know them was speculation; it will appear later, in Chapter 20, along with its counter-poem, "the Prescriptive," and a selection of other verses he wrote in Paris. When the learned man examined its tropes, he admired them greatly and translated them into his own language and went on to have the translation published in a newspaper, a copy of which he brought to the Fāriyāq, saying, "I have had the translation of your poem printed in this newspaper, and the Société Asiatique[520] (the adjective means 'pertaining to Asia') has promised to have the

Arabic original printed among its scientific papers, as you are the first poet to write in praise of Paris in Arabic." The Fāriyāq thanked the man and told him, "I would like a copy of the translation." The man told him, "It's sold at such and such a place for around two-thirds of a franc." So he went and bought a copy himself. A few days later, someone who had read the paper came to him and said, "I read the translation of your poem and I liked it. Would you be willing to exchange lessons with me?" "That's exactly what I want," said the Fāriyāq, and the man continued to visit him for a number of days, during which he introduced him to the well-known scholar Monsieur Quatremère,[521] and that scholar introduced him to Monsieur Caussin de Perceval,[522] the teacher of Arabic. Subsequently, he also became acquainted with the other teacher of Arabic, Monsieur Reinaud.[523] However, his acquaintance with them was like the definite article in the sentence "Go to the market and buy meat!"[524]

Then he was visited by one of those notables whose names are preceded by the article "de," which is a mark of nobility and honor. This was Monsieur de Beaufort, whose sister had a house in which she gave schooling to a number of the daughters of the leading members of society. One night, when it was time for them to be examined, she held a banquet to which she invited the Fāriyāqiyyah and her husband. The Fāriyāq said to his wife, "Here's an example for you of the generosity of these people. For a while now you've complained of being lonely and of the tightfistedness of the people I've come to know, saying, 'They never invite you, and in England everyone invited you, whether they knew you or not, to the point that it often irritated you since it meant you had to change your clothes and the hour at which you ate lunch and deprive yourself of tobacco!' So be happy now that our friends are with virtue furnished." "Indeed," she replied, "every one of them's a vaginal furnace."[525] They spent that evening at the house of the sister of the aforementioned "de" under the most felicitous *conditions* and with the most serene of *dispositions*, and the Fāriyāqiyyah went home in an altogether different mood, saying, "Beaufort was most gracious 4.18.12

and kind, and the Frenchwomen showed me a degree of friendliness and informality I would never have believed! And I liked too all that speaking through their noses and snorting that occurs so much in their speech and to which the French language must owe, in my opinion, its appeal and which is even sweeter and more captivating from the children." The Fāriyāq went on, "I said, 'It seems the ancient Arabs liked that kind of twang too, because my Master the author of the *Qāmūs* says, "*nakhima* or *tanakhkhama* means 'he expelled something from his chest or his nose'" while "*nakhama* means 'he sported, or he sang most excellently.'"' She laughed and said, 'I think your friend must have been in love with a woman who spoke through her nose, and I'm worried you may catch the same infection. I grant that nasality, or even drawling, or even a sharp tongue may be attractive in young boys and girls, but can a young man really stand a sterterous old woman snorting up his nose or a young woman a senile old man wheezing into her nostrils? And I like the way the common people in Paris don't make fun of a foreigner when they see that he's different from them in dress and manners, unlike the London rabble, who lacerate him with their words, one of them sometimes going to the trouble of calling out to him from some distance away till his voice is hoarse just so that he can tell him, "Foreigner, you're a bloody bastard!" though perhaps I'm mistaken in this.' 'On the contrary,' I said, 'you're quite right, for everyone praises the manners of the laborers and other poor people in Paris and their well-spokenness.'"

4.18.13 They went on for a while comparing the good qualities of Paris with those of London. One of the things that the Fāriyāqiyyah hated most about Paris was that the women[526] were licensed to enter houses of whatever kind,[527] and she claimed that the arrangement for houses in London was better in this respect. The Fāriyāq told her, "It cannot be denied that the houses of London are better arranged from the perspective that their stairs and their inhabitants are few and maintain peace and quiet, that their doorsteps are scrubbed every day and that their kitchens hold tasty cuts of meat, that their interiors are well-proportioned and spread with fine carpets, but they are firetraps [?].[528] The houses of Paris, on the other hand, withstand the weather better and look finer on the outside. As for prostitutes being forbidden to enter the former and permitted to enter the latter, this, in my opinion, is evidence of how well-behaved the prostitutes of Paris are, in contrast to those of London, who drink and prostitute themselves shamelessly, which is why they are forbidden to go in to visit the residents. And there is another reason too, which is that the prostitutes of Paris are known to the police stations, where their names are written down. As a result, they don't dare to behave in a depraved or shameless way, even if they are depraved. The prostitutes of London, on the other hand, are left to their own devices."

The Fāriyāqiyyah now went through a period during which she suffered from extremely painful palpitations, which would stay with her for several consecutive days before settling. While this continued, she was invited several times to the house of the "de"'s sister and she'd go with her husband, the two of them being most pleased at this generosity, the like of which they had not met with in Paris. Then the Fāriyāqiyah's sickness took a turn for the worse and she took to her bed, and he brought her two Austrian physicians who treated her for a while, until she got a little better. The "de"'s sister had married a man called Ledos, and when her brother came to visit the Fāriyāq, as he often did, and found the Fāriyāqiyyah moaning and complaining of the pain, he asked her husband, "Have you consulted my brother-in-law about medicine for your wife? He is an expert in the qualities of plants and has cured many of this disease." So the Fāriyāq went to see the man and asked him to go with him to see his wife. The man told him, "I'm not licensed by the Board to treat patients but I won't refuse to go with you, in the hope that your wife may be cured at my hands." Then he went and advised the Fāriyāqiyyah to drink the water of certain herbs, boiled, and sent her six packets of these. When these were used up and the Fāriyāq asked for more, the "de"'s sister, meaning the fake doctor's wife, **4.18.14** came and said, "My husband is charging you fifty francs for the packets." When the Fāriyāqiyyah heard this, her energy returned to her all at once and she asked her, "Aren't you ashamed to ask for such a sum for six packets of herbs when your husband isn't even a doctor?" Her husband then said to her, "But remember that she invited us to drink coffee and tea twice, and provided us, between the one and the other, with confections and cakes, so you mustn't be rude to her." After prolonged discussion and punishing struggle, the "de"'s sister agreed to take half the sum mentioned, which the Fāriyāq paid her, and she left, muttering to herself. After this her brother stopped visiting. A quack of this sort on seeing a foreigner will show him a smiling face, make a fuss of him, invite him to his house, and keep on visiting him until such time as he sees him complaining of a cough or anything of the sort, at which point he prescribes medicine for him. Then he'll charge him an excessive amount for each time they visited one another from the start of their acquaintance, bring neighbors as witnesses that the man used to frequent the man's house, and claim that his disease is chronic. The standard-bearer for this vile regiment was the quack D'Alex, who lived at 61 Berner's Street, Oxford Street, in London.

4.18.15 After this the Austrian doctor resumed his treatment of the Fāriyāqiyyah. When she was convalescing, he recommended that she leave Paris, and they decided to send her to Marseilles. At this, she said to her husband, "I would like now to leave this land in which there is no good to be found. Not one of those acquaintances of yours to whom you brought letters of recommendation from London and whom you then came to know here by virtue of your learning has invited you to sit on a chair in his house. You wrote to that Lamartine, to whom you had transmitted a letter of recommendation from Shaykh Marʿī al-Daḥdāḥ in Marseilles, asking him about something, and he never answered you, though if you were to write to the prime minister of England, he'd certainly give you an answer, whether negative or positive. And that quack, the 'de''s brother-in-law, made us pay twenty-five francs for six packets of herbs, while this Austrian doctor and his friend have treated me for a long time, have taken a lot of trouble with me, and haven't charged you a thing, which is how the doctors of London are, may God reward them well.

"Does everyone except the people of Paris treat the foreigner well and show him kindness? I used to hear that there existed somewhere in this world a tribe of people who were full of artifice,[529] insincere, double-dealing, doublehearted, two-tongued, two-faced, falsehearted, faithless, fickle, hollow-hearted, glib, inconstant, mealy-mouthed, tongue-in-cheek, capricious, hypocritical, treacherous, shifty, sneaky, and backstabbing, but I didn't know which tribe they were. Now, direct experience has taken the place of hearsay and I have discovered that these adjectives that I have listed at such length above are but a few of those that may be applied to the people of this city, for their affection is 'squashy,' meaning that like squash it grows fast and withers quickly, and their engagements are like those of 'Urqūb:[530] How often have they promised and not come *through*, raised false hopes and dashed them, sworn oaths and broken them, given undertakings and proven *untrue*! They're all 'hail-fellow-well-met' to any who's new to them but when he keeps them company they grow *bored* and when he's not among them he's *ignored*. What others settle with a 'yes' or a 'no,' they dither over for days and nights, starting with long *confabulations* and ending with gross *self-contradictions*. 4.18.16

"Their tightfistedness where everything but the dance hall's concerned is proverbial: the fires they light in winter are weaker by far than those of the glowworm (though if they were to light fires like those of the English, you'd find their weather turning darker and grayer than theirs) and in summer they don't light lamps. These are the only seasons they have, so it's either freezing cold or burning hot. Note too that a Frenchman will set the pay of anyone who works for him at the same rate in francs as the English would pay in guineas even though their country has higher prices for staples and so on than London. Did you ever see an Englishman counting 4.18.17

his pennies the way the French do their centimes? Many English don't even know how many pennies they have amongst their small change. Yes indeed—not to mention that one of them (i.e., the Parisians) will write you a letter asking you to do something for him and then not pay you for doing it.

4.18.18 "Among the things that make me laugh at their complacent self-regard is that they eat the most revolting of foods and their stomachs are always full of pig fat. Then, when they attend parties or public places, they go to great lengths to dress up and strut about looking as fine as they can. Also, that many of them close up every chink and window in the summer and never open them, to deceive people into thinking that they've gone to spend that season on some estate in the countryside as do their aristocrats, that many sustain themselves on bread and cheese by day so that they may appear in the theaters and places of entertainment by night, and that their nobility and those with a 'de' before their names eat twice a day and breakfast on shellfish, while everybody else eats three times and the English four. God forbid that all the French are like those of Paris—what a waste it would be if all the praise that has been lavished upon them were to end up like rosewater used to clean a latrine!

4.18.19 "As for the women of Paris and their reputation as examplars of good manners and sophistication, I swear that their front parts stink and they don't wipe themselves properly(1) and most of

(1) *jakhar* is "a foul smell in a woman's front parts, adjective *jakhrā*'"; *ajkhara* means "he washed his back parts and did not clean them well so they continued to stink"; *istawghala* means "he washed his armpits"; the *lijām* is "what a menstruating woman straps on, verb *talajjamat*"; *iʿtarakat* means "she stuffed herself with a piece of cloth"; *shamadhat* means "the woman stuffed her vagina with a piece of cloth lest her womb come out"; *firām* is "a medical preparation" that they use "to make themselves tighter"; the *miʿba'ah* is "the cloth used by the menstruating woman"; *firāṣ* is the plural of *firṣah*, which means "a cloth or piece of cotton with which a woman wipes off the menses" and *thaml*, plural *thamalah*, means the same, as does *rabadhah*; *khadā'il* is the plural of *khadīlah*, which is "something like the *itb* ('a kind of shift open at the sides') made of hide with which menstruating women . . . cover themselves"; *mamāḥī* is the plural of *mimḥāh*, which is "a piece of cloth with which semen and the like are removed."

them don't wash under their arms or use sanitary towels or stuff in a piece of cloth or block it with a rag or wash their bottoms or use vulva-tightening preparations or menstrual cloths or cloths or rags to wipe off the menses or remove semen or menstrual bandages. Based on what one can see of them, the only cleanliness they know is that of the blouse, the handkerchief, and the stockings. That is why you see them forever exposing their legs as they walk in the markets, summer and winter, on the excuse of raising their skirts so that any filth there may be on the ground won't touch them. Those who have good legs show off their legs and their stockings together, and those that have thin shanks show off the second. There are no women in the entire world more haughty, self-admiring, proud, cunning, arrogant, perfidious, competitive, vain, or vainglorious than they, be they ugly or pretty, tall or short (as the majority of them are), old or young, respectable or harlots, bearded and mustached or smooth-cheeked, mannish of aspect and countenance or not (though I have never seen mannish-looking women anywhere but among the women of Paris and London, albeit the latter are not proud and coquettish like Parisian women). They have been driven to this by the extreme lecherousness and lustfulness toward them of the men. You'll see an upstanding young buck walking with his arm around the waist of some hideous she-ghoul and obeying her abjectly. Men of theirs who take wives in our country target black slave girls, as a way of escaping the imperiousness and profligacy of their own women. I have seen women of the common people among them performing *laṭʿ*, which means sucking their fingers after eating, and licking off what is on them.[531] Their noblewomen wash their hands in a cup placed on the table, in the presence of their guests, and rinse their mouths out with water and then spit it into the cup. Is this to be considered a form of good manners or sophistication? Isn't their doing so more disgusting than the belching that happens among us? Only someone whose eye has accustomed itself to them over time could praise their charms or become infatuated with them.

4.18.20 "But even if we suppose, for argument's sake, that the women of Paris are sophisticated and smart, what are we to make of the women who come from the provinces, from the small towns by the river, from the villages and hamlets, from the small rural towns, the country estates, the countryside? Some of these countrywomen cover their heads with a kerchief so that all that can be seen is a few hairs at the temples, while others wear a dunce's cap made of cloth on their heads, with the result that the Parisians can scarcely restrain themselves from laughing when they see one of them, and their accents are uglier still. Many women in Paris sweep the streets and take on men's work. In Boulogne, Calais, Dieppe, Le Havre, and other port cities, you'll find women carrying travelers' baggage on their backs and heads, but there are no female porters to be found anywhere in England except those who carry for men with heavy loads.[532] Their clothes, too, are all the same. How, then, can the French claim that they are all civilized? I swear, were the women in our country to go out into the markets unveiled and show off their feet and waists and legs like the women of Paris, no one would think of mentioning the latter in the same breath when beauty and sophistication were the topic of conversation! To Cairo, to Cairo—the land of fun and *aspiration*! To Syria,[533] to Syria—where virtue and literature are exemplified in *combination*! To Tunis—the best of abodes, where dwells the most generous of the Arab *nation*![534] I have had enough of the treatment I've met with from the Franks, and feel that a day spent with them is like a year. Let me leave these countries that have sickened my body with their food and drink and the chill of their putrid airs!" The Fāriyāq told her, "If you can stand the journey, then let it be as you wish." "Death on the road," she replied, "would be better than staying on forever in the land of the ignoble!" From that moment then, she prepared herself to travel, though the next day she was so weak and in such pain that she could not move—details to follow in the coming chapter.

Chapter 19

A Metropolitan Theft and Miscellaneous Events

When the Christians of Aleppo suffered their calamity[535] and were subjected to that pillaging of their wealth and property and that rapine, their religious leaders met and took the decision to send agents on their behalf to the lands of the Franks to collect aid from the governments and churches there to assure their survival. The Greek Orthodox Church chose Khawājā Fatḥallāh Marrāsh[536] and the Greek Melkite Church chose Metropolitan Atanāsiyūs al-Tutūnjī, author of *Al-Ḥakākah fī l-rakākah* (*The Leavings Pile Concerning Lame Style*),[537] and with him another man, called Khawājā Shukrī ʿAbbūd. These then set off on a tour of the various countries, ending up in the Austrian Empire, from which they collected a significant sum. They had with them a proclamation from the metropolitans of the two aforementioned churches in Aleppo announcing that they were commissioned by the two sects to act in this matter. When they had finished with Austria, the abovementioned Khawājā Fatḥallāh Marrāsh and his colleague Khawājā Shukrī ʿAbbūd went to Paris, taking the proclamation with them, while the metropolitan stayed behind, intending to meet up with them in England. He did not go with them to France, despite his being the delegate of the Melkite church, which is in communion with the French church, because he had committed there, on a former occasion, such breaches of etiquette and oversteppings of the bounds set for such as him that 4.19.1

he had had to be imprisoned and subsequently expelled from the country. He was therefore afraid, things being as they were, that he would be exposed there this time and his bad behavior come back to haunt him. Now, when his colleagues produced their sponsors' proclamation for the Bishop of Paris and asked him for assistance, the latter was surprised to see the name of Metropolitan al-Tutūnjī mentioned therein but not to see his face, and he asked them, "How is it that the delegate of the Melkite church is not in attendance with you?" The two men made excuses for his absence that the aforementioned did not accept and, recalling what al-Tutūnjī had done before, he sent them away empty-handed.

4.19.2 Khawājā Fatḥallāh Marrāsh and his colleague had been paying visits to the Fāriyāq throughout their stay in Paris, the first, however, visiting the more frequently. The Fāriyāq gave him a warm welcome, even though he knew him to be al-Tutūnjī's colleague, because he believed him to be a man of learning and insight, not to mention that he was a married man with children and these rarely resort to cheating and skulduggery, for learning refines the mind and children soften the heart. Then the metropolitan became involved in some shady affair in some town belonging to Austria—Bologna, I think[538]—and was expelled from it at speed and in disgrace and went to England seeking further funds. On the same day, he sent to his two colleagues to join him there. A few days after they had left, the Fāriyāq received a letter from the secretary of the Committee ("committee" meaning "fraternal association"), included with which was a quire from a foreign book that the Fāriyāq had translated into Arabic and which included something displeasing to the Committee. He then realized that one of the metropolitan's two colleagues must have stolen it from his room during one of their visits at the metropolitan's behest, that when he met with him in London he had handed it over to him, and that the metropolitan had given it to the Committee in the hope that its members would inflict some injury on the Fāriyāq. The said Committee, however, being committed to a high standard of conduct, had returned the quire to the Fāriyāq, as they had no reason to keep it. The quire arrived on the same day that the Fāriyāqiyyah had determined to travel, and she became so angry and upset that she took to her bed. As for the metropolitan, he was accosted in London by certain leaders of the Roman church, who forbade him to practice the Sassanian trade.[539] Things got to such a point that his disgrace and notoriety there created difficulties for the others with those whom they were importuning on church business, for these now reckoned that anyone coming to them from the lands of the East must be a hypocrite.

The Fāriyāqiyyah recovered after a few days and insisted on traveling. Her husband therefore wrote her a letter of recommendation to the August Lord Sāmī Pasha the Grand in Constantinople. Then he sent her off, accompanied by the youngest of their children to keep her company. When the time came for them to part, they bade each other farewell and wept and expressed their emotions until, when their eyes ceased to respond with tears—a state known as "dry eye" or "dry cry" or "the unresponsive eye"—he returned home feeling lonely and downcast. She traveled to Marseilles, where her illness left her and she recovered completely, but she did not abandon her intention of going to Islāmbūl,[540] confident that their parting could lead only to their imminent reunion. When she made contact with the aforementioned lord and presented her letter of recommendation to his son, Ṣubḥī Bayk,[541] of noble lineage and line (his father being at that moment absent), he honored her lodgings with a visit and showed her every kindness—and this is another example of Eastern generosity that ought to be conveyed to the ears of the Western, Frankish, princes. While this was going on, the Fāriyāq composed a poem dedicated to the aforementioned person in which he praised him for his generosity and friendship. He also composed verses into which he poured all the loneliness he felt at being so far from her. All of these will be presented in the next chapter, which forms the conclusion to the book.[542] 4.19.3

Next he moved from that house to a room, where he made it his habit to write each day two lines of verse, which he inscribed on its 4.19.4

door. Then the Most Noble Master ʿAbd al-Qādir came to Paris, so he dedicated a poem to him too, and was honored by being invited to attend a gathering in his presence. Then his patience wore out due to loneliness, and some acquaintances persuaded him to play at those decorated pieces of paper,[543] and he joined the gambling fraternity. More than once, however, his ignorance of the game drove his partner to lose his temper with him, so he made do with just being the *ḥurḍah* (the *ḥurḍah* is "the gamblers' record keeper").[544] Then he made the acquaintance of the chief state translator, Conte Desgranges; however, he never crossed the doorstep of any of the other translators, scholars, or teachers of oriental languages because they so begrudged him a share of their milk and honey, their affection, their words, and their meetings that they refused to print his poem in praise of Paris even after they had promised to do so, and their empty promises were made of nothing but envy and bad faith.

Chapter 20

A Selection of Poems and Verses Written by the Fāriyāq in Paris as Previously Alluded To

All hail, the *Fāriyāq*! The time has come to *part*! This is the last chapter of this book of mine, into which I have put enough of your doings to bore me and the readers alike. Had I known before embarking on it that you'd task me with transmitting everything you said and did, I would never have inserted my neck into this noose or taken upon myself such a heavy load. I thought at first that the exiguousness of your body would obviate the need to put together a composition of any great size, such as this, and I swear if you were to tuck it under your arm and walk with it as many steps as it has pages, you'd toss it over your shoulder, complaining of it and of yourself as well since you're the cause of its existence. My friendship for you will not prevent me, should I examine your situation at some later time, from writing another book about you—but mind you don't go in for lots more journeys, or nightly and daily molestation of priests and women, for I have grown very weary of talking about such stuff and all I have gotten in return are trouble and toil. 4.20.1

It remains for me now to transmit, on your authority, some of your poems and verses. Before I start, however, I must say something about my own situation. This year,[545] when I was in London and malign rumors spread of war between the Sublime State and the Russian Empire, I wrote a poem in praise of Our August Lord and Honored Sultan, Sultan ʿAbd al-Majīd—may God remain forever on 4.20.2

his *side* and immortalize his glory and his *pride*!—and presented it to his honorable and ennobled ambassador, Prince Musurus, who sent it on to His Honor, the Pride of Ministers, Rashīd Pasha, may God grant his every desire. Only a few days had passed before the latter sent to the prince-ambassador to inform him that he had presented the poem to the Sultan's Presence at a propitious moment and that it had made a favorable impression, and that a Sublime Command had been issued appointing me to the Imperial Translation Bureau. This was the sweetest news that could come to my ears. I must now therefore make ready to travel and assume the honor of that post.

4.20.3 You must know, however, dear reader, that, since my concern and only desire was to see the book printed before I left for Constantinople and since my sojourn in London required the delaying of my departure (for the parts of the book that had been printed were being sent to me there to make final corrections), Khawājā Rāfā'īl Kaḥlā, who had undertaken to print the book at his expense, suggested that the printing would go faster if I went to Paris myself, and I did so. At that time there was a steamship belonging to the Sublime State in the Port of London that was supposed to set sail soon. I therefore entreated my friend Khawājā Nīnah, who had come with Khawājā Mīkhā'īl Mikhalla' to take care of some business, to let me know when the date of the ship's departure was announced and inform me of that, so that I didn't miss the chance of leaving on it. This Khawājā Nīnah had certain things that he needed and wanted from Paris, most of them related to his wife, and he had commissioned an acquaintance there to buy them. Once that person had bought them, he instructed him to give them to me and wrote me a letter in which he said that the ship was about to leave, so it would be better if I were to return to London quickly. I believed what he said and set off in a hurry for London, worried that the ship might have departed without me, and I left the proofreading I was doing to Khawājā Rāfā'īl to see to. When I reached London, I realized that my friend's advice had not been given because of any need for me to be there but in order to ensure that I would bring his things with me and so save him the usual costs and customs charges and also so that he could adorn his wife with them before they had time to go out of fashion—for the ship remained in the port for a long while to repair its engines, as the one who gave me that advice had known it would. My coming to London this second time resulted, therefore, in a further delay in the printing, since the sheets had to be sent to me to look at before they were printed, as explained above. Were it not for this, the book would have been produced quickly.

Nevertheless, I thank the Almighty that the womanish matters 4.20.4 to which He subjected the book were only such as to delay its printing and not to result in its total cancellation or abrogation, which is something I often worried about, just as the Fāriyāq worried over the misrepresentation of his life story because of similar obstacles. The case lends credence to the Fāriyāqiyyah's statement in chapter 9 of Book Four[546] to the effect that two people may be involved in a marriage, a commercial partnership, or something similar, with one of the two believing privately that he is doing his partner a favor; so whenever, my friend, you are given a piece of advice to listen to by someone, pick it apart and probe its depths to discover whether its goal is to help you specifically, or to help the one who is giving you the advice and only him, or to help the two of you equally (but don't start with this advice of mine since my sole intention in giving it to you is to help you and you alone).

And know, O Fāriyāq, that before your poems and verses are 4.20.5 honored by incorporation into this book, I must honor it and its readers too with the aforementioned poem,[547] which goes

Truth prevails and Right builds.
  Falsehood nullifies and Evil destroys.
Injustice comes to an ugly end, its perpetrator
  To every ruinous iniquity being ever exposed.
The knave's discontent springs from those same blessings with which
  The noble freeborn man's enriched and for which he offers
    thanks.

The Russian tyrants went too far when their large numbers made
them feel hubris and they acted haughtily.
They laid plots, but their scheming has come back to cut their own
throats
For their necks will be slit by sharp swords.
The aggressors, whom no reason can restrain,
The oppressors, the wrongdoers, the debauched,
Violated the agreements (and so was ever their way)
Out of bad faith, and nursed a baseless grudge,
To the point that their leader deemed that violation of rights
Should be counted a glorious deed, but they do wrong who
prefer their own interests.
Does he take the Sublime State to be Sweden
And himself some latter-day Peter?[548]
It is not so! Let him then be deterred and let him know
That its sovereign takes his revenge on whomever he desires!
4.20.6 Muslims, check well,[549] should you hear
A report about the aggressive Russians, and reflect!
Let not the size of their hordes deceive you:
Great armies cannot harm the Truth.
Believers, this is the struggle to which God calls you, so make haste
To volunteer, that you may receive your divine reward!
This is God's struggle, which protects your honor.
Contribute to it with every precious thing you have saved up—
In the words "You will not attain piety until you expend
Of what you love"[550] is the clearest guide—
And hold fast to "the most firm handle"[551] of
Goodly patience in combat and be advised.
"God is greater!" and "There is no god but He!" will relieve you
Of the need to set to against them with trenchant blade.
Meet them, then, with these two cries in struggle and you will
triumph
And fall upon them, take the fight to them, and charge against
them!

Attack them by sea and by land. Mass against them
In companies and troops of horsemen and peck the feathers off their eagle.[552]
Were you but a small band of soldiers,
They would not be overcome[553]—so how can you fail when you are more?
From any bloody tyrant whole nations, nay, fate itself, will be defended
On the day you, O Sultan, bar his path.
You are those who worship God aright, so cleave to 4.20.7
The True Religion, for through you it gains in strength and is restored to its former state.
Protect your households, for the safekeeping of your family
Is a religious duty incumbent upon you that may not be shirked!
Defend your Islam jealously until you raise
Its banners! You must show your pride in it.
Let not the bells be heard in your territories
In place of the call to prayer, and let no mosque pulpit be desecrated!
Let there be heard today in your lands
The cracking of pates by sword blades—or would you be paralyzed?—
For that is sweeter than the song of any singer who entrances
The ears of the people, and they are greedy to hear it.
But God's strong hand that is with you
Will bring you strength, so you will never retreat
No matter how many soldiers of theirs try your strength,
Even should soldiers fill the entire earth.
In the Portioned Narration,[554] your Lord has told you,
"It was ever a duty upon us to help" them,[555] so be reminded!
God will not break his promise to his servants—
They shall remain in his safekeeping, and be victorious.
He was your Lord and has never ceased to be 4.20.8
A stronghold for you. Wherever you may be, He guards.

They may point their lances at you
But never will be able to drive them home.
The cutting sword can do no harm, unless God
Wills. None but Him can induce effect.
Any fire from them, should He wish to extinguish it,
Will turn cold, never to catch again or flare back up.
When He wishes, he will brush aside their throne, and they cannot
Advance that day or delay it.[556]
They attacked protected women of yours
Who for so long had been kept inviolate from any who might debauch them.
Shall some lecherous unbeliever lead them away today in chains
And your swords not drip with blood?
If the touch of it be polluting and filthy,
Then by wading into it, says the law, you may be made clean.
Patience is praiseworthy, but when what is sacrosanct
Is violated, I see no reason for you to be patient.
There is no good in a life that is mingled with humiliation—
Shame on you should you fail or turn your backs!
4.20.9 God has borne witness that He is your Lord
And your supporter, so while praising him, vanquish!
God has promised those of you who struggle on His behalf
"A manifest victory,"[557] in the Book, so be joyful!
He provides the martyrs with the best of abodes—
Gardens of Eternity[558] whose dominion is never eclipsed.
The war between you is an ongoing battle, so stand firm,
And victory is the outcome, so be glad!
In the fighters of Badr[559] is a lesson for you.
O People, let him who would remember remember!
Fight bravely that your Lord may be pleased with you
For he who fights bravely by his detractors is excused.
What a difference between him who comes to the combat as a volunteer
And the one impressed against his will, compelled!

He is led and driven by a master,
Who is coarse, ignoble, tyrannical, unjust
And who can sell him, should he wish, to the slaver,
Along with his son, and take his wife as his concubine.
No honor restrains them nor does any magnanimity
Turn them aside from the debaucheries they inflict on people.
They hasten to commit abominations because 4.20.10
No hope remains that they might be remembered along with men of virtue.
Likewise, the vilest of people, if a praiseworthy deed is beyond them,
Would like to become known by any notorious act.
They have gained fortune, but how often has fortune cut the throat
Of those who win it when they give not thanks.
Maybe their circling eagle[560] will fall
And a light from the crescent moon[561] will rise over it and dazzle.
The wicked shall not flourish so long as they shall live
Nor shall the arrogant so long as they live in luxury, and never shall God ease their way.
Have they not noted what has come down to them concerning those who oppressed men
Before them out of arrogance, and how they were destroyed,
Or do they think God incapable, since He has left them so long to their own devices,
Of taking His people's side that they be victorious,
Or of providing against them an army that may not be seen
Or running galleons that cleave no waves,
Or a wailing wind to uproot them
As they sport in security, their minds oblivious,
Or of loosing against them the "birds in flights"[562] that
Caused their like—may they not be increased!—to perish?
Those who worship the idol can never overcome 4.20.11
A people who are marshaled to the sound of "You we worship."[563]

He among mankind whose sincerity of effort pleases God
Deserves all good.
He who does not lend an ear to the advice of his friend
Is guilty of error, and no warner will be of use to him.
He whom the Lord's gifts have made proud turns violent
In injustice, and out of obstinacy lies and betrays.
He whose God-given allotment of daily bread is not enough to make him rich
And so cranes his neck to look for more loses.
He who foolishly places his trust in an army he has
And not in God will be seized by that against which he was warned.
He who thinks he will be made strong by the force of his intrepidity
And of his weapons and his followers—he is the one who has been duped.
He who challenges the All-Conquering will end up humiliated,
Weakened, and impotent, made abject and defeated.
He who is happy in his day with his disbelief,
The next will receive full measure of the Great Torment.
He who ever should wish for the things of this world
Before those of the next will be carried off by what he prefers.
4.20.12 He whose king among men
Is ʿAbd al-Majīd is the one to whom God grants victory.
Our Most Exalted Sultan, through whom our days
Have been rendered happy and bright—may the ages be his ransom!—
Has spread justice throughout the land. Thus all of us,
In his shadow, feel confidence and joy.
Each nation within his possessions receives aid
From him and gifts that include and embrace all.
His justice and his guarantee of safety never fail them,
Whether they are in hard straits or at ease.
If our enemies take their idol
As master, let us carry out whatever our sultan commands.

We do not hope for proximity to the Merciful
By any means except obedience to him, nor do we pick and choose [which divine commands to obey].
No indeed, nor will we find in anything but service to him
Honor, purity of intention, and justification.
He who pledges allegiance to any but him is an unbeliever, and the aggressor
Against him out of injustice and tyranny is yet more so.
Who is that man who would claim to be like him in exaltedness and glorious feats 4.20.13
And who is it that would deny his most excellent adornments?
Had he demanded [more virtues] from Creation,
He would not have added aught to what we already expect of him.
From the essence of purity was his person shaped
By an All-Capable Lord, who shapes the world according to His wishes.
He put under his charge the affairs of religion and this world together,
For he is imam, ruler, and commander
And he it is whose higher status among other kings
Is honored out of awe and venerated,
And he it is who is beloved among mortals
And exalted and revered and esteemed.
With his name they ward off harm amongst them
And from the pulpits his praise is repeated.
If he speaks, none are exempted from what he says,
And when he acts, he does so as his own master.
The Franks are not partisans of his enemies.
They are not their supporters nor are they their kinsfolk.
Is one who follows the guidance of his Lord 4.20.14
Like one misled, whom an evil sorcerer has seduced?
Or one who possesses a noble character to be compared
To a base pest in nature and to him likened?

Or is one who gives with open hand on the same plane
In beneficence and capability as one who gives grudgingly and is a miser?
More, O Commander of the Believers!—And all who call,
"More, O Commander of the Believers!" are made princes!
Rule in your nobility, excelling in glory all mankind
And any spiteful gelding who hates you![564]
Your all-encompassing rewards have encompassed our most extreme
Requests and all that we could ever think of,
Until our imaginations have become exhausted from
Asking so much, while you still hand out booty and do not grow angry.
The stammerer, when obliged to speak your praise, speaks fluently;
Even the inanimate comes close to being able to express it.
Your glory has illumined the entire universe
To the point that it is as one to the blind and to the sighted.
The tyrants directed at you an envious look,
Then reluctantly retracted it and grieved.
4.20.15 Their army has no right, by God, to menace
Or to devise plots. Verily your Lord's devising is greater!
Craft is impossible if it runs
Contrary to His design, and what is fated will be.
Their horde was but fragments blowing in the wind
And the sun is not hidden by motes.
An epithet of Constantinople. Farūq belongs to no throne but yours; so long as it lives by
The Furqān,[565] it will not become desolate.
You are he the eulogizing of whose form causes cares
To be lifted from us and our horizon to exude perfume,
And dreams of hopes come true on the morrow of the one
Who diverts himself with them, though the times be contrary and harsh.

The stringing of the pearls in praise
Of you cannot match the precious gifts that are scattered from the clouds of your palm.[566]
No speaker is left among mankind
Who does not tell of the gifts of your beneficence.
God protect Your Sublime Excellence and may
Your slaves forever be safe in His protection,
And may He preserve your Sublime State so long as
Stars travel by night and seas, like your liberality, swell!
I have declaimed two Hijri dates[567] in
Concluding my praise of you, which is in itself my best reward:
ʿAbd al-Majīd, may God curse his enemy— In the Year 1270
Our sultan is the best of those who by fortune are assisted. In the Year 1270

4.20.16

The Presumptive Poem[568] in Praise of Paris

Is this Paradise on earth or is it Paris?
Is it angels its inhabitants are, or French?
Are these houris in its pure fastnesses one sees
Or is it that every little while Bilqīs comes sauntering by?

Are these stars that in the darkness of the night chase care
From the mind, should it ever occur, or are they streetlamps?

The Prescriptive Poem in Dispraise of Paris

Is this an abode of the jinn on earth or is it Paris?
Is it rebellious jinn its inhabitants are, or French?
Are these women in its mires one sees
Or is it that every little while a water buffalo comes sauntering by?

Are these sparks that in the darkness of the night attract care
To the mind, should we be able to distinguish them, or are they streetlamps?

Is it the flower of this world that one sees in litters[569] That pass like lightning flickering, or are they peacocks?	Is it the effluvia of this world that one sees in litters That pass like wild donkeys limping, or are they gobs of filth?
Indeed, it is the promised paradise of ease, and my evidence for this Is meadows, a gushing basin, gardens,	Indeed, it is an infernal abode, and my evidence for this Is villains in its squares, wretches,
A river, and a *ʿIlliyyūn*[570] in which are women with jutting breasts On "raised couches,"[571] and cotton mattresses [?][572]	Evildoers, and a *ʿIlliyyūn* in which are debauched women On perfume-bedaubed couches, and menstrual rags
And fruit with flesh of fowl and plenty And wine and sweet-smelling herbs and perfume and ease of life	And food from the *zaqqūm* tree whose taste is foul And drink of foul pus administered by Satan
And pillars below which crawl the clouds And whose foundations have been laid atop the Uplifted Ones.[573]	And pillars where you will find devils And whose foundations have been laid on top of filth.
4.20.17 Good health to him who takes therein a dwelling! Blessing to him to whom it is given to take a bride there!	Toil and trouble to him who takes therein a dwelling! Misery to him to whom it is given to take a bride there!
Should adversity or trouble beset you, Make pilgrimage to it, for it is the comforter of troubles,	Should adversity or trouble beset you There, go far from it for it is an outlet for troubles,

And be delighted by it, it being
like Tunis[574] in bliss
For the two places are as one
in their similarity of form.
And should you some day feel
hopeless over anything,
The sight of it is an answer to
prayers, from which none
are turned away in despair.
In it are objects of desire of every
sort that's pleasing to the eye
And that the soul might desire
or inborn disposition find
sympathetic.
At the mention of it you will feel a
true pleasure
That will lead you to abandon all other, a pleasure
palpable.
It is the well-filled spring that
everyone who thirsts must
come upon,
All that is good to those who
visit it, ever gushing.
It is security from the tyranny of
adversities and no stranger
there
Has call to be on guard against
injustice or distress.
Yea, it is an amulet against the
envy of the age—
No one in straits has ever made
his way there and found
himself facing calamity.

And defecate upon it if you
should fail to find a latrine
For the two places are as one
in their similarity of form.
And should you some day feel
greedy for a thing,
The sight of it will breed
despair of ever obtaining
what was envisioned.
In it is dross of every sort that's
offensive to the eye
And that the soul might hate
or inborn nature find
antipathetic.
At the mention of it one will feel
something vexatious
That will surpass what you
feared, a displeasure
palpable.
It is the poisoned spring
that spells death for the
thirsty
All that is evil for those who
visit it, ever gushing.
It is fear of every adversity and no
stranger there
Finds anything but dangers
and misery.
Yea, it is a mote in the eye of the
age—
No man has ever gone there
who did not find himself
facing calamity.

No comfort there is marred by any envious person
Nor has the purity of its pleasures been mixed with any turbidity

No comfort is there but someone wishes to take it for himself
And nothing desirable that is not mixed with turbidity

Nor is any right taken from any right-holder among the people unjustly.
How beautiful then an abode where no right is infringed!

And it takes from every right-holder his rights.
How ugly then an abode where rights are infringed!

4.20.18 Nothing diminishing there is manifest for the faultfinder [to seize on]
Other than the Destroyer of All Pleasures,[575] against whom there is no potion.

No rest there is manifest for the one who is weary
Other than the Destroyer of All Pleasures, against whom there is no potion.

Over it are the splendor of sovereignty and might and sublimity.
From it the resplendence of glory and pride may be acquired.

Over it are the darkness of unbelief and injustice and fornication.
From it the flames of evildoing and debauchery may be acquired.

To reach such a city—if its like is to be found—
The wise traveler wears out his steed and to it come the well-bred camels.

To escape such a city—if its like is to be found—
The wise traveler wears out his steed and from it flee the well-bred camels.

We speak of life, so savor its perfume in its quarters to the full
For so long as you shall reside there you will be at ease!

We speak of life, so savor its perfume in some other city
For, so long as you shall reside there, you will suffer ill fortune!

And never will you find for it
A substitute, even should you travel so far that Jupiter lies behind you in the sky.[576]
There you will strike the ball of grief
With a mallet of joy, after which there need never again be frowns.
From it you will garner the fruits of hope
For there the root of all useful things is implanted.

Should the garment of life become too tattered for you to mend,
In the new clothes of its favors, in the bloom of life, you will be clothed.
Spend your night there secure and set off early for
Pastures of diversion unspoiled by misgivings.

Do not yearn for other than it, or you will be
Like one afflicted, after happiness, by a geomancer's spell.[577]

And never will you find a city like it
In filth, even should you travel so far that Jupiter lies behind you in the sky.
There you will strike the ball of fate
With a mallet of despair, after which there must always be frowns.
From it you will garner the fruits of grief
For there the root of all forbidden things is implanted.

Should the garment of greatness that you possess be distinctive,
From the loathsomeness of life there, it will end up drab.

Endure the night there and set off early for
The comforts of some other city unspoiled by misgivings.

Do not yearn for it even for one night, or you will be
Like one afflicted, after happiness, by a geomancer's spell.

4.20.19 For your days, as long as you reside there, will be peaceful,
Your worth upheld, your right to be together with your family preserved.
Better a night there than a year in any other city
Even should the night then be dark as pitch
And there can be no doubt that you will grow older by an age
For if you add a zero to it even an odd number becomes divisible by five.[578]
I used to fear death if not in my birthplace
But now it would be good tidings enough for me if I were to be buried there.
How often have I distracted my soul with promise of its ease,
Then spent the night dreaming good dreams, arriving there in the last hours of darkness
And found it too beautiful to describe
For it has no likes and is beyond compare.

For your days, as long as you reside in some other abode, will be peaceful,
Your worth upheld, your right to be together with your family preserved.
Better a night in that other abode than a lifetime in this
Even should the night then be dark as pitch
And there can be no doubt that you will grow older by an age
For if you add a zero to it even an odd number becomes divisible by five.
I used to fear death if not in my birthplace
And ah what distress for me should I be buried there!
How often have I warned my soul against its corruption,
Then spent the night dreaming bad dreams and nightmares
And found it too ugly to describe
For it has no likes and is beyond compare.

Notable men, generous and hon-
   orable, are there,
   Lords, mighty smiters on the
      day of battle, of imperious
      looks.
Affection and loyalty are natural
      gifts
   Among them all; no duplicity
      shall ever mar them.
Verily, if they were preceded by
      aught,
   It was as a shadow precedes a
      body, foreshortened.
In the heavens of scholarship they
      possess a shining sun
   And in their billow-filled
      literature oceans,[579]
For how many a scholar do they
      have, perfectly qualified,
   Who has obliterated, by over-
      writing, the knowledge of
      former generations

And a concise word from whom
      illumines any matter whose
      horizons
   May be dark, be it merely
      whispered
And how many a virtuous,
      upright man there is among
      them
   To set fate straight again
      should it be reversed

Base men are there, foxes,
   Though if invited to dine,
      lions, of imperious looks.

Treachery and coldness are natu-
      ral gifts
   Among them all; let no duplic-
      ity on this point deceive
      you.
Verily, if they precede aught,
   It is as a shadow precedes a
      body, foreshortened.
Into the seas of doubt they have   4.20.20
      waded, and how often
   Have its ocean waves covered
      them in error—
For how many an arrogant claim-
      ant to scholarship do they
      have
   Whose knowledge, from
      former generations,
      has been obliterated by
      overwriting

And a concise word from whom
      darkens any matter whose
      horizons
   May be bright, be it merely
      whispered
And how many a meddler there
      is among them by whose
      meddling
   The straight back of fate is
      bent and inversed

And hold it so that it cannot stray, like balances
Made even between his two hands!
And how many a preacher they have whose pronouncements from atop the pulpit
Bring clarity, even if they are conveyed to you back to front.
Hidden mysteries are glimpsed as a result of what he says,
So that he whose eye is yet unseeing may see them.
How many a good and righteous man there is among them who
Throughout the night says long glorias and hallelujahs
And how many a conqueror there is among them, who never left his home pastures,
His pens and papers being his battalions!
And how many a lion of war among them, when he pounces,
Is bold and has battle-won experience therein—
4.20.21 Death to his enemies if they rise up, life if they fear God;
Lions if their enemies attack—courageous colossi!

And who tries, falsely, to make it bend though never
Can balances be even between his two hands!
And how many a stammerer they have whose pronouncements from atop the pulpit
Are evil, even if they are conveyed to you back to front.
Hidden vices are glimpsed as a result of what he says,
So that he whose eye is yet unseeing may see them.
How many a lecherous fornicator there is among them who
Throughout the night complains of his lot at length and in impurity
And how many a one foolishly greedy for dominion there is among them,
His pens and papers being his battalions!
And how many a scrounger among them at every banquet
Is bold and has battle-won experience therein—
Death [to their visitors] if they are visited, the soul of liveliness if the latter are handing out gifts;
Lions if they taste food—courageous colossi!

When they forgive, they are gentle; when they become zealous, they are cruel.
To compare them with others is to understand how gracious they are.
They possess a vaulting ambition before which that of all mankind falls short.
Their pride in this is as ancient as the days.
The friendly face they show their guest is better than a meal of welcome
And their welcoming meal, even should their guest be late, is provided without delay.
Their hospitality to the stranger is an inborn trait
And he wakes up to find that [a new] family and the comforts [of family support] have made him wealthy.
All who come to them, evening and morning, sing their praises,
And these are passed on by master and by servant.
They have brought honor to this language and its speakers
And it continues to gain favor among them and be studied.

When they beg, they are gentle; when others beg from them, they are cruel.
To compare them with others is to understand how miserly they are.
They possess a greed before which that of all mankind falls short.
Their reputation for this is as ancient as the days.
The friendly face they show their guest is, they claim, as good as a welcoming meal
And their engagements are full of lying, procrastination, and delay.
Their hospitality to the stranger is an inborn trait,
Provided he has a wife and the wife is friendly.
All who come to them, evening and morning, declaim invectives against them,
And these are passed on by master and by servant.
They have no knowledge of this language and its speakers
And it continues to disappear among them, though it is studied.[580]

They have written a large number
    of books on it
And their shaykhs and their
    teaching have achieved
    illustriousness.
In other cities, the young man
    takes pride in wealth;
    Among them, his exercise
    books render wealth
    unnecessary.
Say then to those who would
    engage them to a duel,
    "Challenge others,
For to seek to compete with
    the highest is madness!"

4.20.22 Their motto is Liberty, Equality,
    Fraternity, and all are
    entrusted with upholding
    these.
Thus there is no difference
    between two lowly oppo-
    nents before the courts
And their prince in wealth and
    affluence is treated like any
    ploughman.
You will find that each of them is
    shrewd
And dabbles in scholarship
    and learning, and they
    cannot be outwitted.

They have fabricated a large
    number of myths about it
And their shaykhs and their
    teaching have strayed far
    from it.
In other cities, the young man
    takes pride in scholarship;
    Among them, exercise books
    are of no value.

Say then to those of them who
    issue challenges to duels,
    "I swear, to compete with the
    highest is madness!"

Their motto is Liberty, Equality,
    Fraternity, but that's become
    a lie.

Thus there is no difference
    between two lowly oppo-
    nents before the courts
And their prince in command-
    ing and forbidding is like
    any ploughman.
You will find that each of them is
    arrogant, tyrannical,
And dabbles in government,
    even though they have been
    betrayed.

From the cast of their
countenances
Evidence may be drawn that
goodness to them is no
stranger
And that they have a noble
way of earning their daily
bread, with which they are
satisfied
And they do not stoop to any
purpose that is demeaning.
You would think that each must
dwell in a well-plastered
edifice
Where the greeting he gives
is a salute and a bow with
hands on heart.
Never have I seen among them
one who was servile
Nor one who did not share in
their good things and good
conduct.
I find myself happy and joyful in
their company
And any who has not visited
this sanctuary is unlucky.

From the cast of their
countenances
Evidence may be drawn that
evil to them is no stranger

And that they have a sinful way
of earning their daily
bread, with which they are
satisfied.
They stoop to all that is
demeaning.
You would think that each must
dwell in a house of ill repute
Where the greeting he gives is
scorpions' bites and insults.

Never have I seen among them
one who was virtuous
Nor one who did not share in
their sins and filth.

I find myself gloomy and regretful
in their company
And any who has ever visited
their land is unlucky.

I have excused the days whatever sins they may commit,
For Paris has interceded on their behalf and that of all people.

I am angry with the days, rebuking them for what I have lived through
For Paris has rendered it, and all creation, repugnant.
In my earlier eulogizing of it I was mistaken:
This, then, is atonement for that and is its reverse.

4.20.23 The Poem in Which He Eulogized the Honorable and Ennobled Emir ʿAbd al-Qādir ibn Muḥyī al-Dīn, Celebrated for His Scholarship as for His Struggle on God's Behalf:[581]

So long as your person is absent from my sight,
My mind can pay no mind to pleasure,
O you, love for whom, whether you be close enough to visit or too far,
And longing, fills my heart!
If you—may I be your ransom!—be true to me but once,
Others' treachery can harm me not.
If you are content with me, then all other discontents are paltry,
And if you come to me, I shall ignore any other who may abandon me.
If you should ever benefit me through closeness to you,
I shall never thereafter fear anything that may injure me.
O you who have entranced me with your sweet appeal, your disposition,
Your perfection, and your radiant beauty,
You have carried off my mind and heart! Return them to me
That I may eulogize well qualities in you that bring me joy
And let the disapproving know that I am sincere
In describing the beauty of your sweetness as a poet would.

O you the drowsiness of whose eyelid has made me burn with longing,
Have you before seen anyone burned by what is lukewarm?[582]
O moon of perfection, your love has wracked my heart;
O sun of beauty, you have taken possession of my soul.
O dorcas of companionability, your form has made my eye yearn, 4.20.24
But you have the nature of the shy gazelle.
Did you not feel pity for my state and want to be kind to me
And did you not promise me a tryst, even if in public?
My innards were wounded by the cruelty of your threat
Before we parted that you would treat me harshly
And you split my heart in two with your coldness, deliberately,
So no wonder I said you were my creator.[583]
Is it thus that the beloved should act with his lover,
Or is it that after loving me you have become my rebuker instead of my excuser?
Had you but known what I suffered from your distance,
You would have taken mercy on me and wanted to visit me.
Since I have been separated from you, sleep has turned its back on my eye
Like an apostate who, after finding guidance, renounces his commitment.
My illness has grown worse and my agony has been stirred up,
And all that was hidden in my heart has been revealed through your love.
I swear by your love, which is the thing I most hope for,
And by the resplendence of your blooming, effulgent countenance,
Since the day you first appeared to my eye, nothing has seemed worthy to me
And no beauty has filled my eye.
The beauty of others has never made me yearn— 4.20.25
No indeed, nor has another's look bewitched me.
I love for your sake any who resembles you in his coquettishness—
Not in his outward form, since any such resemblance would be too rare to imagine.

How can I remain patient today, when the set time has passed
    And you refused to make me content by visiting me as a night
        phantom?[584]
My heart I would give to behold him for an hour
    Before I die, embracing me and keeping me company of an
        evening.
Suppose he were to come, he would find me unsleeping—
    And the phantom does not sleep with one who is awake.
You forgot your pledge to me when other love made you turn aside
    When, for as long as I have known you, you have borne me in mind.
As for me, as you know, whether distant
    Or close I am your impassioned lover, never changing.
Two things I cannot endure to be separated from:
    The memory of your love and praise for ʿAbd al-Qādir.
He is that gallant man, to whose proud good works
    All creation bears witness
As well as to his praiseworthy virtues, pleasing traits,
    Good qualities and deeds.

4.20.26 He is that lord whose efforts are praised
    By God and by every praise-sayer.
He is that individual whose deeds
    Are the object of the eulogies of the desert-dweller and the pride of
        the city-dweller.
He is the one who inspires awe among kings for his integrity
    And the one of far-reaching, pure, and noble reputation,
Descended from the nation of the Arabs, ancient of lineage,
    The people of noble deeds, one proud man following another,
Who act according to the precise rules of the Revelation regarding what
    Is permitted and what forbidden—the party of the Assembler,[585]
Men who place their hands on their breasts when they pray and, when
        they hear the call
    "To battle!", cut the throats of all those who would cut theirs,
Men who prefer their poverty and
    Look on this world as something evanescent—

And how many a people have attached importance to their lot
Therein only to see their pleasure pass like ages receding.
In their eyes, to return a greeting is to do a favor
Most great, one great enough to return life to a worm-eaten bone.
He brings his nights to life with prayerful vigil
Then brings death to great masses of his enemies.
An encounter with him strikes such terror into the hearts of men 4.20.27
That they grow too weak to call for help.
In the heart of each hardened warrior is enough fear
To cause every roaring lion to retreat
And in each word of his eloquent speech
Is a consonant to make them flee, like a severing sword-edge.[586]
Virtue is his trait, his mark the fear
Of God and his gaining the wages of those who are patient.
He distributes largesse before he is asked and his joy
At the appearance of visitors is announced with gifts.
He relieves them of the need to ask, when with him,
For some necessity that has led them to him, or for favors.
His long bow-shots put fate to the test and it faltered, while he
Still possessed and had within him the liveliness of a sprightly man.
The eagle may one day fall
And yet afterward return to where birds fly
For God supports those who are zealous on behalf of His religion
And God forsakes every debauched tyrant
And God, may He be exalted, divides the days among mortals
So as to fit both front-runner and laggard.
As the emir became still,[587] his fame flew throughout the world, 4.20.28
And every contemporary related his high deeds.
The non-Arabs are divided among those who venerate and those who revere,
The Arabs among those who boast of him and those who vie in singing his praises.
O you who came to the aid of the Dear Religion and its followers,
O you most patient man most grateful to your Lord,

O best of those who forbid the consumption of what is forbidden
And best of those who command to the path of the good,
Fear not calamity, for your Lord will crush,
At your blessed prayer, the tyrant's army.
Be as you will, for your reward
Is recorded on the Tablet,[588] the most glorious store for any who lay up stores.
You will have, whenever you wish, the care of an Eternal God
That will assure your protection, and the support of an All-capable Lord.
If you settle, you will be the mightiest of lions in their lairs
And if you depart, you will be the most noble of those who travel.

4.20.29 The Poem in Which He Eulogized the Honorable and Ennobled Ṣubḥī Bayk, of Noble Lineage and Line, in Islāmbūl

Methinks Time has dealt kindly with me and is disposed toward a truce
And after keeping me in deprivation has offered me success,
And that Fortune hearkened to me when I called upon it
And Fate's dawn glimmerings appeared before me, from Ṣubḥī.[589]
Across sea and land his kindness reached me
Faster than my petition could reach any magnanimous man.
That was but a prayer, yet he responded to me
As would a twin, when he is to me a master who yet is close.
Had he not taken my side with his bounty against the days in which I live,
I would have risen in misery and spent the evenings in pain
And would have perished from the sorrows of desire, for I have
Been wounded painfully, with a wound more painful than a physical wound.
Thus by day I have the toil of business and a trade
And by night I am imprisoned and deprived of aught to do.

If I am not to complain to him, then to whom, perchance,
Should he who complains of injury and sorrow complain
And whom will you encounter among men who is forbearing
If not he, when the wronged is forced to express his grief?
Virtues [he has] whose praise no description can adequately fulfill
Even should you be the Ḥassān[590] of rhetoric and eloquence.
I feel jealousy on behalf of his brilliant traits that 4.20.30
The traits of any other should have a share in praise alongside them.
My fate guided me to him when I had gone astray
With unprofitable poets, weaklings.
The days made jest with me so I made jest with them.
Then, when they assumed seriousness, I turned away from jest
And my verse acquired élan and polish
And became worthy to be recited in the assembly of the eloquent.
In the market of the non-Arabs my words and my praises
Of them found no buyers and were without profit.
How many a night I spent exhausting myself in writing their praise
Then arose, dizzy, and fell like an exhausted camel
And all my eulogies of them enriched me by not so much as
A lampwick and they merely grew more miserly and stingy.
They paid no expiatory gift for my lies—what I owe is [written] at the top of the board and cannot be erased[591]—
And were I the Racine of my age among them — The greatest poet of the French.
And its Milton, I would get out of them barely enough sustaining water to quench my thirst. — The greatest poet of the English.
But see me now—profited, and no liar 4.20.31
In my praise and commendation, when once I was insulted for it!
Come then, my days, between my triumph and my demands,
If you can, and bring disasters down, once more, upon me and crush me
For I have, with his name, entrée to any affair
And his right hand is the key to happiness and victory.
Should any visit me today who once ridiculed
My state, he'd find my cottage grander than any mansion.

My status and my rank have risen through his noble acts
And I am now ambitious for the furthest prizes.
Should my eyes light upon one whose hopes are thwarted
As mine once were, I'd sift my advice down to the essential
And tell him, "Rejoice that you are a petitioner,
For he who ever calls his name gains wealth!"
He is the glorious, whose repute shall last as long as time,
Ever close to his petitioner, be he near or far.
When distant, his succor is not delayed
And when he is close, he feels no distaste at giving.
4.20.32 He is the resolute, the learned scholar, bold, efficient,
Generous, full of integrity, with the morals of lenient men,
Scion of the greatest of creation, Sāmī of the summits,[592]
Whose brilliant feats need no introduction—
My emir, my noble lord and master,
And he who, after God, is my mountain-like support.
I expected that in you I would find all that is good and generous
And I found what I expected to be true; the soundness of my expectation is before my eyes.
A promise from you reached me that you would host me
In your house, as you were hosting my family, in spacious quarters.
There is no doubt in my mind that your promise will be carried out
And that I shall need, beyond that, no further leave to travel (*fasḥ*).
Here then is a eulogy from me, the service of an honest man.
Be gracious in accepting it, may I be your ransom, and in overlooking its flaws
And remain forever a cave of strength[593] for the abject and a refuge
For those who seek it, so long as night shall fade to morn.

[*fasḥ*:] "A kind of permit." One says, "The emir *fasaḥa lahu* for travel," meaning "The emir wrote him a permit."

AND HE WROTE A EULOGY TO THE VIRTUOUS AND WISE PRIEST GHUBRĀ'ĪL JUBĀRAH AND SENT IT TO HIM IN MARSEILLES FROM PARIS, THIS BEING THE FIRST TIME HE HAD WRITTEN VERSE IN PRAISE OF A PRIEST. 4.20.33

Halt by the orts,[594] if you can, a little while
  And enquire after the company that departed at such fast pace.
They left, and left behind them a loneliness
  That made you choke as though in death, and grief, and emaciation.
A camping place where I knew riotousness and passionate love
  And drank sweet water, cool to the taste,
And dragged the skirts of my robes and cocked a snook at the fates
  And led by the nose those of them that put on airs
And conferred such comforts and pleasures upon
  Love's followers as I myself had tired of!
Alas! When will life return to
  Its courtyards and I take my pleasure there as a resting-place?
Naught remains but the memories of my joys there
  And its life of ease has departed like a bygone day, irretrievable.
Even should time have changed its traces or
  Utterly stripped it of its markers,
Its memory is ever renewed in my mind
  And it remains by their kind company inhabited.
The wind, occasioned by some of those who envy me it,
  Has blown upon it in the morning and at day's end.
It displays tenderness for it, and the moaning of a mother who has lost her child, 4.20.34
  To which I add wails and sighs.
It raises the dust in its empty spaces and seems
  To whirl it high in the air only to deposit it at the Crown.[595]
Strange that, after a tear of mine had wetted it,[596]
  It should appear as though borne upon the reins of the wind,
Or is it that the shifting winds have realized that
  Its best use is to provide the sky with a place to rest,

Or that, like mine, the eyes of Gemini
  Have become rheumy and are seeking a collyrium there?
I would barely have made out its vestiges, were it not for a trace
  Of perfume that acted as a guide to where it was.
The tent-trench of the beloved is to the lover dearer than
  A mansion in his own land to which no friend makes his way
And a brief while with the one you love is longer than
  An age in which you find your brother full of reproof.
My salamander heart burns with the fire of love
  And it is hard for it to forget the phoenix.
By God, how many a suitor is tormented by love
  And how many an innocent killed!
4.20.35 If words could assuage passion, my readers
  Would chant my words in the darkness
Or if it were possible to use weeping to cure people of it,
  I would have cured every head wound that remains uncured.
I tried to turn my heart from the maladies of love,
  But it answered, "You have lost your path.
With me the longing began and with me is
  Its conclusion. It is not my way to shift and turn.
The Lord endowed me with this way, as he endowed
  Ghubrāʾīl with love of noble qualities."
He is that sage of refined moral character
  To which his beauteous form is a sure guide,
Of good stock and noble deeds, whom you will never
  Find anything but a guide and facilitator.
He gives largesse openhandedly and to him
  What others keep largely to themselves is as dry brushwood.[597]
He wears the mantle of continence embroidered
  With a godliness that obviates the need to declare things sinful or allowed—
Of cheerful countenance, with a tongue so fluent
  It frees sorrow from its shackles and sets it free to leave.

The clarity of his discourse sets right what is confused 4.20.36
And with his scholarship he extracts what was unknown.
Men never cease to ask him about every puzzling matter
And any who seeks finds a hoped-for reward.
Clear of conscience, for the solemn assurances of his loyalty
Will never accept either distortion or substitution,
He was always there if close, and if far
Was kindly, full of advice, loving, available to ask.
His counsel was guidance and felicity
For whomever sought counsel, his advice well-chosen.
His prayer in times of hurt is the greatest guardian
You can have, so take comfort from it and be reassured.
Neither he who kneels his camel at his door, despairing, nor
He who solicits his help is disappointed by what he gives.
A lord he is who has pursued abstinence in this world,
Which, had he wanted it, would have come to him without restraint.
Thus his stock is ever a refuge for many a refuge-seeker
Who will find with him what he hopes and requests.
The mending of broken hearts may be requested of any Jubārah[598]
And through his offspring every glory may be gained.
The days allowed me closeness to him for a long while; 4.20.37
They decided that was not good and became miserly once more.
Now, after him, I meet only with stinginess
And those who have achieved great things through his bounty are lesser men than he;
I learned to make this interpretation in the days when eyes were trained on him alone.
I put the age to the test and experienced its adversities
And behold, it is sleeping still, unheeding.
Should it not have come to me and asked before
Departure was decreed, and urgently too?
Can any doubt that a single person
May contain within himself all virtues in fullest form

Or deny that no prominent man may be mentioned
In the same breath with him other than in terms of exiguity?
If I expatiate in mentioning gifts of his
That have poured down upon me, I shall dictate at length—
Good manners, charitableness, constant good cheer,
And a magnanimity that exhausts any analogizing.
4.20.38 I have not exaggerated in my eulogy for him:
I have said but little of what has been said [by others]
And if I could I would string for him every shining star
To sing his praises, or the Scriptures.
Any who tries to speak long about him is
Like one who lights a candle in the forenoon.
Good tidings are his who enjoys proximity to his honorable person
And who kisses, repeatedly, the hem of his garment
And who addresses to him a salutation, and commendation,
And praise and adulation and veneration.

4.20.39 A Poem on Gambling[599]

It brought us[600]—the old men: "the Ace," Cavell, and Farshakh[601] (my partner)— together
In a place where there are no neighbors
To reveal the loser's cries or even a whimper.
One of us[602] was a clever fellow, the other a greenhorn.
My two opponents, a cheat plus a thief.
I never got up from the table a winner, except one night
When my fingernail became like a fishhook for the ace.
My good luck kept getting the better of my bad till
I fancied myself, at gambling, an old hand, a bit of a dog.[603]
And my partner with a will set about hunting louis d'ors[604] he owed[605]—and how he hunted them!
So the wizard of the pack[606] withdrew, at a loss
As to what to do about him, his hand[607] unhelpful,

His features imitating
    In part a seal ring, in part a bezel.[608]
The "game" made him[609] turn serious
    And distracted him from covering for a true friend,[610]
So the one who was playing well
    Took to stinging[611] him with words and pinching him with fingers.
He didn't sleep that night and got up in the morning complaining
    Of a nausea that burned his throat, as well as an upset stomach.
His neighbor, he of the slipups, meaning me, had never 4.20.40
    Made a show, in the cards he played, of a plan to get any poorer
After forty-six[612] and he'd not served him in writing notice of any
        protest.[613]
He didn't care if he won or was beaten
    Or his partner gave him a jab on the temple.
All he thought about was how to fabricate lies concerning
    Some exalted person who wasn't even good for the price of
        whitewash.[614]
He'd spend the night writing eulogies and, when morning
    Came, bellow from the pain of an empty stomach.
If he had been able to leave this
    Land, he wouldn't have stopped till he got to the town of Homs.
Perhaps one day, gullibility[615] will prove to be of benefit
    And excessive caution will do harm to a person.
All he knows about gaming is what he's read in poetry
    About it; all his life long he's been bad at getting out of situations.
Whenever he tried to write poetry with hairs from his mustache[616]
    He'd turn against them and pluck them out
And if someone demanded that he stay up all night [writing eulogies],
    He'd set upon the same hairs in a fury with the scissors.
He hasn't let them grow so long that they're like 4.20.41
    The lick of hair of a pretty young girl with braids and plaits;
Soon their white parts will be dyed[617]
    With ink, or saffron and Indian yellow.

He never stops fretting and complaining
And refusing to be grateful for any blessing.
A partner of his[618] has squatted in the midst of the game[619]
Like a shaykh enumerating the topics of scholarship
Or like one who assays coins for the sultan
Whose job it is to examine closely.
If he finds even a tiny mistake, he cries out and wails
And sets in motion a thorough examination of the give-and-take.
He gives away the ace as though he were spending money but
There's a basic difference between these two ways of spending
Inasmuch as in the first case it is under compulsion and in the
Second by choice, not to win or in expectation of gain.

[*aṣṣī* ("basic") means] "original"

He acquired his knowledge from famous shaykhs
Possessed of sagacity and depth of insight and understanding.
He is not like a certain misleader, graduate of the school of spitters[620]
Who all rely on guesswork.

4.20.42 All [the latter] knows is trickery and cunning
And deceit ill becomes a person.
He picks out the winning cards when "in play" but
Deals with serious matters by shuffling.
Even in Jews' Alley there's none but he
Who permits what is sinful and defies the truth.
He has imitated them in his eating of animals whose legs have cloven hoofs[621]
And in their distinctive cunning.
If he's winning, you'll find he's overjoyed,
Laughing, given to winking, pinching, and dancing.
If his opponent triumphs, he wishes
Every expert player other than he were castrated.
To the one with three, he gives with
Open palms and to the one with eight with his fingertips,
Leaving his mouth agape from raging thirst like one who finds water
But fails to be quenched by it through sucking.

Your cunning today, I swear, will not save
You if you trick our shaykh, or protect you!
Your cunning may have gained you the cards but
Will not save you from an exemplary, choking, punishment.
Some gifts seem sweet and appetizing, 4.20.43
Only to be followed by the bitterness of gall.
What a gang of gamblers! No great critic or master
Of storytelling has found fault with them
Except for the fact that their meeting takes place outside of
My room[622]—for sinfulness looks lively there.
Its shape[623] is that of an egg, which is why
Sins are hatched in its belly.
He who built it made that his testament and all I have to do
Is, every little while, apply the testator's will.

Room Poems[624] 4.20.44

I am the bankrupts' benefactor,
This room of mine a Mecca for the luckless.
Saturn,[625] that pimp, brings them to its door.
Once they're there, the smell of notebooks renders them senseless.

And

Let no one with brains ever enter my dwelling
For it's naught but a haunt for the weak of mind.
Inside, the lies of the panegyric, accompanied by
A female piper or a base and stupid scoundrel, is all they'll find.

And

O you who've climbed steps one hundred in number
To reach me, what would you after such a stunt?
You may want relief after all that action,
But I'm here, quite quiescent, just hoping for cunt.[626]

And

None visit me but the depraved and the bawdy
  So abandon modesty, all ye who enter my place!
Modesty is hypocrisy's brother, and no two friends can relax
  Without some breathing space.

And

Visitor, watch your head—
  From the onslaught of grammar![627]
This apartment of mine
  Hosts no bonesetter.

And

O you who visit me to acquire some knowledge beneficial,
  Don't expect the impossible: I have none left!
My scholarship got lost in my search for Fortune,
  But Fortune's fickle; now of both I'm bereft.

And

People have fire without smoke[628]
  And I have smokes but no fire.
See me offer them today with open hand
  To my guest and chew the cud when I retire.[629]

And

It's a miracle of the righteous that,
  Should they wish to, they can grant vision to the unsighted.
My tobacco's miracles today do the opposite:
  They leave the seeing benighted.

And

My visitors are generous to me but
I reward them with something equal—it's my way to do so:
Their shoes bring me dust from kohl-painted eyes
And I blacken their eyes with a bit of my tobacco.

And

It's true I've a room at the top, but
My star's the lowest of the low.[630]
How then can I bear to climb to its heights
When I carry such a burden of woe?

And

One like me who's of exalted standing[631]
Is best qualified to describe the feats of an elite
By furnishing the gifts of poesy
In the form of feet, feet, feet.

And

All my visitors are males, 4.20.45
Among them there isn't a single female.
Isn't there one female left in the universe
Or even a single she-male?

And

I kept myself from fellow men aloof
And spared myself their falseness through days of darkness.
No wonder then that I should say,
"My room's become a fastness."

And

If I'm visited by some debt-dodger like myself, I feel quite safe
    But if he be in fortune's way, his trickiness I fear
For I'm well-versed in the ways of each unlucky wretch
    And there's not a one of whose state I'm unaware.

And

He who returns
    To an abode as cramped as mine
Will feel chagrin grip his breast
    And hunger round his empty stomach twine.

And

Inside the house I've a dead cat's body,
    Outside, a mighty elephant's renown.
I used to think 'twas by their bones
    Great men and scholars were known.

And

Come, learn from me three things
    That'll teach you to distribute a predicate.[632]
My allotted portion of good things, my body, and my house—
    Each is exiguate, exiguate, exiguate.

And

My house has become a narrow grave
    Though my visitors remain alive—
Despite which I don't find a living soul
    Among them to make me revive.

And

When a gale blows and dust storms rise,
  Heavens thunder and rain bedecks the skies,
When my room's walls shudder and shake—
  I'm about to be honored by a visitor, make no mistake.

And

Bring me your requests, for today
  I'm exalted of status and of staircase!
(If they're broke, they can borrow
  My razor to slit their throats, or my pen case.)

And

They say we're in straits, me and my anus—
  My verse is now lame and its strength is gone.
Yet anything that flows through so narrow a space
  Ought, by rights, to be strong!

And

I live in this room **4.20.46**
  As I can't practice my trade
So any who visits me in it
  Should expect no aid.

And

In my room I became a hostage to my cares
  For all that came to see me were my griefs and my desire.
I see every man has a female to keep him company
  But I have nothing feminine except for my fire.[633]

And

Let none out of greed suppose that
    Because of this room I'm the owner—
That I sit here at a banquet
    And he's due a scoop of what's left over!

And

The host's due from those who visit
    Is that they say "Amen" to whatever truth or lies are told,
But he owes them nothing, even if they bring him
    A camel from Sheba loaded with gold.

And

I've got two trades and am unafraid
    Of having no work while they remain stable:
By night I fashion rhymes,
    In the morning set off to cook for another's table.

And

Cooking stuffed dishes these days is quite common
    While cooking up rhymes is a trade unprofitable.
That's why I'm a cook and I'll not be a poet
    For poetry's something unconscionable.

And

My room holds all my books and my daily bread
    So not to go out is a comfort and a consolation.
When I'm away from it, I think I'm the poorest of men.
    When I come back to it, I'm the king of creation.

And

From my chamber wafts the scent of the grill, plus
    That of poetry and that of the liar[634] bare-faced.
If any's hungry, the first will revive him,
    And if any's a fibber by the second he's braced.

And

In my dreams I see myself fall,
    So exhausted am I, into the like of a cave,
Then wake in my bed but with no strength left.
    No need for a seer—it must be my grave.

And

Between me and my tobacco there's a friendship firm—
    When I sleep, it does; when I don't, it too takes no ease,
And if any come to see me, its smoke covers my eyes
    For it reckons the sight of men a disease.

And

I've a room that's full of the lies that **4.20.47**
    In praise of each and every miser I did coin.
There's not an empty spot left inside it
    Where a visitor or a friend may recline.

And

They said, "We'll visit you: you were our good friend once."
    I answered, "For sure, there's a lie here somewhere.
Gratitude's been trimmed from your natures like fat,
    As from your natural share of virtue, so no censure."

And

I tell my guests, "Wait a little
   While I put on clothes without tatters:
In rags I look debauched
   But in new clothes like a man of letters."

And

My door when opened gives a squeak that's quite terrifying.
   It says to my visitors, "Let me stay shut!
This, the infection of your hand, has passed into me
   But the habit of opening me hasn't infected you a jot!"[635]

And

'Twas once the home of perky-breasted girls, my room.
   Now it's become a mother lode of amorous verse.
Enough of love's perfume still lingers on
   To stir the lover a beloved to embrace.

And

People see me in a wretched cell
   And despise my status frankly.
Do you, good folk, live in grand houses?
   The grandest of dwellings may still house a donkey!

And

He who visits and thinks my place small,
   For his kindness I'll make my welcome grand.
Welcome be he to the fire and the roasting
   Plus the tobacco crumbs! What better lot could he demand?

And

I ringed my door with verses closely written
When it was innocent of any visitor of worth.
Thus what's been scratched through the wrinkled paint by the scraping of nails [?][636]
Has become a treasury of scholarship with none to observe.

And

Steady on, you who come in here to see me
Till I ask you a question about this place where you so often consort!
Has something about it so caught your fancy you've come
To build something like it as a gambling resort?

And

How great an architect, the one who built my cell
Of different shapes and made it geometric!
It's like a triangle plus a rectangle
Plus a pentagon plus a hexagon—extremely symmetric!

And

If any comes to me tired and sees my front door, **4.20.48**
He forgets whatever ails him by way of ills.
People know whom they should visit simply
By directing a glance at its sills.

And

Let no ill-fortuned person come up to see me today
For my ascendant is branded with every form of luck most foul.
Any who's like me has
Of such visitors no need—thus saith the owl.[637]

And

People envy me my room
For it, like their eyes, is mean.
Despite this, it contains a tool
With the length and breadth of a peen.[638]

And

I've gone through the city house by house
And found none like my own noble abode.
It repels the sun, should it enter, disdaining
To see it atop the commode.

And

I have in my room utensils for cooking
Equal to all my teeth in number
And if one of these utensils ever is broken
The break passes on to my teeth instanter.

And

Not with a kick may my door be opened, mayhap,
Nor by pounding, but rather with a gentle tap.
Made of purest glass refined,
It opens only to those who are kind.

And

My residence is first in station
But due to some error came last in the strand.
Turn not, then, away to someplace else
Should you come here, no matter how grand.

And

When I've mounted the stairs to my cell
 And passed the top step, the hardest,
Methinks I've been climbing
 To cry out, muezzin-like, "God is the greatest!"

And

People can't see me up in my chamber
 And I can't see them from up in my room.
The Lord alone knows which finds the separation between us
 To his liking and which one suffers from gloom.

And

Sammū before entering my home[639]
 And don't hasten, after opening the door, to push your way inside.
It's a sanctuary, and holy, even if
 You'll find I have there neither one wife nor wives.

And

When I said, "*Sammū* before entering my place," **4.20.49**
 It wasn't a *samm*[640] that will destroy it that I had in mind.
All I meant you to say was
 "Blessed be God, mighty His name among mankind!"

And

Don't peep, visitor,
 Through my keyhole and look at my stuff!
My stuff's like my honor. If you ogle
 My stuff, you won't escape a rebuff!

And

Glad tidings to him who sees the key in my door—
A sign that I'm at home and wearing my clothes!
If not, then I'm in bed snoring or
I've gone out, God protect me from woes!

And

I live in my room in a state of commotion[641]
From the shaking of carriages running beneath it.
Thank God, though, there's none tramping
Over my head and trying to screw it.[642]

And

To God I complain of what I see beneath my window—
Things it's no longer in my power to bear.
Each day I see a thousand men walking while embracing
A female, while I embrace nothing but care.

And

The room I have's just fine
Except that beneath it run no rivers.[643]
The carriages, though, that run below
Make up for that—the very moons are their passengers' jealous admirers.[644]

And

I wonder at you, good people—that, being such heathens
And given the cold, you don't worship fire.
It must be that you distract yourselves with the heat from those who,
Though they feed you both fire and shame, you admire.

And

The visitor, after eating, should think of
His host and not impede his income
And any who comes of a morning is in danger:
I'll not tell him either "Come in!" or "Welcome!"

And

They saw smoke from my stove ascending, so ran
With water to extinguish the conflagration.
"Are you a blacksmith?" asked one. "Indeed!" said I.
"I forge verses and have a workshop for prevarication."

Poems of Separation[645] 4.20.50

My two friends! Disparage not one needy for love
If you be among those who have known the agony of separation,
And do not reproach me for my passion, for I,
Against my desire, love him without requital.
Who is content that tribulation befall him
Or that he thrive, but with sorrow and insomnia,
And does anyone suffering loneliness enjoy life
When sundered from his own and lacking energy and intention?
The people of my house have gone far from me and in their place I have
Hateful neighbors whose proximity is of no value,
As though my times wished to see me, in every situation,
Alone—and lonely I am indeed!
My past felicity had no like:[646]
In beauty those people surpassed any peer.
What then afflicted me after this good fortune that I had won
When, being close to them, I lived a life of ease?

Why, what would it have harmed my days if
No darkness from their beginnings had infected them to the end?[647]
Is there among men one like me—heart in one place,
Body in another—suffering the pangs of absence?
Others I see *sans* pangs of love, yet living
At ease; his good fortune aids him without effort on his part.
4.20.51 Is there someone who, for the sake of God, will take mercy on an agony
That keeps coming back to me, nay adheres to me like skin?
Is there one who will inform the breeze of me and send this as a greeting
To them, and show them how I long for them?
I am in love with what the ones I love used to see
Even if it be certain inanimate objects or an enemy.
I constantly repeat the words they used to repeat
For to recall them is my *dhikr* and to utter them my *wird*.
Since I am a poet, it is my right to celebrate in verse my love—
For them, not for Hind or Mayyah or Daʿd.[648]
Did I not harbor a hope of meeting them,
I would rather lay my head down, from today, in my grave
But I hope that time will gladden me
With them soon, and this is the dearest of my wishes.
They tell me, "Be patient!" but how can I be patient
When to the light of insight I am not guided?
I swear, the authority of love is overwhelming. From its pitfalls
The right-thinking man is not saved, nor the rightly guided.[649]
Would that my tears had run to where they were standing
And arisen like a barrier at their feet,
To prevent them from moving on and growing more distant
For I have had enough of moving on and of distance.
4.20.52 O you whom we love, is your affection still sound
And do you, like me, still maintain the pledge?

I see the world through you yet see you not in it.[650]
My state today is that of the wise man perplexed.
The Feast brought its joys to all the people
But naught visited me then except care and woe.
How can I not complain when the distance to you is so long,
And what is between cannot be covered with the longest of strides?
And what do I have to hope for after your departure
When ease and toil to me are as one?
How excellent would be the feast of my setting off toward you
Like a thirsty bird being sent off to the water source!
And should your phantom visit me before we meet
And were I to embrace it by night, it would be my fortune.
When my eye spots the mail, my heart
Flutters with apprehension like a banner,
And if I receive a letter from you, I kiss it
And settle it thereafter next to my liver.
Whatever bears with it some trace of you is preferred by me
To eye and to al-ʿĪnayn[651] and to kind and cash
For I have nothing but it today to distract me
And naught else than it do I find to cool my burning heat,
And if there is none, my tears run for what has happened
And I turn from it like the poor man who takes nothing from charity's feast.

And he wrote: **4.20.53**

Have I not today had enough of separation
From those I love and whom it is now too late to meet?
O you who have departed when your place was in my heart
How often I say that you reside now in my guts!
How often I bemoan my bad luck with you
Though my fate does not heed my call!
You departed to be cured of what ailed you;[652]
When shall I, through your closeness, be cured?

And when will the days grant me that I meet with you
  And the hand of destiny unhand me and stop hurting me?
You went east, and I, through the agony of my exile
  In the west am choked and filled with anxiety.
O You who have pity on the wounded and sickly,
  I am wounded, and must constantly take medicine.
Prescribe then for me what you prescribe for those who
  Recover and be cunning in your treatment.
Let not what you see of my clothes deceive you:
  Beneath the clean clothes the limbs are hollow (*ṭahāmil*).
By Him who grants life and annihilates, I cannot be classed
  Either among the perished or among those who are alive!
4.20.54 I, though the ones I love may have forgotten me,
  Do not forget them even in misery and bad times.
Despite my state, I feel pity for any lover
  Like me, even though he be an enemy of mine.
Distance does not extinguish the fire of my love, rather
  Separation from the gazelle causes me to grow hot.
No love after theirs can occupy my heart
  Nor is an abrogation of my fidelity lawful.
Change is the condition of all mankind yet my case
  Is as you see, morning and evening.
My tears can do nothing but run
  And the eye is exempted from slumber
Yet I see those who, like me, once wept at separation
  Now rejoined with the one whose distance afflicted him with weeping.
How strange my fate—it never ceases to keep me under observation
  Yet my emaciation makes me invisible to any watcher!
How strange my tears—in bathing me they sicken me
  While hot water cures all others!
How strange my life—how it grows longer with separation
  While the Earth shrinks too much to hold my hopes!

ṭahmal [sing. of *ṭahāmil*] is "that which, when touched, is found to have no mass."

How strange the night of others—how its morning comes quickly
When my night's morning is always slow in coming!
My thoughts during it build hope upon 4.20.55
A foundation of the impossible, and what worse foundation could there be?
And the longing that dwells within my ribs
Makes me imagine that I am sleeping and they're my bedfellows
Until such time as I awake, when it becomes clear that they were
But ropes of floating dust.
O you whom I hold in affection, in my malady
There is nothing that can infect you so return and fear not my disease.
My languor is from the languid eye and that which makes me thin
Is the slim waist, may what has infected me pass you by!
I shall burden you with naught but the mention of the name of the one
I love—enough for me is such naming!
If my high hopes were good for anything I would today
Be the most fortunate of mankind, the happiest of the happy
For every morning bird utters their name—
Or is that but the deceitful whispering of the air?
Or is it part of what longing creates that it
Should distract me with things that do not exist from those that do?
Would that people's hearts, or effort, were with me—
Should a departure prove painful, they would be committed to commiseration!
Or would that the ones I love might be aware of how I feel
And hasten, out of pity, to rescue me!
God forbid that they should abandon one so fond of them— 4.20.56
Enough for him the deprival that he has known!
With a sympathetic friend, distance seems easy, just as
With unkindness, proximity seems to recede.

Alas, I cry, for a time that has passed and with it
The pleasure I knew with them and my happiness!
For what great sorrow now and disaster
Have the days preserved me—and how evil a preservation!
How can I patiently bear separation when my eye
After so much gazing, sees none that resembles them?
If I complain, I find no one to hear my complaint—
And the gloating of those who hear complaints is the worst of tribulations—
And if I hold my tongue, the thinker will think I am consoled,
Which is something no thinker could reasonably think.
Would that those I love had not turned
From me under pressure of warnings and seduction!
They were too miserly to spare me a fragrant breath from their mouth
That the east wind might have brought me to cure me.
4.20.57 How is it that their hearts have remained like iron
Despite the fire of my love and have not softened to my prayers?
Did they perhaps find some reason to blame me
That allowed them to distinguish the good from the bad?
Even if I did wrong, I now hereby ask forgiveness
And pardon is to be hoped for from the noble.
My cure—their approval—would cost them little,
The near and the far being as one in this.
If it may not be spoken openly, then let
A private thought take its place; that is enough for me.
I am content with your good intentions
Even if what would make me happy has passed me by.

4.20.58 On the same topic he wrote

A letter reached me from a friend—elegantly written,
Each character inscribed with beauty and flair.
I swooned with passion when I sniffed its perfume
And why not, when attar of roses wafted from it?

How lovely that scent and how lovely
  A breeze that brings it to me, outpacing the good tidings!
To God I complain of the separation I have suffered
  And of a heat of ardent love at which I almost gave up the ghost.
I stayed, and my darlings departed by land and by sea
  Against my desire and my family was dispersed.
Since they left, I have not ceased to swear my passion.
  When it is time to take action, I almost drown in tears
For in my captive heart I store up love
  And from my overflowing eye I expend tears.
Melancholy, wasted, pining, longing,
  Alone, sick, lost, and yearning,
I am neither possessed of patience, that I should expect its reward,
  Nor consoled and reconciled.
There is no guarantee that my fate will permit a meeting—
  Has any firm commitment ever been taken from fate?
I yearn, panting, to meet them, **4.20.59**
  When my night companions, the stars, appear, and I am restless,
And if the rim of the sun should appear over the horizon, I am deluded
  Into thinking that it brings me a greeting from them and will speak
For in it I see the marks of their beauty,
  And in all beauty is a reminder to the heart of what it loves.

This trope is stolen from the Fāriyāqiyyah and was alluded to earlier.[653]

I distract a love-maddened heart with hopes
  Though there is nothing left there for the hopeful to believe in.
It flies me, in longing, to them and I
  Am captive to a love for them that is linked to my destiny.
It quivers at the mention of their name
  And it seems to me that my bed quivers at its mention
And I pour out the very tears that I used to when I was close to them
  Though how can that be when the door to union is closed?

When will God unite the lovers for an hour
   And the veils of distance be ripped apart
(Though many a craving distance has resulted in the permanence
      that was
   Hoped for from the lovers' proximity!)?
God possesses secrets whose discovery is painful,
   And fate has phases that both displease and please.

4.20.60 And he wrote

O you who bid me farewell, the tears near parting us,
   Passion's blaze striking terror,
How can there be patience after you, already missed, have departed
   And I remain, neither an object of desire nor a hoped-for goal?
Your absence, even for an hour, used to grieve me
   And I would imagine that it was unlikely that you would return.
Now you have been absent, at a high price to my passion,
   For an age, and long is the night of the afflicted.
If you forget me, I shall remember you, or should you grieve for me,
   I shall thank you; never shall I turn from you as long as time shall
      last.
Would that your phantom would come to me as I sleep
   Or my eye close when I am overcome by night,
For a single visit by it would be dearer to me than
   Love's pleasures with another enjoyed at length.
I was distracted by my twofold love for you[654] from the pain of
      separation,
   And distraction may bring comfort to suitors.
The pupil of my eye you are—yes indeed!—and blood
   Of my heart, and for these two I have no alternative.
Should I use up all my limbs in making you content,
   I would still be niggardly and what I have used up would be little.
4.20.61 I find you pictured in everything that is beautiful
   So I gaze at it at length in contemplation

And if I hear of one unique in beauty
I remain convinced that you have precedence in that.
I pass the night asking the planets of darkness about you
(If such an object of questioning can be of use to such a questioner).
O you who have bewitched me with your winsomeness, no
Distraction whatsoever remains to me in life after you.
No other than you has pleased me and my innermost mind
Has believed no other to be beautiful.
If man's preoccupation is this world,
Then I am the one who is forever preoccupied with you.
In you may be found proof for the oneness of a Creator,
Should the philosopher find it hard to come up with such a proof.
I sent my tears with my letter, knowing full well
That no messenger can take the place of the beloved.
You who condemn love, be not reproachful
For this decrepitude of mine may be attributed to haste.
My heart preceded my eye in love, **4.20.62**
And through it I fell; let my reproacher then be blamed.
Alas for the days of loving union! I wonder,
Can parting, like them, also suffer postponement?
Had I not had their felicity to recall, I would have died
Of passion, and how many a one slain by passion has gone unavenged!
Transformation will never cause me to forget the hours of embracing
Or ever prevent them from recurring to my mind.
Many a day of pleasure will compensate one
For a life made long by the vexations of separation.
Let me then wean the soul from its pleasures
And let wailing sadden me after song!
O denier of the reality of ghouls, know well
That distance is in truth a ghoul!

He who has not tasted the pain of separation
Has no right ever to reproach fate:
Every burden other than this has for the man of good sense
Its consolation and, in mourning, its cure.
O agony of longing, dwell in my heart
So long as contact with the ones I love is missing!
The trembling of my heart at your silence is continuous
Yet mayhap soon my wearing cares will disappear.

4.20.63 This is the last news we have of the Fāriyāq that must be placed at this time within these *pages*, and any who wishes to bless him or curse him shall, when "leg is intertwined with leg" and it is said, "unto thy Lord that day shall be the driving,"[655] receive his *wages*. As for he who prays for the restoration of his marriage before he breathes his last, I guarantee he'll invite you to a banquet around and upon whose table will be set out, in proper order, everything this book mentions that the appetite may *stimulate* or the eye *captivate*, be it presented on couch or on *dinner plate*.

Conclusion

Part One of the Book *Leg over Leg Regarding the Fāriyāq* ends here and will be followed by Part Two once the author through God's favor and generosity has been stoned and crucified.[656] 4.21.1

Amen

In the Name of God the Merciful, the Compassionate[657] 5.1.0

Sīdi[658] Shaykh Muḥammad, *Sayyidna* Metropolitan Buṭrus, *Abūna* Ḥanna, *Abūna* Manqariyūs, *Ṣirna* Abraham, Mister Necton [?], Herr Schmidt, Signor Giuseppe,[659] as you can see I've now made (that is to say written and not printed or bound) this book and placed it before you. I know well that *Sīdi* Shaykh Muḥammad will be laughing at it, if he's read it, because he knows without anyone having to tell him that he could do better and thinks it's a foolish thing even if I have filled it with letters. *Sayyidna*, *Abūna*, and *Ṣirna*, though, could not. In fact, they won't even understand it, and I therefore ask of them that, before they light a fire to burn it, they ask about what's good in it and what's not. If the good outweighs the bad, they should let me keep it; if not, they can burn it with its binding. If, though, they find in it only a few shortcomings, they shouldn't burn it, for we all have many shortcomings and God won't burn us in hellfire just because of them. 5.1.1

Father Ḥanna, I swear to you I don't hate you. I hate only your arrogance and your ignorance: when I greet you you give me your hand to kiss, but how can I kiss it when you're an ignoramus and haven't written a book, or even a hymn, in your life? My dearest Shaykh Muḥammad, I know that books of jurisprudence and grammar are more sublime than this book of mine because when one reads one of those books, one screws up one's face and frowns as one tries to understand what it's about, and you believe that venerability and sublimity are to be found only in frowning. However, 5.1.2

the books of jurisprudence don't say that laughter is a sin or is reprehensible, and you—God protect you from envy!—are quick and intelligent. You've read more books of literature than *Sayyidna* Metropolitan Buṭrus has eaten braised chickens and in every book of literature you'll find a chapter devoted to licentiousness, which they wouldn't have included if licentiousness were against literature.

5.1.3 The easiest of my duties is to say at the end of this book of mine, as others have done, "and I seek God's forgiveness for any excesses of the pen and slips on the path." We are now, God be thanked, at peace with one another. Monsieur, Mister, Herr, and Signor are not obliged to print my book as my words aren't addressed to cattle, donkeys, lions, and tigers[660] but to people—offspring of Adam—and this may be why (though God alone knows) you're angry with me.

END OF THE LETTER

A List of the Synonymous and Lexically Associated Words in This Book[661]

Volume One	**Section**
"assiduous"	[1.14.7]
Gambling and associated words, to which should be added *mukhāḍarah*, meaning "the selling of fruits before their quality is known"	[1.16.5]
Base sense: "to take an omen or an augury"	[1.16.7]
Magic and amulets, to which should be added *raʿb*, meaning "a charm, magic or otherwise" and *ʿunnah*, the noun from *ʿunna l-rajul*, said if "a man is prevented from having intercourse with his wife by magic" or "because the judge made such an order" and *al-sahm al-aswad* ("the black arrow"), i.e., the blessed arrow from which good omens are taken (as though it had been blackened by frequently being touched by the hand) and *tafyīd*, meaning "taking auguries from the call of the *fayyād*" (the male owl)	"
Glue	[1.18.4]
Names of parts of the body	"
Places in Hell, names of devils and jinn, sounds made by jinn, and so on, up to page 265, to which should be added, to the part on jinn, *quṭrub*, meaning "their young"	[1.18.5–11]
Base sense: bad dream	[1.18.12]

Volume Two

5.2.3

Stars and their conditions	[2.1.3]
Some synonyms of "crowding"	[2.1.4]
Instruments of war	[2.1.7–10]
Names of idols, to which should be added *al-Jalsad*, "the name of an idol," *Awāl*, on the pattern of *saḥāb*, an idol of the tribes of Bakr and Taghlib, and *Balj*, "a certain idol, or a name"	[2.1.11–16]

Volume Two	**Section**	
Some star names	[2.1.16]	
Some synonyms of "pushing" and "pressing"	[2.1.23]	
Turbans and hosiery, to which should be added *fidām* ["something the non-Arabs and Magians attach over their mouths when drinking"]	[2.2.1–2]	5.2.4
Women's movements and ways of walking	[2.2.4]	
Base sense: "contracted," to which should be added *iqʿansasa* ["to fall behind, or to withdraw to the back"]	[2.2.5]	
Land conveyances	[2.2.6–7]	
Pulses	[2.2.10]	
Seagoing vessels, to which should be added the *thurtumī* [?][663] and the like	[2.3.6–8]	
Facial characteristics	[2.4.6]	
Facial states, to page 99	[2.4.7–12]	
Describing the city	[2.5.1]	
Phrases related to divorce	[2.13.6]	
Types of beauty, to page 219, continued in Volume Four, page 235	[2.14.8–29] + [4.16.5–12]	5.2.5
Meadows	[2.14.32]	
Names of places, to which should be added *al-Ubullah*, "a place[664] in Basra, one of the paradises of this world"	[2.14.33–42]	
Places in Heaven	[2.14.43]	

Wonders, to which should be added *Hinda Mandu*, "a river in Sijistān into which a thousand rivers empty producing no increase in its waters and from which a thousand rivers branch producing no decrease in its waters," and *al-Jazā'ir al-khālidāt* ["the Immortal Isles"], also called *Jazā'ir al-sa'ādah* ["the Happy Isles"]—"six islands in the ocean over toward where the sun sets from which astrologers begin their measurements of the longitudes of the lands and on which grow every sort of fruit, eastern and western, and every kind of aromatic plant and every flower and grain, without being planted or cultivated" [2.14.44–47]

Games of the Arabs, to which should be added *midād Qays*, "a game" [2.14.48–56]

Musical instruments [2.14.57–58]

Kinds of food, to page 267 [2.14.59–68]

Fungi and kinds of fish [2.14.69–73]

Bread, to which should be added *qizmāz*, which is "bread one prepares and turns in order to place in the ashes" [2.14.74]

Milk [2.14.75]

Sweets [2.14.76–77]

5.2.6 Fruit [2.14.78–81]

Drinks [2.14.82–84]

Base sense: "erectile dysfunction" [2.14.86]

The wife [2.14.88]

Kinds of gems and precious metals [2.16.8–11]

Jewelry and ornaments, to which should be added *sikhāb*, which is "a necklace made of *sukk*[665] and *maḥlab*[666] without gems or precious metals" [2.16.12–19]

Perfumes and aromatic pastes [2.16.20–28]

Volume Two **Section**

Vessels, household articles, and furnishings, to which should be added *ʿālah*, which is "a shade used for protection against the rain" [2.16.29–35]

Trees and minerals [2.16.36–38]

Clothes, mantles, and wraps, to page 363 [2.16.39–63]

Base sense: "to yearn," with words associated with "to turn head over heels," meaning "to strike the heart of" [2.16.71]

Aphrodisiacs [2.19.4]

Volume Three

Sicknesses and defects, to which should be added *qawas*, 5.2.7
meaning "curvature of the back," *ṣarʿ* ["epilepsy"] "a malady too well-known to require definition," *ḥajaz*, a sickness of the stomach, namely rancidness, *qudād*, "a pain in the belly," *saktah*, ["apoplexy"] "a malady too well-known to require definition," and others scarcely worth mentioning [3.1.4–30]

Base sense: "bustle" [3.5.8]

Base sense: "big-buttocked (fem.)" [3.5.17]

Base sense: "fat (fem.)" [3.5.18–21]

Base sense: "kissing" [3.6.3]

Charms of the body [3.6.7]

States and characteristics of the breasts [3.6.8]

Base sense: "hard and strong" and words of similar meaning [3.6.11]

"Alas for Zayd!"[667] [3.12.6]

Base sense: "cosseted" [3.12.6] 5.2.8

	Volume Three	**Section**
	Base sense: “the racing of the pulse”	[3.12.8]
	Base sense: “groping and grasping”	[3.12.8]
	Kinds of wrestling	[3.12.12]
	Base sense: “servants and attendants”	[3.12.18]
	Names of singers, male and female	[3.12.20]
	Acts and motions specific to the small child	[3.12.21–23]
	What a woman does with her child	[3.13.14]
	Women’s postpartum sicknesses	[3.13.15]
5.2.9	Some synonyms of “wind”	[3.18.7]
	Rotten smells	[3.18.7]
	Hapax legomena and the like	[3.18.7]
	Some synonyms of “huffing and puffing”	[3.18.9]
	Base sense: “slave” and “captive”	[3.18.9]
	Defects in a wife	[3.18.10]
	Traits desirable in a wife	[3.18.13]
5.2.10	Base sense: “small-buttocked woman”	[3.19.2]
	Base sense: “short woman”	[3.19.3]
	Base sense: “black (fem.),” including makeup and face paint[668] (meaning “things women use to improve their faces”)	[3.19.4]
	Base sense: “old woman”	[3.19.5]
	Characteristics of the comely woman	[3.19.6]
	Maladies of the neck	[3.19.12]
	Despicable traits of the dissolute woman	[3.19.13]
	Base sense: “iteration” and “occasion”	[3.19.14]

Volume Four	**Section**
Base sense: "chortling"	[4.12.10]
"Looking" and its various forms	[4.15.1]
Praiseworthy traits of women and the various types of the latter	[4.16.5–12]
Base sense: "she moves" and "she oscillates"	[4.16.12]
Base sense: "the condition of being a pander or a wittol"	[4.16.13]
5.2.13 "Traps," "snares," and associated words	[4.17.1]
Base sense: "mainstay"	[4.17.1]
Base sense: "commercial establishment"	[4.17.1]
Base sense: "accounting"	[4.17.1]
Qualities of voice and setting to music	[4.17.2]
Dressing of the hair and its styles	[4.17.2]
Base sense: "with head bowed"	[4.17.3]
Base sense: "full" and "complete"	[4.17.3]
"Limpness" and "rigidity"	[4.17.4]
Base sense: "person with defective vision"	[4.17.12]
Base sense: "insincere friends," "false flatterers," and "those whose friendship cannot be relied on"	[4.18.16]
Things peculiar to women[669]	[4.18.19]
Base sense: "the countryside" and "the provinces"	[4.18.20]
The inability of the eye to respond with tears	[4.19.3]

Appendix to the Book

In Which Are Strung Together the Pearl-like Errors Made by the Great Masters among the Teachers of Arabic Languages[670] in the Schools of Paris

In the opening passage of a book on Persian grammar that he wrote in 1853, Alexandre Chodźko[671] states, "The countries of Europe have long been possessed of everything needed for the study of oriental languages, as they are of libraries and schools and scholars well-qualified to direct them. With regard to the literature of the languages of Asia and their associated philosophy and history, the professors of the Persians, the teachers of the Arabs, and the Brahmans of India now have much to learn from our professors." I declare this claim to be lies, chicanery, mendacity, fakery, falsehood, forgery, slander, empty boasting, implausibility, injustice, farfetchedness, fallacy, fibbing, fabrication, blarney, hyperbole, hokum, and humbuggery and that its author ought to be listed in the chapter on marvels[672] among those who delude themselves, for not only does he delude himself but he leads others to do likewise. 5.3.1

Firstly, he—that is, the writer of the essay in question—does not have the knowledge of oriental languages that would justify the witness he bears to the excellence and mastery of these professors and is unaware of the shallowness of their knowledge, for in transferring the letters[673] in Persian that he has put into his book, he makes many gross mistakes both of copying and of translation. Among these, on page 198, he writes *qāniʿ ṣafṣaf* when the original reads *qāʿ ṣafṣaf*, the quotation being from the words 5.3.2

of the Almighty *wa-yas'alūnaka ʿani l-jibāli qul yansifuhā rabbī nasfan fa-yadharuhā qāʿan ṣafṣafan* ("They ask you about the mountains. Say, 'My lord will scatter them as dust and leave the earth level and bare. . . .'");[674] being ignorant of the meaning, he has changed *qāʿ* ("low-lying land") to *qāniʿ* ("content") and translated it into French by saying, in his words, "and he satisfies himself with the sands of the plain."[675] How could this scholar permit himself to fill the book with sand and be too proud to ask someone knowledgeable what it meant? Such, however, is his custom and that of his predecessors and professors: when they are in doubt as to the meaning, they resort to patching, botching, and concocting.

5.3.3 Secondly, these professors do not get their knowledge from those who are masters of it, such as Shaykh Muḥammad, Molla Ḥasan, or Üstad Saʿdī.[676] They acquire it parasitically and pounce upon it randomly. Those who graduate with some knowledge of the subject do so at the hands of Priest Ḥanna, Monk Tūmā, and Parson Mattā and then stick their heads into confused dreams, or stick confused dreams into their heads, and imagine that they understand things that they do not. Any of them who teaches an oriental language or translates from one you will find flailing around blindly. Anything they are in doubt about they patch up any way they please and anything that lies between doubt and certainty they conjecture or guess at, giving greater weight to the less weighty and preferring the less preferred. This is because there is nobody at hand to take on the task of pointing out their mistakes and helping them to improve. As Abū l-Ṭayyib[677] says

> If a coward finds himself alone in a land
> He calls for war on his own, and for battle.

5.3.4 Because they have invested all their dignity in having people call them by the title of "teacher," they are content to have the name without the doing and without undertaking what is properly meant by being a teacher. He who occupies this sublime position must be truthful in his transmission, cautious in his narration, careful not to give too much credence to the likelihood of what he favors at the expense of what the author intended, thoughtful as to the material's context, to the text that precedes it, and to any delimiting attributes or relevant issues connected to it, and he must be steeped in the lexicon, as also in the grammar, syntax, and literature. Where are such qualities among these professors, who distort the author's manner of expression and impose on it strange meanings unacceptable to both nature and taste, importing, speculatively and recklessly, whatever personal interpretations they fancy? I swear, if they had any shame, they would not occupy these prominent posts and would not make so bold as to produce such patched and faked translations! If, my sandy shaykh,[678] your words concerning these professors were intended seriously, it would be your duty, after reading the list of their appalling mistakes, to retract your ignorant hogwash and hokum and confess your mendacity in the preamble to some other book you may one day write—on Arabic grammar, God willing! If not, the sin of taking pride in a falsehood will be upon your head.

Or if it was said in jest and you intended to poke fun at those prominent professors and celebrated stars, it would be better if they were to answer you, though I notice that they have said nothing to refute you, and it seems that this ill-judged praise of yours has tickled their fancies. You and they are like that fool who fell in love with a woman and was unable to have her and continued thus until his love for her made him sick and crazed, at which point he became incapable of movement. He was then visited by a crafty man such as you who kept congratulating him on having achieved what he wanted from her. "How can this be," asked the fool, "when I am besotted with love for her and the more I long and yearn for her, the more she shuns and rejects me?" Said the other, "With my own eyes I saw you embracing her yesterday, after which you left her house, radiant with joy. Many others saw you too, and if you deny it, they are all ready to bear witness against you," and he stuck to this version of events until he had persuaded him and convinced him to forget about her, and the man recovered from his sickness. Though there is a great difference between you and that crafty man: he used his cunning to do good, while you used yours to do evil. That book of yours may fall into the hands of a statesman who knows nothing of Persian and Arabic and in his ignorance he may think that the shaykhs of Egypt 5.3.5

and the professors of Persia need to acquire knowledge from your friends—and when one of those bigwigs nonchalantly grasps the wrong end of the stick, the hoi polloi, as one, nonchalantly grasp it along with him.

5.3.6 Your statement that the Frankish countries have many libraries seems to imply that these contain books that are not to be found in ours, but this is because the representatives of various nations are buying up the most valuable books from our countries. The presence of books is not, however, evidence of the presence of knowledge. Carrying books around does not make one, God guide you, a scholar, for knowledge is in the mind not in the lines. But tell me: how is it that these professors never write a word in the oriental languages? The extent of their production is that one of them translated from our language *Lughat al-aṭyār wa-l-azhār* (*The Language of the Birds and the Flowers*),[679] filling it with guesses and conjectures. Another translated the correspondence of a Jewish broker with an imbecilic merchant.[680] Another transmogrified the proverbs of Luqmān the Wise into the feeble language used in Algeria[681] and another labored to have printed silly sayings taken from the rabble in Egypt and the Levant,[682] leaving whatever incorrect and corrupt language he found therein as is and seeking to make excuses for himself by saying "*sic*," which he thought would allow him to evade any blame or refutation. What lies behind the craze for translating such books and printing such sayings from our language into French if not the craving of their compilers to join the ranks of authors? And why has none of them gone to the trouble of translating any French books into Arabic to show off his mastery in this area, given that he is supposedly the shaykh of those who study the language and the imam of its imams and when there are very estimable books in French in every field? Even more amazing is the fact that it has occurred to none of them to translate the grammar of their language into ours. Can there be any reason other than their reluctance to expose themselves to verification, refutation, and excoriation? The words of the grammarians and the Arabists would have to be rendered exactly, and it would be no excuse for them in this case to say "*sic*." I wish I knew what was the point of one of these professors writing a book in corrupt, mixed style, on the speech of the people of Aleppo,[683] calling it a "grammar," and recording in it words such as *anjaq* ("barely, scarcely"),[684] *biykaffi* ("it's enough"), *ishlōn* ("what?"), *kēfak* ("how are you?"), *khayyu* ("little brother"), *ha l-kitāb* ("this book"), and *awi ṭayyib* ("very good"). Or of another writing in the dialect of the people of Algeria[685] *kān fī wāḥid il-dār ṭūbāt bi-z-zāf il-ṭūbāt kishāfū* and *kīnākul* and *rāhī* and *antīnā* and *antiyyā* and *naqjam* and *khammim bāsh* and *wāsīt shughl il-mahābil* and *yiwālim* (i.e., *yulā'im*, "it suits") and *mājī* (i.e., *jā'in*, "coming") and *killi* (i.e., *ka'annī*, "as though I") and *ḥirāmi* (i.e., *bustānī*, "my garden") and *is-sittāsh* (i.e., *al-sādis*, "the sixth")[686] and *id-dajājah tirja' twallid zūj 'aẓmāt* and similar kinds of laxative.

5.3.7 How is it, my dear professors, that you do not write books in that corrupt language of your own that you call *patois*, and would you advise an Arab who has taken residence in Marseilles, for example, to talk like the people there or like the people of Paris? If you were to be rational about this activity of yours, you would have to record all the differences and variations present among Arabic speakers, for the people of Damascus use words that the people of Cairo do not and you may extrapolate from that to the rest of the Islamic countries. Indeed, the people of one area may use a variety of different terms. The speech of the Beirutis, for example, is different from that of the people of Mount Lebanon and the speech of the latter is different from that of the people of Damascus. This would lead you into folly and the corruption of this noble language of ours, one of whose distinguishing characteristics is that its rules have remained unchanged and its style fixed in the face of the extinction of all other ancient languages and whose writers of today are in no way inferior to their predecessors who passed away one thousand two hundred years ago. Is it that you envy us this and have been trying to transform the language and bring it into line with your own, in which you cannot understand what was written three hundred years ago?

5.3.8 I would like to know if your authorities would give permission to a man who wanted to open a school for teaching children to do that without taking an examination first. Who, then, examined you and found you qualified for this rank, which is higher than that of a schoolteacher, and who compared what you translated and concocted and botched together with the original? And how did you obtain a license to print it without it first having been checked for correctness? I swear, a teacher who cannot write a single line correctly in the language that he is teaching ought to be sent back to school immediately, despite which some of these professors cannot understand if spoken to, never mind their ignorance of writing, and cannot understand if they read and cannot form the words properly when doing so. I once heard a student reading to his teacher from the *Maqāmāt* of al-Ḥarīrī, and he was barely able to enunciate clearly a single one of the letters that their language is without—*th, ḥ, kh, dh, ṣ, ṭ, ẓ,* ʿ, *gh, q,* and *h*—and his teacher said nothing because he knew that any correction he might make would be wrong. How can anyone who has not heard the language from its native speakers pronounce it well? How can it not be so when any of them who has written anything on the grammar of our language has based it entirely on false ideas? Thus, they transcribe the letter *j* of our tongue with the two letters *d* and *j* of theirs,[687] ignoring the fact that there are no compound letters in Arabic such as exist in Greek, since for a word to begin with a double consonant is unacceptable, if not indeed inadmissible, among the Arabs. Likewise, they transcribe *th* as *ts,* and *dh* and *ẓ* as *tz.* As for the rest of the letters, ʿ, *h,* and *ḥ* are all glottal stops to them, *kh* is *k, ṣ* is *s, ḍ* is *d, ṭ* is *t,* and *q* is *k,* and they pronounce *s* preceded by a vowel as *z.* The preaching metropolitan's "cut off *azbābakum*" mentioned earlier is an example.[688] The glottal stop may occur in their language at the beginnings of words but not in the middle or at the end, and they can only pronounce it as a glide; indeed, most of their writers are unaware that an *alif* at the start of a word has to be pronounced as a stop.

5.3.9 It is not my intention here to teach them how to pronounce the glottal stop with the proper bite—they are already (back) biters enough—but to demonstrate to this ingratiating, toadying sandman,[689] in defense of those shaykhs of mine to whom I owe whatever knowledge I may have acquired, that his shaykhs are not to be considered scholars and that not one of the scholars of Cairo, Tunis, the Maghreb, Damascus, the Hejaz, or Baghdad has need of a single letter from them. True, they have a deep knowledge of literary history. They know, for example, that Abū Tammām and al-Buḥturī were contemporaries and that the second took from the first, and that al-Mutanabbī came after them and that al-Ḥarīrī wrote fifty *maqāmah*s that advanced the *badīʿ* style and so on. They do not, however, understand the books these people wrote and cannot tell fine language from lame or established usage from invention, or recognize well-executed ideational and verbal devices or fine lexical differences or literary or grammatical jokes or poetical terminology. The most that can be said is that they have acquired a shallow knowledge of the scholarship of the Arabs via books written in French—and would they grant that an Arab who had learned their language from books in his own was the equal of their own scholars, or that they needed to be educated by him?

At the same time, it cannot be denied that Monsieur de Sacy acquired through his own efforts enough skill to be able to understand many of our books and even indeed to write in our language. However, "not everything white is a truffle."[690] Despite all of the foregoing he should not, God rest his soul, be placed among the ranks of the most reliable scholars, for he failed to grasp numerous matters in the areas of literature, lexicon, and prosody and I have, I swear, praised his command of the field and lauded his scholarship and merit time and time again. However, when this skill and command of his became a cause of evil—for they it was that emboldened others to take a leading role in teaching our language and seduced this liar into adopting an insolent attitude toward our scholars—I felt it my duty, out of concern for the rights of scholarship and scholars, to delete his name from among those of the shaykhs of the Islamic countries in their entirety as a slap in the face to those who have sheltered behind it and used his scholarship as a cover for false claims and arrogations. Were it not for the monstrous words of this pseudo-erudite blusterer, I would never have taken the time to point out the faults of any of them, as I know that they will never abandon their error and that these words of mine will only make them more arrogant. In contrast, those shaykhs who devote their lives to the pursuit of knowledge hesitate to say what it is that they have achieved, for the more a person's knowledge increases, the more he becomes cognizant of how little he knows. This book of mine may fall into the hands of a Persian or Indian professor and motivate them to take on the task of pointing out their faults in those two languages too, for I am absolutely certain 5.3.10

that they are even more ignorant where those are concerned, since more of them have traveled to the Arab lands than to any others (despite which they have learned nothing from them but lame language and nonsense).

5.3.11 Know, my dear Arab reader, that the only work among all those that they have printed in our language that I have found worthy of close consideration is the *Maqāmāt* of al-Ḥarīrī[691] and, given the limited time available due to my being about to travel, I was able to look only at the verses in the commentary; I have entrusted to others the task of critiquing the rest just as certain scholars entrusted me with that of critiquing the verses. Subsequently, I came across the travels of the scholar and writer Shaykh Muḥammad ibn al-Sayyid ʿUmar al-Tūnusī[692] in the form of a lithograph based on a copy in the hand of Monsieur Perron,[693] who had freighted the whole book with misspellings and mistakes of a sort for which it would be unreasonable to hold even the least of the aforesaid shaykh's students responsible. Is it possible that any student, let alone scholar, could say *jūduhu nāsikhun li-kulli l-wujūd* in place of *li-kulli l-jūd* or write, more than once, *al-ʿaṣā* with a *y*,[694] or, more than twenty times, *aʿlā* as an elative with an *alif*[695] or *najā* with a *yā*ʾ[696] or *ataʿmā l-muʿālimūna ʿani l-ḍiyāʾ* for *ayaʿmā l-ʿālimūna* or *āminīna muṭmaʾinnīna* when these words occur in the nominative[697] or *fallāḥīna Miṣr*[698] or *maḥmūdīna l-sīrah*[699] or *istawzara l-faqīha Mālik*[700] or *lā yaʿṣā*[701] or *lā arā sūʾa raʾyak* for *lā arā siwā raʾyaka* or *yataʿaddā raʾyahu*[702] or *ithnay ʿashara malik*[703] or *min ḥaythu inna abādīmā wa-l-takaniyāwī mutāʿadilayni lam* for *min ḥaythu inna abādīmā wa-l-takaniyāwī mutāʿadilayni*[704] *fa-lam* or *tajidu l-rijāla wa-l-nisāʾa ḥisān*[705] or *daʿā lanā*[706] or *ʿujūbah*[707] or *ṣawāḥibatuhā* and *ṣawāḥibātuhā*[708] or *lughatun fīhā ḥamās*[709] or *innahumā mutaqāribayi l-maʿnā*[710] or *ḥattā taʾtiya arbābu l-māshiyati fa-yaqbiḍūn*[711] or *fa-hal iḥdā minkum*[712] or *yarfaʿūna aṣwātahum bi-dhālika ḥattā yadkhulūn*[713] or *māshiyīn*[714] or *al-musammayayn*[715] or *ḥattā yashuqqūn*[716] or *munḥaniyūn*[717] or *innahum yakūnū*[718] or *lā-ʿtāḍa*[719] or not know the poetic meters, so that he takes *kāmil* for *hazaj*, *ṭawīl* for *madīd*, and so on?

5.3.12 It is amazing that the aforementioned shaykh quotes the following lines[720]

abraku l-ayyāmi yawmun qīla lī
hādhihi Ṭībatu hādhī l-Kuthubū
hādhihi rawḍatu Ṭāhā l-muṣṭafā
hādhihi l-Zarqā'u ladaykum fa-shrabū

(The most blessed of days was that on which it was said to me
"This is Thebes! This is al-Kuthub![721]
This is the garden of Ṭāhā the Chosen![722]
This, before you, is the Bright One,[723] so drink!")

explaining in his commentary that "the *yā'* in *hādhī* is in place of the [second] *hā'*"[724] and yet when a student read them to Monsieur Caussin de Perceval, one of the mighty teachers in question, the latter corrected his pronunciation of Ṭāhā to *waṭ'* ("treading"), explaining it as meaning "the treading of the foot," and changed the [second] *hā'* in the words *hādhihi l-Zarqā'u* to *yā'* because of the words of the shaykh "the *yā'* in *hādhī* is in place of the *hā'*,"[725] throwing the meter off in the process. He also left *al-Zarqā'u* uncorrected (Monsieur Perron having put a *hamzah* after the *alif*),[726] which again broke the meter. *Waṭ'* should properly be written without an *alif*.[727] Observe, then, the copyist and the correcter, and all this confusion, and wonder!

List of Misspelled Arabic Words that I Discovered in the Transcriptions of Letters in Persian in the Book by "the Sandy Shaykh," Alexandre Chodźko

5.4.1

Page	Line	Misspelling	Correct spelling
192	1	*fī mā*	*fīmā* (as in the original)
"	4	*iltiyām*	*ilti'ām* (as in the original)
192	9	*shakhāmat*	*shahāmat* (as in the original)
"	22	*bih mamlakat*	*bi-mamlakat* (as in the original)
193	6	*'azẓām*	*'iẓām* (as in the original)
"	17	*istikhḍār*	*istiḥḍār* (as in the original)
196	23	*janāb aqdasī ilāhī*	*janāb aqdas ilāhī* (as in the original)
"	26	*khilāfan al-Akhfash*	*khilāfan li-l-Akhfash* (as in the original)
197	4	*barā'u l-sā'ah*	*bar'u l-sā'ah* (as in the original)
198	"	*qāni' ṣafṣaf*	*qā' ṣafṣaf* (mentioned above)[728]
200	" (Opening of the epistle)		
		wa-mubārakun sulṭānuhu	*wa-tabāraka* etc. to match *awwalan ta'ālā sha'nuhu*
201	18	*mawlāt*	*mawālāt*

and this despite the fact that I have not gone to the lengths of comparing every one of these epistles with the original, the point being simply to demonstrate the mendacity of his claim, what I have cited being sufficient for that purpose.

Table Showing the Mistakes in the Probative Verses in the *Maqāmāt* of al-Ḥarīrī which Appeared in a Second Edition, with Corrections by the Two Eminent Shaykhs Reinaud and Derenbourg,[729] in 1847 following the Death of de Sacy; the Mistakes in the Commentary Itself are Too Numerous to Count[730]

5.5.1

Page	Line	[Incorrect]	[Correct]
ه	1	تَرب[731] (twice)	تُرب
"	4	المجلَس	المجلِس
"	10	غضابًا	Should be without *tanwīn*, for the rhyme.
ح	4	قالوا العواذل	قال العواذل, as العواذل is the plural of عاذل.[732]
"	9	خَدَرَت	خَدِرَت
"	13	(in the prose) ذميما	دميما
Title page	10	تكتب	نكتب is the more common reading.
6	[17][733]	وان اصدق بيت	The more obvious reading would be احسن بيت.
11	17	الكرا	الكرى because the root is with ى
18	[10]	ثنَّى	ثَنى is the more common reading.

	Page	Line	[Incorrect]	[Correct]
5.5.2	41	[24]	فيُظلمونى	فيَظلمونى
	49	17	ياطلحَ اكرمُ من	اكرمَ من
	51	15	فانه بنَثٍّ	ينُثُّ
	52	[26]	اقترحتُ العشآءَ عليه يوما	اقترحت العشآء يوما عليه
	"	[27]	قال لِىَ آلعشا	لى اَلعشا because he uses the word [and what follows] with the force of a proverb,[734] in which case it does not change, as when one says الصيفَ ضيّعتِ اللبن.[735]
	69	[12]	مبَرّاءَ	مُبرّاءًا
	70	[9]	نراه	تراه
	71	[23]	احسنُ من	احسنَ because it is the predicate of ليس.
5.5.3	75	13	نيل المنا	المُنَى because it is the plural of مُنية.
	76	10	الأَفلاس	الإفلاس
	"	12	فى عَسْر وفى يُسَر	يُسُر
	78	21	سُلَّمًا	سلَّما without *tanwīn* as it is the rhyme word.
	80	8	فى ما	فيما
	"	"	سبيلْ	سبيلُ, and likewise دليل in the second line of verse.
	82	[11]	ركِد	ركَدَ
	84	[26]	وكونْ	Without *tanwīn*.
	86	10	جُمَّة	جَمَّة
	"	"	امرءَ	امرأ
	"	17	فانيًا	فانيا without *tanwīn*.

Page	Line	[Incorrect]	[Correct]
89		ومن يلقَ ما لاقيت لا بد يارقُ ارقتُ فلم تخدع بعينى نعسةٌ ("And he who meets with what I have met with must surely spend the night unsleeping / I spent the night unsleeping, and never a wink of sleep seduced my eye") 5.5.4 The hemistichs should be reversed. The strange thing is that this *naʿsah* ("wink of sleep") closed the eyes of both de Sacy and the other two eminent shaykhs. Did you ever—you Arabs and you nation of men-and-jinn!—hear of a rhyme word (here an imperfect verb) occurring as the last foot of an initial hemistich unless both hemistich-final words are rhymed or of the tanwīn in *naʿsah* or similar words such as *taʿsah* ("an instance of wretchedness"), *ḥamqah* ("an instance of stupidity"), *ḥabqah* ("a fart"), *salḥah* ("a turd"), or *faqḥah* ("an anal orifice") occurring as the rhyming syllable?[736] Do not the words *wa-man yalqa* ("And he who meets with") follow naturally from the first hemistich and are they not proclaimed as having the force of a proverb?	
92	19	البلاقعَ	البلاقعا with prolongation of the vowel for the rhyme.[737]
93	13	بدناً	بدنا without tanwīn. How could these "teachers" not have noticed this, given that the last word of the first hemistich is أنا?[738]
97	22	اليهُم	What could be the cause of such contortedness?[739]
110	18	يغدوا	يَغْدو; in the same line مهموم and مهدوم and كلثوم also occur, all of which should properly be without *tanwīn*.
111	7	ارءف	أَرْأَف
"	9	بْنةُ	آبْنة
"	11	مجذب	مجدب

	Page	Line	[Incorrect]	[Correct]
	113	17	مراحًا . . . مفاحًا	Without *tanwīn*.
	115	[20]	متيَّمٌ اثرُها	اثرَها since how can *tatayyum* ("enslavement to love") be attributed to *ithr* ("after")?[740] Even stranger are the *tanwīn* on متبول and مكبول! How would you deal, my dear professors, with a غول?[741] Do you not observe how such affected erudition draws people into shameful situations? Not to mention that Kaʿb's poem[742] is known to all.
5.5.5	123	11	شيًا	شيّا, to agree with يديّا and حيّا.
	124	[16]	الآدِبُ	الادبَ because it is the object of لا ترى.
	125	[1–11]		All the rhyming syllables of the *qaṣīdah muṣammaṭah*[743] should be "fettered."[744]
	132	[11]	دَنى	دنا, because it is from the root *d-n-w*.
	134	5	كتمانى	كتمانِ
	137	[24]	ناصبٍ	ناصبِ
	146	16	تُثنى	تَثنى
	147	[20]	اَسْفار	اَشْفار ("outer edge of the eyelid"), and what have اسفار ("books") to do with the eye, O you who see well?
	152	[15]	حسرانًا	حسرانا without *tanwīn*.
	158	16	صَناعة	صِناعة
	"	25	مظهرًا	Without *tanwīn*.
5.5.6	159	26	سَنًا	سَنًّى
	169	12	وربُّتْ	وربُّتَ

Page	Line	[Incorrect]	[Correct]	
174	13	خُمْسَ كفّك	خَمْس	
177	[18]	بَكور	بُكور, and in the same line تشميتًا, which is correctly without *tanwīn*.	
179	[15]	فى الدعوةِ_الى الجفوةِ	The pausal form is required.[745]	
183	17	خَيارهم	خِيارهم	
"	18	تَسْئَلْ فَسَلْ	تَسْأَلْ وَسَلْ	
"	21	وصُحبه	وصَحبه	
185	13	المنطَق	المنطِق	
"	16	عنه	منه	
189	[6]	البَصْرِ	البَصَرْ	5.5.7
"	[23]	نجئ (twice)	تجئ	
"	["]	فطورا	وطورا	
"	"	بجميئة	بحماة	
195	13	دنى	دنا	
199	[19]	المِشتاة	المَشتاة	
"	["]	ينتقرُ	ينتقرْ	
204	7	جُمَّة	جَمَّة	
"	[22–23]	غمامٍ_زنامٍ	Without *tanwīn*.	
212	12	لاقِى الاحبَّةِ	لاقَى الاحبَّةَ	
"	15	أَبْغِض	اُبْغِض	5.5.8
"	18	اليهِمُ	Strangely contorted.[746]	
215	[18]	إن	اَن	

	Page	Line	[Incorrect]	[Correct]
	218	24	صروفه	صروفها unless the pronominal suffix refers to something mentioned earlier.[747]
	221	[26]	قُنبُرة	قُبَّرة is preferable (line of verse at the end of the page).
	222	18	يمنعَ_فترتعَ	يمنعُ فترتعُ
	232	17	يصنعُ	يصنع
	"	18	بدوُه	بدؤُه
	236	[17–18]	اَرْبِه_اَدْبِهِ	اَرَبِهْ اَدَبِهْ
	237	[9]	وانَّ منّى لوَّا	وان لوًّا عَناَءً; he seems to have thought that عناء here has the function of a pre-position followed by its object and that putting it after لوّا would upset the meter, so he changed it to منّى and made the suffix singular.
5.5.9	239	13	ياعابِثَ الفقر	اعائب الفقر, though the word عيب in the second hemistich ought to be enough to guide a blind man to the meaning of the line; our good professors, however, are fond of foolishness.[748]
	245	23	اِنَّما	اَنَّما
	247	14	قوسَا	قوسًا
	248	12	منَ آبن	منِ آبن
	"	"	مامة كعبٍ	مامةِ because in construct.
	252	[27]	وَلهًا	وَلَها, i.e., ولها عليه رنين.
	255	11	المقانعَ	المقانعا

Page	Line	[Incorrect]	[Correct]	
258	19	تَسْلمْ مِنْ أَنْ	تَسْلَمْ مِنَ آنْ, the *hamzah* being deleted for the meter.	
258	23	تَجَرَّبْ سبيل القصد	تَجَرّ [سبيل القصد], the word having been misread by everybody, the reason for their error being the poet's use in the following line of the words لم تجرّبْ; the words ولا تُسىءُ الظنا are properly [ولا] تسيء [الظنا]: the former breaks the meter. Also, the words لدى الخَبر should properly be [لدى] الخُبْر, i.e., "on being tested."	
260	[21]	ضَلَّتْ	ضَلَّتِ	
"	[22]	بَرغوثا	بُرغوثا; لولَّت ought to be لَوَلَّتِ; the professors should review the rule. As for *barghūth* with *fatḥah*, it's one of the oddities their like come up with, for there are no words in the language of the pattern *fa'lūl* with the sole exception of *ṣa'fūq*.	
262	[23]	تَهامة	تِهامة	5.5.10
263	7	الكاسِ	الكاسى	
"	8	فانك انت الآكل اللابسُ	[فانك الآكل] اللَّاسِى from لسا meaning "to eat voraciously"; how, mighty teachers, can اللابسُ rhyme with الكاسى, even if they have the same meaning? الكاسى here is from كَسِىَ, which is intransitive; if it were from transitive كسا it would constitute praise, which is not what is required ("Will you not then understand?").[749]	

	Page	Line	[Incorrect]	[Correct]
	"	24	يحفِظ	يحفَظ
	264	18	ممكِّنا	ممكَّنا
	2	18	وهنُ	وهنَ
	269	23	قُلِبَ	قُلِبا
	271	15	شَتّانِ	شتانَ
	276	20	اللّٰهُ	اللّٰهَ
	279	21	قبلُنا	قبلَنا
5.5.11	280	23	The line cannot be scanned properly if one reads وتُنقَب and it must therefore be وتنقب.	
	287	19	وعَمرى	Should be وعُمرى as the poet was not being wordy. [750]
	293	22	وشُرب	وشَرب[751]
	"	24	لجهنَّم	فى جهنَّم; the whole thing should be checked.
	295	16	المُغْزَل	المِغْزَل
	"	1	ويَعرِى استُه	Better, ويُعرى استَه.
	301	"	فانك الطاعم	فانك انت الطاعم
	303	19	والدَرَّ	والدُرَّ
	312	[22]	ضَبارم	ضُبارم
	316	[28]	قبلهُ_بَعْدُهُ	قبلَهُ_بَعْدَهْ (line of verse at the bottom of the page).
5.5.12	319	[12]	دُرْنا دُرْنَى	It would be better to stick with one or the other.[752]
	323	27	جلاجلَ	جلاجلٍ, as Dhū l-Rummah was not one to use contorted language.[753]

Page	Line	[Incorrect]	[Correct]	
324	12	جلاجلَ	The same botched job as before; a parallel form occurs in the first line.[754]	
326	16	ويُسهِرُ	وَيَسْهَرُ; and حَرَّاها should apparently be جَرّاها	
329	17	صئيلة	ضئيلة	
332	19	مَنْجا	مَنْجَى	
338	12	حُنانَيْك	حَنانَيْك	
339	[20]	الى خبيرا	The line cannot be scanned properly thus; it has to be made right with some word such as سوق.	
342	18	مرتهِن	مرتهَن	
343	18	عَرْب	عُرْب	
344	20	فآخَر	فآخِر	5.5.13
346	8	ظفَرت	ظفِرت	
"	9	القرونُ	القرونَ; also, the word مَنآئيا is twisted.[755]	
347	[16–26] Much botched work in the verses of al-Mutanabbī.			
348	[12]	وقبلُك	وقبلَك and this occurs frequently; I have no idea how the good professors think that an adverb can end in *-u*.	
349	[26]	ايُّما	ايَّما; also the word الرزّ should perhaps be الرَزّ (it is the sound of the rain).	
350	5	اَوْ اَشْرَخَ	اَوَ آشْرِخ	
353	[25]	عُنّيت فى الخدر عُشرا	Apparently, غُيّبت فى الخدر عَشْرا.	
353	["]	والأُنس	والإنس	
"	[26]	عنه	منه	

	Page	Line	[Incorrect]	[Correct]
5.5.14	358	21	يغشون حتى ما تهرَّ	[يغشون حتى ما] تهرُّ
	"	"	السُّواد	السَّواد
	361	13	اِنَّ	اَنَّ
	366	[19]	امن تذكرِ جيْرانَ	[امن تذكر] جيْرانٍ
	368	[25]	النُعْما	النعْمى
	370	18	يسلِم	يسلَم
	"	25	اِنى	اَنى
	373	9	ركَبت	ركِبت
	378	[24]	سريعةُ	سريعةِ (line at the bottom of the page).[756]
	387	3	محتِقرا	محتقَرا
5.5.15	"	5	اِنَّ العزّ	اَنَّ [العزّ]
	"	6	بلوغُ	بلوغَ (following *anna*).
	425	21	اغيدَ	اَغْيدٍ, for the meter, and the good professors should have realized that in view of the poet's using احورِ for the rhyme.
	433	12	ظفرِكَ . . . امركَ . . . بقدرِكَ	All should have sukūn on the *kāf*.

Page	Line	[Incorrect]	[Correct]	
"	23	فالنَعْشُ ادنى لها من ان اقول لَعا	فالتَعْسُ [ادنى لها من ان اقول لَعا] is the correct reading. The poet means "It is better for me to say *taʿs* to her than to say *laʿā*." However, the good professors rushed to write what they did because of the earlier occurrence of *naʿsh*, when he says "and one says, 'May there be no *laʿā* to so-and-so,' meaning 'May God not raise so-and-so after stumbling or from his bier!'" Despite this, it is clear enough from the way the verses are written that *laʿā* and *naʿsh* have the same meaning, so how then could he come up with فالنَعْشُ ادنى لها من ان اقول لَعا?	
438	15	نَسبتى	نِسبتى or نُسبتى	
452	31	وحُبَّ بها مقتولةٍ	[وحُبَّ بها] مقتولةً	
"	25	فاُظهِرَ فى الالوان مِنْ أَلدَّمِ الدَّمُ	The expression is grammatically disordered and it is impossible to scan the line as it stands. It must be repaired by inserting the word *dhā* or something of the sort [between *min* and *al-dami*]. Otherwise, how can the *sukūn* on the *nūn* of *min* be accepted, when it is followed by the definite article?	
"	27	آدَمَ	آدَمُ, <u>for the meter</u>; cf. the second hemistich.	
455	5	اُغلى السَّباَءَ	اِغلى [السَّباَءَ]	5.5.16
"	"	خَتامها	خِتامها	
459	19	كَلًّا	كَلَّا	

	Page	Line	[Incorrect]	[Correct]
	463	18	زُبرقان	زِبرقان
	"	[19]	قبلُك	قبلَك, this being the fifth time; are you going to put the blame on the printer as is your wont these days? Compare عَوْلَ.[757]
	477	11	تعاقَبْ	تعاقِبْ
	"	19	الأُنثى	With elision [*al-unthā* instead of *al-ʾunthā*] for the meter.
	480	25	ضُوء	ضَوء
	484	24	البُسَيْطة	البَسِيْطة, the diminutive not being allowed to take the definite article.[758]
	"	25	زَجاج	زُجاج, and the same goes for الضَرّ occurring earlier.
5.5.17	"	28	قبلُه	قبلَه because it's an adverb, because it's an adverb, because it's an adverb! Are you going to put the blame on the printer?
	487	19	يبدو محاسنه	تبدو [محاسنه]
	493	"	مناهِلُ	مناهلْ because it occurs as the rhyme word of the first hemistich; they should review the rule .
	"	[22–23]	The last two lines of verse are botched and seriously contravene the rules of the classical language.	
	494	[11]	The verse by al-Mutanabbī contains unwieldy wording;[759] also ويالكِ من خد اسيل in the other line of verse should read ويالك .	
	501	[9]	اشتوا	شَتَوا; also مثلَ should be مثلُ.

Page	Line	[Incorrect]	[Correct]	
503	13	جَنائِى وخَياره	جناىَ وخِياره	
508	22	لِذُوى الالباب وذى	لذَوى الالباب او ذى	
509	12	والنَّجح	والنُّجح	
"	13	تُقاذف	تَقاذف; originally تتقاذف, with the first *tā'* being dropped to make it lighter.[760]	
"	19	وكلُّ يوم	وكلَّ يوم, in the accusative in the absence of a genitive agent.	5.5.18
515	[29]	خِندَف	خِندِف (line of verse at the bottom of the page).	
516	6	يُفنِى	يَفنى	
"	11	معتَب	معتِب	
"	22	كِثرة	كَثرة	
517	15	بنُ	بنَ	
520	22	فنُّ	فنَّ	
"	29	نُفذت	نَفذت	
532	5	خَدَع	خُدَع	
"	10	وعصرهُ	وعصرِهِ	
535	9	تَساق	تُساق	5.5.19
"	10	مِثلَ فِىءِ	مثلُ فَىْءِ	
535	14	قنَعوا	قنِعوا	
538	[23]	عرَى	عُرْىِ	
"	[24]	الشَّرك تعلِمُه	الشِرك تعلَمُه	
"	["]	عِماها	عَماها; العَمَى is with *a*, you professors![761]	
539	[17]	تُجهَل	تَجهل	

	Page	Line	[Incorrect]	[Correct]
	541	19	كانوا الأكارمُ	كانوا الأكارمَ; also the second line of verse is botched.
	542	[24]	المغيظ المحنَق	المغيظ المحنِق, the second word here meaning *al-ḥāqid* ("the resentful"); *muḥnaq* means the same as *mughḍab* ("vexed") and would therefore have the same sense as *maghīẓ*.
5.5.20	548	[25]	فُمى	فَمى (the line of verse is at the bottom of the page).
	549	9	تَنْكَر	تُنكِر
	"	"	ابتَلَيْت	ابتُلِيْت
	"	19	غدتْ بنتُ	[غدتْ] بنتَ
	"	24	قَبلُ	قبلَ because it's an adverb, because it's an adverb, because it's an adverb! This is the seventh time. Are you going to put the blame on the printer?
	"	25	الزَبْد	الزُبْد; cf. ياعقارُ
	555	[23]	انُْس	إنْس
	"	[24]	يحمُدُ	يحمَدُ; also the word خِمسا in the previous line [is dubious], so it should be checked against the original.
	561	[16]	فوق رؤسِهِمُ	فوق رؤُسِهِم; the book abounds in examples of this sort.
	"	["]	جلّال	إجلال
	566	[6]	لم يَلُذَّ	يَلِذّ, because intransitive geminate verbs have the middle consonant with *i* except in rare cases.

Page	Line	[Incorrect]	[Correct]	
568	[28]	لَاسْقِيهِمْ	لَاسْقِيَهُمْ (the line of verse at the bottom of the page).	5.5.21
569	,,	فيعرُض	فيعرِض	
570	23	كِلامَ	كَلام	
575	14	وزَهْدُ	وزُهْد	
"	[15]	يساوِى	يساوَى	
"	[17]	نحو مبرّد	[نحو] المبرّد	
"	[20]	هاكِها	هاكَها	
"	["]	تطُنّ	تطِنّ	
590	[7]	تفهِموا	تفهَموا	
"	["]	ذُوو	ذَوو; the good professors seem to have formed the plural by analogy with the singular.	
"	[21]	بالِ	بالْ, the rhyme being with an unvoweled consonant throughout.	5.5.22
591	13	تعلِم	تعلَم	
597	[20]	بالمُشرفىّ	بالمَشرفى	
608	23	اَرْحَمْ	اِرْحم	
610	22	ويُحْسَنُ دَلُّها	ويَحْسُنُ دَلُّها	
611	[24]	اكارِعَه	اكارِعُه	
614	11	قبلَ الأَجَلْ	من قبلِ الاجل to allow the verse to scan correctly.	
"	13	لَيْلاً	لَيْلَى	
626	[24]	جُعِلنا عوارِضُ	[جُعِلنا] عوارَضُ (the line of verse at the bottom of the page).	

	Page	Line	[Incorrect]	[Correct]
	627	[11]	يُنْصَحان	يَنْصَحان
5.5.23	"	[12]	واصبُرْ	واصبِرْ and the same in the second [hemistich].
	628	[25]	يجئ	يجى, with elision of the glottal stop for the meter.
	633	10	جَسْم (twice)	جِسْم
	"	[10]	In the final verses, it would be better to treat مسلم as diptote than to break the meter.	
	633	22	بارِد	With *tanwīn*; also الطَّهور not الطُّهور.[762]
	635	15	الاشقِينَ	الاشقَينَ
	"	[26]	مطبَخَه	مَطْبَخُهُ; also ساباطَ should be either ساباطا or ساباطِ.
	639	[12]	نائلكَ	نائلكم because it comes as the last word of the first hemistich.
	641	[22]	سعادٌ	سعادُ, and اثرُها should be اثرَها, which is the second time this mistake has been made.
	645	10	ضَرغام	ضِرغام
5.5.24	"	[13]	مصابحُ	مصابحٌ as it comes as the last word of the first hemistich.
	"	19	دارَ وفارَ	دارْ وفارْ for the rhyme.
	646	[18]	السِعلات	السعلاةِ; also وعمرُو بنُ مسعود شرارُ should be with final *fatḥah* throughout.
	649	15	اربعةٌ	Corr.[763] اربعةً; also فى جبرِئل is botched and نَصْل should be فَصَلَ.
	650	[12]	تزوَّجَ ابنُ	In the authoritative reading, نزوّجُ ابنَ.

Page	Line	[Incorrect]	[Correct]
653	[18]	مُعاذَ اللّٰه	مَعاذ [اللّٰه]
658	[16]	شديدُ	شديدْ
660	[21]	تِريْنَ	ترَيْنَ; also واعلِم should be واعلَم.
"	[26]	من الحرفةِ	من الحِرَفَهْ
662	[9]	وطيًّا	وطيئًا
"	["]	فقَصِّرُكما	فقَصْرُكما meaning "your objective" or "your destiny." 5.5.25
"	["]	وتَلِدَ	وتَلِدا
662	[21]	فتًى هو اَحْيا	In the authoritative reading, كان احيا.
664	[26]	لعلَّ اللّٰهُ	[لعلَّ] اللّٰهَ (the line of verse at the bottom of the page).
668	[11]	يَخزنى	يُخزنى
669	[23]	مزيدَ	مزيدٍ because it occurs as the last word of the first hemistich.
672	[17]	اَحَبُّ	اُحِبُّ
674	[19]	شوامش	شوامس; the second شوامس should be the object of the preposition, with *–i*, or with *alif* to mark the prolongation of the vowel.
678	[20]	خَبْزه	خُبزه
679	14	شيا تُجَرّ	[شيا] يَجْرُ
"	22	اخفُّ	اخفَّ
"	23	وابصرُ	وابصرَ

and the two shaykhs keep on in the same vein to the end of the *maqāmāt*. If one were to investigate every example of error and misspelling in both the text and the commentary, it would amount to a very great quantity, so let what I provide here be sufficient testimony as to the scholarship of the two aforementioned persons and give the lie to their friend's claim. The selections of Monsieur Caussin de Perceval from *Qiṣṣat ʿAntar* (*The Story of ʿAntar*),[764] his writings on the speech of the people of Aleppo, and the transcriptions by others of silly stories in lame language are not worth the time one would waste on them, for they are all bad.

END OF THE APPENDIX

NOTICE: it is the habit of the abovementioned professors and those like them who have written something in Arabic to excuse their terrible mistakes by putting the blame on the printer and typesetter, saying that the mistakes are due to the latter's ignorance of the language, or so I was told by Conte Alix Desgranges,[765] who was reporting the words of Professor Caussin de Perceval. This is an excuse worse than the offense, for the typesetter does exactly what you ask of him and whatever rules you lay down he obeys. Do you not observe that M. Perrault, of Rue de Castellane, 15, Paris, even though he knows nothing about the Arabic language, has followed with the utmost care our instructions in terms of corrections and changes and gone to great lengths to compose the letters correctly and produce an excellent piece of printing, so much so that he has come up, praise God, with the best thing ever printed in our language in Europe? We commend him, therefore, to any who wish to print anything in Arabic; there can be no doubt that they will praise his efforts and be happy with his work, even if he is not with the Imprimerie Nationale, the excellence of the work being its own recommendation. 5.6.1

[END]

Translator's Afterword

This is the first translation into English of Aḥmad Fāris al-Shidyāq's *al-Sāq ʿalā l-sāq*,[766] a work published in Arabic in 1855 and celebrated thereafter both for its importance to the history of Arabic literature and as a "difficult" text. The book's literary and historical significance is the subject of the Foreword (Volume One, ix–xxx). This Afterword deals only with translational issues.

The first element of the work's title is itself often cited as representative of the book's difficulties. The words *al-sāq ʿalā l-sāq* are ambiguous and clearly meant to be so. The common meaning of *sāq* is "shank" and thus by metonymy the leg as a whole; less well-known are the senses "male turtle dove" and "trunk (of a tree)." What it means for a leg to be "over" or "upon" (*ʿalā*) another leg is for the reader to decide. Paul Starkey reminds us that Henri Pérès proposed that the phrase should be understood as "[sitting] cross-legged" and thus evokes "the familiar attitude adopted by a storyteller who, comfortably installed in an armchair, is about to narrate a long story of wonderful adventures."[767] This bland interpretation cannot be entirely excluded, if only on principle: if the title is intended to be ambiguous, more than one possible interpretation is, by definition, required. Pérès's definition is not, however, explicitly reflected in the text; rather, as Starkey also points out, the phrase *al-sāq ʿalā l-sāq* occurs there with sexual innuendo, as when the author writes of a woman's suitor speaking to her of "the bed, of drawing her close, of embracing, of leg over leg, of kissing, of kissing tongue to tongue, of intercourse, and the like" (Volume Three, 3.4.1); similar is the earlier use, during a discussion that exploits the sexual suggestiveness of Arabic grammatical terminology (Volume One, 1.11.9), of the phrase *alladhī yarfaʿu l-sāq* ("the one who raises his leg"). In this translation, therefore, the title has been tilted towards the erotic by the use of the perhaps more suggestive "over" in preference to "upon."

The second element of the English title—"or the Turtle in the Tree"—which builds on the two less common senses of *sāq*, has been introduced to provide a rhyme (an essential element of the title, though achieved differently in the original) and to sensitize the English reader to the ludic nature of the text as a whole.

Turning to the text, it should perhaps be made clear that *al-Sāq ʿalā l-sāq*, despite its reputation, is not always "difficult." As Pierre Cachia has written, the author is capable of expressing himself "with a simplicity and directness that a writer a century later would be pleased to claim for himself."[768] At the same time, however, his writing is characterized by two general features and two specific practices of prose organization that do pose challenges for the translator.

The two general features are a fondness for arcane vocabulary and a verbal playfulness that expresses itself through punning, word games, and humorous allusion. Both are so widely distributed throughout the text as to be numbered among its most fundamental characteristics.

To "give prominence to the oddities of the language, including its rare words" (Volume One, 0.2.1.) is the author's first stated goal for the work. Rare words are present in huge numbers either in the form of lists, which sometimes proclaim their presence with headings such as "Here are the meanings of the rare words mentioned above" (Volume One, 1.16.9) or "An Explanation of the Obscure Words in the Preceding *Maqāmah* and Their Meanings" (Volume Two, 2.14), or else embedded in the general narrative. In the latter case, the author will, on occasion, call attention to the lists by glossing them in the margin (see, e.g., the note on *izāʾ* at 1.4.2 in Volume One). The main challenge posed by such words is the time needed to research them; I must, therefore, acknowledge the help provided by online dictionary sites, without which this translation would have been too time-consuming to be feasible. The sites I used most were www.baheth.info (for, among others, al-Fīrūzābādī's *al-Qāmūs al-muḥīṭ* and Ibn Manẓūr's *Lisān al-ʿArab*) and both www.tyndalearchive.com and http://www.perseus

.tufts.edu for Lane's *Lexicon*. Rare words pose a major obstacle to the translator, however, only when they fail to appear, in an appropriate sense, in any dictionary; fortunately, the number of such items is small.

Puns and allusions pose a greater challenge, partly because they may go unnoticed and partly because, even when they are recognized, native readers themselves may differ as to their meaning. Inevitably, therefore, interpretation sometimes remains speculative. The reference to "the two ks" (Volume One, 1.16.5 and note 235 there) is a case in point: two widely differing understandings of the phrase were put forward by two scholars I consulted; my own, third, interpretation may or may not be correct.

The prose organization practice perhaps most likely to give the translator pause in this work is the use of *sajʿ* (rhymed, rhythmic prose that often involves semantic or syntactic parallelism and that is typically associated with heightened drama or emotion in the text).[769] In *al-Sāq*, *sajʿ* is employed throughout, both over the span of entire chapters and in passages within a chapter that range from a phrase or two to several pages. Patently, Arabic, with its productive morphological classes all of whose members possess, or end in, the same pattern of vowels and consonants, lends itself to this practice. It is enough, in Arabic, to choose as one's rhyme word a Form III verbal noun of the pattern *mufāʿalah*, for example, to access hundreds more words of that pattern, or to deploy, say, the third person masculine plural imperfect verb to have at one's disposal thousands of words ending in *–ūna*. The capacity of English to generate rhymes is more limited and the translator is therefore faced with a "rhyme deficit." Not surprisingly, it has often been the practice of translators faced with *sajʿ* to ignore it, even though this be at the expense of a prominent aesthetic dimension of the original.

This is not an option, however, in the case of *al-Sāq*, if only because the author's use of *sajʿ* is self-conscious and his references to the problems it creates numerous. Thus at one point the author remarks that "Rhymed prose is to the writer as a wooden leg to the walker" (Volume One, 1.10.1), following this observation with a disquisition on the dangers of its overuse and the differences between it and verse (which he claims to be less demanding). Likewise, the difficulty of writing *maqāmah*s, a genre to which *sajʿ* is intrinsic, is a favorite topic of the author's (e.g., Volume One,

1.14.1). Even his tendency, when subjected to the appropriate stimulus, to break into *saj*ʿ in the midst of unrhymed prose may elicit an explicit comment from him on his own writing, as when he exclaims, "God be praised—the mere thought of women produces the urge to write in rhymed prose!" (Volume One, 1.16.2).

The translator is therefore obliged to do the best he can. Given the limitations of English, some latitude is essential. In additional to full rhyme, near rhyme, rime riche, alliteration, and assonance have all been used; occasionally, the order of the Arabic periods has been changed. Likewise, it has not always been possible in the English to rhyme the same words that are rhymed in the Arabic, which has meant a reduction in the "linking and correspondence" that the author regards as an intrinsic element of the technique (Volume One, 1.10.1).[770] It has not always even been possible to produce the same number of rhyming words in any given passage: the number of rhymes in the translation is fewer than in the original. I hope, nevertheless, that at least something of the force and humor of al-Shidyāq's *saj*ʿ has been carried over.

What applies to *saj*ʿ applies equally, of course, to verse, which in the Arabic of this period is entirely monorhymed. In this translation, shorter poems have mainly been rendered into rhymed couplets.[771] Most of the longer poems, such as the Proem (Volume One, 0.4) and the poems at the end of the work (Volume Four, 4.20) have been left unrhymed.

The other challenging fundamental practice in *al-Sāq* is the presentation of large numbers of words, usually rare, in the form of lists. Studies have stressed the "sound effect of the accumulated words"[772] and the "*fonction incantatoire*"[773] of such lists, and to these aspects may be added the distancing effect (amounting, in Peled's view, to a "sense of terror")[774] created by the obscurity (i.e., the quality of their being unknown to and unknowable by the ordinary reader) of the words and, often, their phonetic exoticism. The impact of many of these lists is increased by their great length; one series of interlinked lists (Volume Two, 2.14.8–84) extends, in the original, over more than forty-two pages.

Such lists fall into two categories: those with definitions and those without. Each category calls for a different approach from the translator.

As a preliminary point of reference, the hitherto perhaps under-recognized fact that the words that constitute these lists are taken, largely and perhaps even exclusively, from al-Fīrūzābādī's renowned fifteenth-century dictionary *al-Qāmūs al-muḥīṭ* should be noted. Similarly, the definitions given for these words, where definitions are given, are verbatim transcriptions of the definitions in the same dictionary and they are not of the author's own making or drawn from any other source. Indeed, al-Shidyāq makes this explicit in the Proem when he says, "To me and to the author of the *Qāmūs* must go the credit / Since it is from his fathomless sea that my words have been scooped" (Volume One, 0.4.6) and again when he claims that the *Qāmūs* was "the only book in Arabic I had to refer to or depend on" (Volume One, 1.1.7) during the writing of *al-Sāq*; on occasion too he states explicitly that he is copying a particular list from the *Qāmūs* (Volume Two, 2.4.12). He also refers to the *Qāmūs* in the comments that he occasionally includes within the lists (see, e.g., the entry for *ṭurmūth* in Volume Two at 2.14.74 and for *mumarjal* in Volume Two at 2.16.47).

So thoroughgoing indeed is the author's reliance on the *Qāmūs* that I am tempted to believe that my occasional failure to locate a definition in the *Qāmūs* is more likely to be due to the item's occurring in some entry other than that in which it should, on the basis of root, be found, or to a discrepancy of editions, than to its not in fact occurring there. In the translation, verbatim quotes from the *Qāmūs* occurring in the lists have been placed in quotation marks, while material that could not be found there, and author's comments, are given without quotation marks.

These facts have the important implication that these lists are lexicologically driven and bear only a tenuous and opportunistic relationship to reality. The list of headwear worn in Alexandria (Volume Two, 2.2.1), for example, tells us little about what men actually wore at that time and place; even the few items that may indeed have been present—e.g., "tall pointed hats (*ṭarāṭīr*) and tarbushes (*ṭarābīsh*)"—are included, I would argue, because they, like the other, more obscure, terms, occur in the *Qāmūs*, not because they were worn in Alexandria in the third decade of the nineteenth century. Similarly, a list of foods supposedly eaten in Alexandria (see Volume Two, 2.2.10) and consisting largely of edible vetches but containing few words for whose use in Egypt there is any evidence, tells us nothing about the diet of the inhabitants of that city at that time beyond, perhaps, the fact that it included a lot of pulses. Such lists are not intended to convey information about the world but to impress the reader—firstly, with the inexhaustible resources of the classical Arabic language and secondly, with the author's mastery thereof; perhaps they also simply reflect the author's fascination with words per se, irrespective of any intention to edify or impress.

The lists with definitions, most of which occur in the first half of the work and which can run to over forty pages, do not pose any particular methodological problem for the translator. They are, for the most part, presented by the author in the form of tables, with headwords in one column and definitions in the next.[775] The headwords in these tables must be transcribed, the definitions translated; any other approach results in the nonsense of an English translation of an Arabic word followed by an English translation of its Arabic definition.

The lists without definitions form at least as large a part of the work as the tabular lists but pose a greater challenge. The work opens with one such list—eleven synonyms or near-synonyms for "Be quiet!" (Volume One, 1.1.1)—and they continue to occur throughout. They vary in length from half a dozen to close to three hundred words (e.g., the list of women's ways of looking and walking in Volume Two at 2.2.4). Items in such lists are all synonyms, near-synonyms, or semantically associated words, and are often grouped into rhymed pairs, or series of pairs, which are sometimes also metatheses of each other. These lists pose three main problems: how to circumvent the limitations of English in terms of translational equivalents for the list items; how to deal with the under-specificity of some definitions in the *Qāmūs* (and other dictionaries), which further reduces the options available to the translator; and how to render their "incantatory," recondite, and exotic aspects.

As far as availability of equivalents is concerned, shorter lists may not pose a problem: English may furnish a sufficient number of appropriate synonyms. Even medium-length lists may be susceptible to one-to-one, or near one-to-one, translation (see, e.g., the list of the sounds made by the organ in Volume One at 1.4.6), especially when the author's use of onomatopoeia and other forms of playfulness opens the door for a degree of inventiveness in the English (see e.g., the list of types of metaphor and their fanciful subdivisions in Volume One at 1.11.5). In the case of longer lists, however, English may refuse to yield enough words within a given semantic field, while what words it does possess in that field may fail to match, even approximately, the Arabic items.

A case in point is the list of words describing women's ways of looking and moving referred to above (Volume Two, 2.2.4). It is doubtful that English possesses 288 words in this semantic field and a virtual certainty that what words it does possess will not map exactly onto the words in the text. Further examples are the list of 255 words denoting genitalia and sexual activities occurring near the beginning of the book (Volume One, 1.1.6) and the 65-word list of activities associated with gambling and risk-taking (Volume One, 1.16.5); numerous others could be adduced. In such cases, the translator is faced with a choice between presenting the "untranslatable" words in transcription—in other words, not translating them—and resorting to multi-word glosses (e.g., "her stepping out manfully and her walking proudly in her clothes, her swaggering and her swinging along, her stepping like a pouting pigeon and her rolling gait," etc.). The transcriptional approach would yield nonsense (a "translation" consisting of words in the original language); the use of multi-word glosses, while preferable, would nevertheless threaten one of these lists' most important characteristics, namely their obscurity. Sonority may perhaps be retained through the use of rhyme, alliteration, and so on in the English, but the resources are, again, more limited.

In some cases, the problem is compounded by the under-specificity of definitions in the *Qāmūs*. For example, several of the different kinds of headwear worn in Alexandria (Volume Two, 2.2.1) referred to above are defined in the *Qāmūs* either by the single word *ʿimāmah* (any cloth worn around the head, or "turban") or by the single word *qalansuwah* (any shaped covering for the head, or "cap"). With nothing but these generic definitions to go on, the translator is faced with the possibility of renditions along the lines of "in [Alexandria] you see some people whose heads are covered with . . . turbans . . . some with [other kinds of] turbans . . . some with [further kinds of] turbans . . . and others with [even more kinds of] turbans," etc. The solution in this case, inadequate though it may be, was to associate the Arabic word with the appropriate generic English term: "in [Alexandria] you see some people whose heads are covered with *maqāʿiṭ* turbans . . . some with *aṣnāʿ* turbans . . . some with *madāmīj* turbans . . . some with the turban under the name *mishmadh* and others with the turban under the name *mishwadh*," etc.

Such phrasal glosses and/or the use of generic terminology, while perhaps justifiable in terms of highlighting the lexically driven nature of these lists, may also produce a numbing repetitiveness or a kind of off-list intrusiveness—"turbans . . . turbans . . . turbans . . ." or "some other way of simply walking, the same with a difference of one letter . . . and another way of simply walking with yet another letter changed" or "the vulva said four other ways"—that is very different in impact from the original list.

The translator's strategies for such lists have developed during the course of the work.

In Volumes One and Two, lists without definitions were mainly dealt with by "direct" translation (i.e., by using one-word equivalents conveying, in principle, the exact meaning of the Arabic word, such as "her strutting, her galloping"). When such equivalents proved impossible to find (as was often the case), I resorted to phrases ("her walking with her thighs far apart kicking up her feet"). Such phrasal equivalents, however, while perhaps accurately conveying the meaning of the word, betray the nature of the original text by making the translation wordier.

Starting in Volume Two, therefore, with this in mind, I also used some indirect strategies. For example, the list of forty-eight monosyllabic rhyming words (*al-azz wa-l-baḥz wa-l-bakhz* etc.) denoting a blow resulting in implicit or explicit injury (Volume Two, 2.1.23) reproduces all the monosyllabic words in the same semantic field found in *Roget's Thesaurus*, without regard for one-to-one correspondence between the Arabic and the English; the result is closer to my mind to the effect of the Arabic than a translation that sacrifices percussive sound in a search for semantically accurate correspondence. Similarly, the series of notes relating to ugliness in women (which are themselves lists) that interrupt the tabular lists on women's charms (Volume Two, 2.14.12–29) were translated using various tools: the first (2.14.13) uses mainly medical, or pseudo-medical, terms gleaned from the Internet ("nanoid, endomorphic, adipose," etc.); the second (2.14.18: "dirty crockadillapigs, shorties, runts," etc.) was compiled from http://onlineslangdictionary.com/thesaurus; the third (2.14.26: "women who have dilated dugs or deflated bellies, who are blubber-lipped," etc.) depends on *Roget's Thesaurus* and other nonspecialized lexical lists; and the fourth (2.14.29: "brevo-turpicular, magno-pinguicular, vasto-oricular," etc.) uses Google's Latin translation facility to create nonexistent terms imitative of the orotund Arabic. Again, the goal of such translations is to escape one-to-one equivalence in favor of similarity of effect.

In Volumes Three and Four, a thesaurus-based method of translating all lists too long or too generic to allow for one-to-one lexical equivalence was applied systematically. Each of the items in the given list was looked up in the *Qāmūs* and the definitions found there were assembled into a working list; the definitions were then grouped by semantic subfield based on the critical term used in the definition in the *Qāmūs*. A list of words relating to insincerity, for example, might contain twenty-four items, a number of which are defined in terms of glibness,[776] a number in terms of fickleness, and others in terms of hypocrisy. "Glibness," etc. were then looked up in Roget's Thesaurus and their synonyms organized into a new list, attention being given where possible to reproduction of nonlexical elements such as rhyme, alliteration, and rhythm as well as rarity or reconditeness. The resulting English list is thus a representation and not a translation of the original Arabic list. Since this approach violates the reader's presumed expectations of translation as a system of (more or less) one-to-one equivalency, I give notice of such "representations" in the endnotes, in a spirit of transparency.

Theoretically, this method of "representation" rather than "translation" could be extended further. If, for example, the works of Rabelais—another list maker and lover of recondite words—or of Thomas Burton, or of any other writer with a sensibility similar to al-Shidyāq's, had been found to contain word lists resembling those in *al-Sāq* and if these were culturally plausible (i.e., did not produce distractingly European resonances), it might have been appropriate or even desirable to transfer these, lock, stock, and barrel, into the English text. In the event, no lists that matched the Arabic sufficiently closely were found.

Finally, a word on chapter titles. The use of *fī* ("on, concerning") in the title of each chapter of *al-Sāq* has been said to embody an intentionally created "gap between the titular imperative . . . and its claim to an exposition of the subject that follows, and the narrative, that has nothing at all to do with the title."[777] This insight, if accepted, would call for retention of "on" in the translated chapter titles. We have, however, decided not to apply this principle for two reasons. The first is that the use of "on" in English risks distorting the meaning of most chapter titles: to translate *Fī nawādir mukhtalifah* (Volume One, 1.3), for example, as "On Various Amusing Anecdotes" would be to imply that the chapter consisted of a discussion or study of such anecdotes, whereas in reality it consists of anecdotes tout court; the same applies to many other chapters, such as "The Priest's Tale" (Volume One, 1.15), which is a tale told by a priest rather than a discussion of a tale, or "A Description of Cairo" (Volume Two, 2.5, 2.7), likewise. The second is that the use of *fī* to introduce chapter titles is a common feature of older works in the Arabic belles lettres tradition and not specific to *al-Sāq*. Thus one finds *fī* used in the title of every chapter of (by way of random example) the *Thimār al-qulūb* of al-Thaʿālibī (died 429/1038) and the *Ḥalabat al-kumayt* of al-Nawājī (died 859/1455). I have preferred, therefore, to regard *fī* as a conventional element of Arabic title headings requiring no equivalent in English.

Wahiduddin Khan's translation of the Qurʾān is that mostly used in the text and endnotes, in accordance with series policy, but Arberry's and Yusuf Ali's translations were preferred in a few cases for a better fit with the context; all these were accessed via the Tanzil website (http://tanzil.net). The King James (Authorized) version is that used for translations from the Bible, in the version available at the University of Michigan's site (http://quod.lib.umich.edu).

This translation is exploratory, an attempt to map the highly varied terrain of al-Shidyāq's masterpiece and not only to reveal something of its many pleasing landscapes but also to mark where the figurative dragons are to be found. It may also be that the presence of the text side by side with the translation in the original bilingual edition and the awareness that some readers would be comparing the two word for word have made the translation more conservative (outside, at least, the realm of rhymed prose and the lists without definitions) than the translator would otherwise have preferred; this is especially true of the long poems. In any case, others may wish to suggest different strategies for addressing general problems, such as that of the lists without definitions, for filling in gaps with regard to historical detail (such as the real names of figures who are referred to in code), or for reinterpreting some of the author's teasingly gnomic allusions. Others too may prove more talented at the conversion of rhymed prose and long monorhymed poems into English. I hope, nevertheless, that the appearance of *al-Sāq* in English will serve to alert a wider audience to its importance and its many rewards.

It remains for me to acknowledge the generous help of Mohammed Alwan, Ahmed Alwishah, Julia Bray, Phillippe Chevrant, Robert Dankoff, Hugh Davies, Madiha Doss, Ekmeleddin Ihsanoglu, the Research Centre for Islamic History, Art, and Culture (IRCICA), Ahmet T. Karamustafa, Matthew Keegan, Jerôme Lentin, Joseph Lowry, Ussama Makdisi, Ulrich Marzolph, Simon Mercieca, James Montgomery, Mansur Mustarih, Everett Rowson, Ahmed Shawket, Adam Talib, Yassine Temlali, Shawkat Toorawa, Geert Jan van Gelder, Emmanuel Varlet, and, especially, Geoffrey Roper. Thanks are due too to the Project Committee and staff of the Library of Arabic Literature for their support and flexibility, and particularly to my Project Editor, Michael Cooperson, for his careful review of both text and translation and his numerous helpful comments and suggestions, to Chip Rossetti, Managing Editor, for his incisive direction, to Gemma Juan-Simó for her unfailing adminstrative support, and to Stuart Brown, the typesetter, for his skill and meticulousness in finding solutions to the multiple challenges posed by the layout. Above all, however, thanks are due to my Cairo-based colleague Ahmed Seddik for the many hours he spent with me discussing details of the text and offering always-plausible solutions to many of its knottier problems.

Chronology: al-Shidyāq, the Fāriyāq, and *Leg over Leg*

Though it is not suggested that *Leg over Leg* should be read primarily as autobiography, it may be of interest to readers to know at what points the Fāriyāq's life as described in the work coincide with what is known of al-Shidyāq's; the following table therefore attempts to correlate the two. Much about al-Shidyāq's life (especially his earliest years) is the subject of debate, and the work itself is studiously unspecific where dates, for example, are concerned, just as it obfuscates the identity of individuals by using coded names. The following table relies to a great extent on information kindly supplied by Geoffrey Roper, who has studied contemporary primary sources, including those of the missionary organizations for which al-Shidyāq worked.[778] I have also consulted the work of Muḥammad al-Hādī al-Maṭwī[779] and of Simon Mercieca.[780] Material not in square brackets derives from the work itself; the material in square brackets comes from other sources, as do the dates. Numbers in the format (1.1.13) refer to the numbered sections of the text and translation.

Event	**Year**
Volume One	
The Fāriyāq [Fāris al-Shidyāq] is born [probably in his ancestral village of ʿAshqūt in the Kasrawān district of Mount Lebanon] (1.1.13).	1805 or 1806[781]

Event	Year
He attends school (1.1.13 (end), 1.1.14, 1.1.20) [probably in the village of al-Ḥadath, near Beirut, to which the family is said to have moved in 1809].	Second decade of the 19th century
His father joins a revolt against the ruler of Mount Lebanon [Bashīr II ibn Qāsim al-Shihābī, reigned 1788 to 1842] which is crushed, leading to the father's flight to Damascus; his house, where Fāris and his mother are living, is looted [by troops under the command of Ḥaydar ibn Aḥmad al-Shihābī, the ruler's cousin] (1.4.4).	1820
His father dies in Damascus (1.4.8).	1821
He works mainly as a copyist, both at home (1.4.8) and for an emir (1.5.2) [the same Emir Ḥaydar whose troops looted his home], but also [seeking employment] visits one of his brothers [presumably the eldest, Ṭannūs], who is working for a Druze emir (1.6), and later, with a partner, tries his hand first at selling cloth as an itinerant merchant among the villages of Mount Lebanon (1.7), then at innkeeping (1.8). Subsequently, he becomes tutor to an emir's daughter (1.10) but later resumes work as copyist for an emir (1.11); he also tries, and fails, to make money by writing a eulogy for an emir (1.18.15).	ca. 1820–25
He meets his first "Bag-man" [an American Protestant missionary working for the Board of Commissioners of Foreign Missions, in Beirut, referred to in the text as a "peddler . . . [who had] hot-footed it over bringing with him a large saddlebag"] (1.18.19) and eventually declares his adherence to Protestantism (1.19.5). [His elder brother As'ad, a convert to Protestantism, is arrested and eventually	1826

Event	Year
imprisoned by the Maronite Patriarch at his residence at Qannūbīn; Asʿad will die there in 1830 (cf. 1.19.11–14).]	
He leaves Lebanon for Alexandria (1.19.6) [embarking at Tyre, from which he is smuggled by the missionaries amid fears for his safety.]	December 2, 1826

Volume Two

Event	Year
First stay in Alexandria (2.2).	December 1826 to early 1827
He moves from Egypt to Malta (2.3) where he works for [American and subsequently British] missionaries [in the latter case, those of the Church Missionary Society (CMS)].	Early 1827
He returns from Malta to Alexandria (2.3.19), where he stays with a missionary (2.4.1).	Mid-October 1828
Subsequently he moves to Cairo (2.4.2) [where he is employed by the CMS].	November or December 1828
He quarrels with the missionaries (2.4.16) and decides to find other employment (2.8.1). He is directed (2.8.2) to a Christian poet [Naṣr al-Dīn al-Ṭarābulusī] (2.8.3), whom he eventually meets and who suggests he work for the "Panegyricon" [Egypt's official gazette, *al-Waqaʾiʿ al-Miṣriyyah*] as a translator of eulogies in praise of a "rich prince" [the viceroy, Muḥammad ʿAlī] (2.11.5).	December 1828
He leaves the employ of the missionaries (2.12.1) and enters that of the "Panegyricon" (2.12).	January 1829

Event	Year
[He continues to lodge with a German missionary, Theodor Müller, and presumably continues to work for *al-Waqāʾiʿ al-Miṣriyyah*; in May 1829 he approaches the CMS with a proposal to reenter its employ at a higher salary but is refused; finally he is evicted by Müller.]	1829 to October 1830
During this period, he studies the linguistic sciences with Egyptian scholars in order to better perform his duties at the Panegyricon (2.18.1) and suffers a series of illnesses (2.18.1–7) [including tuberculosis, contracted in Malta, and a venereal disease (the latter the reason for his eviction by Müller)]. Eventually he takes a job teaching Arabic to the son of a French physician in return for treatment (2.18.7 and 2.19.8). [It is unclear whether this last is in parallel to or replaces his employment by *al-Waqāʾiʿ al-Miṣriyyah.*]	1829 to April or May 1832
He resumes work with the missionaries [being employed at the CMS seminary] (2.19.9).	April or May 1832

Volume Three

Event	Year
He courts the daughter [Wardah al-Ṣūlī] of a Syrian Roman Catholic merchant (3.2.1–6); during this process, he is inspired to write verses in a "strange new style" (3.2.9–10; also 3.2.27–48).	1832–35
He is invited [by the CMS] to return to Malta and teach Arabic there and to work as a "dream interpreter" [translator] in the "Oneiromancer's Chamber" [the premises of the CMS translation project] (3.4.4). [*Leg over Leg* presents some of the events	November 1835[783]

Event	Year
outlined in this and the following segment in reverse order.]	
Eventually, the courtship of Fāris and Wardah is discovered and, despite attempts by the family to thwart their union, the couple marries, after he agrees to convert to Roman Catholicism for one day (3.2.24–26). After a brief stay in Alexandria (3.5.1), they leave on a steamship for Malta, where, on arrival, and after thirty days in quarantine, they find lodgings [in Marsamxett in Valletta] (3.5.22).	December 1835[784]
The Fāriyāq works as an interpreter of the dreams of the master of the Oneiromancer's Chamber (3.8–10). [i.e., translates texts in collaboration with the head of the CMS office in Malta, Christoph Schlienz. Starting in 1838, Schlienz employs the author principally on the project for the translation of the Bible, though at times the work is suspended due to Schlienz's intermittent bouts of mental illness due to having been hit on the head by a barge-pole in Egypt in 1838.][785]	1836–May 1842[786]
In tandem with his work for the CMS, the Fāriyāq is hired by the island's ruler [the British Governor] to "physic the foul of breath" [to teach Arabic to Maltese students at the University of Malta, at the Lyceum, and at a primary school] (3.11.1-2).	1836–38[787]
The master of the Oneiromancer's Chamber [Schlienz] invites the Fāriyāq to accompany him and his wife on a trip to Syria, he obtains permission from the university to do so (3.12.1), and they set sail for Beirut.	April 1840[788]

Event	Year
The travelers arrive in Beirut, which is in a state of upheaval due to an uprising against Egyptian rule [which began in 1831 when Ibrāhīm Pasha invaded the Levant as part of his campaign against the Ottoman Empire] (3.12.14). From there, the Fāriyāq makes a visit to his family in Mount Lebanon (3.12.14–25) [either in the village of ʿAshqūt or al-Ḥadath].[789]	After April 1840
Later, the party leaves Beirut to stay in a Greek Orthodox monastery [probably that of Mār Ilyās at El Qraye] (3.14.1). Against a background of danger and starvation caused by the presence of Egyptian troops and in the face of his wife's infidelity, the master starts to show renewed signs of insanity (3.14.5).	October 1840[790]
Following the withdrawal of the Egyptian troops, the master recovers and decides to set off for Damascus via Baalbek (3.14.5). Between Damascus and Baalbek, the Fāriyāq is injured in a riding accident (3.15.1). In Damascus, he convalesces, staying at a caravanserai (3.15.3). Recovered, he travels with an unnamed companion to Beirut and thence to Jaffa, Alexandria, and finally Malta (3.15.6) [where he resumes his work on the translation of the Bible].	October 1840?[791]
During the university's summer vacation, the author makes a trip to Tunis (3.18.3–5). [*Leg over Leg* presents the events outlined in this and the following segment in reverse order.]	Summer 1841[792]
The master [Schlienz] has a particularly bad relapse into madness, during which he incites his fellows to discard their clothes (3.17.2).	December 1841[793]

Event	Year
On February 5, 1842, he writes a eulogy in praise of the ruler of Tunis (3.18.6; the letter is dated in the text). Machinations by Metropolitan Atānāsiyūs al-Tutūnjī result in the latter's taking over the Bible translation project; this leads to the closure of the CMS office in Malta, leaving the Fāriyāq with no income apart from that from his "physicking" [Arabic teaching] (3.18.1). [Representations to the Committee in London by Metropolitan Atānāsiyūs al-Tutūnjī, a Greek Melkite bishop, in early 1842, to the effect that the Fāriyāq's translation style is "too high" result in him being dismissed from the Bible translation project and the work being assigned to al-Tutūnjī instead.[794] He is assigned to translate another work. In May 1842, the CMS closes its operations in Malta due to a financial crisis and in June the author is dismissed.][795]	February to June 1842[796]
The author complains to the Society for the Promotion of Christian Knowledge (SPCK) (3.18.7). He renews contact with Sāmī Pasha, an Ottoman official and former head of *al-Waqāʾiʿ al-Miṣriyyah,* who visits the island (3.18.8) and takes him on a trip to Italy (3.18.17).	1844
Eventually, the Fāriyāq's complaints to the SPCK bear fruit, al-Tutūnjī is exposed, and the Fāriyāq is invited by the SPCK to go to England to work on the translation of the *Book of Common Prayer* there [the date given is that of the minutes of the SPCK meeting at which this decision is taken]. He prepares to travel and his wife rejoins him in Malta (3.20.6).	January 28, 1845

Event	Year
Volume Four	
Leaving his wife in Malta, the Fāriyāq travels via Italy, Marseilles, and Paris to London, and thence to a village [Barley, in Hertfordshire, close to Cambridge, where Samuel Lee, the author's collaborator, is rector; the work is carried out at the rectory][797] (4.3.9–11). After two months,[798] the Fāriyāq moves to Cambridge (4.4.2). During his stay there, he visits London for a month (4.5.7). He returns from London, via Paris and Marseilles, to Malta (4.6.1) and resumes, unhappily, his "physicking" of "the foul of breath" [his teaching Arabic to Maltese].	January to November 1845[799]
The Fāriyāq is invited by the ruler of Tunis to visit that country (4.8.1) with his family (4.8.2) [in response to a second eulogy of its ruler, written on the occasion of the latter's visit to France (November 5 to December 31, 1846)]. They go, are entertained generously by the ruler (4.8.3), and return to Malta (4.8.11).	January or February 1847[800]
The Fāriyāq plans to return to Tunis (4.9.1), but is forestalled by an invitation from "the Committee" [of the SPCK] to return, this time with his family, to England [to work on the translation of the Bible] (4.9.15). They travel to London via Leghorn, Genoa, Marseilles, and Paris, where the Fāriyāq meets Lamartine (4.10.1). After a day in London, they move to the countryside [the village of Barley, as before]. During their stay in that village, they lose their two-year-old son [Asʿad] to illness (4.14.4–5). To escape the memory of this tragedy, they move to Cambridge (4.15.1). The Fāriyāq finishes the	September 1848 to December 1850[801]

Event	Year
translation of the Bible, (4.16.1). Loath to return to Malta, he seeks employment at the University of Oxford (4.16.2) [and other institutions] but is unsuccessful and returns to London, from where he resigns his post in Malta (4.16.3).	
The Fāriyāq and his wife, both of whom have succumbed to illness in England, move to Paris for the sake of their health (4.16.4). In Paris, the author [works primarily on the correction of the proofs of his translation of the Bible though he also] establishes a language exchange arrangement with a French student and writes a poem in praise of Paris at the behest of an unnamed French scholar (4.18.11).	December 1850 to June 1853[802]
Eventually, the Fāriyāqiyyah is ordered by her doctors to leave Paris for Marseilles (4.18.15). Al-Tutūnjī, however, who is visiting Paris, once again attempts to blacken the Fāriyāq's reputation with the SPCK and is once again foiled (4.19.2). The Fāriyāqiyyah leaves for Marseilles and from there goes to Constantinople (Istanbul) where she is welcomed and hosted by Ṣubḥī Bayk, Sāmī Pasha's son (4.19.3). The Fāriyāq moves into a room on his own in Paris, meets 'Abd al-Qādir al-Jazā'irī, makes the acquaintance of leading French Orientalists, and becomes involved in gambling (4.19.4); he may also have worked as a cook (see the fifth and sixth poems in 4.20.46). [During this period, al-Shidyāq's wife apparently died.]	Same time period
[Having visited London on several occasions during the preceding period, he becomes a permanent	June 1853 to summer 1857[803]

Event	Year
resident there starting in June 1853.] The author ends by describing how a poem of his dedicated to the Ottoman sultan and expressing his support in the face of the looming war with Russia [the Crimean War] finds favor in the sultan's eyes and how the author is then offered a post with the Imperial Translation Bureau in Istanbul (4.20.2). He delays his departure, however, to oversee the last stages of the production of *Leg over Leg* and makes a trip to Paris, where the book is being printed; due to the machinations of a selfish acquaintance he returns to London prematurely, resulting in a delay in the book's publication. As the book ends, he prepares to leave on a steamer for Turkey (4.20.3). [In the event, his departure for Turkey is thwarted by the outbreak of the Crimean War (1854-1856) and he remains in London (until June 1857, when he departs with his family for Tunis).]	

As an appendage to the above, we note that the date of 1857 or 1858 that is sometimes given for al-Shidyāq's conversion to Islam[804] appears to be contradicted by language used in *Leg over Leg*, such as the author's comment regarding a Christian woman, that "she had converted to Islam, praise be to God, Lord of the Worlds" (Volume Two, 2.4.16) (unless this is meant ironically, which seems unlikely: nowhere else does the author use language in any way derogatory of Islam).

Notes

1 "these twenty-eight letters": i.e., of the Arabic alphabet.

2 "venereal disease, for which our noble language has no word" (*al-dāʾ al-zarnabī mimmā khalat ʿanhu lughatunā l-sharīfah*): the adjective *zarnabī* (from *zarnab* "vulva") is probably the author's coinage, though not one that was adopted (the current term for "venereal" is *zuharī*), and the specific disease he had in mind is probably syphilis, introduced from the New World, hence absent from the classical lexicon. The disease was rampant in Egypt from at least the time of the visit of the Turkish traveler Evliya Çelebi in the seventeenth century (Dankoff, "Ayıp değil!"). In the nineteenth century, terms for syphilis appear to have included *al-tashwīsh* (Spiro, *Arabic-English Vocabulary*, where it is defined as "sickness, illness, venereal disease"), which the author may have regarded as not belonging to the true Arab lexicon since it appears in the classical dictionaries only in the sense of "confusion" (the semantic progression being from "confusion" to "disorder, sickness" to (perhaps as a euphemism) "venereal disease") and in the colloquial as *al-ʿaya* (= *al-ʿayāʾ*) *al-afranjī* ("the Frankish disease") (Spiro, *Arabic-English Vocabulary*).

3 "the author like me of lunatics" (*al-muʾallifu mithlī mina l-majānīn*): up to the word *al-majānīn*, the sentence may be understood as meaning "the author, like me a lunatic," with *min* as a partitive; thereafter it reveals itself as parallel to the preceding clauses.

4 "the farter" (*al-khaḍfā*), etc.: the following adjectives are vowelled in the Arabic as though feminine, perhaps implying intensification of the insult; however, it is also possible that the vowelling is in error for the

masculine intensive form *fiʿillā* (cf., e.g., in the *Qāmūs*, "*khibbiqā* on the pattern of *zimikkā*").

5 Cf. Mal. 2:10: "Have we not all one father? Hath not one God created us? Why do we deal treacherously every man against his brother, by profaning the covenant of our fathers?"

6 Ps. 133:1–2.

7 "prize" (*maghnam*): i.e., marriage.

8 "to 'ties of kinship' is *applied*" (*ʿalā l-ansābi nṭabaqat*): this is an extended sense of *arḥām*.

9 "you Orientals . . . the Occidentals": (*minkum fī l-sharq . . . ahl al-gharb*): probably meaning "any two groups of people from different parts of the world" (cf., e.g., *mashāriq al-arḍ wa-maghāribuhā*, "the entire world").

10 The merchant's last name was al-Ṣūlī, he was a Catholic from Damascus, and his daughter's name was Wardah (al-Maṭwī, *Aḥmad*, 1:82).

11 "it was not to be imagined that anyone else could have been exhibited to her": i.e., the girl's family was too respectable to have allowed her to meet any other man.

12 "the 'twisting of the side-tresses'" (*al-haṣr bi-l-fawdayn*): the reference is to the *muʿallaqah* ("suspended ode") which, in this version (other versions have a different first hemistich), reads *haṣartu bi-fawday raʾsihā fa-tamāyalat * ʿalayya haḍīma l-kashḥi rayyā l-mukhalkhali* ("I twisted her side-tresses to me, and she leaned over me; slender-waisted she was, and tenderly plump her ankles") (translation: Arberry, *Seven Odes*, 63).

13 Prov. 5:19.

14 I.e., in chapter 7 of Volume One.

15 "regarded their wives as chattel" (*kāna ḍayzanan lahu ʿalā l-māʾidah*): literally, "wanted too much of their share at table," to be understood in the context of the contrasting phrase below (3.2.7): "no man will jostle me for her affections" (*wa-lā yuzāḥimunī fīhā l-rijāl*).

16 "shifts would be ripped from in front and from the rear" (*wa-qudda l-qamīṣāni min qubulin wa-min dubur*): an echo of Q Yūsuf 12:25, 28 *wa-qaddat qamīsahu min duburin . . . fa-lammā raʾā qamīṣahu qudda*

min duburin "she tore his shirt at the back. . . . When he saw his shirt was torn from the rear. . . ."

17 Located at the end of this chapter.

18 "My shaft . . . your luckless stick" (*qidḥī . . . qidḥuka l-safīḥ*): *qidḥ* may be taken to mean "horse," thus extending the metaphor of the preceding line, or "arrow-shaft" (as used in the ancient Arabian gambling game of *maysar*), a possibility strengthened by the use of the term *safīḥ*, meaning "an arrow-shaft used in *maysar* that has no good luck" (*Qāmūs*).

19 "single verses" (*abyāt mufradah*): i.e., of self-contained, one-line (two-hemistich) unrhymed poems.

20 "Some count among this last kind the *sarābātiyyah*" etc: meaning, perhaps, that latrine cleaners are held up by some (presumably sarcastically) as examples of people so devoted to their fellow men that they will collect their night soil, while others see them merely as persons who have to earn a living.

21 "a sun . . .": *mahāt* means both "sun" and "female oryx"; thus the meaning is that separation from the beloved does not result in her being seen simply as a beautiful object, but rather makes the lover's feelings more intense.

22 "of her and of me": perhaps because in so doing the grateful lover would give precedence to the beloved for his happiness, thus fitting the conceit more closely to the sense of the preceding passage.

23 "something else that comes from her": *ʿadhirah* (with identical ductus to *ʿadhrah*) means "feces."

24 "who suffers from diochism" (*bihi sīfanniyyah*): see the author's note that follows, which refers to the bird itself, the *sīfannah*; the allusion may be to the dioch (*Quelea quelea*), a bird that forms flocks of thousands and is known to strip trees entirely; though not found now in Egypt, the dioch is common in Sudan and the reference in the note to Egypt may be loose.

25 "the two honey-seekers" (*al-mustaʿsilayn*): or, punningly, "the two seekers after intercourse" (see 3.2.11).

26 "Reproach me not, for reproach is a spur" (*daʿ ʿanka lawmī fa-inna l-lawma ighrāʾū*): Abū Nuwās, *Dīwān*, 7.

27 “this manifest victory” (*hādhā l-fatḥ al-mubīn*): a Qur’anic reference (Q Fatḥ 48:1) but capable also of being read as “this demonstrated opening.”

28 “The Two Titter-Making Poems” (*al-qaṣīdatān al-ṭīkhiyyatān*): one likely reason for the author’s calling them by this name is to be found in the third and fourth lines, where much of the vocabulary used is open to two interpretations, one respectable (and to be found in the dictionaries) and the other vulgar (and primarily vernacular). Thus, in line 3, *muzabbiban*, according to the definition of the *Qāmūs* which the author is at pains to reproduce in a marginal note, means “talking too much” or “having the sides of his mouth filled with saliva”; most readers, however, will immediately relate the word to *zubb*, meaning “penis,” so that it might be interpreted as “touching my penis”; similarly, *mutakassisan*, again according to the marginal note quoting the *Qāmūs*, means “putting on airs,” whereas most readers will be reminded of *kuss* (“cunt”), thus allowing a reading of “cunt-obsessed.” In the same vein, the two following words (*mustaqbilan mustadbiran*) might be understood as “approaching from the front, approaching from the rear.” Similarly, in the next line, *tajmīsh*, which the *Qāmūs* defines as “flirting” (*al-mughāzalah*), commonly occurs in Abbasid poetry in the sense of “(sexually) groping, fondling.” Another feature that might be perceived as “strange” (see 3.2.9) is the piling up of unusual lexical items in lists, a feature carried over by the author from the prose passages of the book.

29 “A jinni-possessed poet” (*shāʿir dhū jinnah*): the belief that poets were inspired by jinnis was widespread in pre-Islamic Arabia.

30 “my two little friends” (*ṣuwayḥibayya*): i.e., his poetic familiars.

31 “Ask her, ‘Does the oven burn hot as it should/Each month, or is it late some months?’”: meaning “Is she not, despite her pretensions to glory, a mere woman who menstruates and gets pregnant?”

32 “He-of-the-Two-Horns” (*Dhū l-Qarnayn*): an epithet of Alexander the Great.

33 I.e., the beloved.

34 "Yūsuf . . . prison": in Islam, Yūsuf (biblical Joseph) represents young male beauty and virtue; according to the Qur'an, Yūsuf was imprisoned when falsely accused of assault by Pharaoh's wife (Q Yūsuf 12:35 and passim).

35 Rashā: poetic license for Rasha', which, in addition to being a female given name, means "young gazelle."

36 Suʻād: a woman's name often given the beloved by poets (mostly famously by Kaʻb ibn Zuhayr in the opening line of a poem dedicated to the Prophet Muḥammad); thus the author asks in effect, "Who is this Suʻād? It is you who are the true angel?" etc.

37 See Volume One, 1.13.10.

38 "thrusting the soles of his feet toward the face of the person sitting with him": it is considered insulting to deliberately show the soles of one's shoes.

39 "*Fulān shamma l-narjisa wa-ḥabaq*" etc.: these appear to be distorted versions of the saying *man sabaq shamma l-ḥabaq* ("he who arrives first, smells the basil," i.e., "the early bird catches the worm") that exploit the shared senses of *ḥabaq* as "basil" and "he farted"; Franks would, presumably, be ignorant of the saying itself and a fortiori be oblivious to the grammatical and semantic solecisms.

40 *The Thistle and the Cedar of Lebanon* by Habeeb Risk Allah (Ḥabīb Rizqallah) (London, first edition 1843, second edition 1853) includes a description of *feasts* (pp. 28–33), not a wedding, that he attended in Damascus at which poems such as that quoted would sometimes end the festivities. Risk Allah glosses "feast" as *faraḥ*, a word used colloquially to mean "wedding," which may explain al-Shidyāq's confusion. While it would obviously be regarded as ill-omened to sing a funeral lament at a wedding, it might have been more acceptable at a party at which the arts were on display, and it remains an open question whether al-Shidyāq's criticism was reasonable or deliberate obfuscation. The verses form the second stanza of the longer poem quoted by Risk Allah, and in Risk Allah's version go, "Tell me, O Grave, tell me, is her incomparable beauty gone? Has she, too, faded as the petals fall

from the sweetest flower, and her lovely face changed—changed and gone! Thou art not a garden, O Grave; nor yet heaven; still all the fairest flowers and brightest plants are culled by thee"; similar verses are quoted anonymously in ʿAbbās b. Muḥammad al-Qurashī, *Ḥamāsat al-Qurashī* (ed. Khayr al-Dīn Maḥmūd Qablāwī, Damascus: Manshūrāt Wizārat al-Thaqāfah, 1995), 245, no. 78.

41 "two assemblies, one for the common people and another for the elite" (*majlisayni aḥaduhumā ʿāmmiyyūna wa-aḥaduhumā khāṣṣī*): the account of the assembly for the common people is written in colloquial Arabic.

42 "transmitter of poetry" (*rāwī*): premodern Arabic poetry was passed from generation to generation orally via persons who preserved and recited a poet's works and taught them to others.

43 "smacks to the back of the neck" (*al-ṣafʿ*): to slap oneself on the back of the neck (or the cheeks) is a ritual expression of mourning.

44 "his anterior and his posterior" (*quddāmuhu wa-khalfuhu*): probably an allusion to his "pantaloons that are big both in front and behind" (*sarwīlātuhu l-mufarsakhah*) above (3.3.8).

45 Perhaps a reference to Judaeo-Spanish (Ladino), brought to the Ottoman Empire by Jews expelled from al-Andalus at the end of the fifteenth century.

46 "from the furthest west and . . . from the further east" (*min aqṣā l-maghrib . . . min aqṣā l-mashriq*): i.e., from Morocco and from Iraq.

47 "the emir of al-Quffah": either the emir of a place called al-Quffah (unidentified) or "the emir of the basket," in which case the reference is equally obscure.

48 "in this case": i.e., in the case of the display of the bride's blood, which the author treats as an exercise in rubbing the beholders' noses in the groom's good luck at having married a virgin, or perhaps at having married at all.

49 "testing for *virginity* leads mostly to *sterility*" (*al-ʿuqru yakūnu ghāliban sababan fī l-ʿuqr*): the definition used in the translation of the author's note ("the exploration . . .") is taken from Lane's *Lexicon* (s.v. *ʿuqr*); Lane comments, "Perhaps it is a meaning inferred from . . . *bayḍat*

al-ʿuqr [meaning] '*That [egg] with which a woman is tested on the occasion of devirgination.*'"

50 "penetration" (*baṣīrah*): punning on the two meanings of the word, i.e., "insight, acumen" and "bloody proof."

51 "the baker's oven flared up, the heated pot boiled over" (*qad fāra l-tannūr wa-fāḍa l-masjūr*): i.e., the bride was menstruating.

52 "to the Island of the Foul of Breath" (*jazīrat al-bukhr*) etc.: i.e., Malta (see Volume Two, 2.3.16 and below, 3.11.2).

53 "dream interpreter" (*muʿabbir li-l-aḥlām*): the author was in fact engaged by the Church Missionary Society, for whom he was already working in Cairo as a teacher, to go to Malta in the capacity of a translator (Roper, *Fāris al-Shidyāq as Translator and Editor*). The non-figurative key to the ironic substitution of dream interpretation for translation lies in the fact that while the root *ʿ-b-r* means "to interpret (dreams)," reversal of the second two consonants results in *ʿ-r-b*, from which *taʿrīb* "to translate into Arabic." The author has already in this work (Volume One, 0.2.3) shown his interest in metathesis and later was to write a book—*Sirr al-layāl fī l-qalb wa-l-ibdāl* (*The Secrets of Morphology and Metathesis*, 1884)—devoted to this form of word play.

54 "a man is tied by his tongue" (*al-rajulu yurbaṭu bi-lisānihi*): i.e., a man must honor his word.

55 "make for the back of that Friend of God" (*yaqṣidna ẓahra hādhā l-walī*): i.e., go for a boat ride; the speaker likens the sea to one of God's chosen "friends" among men, to whom He grants the power to perform wonders.

56 "the two sweetest things" (*al-aʿdhabayn*): i.e., food and coitus.

57 "He had triumphed and succeeded—and with what triumph and what success!": presumably meaning that he felt that his sexual performance on what was in effect his honeymoon had been more than adequate.

58 "the fire-ship" (*safīnat al-nār*): i.e., the steamer; the implications of the Arabic term are the topic of further discussion below (3.5.6).

59 "Angering Women Who Dart Sideways Looks, and Claws like Hooks": i.e., Volume One, chapter 10, where the author says, for example, "if

[women] set their hearts on reading, who knows where it will end?" (1.10.10)

60 "the *al-*" (*al-alif wa-l-lām*): i.e., the Arabic article, often translatable as "the."

61 "generic or referential" (*al-jinsī aw al-dhihnī*): i.e., whether the poet meant that the beloved's rump was incapable of passing through any door or only of passing through some specific door that was in the mind of the poet and his readers.

62 Imam al-Zawzanī: al-Ḥusayn ibn Aḥmad ibn al-Ḥusayn al-Zawzanī (d. 468/1093), a noted philologist and man of letters best known for his commentary on the seven "suspended odes," entitled *Sharḥ al-qaṣā'id* (or *al-mu'allaqāt*) *al-sab'*.

63 "for a man's eye, despite its small size" (*fa-'inna 'ayna bni 'ādama ma'a kawnihā ḍayyiqah*): also, punningly, in allusion to the Lebanese idiom *'ēnu ḍayyiqah*, "for a man, despite the limitations of his imagination."

64 "six-letter verbs . . ." (*al-af'āl al-sudāsiyyah . . .*): by "six-letter verbs" the author means those called in English-language grammars of Arabic "Form X verbs," which are formed by prefixing to the three root consonants the three-letter formative element *ist-*, which, as a substantive, means "anus"; Form X verbs may "express the taking, seeking, asking for, or demanding, what is meant by the first [form]" (e.g., *istaghfara* "to ask pardon"), as also that "a person thinks that a certain thing possesses . . . the quality expressed by the first form" (e.g., *istathqala* "to find (s.th.) heavy") (Wright, *Grammar*, I:44, 45).

65 "'bearing,' as some poets would have it" (*ḥāmilah kamā dhahaba ilayhi ba'ḍu l-shu'arā'*): no description in poetry of the posterior as "bearing" has been found.

66 "the Most Beauteous Names" (*al-asmā' al-ḥusnā*): the names, or epithets, of God, e.g., "the Satisfier of All Needs," "the Opener," "the Patient," etc.

67 "they encompass both front and back" (*ma'a ḥtiwā'ihimā 'alā l-qubuli wa-l-dubur*): i.e., "even though the anus and the vagina, in animals, are located in close proximity to one another between the buttocks."

68 "what is concave" (*al-mujawwaf*): perhaps meaning the small of the back.

69 Al-Ḥusayn ibn Aḥmad ibn Khālawayh (d. 370/980–81) was a leading philologist of Baghdad. The reference is to his work *Laysa fī kalām al-ʿArab* (*Not to Be Found in the Speech of the Arabs*) (p. 267); Ibn Khālawayh does not otherwise gloss *al-ṣawfaqatān* and the word is not to be found in the lexica.

70 *mirfad*: "the bustle by which a flat-buttocked woman enlarges herself" (*Lisān*).

71 "no matter how you switch them around, they'll give you a new meaning each time" (*kayfamā qalabtahā ẓahara laka minhā ayḍan maʿnā*): i.e., the consonants *d-b-r* that form *dubur* ("backside") may be arranged in different combinations to produce new words (e.g., *radb* ["dead-end road"], *rabada* ["to erect"], *badr* ["full moon; beautiful girl or boy"], *bard* ["cold"]).

72 "according to their numerical values" (*bi-ḥisāb al-jummal*): i.e., according to the counting system that allots a numerical value to each letter of the Arabic alphabet; *dubr* yields the values 4 (*d*), 2 (*b*), and 200 (*r*), any two of which add up, of course, to an even number.

73 "the two '*u*'s imply ponderousness and gravity" (*al-ḍammatayni ishāratun ilā l-thiqal wa-l-razānah*): the *ḍammah* or "u," as in *dubur*, is conventionally described as a "heavy vowel" (*ḥarakah thaqīlah*); the author exploits the literal sense of the terminology.

74 "at the end of the month" (*dubura l-shahr*): *dubura* is simply a noun used as a preposition and it makes no sense, as the author knows, to posit it as the etymon of the noun (Wright, *Grammar*, I:280 [357]).

75 "the question of its derivation from 'the afterpart of anything'" (*al-khilāfu fī shtiqāqihā min ʿaqibi l-shayʾ*): the author appears to willfully misunderstand the formulation that he has quoted earlier from the *Qāmūs* (see 3.5.13, last sentence), where the words *wa-min kulli shayʾin ʿaqibuhu* (literally, "and [*al-dubr* and *al-dubur* also] mean 'the afterpart . . . of anything'"), as though the lexicographer had written *wa-l-dubr wa-l-dubur min ʿaqibi l-shayʾ* ("*al-dubr* and *al-dubur* are [derived] from the *ʿaqib* of anything"), which is, of course, nonsense,

but of a piece with his reasoning concerning *dubura l-shay'* (see preceding endnote).

76 "they [would certainly] turn their backs" (*[la-]wallawu l-adbāra*): cf. Q Fatḥ 48:22.

77 On Metropolitan Atanāsiyūs al-Tutūnjī and *Al-Ḥakākah fī l-rakākah*, see Volume Two, 2.3.5 and 2.9.3; this volume, chapter 20; and Volume Four, chapter 19.

78 "Raising a Storm" (*Fī Ithārat al-Riyāḥ*): i.e., Volume One, chapter 1 (see 1.1.6., pp. 45–47).

79 Umm Suwayd, Umm al-ʿIzm, and Umm Khinnawr: epithets (i.e., *kunyas*, or descriptive labels consisting of either *abū* ("father of") or *umm* ("mother of"), in the sense of "possessed of," followed by a noun) are often nontransparent or ambiguous; thus Umm Suwayd might be translated as "Mother of a Little Black Thing," Umm al-ʿIzm has no clear meaning, and Umm Khinnawr may denote "Mother of a Hyena," or "of a Cow," etc.

80 "had they not held it in the same esteem" etc.: i.e., since the Arabs typically allocated heroic descriptive epithets to lions, etc. and since they did the same for the backside, they must have viewed them as being on a par.

81 "a possessor of Umm Suwayd" (*umm Umm Suwayd*): i.e., a woman, which the cat resembles in its fertility, playfulness, etc.

82 "or that they may be used as a means to get hold of one" (*aw annahā takūnu dharīʿatan lahā*): i.e., as a go-between with access to women's quarters, a common theme in Arabic romances and one to which the author refers again below (3.15.4).

83 "another book": unidentified.

84 "the massively uddered": thus the *Qāmūs* (*al-ʿaẓīmatu l-ḍarʿ*), though the word seems out of place in this list.

85 *balkhā'*: feminine singular of *bilākh*.

86 Most of the words in the following table were cited in an earlier list (Volume Two, 2.14.8ff.).

87 "this custom" (*hādhihi l-ʿādah*): i.e., that of a woman's turning her backside toward her husband (see 3.5.7 above).

88 "the city": Valletta.

89 "Steven": probably William *Stevens*, a notary and solicitor, who worked in Valletta from 1803 to his death in 1854, when he left behind him six sons and seven daughters (see 3.6.5 below); he lived at Pieta, which would have been most easily reached from the Marsamxett side of Valletta, where the author and his wife were staying, by boat; one of William's sons—William John—also worked in Malta from 1831 to 1878 but his place of residence does not fit the author's description (personal communication from Dr. Simon Mercieca, University of Malta). That Stevens was a lawyer explains the author's apparently mocking allusions to him by the Islamic terms *faqīh* ("jurisprudent") and (3.6.2 below) *faraḍī* ("expert on the division of inheritances").

90 "in Across the Sea" (*fī ʿIbra l-Baḥr*): the odd wording may reflect the Maltese expression *jaqsam il-baħar* ("to cross the sea"), used of crossing either of the two harbors that flank Valletta (personal communication from Dr. Simon Mercieca, University of Malta); if that is the case, the author seems to have mistaken the phrase for a place-name.

91 "for both orientation and osculation" (*fī l-qiblah wa-l-qublah*): i.e., by virtue of having the *qiblah* (the place—Mecca—to which Muslims direct themselves in prayer) in their lands and by virtue of their excellence in kissing.

92 "the same downfall had befallen them as befell the Barāmikah" (*nazala bihinna nakbatu l-barāmikah*): the Barāmikah family held high office at the court of the early Abbasid caliphs and became known for the extravagance of their lifestyle. In 187/803, they were imprisoned and had their possessions confiscated by Hārūn al-Rashīd.

93 "*khawals*": Lane calls these "dancing-men" (see Lane, *Description*, 381–82).

94 "The Fāriyāq went on" (*qāla*): many of the Fāriyāq's discussions with his wife begin by being reported in the third person (i.e., putatively by the author) and shift to being reported in the first person by the Fāriyāq himself.

95 The final word in the author's note does not in fact occur in the text.

96 "the protuberance of her two breasts and their perkiness . . ." (*burūz al-nahdayni wa-nuhūduhumā . . .*): the following list of words related to breasts is shorter than that in the original and is intended as a representation, not a one-to-one translation, of the latter, using words from the same semantic areas drawn from thesauri, dictionaries, and other lexical resources; see further Volume Four, Translator's Afterword.

97 *saʿdān*: a creeping desert plant, *Neurada procumbens*, that has conical prickles.

98 "*ra . . .*": the first syllable of the word *rajīm* ("the lapidated"), which follows *al-shayṭān* in the pious formula *aʿūdhu bi-llāhi mina l-shayṭān al-rajīm*, and also of *rajul* meaning "man"; in the following sentence, reference is to the phrase *bi-smi llāhi r-raḥmāni r-raḥīm* ("In the name of God, the merciful, the compassionate").

99 "and the fact of his being strong and hard" (*wa-kawnuhu qawiyyan shadīdan*): the following list of words related to being strong and being hard is shorter than that in the original and is intended as a representation, not a one-to-one translation, of the latter, using words from the same semantic areas drawn from thesauri, dictionaries, and other lexical resources; see further Volume Four, Translator's Afterword.

100 "al-Suyūṭī . . . suits . . . sots" (*al-Suyūṭī . . . al-sawṭiyyīn . . . al-miswaṭiyyīn*): the Fāriyāqiyyah believes that the name al-Suyūṭī ("from al-Asyūṭ," referring to the town in Upper Egypt) is related to the word *sawṭ* meaning "whip" and the Fāriyāq carries the joke further by invoking a further related word, *miswaṭ*, meaning the same; this purely phonetic play has been realized here in a different form.

101 "splitting it into hemistichs and inserting between them others of her own or building new stanzas based on what I've already written" (*shaṭṭarathu wa-khammasathu*): *tashṭīr* and *takhmīs* are practices by which existing, usually well-known, poems are expanded by a later poet; *tashṭīr*, strictly interpreted, consists of inserting a new hemistich after the first and before the second hemistich of the original, resulting in two lines where before there was one; *takhmīs* consists of the "expansion of a given poem into a strophic poem of five-line stanzas in which the last two lines consist of one line (two hemistichs)

from the original poem, and the three new lines at the beginning rhyme with the first hemistich" (Meisami and Starkey, *Encyclopedia*, I:82).

102 "Postscript" (*ḥāshiyah*): Having exhausted the resources available to him (see n. 95, above), the translator is unable to provide equivalents for the further ninety-seven synonyms for "strong and vigorous" and "hard and tough" listed here and invites readers to read the transcribed Arabic to themselves and experience its purely phonic aspects; see further Volume Four, Translator's Afterword.

103 "scraps of paper . . . scrap of food" (*ṣaḥfatun min ṣuḥufi ṭ-ṭaʿām*): the double entendre depends in the Arabic on the fact that *ṣuḥuf* may be used as the plural of both *ṣaḥīfah* ("leaf, page") and *ṣaḥfah* ("large eating bowl").

104 "the head of the Chamber" (*raʾīs al-muʿabbar*): i.e., Christoph Schlienz, a German missionary recruited by the Church Missionary Society soon before the author's first visit to Malta and to whom he had, during that stay, taught Arabic (Roper, *Fāris al-Shidyāq as Translator and Editor*). "In 1838 Schlienz was hit on the head by a barge-pole while in Egypt, which rendered him intermittently insane for the next three or more years. In December 1841 he suffered a particularly bad relapse. This took the form of an insistence on undressing and walking naked in the street, so that he had to be forcibly re-dressed. This incident was recorded in a report now in the CMS archives" (personal communication from Geoffrey Roper). The incident is described in chapter 17 below.

105 "The rest of the dream is self-explanatory": the author hints that the wife retained two lovers (two "branches") and returns to this theme later (3.14.5 and 3.15 passim).

106 *kuʿkubbah*: this almost comically strange-sounding word is defined in the *Qāmūs* as "four lengths of hair braided so that they intertwine with one another."

107 "wipe her nose" (*yuraʿʿimahā*): exactly what is implied here is unclear, but see the author's comments on the same word below (3.12.21, *wa-lā turaʿʿimuhu*, sixth item in table).

108 "figure 2 . . . two strokes" (*ʿadada thnayn*): i.e., she wrote the Arabic figure ٢, which consists of a lateral stroke and a vertical stroke; when the first is removed, something resembling a figure ١ is left.

109 "*rafḍ . . . farḍ . . . ʿirḍ . . . ʿarḍ*": i.e., if the husband substitutes refusal (*rafḍ*) for religious duty (*farḍ*), his wife will trade in her honor as a woman (*ʿirḍ*) for the exposure (*ʿarḍ*) of his failure as a man.

110 "its circularity": the idea of the repetition of worldly events (such as the rise and fall of nations) over time is a well-established trope.

111 "figure 3 . . . two teeth . . . a crooked figure 1" (*ʿadada thalāthatin . . . sinnayn . . . wāḥidan dhā ʿawaj*): as with the "figure 2" above, except that the lateral stroke of the Arabic figure 3 (٣) consists of two joined "teeth," or small peaks.

112 "a people with breath so foul" etc.: the author says earlier of the inhabitants of the island (i.e., the Maltese) that "they speak a language so filthy, dirty, and rotten that the speaker's mouth gives off a bad smell as soon as he opens it" (Volume Two, 2.3.16). Al-Shidyāq considered Maltese a dialect of Arabic, although some modern linguists consider it a mixed language. It is descended from eleventh-century Sicilian Arabic but contains a preponderance of elements from Sicilian Romance, standard Italian, and English (Brincat, *Maltese and Other Languages*). Decoded, al-Shidyāq's "treating the foul of breath" may be taken to mean teaching formal Arabic to Maltese speakers.

113 "cap . . . tail" (*raʾs . . . dhanab*): a play on the word *raʾsmāl*, meaning "(financial) capital" (literally, "the head, or greater part, of wealth").

114 "the rope . . . the knot" (*al-ʿiqd . . . al-ʿaqd*): a play on two similar-sounding words, both derived from the root for "tying"; by the second (literally, "contract") he means the tie of marriage.

115 *bihim . . . bihā*: in using plural concord to refer to "earnings" (*darāhim*, literally "silver coins"), the wife is following colloquial rules, which allow the use of plural concord with inanimate objects; literary Arabic prefers feminine singular concord in such cases, reserving plural concord for persons.

116 "matron . . . patron" (*ḥayzabūn . . . zabūn*): the wife mishears the little-known word *ḥayzabūn* (literally "old woman, hag") as the common

word *zabūn*, "patron, customer." The patron the Fāriyāqiyyah has in mind would no doubt be one of the "foul of breath," come for a lesson; see again 3.12.3, at the end.

117 "If you'd 'opened' the *ṣād* . . . a perfect line of verse" (*law fataḥti l-ṣāda . . . baytan muṭlaqan*): i.e., if she had ended the last word of each hemistich with an *a* vowel (*fatḥah*), mark of the accusative case (i.e., *al-raqṣ-ā . . . al-naqṣ-ā*), she would have turned her words into properly metered (*rajaz*) and rhymed verse; at the same time, *baytan muṭlaqan* may be understood in its technical meaning of "a line of verse whose final short vowel is converted into a long vowel, according to the convention."

118 "such a thing": the wife is scandalized because the letter *ṣād* is used in poetry as a code for the vagina (see Volume Two, 2.4.15).

119 "Dah-da-dah-dah dah-da-dah! Dah-da-dah-da dah-da-dah!" (*fāʿilātun fāʿilūn fāʿilūna fāʿilāt*): the Fāriyāq mimics his wife's words, employing the mnemonic forms (constructed from the root *f-ʿ-l* "to do") used to fix the patterns of long and short vowels from which the meters of classical Arabic poetry, which are quantitative, are constructed; in this case the meter seems close to *majzūʾ al-madīd*. At the same time, the mnemonics may be understood literally, i.e., as feminine and masculine plural active participles of the verb *faʿala* ("to do"), here used in a sexual sense, so that the Fāriyāq is also saying "women having sex and men having sex, men having sex and women having sex." See 3.19.10 below for a similar conceit.

120 See Volume Two, chapter 12.

121 "the companion of madmen": probably referring to the Bag-man who thought he could revive the dead, in Book Two, chapter 20.

122 "monk": i.e., here, "saint."

123 "*mufāqamah, mubāḍaʿah, muwāqaʿah*, and similar forms": i.e., these verbs, all of which mean "to have sexual intercourse," are of the pattern *mufāʿalah*, with which "the ideas of effort and reciprocity are always more or less clearly implied" (Wright, *Grammar*, I:33 D).

124 "'What's "conserve you" mean?' 'Nothing at all,' I replied": in the phrase *ḥayyāki llāhu wa-bayyāki*, rendered here as "May God preserve

you and conserve you," the element *bayyāki* is regarded by some lexicographers simply as an imitative element serving to increase the rhetorical force of the formula.

125 "*je t'adore!* . . . There's no one there" (*qultu li-llāhi ʿalaykī mā arā lī min yadayki manjā . . . mā jāʾa aḥad*: the Fāriyāqiyyah understands *manjā* ("place of escape") as *man jā* ("who came?"), the glottal stop being dropped as in the colloquial; in the translation, the locus of the misunderstanding has been shifted to the phrase *li-llāhi ʿalayki* (approx. "What a caution you are!").

126 "patrons" (*al-zabūn*): a reference to an earlier, similar joke (see 3.11.3 at the end).

127 "How I wish that he" (*alā laytuhu*); *ḥabīb* ("beloved"), the grammatical referent of the pronoun, is always masculine in Arabic, even when, as here, the actual referent is unambiguously female.

128 "meaning her" (*bi-hi ay bi-hā*): a reminder to the reader that, though the Fāriyāq is following the convention of referring to the beloved in the masculine, he means the feminine; see preceding note.

129 ʿAbd Allāh ibn al-Muʿtazz (247–96/861–908), son of the thirteenth Abbasid caliph and himself caliph for one day before being assassinated, was a poet, "[t]he rhetorical brilliance and originality of [whose] conceits, especially in his descriptive verses . . . have been greatly admired by medieval critics" (Meisami and Starkey, *Encyclopedia*, I:354–55).

130 "not every slave is an ʿAbd Allāh": the author plays with the original meaning of *ʿabd*, namely "slave," a usage often extended to mean "mortal man" and used in proper names of the form "Slave of the [name of God]" (e.g., ʿAbd al-Raḥmān (Slave of the Compassionate), etc.).

131 "the monster" (*al-waḥsh*): i.e., the dream of the monster, see 3.11.5.

132 In 1831, Egypt invaded Syria and Lebanon and threatened the Ottoman state; in 1840, the time of this journey, Egypt was being forced out of the Levant under pressure from both the Western powers and local uprisings.

133 "though adding nothing thereby to that of the terrifier" (*wa-lam yazid qalba l-muhawwili shayʾan*): the assumption apparently being that the

more heart one has, the more one feels fear; in this case, the soldier remained unaffected by the shot that terrified the Fāriyāq.

134 "some staying at home" (*al-barthaṭah*): the author appears to have allowed his list of verbs describing ways of "sitting" (*qiʿdah*) to be contaminated by one relating to the radically related concept of "staying" (*quʿūd*), for the *Qāmūs* defines *al-barthaṭah* as "to remain unmoving in one's house and to stick to it" (*thabata fī baytihi wa-lazimahu*).

135 *ṭanṭūr*: a cone-shaped headdress worn by women (see Volume One, 1.2.4, n. 123.)

136 "thrower of the palm-branch javelin" (*rāmī al-jarīd*): i.e., as a sport and a martial art.

137 Maʿbad . . . Ibrāhīm al-Mawṣilī: singers of the early to high Islamic period.

138 "*akl* ('eating') would mean *taʿām* ('food')": this would not be surprising since, though *akl* is in origin a verbal noun ("eating"), it is widely used in speech as a substantive.

139 "*ta'ta'ah* is onomatopoeic" (*al-ta'ta'ah ḥikāyatu ṣawtin*): though al-Shidyāq does not specify what *al-ta'ta'ah* imitates, the entry in the *Qāmūs* implies that it is the sound of stuttering, and specifically the repetition of the letter *t*.

140 "two strange words that have no like in terms of structure in the entire language": *ṣaṣaṣ* and *qaqaq* are unique in having the same consonant for each radical.

141 See Volume One, 1.13.2 n. 219.

142 "'Wife' is a form that's used" (*qad yuqālu zawjah*): *zawj*, meaning "one of a pair" and hence "spouse (of either sex)" has higher authority than *zawjah*, with the feminine marker *-ah*, the latter form having been introduced, according to some lexicographers, simply "for the sake of perspicuity, fearing to confound the male with the female" (Lane, *Lexicon*).

143 "your regret / for the one you lost is plainly displayed" (*wa-ʿalā lladhī bāyanta ḥuznuka bādī*): perhaps meaning that the regret felt by a woman at foregoing promiscuity leads her to commit other offenses.

144 "food and copulation" (*al-aṭyabayn*): literally, "the two best things."

145 I.e., Būrān bint al-Ḥasan ibn Sahl, wife of the Abbasid caliph al-Ma'mūn.

146 "the palace of Ghumdān": a fabled palace in Yemen (see Volume Two, 2.14.41).

147 "the one who'd attacked women without distinction" (*alladhī hajā l-nisā'a jamī'an*): see 3.13.8 and the reference to the man who "cast on women a wholesale blot" (*hajā l-nisā'a ṭurran*).

148 "cleans them . . . gripes them . . . preens them" (*tarḍi'uhu . . . wa-tuṭawwisuhu . . . wa-tuzahni'uhu*): the following list, preceding and following the table, of words and expressions related to child rearing is shorter than that in the original and is intended as a representation, not a one-to-one translation, of the latter using words from the same semantic areas drawn from thesauri, dictionaries, and other lexical resources; see further Volume Four, Translator's Afterword.

149 See 3.12.21 (*tubāghim/bāghamahu*).

150 See 3.12.21 (*tura''im/ra''amuhu*).

151 See 3.12.21 (*tuqarrim/taqrīm*).

152 See Volume One, 1.16.10.

153 "lactation though not pregnant . . . postpartum prolapse . . . morning sickness" (*wa-l-diḥāq . . . wa-l-tafarruth*): the author's note, which consists simply of the definitions of these words as given in the *Qāmūs* and which has been followed in the translation verbatim, has been omitted to avoid repetition.

154 "requiring a female neighbor to suck on it a couple of times to make it drain" (*al-'ayfah*): Lane says that *'ayfah* "is a term employed in the case when a woman brings forth and her milk is suppressed in her breast, wherefore her fellow-wife, or female neighbour, draws it, by the single sucking and the two suckings" (*Lexicon*); he also mentions that the definition in the *Qāmūs*, quoted by the author in his note, should read *fa-tarḍi'uhu* for *fa-tarḍi'uhā*.

155 *'iddah*: in Islam a divorced woman who is pregnant is forbidden to remarry for forty days following childbirth.

156 "Not for nothing did Qaṣīr cut off his nose" (*li-amrin jada'a Qaṣīrun anfahu*): the story goes that in the third century AD, during the rivalry

between the Arab cities of al-Ḥīrah and Tadmur (Palmyra), a certain Qaṣīr ibn Saʿd of al-Ḥīrah cut off his nose in order to convince al-Zabbāʾ (Zenobia), queen of Tadmur, that he had been unjustly punished by the ruler of his city; this, along with a series of other maneuvers, allowed him to gain her confidence and, eventually, bring about her death in revenge for her murder of al-Ḥīrah's former king (see al-Maydānī, *Majmaʿ*, I:158–59). The saying, attributed to al-Zabbāʾ, became proverbial for extreme determination in pursuit of a goal.

157 "the boon companion abandoned the one to whom he'd been so close": an allusion to the speaker's leaving his wife, as described in 3.13.1 above.

158 "neither his body nor his mind": the significance of the reference to the mind is made clear in chapter 17, below.

159 The monastery in question was probably that of Mār Ilyās (Roper, *Fāris al-Shidyāq as Translator and Editor*) near El Qraye, Mount Lebanon.

160 "or vice versa" (*aw bi-l-ʿaks*): i.e., it may be the monks that appeal to women, or it may be the challenge of their seduction that is uppermost in their minds.

161 "Shitter Bāy" (*Bāʿir Bāy*): while, at first glance, the name seems reminiscent of the code used earlier in references to Amīr (Emir) Ḥaydar as Baʿīr Bayʿar (see Volume One, 1.5.2, n. 148), in which case it might be read as standing for, for example, "Māhir Bāy" or "Tāmir Bāy," it appears more likely that here the author is simply exploiting, for comedic purposes, the root *b-ʿ-r*, which has associations with "dung" (also significant, as Geoffrey Roper has pointed out, in the earlier case); thus the meaning of Bāʿir Bāy would be "Shitter Bāy" (on the title Bāy, see below 3.18.6, n. 229) and the doors that cannot be closed would be those of latrines (on which theme see further Volume Four, 4.18.3).

162 "darnel" (*al-zuʾān*): a weed, hard to distinguish from wheat, that can be infected by an intoxicating fungus.

163 Taftāzān: a town in Khorosan, birthplace of Masʿūd ibn ʿUmar al-Taftāzānī (died between 791/1389 and 797/1395), whose works on

rhetoric were "widely accepted as the primary authoritative texts" in that field (Meisami and Starkey, *Encyclopedia*).

164 "Zayd struck ʿAmr": a conventional sentence used to illustrate a certain grammatical rule; see Volume One, 1.11.2.

165 "Which of you could bestow such blessings?" (*min ayyikum yaḥṣulu dhālik*): i.e., which of you, who are supposedly celibate, could provide such blessings (to be understood here as meaning "a bit of slap and tickle" or the like), this in turn being a veiled invitation to the lady to avail herself of the blessings that the non-celibate Fāriyāq was qualified to provide.

166 "a branch from the first dream": i.e., one of the Bag-man's wife's lovers (see 3.8.6), whom the narrator will henceforth refer to as "the Branch." Though it is impossible to be certain of the identity of "the Branch," there are some pointers: in the (admittedly obscure) poem in which the author recapitulates these events (3.17.7–9), he refers to a certain Ḥannā in a way that suggests that he might be the Bag-man's wife's lover, while Ferdinand Christian Ewald, a missionary who passed through Malta, writing of his visit to the Schlienz household on 3 January, 1842, states that he met there "a converted Persian . . . another convert from Egypt, and a young Greek from Beyrout" (Ewald, *Journal*, 11; I am indebted to Geoffrey Roper for bringing Ewald's statement to my attention); the convert from Egypt was likely Ḥannā al-Jawālī, a Copt who had been brought over from Egypt to assist with the translation project (Roper, *Fāris al-Shidyāq as Translator and Editor*). Al-Jawālī, who had attended the Protestant school in Cairo since the age of eight or nine, was in Malta between 1838 and 1842 (personal communication from Geoffrey Roper). Church Missionary Society records relating to Schlienz's trip to Syria mention that he was accompanied by al-Shidyāq but make no mention of al-Jawālī. However, they do not state that he did not go and al-Shidyāq here explicitly links "the Branch" to dreams Schlienz dreamed while in Malta. It does therefore seem possible that Ḥanna al-Jawālī was "the Branch." The "converted Persian" appears in chapter 17, below.

167 "his companion": it is not clear who is intended; the likeliest candidate is the Bag-man (which may explain why the two were received so hospitably by the British vice-consul, see 3.15.6 below), though in that case the question of the whereabouts of his wife arises; this would imply that "the Branch" stayed on in Syria for a while, perhaps as a result of his accident, which would be consonant with the terms in which his reappearance is described later (see 3.17.3).

168 "the *ḥabar* of the women of Egypt": a mantle of black (for married ladies) or white (for the unmarried) silk covering the head and body and open in front; see Lane, *Description*, 45 and 46 (illustration).

169 "eloquent" (*manāṭīq*): or, punningly, "had such stuffing to emphasize the size of the buttocks" (*Qāmūs*).

170 "a drunk" (*nāhib*): literally, "a thief."

171 "the Turkish *jīm*": i.e., "j" as in "James"; *anjaq* is Turkish *ancak*.

172 *yitqallanu*: from *kullanmak*, "to use."

173 *khōsh khuy*: apparently, *hoşhuy* ("good-natured").

174 "the deputy to the British consul (who was *not* the skilled and sagacious Khawājā Asʿad al-Khayyāṭ)": according to his own account (Kayat, *A Voice*, 265–66), Asʿad al-Khayyāṭ actually joined Schlienz's party in Lebanon, though al-Khayyāṭ makes no mention of the author and the author refers to al-Khayyāṭ only in this oblique fashion. Al-Khayyāṭ was in fact appointed consul in Jaffa in May 1847 (List of Consuls-General, Consuls, Vice-Consuls, Consular Agents and Consular Assistants in H.M. Service Presented to the House of Commons on 6th of June 1848, [989] XXXIX, 307, p. 7) and the sentence should presumably be understood to mean "the British vice-consul (who was not *at that time* the skilled and sagacious Khawājā Asʿad al-Khayyāṭ)."

175 "the smell of Umm Dafār": according to the *Qāmūs*, Umm Dafār means both this world, or life itself (*al-dunyā*), and "a slave girl" (*amah*); in other words, the author seems to be saying, the smell of a woman is both another name for ecstasy, and life itself.

176 "The two of them": i.e, the Fāriyāq and his companion referred to above (3.15.3, 3.15.6); see also n. 166 above.

177 "bringing with him the delirious promise of delicious fruit and a sturdy trunk" (*wa-huwa mutarjimun ʿan janyin shahiyyin wa-jidhʿ qawī*): the unusual use of *mutarjim*, active participle of *tarjama* "to translate," may reflect the colloquial usage *yitarjim bil-lisān*, "to speak in unknown tongues, jabber" (see Davies, *Lexicon*); at the same time, the author may be hinting at the identity of "the Branch," if the identification of the latter with the translator Ḥannā al-Jawālī is correct (see n. 165), and a second reading may be intended as well, as though the author were saying "he being a *mutarjim* ['translator'] (by which of course I mean a *mutarjim* ['a jabberer']) about . . ."

178 Dhāt al-Niḥyayn: literally, "She of the Two Butterskins." The story is told that this woman sold butter at the market of ʿUkāẓ near Mecca in the period immediately preceding Islam and was tricked by a man into holding two skins that he pretended he wanted to buy; while she was thus encumbered, the man had his way with her.

179 "particles of attraction" (*ḥurūf al-jarr*): the Arabic term for "prepositions."

180 "But you omitted 'particles' . . . They're still there" (*qad ḥadhafti l-ḥurūf . . . bal hiya bāqiyah*): the point is obscure; perhaps the Fāriyāqiyyah understands *ḥurūf* in the sense of "edges" and gives the word a sexual connotation (i.e., "edges of the vagina").

181 "theology . . . talking" (*al-kalām . . . al-kalām*): "theology" is referred to as *kalām*, literally, "talk"; the Fāriyāqiyyah recognizes the word only in its literal sense.

182 "the Hairy One" (*al-Ashʿarī*): ʿAlī ibn Ismāʿīl al-Ashʿarī (260–324/873–936), whose last name might be taken to mean "hairy" (albeit its real sense is "affiliate of the Banū Ashʿar"), was the founder of an influential school of theology "famed for its adoption of rational argumentation" (Meisami and Starkey, *Encyclopedia*); again the Fāriyāqiyyah recognizes the word only in its literal sense.

183 "seminary talk . . . semen" (*kalāmaki hādhā l-maʿṣūd . . . al-ʿaṣd*): in the Arabic, "twisted talk."

184 "for reasons that will be explained" (*li-asbābin yaʾtī bayānuhā*): presumably, a reference to the account given in 3.17.7.

185 The poem that follows poses so many problems that this translation must be considered tentative, literal, and incomplete. The poem employs a style that the author uses only rarely (another example is the "Qaṣīdah Qimāriyyah" ("A Poem on Gambling") in Volume Four, 4.20.39). Both poems allude to and satirically retell past events but deal with these elliptically, use coded references to persons who may or may not have been mentioned earlier in the work, and rely heavily on puns and the multiple meanings of single words. In this case, the events seem to be those of chapter 15 above ("The Journey from the Monastery"), which presents the Bag-man, his wife, and her lover ("the Branch") in a triangle of deceit and hidden passions, and those of the present chapter, with its account of the Bag-man's madness; the poet appears to imply a link between the two. The first part of the poem appears to be addressed to the mentally unstable missionary Christoph Schlienz (see n. 97); then, from 3.17.8 on, to the Persian convert.

186 Ḥannā: see n. 147 above.

187 "sick, depleted" (*marīḍun mannā*): from *manna* (root *m-n-n*) "to become diminished" (*Qāmūs*: *naqaṣa*) but also, punningly, "sick, from masturbating," from *mannā* (root *m-n-y*).

188 "some lecher" (*fāsiq*): presumably meaning the Bag-man himself, given that he, along with his wife, was the only member of the party to have ridden a horse rather than a mule (see 3.15.1).

189 "his joints go weak" (*zannā*): from roots *z-n-n* and *z-n-w* or, punningly, "he oppressed [us]," from *z-n-'*, or "he called us fornicators," from *z-n-y*.

190 "from any tormentor who may hurt him" (*min kulli muʿannin ʿannā*): from root *ʿ-n-y*, or "from any person curious about us," from root *ʿ-n-n*.

191 "the whickering doe, the snickering buck" (*wa-l-ghannā'a wa-l-aghannā*): i.e., the wife and her lover, or perhaps amorous couples in general.

192 "a preacher who went mad— / And from one who goes around here—and who wept" (*min nadhīrin janna/wa-min ṭawwāfin hāhunā wa-hannā*): the preacher presumably is Schlienz; the identity of "one who goes around here" is not obvious.

193 “The loving couple” (*al-muḥibbayn*): presumably Mrs. Schlienz and “the Branch.”

194 “Madmen who have exposed their willies” (*fa-min majānīna abānū l-hannā*): presumably a reference to Schlienz.

195 “One afflicted . . . and a sickly invalid who moans” (*wa-min muṣābin . . . wa-min ʿalīlin qad annā*): both may stand for the Fāriyāq (see 3.15.2–3 above).

196 “a crabbed little man” (*khubunnan*): probably meaning the Fāriyāq / author.

197 “His devil” (*shayṭānuhu*): i.e., presumably, the poet’s demon.

198 “a book”: during the period of his first visit to England, in 1845, the author was involved in the translation of both the Bible and the Psalms (Roper, *Fāris al-Shidyāq as Translator and Editor*).

199 “the Committee” (*al-lajnah*): i.e., the governing board of either the Church Missionary Society or the Society for the Propagation of Christian Knowledge, both of which were involved in the project for the translation of the Bible.

200 “the Christians”: i.e, the Christians of the Arab world at whom the translation was targeted.

201 This insertion of a poem into the middle of a sentence that begins and ends as prose is certainly unusual and may be unique in Arabic letters.

202 “the richness of their solecisms in speaking . . .” (*ghanāʾa l-laḥni fī l-qawli ʿindahum . . .*): the poet appears to be saying that (from a classical literary perspective) Christians make a lot of mistakes in speaking but that they are happy with that because the way they speak sounds musical to them.

203 “al-Mawlā in reference to God”: literally, “the Lord, the Master”; presumably al-Tutūnjī favored *al-rabb*.

204 “*wallawu l-adbāra*”: the phrase means “they turned their backs” and occurs in the Qurʾān (Q Fatḥ 48:22); the metropolitan may have wanted to pronounce *wallawu* as *wallū* in keeping with colloquial paradigms.

205 “*tukāh . . . muttaki*ʾ”: the root *w-k-ʾ/t-k-ʾ* does not form a (Form I) verb **wakaʾa/takaʾa*; hence **tukāh*, putative plural of an active

participle **tāki'*, does not exist, the correct form being (Form VIII) *muttaki'*.

206 "*maṣūn . . . muṣān*": the first means "sheltered, chaste"; the second wrongly assumes the existence of a verb **aṣāna* from the same root.

207 "*shaʿb . . . qawm*": both words refer to collectivities of people but the former has connotations related to the concept of "nation" that are lacking in the second.

208 "*malak . . . malāk*": both mean "angel" but the former belongs to the literary lexicon, the latter to the colloquial.

209 "*ʿabīd . . . ʿibād*": both mean "slaves" but only the second is used in the phrase *ʿibād allāh* ("slaves of God, humankind").

210 "*ʿadhāb . . . rakākāt*": the plural of *ʿadhāb* ("torment") is *aʿdhibah*, and not **ʿadhābāt*; *rakākāt* means "leavings" or "lame forms."

211 "*sā'ir* is not a synonym of *bāqī*": it is usually considered to be so.

212 "*wāʿiẓīhā . . . mūʿiẓīnahā*": the first means "those who preach to them," the second wrongly assumes the existence of a verb **awʿaẓa* from the same root; should it exist, the correct form would be **mūʿiẓīhā*.

213 "*addaw . . . waddaw*": the first word is correct according to literary norms, the latter is its colloquial equivalent.

214 "*radda . . . muridd*": the active participle of the verb *radda* ("to send back") is *rādd* or *rādid*; *muridd* assumes a nonexistent verb **aradda*.

215 "*yaẓharu . . . yabānu*": while the roots *ẓ-h-r* and *b-y-n* both refer to "appearing, becoming distinct," the imperfect form of the latter (Form I) is *yabīnu*.

216 "*ṣirnā banīnan bi-tadhakhkhur*" ("and we became children by laying up" [?]): the error is *banīnan* for *banīna*, the sound plural not taking *tanwīn*; the sense of *al-tadhakhkhur* is not obvious and the verse is unidentified though reminiscent of Prov. 13:22, *al-ṣāliḥu yūrithu banī l-banīna wa-tharwatu l-khāṭi' tudhkharu li-l-ṣiddīq* ("A good man leaveth an inheritance to his children's children: and the wealth of the sinner is laid up for the just").

217 "a *maṣaff* gathered glorifying God": *maṣaff* is used here in the sense of "row" (*ṣaff*), whereas its correct meaning is "the place where a row is formed" (*mawḍiʿ al-ṣaff*) (*Qāmūs*).

218 "that a *wāw* immediately follows *ka-mā* used as a conjunction" (*wa-baʿda ka-mā li-l-ʿatfi wāwun tubāshiru*): though not apparently documented in older Middle Arabic texts (the translator is indebted to Jérôme Lentin for this information), the use of the redundant *wāw* is frequently met with on the Internet in phrases such as *ka-mā wa-yuḥabbadhu* ("just as it is to be preferred that") (http://www.bakhdida.com/BehnamAtallah/MasrahDoma.htm) and *qaṭarāt al-nadā wa-jamāluhā r-rāʾiʿ ka-mā wa-lam tushāhidhā min qabl* ("dewdrops and their amazing beauty as you have never seen them before") (http://www.forum.ennaharonline.com/thread24136.html).

219 "*idh* must take the jussive": *idh* ("since") should be followed by the indicative.

220 "*alladhī* after the dual": invariable *alladhī* following referents of different number and case is a common feature of Middle Arabic.

221 "writing imperative –*ī* with the weak verb": i.e., writing أعطي for أعْطِ ("give!").

222 "that modern, the priest of Choueir" (*qass al-Shuwayr al-muʿāṣir*): the village of Choueir, or Dhour el Choueir, is located in the Matn region of Lebanon; the priest is ʿAbd Allāh Zākhir (1684–1748), a Melkite Catholic of the Basilian Choueirite Order credited with the establishment, in 1733, of the first printing press in the Middle East to use movable Arabic type, and a writer (see also next line).

223 "retention of the *nūn* of *-ūna* following *kay* and *an*": i.e., use of the indicative in place of the subjunctive following *kay* ("in order to") and *an* (conjunctive "that") (e.g., **kay yaktubūna* for *kay yaktubū* ["that they may write"] or **arādū an yadhhabūna* for *arādū an yadhhabū*["they wanted to go"]).

224 "after *yuʿṭā* to put the subject supplying the agent in the accusative is / A necessity": i.e., when a subject supplying the place of an agent (here, *nāʾib fāʿil*; see Wright, *Grammar*, II269 D) follows a passive verb, as in the sentence *yuʿṭā l-kitāb* ("the book is given"), the subject must be in the accusative (though correct usage requires the nominative).

225 "the story of al-Ma'mūn and the jurisprudent 'Allawayh": in this much-recorded anecdote, the caliph al-Ma'mūn demonstrates to his companions, at the expense of a certain *faqīh* called "Ḥamdawayh, known as 'Allawayh," that "a man's brain shrinks as his beard grows" (see, e.g., Muḥammad al-Munāwī, *Fayḍ al-qadīr fi sharḥ al-Jāmi' al-ṣaghīr* [Lebanon: Dār al-Kutub al-'Ilmiyyah, 1994], 5).

226 "one of those natives of the island who are between the Market-men and the Bag-men, and sometimes between the latter and the philosophers": one might hazard that the author means the Anglicans.

227 I.e., either out of respect for Friday as the Muslim Sabbath or the contrary.

228 "The latter had borrowed. . . .": a swipe, presumably, at the man's rudeness in not returning so necessary an item sooner and/or his miserliness in not buying his own, despite being "the son of an officer in the army of the Pope"; "phosphoric matches" (*nabakhāt*) were a recent invention and little known at the time in the Levant (see Kayat, *Voice*, 255).

229 "Counselor" (*mushīr*): a title awarded the ruler of Tunis by his nominal suzerain, the Ottoman sultan.

230 Bāy is a variant of the Turkish honorific that is realized more frequently in the eastern Arab countries as Bayk or Bayh and was appended to the names of all rulers of the Husainid dynasty of Tunis.

231 I.e. February 5, 1842 AD.

232 "dust-laden . . . harmattan" (*ḥāṣib . . . sāfiyā'*): the following list of words related to wind is shorter than that in the original and is intended as a representation, not a one-to-one translation, of the latter using words from the same semantic areas drawn from thesauri, dictionaries, and other lexical resources; see further Volume Four, Translator's Afterword.

233 "odors overpowering . . . and oro-dyslalic" (*rawā'iḥ hanbiyyah . . . najwiyyah*): the following list of words, most of which are related to foul smells, with others related to effeminacy and to impaired speech, is shorter than that in the original and is intended as a representation,

not a one-to-one translation, of the latter using words from the same semantic areas drawn from thesauri, dictionaries, and other lexical resources; see further Volume Four, Translator's Afterword.

234 "schwa-ations" (*al-qalqalāniyyah*): it is assumed here that the word, which is not to be found in the lexica, is to be taken as equivalent to *qalqalah*, meaning "the insertion of /ə/ [the neutral vowel schwa] after syllable-final /q/, /d/, /ṭ/, and /j/" in the recitation of the Qur'ān (Nelson, *Art*, 22).

235 "sibillations" (*al-kaskasiyyah*): "the adding of /s/ following the feminine suffix /k/ . . . at the end of an utterance" (*Lisān*).

236 "shibillations" (*al-kashkashiyyah*): "substitution of /sh/ for the feminine second-person suffix /k/" (*Lisān*).

237 "how to clean out the mud" (*taṣlīḥ al-ṭabaʿ*): or, reading *al-ṭabʿ*, "how to correct the proofs."

238 "reclusion" (*al-iʿtizāl*): the Fāriyāq has used the same word in its contemporary sense of "quarantine," but the Fāriyāqiyyah takes it in its root sense of "holding oneself aloof," with, in this context, a sexual connotation.

239 "Will he be with one of his wives?" (*amaʿa jārin lahu*): the Fāriyāqiyyah appears to be questioning whether Sāmī Pasha will be making the same sacrifice of female companionship that he is demanding of the Fāriyāq.

240 "If the name were enough . . .": i.e., if a name were enough to compensate a woman for what she will miss by way of lovemaking when her husband is summoned by his emir, she could simply write "emir" on her body.

241 "and treat her frivolously . . ." (*wa-yuʿāmiluhā bil-khayʿarah . . .*): the following list of words, most of which are related to levity and unsteadiness, anger, disordered speech, rudeness and coarseness, physical violence, and infidelity, is shorter than that in the original and is intended as a representation, not a one-to-one translation, of the latter using words from the same semantic areas drawn from thesauri, dictionaries, and other lexical resources; see further Volume Four, Translator's Afterword.

242 *ghabūq*: defined by the *Qāmūs* as "what (i.e., of camel's milk) is drunk in the evening" and by Lane as "a she-camel whose milk one drinks in the evening," the relevance being, in either case, obscure.

243 "an intelligent man skilled at his work" (*al-ṭabb*): this, and most of the other words in this and the following lists, have multiple meanings and/or vowelings, and it is not always obvious which the author has in mind.

244 "*basṭ . . . sharḥ*": here, as in some further items in this list, the "conformity" is semantic rather than formal (as each comes from a different root), with both having the underlying sense of "opening up" and similar figurative uses (note *shariḥa ṣadruhu*, "his breast became open" or "he became glad").

245 "Every other difficulty pales into insignificance next to such things" (*kullu ṣaʿbin fī janbi dhāka yahūn*): i.e., next to the difficulties of the Arabic language.

246 "assy-nonymous" (*ardāfiyyah*): i.e., *mutarādifah* meaning "synonymous," though the Fāriyāqiyyah confuses the word with *ardāf*, from the same root, meaning "buttocks."

247 "Multiply and fill the earth": cf. "be fruitful, and multiply upon the earth" (Gen. 8:17) .

248 Cf. (1 Tim. 2:15): ". . . she shall be saved in childbearing, if they continue in faith and charity and holiness with sobriety."

249 "This bitty-buttocked . . ." (*hādhihi . . . al-rasḥāʾ . . .*): the following list of words related to having insufficient flesh on the backside, the thighs, the calves, the breasts, or the arms is shorter than that in the original and is intended as a representation, not a one-to-one translation, of the latter using words from the same semantic areas drawn from thesauri, dictionaries, and other lexical resources; see further Volume Four, Translator's Afterword.

250 "This short, little . . ." (*hādhihi . . . al-bultūqah al-duʿshūqah . . .*): the following list of words related to shortness of stature is shorter than that in the original and is intended as a representation, not a one-to-one translation, of the latter using words from the same semantic areas

drawn from thesauri, dictionaries, and other lexical resources; see further Volume Four, Translator's Afterword.

251 "This black, sable . . ." (*hādhihi . . . al-sawdā' al-musakhkhamah . . .*): the following list of words related to blackness is shorter than that in the original and is intended as a representation, not a one-to-one translation, of the latter using words from the same semantic areas drawn from thesauri, dictionaries, and other lexical resources; see further Volume Four, Translator's Afterword.

252 "This old, aged . . .": (*hādhihi . . . al-ʿajūz al-mutahaddimah . . .*): the following list of words related to old age and decrepitude is shorter than that in the original and is intended as a representation, not a one-to-one translation, of the latter using words from the same semantic areas drawn from thesauri, dictionaries, and other lexical resources; see further Volume Four, Translator's Afterword.

253 "*dustūr*": "The great wezeer . . . to whom recourse is had [by the King] with respect to what he may prescribe concerning the circumstances of the people" (Lane, *Lexicon*); see also following note.

254 "*dussa tawrun*": "a messenger was secretly sent"; as usual in such word puzzles, it is the unvowelled ductus that is in play; thus دستور may be broken down into دس and تور, re-vowelled, and reconstructed as given (دُسَّ تَوْرٌ).

255 "Two parts to which the male can lay no claim" (*ḥaẓẓāni lā li-l-dhakar*): an echo of Q Nisāʾ 4:11, where, in stipulating inheritance shares, God says, "a male should receive a share equivalent to that of two females" (*li-l-dhakari mithlu ḥazzi l-unthayayn*); the conceit inverts the allocation.

256 "in a state of sin" (*nukran*): and also perhaps, punningly, "as a cipher" or "one unknown," or even "in a state of indefiniteness" (cf. *nukirah* "indefinite noun").

257 "precedence of the masculine" (*taghlīb al-mudhakkar*): on *taghlīb*, see Volume Two, 2.12.7 n. 140; the "precedence" referred to here is that implied by the grammatical rule that a masculine plural form may be taken to refer to persons of both sexes, whereas a feminine plural form can refer to women only, e.g. *yarawna* ("they (masculine

and possibly feminine) see") and *yarayna* ("they (feminine only) see.")

258 "crawling" (*ziḥāf*): a pun combining the nontechnical sense of the word and its technical use in the science of prosody, where it refers to certain metrically acceptable changes to a two-consonant syllable (*sabab*) as a component of a foot.

259 "propping" (*sināduhu*): again, a pun combining the nontechnical sense of the word and its technical use in the science of prosody, where it refers to "dissimilarity of two *ridf*s in verse" (*ikhtilāf al-ridfayni fī l-shiʿr*), the *ridf* being "one of the letters of prolongation ا, ى or و, when it immediately precedes the *rawī*" (Wright, *Grammar*, II:353); dissimilarity would mean the permissible rhyming of, e.g., *qarīḥ* with *ṭarūb*, since "the long vowel *ā* remains invariable" (*idem*).

260 "I want pussy, I want pussy, I want pussee!" (*mustafʿilun mustafʿilun mustafʿilū*): forms based on the root *f-ʿ-l* are used to represent the combinations of short and long syllables from which the sixteen quantitative meters of Arabic verse are formed; thus *mustafʿilun* (*mustafʿilū* in the final foot) represents the combination LLSL, a variant of the meter called *al-kāmil* (see Wright, *Grammar*, II:359). However, *mustafʿilun* may also be interpreted as the active participle of the desiderative form of the verb (see Wright, *Grammar*, I:45 [63]), deriving its sense here from *fiʿl*, meaning "the vulva of any female" (*Qāmūs*). A similar conceit is used in 3.11.4 above.

261 "your 'shame' inspires me to worship and to insane passion" (*ḥayāʾuki taʾlīhī wa-tawlīhī*): *ḥayāʾuki* may be interpreted as either "your shame/modesty" or "your vagina"; this allows for the possibility that *taʾlīhī* ("my considering you divine") is intended to evoke the first meaning ("your shame/modesty") while *tawlīhī* ("my being driven insane by passion") evokes the second, according to the rhetorical figure known as *istikhdām* ("employing (both meanings of a homonym)") (see Meisami and Starkey, *Encyclopedia*, II:657).

262 "growths, lumps . . . necrosities" (*al-waram wa-l-nuffākh . . . al-khunāq*): the following list of words related to maladies affecting the neck, throat, and face, or more generally the skin is shorter than that in the

original and is intended as a representation, not a one-to-one translation, of the latter using words from the same semantic areas drawn from thesauri, dictionaries, and other lexical resources; see further Volume Four, Translator's Afterword.

263 "man-mannered, ill-natured. . . ." (*al-zanmardah al-ʿanjarid . . .*): the following list of words related to shamelessness, foulmouthedness, promiscuity, and the display of sexual desire is shorter than that in the original and is intended as a representation, not a one-to-one translation, of the latter using words from the same semantic areas drawn from thesauri, dictionaries, and other lexical resources; see further Volume Four, Translator's Afterword.

264 "to look lively and apply himself to intercourse . . ." (*ilā l-tamshīr . . .*): the following list of words related to sexual activity is shorter than that in the original and is intended as a representation, not a one-to-one translation, of the latter using words from the same semantic areas drawn from thesauri, dictionaries, and other lexical resources; see further Volume Four, Translator's Afterword.

265 "your teacher": i.e., her husband, the Fāriyāq.

266 "the windy day . . . when" (*wa-yawma . . . wa-ḥīnata*): each of the next several sentences begins with a word meaning "on the day (or at another point in time) when"; the original list comprises thirteen separate words for point of time or time periods but these can be matched by only ten expressions for time in the English; see further Volume Four, Translator's Afterword.

267 "sent your servingman . . . dispatched your serving girl": i.e. to take someone a billet-doux.

268 "you tied a piece of string around your finger" (*artamti*): perhaps as a reminder of an assignation.

269 "toiled and moiled . . ." (*taʿannā wa-taʿammala . . .*): the following list of words related to hard work, failure to complete or to properly carry out work, lying, confusion, and conceitedness is shorter than that in the original and is intended as a representation, not a one-to-one translation, of the latter using words from the same semantic areas drawn from thesauri, dictionaries, and other lexical resources; see

further Volume Four, Translator's Afterword. On *takassus* and *tazabbub*, see also the author's marginal note to 3.2.27.

270 "Is there in the universe no glass . . ." (*a-laysa fī l-kawni min mir'āh . . .*): the following list of words related to mirrors is shorter than that in the original and is intended as a representation, not a one-to-one translation, of the latter using words from the same semantic areas drawn from thesauri, dictionaries, and other lexical resources; see further Volume Four, Translator's Afterword. The term *māriyyah* is defined in the printed editions of the *Qāmūs* as *al-mar'ah al-bayḍā' al-barrāqah* ("a shining white woman") and its presence in the list reflects either the author's misreading of *mar'ah* as *mir'āh* or an incorrect vowelling of the word in a printed edition of the *Qāmūs*.

271 "Syrian Tripoli" (*Ṭarābulus al-Shām*): i.e., the city that today is in Lebanon, as distinct from Libyan Tripoli.

272 "His reading in grammar . . ." (*fa-ghāyatu mā ʿalimahu mina l-naḥw . . .*): here and in the following clauses the author uses terms that may be interpreted either technically, according to the field in question, or according to their base senses, in which case they are also open to a sexual or vulgar interpretation. Thus *al-fāʿil wa-l-mafʿūl* are "subject and object" in grammatical terms but "the doer and the done" in their basic senses and "the fucker and the fucked" when used sexually.

273 "the figure of 'stripping'" (*nawʿ al-tajrīd*): in the field of rhetoric, "abstraction," i.e. "'abstracting a general attribute from an individual' according to the pattern of 'in him (individual) I have a true friend (general attribute)'" (Meisami and Starkey, *Encyclopedia*, II:659); the base sense is "stripping off (of clothes)."

274 "the movable peg" (*al-watid al-mutaḥarrik*): in the science of prosody, the *watid* (literally "peg") is a three-consonant syllable as a constituent of a metrical foot; when a *watid* ends in a consonant followed by a vowel it is said to be "moving" (*mutaḥarrik*) (see Wright, *Grammar*, II:358D and 355B); its base sense is "peg," commonly used for "penis."

275 "having the buttock echo the breast" (*radd al-ʿajuz ʿalā l-ṣadr*): i.e., "repeating the rhyme word in the first hemistich, often at the beginning of the line, or sometimes at the start of the second hemistich"

(Meisami and Starkey, *Encyclopedia*, II:660); the technical sense of *ʿajuz* is "the last foot," that of *ṣadr* "the first foot of the first hemistich," of a line of verse; their base senses are as given in the translation.

276 "pipe stems" (*qaṣab al-tibgh*): tobacco pipes of the period consisted of a small earthenware bowl fitted to the end of a long stem, and these stems were stored on racks on the walls.

277 "dear shame-faced abstainer" (*yā rāqiʾan*): i.e., *yā rāqiʾan ʿalā ẓalʿika*, see Volume One, 1.1.2, n. 35.

278 "Dear blind-eye turner" (*yā ʿāmisan*): i.e., "turner of a blind eye to one's own faults" though also, punningly, "dear peruser (of this book)." The reader will note too that in Arabic, not only do the four preceding words rhyme but the first and third and the second and fourth are examples of "perfect paronomasia," i.e., each consists of the same letters in different order.

279 "Were the Almighty to call his servants to account for their thoughtless words as severely as you do" (*law inna llāha taʿālā yuʿākhidhu l-ʿibāda fī-l-laghwi mithlukum*): an echo of Q Baqarah 2:225 *lā yuʾākhidhukumu llāhu fi l-laghwi fī aymānikum* ("God will not call you to account for thoughtlessness in your oaths") (trans. Yūsuf ʿAlī), and similarly Māʾidah 5:89.

280 "That . . . goes with the other!" (*wa-hādhā ayḍan min dhāk*): the Fāriyāq seems to mean that the Fāriyāqiyyah's last remark is an example of the fact that "our language . . . is so wide that it allows every expression to bear numerous possible meanings"; the Fāriyāqiyyah, however, lends a sexual innuendo to "that" and "this." Here and throughout the exchange the language is elusive and open to more than one interpretation, and the translation offered here—for which I am indebted in part to the suggestions of Michael Cooperson and Gerald Van Gelder—is tentative; for a different interpretation, see Khawam, *Jambe*, 554.

281 "In one of the two meanings": as already mentioned (3.18.14, in the middle), the *Qāmūs* defines *rajul* as "too well-known to require definition [i.e., 'man, a male of the human species']; also, one who has frequent intercourse."

282 "the dismemberment of our relationship . . . the dehydration of your member" (*al-inbitāt . . . al-inbitāt*): the joke lies in each phrase using the same word in a different way; thus the verb *inbatta* may mean either "[i]t was . . . cut off [of] a thing . . . and a tie . . . between two persons" or "[h]is . . . seminal fluid became cut off . . ." (Lane, *Lexicon*), the Fāriyāqiyyah presumably meaning that he will never find another woman to have sex with.

283 "rooftop . . . top[ling] . . . top[ling]" (*al-saṭḥ . . . al-saṭḥ . . . al-saṭḥ*): after the Fāriyāq evokes the "rooftop" (*al-saṭḥ*) that witnessed their falling in love (3.2.1), the Fāriyāqiyyah uses the opportunity to (mis)understand the word in another of its senses, namely "to bed."

284 "*ḍighn* . . . 'yearning'": according to the *Qamūs*, *ḍighn* means both "yearning" and "malice."

285 "*ʿIqyawn*": "a sea of wind beneath the Throne in which there are angels of wind with spears of wind gazing at the Throne whose Magnificat is 'Glory to Our Lord Most High!'" (*Qāmūs*); see Volume Two, 2.14.43.

286 "*fiṭaḥl*": "the preadamic period" (see 3.12.2).

287 "*ḥabrah*": "yellowness of the teeth" (*Qāmūs*); in fact, the word has not occurred in precisely this form before; however, *ḥabar*, the verbal noun from which it derives, is used in the list of maladies affecting the neck and adjacent parts of the body in 3.19.12.

288 "its closeness to *ʿiqyān . . . faḥl . . . ḥibarah*": i.e., the Fāriyāqiyyah was able to memorize these abstruse words because of their resemblance to other words describing things dear to her heart.

289 "She replied, 'And they also say that *tasdīd* ("the plugging of holes") is from *sadād* ("proper behavior") . . .'" (*qālat wa-qālū . . .*): the following passage poses numerous problems and the translation advanced above is tentative and does not claim to reveal the underlying argument.

290 I.e., he sent further examples of the metropolitan's grammatical errors.

291 "a book on the state of the island's inhabitants": in 1834, al-Shidyāq published *al-Riḥlah al-mawsūmah bi-l-Wāsiṭah bi-maʿrifat aḥwāl Māliṭah* (*The Book of Travel Entitled Means to a Knowledge of the State*

of Malta) (Beirut: al-Muʾassasah al-ʿArabiyyah li-l-Dirāsāt wa-l-Nashr, 2004).

292 "the head of the infirmary for the foul of breath" (*raʾīs maṣlaḥ al-bukhr*): i.e., the director of the school for teaching Arabic to the Maltese (see 3.11.2).

293 Mr. Drummond: unidentified but likely a member of the gentry of the village in which the Fāriyāq was "fated to reside" (see further n55).

294 "amber": i.e., such as that used to make mouthpieces for pipes.

295 "for whose typeface I take no responsibility": elsewhere, the author describes the font used in the first edition, which was made in Paris by the printer, as being "of alien form" (see "A Note on the Arabic Text," Volume One, p.xxxiii n78).

296 "turnips": the author uses the word *qulqās*, which means "taro" or "elephant's ear" (an edible tuber); since the latter is not grown widely in England, it seems likely that he had in mind turnips, which somewhat resemble taro.

297 "a quarter of a language": a reference to the supposed propensity of the author's countrymen for learning only the rude words in any language (see 4.1.3).

298 The narrative of the Fāriyāq's travels now resumes at the point where we left it at the end of the previous volume (Volume Three, 3.20.6), while the repartee that follows is in essence a continuation of that between him and his wife that preceded her own departure earlier for Cairo (Volume Three, 3.20.1–4).

299 "Half the latter and half the former" (*niṣfun min hādhā wa-niṣfun min dhāk*): the Fāriyāqiyyah probably means no more than "a bit of both" but the Fāriyāq takes her words literally (see what follows).

300 "Application of *naḥt* brings us back to the first" (*yurjiʿunā l-naḥtu ilā l-awwal*): *naḥt* means taking parts of two words and creating from them a third; here, the Fāriyāq takes the first half of the first word in his question (*nākir*) and the second half of the second (*shākir*) and finds himself (since the second half of each word is identical) back at the first, i.e., *nākir* ("hatefully").

301 "or the first brings us back to another meaning of *naḥt*" (*aw yurjiʿunā l-awwalu ilā n-naḥt*): the *Qāmūs* gives "intercourse" as one of the meanings of *naḥt*, and the first half of the first word in the Fāriyāq's question, i.e., *nākir*, is *nāk*, which means "to fuck."

302 "Which first did you have in mind?" (*ayyu awwalin aḍmarti*): i.e., "were you thinking of the first part of *nākir* (see preceding note) or of *shākir*," the first part of *shākir* being interpretable as *shākk*, i.e., "doubting."

303 "You forbade me before to deal with you on the basis of suspicion" (*innaki kunti nahaytinī ʿani l-muʿāmalah bi-l-qasm*): here, as in an earlier passage (Volume Three, 3.20.1: "dealing . . . on a basis of conjecture and suspicion"), the author puns on two senses of *qasm*, namely "doubt" and "definition by division" or "logic chopping."

304 "I'm the one sinned against" (*huwa ya'tīnī*): because her husband's questions imply doubt.

305 "Does the word 'no' have no place in your mouth?" (*a-mā fī fīki lafẓatu lā*): presumably meaning, "I would have preferred it if you had simply said, 'No, I won't' in answer to my request that you explain what you meant."

306 "It used to be pronounced 'yes'" (*kānat naʿam*): perhaps meaning, "When we were first married, I never said no to you."

307 "A no from a woman is a boon" (*inna lā mina l-mar'ati ilan*): perhaps implying that the Fāriyāq found his wife's demands exhausting

308 "If a woman doesn't fit properly she'll never give birth" (*wa-lā talidu man lā talīq*): the verb *yalīq* means "to be proper, fitting" (as in the Fāriyāq's statement) and also "to stick, to cling, to fit tightly," as in the Fāriyāqiyyah's.

309 "the same Matter . . . different Forms" (*māddah . . . ikhtilāf al-ṣuwar*): the banter now draws on the terminology of Aristotelian logic, as in an earlier passage (see Volume One, 1.6.4.). In their Aristotelian senses the *māddah* (literally, "matter") is the substratum of which any entity consists and the *ṣūrah* ("picture, shape") is the form in which it is manifested; here, the Fāriyāq argues that the Matter (i.e., sexual

intercourse) is the same in essence under all circumstances (and a woman should not therefore need more than one lover) while the Fāriyāqiyyah exploits the Aristotelian idea that Matter must possess a certain degree of consistency to manifest itself to argue that if the Matter is not "copious and inseparable" (*ziyādah muttaṣilah*), it will manifest itself in a variety of Forms, i.e., if a woman does not enjoy sufficient and regular intercourse she will seek a variety of lovers.

310 "in certain circumstances . . . where the circumstances of certain people are concerned" (*fī baʿḍi l-aḥwāl . . . aḥwāli l-baʿḍ*): the Fāriyāqiyyah seems to imply that the Fāriyāq makes an exception, in the case of certain women he knows, from the preference for monogamy that he has just expressed.

311 "*ghāniyah*": literally, "she who dispenses (with something)"; see further Volume One, 1.1.11n105.

312 "*ʿawānī*": plural active participle of the verb *ʿanā* ("to be subservient; to be taken by force"); the Fāriyāqiyyah is reminded of the word because of its resemblance to *ghawānī*, plural of *ghāniyah*, from which it differs, as she goes on to say, by a single dot.

313 "though the dot on the one ought to put in a good word for the other" (*hādhihi n-nuqṭatu shafaʿat fī tilk*): i.e., the dot that produces a word (*ghawānī*) meaning women ought to intercede to prevent those referred to by an otherwise identical word (*ʿawānī*) from being taken captive.

314 "dotting" (*al-tanqīṭ*): the word may be taken to mean either "placing dots over letters" or "dripping, spotting."

315 "scripting" (*al-taḥrīf*): in the surface context of the discussion of writing, the word may be taken to mean "creating written characters," in that of the sexual subtext as "rubbing against the edge (*ḥarf*)," and in the broader context of men's disingenuousness regarding women as "distorting the meaning (of a word)."

316 "and the woman who chases men ends up unchased" (*wa-l-ṭālibatu taʿūdu ghayra maṭlūbah*): i.e., undesired by her husband because she has entertained a suitor and undesired by her suitor because she has not acceded to his wishes.

317 “*martyrs . . . medulla oblongarters*” (*al-aḥwāl . . . al-abwāl*): the Fāriyāqiyyah means to say, “were it not for the necessity of circumstances, they wouldn’t worry their heads about such things”; however, knowing that the singular of *aḥwāl* (literally, “state, condition”) is *ḥāl*, she assumes that the plural of *bāl* (“mind, intellect”) is *abwāl*, which, in fact, is the plural of *bawl* (“urine”). The translation substitutes a different distortion.

318 “no conformity between male and female or between female and male” (*lam takun munāsabatun bayna l-dhakari wa-l-unthā wa-bayna l-unthā wa-l-dhakar*): perhaps meaning that there would be no words such as *qafā* (“back of the neck”) and *kabid* (“liver”) that may be treated as either masculine or feminine (for a list see Hava, *al-Farā'id*, v [unnumbered in the original]).

319 “the masculinization of the true feminine” (*tadhkīr ḥaqīqat al-ta'nīth*): perhaps meaning the formation of words such as *ʿajūz* (“old woman”) and *ḥāmil* (“pregnant”) that are masculine in form but feminine in meaning (for a list see Hava, *al-Farā'id*, v [unnumbered in the original]).

320 “the feminization of words that have no equivalent” (*wa-ta'nīthi mā huwa ghayru muqābilin bi-mithlihi*): perhaps meaning that assignment of feminine gender to certain words such as *shams* (“sun”) and *ka's* (“cup”) that are often described as being feminine simply by usage is in fact due to their lack of any formally feminine equivalent (i.e., there is no *shamsah* or *ka'sah*).

321 “the Syrians” (*al-shāmiyyīn*): a term that here would signify Levantines in general.

322 “Would that I had . . . two hearts to devote to these concerns of ours” (*layta lī qalbayni fī shughlinā*): meaning perhaps, “Would that I could deal with the world (or perhaps specifically the world as it affects ‘us,’ i.e., us women) as both a woman and (in the terms described in the preceding passage) a man.”

323 “in part by design and in part through preference and predilection” (*baʿḍuhu bi-l-takhṣīṣi wa-baʿḍuhu bi-l-tafḍīli wa-l-īthār*): meaning perhaps that some things (e.g., feminine charms) belong to women by

divine design while others (e.g., wealth) do so because men cede them to them.

324 "Judges, chapter 19": the chapter relates how a man, staying overnight in the village of Gibeah, is forced to hand over his concubine to local men and how "they knew her, and abused her all the night until the morning. . . . Then came the woman in the dawning of the day, and fell down at the door of the man's house where her lord was. . . . And her lord rose up in the morning, and opened the doors of the house, and went out to go his way: and, behold, the woman his concubine was fallen down at the door of the house, and her hands were upon the threshold. And he said unto her, Up, and let us be going. But none answered." (Judges 19:25–28)

325 The following definitions in quotation marks are taken by the author directly from the *Qāmūs*.

326 "the sworn virgin, who 'abstains completely from intercourse'" (*al-shafīratu wa-hiya l-qāniʿatu mina l-biʿāli bi-aysarihi*): the author ignores, either carelessly or teasingly, the second and more contextually appropriate meaning of *shafīrah* given in the *Qāmūs*, which is "she who finds her pleasure in the edges of her vagina and therefore comes quickly."

327 4.2.13–16: as in an earlier passage (see 4.2.2), many of the terms used in this debate are taken from the vocabulary of theology (*kalām*) and philosophy (*falsafah*); of note here are *ziyādah* ("increase"), *nuqṣān* ("diminution"), *ṣifah* ("distinguishing characteristic"), *ʿāmm* ("general, universal"), *khāṣṣ* ("particular"), and *q-s-m* "definition by division."

328 "the two last characteristic abilities" (*al-ṣifatān al-madhkūratān*): reference appears to be to keeping going longer, penetrating more deeply, and maintaining a harder erection, with the author either regarding one of these three as subsidiary to one of the others or miscounting.

329 The term *taṣawwur*, meaning how the mind perceives things outside of the soul, is typically translated as "conceptualization" in philosophical contexts such as this. However, given the emphasis on the visual

aspect of what is conceptualized elsewhere in the work (see 4.2.8, 4.4.5, 4.6.5, and 4.9.8), "visualization" has sometimes also been used.

330 Ya'qūb: the reference is perhaps to Ya'qūb (Jacob) sleeping with Leah when he supposed he was sleeping with Rachel (Gen. 29:23–25).

331 I.e., a woman will "visualize" various men in the hope of selecting from each some physical characteristic that will be passed on to her children.

332 I.e., a man's infidelities, unlike a woman's, do not serve the useful purpose of making their children better-looking since if a woman is unfaithful then her children will be better-looking than if they were fathered by her husband (it being assumed here that husbands are ugly), whereas if her husband is unfaithful his infidelity will (obviously) have no impact upon the looks of her children.

333 "the different ways in which the father and the mother visualize": the implication appears to be that men have no impact on the form of their offspring because they visualize women purely in terms of their sexual traits, while women do have such an impact because they think of men in terms of discrete and not directly sexual attributes; as a rider, it is added that proof that men do not affect the form of their offspring lies in the fact that, if they did, given their narrow obsession with sexual attributes, all their children would be females, etc.

334 "frontward is better" (*al-ṭardu awlā*): the translation reflects the meaning of *al-ṭard* when it occurs in context with *al-'aks* ("backward"); alone, however, *al-ṭard* has the also relevant sense of "ejection/ejaculation."

335 "Unitarians . . ." (*al-muwaḥḥidūn . . .*): the Fāriyāqiyyah, in inventing words to describe those who perform once, etc., has hit on the names of various religious sects, for which the Fāriyāq makes fun of her by invoking further real sects whose names can be similarly interpreted; thus the Mu'tazilites were practitioners of speculative dogmatism but the word can be taken to mean "those who withdraw," while the Mu'aṭṭilites were deniers of the divine attributes but the word can be taken as meaning "those who go on strike."

336 "without redeeming qualities" etc.: the Fāriyāqiyyah, being ignorant of the specialized meaning of the word (see preceding note), takes it in its literal sense of "strikers" (i.e., men who down tools).

337 "'My sense of feeling,' I said, 'is in my head'" (*ḥissī fī ra'sī*): though the author appears at first to be alluding to the opposition of heart vs. head, it emerges that by "head" he means "tip" (of the male member).

338 "Try then to break it" (*ḥāwil idhan fakkahu*): the surface meaning seems to be an appeal to the Fāriyāq to break the closed circle of their argument; however, it may also be read as a request to restore their amicable relationship by initiating sexual intercourse.

339 "I reject such a characterization" (*lā arḍā bi-hādhihi ṣ-ṣifah*): the Fāriyāq (presumably willfully) mishears *al-ʿaqd* ("contract") as *al-ʿaqid*, which can mean (of a dog) "[having its] penis . . . *compressus in coitu, et extremitate turgens*" (Lane, *Lexicon*).

340 "Was the contract over the condition?" (*hal kāna al-ʿaqdu fī l-sharṭ*): meaning either, "Was the contract (between us) dependent on the condition (*sharṭ*) (that we remain faithful to one another)?" or "Was the contract between us dependent on the slit (also *sharṭ*)?"

341 "And was the condition without a contract?" (*wa-hal kāna l-sharṭu bi-lā ʿaqd*): or "and was the slit without a contract?", i.e., "and could you have [access to] the slit without a [marriage] contract?"

342 "that lunatic": i.e., the Bag-man who went insane and stripped off his clothes (see Volume Three, 3.17.2).

343 "utmost goal" (*muhwa'annahā*): defined in the *Lisān* as "distant place" (*makān baʿīd*) and "broad desert" (*ṣaḥrā' wāsiʿ*) , the word is not found in the *Qāmūs* and seems out of place here; the translation is speculative.

344 "The king's heart is in the hand of the Lord": not in fact Psalms but Proverbs 21:1.

345 "he was 'rubbing' him" (*yatamassaḥu bihi*): on the practice of drawing the hands over the accoutrements of venerated persons, see Volume One, 1.16.7n245.

346 "the Sublime State" (*al-dawlah al-ʿaliyyah*): the Ottoman Empire.

347 "that village": i.e., Barley in Hertfordshire, where the Reverend Samuel Lee, professor of Hebrew and formerly of Arabic at Cambridge and with whom the author was engaged in the translation of the Bible, was rector; the work was carried out at the rectory (see Roper, "Aḥmad Fāris" 236).

348 "the book referred to earlier": i.e., the Bible; see Volume Three, 3.18.1n198.

349 "the *ḥadanbadā* chapter": i.e. Volume Three, chapter 19, of which *ḥadanbadā* ("marvel") is the second word.

350 "the element of discussion" (*rukn al-dhikr*): see 4.2.16.

351 "for the pressing . . ." (*lil-nabrah . . .*): in the first item of each of the following pairs, the word in question is used in its nontechnical sense, while in the second it is used in its technical sense according to the lexicon of phonetics and/or Qur'anic recitation; thus *nabrah*, as the second term, means stress or accent, *hamzah* means a glottal stop, *ḥarakah* a vowel (because a consonant followed by a vowel is said to be "in motion"), *sukūn* a consonant not followed by a vowel (because such letters are said to be "inert"), *madd* the prolongation of *a* to *ā* in a variety of vocalic contexts (see Wright: *Grammar* I/24–25), *hadhdh* a rapid quickening of pace in the recitation of the Qur'ān (considered inappropriate), *tarkhīm* the omission of one or more of the final letters of a noun in the vocative indicating a low level of energy in the uttering of the word, *tarassul* a slowing of the pace of a reading.

352 "doubling of the letter *dhāl*" (*al-tashdīd ʿalā l-dhāl*): perhaps meaning specifically in the word *al-dhakar* ("the penis"). As a "sun" letter, *dhāl* (/*dh*/) is assimilated to the *lām* (/*l*/) of the definite article; thus *al-dhakar* is pronounced *adh-dhakar*, providing the speaker, in this case, with an opportunity to give extra prominence to the word.

353 "The best way to mend a slit is to sew it up" (*inna dawāʾa l-shaqqi an taḥūṣahu*): proverbial (see the *Qāmūs* s.v. *ḥ-w-ṣ*).

354 Ibn Alghaz: the name of a man of whom it is said that he was "much given to copulation and intercourse; he would lie down and get an erection, and the young camels would come and rub themselves against his penis, taking it for a scratching post" (*Qāmūs*).

355 the Banū Adhlagh: a tribe "characterized by intercourse" (*Qāmūs*).

356 "If at first you don't succeed . . ." (*al-ʿawdu aḥmad*): a proverb; literally, "A second, or subsequent, attempt (after a failure) is more likely to succeed because of the experience gained" (al-Maydānī, *Majmaʿ* I:324).

357 "Always count twice" (*man ʿadda ʿād*): the proverb has not been found in the sources and the relevance in this context is not obvious.

358 "Come early as the crow" (*bakkir bukūra l-ghurāb*): the crow being, proverbially, the first bird to wake (al-Maydānī, *Majmaʿ* I:79).

359 "turning disdainfully to one side . . . like a mirage dissipating" (*al-ṣufūḥ . . . muzlaʾimmah*): the following list of words related to shying and fleeing is shorter than that in the original and is intended as a representation, not a one-to-one translation, of the latter, using words from the same semantic areas drawn from thesauri, dictionaries, and other lexical resources; see further Volume Four, Translator's Afterword.

360 "an agitation . . . a rattling of the jaw" (*al-qushaʿrīrah . . . al-qafqafah*): the list of thirty-seven words in the original relating to *riʿdah* ("shaking"), *qushaʿrīrah* ("shivering"), and *ḥāʾir bāʾir* ("dizzy-headedness") (see 5.2.11) is represented here by twenty-nine English words or phrases selected from *Roget's Thesaurus* (see Translator's Afterword); *ʿusūm* is, according to the *Qāmūs,* the verbal noun of *ʿasama* "to gain," but the author appears to use it as the verbal noun of *ʿasima* "to suffer stiffness of the wrist or ankle joint," for which the correct form, according to the *Qāmūs*, is *ʿasam.*

361 "the four humors . . . each mix" (*al-akhlāṭu l-arbaʿatu . . . kullu khilṭ*): according to the Galenic system, varying combinations of the four humors (blood, black bile, yellow bile, and phlegm) in the body result in different moods (sanguine, melancholic, choleric, and phlegmatic).

362 "euphorbia fruit" (*qurmūṭah*): the comparison of euphorbia fruit, or red scrub berries, to women's breasts is conventional; see Volume Three, 3.6.8.

363 "Joshua would not have been able to enter the Promised Land": the reference is to Rahab the harlot (Josh. 2).

364 "Abraham would not have found favor with the King of Egypt": the reference is to Sarai, wife of Abram (i.e., Sarah, wife of Abraham), see Gen. 12:14–16.

365 "David ... an image in his bed": "Saul also sent messengers unto David's house, to watch him, and to slay him in the morning: and Michal David's wife told him, saying, If thou save not thy life to night, to morrow thou shalt be slain. So Michal let David down through a window: and he went, and fled, and escaped. And Michal took an image, and laid it in the bed, and put a pillow of goats' hair for his bolster, and covered it with a cloth" (1 Sam. 19:11–13).

366 "the wife of Nabal": i.e., Abigail (1 Sam. 25).

367 "Bathsheba's stratagem against David": 1 Kings 1:11–14.

368 "the Anglican sect" (*madhhab al-inkilīz*): referring, presumably, to Queen Elizabeth I (cf. Volume Two, 2.14.89).

369 "the *ḍād* ... the *ḍa'd*": the letter *ḍād* is supposedly unique to Arabic, which is often referred to as *lughat al-ḍād* ("the language of the *ḍād*"); *ḍa'd*, a variant of *ḍād*, also means "the vagina," probably because of the shape of the letter (ض), as is the case with the letter *ṣād* (ص), from which it differs only in having a dot (see similarly Volume Two, 2.4.15n79).

370 "the *mīm*": i.e., the letter *mīm* (م), which stands for the anus (see similarly Volume Two, 2.4.15n79).

371 "because the more bitter cold required that" (*li-kawni ziyādati qarṣati l-bardi awjaba dhālik*): meaning, presumably, that the women had been forced to put on thicker clothing.

372 "for everything that falls there's something to pick it up" (*li-kulli sāqiṭah lāqiṭah*): i.e., approx. "every Jack has his Jill," it being noted that *sāqiṭah* may also be understood to mean "fallen woman."

373 "When you enter the land of al-Ḥuṣayb, run" (*idhā ji'ta arḍa l-Ḥuṣaybi fa-harwil*): according to the *Qāmūs*, al-Ḥuṣayb is a place in Yemen "whose women are of surpassing beauty."

374 "Londra": the author alternates throughout the text between this Italian- (or possibly French-) derived form, which was that used at the time in Lebanon, and "London."

375 “hips”: in the Arabic, “forearms” (*al-sāʿidayn*).

376 “with undoing, dresses” (*wa-mina l-ḥalli ḥulal*): presumably meaning that a woman’s acquiescence to a man’s demands leads to her acquisition of dresses.

377 “with this trait” (*bi-hādhihi l-ḥilyah*): i.e., with the trait of contrariness and refusal to compromise.

378 “‘A woman’s eyes,’ she declared . . . the situation I have described will come about” (*qālat inna ʿaynay al-marʾah . . . fa-waqaʿa mā qult*): i.e., if a woman does not keep track of how distant or close she and her husband are, the balance between the two will be disturbed (to her disadvantage).

379 “O delight of my eye!” (*yā qurrata l-ʿayn*): i.e., why do people use this phrase that implies that the eye is given to content rather than discontent?

380 “Prevention of your neighbor from visiting your house”: to be taken in the context of his later reference to a handsome young neighbor who is always dropping by (4.7.4).

381 “the hair on the lower sprouts before the hair on the upper” (*shaʿru l-aʿlā yanbitu qabla l-asfal*): apparently “the hair on the upper” means the facial hair, even though the Fāriyāqiyyah subsequently talks of head hair.

382 “the first category”: i.e., to the physical rather than the moral difference between men and women.

383 “trenches . . . firestones, campsites . . . women in camel litters” (*nuʾy . . . athāfī . . . dawāris . . . ẓawāʿin*): all these items are frequently referred to in pre-Islamic poetry; *nuʾy* are trenches dug around a tent pitched in the desert to take runoff from rain water; the *athāfī* are the three stones placed under a cooking pot as trivets; *dawāris* are the traces of a campsite (such as that formerly containing the beloved); *ẓawāʿin* are covered camel litters in which women ride.

384 “in origin they mean ‘of unpleasant appearance’”: the *Qāmūs* says: “*al-basl* [sic] means . . . the man who is of unpleasant appearance.”

385 “All good things come to those who wait. . . . And every good thing should make love” (*kullu ātin qarīb . . . wa-kullu qarībin ātin*): the

first phrase (literally, "everything that is near is coming") is a proverb, which the Fāriyāqiyyah then twists by taking *ātin*, active participle of *atā* "to come," in another of its senses, namely, "to have intercourse with" (cf. Q Shuʿarāʾ 26:165).

386 "such a 'universal' statement" (*bi-hādhihi l-kulliyyah*): as earlier (see Volume Two, 2.18.4n280), Aristotelian logic is invoked.

387 "all" (*jamīʿan*): i.e., the Fāriyāq, the Fāriyāqiyyah, and their child.

388 "the greatest of their poets": from the *muʿallaqah*, or "suspended ode," of Imruʾ al-Qays (translation: Arberry, *Seven Odes*, 63).

389 "the quintessence and best part of blood is of that color" (*khulāṣata l-dami wa-ṣafwatahu huwa fī dhālika l-lawn*): according to Aristotle, semen is formed from blood.

390 "So that's the reason!" (*fa-hādhā huwa l-sababu idhan*): i.e., the people of London like the color white because it is the color of semen.

391 "Now the truth has come to light" (*al-āna qad ḥaṣḥaṣa l-ḥaqq*): Q Yūsuf 12:51.

392 "the red" (*al-aḥmar*): presumably meaning, in light of the preceding, "semen."

393 "Great indeed / is women's guile" (*īnna kayda l-nisāʾi kāna ʿaẓīman*): reminiscent of Q Yūsuf 12:28.

394 "even if their promenading is leading them at that very moment to trial and litigation before His Honor the Judge": i.e., "even if they are in the process of taking one another to court."

395 "seeking to 'mix the rough with the smooth'" (*ṭalaban li-l-murāzamah*): perhaps to be taken in the sense of the saying of ʿUmar ibn al-Khaṭṭāb *idhā akaltum rāzimū* ("When ye eat . . . mix ye, in your eating, what is soft with what is hard") (Lane, *Lexicon*), the emphasis here being not on texture, however, but on variety.

396 "food for two will satisfy three" (*ṭaʿāma thnayni yushbiʿu thalāthah*): reminiscent of the hadith *ṭaʿāmu thnayni kāfī thalāthah wa-ṭaʿāmu l-thalāthati kāfī l-arbaʿah* ("the food of two is enough for three and the food of three for four").

397 "and give him hope" (*wa-tumannīhi*): or, punningly, "make him produce semen."

398 I.e., "When the husband hears that his neighbor devours his (i.e., his neighbor's) wife's lips and lies with her under her shift, so that she (the husband's wife) neither dreams of the neighbor nor he (the neighbor) of her (the husband's wife)."

399 "the swooning prude" (*al-rabūkh*): "the woman who faints during intercourse" (*Qāmūs*).

400 "back-passage bleeder" (*al-salaqlaq*): "the woman who menstruates through her anus" (*Qāmūs*).

401 "the single-barreled bawd" (*al-sharīm*): "the woman who has had so much intercourse that her two passages [the vagina and the rectum] have become one" (*Qāmūs*).

402 "play the mooning she-camel that lives its false calf to lick, for I see curly shavings on the fire stick" (*fa-ttakhidhī mudhi l-yawmi ẓīrā fa-'innī arā fī l-zan(a)di īrā*): a *ẓīr* is "one [esp. a she-camel] *that inclines to*, or *affects, the young one of another, and suckles* [or *fosters*] *it*" (Lane, *Lexicon*, quoting the *Qāmūs*); *zand* ("fire stick") may also be read as *zanad* ("a stone wrapped up in pieces of rag . . . which is stuffed into a she-camel's vulva, when she is made to take a liking to the young one of another" [Lane, *Lexicon*, quoting the *Qāmūs*]); *īr* "shavings" may also be read as *ayr* ("penis"), in which case the second clause may be taken to mean "for I see a penis in [place of] the stone wrapped in rags that takes the place, etc."

403 In 1850 the author sent Queen Victoria an ode in her praise which he also had translated into English and published at his own expense as a broadsheet; however, he received neither acknowledgment nor reward for his pains (see Arberry, "Fresh Light" and *Arabic Poetry*, 136ff, both of which reproduce the Arabic text and Arberry's translation).

404 "the Austrians of Schiller": Schiller was born and died in states that were part of the Holy Roman Empire and he might be better described as German; perhaps the author was influenced by the fact that during the period covered by this book, the Austrian Empire (1804–67) was the largest and strongest member of the German Confederation, ergo the most prominent German-speaking state.

405 "rhyme-consonants and rhymes" (*al-rawīy wa-l-qāfiyah*): the *rawīy* is the final consonant at the end of a line of verse and thus "the essential part of the rhyme" (Wright: *Grammar* II:352); the *qāfiyah* is the combination of consonants and vowels that constitute the sonic effect. Both are governed by complex rules.

406 The author appears to have in mind the license required (in England, for instance, from the Lord Chamberlain) before writers such as Shakespeare could perform their works.

407 From the *muʿallaqah* ("suspended ode") of Imruʾ al-Qays (mid-sixth century AD; translation Arberry, *Seven Odes*, 62); the reference is to a woman who tends to her baby while having intercourse with the poet.

408 From the *muʿallaqah* ("suspended ode") of ʿAntarah ibn Shaddād (mid-sixth century AD; translation Arberry, *Seven Odes*, 182).

409 "the August Master": i.e., the ruler of Tunis.

410 "my eulogy of Our Lord the Emir": i.e., of the ruler of Tunis (this eulogy is not reproduced in the book).

411 "One of those ancient delusions of yours" (*min ḍalālika l-qadīm*): cf. Q Ṭā Hā 20:95 *qālū ta-llāhi innaka la-fī ḍalālika l-qadīm* ("They said, 'By God, you still persist in your old delusions!'"), said by the sons of Yaʿqūb (Jacob) to the latter when he persisted in believing that Yūsuf (Joseph) would return.

412 "the three": i.e., sensual pleasure, this world, and the next.

413 "*hakhakah*": "copiousness of intercourse" (*Qāmūs*).

414 "a reduplicative formed from *hakka hakka*" (*muḍāʿif hakka hakka*): Arabic allows the formation of new, quadriliteral, verbs from simple geminate verbs such as *hakka* ("to have sexual intercourse with a woman with force or with frequency") (*Qāmūs*) with intensifying effect; the other verbs that follow all mean "to have sexual intercourse with" (though *hanā* has not been found in the lexica, it presumably derives from *han(ah)*, "thing" or "vagina").

415 "the ones that preceded it": i.e., the verbs meaning "(plain, one-go-per-session) intercourse" (*biʿāl, mubāʿalah*) cited above.

416 "corruption" (*khamaj*): or, punningly, "lassitude."

417 "those things the Franks wear down to their waists" (*hādhihi llatī talbisuhā l-ifrinju ʿilā khuṣurihim*): i.e., jackets.

418 "a bin . . . platter" (*al-quffah . . . al-ṣaffūt*): the following list is shorter than that of words meaning kinds of basket or other containers (see 5.2.11) in the original and is intended as a representation, not a one-to-one translation, of the latter using words from the same semantic areas drawn from thesauri, dictionaries, and other lexical resources; see further Volume Four, Translator's Afterword.

419 "though not in terms of his specific attributes but as an example of the attributes of the absolute" (*lā bi-l-ṣifati l-ʿayyinati bal bi-l-ṣifati l-muṭlaqah*): i.e., as a representative of his sex in general, not because of his individual traits.

420 "her bedmate . . . her intimate" (*kamīʿahā . . . wa-khalīlahā*): the following list is shorter than that of words of the highly productive *faʿīl* pattern (see 5.2.12) in the original and is intended as a representation, not a one-to-one translation, of the latter using words from the same semantic areas drawn from thesauri, dictionaries, and other lexical resources; see further Volume Four, Translator's Afterword.

421 "clapper-board" (*nāqūs*): a wooden board or plank functioning, when struck with a mallet, as a gong.

422 Cf. the *Qāmūs*, III:377.

423 "Your friend" (*ṣāḥibuka*): the Fāriyāqiyyah picks up on the Fāriyāq's earlier reference to "the author of the *Qāmūs*" as *ṣāḥib al-Qāmūs* but understands the word in its more vernacular meaning of "friend."

424 "language is a female" (*al-lughatu unthā*): the Fāriyāqiyyah appears to be unaware that the word for "feminine" as a grammatical gender category is *mu'annath* while *unthā* refers to sexual gender.

425 "which are neither voweled nor unvoweled" (*wa-hiya laysat mina l-ḥarakati wa-lā l-sukūn*): meaning perhaps, "which are free of the male-constructed constraints of language."

426 "Conversation's carpet . . . reach its end . . . End of Days" (*fa-ʾinnamā huwa bisāṭ ḥadīth qad nushira fa-lā yuṭwā ḥattā naṣila ilā ākhirihā*): in the Arabic, the pun turns on the two meanings of the verb *nashara*: "to unroll" and "to resurrect."

427 "desert rose" (*jarāz*): a plant (Adenium obesum) distinguished by its "stout, swollen basal caudex" (http://en.wikipedia.org/wiki/Adenium_obesum).

428 "removing facial hair using a thread" (*al-taḥaffuf*): probably meaning the use of a doubled thread, looped around the fingers, whose ends are held between the beautician's teeth and which is worked by moving the head back and forth, causing the threads to revolve and thus catch and pluck out the hairs, as practiced in Egypt today.

429 "the pelvic egg" (*bayḍat al-ʿuqr*): according to the *Lisān*, an egg laid by a cockerel, used, because of its softness and delicacy, to test the virginity of slave girls.

430 "such things not being considered speech by the grammarians" (*wa-hwa ʿinda l-nuḥāti laysa bi-kalām*): in grammatical theory, the term *kalām* ("speech") is properly bestowed only on statements that are *mufīdah* ("information-bearing"), i.e., that convey a complete thought and are thus meaningful; the author misrepresents this concept to include within it statements such as his earlier ones concerning women that are, according to his assertion, too banal and obvious to be regarded as information-bearing, and which fail, therefore, to qualify as true speech.

431 "[having] a clean-plucked beard and a pocket with a hole in it" (*mantūf al-liḥyah mukharraq al-jayb*): perhaps meaning "destitute, taken to the cleaners" (by his wife).

432 "our friend" (*ṣāḥibinā*): i.e., his future employer, for whom they are bound.

433 "Perhaps . . . excitement" (*laʿalla . . . al-tashwīq*): meaning perhaps that the thought of finding men (even mad ones) out on the streets in England and not closeted in their houses is responsible for her excitement at being there.

434 " a city thronging with men": i.e., Cambridge (cf. 4.4.2 and 4.5.7).

435 "the village for which they were bound": see 4.10.7n55.

436 "Man is a creature of haste" (*khuliqa l-inṣanu min ʿajal*): Q Anbiyāʾ 21:37.

437 "Would you be kind enough to explain them to me?" (*fa-hal laka an tuwaqqifanī ʿalayh*): in his response, the Fāriyāq pretends to

understand these words in an alternative sense: "Would you be kind enough to stick me on it?"

438 "cheap girls who laugh till they're fit to bust . . . the unjust" (*al-tāghiyāt . . . al-ṭāghiyāt*): the Fāriyāqiyyah mishears the *t* of *tāghiyāt* ("slave girls who try to hide their laughter but are overcome by it") as the *ṭ* of *ṭāghiyāt* ("[female] oppressors").

439 "snacking . . . unenthusiastically" (*na'j . . . tamaṣṣuṣ*): the following list of words referring to "tasting" and "sipping" (see 5.2.12) is shorter than that in the original and is intended as a representation, not a one-to-one translation, of the latter using words from the same semantic areas drawn from thesauri, dictionaries, and other lexical resources; see further Volume Four, Translator's Afterword.

440 "sedateness . . . sanctimony" (*al-tarazzun . . . al-tanaẓẓuf*): the following list of words referring to "reticence," "wariness," and "caution" (see 5.2.12) is shorter than that in the original and is intended as a representation, not a one-to-one translation, of the latter using words from the same semantic areas drawn from thesauri, dictionaries, and other lexical resources; see further Volume Four, Translator's Afterword.

441 "expose their backsides to warm them up" (*kashf adbārihim li-l-iṣṭilā'*): the image evoked is that of a man standing in front of a fireplace and raising his coattails.

442 "my armpit when he stretched out his body" (*rufghī idhā mā sbaṭarrā*): or, "my cunny when he lay down flat" (see the *Qāmūs*: *al-rufgh* "the armpit, or the area around a woman's vulva" and *isbaṭarrā* "he laid down, or extended himself" and *sibaṭr* "the lion when it extends its body on leaping").

443 "their hands concealed / In skins" (*wa-l-rāḥu minhunna bi-l-jildi mustatirātun*): i.e., "wearing gloves."

444 "she spears" (*wa-ta'khudhu . . . bi-l-mishakkah*): presumably meaning the old woman referred to at the start of the poem, the abruptness of the shift of subject being attributable to the missing lines.

445 "privacy . . . wife" (*ḥurmatahu*): *ḥurmah* means both "sanctity, inviolability" and "wife."

446 "our friends": i.e., the English.

447 The Fāriyāq's translation appears to assume that the verses are addressed by a woman to a man, though the switch from first person (*su'lī 'indak*) to third (*wa-blugh . . . minhā*) is problematic; some elements of the equally baffling English are missing from the Fāriyāq's translation.

448 "he's complaining of himself" (*huwa yashkū min nafsih*): apparently meaning that the poet is implying that he is incapable of satisfying the woman.

449 "turnips" (*qulqās*): see 4.1.10n4.

450 Cf. Deut. 7:13 "And he will love thee, and bless thee, and multiply thee: he will also bless the fruit of thy womb, and the fruit of thy land, thy corn, and thy wine, and thine oil, the increase of thy kine, and the flocks of thy sheep, in the land which he sware unto thy fathers to give thee."

451 Jephthah the Gileadite: see Judg. 11:1 "Now Jephthah the Gileadite was a mighty man of valor, and he was the son of an harlot" and 11:29ff.

452 "or so the theologians assert" (*kamā afādahu l-mutakallimūn*): the allusion is to the discussion among theologians of who—God or man—is responsible for evil, the Muʿtazilites, for example, claiming that man is responsible, the Ashʿarites, God, although the author appears to have either forgotten that the standard terms are *ḥasan* (rather than *jamīl*) for "good" and *qabīḥ* for "evil," or else has adapted the argument to his ongoing concern with the physically beautiful (*jamīl*) and the ugly (*qabīḥ*).

453 "well-endowed in both senses" (*al-jihāzān*): *jihāz* means both "dowry" and "genitalia."

454 "nothing of that greenness brings a flush of good cheer" (*lā shay'a min hādhihi l-khuḍrati yubayyiḍu l-wajh*): literally, "nothing of that greenness whitens the face," "whitening of the face" being a familiar trope.

455 See Volume One, 1.13.2n219.

456 "confines himself to 'the little nest'" (*yuḥaffishu*): the author appears to be reading the laconic definition of *taḥfīsh* that he quotes (from the *Qāmūs*) in the light of another found in the same entry there, namely, *ḥifsh*, meaning "vagina."

457 "a fastness . . . dry" (*manzahan . . . al-mā'*): a basic meaning of the root *n-z-h* is "to be distant" and especially "to be distant from anything unpleasant"; however, the *Qāmūs* highlights certain collocations in which the sense is specifically "to be distant from water."

458 "viceroy to the Creator of Nations" (*khalīfat bārī l-umam*): i.e., the Ottoman caliph.

459 "hands free, his cuffs unsoiled" (*yaduhu khafīfah rānifatuhu naẓīfah*): probably meaning that he can go home without passing by the market first to burden himself with food items demanded by his wife and getting his cuffs dirty.

460 "like a bad penny" (*sayra l-ʿajāj fī kulli fujāj*): literally, "like flying dust in every mountain pass."

461 The poem that follows only gets around to comparing the married state with bachelorhood in its last lines (4.13.8), perhaps not surprisingly given that it was not written as a response to al-Hāwif ibn Hifām's question; earlier lines seem to reflect the Fāriyāq's anxieties about the pressures to which his own marriage was subject in foreign environments.

462 "his money" (*filsihi*): or, colloquially and punningly, "his anus."

463 "his spine, / His resuscitator from misery": alluding to the belief that semen is generated in the spine.

464 "The stranger . . . folk" (*inna l-gharība . . . jinsihi*): the "stranger" is presumably the one, referred to above, who marries in a small village, i.e., not in his hometown, but the wider meaning remains elusive.

465 "So long as the advantages of starting over at it / Do not damage the ending of what was good" (*mā in yaḍurra khitāma mā / qad ṭāba nāfiʿu rassihi*): perhaps meaning "Do not become so attracted to the pleasures of initiating new marriages that you end earlier ones badly."

466 "And many a mother and child . . ." (*wa-rubba ummin wa-ṭiflin . . .*): the quotation is from an elegy for al-Andalus written by Abū l-Baqā' al-Rundī (601/1204 to 684/1285).

467 Num. 31:15–17: "And Moses said unto them . . . Now therefore kill every male among the little ones."

468 "Death's rule on Man's imposed. . . . This world for permanence can furnish no abode" (*ḥukmu l-maniyyati fī l-barriyyati jārī. . . . mā hādhihi l-dunyā bi-dāri qarārī*): these two hemistichs, here separated from each other and used as the second half of each of two verses, are taken from and together originally form the first verse of a poem by Abū l-Ḥasan al-Tihāmī al-Ḥasanī (d. 416/1025) composed to mourn the death of the poet's son at the age of fourteen; al-Shidyāq goes on to quote another well-known verse from the same poem below ("I kept company with my neighbors, he with His Lord— / And how different his neighbors from mine!"—see 4.14.8).

469 "the Fāriyāq had no choice but to live close to that ill-fated village": because it was where he was working; see 4.4.1n55.

470 "Two weak things will conquer a stronger" (*wa-ḍaʿīfāni yaghlibāni qawiyyan*): the words are by Ṣafī al-Dīn al-Ḥillī (667/1278 to ca. 750/1349) (in the original *fa-ḍaʿīfāni*); the preceding hemistich runs *lā tuḥārib bi-nāẓirayka fuʾādī* ("Do not wage war with your eyes on my heart").

471 "to peer . . . meditate" (*al-ṣaʾṣaʾah . . . al-tarannī*): the following list of words relating to "looking and its various forms" (see 5.2.12) is shorter than that in the original and is intended as a representation, not a one-to-one translation, of the latter using words from the same semantic areas drawn from thesauri, dictionaries, and other lexical resources; see further Volume Four, Translator's Afterword.

472 "from a drop of mingled fluid" (*min nuṭfatin amshājin*): cf. Q Insān 76:2.

473 Ashʿab: i.e., Ashʿab ibn Jubayr (born 9/630–31, died during the reign of al-Mahdī, 158/775 to 169/785), whose greed became the subject of many anecdotes.

474 *qalb* ("heart") is from the same root as the verbs meaning "to turn, transmute," etc., a fact of which the author has already made full use in this passage, as have numerous poets and writers before him.

475 Hind and Daʿd: stereotypical names of the beloved woman.

476 "The Fāriyāq resumed": the author appears to have forgotten that the Fāriyāq has not been described earlier as speaking.

477 "*aḥaddahā* or *ḥaddadahā . . . taḥiddu*": these words are taken from the *Qāmūs*.

478 "and you know better than I the full sense of that word" (*wa-nta bi-tamāmi l-maʿnā adrā*): *sabd* (which is the voweling in the Arabic text) may mean, in addition to the meanings already noted by the author, "wolf" and "calamity"; however, it seems likely that he has in mind the form *subad* (indistinguishable from the former when short vowels are not written), meaning "the pubes" (*al-ʿānah*).

479 "a large musical instrument" (*ālatu ṭarabin ʿaẓīmah*): *ālah* ("instrument, tool") is frequently used in a sexual sense.

480 "to vie with me in quoting poetry" (*tushāʿiranī*): or, punningly, "to sleep under the same blanket with me."

481 "for I possess the very source from which relief (*faraj*) is derived" (*fa-inna ʿindī maṣdara shtiqāqi l-faraj*): the author plays with the fact that the verbal noun (*maṣdar*, lit. "source") of *faraja* ("to provide relief to someone [of God]") is *farj*, which also has the sense of "vagina."

482 "if he hadn't at first succeeded, he wouldn't if he tried again" (*inna l-ʿawda ilayhā ghayru aḥmad*): a play on the proverb *al-ʿawdu aḥmad* (see 4.4.6n64).

483 "no metropolitan or monk": presumably another dig at Metropolitan Atanāsiyūs al-Tutūnjī (see Volume Two, 2.3.5n66 and 2.9.3 and, in this volume, 4.19).

484 "William Scoltock": matriculated at Christ Church, Oxford in 1842 aged 19, became an inspector of schools, and died 1886. "Williams" in the Arabic is the author's error.

485 "mature horses run ever longer heats" (*jaryu l-mudhakkiyāti ghilāʾ*): see al-Maydānī 1:106 (s.v. *jaryu . . . ghilāb*).

486 "swan-necked" (*al-jūd*): in view of the context, this may be a misprint for *al-ḥūr* ("having eyes like those of gazelles and of cows") (Lane, *Lexicon*).

487 "the scrubbers" (*al-ḥakkākāt*): the true significance of this word becomes clear only at the end of this list (4.16.5).

488 "vibrating . . . scudding" (*tatadhabdhabu . . . taṣrā*): the following list of words meaning "she moves" and/or "she oscillates" (see 5.2.12) is

shorter than that in the original and is intended as a representation, not a one-to-one translation, of the latter using words from the same semantic areas drawn from thesauri, dictionaries, and other lexical resources; see further Volume Four, Translator's Afterword.

489 "What a monstrous thing to say!" (*laqad kabura qawlan*): an echo of the Qur'ān's *kaburat kalimatan takhruju min afwāhihim* ("What they say is monstrous; they are merely uttering falsehoods!" (Q Kahf 18:5).

490 "panderation . . . cuckoldism" (*daybūbiyyah . . . arfaḥiyyah*): the following list of words related to "the condition of being a pander or a wittol" (see 5.2.12) is shorter than that in the original and is intended as a representation, not a one-to-one translation, of the latter using words from the same semantic areas drawn from thesauri, dictionaries, and other lexical resources; see further Volume Four, Translator's Afterword.

491 "as it does in this noble language of ours": according to the *Lisān*, the (ancient) Arabs used the word *ʿatabah* ("doorstep") as an epithet for a woman.

492 "sprinkle white ashes on their heads": i.e., wear powdered wigs.

493 "slipways . . . hides" (*al-mazālij . . . al-maṣālī*): the following list of words related to "traps, snares, and associated words" (see 5.2.13) is shorter than that in the original and is intended as a representation, not a one-to-one translation, of the latter using words from the same semantic areas drawn from thesauri, dictionaries, and other lexical resources; see further Volume Four, Translator's Afterword.

494 "liquid account" (*sayyāl*): defined by the *Qāmūs* simply as "a kind of account/calculation" and not found elsewhere; the translation derives from the base sense of the root.

495 "precautionary blank-filling" (*al-tarqīm wa-l-tarqīn*): Lane, *Lexicon*: "A certain sign, or mark, of the keepers of the register of the [tax . . .] conventionally used by them, put upon . . . accounts, or reckonings, lest it should be imagined that a blank has been left [to be afterwards filled up], in order that no account be put down therein."

496 "under the letter *yā'*" (*fī bāb al-yā'*): the primary organizing element of the *Qāmūs* is the final root consonant; thus words of the root *j-dh-y*, such as *judhā'*, ought to appear there under *yā'*.

497 "nasality . . . movingly" (*bi-l-ghunnah . . . wa-l-tarniyah*): the following list of words relating to "qualities of voice and setting to music" (see 5.2.13) is shorter than that in the original and is intended as a representation, not a one-to-one translation, of the latter using words from the same semantic areas drawn from thesauri, dictionaries, and other lexical resources; see further Volume Four, Translator's Afterword. The list includes a number of technical terms from Arabic phonetics and prosody and the science of Qur'anic recitation that by definition have no equivalents in English.

498 "the curling of the hair, its . . . rumpling" (*taqṣību l-sha'r . . . wa-taghbiyatuhu*): the following list of words relating to "hair dressing and its styles" (see 5.2.13) is shorter than that in the original and is intended as a representation, not a one-to-one translation, of the latter using words from the same semantic areas drawn from thesauri, dictionaries, and other lexical resources; see further Volume Four, Translator's Afterword.

499 "the *ku'kubbah* and the *muqaddimah*": the *ku'kubbah* is a way of wearing braids (see Volume Three, 3.9.1n106); the *muqaddimah* is defined in the *Qāmūs* as "a way of combing the hair."

500 "*rigadoon*" (*rīdūqā*): the identification is tentative.

501 "in abject submission" (*qalbuhu bayna rijlayhā*): the literal meaning of the phrase is "with his heart between her legs" and both reverses the standard expression *bayna yaday* . . . (lit. "between the hands of . . ." meaning "in front of . . . , before . . .") and allows an obvious sexual reading.

502 "they drop the ends of all the masculine words and pronounce them in the feminine" (*yaḥdhifūna fī l-lafẓi awākhira jamī'i l-alfāẓi l-mudhakkari wa-yanṭuqūna bi-hā fī l-mu'annath*): the author was perhaps thinking of a situation such as *épicier* ("male grocer") versus *épicière* ("female grocer"), where the "r" is heard only in the second.

503 "the masculine should take precedence over the feminine" (*taghlīb al-mudhakkar 'alā l-mu'annath*): probably a reference to the rule that in any plural group, if even one masculine element is introduced, the entire group is treated as masculine plural (example: *les filles et les garçons sont venus* ["the girls and boys have come"]), where *venus* has the masculine form.

504 "languorousness . . . litheness" (*al-wanā . . . al-inthiṭā'*): the following list of words relating to "limpness and rigidity" (see 5.2.13) is shorter than that in the original and is intended as a representation, not a one-to-one translation, of the latter using words from the same semantic areas drawn from thesauri, dictionaries, and other lexical resources; see further Volume Four, Translator's Afterword.

505 "that other quality mentioned by Abū Nuwās in his poem rhyming in the glottal stop": the poet has several poems with this rhyme letter; a likely candidate is the one that begins *da' 'anka lawmī fa-l-lawmu ighrā'u / wa-dāwinī bi-llatī kānat hiya l-dā'u* ("Leave off your blaming of me, for blame is itself an incitement / And treat me with that which was the very disease [of which you accuse me]!"); in this case, the quality attributed to some of the women of Paris would be, presumably, a willingness to engage in anal intercourse as, in line 3 of this poem, Abū Nuwās speaks of receiving wine *min kaffi dhāti ḥirin fī ziyyi dhī dhakarin / lahā muḥibbāni lūṭiyyun wa-zannā'ū* ("from the hand of one with a vagina in the dress of one with a penis, who has two lovers, one a sodomite, the other an adulterer") (Abū Nuwās, *Dīwān*, 7).

506 "is no insult" (*laysa mina l-sabbi fī say'*): an acquaintance seems to be assumed with the following entry in the *Qamūs* under *b-ẓ-r*: *huwa yumiṣṣuhu wa-yubaẓẓiruhu ay qāla lahu umṣuṣ baẓrata fulānah* ("*yumiṣṣuhu* and *yubaẓẓiruhu* mean, 'He tells him, "Suck such and such a woman's clitoris!"'"), in which *umṣuṣ* etc. seems to have the force of an insult; the point here, of course, is that it is no insult to say this in Paris because its "old experienced men" do indeed practice cunnilingus.

507 See the deuterocanonical Book of Baruch (Epistle of Jeremiah) 6:43: "The women also with cords about them, sitting in the ways, burn bran for perfume: but if any of them, drawn by some that passeth by, lie with him, she reproacheth her fellow, that she was not thought as worthy as herself, nor her cord broken."

508 "thou art among those thankful to her" (*wa-nta lahā mina l-shākirīn*): echoes a Qur'anic phrase (without *lahā*) (Q An'ām 6:63, A'rāf 7:144).

509 "Yet how can a man agree to protect his dependents / With both hanger and horn?" (*wa-kayfa yarḍā mra'un yaḥmī... bi-l-qirni wa-l-qarni*): i.e., how can a husband be expected to protect his dependents with his hanger (a type of sword) if his wife's conduct has rendered him a cuckold with a horn?

510 Umm Khārijah: lit., "the Mother of Khārijah," a woman from whom many tribes descended and of whom it is said that if any man said to her, "Marry me?" she replied, "Done!" The identity of the father of her son Khārijah, which means "One Who Goes Out Much," was unknown. The wit of the Arabic comes from its exploitation of the contrasts between *dākhilat al-insān* ("man's *inner* state"), *Umm Khārijah* ("Mother of Him Who Goes *Out*"), *wa-yakhruju 'anhu l-ḥilm* ("[and] all sense of proportion will leave him [lit., '*go out* from him']"), and *wālijah* ("where she's *gone in*" or "is being *entered*").

511 "Paris is heaven for women, purgatory for men, and hell for horses": Louis-Sébastien Mercier (1749–1814), French dramatist and commentator, attributes the description of Paris as being *le paradis des femmes, le purgatoire des hommes, et l'enfer des chevaux* to "the common people" (*le petit peuple*) (Mercier, *Tableau de Paris*).

512 "here... they're forever being touched" (*sha'nahunna dawāmu l-ṭamth*): echoes the Qur'ān's *ḥūrun maqṣūrātun fī l-khiyāmi... lam yaṭmithhunna insun... wa-lā jānn* ("[in Paradise are] pure companions sheltered in pavilions... whom neither a man nor a jinn... has ever touched" (Q Raḥmān 55:72/Muddaththir 74:72).

513 "squint-eyed... pinguecula" (*aḥwal... mudanqishan*): the following list of words relating to "persons with defective vision" (see 5.2.13) is shorter than that in the original and is intended as a representation,

not a one-to-one translation, of the latter using words from the same semantic areas drawn from thesauri, dictionaries, and other lexical resources; see further Volume Four, Translator's Afterword.

514 "skin flap" (*zanamah*): the author returns to a figurative conceit used in Volume Two (see 2.9.1).

515 "A Complaint and Complaints" (*Fī shakāh wa-shakwā*): the two words derive from the same root and are essentially synonymous, but the first must be used here in a medical sense and refer to the Fāriyāqiyyah's sore feet (4.18.1) and the second to her complaints about Paris (4.18.2ff).

516 "and what shall teach thee what is 'the Maid'?" (*wa-mā adrāka mā l-khādimah*): an ironic play on a rhetorical device occurring in passages in the Qur'ān such as *wa-ma adrāk mā l-ḥāqqah* ("And what shall teach thee what is the Indubitable?") (Q Ḥāqqah 69:3; trans. Arberry, *Koran*) in which a term deemed significant but little known is highlighted.

517 "Cremorne, Vauxhall . . . Rosherville": Cremorne Gardens, a proprietary place of entertainment on the Thames in Chelsea, opened in 1845 and closed in 1877; Vauxhall Gardens, on the south bank of the Thames at Vauxhall, opened before 1660 and closed in 1859 and was the best-known pleasure garden in London; Rosherville Gardens, at Gravesend, Kent, on the Thames, opened in 1837 and closed in 1911.

518 "the woman with lupus" (*al-dha'bah*): the word is problematic: as spelled in the Arabic text, it does not appear in the lexica; however, the term *al-dhi'bah* is used in modern medicine (but only since the early twentieth century, according to Arabic Wikipedia) in the sense of "lupus" (an autoimmune connective tissue disease that affects women more than men and leaves disfiguring scars, often on the face). I have read it tentatively as *al-dha'ibah* meaning, by analogy, "the woman with lupus."

519 "*pissoirs* . . . tent pegs" (*al-manāṣi' . . . al-manādif*): the *mindaf* referred to in the Arabic is a "cotton-carder's bow," i.e., a device resembling a single-stringed harp, about a meter in length and held between the carder's thighs.

520 the Société Asiatique: established in 1822, the society publishes the *Journal asiatique*.

521 Étienne Marc Quatremère (1782–1857), student of Silvestre de Sacy, philologist and prolific translator and editor of Arabic texts, and frequent contributor to the Journal asiatique.

522 Armand-Pierre Caussin de Perceval (1795–1871) became professor of modern Arabic at the École spéciale des langues orientales in 1821 and professor of Arabic at the Collège de France in 1833. Earlier, he had worked as a dragoman in Aleppo; in 1828, he published a *Grammaire arabe vulgaire* based on the dialect of that city.

523 Joseph Toussaint Reinaud (not *Reineaud* as in the Arabic) (1795–1867) succeeded to Silvestre de Sacy's chair at the École spéciale des langues orientales on the latter's death in 1838; see also 5.5 below.

524 "like the definite article in the sentence 'Go to the market and buy meat'" (*ka-adāti l-taʿrīfi fī qawlika idhhab ilā l-sūqi wa-shtiri l-laḥm*): i.e., his acquaintance with these French scholars was nonspecific, or impersonal, just as the definite articles preceding *sūq* and *laḥm* serve to indicate that the following noun is generic (i.e., "Go to any market and buy any meat").

525 "with virtue furnished . . . a vaginal furnace" (*bi-l-khayri qamīnuna ḥariyyūn . . . qamīnun ḥiriyy*): the phrases *qamīnun bi-* and *ḥariyyun bi-* both mean "capable of" while *qamīn* means "a bathhouse furnace" and *ḥiriyy* is an adjective derived from *ḥir* ("vagina"); the consonantal ductus is the same in both senses.

526 "the women" (*al-nisāʾ*): "women" has to be understood as "public women" (see below).

527 "of whatever kind" (*min takhālufi anwāʿihā*): meaning apparently "whether private houses or brothels."

528 "firetraps" (*balw al-nār*): the translation is tentative.

529 "full of artifice . . . treacherous" (*al-mallādhūn . . . al-badhlākhiyyūn*): the following list of words relating to "insincere friends," "false flatterers," and "those whose friendship cannot be relied upon" (see 5.2.13) is shorter than that in the original and is intended as a representation,

not a one-to-one translation, of the latter using words from the same semantic areas drawn from thesauri, dictionaries, and other lexical resources; see further Volume Four, Translator's Afterword.

530 'Urqūb: a giant, 'Urqūb ibn Ma'bad ibn Asad, who was known as the biggest liar of his day; according to the *Qāmūs*, "Once a man came to him for alms and he said, 'When my palm trees grow,' and when the palm trees grew, he said, 'When they put forth dates,' and when they put forth dates, he said, 'When they flower,' and when they flowered, he said, 'When they soften,' and when they softened, he said, 'When they dry,' and when they dried, he cut them at night and gave the man nothing."

531 "sucking their fingers after eating, and licking off what is on them" (*yamṣuṣna aṣābi'ahunna ba'da l-akli wa-yalḥasna mā 'ahayhā*): the definition is quoted from the *Qāmūs* (s.v. *rajul laṭṭā'*).

532 "men with heavy loads" (*aṣḥāb al-athqāl*): this apparently contradictory statement should perhaps be understood as sexual innuendo.

533 Syria (*al-Shām*): the word may denote either the city of Damascus or the surrounding lands over which it traditionally has held sway.

534 "the most generous of the Arab nation" (*akram al-'arab*): an allusion to the ruler of Tunis, Aḥmad Bāy, who had earlier, in response to poems written in his praise by the Fāriyāq (i.e., the author), sent him a gift of diamonds (Volume Three, 3.18.6) and subsequently hosted him and his family in Tunis (4.8.1–7).

535 "When the Christians of Aleppo suffered their calamity" (*lammā nukibat naṣārā Ḥalab*): in October of 1850, a Muslim mob turned on the Christian quarters of Aleppo and up to seventy persons died; a further five thousand Aleppines died as a result of bombardment by Ottoman forces seeking to retake the city.

536 Fatḥallāh Marrāsh: presumably the father of Faransīs Fatḥallāh Marrāsh (1836–73), who was a leading intellectual and writer of his day and whom the author later met (see Volume One, Foreword, p. xv).

537 Metropolitan Atanāsiyūs al-Tutūnjī: see further Volume Two, 2.3.5n66, 2.9.3.

538 "some town belonging to Austria—Bologna, I think" (*baladun min bilādi ūstiriyā wa-hwa fī-mā aẓunnu Būlūniyā*): Bologna, though at this time a Papal Legation, was garrisoned by Austrian soldiers.

539 "the Sassanian trade" (*al-ḥirfah al-Sāsāniyyah*): i.e., the trade of the Banū Sāsān ("Sons of Sāsān"), a name applied in medieval Islam to charlatans, vagabonds, and thieves, supposedly because of their original allegiance to a mythical "Shaykh Sāsān."

540 Islāmbūl: literally, "Find Islam," a folk-etymological adaptation of Istanbul introduced following the Muslim conquest of the city in 1453 to emphasize the centrality of the city, in its rulers' eyes, to the Islamic nation.

541 Ṣubḥī Bayk: later to hold, as Ṣubḥī Pasha, the posts of minister of education and governor of Syria; the author benefited from this contact when he himself settled in Istanbul (al-Maṭwī, *Aḥmad*, II:902).

542 For the poem in praise of Ṣubḥī Bayk, see 4.20.29–32; for those describing his longing for his wife, see 4.20.50–62.

543 "those decorated pieces of paper" (*hādhihi l-awrāq al-muzawwaqah*): i.e., playing cards; from the references to gambling and a partner that follow (and that are elaborated in his later poem on the subject, see 4.20.39–43), he likely played whist, a popular game with gamblers in Paris at the time (see, e.g., Balzac's *Le Père Goriot*, first published in 1835).

544 "the gamblers' record keeper" (*amīn al-muqāmirīn*): the definition is from the *Qāmūs*.

545 I.e., 1853, the year of the outbreak of the Crimean War, which began in October.

546 See 4.9.10.

547 "the aforementioned poem": i.e., that presented by the author to Prince Musurus (see 4.20.2).

548 "Sweden ... some latter-day Peter": in the Great Northern War (1700–21), Peter the Great of Russia successfully contested the hegemony of the Swedish Empire in northern Europe.

549 "Muslims, check well ..." (*yā muslimūna tathabbatū ...*): cf Q Ḥujurāt 49:6 *yā ayyuhā lladhīna āmanū in jā'akum fāsiqun bi-naba'in*

fa-tabayyanū ("Believers, if an evildoer brings you news, ascertain the correctness of the report fully").

550 "You will not attain piety until you expend / Of what you love" (*lan tanālū l-birra ḥattā tunfiqū / mimmā tuḥibbūn*): Q Āl ʿImrān 3:92 (trans. Arberry, *Koran*, 57).

551 "the most firm handle" (*al-ʿurwah al-wuthqā*): "So whosoever disbelieves in idols and believes in God has laid hold of the most firm handle" (Q Baqarah 2:256; similarly Luqmān 31:22).

552 "and peck the feathers off their eagle" (*wa-nisrahumu nsurū*): an allusion to the double eagle of the imperial Russian insignia.

553 "Were you but a small band of soldiers, / They would not be overcome" (*law lam yakun minkum siwā nafarin lamā / ghulibū*): cf Q Anfāl 8:65 *wa-in yakun minkum miʾatun yaghlibū alfan* ("and if there are a hundred of you, they will overcome a thousand").

554 "the Portioned Narration" (*al-dhikr al-mufaṣṣal*): "an appellation of *The portion of the Kur-án from [the chapter entitled]* الحُجُرَات *[i. e. ch. xlix.] to the end; according to the most correct opinion* . . . ; this portion is thus called because of its many divisions between its chapters . . . or because of the few abrogations therein" (Lane, *Lexicon*, s.v. *mufaṣṣal*).

555 "It was ever a duty upon us to help them" (*haqqan ʿalaynā naṣruhum*): cf. *wa-kāna haqqan ʿalaynā naṣru l-muʾminīn* ("And it was ever a duty upon us, to help the believers") (Q Rūm 30:47).

556 "and they cannot / Advance that day or delay it" (*fa-lan / yastaqdimū ʿanhu wa-lan yastaʾkhirū*): cf. Q Naḥl 16:61 *fa-idhā jāʾahum ajaluhum lā yastaʾkhirūna sāʿatan wa-lā yastaqdimūn* ("when their time [i.e., the time of living creatures] comes they cannot delay it for an hour, nor can they bring it forward").

557 "A manifest victory" (*fatḥan mubīnan*): Q Fatḥ 48:1.

558 "Gardens of Eternity" (*jannātu ʿadan*): Q Tawbah 9:72 and passim.

559 Badr: site of a battle (2/624) between the Muslim forces and the much larger army of the Prophet's opponents; the Muslims' victory was a turning point in their fortunes and is often attributed to divine intervention.

560 "their circling eagle" (*nisruhum al-mudawwimu*): see 4.20.6n260.

561 "the crescent moon" (*al-hilāl*): an allusion to the crescent of the imperial Ottoman insignia.

562 "birds in flights" (*al-ṭayr al-abābīl*): the reference is to God's destruction of an Ethiopian army that sought to take Mecca in the days before Islam (Q Fīl 105:3).

563 "You we worship" (*iyyāka naʿbudu*): the words are taken from the opening *sūrah* ("chapter") of the Qur'ān, often recited at the initiation of an enterprise.

564 "And any spiteful gelding who hates you" (*wa-shāni'uka l-baghīḍu l-abtarū*): echoes Q Kawthar 108:3.

565 "Farūq . . . the Furqān": the epithet Farūq probably means "sharply dividing" (by analogy with other intensive adjectives of this form such as *laʿūb* ["very playful"] and *ḥasūd* ["very envious"]), though the dictionaries do not give it this sense, and reflects the idea that, previous to its conquest by the Ottomans, the city represented the divide between the Christian and Muslim worlds; the author appears to share this view as he derives it from al-Furqān, an epithet of the Qur'ān, so called because it "makes a separation . . . between truth and falsity" (Lane, *Lexicon*).

566 "The stringing of the pearls . . . your palm" (*mā in yafī naẓmu l-la'āli'i . . . tuntharū*): i.e., using conventional imagery, "The arrangement of lines of verses into a eulogy for you cannot match the gifts that are dispensed from your hand's generous supply."

567 "two Hijri dates" (*tārīkhayni hijriyyayni*): i.e., the author has used the system known as *ḥisāb al-jummal*, which allots a numerical value to each letter of the alphabet, to construct the final line of the poem, each of whose hemistichs consists of letters whose values add up to 1270 (the Hijri year that began on 4 October 1853), as follows: *ʿAbd* (70 + 2 + 4 = 76) + *al-Majīd* (1 + 30 + 40 + 3 + 10 + 4=88) + *Allāh* (1 + 30 + 30 + 5 = 66) + *arkā* (1 + 200 + 20 + 10 = 231) + *ḍiddahu* (800 + 9 = 809) = 1270 and so on for the remaining hemistich; *hisāb al-jummal* values may be found in Hava, *al-Farā'id*, 4 (unnumbered).

568 "The Presumptive Poem . . . The Prescriptive Poem" (*al-Qaṣīdah al-Harfiyyah . . . al-Qaṣīdah al-Ḥarfiyyah*): see 4.18.6 above.

569 "litters" (*hawādij*): throughout these two poems, the author presses words from the early Arabic lexicon, including Qur'anic terms, into the service of contemporary purposes; here, presumably, the women's camel litter stands for the enclosed carriage.

570 "a 'Illiyyūn": a word used in the Qur'ān (Q Muṭaffifīn 83:19) and said to mean "a place in the Seventh Heaven, to which ascend the souls of the believers" (*Qāmūs*).

571 "raised couches" (*surur marfūʿah*): cf. Q Ghāshiyah 88:13.

572 "cotton mattresses" (*aʿārīs*): the translation is tentative; the word appears not to be attested in the lexica but may be an invented plural of the plural *ʿarānīs* (a word which according to Ibn ʿAbbād has no singular) meaning something like "things made by women out of cotton" and associated with beds: see al-ʿUbāb al-Zākhir in http://www.baheth.info, s.v. *ʿirnās* (*ʿirnās al-mar'ah mawḍiʿu sabā'ikh quṭnihā*) and Lane, *Lexicon*, s.v. *sabīkh*, at end.

573 "the Uplifted Ones" (*al-simākayn*): Arcturus and Spica, two unusually bright stars.

574 "be delighted . . . Tunis" (*fa-tu'nasu minhā wa-hiya Tūnusu ghibṭatan*): a pun based on the identical forms of the words *tu'nasu* ("may you be delighted") and *Tūnusu* ("Tunis") when written without vowels.

575 "the Destroyer of All Pleasures" (*hādim al-ladhdhāt*): i.e., death.

576 "even should you travel so far that Jupiter lies behind you in the sky" (*wa-law amsā warā'aka Birjīsū*): perhaps an allusion to the use of Jupiter as a reference point in celestial navigation.

577 "a geomancer's spell" (*inkīs*): literally, a certain sign used by geomancers (see Volume One, 1.16.9).

578 "For if you add a zero to it, even an odd number becomes divisible by five" (*fa-fī ṣ-ṣifri li-l-fardi l-ʿaqīmi takhāmīsū*): perhaps meaning "so too an hour in Paris will make your life longer (for better or for worse) by orders of magnitude."

579 "oceans" (*qawāmīs*): and, punningly, "dictionaries."

580 "though it is studied" (*wa-hwa madrūsū*): or, punningly, "and has been erased."

581 The poem is referred to earlier as having been written on the occasion of a visit by Emir ʿAbd al-Qādir to Paris, when the author "was honored by being invited to attend a gathering in his presence" (4.19.4); however, from references within the poem, it would seem that the relationship was more extended and included the emir's standing the author up on at least one occasion.

582 "drowsiness . . . lukewarm" (*bi-fātir . . . bil-fātir*): seductive faces are conventionally described as having "drowsy" eyes or eyelids, using the same word as for "lukewarm, neither hot nor cold."

583 "my creator" (*fāṭirī*): an apparent reference to the Qurʾanic verses "then we split the earth in fissures / and therein made the grass to grow" (*thumma shaqaqna l-arḍa shaqqan / fa-nbatnā fīhā ḥabban*), Q ʿAbasa 80:26–27, which is preceded by references to God's role as creator, e.g., "Of a sperm-drop He created him" (*min nuṭfatin khalaqahu*), 80:19.

584 "night phantom" (*ṭayf*): the appearance of the beloved as a shimmering figure in the lover's dreams is a standard trope.

585 "the Assembler" (*al-ḥāshir*): i.e., God, who will assemble men for judgment on the Last Day.

586 "word . . . consonant . . . sword-edge" (*ḥarf . . . ḥarf . . . ḥarf*): a triple pun.

587 "the emir became still" (*sakana l-amīr*): by the time the author met Emir ʿAbd al-Qādir, the latter had abandoned his struggle against the French colonization of Algeria and was living in exile.

588 "the Tablet" (*al-lawḥ*): "the Preserved Tablet" (*al-lawḥ al-maḥfūẓ*), on which God has written divine destiny.

589 "from Ṣubḥī" (*min Ṣubḥī*): or, punningly, "from my [rising in the] morning."

590 Ḥassān: i.e., Ḥassān ibn Thābit al-Anṣārī (d. probably before 40/661), the poet most associated with the Prophet Muḥammad, on whom he wrote eulogies.

591 "what I owe is [written] at the top of the board and cannot be erased" (*alladhī ʿalay-ya bi-aʿlā l-lawḥi mā huwa bi-l-mamḥī*): perhaps

meaning "the sins (of eulogizing unworthy persons) for which I must pay expiation are plain for all to see."

592 "Sāmī of the Summits" (*Sāmī al-dhurā*): a reference to Ṣubḥī Bayk's father, Sāmī Pasha; however, since *sāmī* means "elevated," the phrase may also be read as "high-peaked."

593 "a cave of strength" (*kahfa ʿizzin*): the image, conventional in poetry, echoes references in the Qur'ān to God's protection of believing young men in a cave, e.g., *fa-'wū ilā l-kahfi yanshur lakum rabbukum min raḥmatihi wa-yuhayyi' min amrikum mirfaqan* ("Take refuge in the cave; your Lord will extend his mercy to you and will make fitting provision for you in your situation") (Q Kahf 18:16).

594 "Halt" (*qif*): the poem uses the conventions of the pre-Islamic ode in opening by apostrophizing an unnamed companion, who is asked to halt his camel at the abandoned campsite, identifiable by the "orts" (*al-ṭulūl*) (the remains of the eating, drinking, and sleeping places) of the poet's beloved's clan; thereafter, the poet shifts his attention from his companion to himself, which explains the shift of subject from second to first person ("Halt . . . I knew . . . I dragged" etc.).

595 "the Crown" (*al-iklīlā*): defined in the *Qāmūs* as "a mansion of the moon—four aligned stars."

596 "after a tear of mine had wetted it" (*wa-qad ballathu minnī ʿabratun*): the poet appears to picture himself peering through his tears and finding the campsite "borne upon the reins of the wind."

597 "as dry brushwood" (*ka-l-jazl*): i.e., of no importance.

598 "The mending of broken hearts may be requested of any Jubārah" (*jabru l-khawāṭiri min jubāratin yurtajā*): i.e., anyone called Jubārah (or anyone of the Jubārah family) may be asked to mend hearts because the root consonants of his name, i.e., *j-b-r*, are associated with "restoring, bringing things back to normal, helping back on one's feet, setting (broken bones)."

599 "A Poem on Gambling" (*al-qaṣīdah al-qimāriyyah*): the poem seemingly alludes to events referred to earlier (4.19.4). Its vocabulary and syntax are unusually difficult and the translation is in places tentative;

choices made in the translation have therefore been more thoroughly endnoted here than elsewhere.

600 "It brought us . . . together" (*jamaʿatnā*): it is assumed here that the unexpressed subject of the verb is *al-luʿbah* ("the game") or a similar word.

601 "'the Ace,' Cavell, and Farshakh" (*al-Āṣ wa-Kawall (?) wa-Farshakh*): *āṣ* presumably means "ace," from the French, and is so used in line 4 of the poem, but here must be a nickname; *Kawall* is credible as the French/British surname "Cavell"; *Farshakh* appears to exist as a family name in Lebanon.

602 "One of us" (*baʿḍunā*): i.e., we were a pair, consisting of a practiced cardplayer and a greenhorn (the poet).

603 "a bit of a dog" (*ibn baʿṣī*): for *baʿṣ* the *Qāmūs* gives the meanings "leanness of body" and "disturbance"; however, usage on the Internet indicates that it has the same meaning as (Egyptian) colloquial *baʿbaṣah* "goosing." The translation is contextual.

604 "louis d'ors" (*mulūk*): literally "kings" but perhaps here "coins with a king's head on them," i.e., "sovereigns," or, given the French setting, as translated above.

605 "he owed" (*yudīnuhā*): i.e., perhaps, winning back debts he'd incurred.

606 "the pack" (*al-muzawwaq*): literally, "the decorated thing," cf. *al-awrāq al-muzawwaqah* ("[decorated] playing cards") above (4.19.4).

607 "his hand" (*taʾlīfu*): literally, "his blend, his mixture."

608 "In part a seal ring, in part a bezel" (*baʿḍuhu khātaman baʿḍuhu ka-faṣṣī*): meaning perhaps "part flat but engraved (like an inscribed seal ring; i.e., etched with anger), part bulging (like a curved stone set in a ring; i.e., bulging with fury)."

609 "him" (*minhu*): reference apparently switches from "the wizard of the pack" to the poet's overenthusiastic partner on his winning streak.

610 "a true friend" (*khilṣī*): i.e., his partner, the poet, who would need "covering for" if he is the "greenhorn" referred to at the start of the poem.

611 "stinging" (*yaqruṣu*): punning on the meanings "to sting" (like an insect) and hence "to speak bitingly," and "to pinch" (with the fingers).

612 "After forty-six" (*baʿda sittin wa-arbaʿīn*): i.e., presumably, "after reaching the age of forty-six," an age that, given his likely birth date of 1805 or 1806 (see Chronology, n488), accords with his stay in Paris between December 1850 and June 1853 (al-Maṭwī, *Aḥmad*, I:116); thus the meaning may be that the poet viewed unenthusiastically the prospect of living the rest of his life in poverty as a result of gambling.

613 "he'd not served him in writing notice of any protest" (*wa-lam yublighhu ʿan bandati ḥtijājin bi-naṣṣī*): the meaning of *bandah* is not obvious; *iḥtijāj* is taken here in the sense of "protest regarding nonpayment of a bill"; it is assumed that the subject of "served" is the player who failed to cover for the poet, who therefore by implication involved the pair in losses; the whole may mean that while the poet, though not a skilled player, had joined in the game, he had not expected to become liable for any debts that he and his partner might incur.

614 "All he thought about . . . whitewash" (*fikruhu fī . . . bi-jiṣṣī*): i.e., he was completely preoccupied with the writing of eulogies for persons of elevated station who paid him too little even to allow him to whitewash his room.

615 "gullibility . . . person" (*rubbamā . . . hirṣī*): i.e., perhaps the actual order of the world will be reversed one day and naïve but cautious persons, such as the poet, will in fact benefit from their virtues (but, it is implied, this is not likely to happen soon).

616 "Whenever he tried to write poetry with hairs from his mustache" (*wa-bi-shaʿrin min shāribayhi idhā ḥā/wala shiʿran*): the image of the poet twisting his mustache when deep in thought was used earlier in the work (see Volume Three, 3.8.5: "he set about playing with his mustache, as was his custom . . . until he was guided to an understanding of its meaning"). The subsequent use of the feminine pronoun apparently in reference to the hairs of the mustache (*yunḥī ʿalayhā . . . atāhā*) is problematic; perhaps the poet is evoking an unstated plural (*ashʿār*).

617 "soon . . . yellow" (*ʿan qarībin . . . ḥurṣī*): i.e., soon the white hairs in his mustache will be colored black with ink or yellow with nicotine.

618 "A partner of his" (*wa-sharīkun lahu*): presumably "Farshakh" (see the opening line of the poem); this and the following lines appear to picture the author's partner calculating the pair's winnings and losses.

619 "the game" (*al-dast*): or, punningly, "the gathering place, the divan."

620 "spitters" (*bassāqīna*): the reference is unclear.

621 "cloven hoofs" (*dhāt ẓilf*): Jewish dietary law permits the eating of animals that have cloven hoofs (and chew the cud).

622 "No great critic . . . my room" (*mā ʿābahā jihbidhun . . . ghurfatī*): meaning perhaps that the occurrence of the game anywhere but inside his room would be considered by the critics so unlikely as to constitute a challenge to the readers' credulity and hence a literary flaw.

623 "Its shape" (*shakluhā*): i.e., the shape of the room.

624 "Room Poems" (*al-Ghurfiyyāt*): the name refers to the author's habit of writing poems on the door of the room he rented while in Paris (see above 4.19.4).

625 Saturn (*Zuḥal*): associated elsewhere by the author with bad luck (Volume Two, 2.9.5).

626 "repose . . . quiescent . . . cunt" (*farajan . . . bi-sukūnin . . . al-farj*): the author exploits the fact that *faraj* ("relief") differs from *farj* ("vagina") only by a single additional vowel and that *sukūn* means both "inactivity" and "quiescence (i.e., vowellessness)" of a consonant.

627 "Against the onslaught of grammar" (*min ḍarbi Zaydin wa-ʿAmr*): literally, "against the beatings of Zayd and ʿAmr," the latter being generic names used in teaching the rules of grammar through exemplary sentences such as *ḍaraba Zaydun ʿAmran* ("Zayd beat ʿAmr").

628 "People have fire without smoke" (*li-l-nāsi nārun bi-lā dukhānī*): perhaps meaning, "People (such as those who come and sponge off me) have matches but no tobacco," i.e., expect me to supply the latter.

629 "chew the cud when I retire" (*wa-abītu qārī*): i.e., in the absence of a friend with matches, the poet is forced, at the end of the evening, to chew his tobacco.

630 "the lowest of the low" (*bi-asfali sāfilīna*): cf. Q Tīn 95:5 "then we cast him down as the lowest of the low."

631 "of exalted standing" (*rafīʿ al-darajāt*): or, punningly, "elevated in terms of stairs."

632 "distribute a predicate" (*murāʿāt al-naẓīr*): in rhetoric, applying to each member of a series a predication appropriate to it.

633 "my fire" (*nārī*): *nār* ("fire") is feminine in gender.

634 "liar" (*mayyān*): here and often elsewhere in the author's verse, references to lying and liars are to be taken in the context of his reference to "the lies of panegyric" above (4.20.44, second poem).

635 "This, the infection of your hand . . . has infected you not" (*fa-hādhihi ʿadwā kaffikum . . . muṭlaqan*): perhaps meaning that though the door is sick of being opened by visitors, the visitors have never grown sick of opening it.

636 "what's been scratched through the wrinkled paint by the scraping of nails" (*tanqīru aẓfārihi fī-naqri aẓfārī*): the translation is tentative and depends on understanding the first *aẓfār* as meaning "the creased parts of a skin" (see Lane, *Lexicon*, s.v. *ẓufr*).

637 "thus saith the owl" (*qālahu l-būmū*): the owl is popularly considered a harbinger of bad luck.

638 "a peen" (*al-shīqā*): in the Arabic, "a mountaintop" or, punningly, "the head of a penis."

639 "*Sammū* before entering my home" (*sammū ʿalā manzilī qabla l-dukhūlī*): i.e., "Invoke the name (*sammū*) of God (using some conventional formula)," as it is normal for a man not of the family to do before entering a house so as to warn its female inhabitants of his presence.

640 "*Sammū . . . samm*": the author exploits the coincidental identicality of ductus of *sammū* ("invoke the name of God!") (*s-m-w*) and *summū* ("poison!") (*s-m-m*).

641 "I live in my room in a state of commotion" (*anā sākinun fī ghurfatī mutaḥarrikun*): or, punningly, "I am both 'quiet' (*sākinun*) in my room and 'in motion' (*mutaḥarrikun*)" with a further resonance of "I

am a quiescent (i.e., vowelless) letter (*sākinun*) that is also voweled (*mutaḥarrikun*)."

642 "trying to screw it" (*yuḥāwilu naḥtahā*): *naḥt* means "to exhaust" as well as "to have intercourse with."

643 "Except that beneath it run no rivers" (*siwā an laysa tajrī taḥtahā l-anhārū*): cf. the phrase *tajrī taḥtahā l-anhārū* ("beneath it run rivers") much used in the Qurʾān to describe Paradise (e.g., Q Baqarah 2:25, 266, Āl ʿImrān 3:15, etc.).

644 "the very moons" (*al-aqmārū*): "moon" is a conventional trope for a beautiful person.

645 "Poems of Separation" (*al-Firāqiyyāt*): i.e., of separation from his wife and children when they left him in Paris and went to Istanbul.

646 "My past felicity had no like" (*fa-māḍī naʿīmī lam yakun min muḍāriʿin lahu*): or, punningly, "The perfect tense of my felicity had no imperfect," i.e., "was destined not to last."

647 "Why, what would it have harmed . . . to the end?" (*wa-mādhā ʿalā . . . ṭūlahā*): the author asks why the ill fortune of his earlier days should have been allowed to affect his later, happily married, life.

648 Hind . . . Mayyah . . . Daʿd: women's names often used nonspecifically in poetry.

649 "The right-thinking man . . . the rightly guided" (*al-rashīd . . . al-mahdī*): or, punningly, the caliphs (Hārūn) al-Rashīd and Muḥammad al-Mahdī.

650 "do not see you in it" (*wa-lastu arākumu/bi-hā*): meant either literally (because the poet is in Paris while his family is in Istanbul) or in the sense that "I do not see you as worldly creatures."

651 al-ʿĪnayn: a mountain at Uḥud near Mecca (site of a battle between the first Muslims and the idolaters of the city) from whose summit the devil is said to have proclaimed, falsely, that the Prophet Muḥammad had been killed (*Qāmūs*); presumably, it is the value of its association with the Prophet that makes it something to be cherished in the poet's eyes, along with the assonance between this and the preceding and following words (*al-ʿayn, al-ʿayn*).

652 "You departed to be cured of what ailed you" (*sāfartum li-l-bar'i mimmā nālakum*): a reference to his wife's illness and subsequent departure (see 4.18.15).

653 See 4.9.7: "for everything pulchritudinous reminds [a woman] of a handsome man" (*wa-kullu ḥusnin innamā yudhakkiru bi-l-ḥasan*).

654 "my twofold love for you" (*ḥubbayka*): perhaps meaning his love for the beloved both before separation and after it.

655 "when 'leg is intertwined with leg . . . unto thy Lord that day shall be the driving'" (*yawma taltaffu l-sāqu bi-l-sāq . . . ilā rabbika yawma'idhin al-masāq*): i.e., the Day of Judgment (Q Qiyāmah 75:29–30; trans. Arberry, *Koran*, 620).

656 "Part One . . . Part Two" (*al-juz' al-awwal . . . al-juz' al-thānī*): according to the translator's first reading of the text, this statement would indicate a humorously lopsided (709 pages in Part One versus 33 in Part Two in the 1855 edition) division of the work into two parts (see Volume One, xxxi–xxxii); it now seems more likely to him that "Part Two of the work will follow after the author has been stoned and crucified" should be understood to mean "once the critics have had their say." That the author gave at least half-serious thought to writing a continuation of *Leg over Leg* is indicated by his earlier statement, "My friendship for you [the Fāriyāq] will not prevent me, should I examine your situation at some later time, from writing another book about you" (4.20.1).

657 The letter that follows is written in Egyptian dialect, an unusual choice at that date (for context, see Davies and Doss, *al-ʿĀmmiyyah*) and one for which the author gives no explanation; Michael Cooperson suggests that the author may have chosen colloquial to make the point that the addressees ("Shaykh Muḥammad" presumably excepted) were likely to be ignorant of literary Arabic.

658 "*Sīdi*" etc.: in keeping with the colloquial nature of the letter, titles (*Sīdi*, etc.) have been given in their colloquial forms; *Sīdi* means literally "My Master" and *Sayyidna* "Our Master," while *Ṣirna* ("Our Sir") is a humorous adaptation of "Sir" to Egyptian titling norms.

659 "*Sīdi* Shaykh Muḥammad, *Sayyidna* Metropolitan Buṭrus," etc.: attempts have been made to identify at least some of these persons (see, e.g., al-Maṭwī, *Aḥmad*, I:80); however, it seems more likely that they represent categories of person, i.e., the Muslim scholar ("Shaykh Muḥammad"), Christian clergymen ("Metropolitan Buṭrus," etc.), and Europeans of various nationalities. For further examples of "Shaykh Muḥammad" used generically, see Volume Two (2.18.1n272) and 5.2.4 below, and for a similar roll call of European titles, see Volume Three, 3.12.25.

660 "my words aren't addressed to / cattle, donkeys, lions, and tigers" (*kalāmī mā hūsh ʿala l-baqar wi-l-ḥimīr wi-l-usūd wi-l-numūr*): Rastegar suggests that "the animals . . . are perhaps a reference to the orientalists, religious scholars, colonial officials, and others with whom Shidyaq was compelled to work (and who, outside the small exilic Arab population, were the only possible audience for an Arabic text published in Europe)" (Rastegar, *Literary Modernity*, 118).

661 Long as this list of lists is, it is not complete. To cite but one example, the list of "despicable traits of the dissolute woman" in Volume Three, at 3.19.13, is succeeded in the same paragraph by a brief list of words for types of city streets, followed by another long list of words relating to sexual intercourse, which is itself followed by a brief list of words relating to inappropriate behavior by women; the last three are not listed here. In addition, the semantic range covered in the text is sometimes wider than that suggested by the particular word or words the author has chosen to represent it in this list.

662 "Doublets": i.e., two-part exclamations such as *marḥā marḥā* ("Bravo! Bravo!").

663 "*thurtumī* [?]": the meaning of *thurtum* is "food or condiments left in the dish" (*Qāmūs*), in which sense it occurs a few lines before this list of vessels (Volume Two, 2.3.5).

664 "a place": the Arabic text, quoting the *Qāmūs*, uses the abbreviation ع for موضع (*mawḍiʿ*, "place, locality").

665 "*sukk*": discs made from an aromatic, musk-based substance called *rāmik* (see Volume Two, 2.16.25n252) that are strung on a string of

hemp and left for a year and of which the *Qāmūs* says "the older they get, the better they smell."

666 "*maḥlab*": a kind of plum (*Prunus mahaleb*); presumably the stones are what are used.

667 "Alas for Zayd" (*wayḥan li-Zayd*): the passage cited contains a list of six words meaning "Alas!"; the words "for Zayd" seem to be added to situate the phrases within a spuriously scholastic context, "Zayd" being a name conventionally used in examples by teachers of grammar.

668 "makeup and face paint" (*al-khumrah wa-l-ghumrah*): the relationship between the two words as used here is ambiguous: the *Qāmūs* defines *khumrah* as above and defines *ghumrah* simply as "saffron," which is one of the substances listed among those used as makeup in Volume Three, at 3.19.4; to the *Lisān, khumrah* is a variant of (*lughatun fī-*) *ghumrah*.

669 "Things peculiar to women " (*ashyā'un khāṣṣatun bi-l-nisā'*): in fact, the text refers only to the women of Paris.

670 "Arabic languages" (*al-lughāt al-ʿarabiyyah*): meaning, perhaps, Arabic in all its literary and dialectal varieties; note the discussion of diversity in Arabic at 5.3.7.

671 In his *Grammaire Persane, ou, Principes de l'Iranien Moderne* (Imprimerie Nationale, Paris, 1852), Chodźko writes, "L'Europe est depuis longtemps en possession de tout ce qui est nécessaire pour l'étude des langues orientales; elle a des bibliothèques, des écoles et des savants parfaitement en état de les diriger: aussi, sous le rapport de la philologie, de la philosophie et de l'histoire des langues d'Asie, un ustad persan, un muéllim arabe ou un brahmane hindou auraient beaucoup à apprendre de nos professeurs" (p.i).

672 "the chapter on marvels" (*faṣl ḥadanbadā*): Volume Three, chapter 19.

673 "the letters" (*al-rasā'il*): the *Grammaire Persane* contains a number of letters as exemplars of epistolary style.

674 Q Ṭā Hā 20:106.

675 "and he satisfies himself with the sands of the plain": in the French (p. 201) *Ils se contentent du sable des déserts* [*sic*; the French uses the plural ("they satisfy themselves")].

676 "Shaykh Muḥammad, Molla Ḥasan, or Üstad Saʿdī": i.e., from an Arab, a Persian, or a Turkish scholar.

677 Abū l-Ṭayyib: i.e., Abū l-Ṭayyib al-Mutanabbī; see Glossary.

678 "my sandy shaykh" (*ayyuhā l-shaykhu l-ramlī*): see 5.3.2n383.

679 *Lughat al-aṭyār wa-l-azhār* (*The Language of the Birds and the Flowers*): the Sufi work *Kashf al-asrār ʿan ḥikam al-ṭuyūr wa-l-azhār* (*The Uncovering of the Secrets Concerning the Wise Sayings of the Birds and the Flowers*) by ʿIzz al-Dīn ʿAbd al-Salām ibn Aḥmad ibn Ghānim al-Maqdisī (d. 678/1279) was published in Arabic in 1821 along with a translation by Joseph-Héliodore-Sagesse-Virtu Garcin de Tassy (1794–1878) under the French title *Les oiseaux et les fleurs: allégories morales* (Paris, Imprimerie Royale).

680 "the correspondence of a Jewish broker with an imbecilic merchant" (*muḥāwarat simsār yahūdī wa-aḥmaq mina l-tujjār*): the reference may be to Louis Jacques Bresnier's *Cours pratique et théorique de langue arabe . . . accompagné d'un traité du langage arabe usual et de ses divers dialectes en Algérie*, Alger, Bastide, 1855 (second edition), which includes (pp. 465, 467) an example of Jewish Arabic in the form of a letter from a Jewish businessman to a cloth merchant. According to Bresnier (p. xi), "Nous publiâmes . . . en 1846 la première édition de cet ouvrage, que l'insuffisance des resources typographiques nous contraignait à autographier nous-même" and it may be that this was the edition that the author saw. However, the second, more formal, edition was published in Paris in the same year as *al-Sāq ʿalā l-sāq* and by the same publisher (Benjamin Duprat) and he may have seen it then.

681 "the proverbs of Luqmān the Wise [in] the feeble language used in Algeria" (*amthāl Luqmān al-ḥakīm [fī] al-kalām al-rakīk al-mutʿāraf fī l-Jazāʾir*): in all likelihood, *Fables de Lokman, adaptées à l'idiome arabe en usage dans la régence d'Alger; suivies du mot à mot et de la prononciation interlinéaire* by J. H. Delaporte fils ("secrétaire interprète de l'intendance civile"), Algiers, Imprimerie du Gouvernement, 1835 (see Chauvin, *Bibliographie*, III:16 [21]).

682 "silly sayings taken from the rabble in Egypt and the Levant" (*aqwāl sakhīfah min raʿāʿ al-ʿāmmah fī Miṣr wa-l-Shām*): if *aqwāl* ("sayings")

here is to be taken to mean "utterances," a possible candidate would be Berggren, *Guide français-arabe vulgaire des voyageurs et des francs en Syrie et en Égypte: avec carte physique et géographique de la Syrie et plan géométrique de Jérusalem ancien et moderne, comme supplément aux Voyages en Orient* (Uppsala, 1844), which is a French-Arabic dictionary of the dialects in question with an appended grammar; if the author intended "proverbs," the choice is less clear: many collections of Arabic proverbs were compiled by French writers during the late eighteenth and early nineteenth centuries (see Chauvin, *Bibliographie*, I) but none apparently cover both Egypt and the Levant. It may seem unlikely that the author would direct his criticism in this passage at a Swedish writer, albeit one writing in French, but Berggren was a corresponding member of the Société Asiatique (personal communication from Geoffrey Roper) and al-Shidyāq may have seen his book there.

683 "a book . . . on the speech of the people of Aleppo": presumably Caussin de Perceval's *Grammaire arabe vulgaire* (see 4.18.11n230).

684 "*anjaq*": see further Volume Three, 3.15.5.

685 "the dialect of the people of Algeria" (*lisān ahl al-jazā'ir*): *kān fī wāḥid il-dār ṭūbāt bi-z-zāf il-ṭūbāt kishāfū* "In a house there were many rats (*ṭubbāt*, sing. *ṭubbah*). The rats, when they saw. . . ." and *kīnākul* "When I eat" and *rāhī* "She is (now) . . ." and *antīnā* (= *ntīna*) "you (fem. sing.)" and *antiyyā* (= *ntiyya*) "ditto" and *naqjam* "I joke" and *khammim bāsh* "he thought he would . . ." and *wāsīt shughl il-mahābil* "I did something crazy" . . . and *il-dajājah tirjaʿ tiwallid* [= *tūld*] *zūj ʿaẓmāt* "the hen now lays two eggs." Some of the preceding is open to more than one interpretation and the sectioning sometimes results in incomplete utterances; different Algerian regional dialects may also be represented. Though one might expect al-Shidyāq to have taken this material from Bresnier's grammar (see 5.3.6n388), only some of the individual words occur there.

686 "(i.e., *al-sādis*, 'the sixth')": an error for "the sixteenth."

687 "they transcribe *j* . . . with . . . *d* and *j*": the Arabic letter *jīm* is pronounced in literary usage like the *j* in *Jack*. As in French orthography *j*

is not pronounced like this, but like the *s* in *measure*, traditional French transcription employs *dj* for *jīm* (e.g., *Djerba*) to avoid misrepresentation of that letter by French *j*.

688 "The preaching metropolitan's 'cut off *azbābakum*'": see Volume Two (2.3.3, last sentence, Arabic), where the preacher (who is not, as here, identified as a metropolitan) says *azbābakum* ("your pricks") for *asbābakum* ("your ties to this world").

689 "this . . . sandman" (*hādhā l-ramlī*): see above 5.3.2n383.

690 "not everything white is a truffle" (*mā kullu bayḍā'a shaḥmah*): i.e., "appearances can be deceptive" (see al-Maydānī, *Majma'*, II:156).

691 "the *Maqāmāt* of al-Ḥarīrī": Silvestre de Sacy's edition was first published in 1822; the author critiques aspects of the second edition (1847) below (5.5).

692 "the travels of the scholar and writer Shaykh Muḥammad ibn al-Sayyid 'Umar al-Tūnusī": i.e., *Tashḥīdh al-adhhān bi-sīrat bilād al-'Arab wa-l-Sūdān* (*The Honing of Minds through an Account of the History of the Lands of the Arabs and the Blacks*), published in a lithographic edition by Kaeplin in Paris in 1850 or 1851 and in a critical edition by Khalīl Maḥmūd 'Asākir and Muṣṭafā Muḥammad Mus'ad in 1965 (al-Tūnusī, *Tashḥīdh*).

693 Nicolas Perron and Muḥammad ibn 'Umar al-Tūnusī met when working at the veterinary school at Abū Za'bal, where Perron took lessons in Arabic from al-Tūnusī, and their association continued after Perron became director of the Abū Za'bal medical school and hospital. That the lithographic edition of al-Tūnusī's work is in Perron's handwriting is stated in the work's colophon. However, the editors of the printed edition believe that the lithograph was based on the author's manuscript and, given the lengthy list of errata at its end, must have been checked and approved by the author (al-Tūnusī, *Tashḥīdh*, 15–19).

694 "*al-'aṣā* with a *y*": i.e., عصى for عصا, as though the root were *'-ṣ-y* rather than *'-ṣ-w*.

695 "*a'lā* as an elative with an *alif*": i.e., اعلا for اعلى.

696 "*najā* with a *yā'*": i.e., نجى for نجا, as though the root were *n-j-y* rather than *n-j-w*.

697 I.e., when they should be written *āminūna muṭma'innūna*.

698 "*fallāḥīna Miṣr*": for *fallāḥī Miṣr* ("the peasants of Egypt," *iḍāfah*).

699 *maḥmūdīna l-sīrah*: for *maḥmūdī l-sīrah* ("those of praiseworthy conduct," *iḍāfah*).

700 "*istawzara l-faqīha Mālik*": for *istawzara l-faqīha Mālikan* ("he appointed the jurisprudent Mālik as minister," Mālik being in the accusative and triptote).

701 "*lā yaʿṣā*": for *lā yaʿṣī* ("he does not disobey").

702 I.e., يتعدا for يتعدى.

703 "*ithnay ʿashara malik*": for *ithnay ʿashara malikan*.

704 "*abādīmā wa-l-takaniyāwī mutaʿādilayni*": the error lies in writing *mutaʿādilayni* for *mutaʿādilāni*; *al-takaniyāwī* is the title of the holder of a certain office in the Darfur sultanate (al-Tūnusī, *Tashḥīdh*, 91 by the translator's count: the pages are unnumbered); *abādīmā* was not identified.

705 "*tajidu l-rijāla wa-l-nisā'a ḥisān*": for *tajidu l-rijāla wa-l-nisā'a ḥisānan*.

706 "*daʿā lanā*": i.e., دعى لنا for دعا لنا.

707 "*ʿujūbah*": i.e., for *uʿjūbah*.

708 "*ṣawāḥibatuhā* and *ṣawāḥibātuhā*": the feminine endings *-at* (singular) and *-āt* (plural) cannot be added to a broken plural.

709 "*lughatun fīhā ḥamās*": the phrase as it stands is not ungrammatical; perhaps the original (which was not found in the text) read *lughatun fī ḥamās* ("a dialectal variant of [the word] *ḥamās*").

710 "*innahumā mutaqāribayi l-maʿnā*": for *innahumā mutaqāribā l-maʿnā*.

711 "*ḥattā ta'tiya arbābu l-māshiyati fa-yaqbiḍūn*": for *ḥattā ta'tiya arbābu l-māshiyati fa-yaqbiḍū*.

712 "*fa-hal iḥdā minkum*": for *fa-hal aḥadun minkum*.

713 "*yarfaʿūna aṣwātahum bi-dhālika ḥattā yadkhulūn*": for *yarfaʿūna aṣwātahum bi-dhālika ḥattā yadkhulū*.

714 "*māshiyīn*": for *māshīn*.

715 "*al-musammayayn*": for *al-musammayn*.

716 "*ḥattā yashuqqūn*": for *ḥattā yashhuqqū*.

717 "*munḥaniyūn*": for *munḥanūn*.

718 "*innahum yakūnū*": for *innahum yakūnūn*.

719 “*lā-ʿtāḍa*”: for *la-ʿtāḍa*.

720 al-Tūnusī, *Tashḥīdh*, 11.

721 “al-Kuthub” (literally, “the sand dunes”): thus clearly in the original work, but perhaps an error for “al-Kushub,” the name of a mountain (*Qāmūs*).

722 Ṭāhā: a name given to the Prophet Muḥammad; the contracted spelling—Ṭh—explains the mistake made by de Perceval (see further down in 5.3.12).

723 “the Bright One” (*al-Zarqāʾ*): literally, “the Blue One,” meaning here both the city of that name (today in Jordan) and “wine” (because, according to the dictionaries, of its clearness).

724 “the *yāʾ* in *hādhī* is in place of the [second] *hāʾ*”: i.e., the poet used the form *hādhī*, a variant of *hādhihi* (see Wright, *Grammar*, I:268B).

725 “He also changed the [second] *hāʾ* . . .”: i.e., he generalized from the shaykh’s use of the variant, thus changing the scansion from a long syllable followed by two short syllables (*hādhihi*) to two long syllables (*hādhī*) and throwing off the meter (*al-ramal*).

726 “He also left *al-Zarqāʾu* uncorrected (Monsieur Perron having put a *hamzah* after the *alif*)”: i.e., though al-Zarqāʾ is so pronounced in prose, the meter here calls for omission of the *hamzah* for the sake of the meter, a subtlety the copyist failed to notice.

727 “*Waṭʾ* should properly be written without an *alif*”: i.e., should be written وَطْء and not, as de Perceval presumably had it, وطا.

728 See 5.3.3.

729 Derenbourg: not Darenbourg as in the Arabic.

730 The commentary was written by de Sacy based on the best-regarded Arabic commentaries. The verses analyzed here occur in both the primary text and the commentary.

731 Though Arabic words normally have been transcribed in this translation, the Arabic is retained here since a number of the items cited involve orthographic issues.

732 “قال العواذل” etc.: i.e., *ʿawādhil*, as a plural noun, cannot be preceded by a plural verb of which it is the subject; additionally, as *ʿawādhil* is the plural of a feminine noun, the words cannot be understood as an

appositional phrase ("they said, the censurers") which should rather be قلن العواذل.

733 "[17]": the two dots that appear here and frequently elsewhere in the second column of the original table (as well as the occasional blank) are assumed to be the equivalent of an ellipsis, marking references that the author had not recorded in full and was unable to supply later; the relevant line number is therefore supplied here in square brackets.

734 "with the force of a proverb" (*makhraja l-amthāl*): i.e., and therefore as a self-standing utterance unaffected by the phonetic context.

735 "الصيفَ ضيّعتِ اللبن" (*'al-ṣayfa ḍayya'ti l-laban*): "in the summer you wasted the milk"—a proverb about an opportunity willfully wasted or a good foregone; the grammatical point is presumably that the first word is pronounced with an initial glottal stop for the same reason as that of the preceding example.

736 "the *tanwīn* . . . occurring as the rhyming syllable" (*al-tanwīna . . . yaqa'u qāfiyah*): for the rule see Wright, *Grammar*, II:352B.

737 "with prolongation of the vowel for the rhyme" (*bi-l-iṭlāq li-l-qāfiyah*): for the rule see Wright, *Grammar*, II:352D Rem.a.

738 " بدنا without *tanwīn* . . . أنا": the main rule involved is that *tanwīn* ("nunation") is never used in rhyme; additionally, the editors should have been alerted to the need to read بدنا rather than بدنًا by the occurrence of أنا as the last word of the first hemistich, which should rhyme with the last word of the second hemistich when the line is the first in a poem (Wright, *Grammar*, II:351 C).

739 The correct form is, of course, *ilayhim* rather than, as de Sacy etc. have it, *ilayhum*, which breaks a fundamental rule of the harmonization of the front vowel in this situation.

740 "how can *tatayyum* ("enslavement to love") be attributed to *ithr*": de Sacy's reading (*ithruhā*) would require that the word be read as a noun ("mark, trace"), yielding "her mark is enslaved to love"; in fact it is here used as a preposition, thus "(my heart) is enslaved to love. After her. . . ."

741 "How would you deal, my dear professors, with a غول?" (*wa-kayfa taf'alūna yā asātīdhu bi-l-ghūl*): a sarcastic jab, exploiting the rhymes

makbūl, *matbūl*, and *ghūl*, the last meaning "ghoul"; the sense is thus something like "How would you deal, my dear professors, with something really scary (i.e. difficult)?"

742 "Kaʿb's poem": i.e., the ode by Kaʿb ibn Zuhayr (first/seventh century) in which he apologizes to the Prophet Muḥammad for having satirized Islam and which became "one of the most famous Arabic poems" (Meisami and Starkey, *Encyclopedia*, 1:421).

743 *qaṣīdah musammaṭah*: a poem in which the two hemistichs of each line rhyme but each line has a different rhyme.

744 "fettered" (*muqayyadah*): i.e., the rhyming syllables should all end in a vowelless consonant.

745 "The pausal form is required" (*al-ṣawābu l-wuqūfu ʿalā l-hāʾ*): i.e., دعوهْ. . .جفوهْ.

746 "Strangely contorted" (*hiya mina l-tabaltuʿi bi-makān*): apparently meaning that the writing of the *kasrah* and the *ḍammah* is superfluous.

747 "unless the pronominal suffix refers to something mentioned earlier" (*illā idhā kāna l-ḍamīru yarjiʿu ilā madhkūrin qablahu*): the hemistich in question runs *ʿadhīrī mina l-ayyāmi maddat ṣurūfuhu* but it is more natural to read *ṣurūfuhā* ("days whose vicissitudes have passed") than "my advocate (*ʿadhīrī*) whose vicissitudes have passed."

748 "are fond of foolishness" (*yuḥibbūna l-ʿabath*): the author exploits the meaning of the mistakenly written *ʿābith*.

749 "Will you not then understand?" (*a-fa-lā tashʿurūn*): reminiscent of Qurʾan *law tashʿurūn* ("if only you could understand") (Q Shuʿarāʾ 26:113) and similar phrases.

750 "Should be وعُمري as the poet was not being wordy" (*al-ūlā bi-l-ḍammi fa-inna l-shāʿira ghayru mutanaṭṭiʿ*): i.e., the poet says "and my life . . ." and is not using the oath *la-ʿumrī*, which might be considered unnecessary and thus "wordy."

751 وشُرب: the author has misread de Sacy's edition, which does in fact read وشَرْبُ.

752 "It would be better to stick with one or the other" (*al-awlā l-iqtiṣāru ʿalā iḥdāhumā*): de Sacy says in his commentary that *durnā*, with upright *alif*, is a noun of place (de Sacy, *Maqāmāt*, I:319 line 13), then

quotes a verse in support of this in which he uses the same word with *alif*-in-the-form-of-*yāʾ*.

753 "Dhū l-Rummah was not one to use contorted language": i.e., the meter requires a long syllable in this position, and the normally diptote form *jalājila*, ending in a short vowel, has to be read as triptote.

754 "a parallel form occurs in the first line" (*wa-fī l-bayt al-awwal naẓar*): the final word of the first hemistich of the first line of the probative verse quoted here is *bi-qafratin*, also with *tanwīn*, which should have alerted the editors.

755 "the word مَنَآئِيا is twisted": the reference is to the line above, where مَنَآئِيا is an error for امانيا.

756 "line at the bottom of the page": in fact, the line before the line at the bottom of the page.

757 "compare عَوْلَ": according to some lexicographers, this word is invariable (see Lane, *Lexicon*).

758 "the diminutive not being allowed to take the definite article": the words *al-basīṭah* and *busayṭah* (diminutive of the former) both mean "the earth" but the latter is always without the definite article, being treated as a proper name.

759 "unwieldy wording" (*al-tanaṭṭuʿ*): de Sacy's version of the second hemistich of the verse runs *wa-bi-nafsī rtafaʿtu lā bi-judūdī*; more authoritative versions have the shorter *fakhartu* for *irtafaʿtu*.

760 "the first *tāʾ* being dropped to make it lighter" (*ḥudhifat al-tāʾu l-ūlā li-l-takhfīf*): on omission of *ta-* from the imperfect of Form V and VI verbs, see Wright, *Grammar*, I:65B.

761 "العمى is with *a*, you professors!" (*al-ʿamā bi-l-fatḥ yā asātīdh*): also, punningly, "Damn that *a*, you professors!" from the Lebanese colloquial expression *il-ʿama* ("Damn!").

762 "also الطهور not الطُهور": الطهور appears in the last line on p. 633.

763 "Corr.": in the Arabic ص (*ṣ*) is used apparently as an abbreviation of صوابه (*ṣawābuhu*), meaning "the correct form being . . ."

764 "*Qiṣṣat ʿAntar* (*The Story of ʿAntar*)": a popular romance relating a mythologized version of the life of the pre-Islamic poet ʿAntarah ibn Shaddād al-ʿAbsī; dating to the eleventh or twelth century AD,

it employs a language with oral features and "drew the interest of nineteenth-century Orientalists, who saw ʿAntar as the paramount Bedouin hero" (Meisami and Starkey, *Encyclopedia*, I:93). Caussin de Perceval's *Notice et extrait du roman d'Antar* was published at the Imprimerie Royale in Paris in 1833.

765 Conte Alix Desgranges: not "Desgrange" as in the Arabic.

766 The only other translation of which I am aware is René Khawam's into French (Faris Chidyaq, *La jambe sur la jambe*). This does not, however, pretend to be complete, since the translator asserts, without offering evidence, that much of the Arabic text was originally written separately and included in *al-Sāq* simply to take advantage of the availability of funds for publication; the translator has omitted this extraneous material and thus, according to his claim, presents the book, for the first time, "dans toute son originalité" (Chidyaq, Jambe, 19). Khawam does not specify exactly what he has omitted, but examples include the "Memorandum from the Writer of These Characters" in its entirety (Volume One, 1.19.11–23) and, more surprising in its selectivity, many but not all items of certain lexical lists (e.g., forty-three items omitted out of an original fifty-six between *Shiʿb Bawwān* (Volume Two, 2.14.42) and *bint ṭabaq* (Volume Two, 2.14.46) in the list of things incapable of preventing a man from shrieking "I want a woman!"; see Chidyaq, *Jambe*, 311). Khawam also omits the Appendix (Volume Four, 5.3.1 to 5.3.12). The result is a radical shortening of the text that appears to run counter to the author's wishes as expressed in the warning in the Proem (also omitted by Khawam), "Beware, though, lest you add to it or / Think of using it in abbreviated form, / For no place in it is susceptible / To abbreviation, or to addition, to make it better." (Volume One, 0.4.12.).

767 Starkey, "Fact," 32.

768 Cachia, "Development," 68.

769 On *sajʿ* in general, see Meisami and Starkey, *Encyclopedia*; for a discussion of *sajʿ* in *al-Sāq ʿalā l-Sāq*, see *Jubran*, "Function."

770 This loss of "linking and correspondence"—by which I take the author to mean strict parallelism—would probably have particularly upset

him: in a eulogy of *saj'* written later he writes, "And what shall teach thee what is *saj'*? Well-matched words to which man cleaves by *disposition* and to whose sound his heart must yield in passionate *submission*, so that they become impressed upon his memory, and how effective that *impression*—especially when adorned with some of those beauties of the elaborate rhetorical *style* that employ orthographic and morphological *guile*.... This is the miracle with which no non-Arab can vie or to whose peaks draw *nigh*!" (al-Shidyāq, *Sirr*, 3–4).

771 Again, the author would not have been best pleased at the sacrifice of monorhyme: "As for the poetry of foreign languages, it consists of no more than farfetched figures and convoluted exaggerations and it is impossible to write a whole poem in them with a single rhyme throughout. You find them varying the rhyme and introducing little-used and uncouth words; and despite that, because of their inability to follow this system [of monorhyme], they say that a poem with only one rhyme is to be regarded as ugly. What hideous words and what appalling ignorance!" (al-Shidyāq, *Sirr*, 4).

772 Peled, "Enumerative," 129.

773 Zakharia, "Aḥmad," 510.

774 Peled, "Enumerative," 139.

775 The author appears to have developed the preferred format for the presentation of such lists in stages. Thus, at the occurrence of the first such list (104 words related to augury and superstition, Volume One, 1.16.7), he first provides the list of words without definitions, then some lines later repeats all but fifteen items (those omitted being presumably the most familiar and thus the least in need of definition) in the form of a table, with headwords in one column and definitions in another (Volume One, 1.16.9), in effect rendering the first list redundant; to avoid reproducing two identical lists in the translation, the first iteration is reproduced there in transcription, resulting in the spectacle, possibly bizarre in a translation, of a block of text consisting entirely of Arabic. Thereafter the two-column table format prevails. Further, this first tabular list is not integrated syntactically into the narrative while most of those that follow are (exceptions

include the "five work groups," Volume Two, 2.16.8–63). The alphabetical principle applied to the tables also varies, with some arranged by first letter (e.g., Volume One, 1.16.9–18) and others by last letter (e.g., Volume Two, 2.1.11–16), with occasional anomalies. Even after arriving at the two-column table format, the author continues to ring changes on it. Thus, after a short table of words and definitions relating to attractiveness of the face (Volume Two, 2.4.6), he switches to a non-tabular format (Volume Two, 2.4.7 to 2.4.12), which allows him to group together words with the same root or that are metatheses of one another, while continuing to provide definitions, e.g., "and her *ladīds* have a *ladūd* (the *ladīds* are 'the sides of the neck below the ears' and the *ladūd* is 'a pain that affects the mouth and throat')" (Volume Two, 2.4.11). Later, he interrupts tables with "notes" (see, e.g., Volume Two, 2.14.13), a technique that allows him to enrich the lexical mix by introducing antonyms to the words in the tables.

776 The *Historical Thesaurus of the Oxford English Dictionary*, of which I became aware, unfortunately, only very late in the translation process, was also used to a limited degree. It has the benefit of offering a selection of words many of which are as rare and recondite as those in *al-Sāq* and might provide the best starting point for any future renditions of these lists.

777 Rastegar, "On Nothing," 108. On the relationship between title and contents, the author himself says, "Every one of these chapters, I declare, has a title that points to its contents as unambiguously as smoke does to fire; anyone who knows what the title is knows what the whole chapter is about" (Volume One, 1.17.3.). Though the author may be teasing the reader a little here, the majority of titles do in fact reflect the topic dealth with ("The Priest's Tale," Volume One, 1.15; "A Description of Cairo," Volume Two, 2.5, 2.7; etc.), while others either allude to the governing concept of the chapter (e.g., "Raising a Storm," Volume One, 1.1) or—and this is especially true when the chapter ranges over a variety of topics—consist of or contain a word that is to be found within the chapter (e.g., "Snow," Volume One, 1.17, or "Throne" in "A Throne to Gain Which Man Must Make Moan,"

Volume Two, 2.4) in a manner reminiscent of the names of certain *sūrahs* of the Qur'ān.

778 Relying largely on Geoffrey Roper, "Fāris al-Shidyāq as Translator and Editor," in *A Life in Praise of Words: Aḥmad Fāris al-Shidyāq and the Nineteenth Century*, edited by Nadia al-Baghdadi, Fawwaz Traboulsi, and Barbara Winkler. Wiesbaden: Reichert (Litkon 37) (forthcoming; details are provisional) and personal communications.

779 Muḥammad al-Hādi al-Maṭwī, *Aḥmad Fāris al-Shidyāq 1801–1887: ḥayātuhu wa-āthāruhu wa-ārā'uhu fī l-nahḍah al-ʿarabiyyah al-ḥadīthah*. 2 vols. Beirut: Dār al-Gharb al-Islāmī, 1989.

780 Simon Mercieca, "An Italian Connection? Malta, the Italian Risorgimento and Al-Shidyaq's Political Thought." Unpublished paper.

781 The birth date 1805 or 1806 (rather than, as in many sources, 1801 or 1804) is based on a declaration in the author's hand dated 6 August 1851 accompanying his application for British nationality in which he gives his age as 45 (National Archives, Kew, ref. H01/41/1278A) (Roper, personal communication). The plausibility of this date is reinforced by the statement of a visitor to Malta in 1828, who met "Pharez . . . a most interesting youth, about 22 years of age" (Woodruff, *Journal*, 47).

782 Roper, "Translator," 5.

783 Roper, "Translator," 5.

784 Roper, "Translator," 5.

785 Roper, personal communication.

786 Roper, "Translator," 5, 8.

787 Mercieca, "Italian Connection," 13.

788 Roper, "Translator," 7.

789 al-Maṭwī, *Aḥmad*, 91.

790 al-Maṭwī, *Aḥmad*, 92.

791 Egypt did not finally withdraw from Lebanon until February 1841. If al-Maṭwī is correct in believing that al-Shidyāq returned to Malta in October 1840 (for the start of the academic year at the University of Malta) (al-Maṭwī, *Aḥmad*, 92), the author's words *fa-sārat al-ʿasākir mina l-bilād* ("and the soldiers left the country") (3.14.5) would have to be understood as meaning that they withdrew from Mount Lebanon

to the coast. Al-Maṭwī's timetable would also require the author to have left Qraye after 10 October (the date of the defeat of the Egyptian fleet), traveled to Damascus, stayed there long enough to recover from his accident, go on to Jaffa, and return to Malta all in twenty days, which, while not perhaps impossible, seems unlikely.

792 al-Maṭwī, *Aḥmad*, 125.

793 Roper, personal communication.

794 Roper, "Translator," 8.

795 Roper, "Translator," 8.

796 The author wrote at least twice to the joint committee of the SPCK and CMS complaining of his treatment; the letter referred to in the text is probably that send by al-Shidyāq in March 1844 (Roper, "Translator," 8), which resulted in his eventual reinstatement (*idem* 9).

797 Roper, personal communication.

798 al-Maṭwī, *Aḥmad*, 103

799 al-Maṭwī, *Aḥmad*, 103.

800 al-Maṭwī, *Aḥmad*, 126.

801 al-Maṭwī, *Aḥmad*, 105.

802 al-Maṭwī, *Aḥmad*, 109.

803 al-Maṭwī, *Aḥmad*, 110.

804 al-Maṭwī, *Aḥmad*, 137–38.

Glossary

ʿAbd al-Majīd, Sultan thirty-first Ottoman sultan, reigned 1839–61.

ʿAbd al-Qādir (ibn Muḥyī l-Dīn al-Jazāʾirī), Emir (1808–83) from 1834 the most successful leader of resistance to French rule in Algeria; exiled to France in 1847.

Abū l-Ḥasan al-Tihāmī al-Ḥasanī a poet of Arabian origin who died (416/1025) in Cairo.

Abū Nuwās Abū Nuwās Al-Ḥasan ibn Hāniʾ al-Ḥakamī (ca. 140–ca. 198/755–813), Abbasid poet, best known for his poetry in praise of wine and boys.

Abū Tammām Abū Tammām Ḥabīb ibn Aws al-Ṭāʾī (ca. 189/805 to ca. 232/845), Abbasid court poet and anthologist, teacher and rival of al-Buḥturī.

Aḥmad Pasha Bāy Aḥmad I ibn Muṣṭafā (r. 1837–55).

Akhfash (al-) ʿAbd al-Ḥamīd ibn ʿAbd al-Majīd al-Akhfash al-Akbar (d. 177/793), a noted grammarian of the school of Basra, teacher of Sībawayh and others.

ʿAmr ibn Kulthūm a pre-Islamic poet and tribal chieftain (sixth century AD), whose only surviving poem is that included among the *muʿallaqāt* (the "suspended odes").

Andalus (al-) those parts of the Iberian Peninsula that were under Islamic rule from the seventh to the fifteenth centuries.

Ashʿarī (al-) ʿAlī ibn Ismāʿīl al-Ashʿarī (260–324/873–936), a theologian famed for his rational argumentation in the defense of Islamic orthodoxy.

Ashmūnī (al-) ʿAli ibn Muḥammad al-Ashmūnī (838–918/1434–35—1512–13), author of a well-known commentary on Ibn Mālik's *Alfiyyah*, a poem of a thousand lines containing the principal rules of Arabic grammar.

ʿAyn Tirāz a village in Mount Lebanon ("Ain Traz") southeast of Beirut and the site, from 1790 to 1870, of a Greek Melkite seminary.

Baalbek a town in Lebanon's Beqaa Valley, east of the Litani River, site of the celebrated ruins of a Roman temple dedicated to Jupiter-Baal.

badīʿ an innovative style appearing in poetry starting in the third/ninth centuries featuring complex wordplay; eventually, the term evolved to mean "rhetorical figures" collectively.

Bag-men (khurjiyyūn) the author's term for Protestant missionaries in the Middle East, whether the American Congregationalists of the Board of Commissioners of Foreign Missions with whom he first came into contact in Beirut or the British Anglicans of the Church Missionary Society for whom he worked later in Malta, Egypt, and London. The Congregationalists established their first mission station in Beirut in 1823 (Makdisi, *Artillery*, 81, 83). In December 1823, when their intention to proselytize became clear, Maronite patriarch Yūsuf Ḥubaysh (1787–1845), who had initially received them cordially, ordered his flock to avoid all contact with what he referred to as "the Liberati" or "Biblemen" (Makdisi, *Artillery*, 95–97).

Barāmikah the Barāmikah family held high office at the court of the early Abbasid caliphs and became known for the extravagance of their lifestyle.

Bilqīs Queen of Sabaʾ (Sheba) in Yemen, the story of whose visit to Sulaymān (Solomon) is told in the Qurʾān (Q Naml 27:22–44).

Buḥturī (al-) Abū ʿUbādah al-Walīd ibn ʿUbayd (Allāh) al-Buḥturī (206/821 to 284/897), Abbasid court poet, student and rival of Abū Tammām.

Būlāq Cairo's river port.

Chodźko, Alexandre Aleksander Borejko Chodźko (1804–91), Polish poet, Slavist, and Iranologist, who worked for the French ministry of foreign affairs from 1852 to 1855 and was later appointed to the chair of Slavic languages at the Collège de France.

Church Missionary Society an evangelical Protestant missionary society founded in London in 1799 and active in Egypt (as a mission to the Copts) as of 1825.

Committee, the the Society for the Promotion of Christian Knowledge, which oversaw many of the translation projects, including that of the Bible, in which al-Shidyāq was involved.

Dayr al-Qamar a village in south-central Lebanon, site of the residence of the governors of Lebanon from the sixteenth to the eighteenth century.

Derenbourg, Joseph (1811–95) a Hebraist and Arabist.

de Sacy see Silvestre de Sacy.

Desgranges, Conte Alix Desgranges (d. 1854) held the post of *secrétaire interprète* to the French state, in addition to being, as of 1833, professor of Turkish at the Collège de France; in his former capacity "he welcomes and escorts all Orientals who pass through Paris " (Pouillon, *Dictionnaire*, 292).

dhikr the repetition of the name of God as an exercise intended to bring the one who pronounces it closer to Him.

Dhū l-Rummah nickname ("He of the Frayed Cord") of Abū Ḥārith Ghaylān ibn ʿUqba, an Umayyad poet (d. 117/735?).

emir (amīr) a title (literally, "commander" or "prince") assumed by local leaders in the Arab world; as used in this work, the term most often refers to the emirs of the Shihābī dynasty of Mount Lebanon.

Fāriyāq, the the hero of the events described in the book and the author's alter ego, the name itself being a contraction of Fāri(s al-Shid)yāq.

Fātiḥah, the the opening *sūrah* ("chapter") of the Qur'ān.

Fīrūzābādī (al-) Muḥammad ibn Yaʿqūb al-Fīrūzābādī (d. 817/1415), compiler of the *Qāmūs* (q.v.).

Ḥalq al-Wād the port of Tunis, also known as La Goulette.

Ḥarīrī (al-) Abū Muḥammad al-Qāsim ibn ʿAli al-Ḥarīrī (446/1054 to 516/1122), Iraqi poet, man of letters, and official, best known for his collection of fifty *maqāmāt* (see *maqāmah*).

Ḥimṣ Homs, a city between Damascus and Aleppo.

Ibn Abī ʿAtīq Muḥammad ibn ʿAbd al-Raḥmān ibn Abī Bakr (1st–2nd/7th–8th century), usually referred to as Ibn Abī ʿAtīq, was the great-grandson of the caliph Abū Bakr al-Ṣiddīq and "a friend of many poets and singers, who appears in many stories and anecdotes as a kind of wit" (Van Gelder, *Classical*, 379, 460); it is not obvious why the author brackets him with Ibn Ḥajjāj (q.v.), as unlike the latter he was irreverent rather than foulmouthed.

Ibn al-Fāriḍ ʿUmar ibn ʿAlī ibn al-Fāriḍ (576–632/1181–1235), an important Egyptian Sufi poet, celebrated for his blending of erotic and divine imagery.

Ibn Ḥajjāj al-Ḥusayn ibn Aḥmad Ibn (al-)Ḥajjāj (ca. 333–91/941–1000): a Baghdadi poet best known for his obscene poetry.

Ibn Khālawayh, Aḥmad ibn al-Ḥusayn (d. 370/980–81) a leading philologist of Baghdad.

Ibn Mālik Muḥammad ibn Mālik (600 or 601 to 672/1203 or 1205 to 1274), a scholar best known for his *Alfiyyah* (*Thousand-Line Poem*), in which he presents the rules of Arabic grammar.

Ibn Nubātah Jamāl al-Dīn Muḥammad ibn Shams al-Dīn (686/1287 to 768/1366), an Egyptian poet.

Ibn Ṣarīʿ al-Dilāʾ Abū l-Ḥasan ʿAlī ibn ʿAbd al-Wāhid (d. 412/1021), a poet of Baghdadi origin whose later life was spent in Cairo. Ibn Khallikān refers to him as a poet of *mujūn* ("license").

Imruʾ al-Qays Imruʾ al-Qays ibn Ḥujr (sixth century AD), a pre-Islamic poet, author of one of the *muʿallaqāt* ("suspended odes").

ʿĪsā Jesus.

Islāmbūl Istanbul.

Jubārah, Ghubrāʾīl one of a group of Levantines who supported the author financially and morally during his years in Paris and London; on May 1, 1851 he took the author with him from Paris to London for the opening of the Great Exhibition as a translator and guide.

jubbah an open-fronted mantle with wide sleeves.

Kaḥlā, Rāfāʾīl litterateur and collaborator of al-Shidyāq's in Paris, who paid for the publication of *Al-Sāq ʿalā l-sāq* and contributed to it a publisher's introduction (Volume One, 0.3).

Khawājā a title of reverence and address afforded to Christians of substance.

Majnūn Laylā Qays ibn al-Muwallaḥ (first/seventh century), known as Majnūn Laylā, said to have gone insane (*majnūn*) when his childhood love, Laylā, was married off to another; he came to epitomize obsessive devotion to the beloved and its expression in verse.

maqāmah, plural *maqāmāt* "short independent prose narrations written in ornamented rhymed prose (*saj*ʿ) with verse insertions which share a common plot scheme and two constant protagonists: the narrator and the hero" (Meisami and Starkey, *Encyclopedia,* 2/507). The thirteenth chapter of each volume of the present work is described by the author as a *maqāmah,* the plot scheme in these *maqāmāt* being a debate. See, further, Zakharia: "Aḥmad Fāris al-Šidyāq."

Maronite of or pertaining to the Maronite Christian community, whose historical roots lie in northern Syria and Lebanon and whose church, while using Syriac as a liturgical language, is in communion with the Roman Catholic church.

Market-men (sūqiyyūn) the author's term for the Maronite and Roman Catholic clergy, or the Maronite and Roman Catholic churches in general.

mawāliyā a nonclassical (i.e., not monorhymed) verse form that lends itself to both non-colloquial and colloquial varieties of the language.

Mikhallaʿ (al-), Mikhāʾīl one of the group of Levantines who assisted the author financially and morally during his years in Paris and London, and an early convert to Protestantism.

Mountain (the) Mount Lebanon, a mountain range in Lebanon extending for 170 kilometers parallel to the Mediterranean coast and the historical homeland of both the Maronite and Druze Lebanese communities.

Mūsā Moses.

Muṣṭafā Pasha Muṣṭafā Pasha Khāzindār (1817–78), a Greek slave raised at the Tunisian court who married the sister of the ruler Aḥmad I Muṣṭafā and became treasurer (*khāzindār*) and eventually prime minister of the Tunisian state.

Musurus, Prince Kostaki Musurus (1814 or 1815 to 1891) served as Ottoman ambassador to London without interruption from 1851 until 1885; he translated Dante's *Divine Comedy* into Turkish and Greek.

Mutanabbī (al-) Abū l-Ṭayyib Aḥmad ibn Ḥusayn al-Mutanabbī (ca. 303–54/915–65), a poet renowned for his virtuosity and innovation, which he often deployed in praise of the rulers of the day.

Nakhaʿī (al-) the name of a number of related Traditionists, of whom the best known is perhaps Ibrāhīm al-Nakhaʿī (AD 666–71).

Perron, Nicolas (1798–1876) French physician, Arabist, and Saint-Simonist. Perron studied medicine and also took courses at the École des langues orientales, especially those given by Caussin de Perceval. Later he became director of the hospital of Abū Zaʿbal, near Cairo, Egypt's first health facility based on a Western model.

Qāmūs (al-) *Al-Qāmūs al-muḥīṭ* (*The Encompassing Ocean*), a dictionary compiled by Muḥammad ibn Yaʿqūb al-Fīrūzābādī (d. 817/1415) that became so influential that *qāmūs* ("ocean") eventually came to mean simply "dictionary." The author later published a study of the *Qāmūs* entitled *Al-jāsūs ʿalā l-Qāmūs* (*The Spy on the Qāmūs*).

Rashīd Pasha, Muṣṭafā (ca. 1800–58) Ottoman politician, diplomat, reformer, litterateur, and traveler. Ambassador to Paris and London, then foreign minister and later chief minister, he met al-Shidyāq during his second tenure as ambassador to Paris and was later instrumental in bringing him to Constantinople.

Reinaud, Joseph Toussaint (1795–1867) French Orientalist; Toussaint succeeded to Silvestre de Sacy's chair at the École des langues orientales on the latter's death.

Sāmī Pasha, ʿAbd al-Raḥmān an Ottoman reformer, born in the Peloponnese. He entered Egyptian service in 1821, was appointed director in 1828 of the official gazette, *al-Waqāʾiʿ al-Miṣriyyah* (where al-Shidyāq may have made his acquaintance), and became the Ottoman Empire's first minister of education in 1856. He wrote prose and verse in Turkish (al-Maṭwī, *Aḥmad*, 898–99).

Sayyid al-Raḍī (al-) see Sharīf al-Raḍī (al-).

Sharīf al-Raḍī (al-) Muḥammad ibn Abī Ṭāhir al-Ḥusayn ibn Mūsā (359–406/970–1015), poet and syndic of the descendents of ʿAlī ibn Ṭālib at the Buyid court.

Sībawayhi ʿAmr ibn ʿUthmān ibn Qanbar Sībawayhi (second/eighth century), the creator of systematic Arabic grammar.

Silvestre de Sacy, Antoine Isaac (1758–1838) prominent French philologist who wrote grammars of Arabic and edited a number of Arabic texts, including al-Ḥarīrī's *Maqāmāt*.

Ṣubḥī Bayk son of ʿAbd al-Raḥmān Sāmī Pasha (q.v.) and later himself also Ottoman minister of education and then governor of Syria (al-Maṭwī, *Aḥmad*, 902).

Sublime State, the the Ottoman Empire.

Sulaymān Solomon.

tanwīn pronunciation of word-final short vowels followed by *-n*, thus *-un*, *-an*, *-in*; also called "nunation."

Tūnusī (al-), Muḥammad ibn al-Sayyid ʿUmar (ibn Sulaymān) an interpreter at the Abū Zaʿbal medical school who wrote an account of his travels in Darfur in the early nineteenth century.

ʿUdhrī pertaining to the Banū ʿUdhra, a Yemeni tribe, and applied to a type of elegiac love poetry that flourished during the Umayyad period.

wird a section of the Qurʾān specified for recitation at a certain time of day or night or for use in private prayer.

Yāzijī (al-), Sheikh Nāṣīf Nāṣīf al-Yāzijī (1800–71), a leading Maronite scholar of Arabic, prolific author and translator, and contemporary of the author, with whom he was later to maintain a celebrated feud over linguistic issues that was inherited by al-Yāzijī's son Ibrāhīm after his father's death (see, e.g., Patel, *Arab Nahdah*, 103ff).

Yūsuf the Prophet Joseph, whose story is told in the Qurʾān (*Sūrah* 12) and who is often invoked in verse as the epitome of young male beauty and virtue.

zaqqūm tree a tree mentioned in the Qurʾān as growing in hell and bearing exceedingly bitter fruit.

Bibliography

Abū Nuwās, al-Ḥasan ibn Hāniʾ. *Dīwān*. Beirut: Dār Ṣādir and Dār Bayrūt, 1962.

Alwan, Mohammed Bakir. *Aḥmad Fāris ash-Shidyāq and the West*. Unpublished PhD Dissertation. Indiana University, 1970.

Amīn, Aḥmad. *Qāmūs al-ʿādāt wa-l-taqālīd wa-l-taʿābīr al-miṣriyyah*. Cairo: Lajnat al-Taʾlīf wa-l-Tarjamah wa-l-Nashr, 1953.

Arberry, Arthur J. *Arabic Poetry: A primer for students*. Cambridge: Cambridge University Press, 1965.

Arberry, Arthur J. "Fresh Light on Ahmad Faris al-Shidyaq." *Islamic Culture*, 26 (1952), 155–68.

Arberry, Arthur J. *The Koran Interpreted*. Oxford World's Classics. Oxford: Oxford University Press, 1982.

Arberry, Arthur J. *The Seven Odes: The first chapter in Arabic literature*. London: George Allen and Unwin, 1957.

ʿĀshūr, Raḍwā. *Al-ḥadāthah al-mumkinah, al-Shidyāq wa-l-sāq ʿalā l-sāq, al-riwāyah al-ūlā fī-l-adab al-ʿarabī al-ḥadīth*. Cairo: Dār al-Shurūq, 2009.

Badawi, El-Said and Martin Hinds. *A Dictionary of Egyptian Arabic, Arabic–English*. Beirut: Librairie du Liban, 1986.

Baghdādī, ʿAbd al-Laṭīf al-. *Al-ifādah wa-l-iʿtibār fī-l-umūr wa-l-ḥawādith al-muʿāyanah bi-arḍ Miṣr*, edited by Salāma Mūsā. Cairo: Maṭbaʿat al-Majallah al-Jadīdah, n.d.

Brincat, Joseph F. *Maltese and Other Languages: A linguistic history of Malta*. Santa Venera: Midsea Books, 2011.

Brustad, Kristen. "Jirmānūs Jibrīl Farḥāt." In *Essays in Arabic Literary Biography* 1350–1850, edited by Joseph Lowry and Devin J. Stewart, 242–51. Wiesbaden: Harrassowitz Verlag, 2009.

Cachia, Pierre. "The Development of a Modern Prose Style in Arabic Literature." *Bulletin of the School of Oriental and African Studies*, University of London 52, no. 1 (1989):65–76.

Chateaubriand, François-René. *Oeuvres complètes de Chateaubriand.* Vol. VI: *Voyages en Amérique, en Italie, au Mont Blanc. Mélanges littéraires.* Paris: Garnier, [1861].

Chauvin, Victor. *Bibliographie des ouvrages arabes ou relatifs aux arabes publiés dans l'Europe chrétienne de 1810 à 1885.* 3 vols. Liège: H. Vaillant-Carmanne and Leipzig, O. Harrassowitz, 1882–85.

Dankoff, Robert. "Ayıp değil! (No Disgrace!)." *Journal of Turkish Literature* 5 (2008):77–90.

Dozy, R.P.A. *Dictionnaire détaillé des noms des vêtements chez les arabes.* Amsterdam: Jean Müller, 1843 (offset, Beirut: Librairie du Liban, n.d.).

——— *Supplément aux dictionnaires arabes.* 2 Vols. Leiden: E.J. Brill, 1881 (offset, Beirut: Librairie du Liban, 1968)

EI2 = *Encyclopaedia of Islam*, edited by P.J. Bearman, Th. Bianquis, C.E. Bosworth, E. van Donzel and W.P. Heinrichs et al., 2nd Edition., 12 vols. with indexes and etc., Leiden: E. J. Brill, 1960–2005.

El Mouelhy, Ibrahim. "Le Qirmeh en Égypte." Bulletin de l'Institut d'Égypte, 24 (1946–47): 51–82.

Ewald, Ferdinand Christian. *Journal of Missionary Labours in the City of Jerusalem during the Years 1841-2-3.* 1st edition. London: B. Wertheim, 1845.

Fīrūzābādhī [=Fīrūzābādī] (al-), Muḥammad ibn Yaʿqūb. *Al-Qāmūs al-muḥīṭ.* 4 volumes. 2nd edition. Cairo: al-Maṭbaʿah al-Ḥusayniyyah, 1344 H, also accessed at http://www.baheth.info/.

Flaubert, Gustave. *Flaubert in Egypt*, translated and edited by Francis Steemuller. 2nd edition. Chicago: Academy Chicago, 1987.

Graf, Georg. *Geschichte der christlichen arabischen Literatur.* 5 vols. Vatican: Biblioteca apostolica vaticana, 1944–53.

Hava, J. G. *Al-Farā'id al-durriyyah fī l-lughatayn al-'arabiyyah wa-l-inkilīziyyah*. Beirut: Catholic Press, n.d.

Ḥillī, Ṣafī al-Dīn al-. *Sharḥ al-kāfiyyah al-badī'iyyah*, edited by Nasīb Nashāwī. Damascus, 1983.

Ibn al-Athīr, Majd al-Dīn Abū l-Sa'ādāt al-Mubārak ibn Muḥammad. *Kitāb al-nihāyah fī gharīb al-ḥadīth wa-l-athar*. 4 vols. Cairo: al-Maṭba'ah al-'Uthmāniyyah, 1311 H.

Ibn al-Fāriḍ, 'Umar ibn 'Alī. *Dīwān*. Cairo: Maktabat al-Qāhirah, 1951.

Ibn Khālawayh, al-Ḥusayn ibn Aḥmad. *Laysa fī kalām al-'Arab*, edited by Aḥmad 'Abd al-Ghafūr 'Aṭṭār. 2nd edition. Mecca, 1399/1979 .

Ibn Manẓūr, Jamāl al-Dīn Muḥammad ibn Mukarram al-'Ifrīqī. *Lisān al-'Arab*. Accessed at http://www. baheth.info/.

Jubran, Suleiman. "The Function of Rhyming Prose in 'Al-Sāq 'alā al-Sāq'." *Journal of Arabic Literature*, 20, no. 2 (Sep. 1989): 148–58.

Karamustafa, Ahmet T. *God's Unruly Friends: Dervish Groups in the Islamic Later Middle Period 1200–1550*. Salt Lake City: University of Utah Press, 1994.

Kayat, Assaad Y. [= Khayyāṭ, As'ad Ya'qūb]. *A Voice from Lebanon*. London: Madden & Co., 1847.

Khawam, René. *La Jambe sur la jambe*. Paris: Phébus, 1991.

Lamartine, Alphonse de. *Oeuvres de A. de Lamartine: Méditations poétiques*. Paris: Charles Gosselin, 1838.

Lane, Edward. *An Arabic-English Lexicon*. 8 vols. London: Williams and Norgate, 1863 (offset edition Beirut: Librairie du Liban, 1968).

———. *Manners and Customs of the Modern Egyptians*. 5th edition. Cairo: American University in Cairo Press, 2003.

Levey, Martin. "Medieval Arabic Toxicology: The Book on Poisons of ibn Wahshīya and its relation to early Indian and Greek texts." Transactions of the *American Philosophical Society*, New Series, 56, no. 7 (1966): 1–130.

Lisān see Ibn Manẓūr.

Makdisi, Ussama. *The Artillery of Heaven: American missionaries and the failed conversion of the Middle East*. Ithaca, NY/London: Cornell University Press, 2008.

Maṭwī, Muḥammad al-Hādi al-. *Aḥmad Fāris al-Shidyāq 1801–1887: ḥayātuhu wa-āthāruhu wa-ārā'uhu fī l-nahḍah al-'arabiyyah al-ḥadīthah.* 2 vols. Beirut: Dār al-Gharb al-Islāmī, 1989.

Maydānī, Aḥmad ibn Muḥammad al-. *Majma' al-amthāl.* 2 vols. Cairo: al-Maṭba'ah al-Khayriyyah, 1310 H .

Meisami, Julie Scott & Paul Starkey (eds.). *Encyclopedia of Arabic Literature*, 2 vols. London and New York: Routledge, 1998.

Mercieca, Simon. "An Italian Connection? Malta, the Italian Risorgimento and Al-Shidyaq's Political Thought." Unpublished paper.

Mutanabbī, Abū l-Ṭayyib al-. *Dīwān Abī l-Ṭayyib al-Mutanabbī*, edited by 'Abd al-Wahhāb 'Azzām. *Al-Dhakhā'ir* 1. Cairo: al-Hay'ah al-'Āmmah li-Quṣūr al-Thaqāfah, n.d.

Mu'āmilī, Shawqī Muḥammad al-. *Al-ittijāh al-sākhir fī adab al-Shidyāq.* Cairo: Maktabat al-Nahḍah al-Miṣriyyah, n.d. [1988].

Nelson, Kristina. *The Art of Reciting the Qur'an.* Cairo/New York: American University in Cairo Press, 2001.

Nīsābūrī, al-Ḥasan ibn Muḥammad ibn Ḥabīb al-. *'Uqalā' al-majānīn*, edited by Fāris al-Kīlānī. Cairo: al-Maṭba'ah al-'Arabiyyah, 1924.

Patel, Abdulrazzak. *The Arab Nahdah: The Making of the Intellectual and Humanist Movement.* Edinburgh: Edinburgh University Press, 2013.

Peled, Mattityahu. "The Enumerative Style in 'Al-Sāq 'alā al-sāq'." *Journal of Arabic Literature*, 22, no. 2 (Sep. 1991): 127–45.

Qāmūs see Fīrūzābādhī al-.

Rastegar, Kamran. *Literary Modernity between the Middle East and Europe: Textual transactions in nineteenth-century Arabic, English, and Persian literatures.* London and New York: Routledge, 2007.

Roget, Peter Mark. *Roget's International Thesaurus*, 4th edition, revised by Robert L. Chapman. New York: Thomas Y. Crowell, 1977.

Roper, Geoffrey. "Aḥmad Fāris al-Shidyāq and the libraries of Europe and the Ottoman Empire." In *Libraries and Culture*, 33, no. 3 (1998): 233–48.

———. "Faris al-Shidyaq (d. 1887) and the transition from scribal to print culture." In *The Book in the Islamic World*, edited by G.N. Atiyeh, 209–32. Albany, NY: SUNY Press, 1995.

———. "Fāris al-Shidyāq as translator and editor." In *A Life in Praise of Words: Aḥmad Fāris al-Shidyāq and the nineteenth century*, edited by Nadia al-Baghdadi, Fawwaz Traboulsi, and Barbara Winkler. Wiesbaden: Reichert (Litkon 37) (forthcoming).

Rosenthal, Franz. *Humor in Early Islam*. Leiden/Boston: Brill, 2011.

Rowson, Everett. "The Effeminates of Early Medina." *Journal of the American Oriental Society* 111 (1991): 671–93.

Sale, George. *The Koran: Commonly called the Alcoran of Mohammed*. London: William Tegg, 1850.

Sayyid (al-) al-Raḍī. *Dīwān*. Baghdad (?): *Maṭbaʿat Nukhbat al-Akhyār*, 1306/1888–89.

Sharīf (al-) al-Raḍī, Muḥammad ibn Abū Ṭāhir al-Ḥusayn ibn Mūsā *see* al-Sayyid al-Raḍī .

Shidyāq (al-), Aḥmad Fāris al-. *Kitāb al-jāsūs ʿalā l-qāmūs*. 2nd edition. Constantinople: Maṭbaʿat al-Jawāʾib, 1299 [1860-61]; reprinted, Beirut: al-Muʾassasah al-ʿArabiyyah li-l-Dirāsāt wa-l-Nashr, 2004.

———. *Kitāb sirr al-layāl fī l-qalb wa-l-ibdāl*. Al-Āsitānah [Istanbul]: al-Maṭbaʿah al-ʿĀmirah al-Sulṭāniyyah, 1284 [1867].

[Shidyāq (al-)], Aḥmad Fāris Afandī. *Al-Wāsiṭah fī maʿrifat aḥwāl Māliṭah*. 2nd revised edition (in the same volume: *Kashf al-mukhabbā ʿan funūn Urubbā*). Constantinople: Maṭbaʿat al-Jawāʾib, 1299/1881.

Spiro, Socrates. *An Arabic-English Vocabulary of the Colloquial Arabic of Egypt*. Cairo: al-Mokattam Printing Office, 1895. [Offset with title changed to *An Arabic-English Dictionary* etc., Beirut: Librairie du Liban, 1973.]

Starkey, Paul. "Fact and Fiction in al-Sāq ʿalā l-Sāq." In *Writing the Self: Autobiographical Writing in Modern Arabic Literature*, edited by Robin Ostle, Ed de Moor and Stephan Wild, 30–38. London: Saqi Books, 1998.

Sterne, Laurence. *The Life and Opinions of Tristram Shandy, Gentleman*. Mineola: Dover Publications, 2007 .

Stewart, Devin. "The Maqāma." In *Arabic Literature in the Post-Classical Period* (The Cambridge History of Arabic Literature, Vol. 6.), edited by Roger Allen and D. S. Richards, 145–58. Cambridge, New York: Cambridge University Press, 2008.

Ṣulḥ (al-), ʿImād. *Iʿtirāfāt al-Shidyāq fī kitāb al-Sāq ʿalā l-sāq*. Dār al-Rāʾid al-ʿArabī: Beirut, 1982.

Täckholm, Vivi. *A Students' Flora of Egypt*. Beirut: Cooperative Printing Co., 1974.

Tāj see Zabīdī (al-).

Tūnusī, Muhammad ibn ʿUmar al-. *Tashḥīdh al-adhhān bi-sīrat bilād al-ʿArab wa-l-Sūdān*, edited by Khalīl Maḥmūd ʿAsākir and Muṣṭafā Muḥammad Musʿad. Cairo: al-Muʾassasah al-Miṣriyyah al-ʿĀmmah li-l-Taʾlīf wa-l-Anbāʾ wa-l-Nashr, 1965.

Van Gelder, Geert Jan. *Classical Arabic Literature: A Library of Arabic Literature Anthology*. New York: New York University Press, 2013.

Watt, W. M. Bell's *Introduction to the Qurʾān*. Edinburgh: Edinburgh University Press, 1970.

Woodruff, Samuel. *Journal of a Tour to Malta . . . in 1828*. Hartford: Cooke & Co., 1831.

Wright, W. A. *Grammar of the Arabic Language*. 3rd edition, revised by W. Robertson Smith and M. J. de Goeje. 2 vols. Cambridge: Cambridge University Press, 1951.

Zabīdī (al-), al-Sayyid Abū l-Fayḍ Muḥammad ibn Muḥammad ibn ʿAbd al-Razzāq al-Murtaḍā. *Tāj al-ʿarūs min jawāhir al-qāmūs*. Accessed at http://www.shamela.ws.

Zakharia, Katia. "Aḥmad Fāris al-Šidyāq, auteur de 'Maqāmāt'." *Arabica*, T. 52, Fasc. 4 (Oct. 2005): 496–521.

Further Reading

'Abbūd, Mārūn. "'Ālim an-nahḍah al-ḥadīth: Aḥmad Fāris al-Shidyāq 1804–1887." *Al-kitab* 2 (1946): 587–606.

———. *Ṣaqr Lubnān, baḥth fī l-nahḍah al-'arabiyyah al-ḥadīthah wa-rajuliha al-*
awwal Aḥmad Fāris al-Shidyāq. Beirut: Dar al-Makshūf, 1950.

Agius, Dionysius. "Arabic under Shidyaq in Malta 1833–1848." *Journal of Maltese Studies* 19–20 (1989–90): 52–57.

'Akkāwī, Riḥāb. *Al-Fāryāq, Aḥmad Fāris al-Shidyāq*. Beirut: Dār al-Fikr al-'Arabī, 2003.

Alwan, Mohammed. "The History and Publications of Al-Jawa'ib Press." *MELA Notes* 11 (1977), pp. 4–7.

Āṣāf, Yūsuf. *Huwa l-bāqī*. Cairo: Maṭba'at al-Qāhirah al-Ḥurrah, 1305/1885.

'Āshūr, Raḍwā. *Al-ḥadāthah al-mumkinah, al-Shidyāq wa-l-sāq 'alā l-sāq, al-riwāyah al-ūlā fī-l-adab al-'arabī al-ḥadīth*. Cairo, Dār al-Shurūq, 2009.

Abu-Lughod, Ibrahim. *The Arab Rediscovery of Europe: A Study in Cultural Encounters*. Princeton, NJ: Princeton University Press, 1963.

Al-Bagdadi, Nadia. "The Cultural Function of Fiction: From the Bible to Libertine Literature: Historical Criticism and Social Critique in Aḥmad Fāris al-Šidyāq." *Arabica*, T. 46, Fasc. 3 (1999): 375–401.

Arberry, A. J. "Fresh Light on Ahmad Faris al-Shidyaq." *Islamic Culture* 26 (1952): 155–68.

Bayham, Muḥammad Jamāl. "A'lām al-lughah: Aḥmad Fāris al-Shidyāq." *Al-lisān al-'arabī* (Rabāṭ), 8/1, January 1975.

Bustānī, Fu'ad Ifrām al-. "Fī l-Nahḍah al-adabiyyah: Nāṣif al-Yāzijī wa-Fāris al-Shidyāq." *Al-mashriq* 34, 1936: 443–47.

Cachia, Pierre. "An Arab's View of XIXth Century Malta: Shidyaq's '*Al-Wasitah fi ma`rifat ahwal Malitah*.'" *Maltese Folklore Review* 1 (1962–66), pp. 62–69, 110–16, and 232–43.

———. "The Development of a Modern Prose Style in Arabic Literature." *Bulletin of the School of Oriental and African Studies, University of London*, Vol. 52, No. 1 (1989): 65–76.

Cassar, Francis Xavier, trans. *Al-Wāsiṭah fī ma'rifat aḥwāl Mālitā. El-Wasita. Tagħrif dwar Malta tas-Seklu 19*. Paola: Centru Kulturali Islamiku F'Malta, 1988.

Ḍāwī, Aḥmad 'Arafāt. *Dirāsah fī adab: Aḥmad Fāris al-Shidyāq wa-ṣūrat al-gharb fīh*. Amman: Wizārat al-Thaqāfah, 1994.

Dāyah, Jān. "Aḥmad Fāris al-Shidyāq fī l-qiṣṣah al-qaṣīrah." *Fikr* (Beirut), Issues 27–28, December 1978–January 1979.

El-Ariss, Tarek. *Trials of Arab modernity: literary affects and the new political*. New York: Fordham University Press, 2013.

Hajrasī, Maḥmūd. "Al-Sāq 'alā l-Sāq." *Majmū'at turāth al-insāniyyah* (Egypt), 5, n.d.

Hārūn, Jiyurj. "Al-Shidyāq rā'id al-ḥurriyyāt fī fikrina al-ḥadīth." *Ḥiwār* (Beirut), 1 September–October 1963, 79–87.

Ḥasan, Muḥammad 'Abd al-Ghanī. *Aḥmad Fāris al-Shidyāq*. Cairo: al-Dār al-Miṣriyyah li-l-Ta'līf wa-l-Tarjamah, n.d.

Ibn 'Āshūr, Muḥammad al-Fāḍil. "Athar Tūnus fī ḥayāt Fāris al-Shidyāq." *Al-Zamān* (Tunis), Year 10, Issue 462, 12 January 1979.

Ibn Maḥmūd, Nūr al-Dīn. "Fāris al-Shidyāq fī Tūnus." *Al-nahḍah* (Tunis), 2, May 1937.

Jabrī, Shafīq. "Sukhriyyat al-Shidyāq." *Majallat al-majma' al-'ilmī al-'arabī bi-Dimashq*, 2/34, April 1959.

———. "Lughat al-Shidyāq." *Al-mawrid*, 4/3, 1974.

Jubran, Sulaiman. "The Function of Rhyming Prose in 'Al-Sāq 'alā al-Sāq'." *Journal of Arabic Literature*, Vol. 20, No. 2, September 1989: 148–58.

Jubrān, Sulaymān. *Al-mabnā wa-l-uslūb wa-l-sukhriyyah fī kitāb al-sāq 'alā l-sāq fī-mā huwa l-Fāryāq li-Aḥmad Fāris al-Shidyāq*. Cairo: Qaḍāyā Fikriyyah li-l-Nashr wa-l-Tawzī', 1993.

Karam, A. G. "Faris al-Shidyak," in *The Encyclopaedia of Islam*, vol. II: 800–2. 2nd edition. Edited by B. Lewis, C. Pellat, and J. Schacht. Leiden: Brill, 1965.

Khalaf Allāh, Muḥammad Aḥmad. *Aḥmad Fāris al-Shidyāq wa-ārā'uh al-lughawiyyah wa-l-adabiyyah*. Cairo: Maṭba'at al-Risālah, 1955.

Khayr al-Dīn, Tāhir. "Ḥawla Fāris al-Shidyāq fī Tūnis" *Al-nahḍah* (Tunis), 16 May 1937.

Khūrshīd, Fārūq. "Miṣr fī adab al-Shidyāq." *Al-hilāl*, February 1979.

Ma'lūf, Amīn al-. "Khamsūna sanah 'alā wafāt al-Shidyāq." *Majallat al-muqtaṭaf*, 3/91, October 1937.

Maṭwī, Muḥammad al-Hādi al-. *Aḥmad Fāris al-Shidyāq 1801–1887: ḥayātuhu wa-āthāruhu wa-ārā'uhu fī l-nahḍah al-'arabiyyah al-ḥadīthah*. 2 vols. Beirut: Dār al-Gharb al-Islāmī, 1989.

Mu'āmilī, Shawqī Muḥammad al-. *Al-ittijāh al-sākhir fī adab al-Shidyāq*. Cairo: Maktabat al-Nahḍah al-Miṣriyyah, 1988.

Mus'ad, Būlus. *Fāris al-Shidyāq*. Cairo: Maṭba'at al-Ikhā', 1934.

Najārī, 'Alī Ḥaydar al-. "Aḥmad Fāris al-Shidyāq wa-qaṣīdatān makhṭūtatān la-hu." *Al-adīb* (Beirut), Year 27, February 1978.

Naṣṣār, 'Iṣmat. *Aḥmad Fāris al-Shidyāq: qirā'ah fī ṣafā'iḥ al-muqāwamah*. [Cairo]: Dar al-Hidāyah, [2005].

Paniconi, Maria Elena. "La Thématisation de depart et la (trans) formation du personage fictionnel dans Al-sāq 'alā l-sāq d'Aḥmad Fāris al-Šidyāq." *Annali di Ca' Foscari: Rivisti della Facoltà di Lingue e Letterature Straniere dell'Università Ca' Foscari di Venezia*, 48 iii (Serie 40), 2009 (2010): 241–59.

Peled, Mattityahu. "al-Sāq 'Alā al-Sāq: A Generic Definition." *Arabica*, T. 32, Fasc. 1 (Mar., 1985): 31–46.

———. "The Enumerative Style in 'Al-Sāq 'alā al-sāq'." *Journal of Arabic Literature*, Vol. 22, No. 2 (Sep., 1991): 127–45.

Pérès, Henri. "Les Premières manifestations de la renaissance littéraire arabe en Orient au XIXe siècle. Nasif al-Yazigi et Faris ash-Shidyak." *Annales de l'Institut d'Études Orientales* 1 (1934–35): 232–56.

———. "Voyageurs musulmans en Europe aux XIXe et XXe siècles," in *Melanges Maspero*, Vol. III: 185–95. Cairo: Imprimérie de l'Institut Français d'Archéologie Orientale, 1940.

Qāsimī, Ẓāfir al-. "Musṭalaḥāt Shidyāqiyyah." *Majallat al-majmaʿ al-ʿilmī al-ʿarabī bi-Dimashq*, 2/40, April 1965: 431–51.

Rastegar, Kamran. *Literary Modernity between the Middle East and Europe: Textual transactions in nineteenth-century Arabic, English, and Persian literatures*. London and New York: Routledge, 2007.

Roper, Geoffrey. "Aḥmad Fāris al-Shidyāq and the Libraries of Europe and the Ottoman Empire." *Libraries & Culture* 33/3 (Summer 1998): 233–48.

———. "Arabic printing in Malta 1825–1845: Its history and its place in the development of print culture in the Arab Middle East. " Doctoral thesis, Durham University, 1988.

———. "Faris al-Shidyaq and the Transition from Scribal to Print Culture in the Middle East." In *The Book in the Islamic World: the written word and communication in the Middle East*. Edited by George N. Atiyeh. Albany, State University of New York Press, 1995.

———. "Fāris al-Shidyāq as Translator and Editor." In *A Life in Praise of Words: Aḥmad Fāris al-Shidyāq and the nineteenth century*. Edited by Nadia al-Baghdadi, Fawwaz Traboulsi, and Barbara Winkler. Wiesbaden: Reichert (Litkon 37) (forthcoming).

———. "National Awareness, Civic Rights and the Role of the Printing Press in the 19th Century: The Careers and Opinions of Faris al-Shidyaq, His Colleagues and Patrons." In *Democracy in the Middle East. Proceedings of the Annual Conference of the British Society for Middle Eastern Studies*. St. Andrews: University of St. Andrews [for the British Society for Middle Eastern Studies], 1992.

Ṣawāyā, Mīkhā'īl. *Aḥmad Fāris al-Shidyāq, ḥayātuhu, āthāruhu*. Beirut: Dar al-Sharq al-Jadīd, 1962.

Starkey, Paul. "Fact and Fiction in al-Sāq ʿalā l-Sāq." In *Writing the Self: Autobiographical Writing in Modern Arabic Literature*, 30–38. Edited by Robin Ostle, Ed de Moor and Stephan Wild. London: Saqi Books, 1998.

———. "Voyages of Self-definition: The Case of [Ahmad] Faris al-Shidyaq." In *Sensibilities of the Islamic Mediterranean: Self-Expression in a Muslim Culture from Post-Classical Times to the Present Day*, 118–32. Edited by Robin Ostle. London, I.B. Tauris, 2008.

Ṣulḥ, ʿImād al-. *Aḥmad Fāris al-Shidyāq: āthāruhu wa-ʿaṣruhu*. Beirut: Dār al-Nahār li-l-Nashr, 1980.

———. "Shakhṣiyyāt Tūnusiyyah fī-ḥayāt al-Shidyāq." *Majallat al-Fayṣal*, 31, December 1979.

Traboulsi, Fawwaz. "Ahmad Fâris al-Chidyâq (1804-1887)". In *Liban: figures comtemporaines. Essais rassemblées et présentées par Farouk Mardam-Bey*, 11–24. Paris: Institut du Monde Arabe/Circé, 1999.

Yāghī, Hāshim. "Jawānib min Aḥmad Fāris al-Shidyāq al-nāqid." *Majallat al-afkār* (Jordan), 1/1. June 1966.

Zakharia, Katia. "Aḥmad Fāris al-Šidyāq, auteur de 'Maqāmāt'." *Arabica*, T. 52, Fasc. 4 (Oct. 2005): 496–521.

Zaydān, Jurjī. "Aḥmad Fāris." *Al-hilāl*, 14 (15 March 1894) and 15 (1 April 1894).

Index

witness, 220; the Bible, 236, 237, 317, 531n348, 548n507; burning, 24; in Cairo, 79; of the Fāriyāq, 31, 103, 187–88, 202–3, 512n198, 523n291; the Fāriyāq as translator, 174–76, 201–2, 512n198; by Franks, 166; on Franks, 67–72; God's Book, 376; 231, 332, 350, 369, 371–73, 427–30, 445, 468, 475, 537n410; of Jews, 73; of judges, 23; lending, 209; metropolitan as translator, 179; mirrors of the mind, 196; owning, 210, 215, 237, 252, 276, 278, 410, 442; on Persian grammar, 439–42; printing, 208, 372–73, 430, 442; reading, 81, 100, 137, 143, 228, 235, 252, 255, 260, 304, 356, 444, 445; translating, 209, 215, 236, 281, 283, 287, 368, 442, 574n765; used for evidence, 168; writing, 24, 77, 100, 133, 181, 187–88, 197, 208, 211–12, 215, 220, 234, 245, 290, 315, 371, 390, 429–30, 441, 443–44, 563n656, 568n692
Book of Psalms, 29
Boulogne, 366
Brahmans, 439, 565n671
Branch, the (the Bag-man's wife's lover), 161, 162, 163, 169, 508–9n166, 509n167, 510n177, 511n185, 512n193
breasts, augmentation, 33, 189; curative qualities, 164; descriptions, 98–99, 181, 182, 190, 192–93; display, 136; retention of milk, 154; size, 33, 47, 91–92
British, 166, 509n174
al-Buḥturī, 444
Būlāq, 79, 82, 580
bustle, bustles, 33, 33, 83, 108, 109, 257, 435, 497n70, alluring, 240–41, 256; and Englishwomen 239–40, 332, 338; and Frankish women, 275, 342; praising, 292–93. See also backside, backsides; buttock, buttocks; posterior; rump
buttock, buttocks, Arabic eloquence concerning, 87–92, 197, 517n246; defects and diseases, 11, 20, 21, 22, 182, 189; manner of sitting, 332; in men, display of, 96; size, 50, 86, 138, 189, 190, 197, 509n169; in women, attractiveness of, 84–87, 164. See also backside, backsides; bustle, bustles; posterior; rump
Byron, 135, 267
Cairo, 78–79, 80, 199, 201; travel to 306, 366, 524n298; scholars of, 330, 444, 478, 568n692; people of 443; A Description of, 477
Calais, 366
Cambridge; city, 236, 242–43, 246, 324, 330, 539n434; University and colleges, 236, 243, 246, 531n347
Caussin de Perceval, 550n522, 569n683, correcting pronunciation, 447, 570n727, 570n722; introduced to, 359; and Qiṣṣat ʿAntar, 466, 573n763; words of 467
child, children, 217, 233, 267, 315, 322, 354, 368, 436, 542n466; affection, 39; appearance of, 226, 251, 260, 316, 529n331, 529n332, 529n333; bearing of, 302–4; and books, 208, 211; brains of, 66; defects and diseases, 17, 154; dying 317–18, 322–23, 399; and education, 215, 443; English, 95; and exploitation of, 301;

child, children, (cont.)
and the Fāriyāq, 369, 535n387, 362n645; the Fāriyāq's plea to the emirs of the Mountain concerning, 138–44; Frankish, 67, 138; illegitimate, 302; love for, 9, 38; natural disposition towards red, 254; pregnancy and childbirth, 78, 121, 154, 170, 180, 185, 187; protection, 23; raising, 215–16, 232, 260, 263, 300, 303, 316, 322, 346; singing, 207–8; speaking French, 360; violence toward, 28; words related to, 140–42, 152–53, yearning for, 244
Chodźko, Alexandre, 439, 448, 365n671
Christian, Christians, 273, 564n59; of Aleppo; 367, 551n535; of Aleppo and Damascus, comparison between, 163–66; beliefs concerning Jews, 177; "bloody proof," adoption from Jews, 73–74; conversion from Islam, 168–69; divorce, 177–76; in Egypt, treatment of wives, 119–23; of Malta, 202; omens and portents, 69; oriental and occidental, 73–74, 78; style of discourse, 174, 175, 512n200, 512n202, of Syria, 221
city, cities; costs for cleaning, paid for by a rich merchant in a hypothetical, 215; of England, 212, 231, 235–36, 244, 247, 248–49, 283, 287, 299–300, 330–32, 350, 354–55, 539n434; of France, 235, 279, 339, 344–46, 349–52, 355–58, 363–64; great, 209, 236, 390; of Jordan (al-Zarqā'), 570n723; of a king, 232; leaving one's own, 208; one's own, 394, 414; in the Papal states, 234; port, 366; of Syria, 550n522, 551n532, 551n535; of Tunis, 269; of Turkey, 552n540, 554n565; visiting others, 213, 322, 325, 384–86; words for, 433, 564n661
civilization, 302–3, 338
Cleland, John, 290
clergy, clergyman, 236, 301, 330–31, 564n659
committee, 281, 368, 578n794
Committee, the, 174, 175, 180, 202, 512n199
conceptualization, 225, 528n329. See also visualize
Constantinople, 369, 372, 380
consul, 231, 234, 282
countryside, countrywomen, 438; difficulty of life, 287, 299, 366; and good air, 346; mansions in, 209, 364–65; and parks, 354–55; and well-endowed men, 344
Cremorne Gardens, 356, 549n517
customs; customs authority, 282, 373; customs charges, 373, customs office, officers, 235, 282; customs (traditions) 208, 221, 232, 245, 284, 292, 327, 338
al-Daḥdāḥ, Mar'ī, 362
Daḥmān al-Ashqar, 139, 505n137
al-Dalāl ibn ʿAbd al-Naʿīm, 139, 505n137
D'Alex, 362
Damascus, 551n532; compared with Aleppo, 165–66; the Fāriyāq's travel to, 160, 162–65, 306, 577n790; girls, 80, 163–65; people of, 443; scholars of 444; wedding in, 67–72

dance, 308, 349; dance floors and dance halls, 257, 340, 345, 357, 363; horizontal dance, 286; in place of entertainment, 231
David, 244, 533n365, 533n367
Dayr al-Qamar, 73, 581
the Days of Barbarism, 267
de Beaufort, 359–60
De Sacy, 445, 452, 550n521, 550n523, 568n691, 570n730, 571n739, 571n740, 572n751, 573n758
Derenbourg, 570n729
Desgranges, 370, 467, 573n764
Dieppe, 366
Dhāt al-Niḥyayn, 169, 510n178
dialect, 135, 166
disease, diseases, in Cairo, 79; hardship, 9; list of, 10–23, 489n2; love as, 25, 61; suffered by the Fāriyāq, 31, 172, 512n195
doctor, doctors, 25, 53, 78, 125, 164, 315, 317, 330, 362–63
dogs, 243, 294, 402, 530n339, 558n603
doorkeeper, 354, 355
dream, dreams, the Fāriyāq as dream interpreter, 77, 102, 103–6, 107–9, 110–15, 116, 118, 124, 134, 150, 160–61, 168, 169, 174, 495n53, 504n131; love, 63, 147; of women, 178
dress, 275, 278, 299, 340, 360, 431, 547n505; dressing up, 309; exposing calves, 257; the Fāriyāq's, 242; of the Franks, 275, 327, 343, 364; mourning dress, 326–27, 329; red dresses, 254, 257; silk brocade 265; trying on, 264; of Tunisians 273; undoing, 248, 270, 534n376
Drummond, 210, 524n293
Dubays, 139, 505n137
Egypt, Egyptian, Egyptians, 539n428, 563n658, 569n698, 577n789; Christians, treatment of wives, 119–23; dress, 33, 93, 164; *khawals* (dancing men), 97; King of, 244, 533n364; language of, 442, 473, 558n603, 563n657, 566n682; marriage, 47–48; *mawāliyā* (verse form), 42; rebellion of the people of the Mountain against, 135, 157, 504n132, return from, 249; shaykhs of, 441; travel to, 244; women of, 275;
emir, emirs, appearance, 44; backsides, attraction to, 85; compared with poor men, 143; definition, 398; English reverence for, 176; the Fāriyāq and, 188, 199; Fāriyāq's opinion of, 358, 395, 398, 556n581, 556n587 Frankish, 138; friendship with, credibility gained by, 70; high rank of, 180, 191, 516n240; honorifics, 92; monitoring by, 251; of the Mountain, avoidance of women, 137–38; poem in praise of, 234, 392, 395, 398, 556n581; rule of, 23, 33–34; of Tunis, 270, 537n410; in service of, 280;
wife of, 160–61
Emir of al-Quffah, 73, 494n47
England, 524n296, 539n433; conquered by William the Conqueror, 302; correspondence with prime minister of, 362; Fāriyāq's travels to, 212, 327, 359–60; female porters in, 366; Atanāsiyūs al-Tutūnjī in, 367–68; prose writers in, 267, 537n406; railway tracks in, 287; villages of, 236, 317

English, Englishman, commoners' attitudes toward, 69; customs regarding children, 95; *faqīhs*, 72; and the Fāriyāq, 174, 179; kissing among, 93–95; language, 68; reverence for titles, 176; trust in books, 69, 72. See also Franks, Frankish
English (language); books written in 245; capacity for rhymes, 470, 478; learning, 269, 355; Milton, greatest poet of, 397; of Shakespeare, Milton, and Myron, 267; translation into, 468, 471, 473–78, 532n360, 536n403, 541n447, 546n497, 575n775; writers, 304
English (people); avoiding hotels for, in France, 283; clergymen 236; decency of young men, 357; eating four times a day, 364; expenses of husband on clothes, 348; fires of, 363; impressions of, 298; king of the, 231; poor behavior of, 331; prostitute, 349; setting the pay of workers, 363; women 237–40, 246, 252, 343, 347,
the Fāriyāq (protagonist of *Leg over Leg*), in Across the Sea, 93–96; in Alexandria, 80; Arabic language, 220, 242, 271–72, 358, 538n424; arguing, 51; author's commentary upon, intrusiveness of, 102; Bag-man/Bag-men, 31, 46, 77–79, 80, 82, 92, 169; Bag-man's wife, 135; at banquets, 230 ; on beauty, 239–41, 247, 252; on colors, 254–55; courtship, 31, 36, 46, 48; at a dance, 118; dream interpretation, 102, 103–5, 109, 112–15, 116, 117, 124, 134, 168, 174; on dress, 273–77, 327–29, 543n476; on English, 288–90, 296–97, 337–38, 539n437, 541n447; on the English, 290–94; 295–300, 304–7; in English villages, 210, 236–37, 288, 324, 524n293, 543n469; the foul of breath, physicking, 118–17, 168, 265; identity, 581; illness, 163–64; on infidelity, 181, 221–29, 237, 249–53, 270–71, 273, 529n335, 530n339;; jealousy, 158; kissing in public, attitude toward, 94–95; on London, 247, 252–53, 283–85, 300–2, 337, 350, 353–57, 360–61, 363, 365; in Malta, 93; Malta's inhabitants, book on the customs of, 202–3; marriage, advice concerning, 154–56; Master of the Chamber, 168, 171–73; Metropolitan al-Tutūnjī, 179; at the monastery, 157, 159–60; at the Mountain, 136–37; mourning his son, 317–18, 324; Paris, 331, 337, 349–361, 363–66, 368–70, 381–92; poetry of, 240–43, 265, 269, 312–13, 341, 349–50, 381–406, 542n461, 551n534; the Persian, a convert to Christianity, 168–71; return to Beirut, 144; ruler of Tunis, ode in praise of, 120–21; Sāmī Pasha, 180, 188, 199; on sorrow and loneliness, 132–35; translation, 174–76, 179, 202–3; travel to and in England, 212, 217, 235, 282–83, 287, 330–31, 524n298; travel to France, 235, 249; travel to Malta, 77–79, 92, 165–66; travel to the Mountain, 136; travel to Syria, 124, 162–63; travel to Tunis, 176–79, 266, 269, 551n534; wedding, 46; wedding night,

46–48; wife, 80–82, 92, 97, 117, 118, 120–23, 124, 166, 180, 181, 188, 199; on wives and marriage, 244–45, 254–64, 277–81, 301–5, 417–26, 524n300, 524n301, 525n308, 526n310, 530n338, 532n361; on women, 284–87, 311–14, 332–37, 341
the Fāriyāqiyyah (protagonist of *Leg over Leg*), 93, 94, 169, 203; arguing, 230, 270; on colors, 254; discussing Arabic, 220–21, 271–72, 527n317, 527n323, 538n424; on dress, 273–77; on the English, 290–94; 295–300, 304–7; learning English, 288–90, 297, 330, 540n438; on husbands and marriage, 217–18, 255–56, 302–5, 373, 423–24, 524n299, 525n308, 526n310, 526n312; on infidelity, 221–29, 238, 249–52, 269–71, 278–81, 529n335, 530n336, 534n385; invitations, 266; on London, 283–84, 301, 353–57, 363, 365; on men, 284–87, 534n381; Paris, 351–61, 363–66, 549n515; sick, 330–31, 361–63, 368–69, 549n515; vociferate, 265
Farūq, 380, 554n565
father, fathers, fatherhood, 541n450, 548n510, 551n536; becoming, 317; in the Bible, 28, 490n5; children, 28, 38, 152, 183; children, appearance, 170–71; children honoring, 216; effect on the fetus of his visualization, 227, 529n333; daughters, finding husbands for, 76, 95; the Fāriyāq as, 318; of the Fāriyāq, 164; in oaths, 75, 139; strictness, 101; Father Ḥanna, 429; gaining through commendation, 297; giving away for a woman, 327; husband as, to his wife, 277; lamenting death of child, 318; love for children, 315–18, 322; mourning death of, 327; not giving education, 211; of Subḥī Bayk, 369, 557n592; visiting one's, 233, wives, infidelity of, 154; wives, spending on, 117
females, 41, 76, 77, 180. children, 227; hens, 311; keeping men company, 409, 416; in language and grammar, 220–21, 278, 341, 527n318, 538n424, 546n502; oppressors, 540n438; polygamy with, 228; porters, 366; pipers, 405; reprobates, 281; searching for men, 356, 247, 280, 529n333; singers, 231, 435; visitors 407, 561n639. See also girl, girls; woman, women, womenfolk
feminine; charms 527n323; fire being, 409, 561n633; masculine, taking precedence over, 341, 547n503; masculinization of, 221, 527n318, 527n319; plurals, 569n708, 570n732; pronouns, 559n616; pronunciation, 341, 546n502; words, in gender, 271, 527n320, 538n424
fire-ship, 80, 82, 92, 495n58
al-Fīrūzābādī, 90, 581
Flummox son of Lummox, 105, 109, 113, 114
food, foods, cooked by a wife, 263, 532n359; dipped in the curses of the poor, 300; dying from too much, 251; eating slowly, 251; in England, 212, 236, 300, 356, 366; enjoying the tastiness of, 305; "for two will satisfy three," 259,

food, foods (cont.)
535n396; in France, 221, 341, 344, 348–49, 364, 366; hot, heats the blood, 292; liquid 306; lions tasting, 388; offered to guests, 293, 295, 338, 348; of offspring, 315–17; for seafarers, 207; not serving, to the ill, 210; sweet, made by small feet, 342; taking one's, surreptitiously, 237, 243; tastier, of the bachelor, 311, 314; unpalatable, 279; varieties of, 434, 472, 564n663; waistbands preventing the digestion of, 275; from the *zaqqūm* tree, 382
the foul of breath, 265
France; Collège de, 550n522; consuls of, 234; hotels for the English, 283; poets in, 267; travel to, 265, 367
Franks, Frankish, having books for women and children, 211; Christian agents sent to lands of, 367; commoners' attitudes toward, 69; court protocol, 117; dancing, 118; dress, 33, 66, 274–75, 538n417; good qualities, 67; honeymoon, 37; imitation by Arabs, 66–67; kissing among, 94–95; land of, finding loneliness and adversity, 306; language teachers, 203; libraries, 442; love of black, 329; and mourning, 327; notables of, 267, 279; old women, 246; platonic love, 41; and poetry, 267; princes, 369; proof of virginity among, 72–75; style of description, 33; ways of, 221, 295–97, 316, 338, 366, 379; women, 340; women, jealousy concerning, 45, 134, 138; women in public, 118–19, 138. See also English, Englishmen
French, Frenchman, Frenchmen; bad habits of, 364–66; church, 367; colonization of Algeria, 556n587; dictionaries, 566n682; Frenchwomen, 343, 347, 349, 360; harlot, 349; and hygiene, 353; language, 269, 341, 360, 440, 442, 445, 533n374, 558n601, 565n675, 567n687, 568n693, 574n765; poets, 283, 342; proverbs of, 348, 381–82, 548n511; and Rabelais, 290; boasting of Racine and Molière, 267; scholars, 550n524; setting the pay of workers, 363; using servants, 337; slurping feces, 344; sovereign, 558n604; youths, 357
Friend of God, 78, 495n55
funeral lament, 68, 493n40
gambling, 413 432, 474, 559n612; being an old hand, 402; joining the fraternity, 370, 552n543; words related to, 432, 474, 557n599
generosity; of the Arabs, 266–68, 306; 551n534; celebrated for 240; Eastern, 369; of the French, 297, 538–39, 361, 370; of God, 427; of the host, 294, 295
Genoa, 234, 282
girl, girls, attractive with nasality, 360; attractiveness of, 35, 51, 76, 87, 89, 96, 138, 169; giving birth, 303; being counted among the cheap, 291; crowding around casements, 214; of the desert, 88; English, 246, 300–2, 332–33, 357; encouraging infatuation, 342; tempting the Fāriyāq, 236–37; the Fāriyāq's courtship and marriage, 31–32, 46–48; forced into intercourse,

301; French, 246, 344–46, 422; hair of, 403; ignorance, 80–82; jealousy regarding, 213, 303; kissing of, among Franks, 94–95; loving bachelors, 310; in an undesirable marriage, 279; as mistresses, 338; neighbor, 259, 291; seduction of, 92; slave and serving girls, 41, 122–23, 184, 185, 190, 285, 291, 365, 539n429; smart-talking, 252; virginity, 47–48, 74–75; wiles, 81, 187; becomes a woman, 211; words related to, 335–36, 540n438, 547n503; young, marriage to, 120–22. See also females; woman, women, womenfolk

God; belief in, 553n551; calling one to a struggle, 374; choice of, 320; consulting, by divination, 331; creating, 275, 283, 556n583; failing to inspire, 276; giving sons to the Fāriyāq, 317; fearing, 237, 346, 353, 388, 395; grace of, 208; imposing duties, 211; invoking, 211, 216, 224–26, 229, 232, 244, 253–55, 269–70, 281, 283, 285, 288, 309–10, 318, 326, 328, 332, 354, 364, 371–72, 374, 380–81, 394–95, 400, 415–16, 416–18, 421, 423, 427–29, 441–42, 445, 459, 467, 471, 545n491, 561n639, 561n640; law of, 271; Lord of Death and Life, 317; merciful, 429–30, 557n593; as perfect, 297; pleasing, 378; rendering judgments of the king infallible, 232; responsible for evil, 541n452; rewarding, 211, 249, 265, 300, 303, 325, 363, 375–78, 395, 398, 554n481, 554n562, 556n585; temple of, 244; struggle on behalf of, 392; things known only to, 237, 338, 424, 535n389; servants of, creatures of, 274, 298–99

Gospels, 237

Greek, Greeks, 267, 444

Greek Melkite Church, 367

Greek Orthodox, 157, 367

al-Ḥakākah fī l-rakākah (*The Leavings Pile concerning Lame Style*) (Atanāsiyūs al-Tutūnjī), 88, 174, 367, 498n77

Ḥakam al-Wādī, 140, 505n137

Ḥalq al-Wād, 176, 581, 266

al-Ḥarīrī, 444–46, 568n691

harlot, harlots, 290, 349, 365, 532n363, 541n451

Hāshim ibn Sulaymān, 139, 505n137

Ḥassān, 397, 556n590

al-Hāwif ibn Hifām (character in *Leg over Leg*), 145, 154, 156, 308, 312–14, 542n461

He-of-the-Two-Horns (Alexander the Great), 51

Hejaz, 444

Hill, Fanny, 290

Homer, 267

horn, horns, in dreams, 103–6, 119, 120; male genitalia, 26–27, 51, 78, 148, 161; of Satan, 26–27, 161; symbol of submission to wife, 51, 78; symbol of cuckoldry, 103–5, 172, 195

hunger, 9, 25, 74, 155, 158, 159, 169, 173

husband, husbands, anxieties, 25; not arousing the jealousy of, 296; benefits of a stupid, 255; death of, 327; in dreams, 112–15; the Fāriyāq as, 102; the Fāriyāq to the Fāriyāqiyyah, 288–90, 298, 257–59,

Island of the Foul of Breath, 77, 495n52. See also Malta
Italians, 267, 533n374
Jamāl al-Dīn ibn Nubātah, 343
al-Jarādatān, 139, 505n137
jealousy, 213, 218, 397
Jephthah the Gileadite, 302, 541n451
Jerusalem, 244
Jesus, 244. See also ʿĪsā
Jew, Jews, Jewesses, 73, 177–78, 223, 244, 273, 292, 404, 442, 560n621, 566n680
Jirmānūs Farḥāt, 165
Joshua, 244, 532n363
jubbah, 275
Jubārah, Ghubrāʾīl, 399, 401
judge, judges, friendship with, credibility gained by, 70; honorifics, 92; judging, 73; women, attraction to, 23, 85, 191
Kaaba, 165
Kaḥlā, Rāfāʾīl 372
Khalīlān, 139, 505n137
Khān Fāris, 164
Khawājā (term of address), 69, 166, 582
*khawal*s, 97, 499n93
king, kings, 84, 86, 178; ʿAbd al-Majīd as, 378; of beauty, 341; caution of, 358; on coins, 558n604; council of, 212; of creation, 410; customs of, 232; of Egypt, 244, 533n364; of the English 231; eulogy of, 267; heart of, in the hand of God, 232, 530n344; inspiring awe among, 394; obeying, 346; palaces of, 207, 299; sending horses on ships, 305; sending a warship for a poet, 267; subject to God, 379; vizier of, 310
kiss, kissing, among Arabs, 94; the backside, 86; children, 139; among Franks, 67, 94; between lovers/spouses, 41, 59, 76, 86, 191, 195, 199–200; withheld by husband, 120
knowledge; amount of, decreed by fate, 269; and books, 442; buying, 210–11; as the cause of numbness, 304; lack of, 389, 439–42, 444; about one's neighbors, 346; obliterating that of former generations, 387; pursuit of, 216, 304, 404, 406, 440–42, 444–45; raising offspring with, 211; of the ways and languages of others, 221, 295–96
Lamartine, 283, 362
lament, 68–72, 493n40
landlady, landladies, 296, 355
language, languages; Arabic, 238, 269, 290, 327, 330–31, 337, 389, 442–43, 446, 455, 460, 533n369, 543n491, 565n670; of the body, 283; contorted use, 456, 524n297, 572n752; corrupt dialects, 442–43, 565n670, 566n681; created by men to oppress women, 278, 538n425; English, 288–90, 304, 337–38, 355; excessive use of, 226; of the Fāriyāq, 266, 269; as female, 278, 341, 538n424; French, 283, 341, 355, 358–60; ignorance of foreign, 208, 212, 355, 467; knowledge of that of the Franks, 221, 444; lame 466, 573n763, 574n770; learning foreign, 209, 211, 222, 288, 330, 355, 358, 442, 444–45; oddities of, in *Leg over Leg*, 468, 473; oriental, 370; speaking one's own, 304–6
latrine, latrines, 293, 352–53, 364, 383

Le Havre, 366
Ledos, 361
Leghorn, 234, 336
Levant, Levantines, 47, 73, 120, 287, 442, 566n682
London, 197; amazing sights in, 299, 355, 256–57, 549n517; customs of, 301; description of, by the Fāriyāq, 252–53, 533n374; doctors of, 363; the Fāriyāq meeting with the metropolitan in, 368; letters of recommendation from, 362; living in, 281, 332, 362, 371–72; as compared to Paris, 331, 351–57, 360–61, 365; people of, 254, 290, 301, 337, 360, 535n389; prices in, 363; thoughts of, 253; travel to, 235, 246, 282, 318, 330–31, 373; women of, 346–47, 350, 357, 361, 365
Londra, 247, 533n374. See also London
love, 37–46; of a bachelor, 311; of the beloved, 398–401, 412, 417–26, 563n654; among blacks, 99; for children, 263, 315, 348; of cloaks, 340; of color, 254–57, 329; of conversation, 224; desire for, when seeing adornments, 276; of "dotting," 219; becoming ensnared by, 347, 452, 571n740; every good thing should make, 253, 534n385; falling in, 219, 231, 271, 286; the Fāriyāq in, 31–32, 47, 77, 117; among Franks, 73; for one's husband, 224, 346–47; for someone other than one's husband, 222–23, 224, 229, 255, 260, 279–81; infidelity, 181, 186; of intercourse, 254; longer of, women, 286; mechanism of control, 71; nature, 37–46, 81, 95; pain of, 251; physical effects, 195; platonic, 41; poetry, 269, 326, 374, 392–94, 418; 558n607; of praise and flattery, 358; promiscuity, as conducive to, 225, 260, 277; separation, 126–29, 135; regarding imitation in as shameful, 343; sickness, 25; sincere in, 305; songs, 54–65; of strangers, 296; Titter-Making Poems, 48–54; ʿUdhrī, 41; in women, 122, 157, 181, 183, 186; of women, 147, 150, 181, 183, 186; talk of, between women, 224; of talking, 297; for one's wife, 218, 222, 256, 302, 305; for someone other than one's wife, 222, 240, 247, 279, 342, 345, 360, 441; words for, 431, 452, 571n740; words related to, 140–41
lover, lovers, celibacy, 35; degrees of love, 38; the Fāriyāq as, 32, 199; letters, 101; multiple, 122; pleasure, 94; poems and songs, 48–49, 55–56, 58, 62, 63, 87, 192, 193; rejection, 40; requited love, 42; separation, 28, 126–31, 134; tricks to bring together, 163; types, 43–46; women, sexual appetite of, 148, 150–51, 155
Luqmān the Wise, 442, 566n681
Maʿbad, 139, 505n137
Madame Ditzia, 113, 114
Maghreb, 444
maid(s), 213, 236, 261, 267, 274, 337–38, 355, 549n516
Majnūn Laylā, 41, 583
male, males; attendants, 40–41, 76, 180, 309, 338; conformity with

female, 220–21, 527n318; constraints of language, constructed by, 538n425; created, for women, 223; entering into the mind of women, 276; entering into rooms with women, 353; jealous, 308; judge, 285; owl, 432; reprobates, 356; singers, 231, 436; visitors, 407; women talking about, 271; young admirers, 258. See also man, men, menfolk
Malta, 197, 495n52. See also The Island of the Foul of Breath
Mamdūd ibn ʻAbd al-Wāsiṭ al-Rabbānī, 139, 505n137
al-Ma'mūn, 176, 515n225
man, men, menfolk, 23–30; beards, 95–96, 99, 188; Christian, attitude toward wives, 120–21; definition, 186, 200; diseases, 66; disharmony, al-Fāriyāq's warnings against, 25–30; dress, 93; impotence, 186–87, 192; infidelity, 125, 128–31, 134–35, 181, 186; jealousy, 45, 74; Jewish, 178; kissing, 94; love, 37–46, 48–54, 63; marriage, 31, 36, 46, 74–75, 105, 151, 170; marriage, arrangement of, 46–48, 96; marriage to young girls, 121; Muslim and Christian, 163–64; nature, 125; poverty, 73, 143; promises, 78, 495n54; seduction, 127–32; suffering, 9, 23–24, 28; turning into women upon marriage, 77; on the verge of marriage, description of, 33–37; wealth, 73; wives, bad behavior toward, 120–23; wives, spending on, 117; women, dancing with, 118; women, dislike for, 146–49; women, equals of men, 81; women, need for, 49; women, men's position over, 50, 131, 154, 180–83; women, cause of sin, 51; women's attraction to, 45–46, 80–81, 97–100, 137, 155; women's backsides, attraction to, 85–86, 90; women's flirtation with, 76, 190; women's knowledge of, 80–82; women's wiles, victims of, 149–50
maqāmah, *maqāmah*s, 66, 133, 144, 583
Maqāmāt of al-Ḥarīrī, 444–46, 465, 568n691
Market-man, Market-woman, Market-men (Maronite and Roman Catholic clergy), 29, 46, 165, 176, 583
markets, 213–14, 246, 253, 299–300, 340, 350, 365–66
Marrāsh, Fatḥallāh 367–68, 551n536
marriage, married, adversities of, 313; age of, 280; alliance, 30; benefits of, 313; benefits of, to an ugly woman, 251; A Book on the Laws of, 245; couples, 354, 525n306; consummation, 74; description of man on the verge of, 33–37; dissolution, 186–88; among Egyptian Christians, 120; of the Fāriyāq, 31, 46, 77–79, 82; among Franks, 74; of handsome young men to ugly middle-aged women, 302; legitimate, 301, 348; madness, leading to, 229; a man doing a woman a favor by, 278, 373; men, 218, 256, 285, 308, 315, 361, 368, 426; obligations, 169; in Paris, 346, 348; pleasure, 123; to a pretty woman, 325;

marriage, married (cont.)
reasons for, 302, 542n461, 542n465, 562n647; re-consummate, 249; social good, 82, speaking of, 313; by villagers, 288, 542n464; words for, 277
Marseilles, 235, 249, 265, 282, 362, 369, 399, 443
masculine, 271, 341, 470, 527n318, 527n319, 546n503, 547n503
al-Mashdūd, 139, 505n137
Master of the Chamber, dream interpretation, 105; incitement to public nudity, 170–71; letter to the Fāriyāq's wife, 124; travel to Damascus, 161, 162; visit from the Persian, 168
Melkite, 367–68
men; books useful to, 208; chased by women, 219, 237, 262, 280, 283, 329, 344, 356, 526n316, 529n331, 539n433; created to serve the needs of women, 251; desiring women, 219, 225, 259, 290, 301, 341, 343–49, 365, 528n324, 547n506, 551n532; dress of, 274–75, 350, 472; of England, 212; expressing the thoughts of, 208; generality of, 227; great, 302–4, 338, 378, 408; love of "scripting," 219; making excuses, 368; married, 218, 223, 228, 249, 279, 285, 302; morals of, 211, 220, 242, 254–55, 263, 326, 377, 387, 394, 396, 399, 530n336, 534n382; outnumber women, 253, 287, 539n434; outnumbered by women, 252; in poetry, 212; scholarly, 254, 358; strive in pursuit of bliss, 248; ways of, 222, 224, 256, 262–63, 271, 285–86, 293–94, 302–3, 304–5, 377, 354–55, 395, 401–3, 407, 410–11, 416–17, 451, 527n323; words for, 277. See also husband(s)
merchant, 215, 231, 442, 566n680
metropolitan, metropolitans (religious leader), Atanāsiyūs al-Tutūnjī, 88, 174–79, 197, 202–3, 235, 331, 367–69, 429, 444, 544n483, 551n537, 564n659, 568n688; books, banned, 160; celibacy, 143; Jirmānūs Farḥāt, 165–66; occupation, 187; reverence for among the English, 176–77
Midian, children of, 317
Mikhalla', Mīkhā'īl, 372
Milton, 267, 397
ministers, 23, 70
Molière, 267
monastery, monasteries, 133, 157, 159, 160, 287, 507n159
monk, monks, celibacy, 121, 133, 160, 216, 236, 256, 317, 331, 440, 544n483; cells of (term for buttocks), 87; in a dream, 160; false statements concerning, 165; the Fāriyāq at the monastery, 159–60; occupation, 187; scholarship, 133; women's love for, 157
Moses, 244, 317, 542n467
mother, mothers, 211, 227, 233, 297, 315–16, 327–28, 399, 412, 529n333, 542n466, 548n510; in the Bible, 28; children, appearance, 170; children, love for, 38; children, marriage of, 47, 76, 95, 183; children's spouses, spying on, 45; in Damascus and Cairo, 80–81; of the Fāriyāq's wife, 46–48, 77–78,

pleasure, pleasures, of animals, 251; denying, 328, 392, 395; of the Fāriyāqiyyah, 281; in jewelry, 210; in language and grammar, 271; of men, 217, 299, 309–10, 315, 383–4, 423, 542n465; from others, 306, 308; of Paris, 349; physical, 212; places of, 248, 303, 399, 422, 424, 549n517; of the rich, 303; sensual 216, 225, 270–71, 537n412; of women, 225–27, 238–39, 266, 286, 343, 528n326
poetry, poet, poets poems, amatory verses, 99, 135, 193; anxieties, 24; Arab, Arabic, 254, 267–68, 290, 294, 343, 359, 534n383, 535n388, 537n407, 543n468, 547n505, 571n741, 572n742; of asceticism, 269; Austrian, 267; backsides, attraction to, 83, 84; of children, 316; confidant, 25; criticism, 200; in a dream, 111–12; English, 267, 290, 397; meeting of the Fāriyāq with, 149, 156; French, 267, 283, 397; on gambling, 402–5, 552n543, 557–58n599, 558n602, 558n609, 559n612, 559n613, 560n618; Greek, 397; Italian, 397; love, 225, 240, 245–47, 269, 289, 297, 326, 348, 417, 541n448, 542n461, 562n645, 565n650, 562n651; the Persian, 168; poetic formulations, 86, 95; poetic license, 160–61; possession by jinn, 49; praise, 234, 239, 266–67, 326, 358–59, 369–71, 381, 392–93, 397, 551n534, 552n541, 552n547, 556n581, 556n590; quoting, 328, 544n480; Roman, 267; success of, 265, 268, 397, 407; techniques of, 230, 240, 407, 445, 446, 455–56, 458–59, 543n474, 554n567, 555n569, 557n593, 557n594, 557n596, 557n599–600, 559n616, 562n648, 570n724, 571n738, 572n749, 573n763, 574–75n770; translation of, 359, 471, 477–78; truthfulness, 134–35
poor, poverty; and books, 410; compassion towards, 296, 300; disaster of, 267; equal to the rich, 233–34, 303–4, 323; of France, 265, 353, 360; and gambling, 402–3, 559n612; good coming from, 250, 394; indifference towards, 300–3; women, 303, 328–29, 347
Pope, 178
Port of London, 372
posterior, 13, 72, 86, 88, 98. See also backside, backsides; bustle, bustles; buttock, buttocks; rump
preacher, 28, 111, 112, 114, 172, 511n192
priest, priests, anxieties, 24, 290, 299, 309, 329, 371, 399, 431, 440, 477; backsides, attraction to, 84; of Choueir, 175; dress, 97; false statements concerning, 165; al-Fāriyāq as, 116; marriages, assistance in arrangement of, 8147–48 remarriage, views on, 187; women, Jewish, views on, 177
printing presses, 208, 210, 216
prostitute, prostitutes, 288, 345–47, 349, 353, 357, 361
proverb, 74, 78, 201
Proverbs, 33
pulchritude, 276, 332
Qāmūs (al-Firūzābādī), 584; on bodily acts, 360, 525n301, 531n354,

532n355, 532n360, 537n413, 537n414, 540n442, 547n506; deficiencies of, 340, 530n343; disagreements with, 140; al-Fāriyāq, copy owned by, 203; the Fāriyāq packing, 217, 281–82, 538n423; on food, 564n663; on gambling, 552n544, 558n603; on herbs, 565n668; important in *Leg over Leg*, 472–76, 528n325, 544n477; items in, 88, 94, 184, 186; items overlooked in, 87, 90, 99, on math, 339, 545n494; on men, 534n384, 551n530; on the moon, 557n595; on the Prophet Muḥammad, 562n651; organization of, 546n496; on proverbs, 564–65n665; on water, 542n457; on women, 219, 277, 528n326, 533n373, 536n399, 536n400, 536n401, 536n402, 541n456, 546n499, 551n531
Qaṣīr, 155, 507n156
Qiṣṣat ʿAntar, 466, 573n764
quarantine, 92, 166, 168, 180, 188
Quatremère, 359, 550n521
Qur'anic, 145
Qurʾān, 88, 493n34, 512n204
Rabelais, 290, 476
Racine, 267, 397
railway, 211, 243, 287
Raqīq, 139, 505n137
Rashīd Pasha, 235, 372
red, 240, 242, 254–57, 260, 318, 333, 350, 532n362, 535n392
Reinaud, 359, 550n523
religion, religions, 57, 143, 183, 199, 222, 228, 244, 375, 379, 395
rich, 208, 215, 232, 246, 293, 299–303, 337, 344, 350, 378
River Thames, 354, 549n517
Roman church, 369, 536n404
Romans, 267
Rome, 197
Rosherville, 356, 549n517
the Royal Park, 213
rump, 84, 87. See also backside, backsides; bustle, bustles; buttock, buttocks; posterior
Russian Empire, Russians, 371, 374, 553n552
Sabbath, 292
Sallāmah, 139, 505n137
Sāmī Pasha, 180, 584, 235, 249, 369, 398, 557n592
Saul, 244, 533n365
Schiller, 267, 536n404
scholarship, scholar, scholars; Arab, 330, 444–46, 564n659, 566n676, 568n692; Arabic language, views on, 185; backsides, attraction to, 83, 84; books, 196; childbirth, views on, 154; dedicated, 230, 254, 351, 390, 392, 398, 401, 408, 413, 445; depravity, occurring to, 344; English, 202; enumerating the topics of, 404; of Europe, 439–40, 445–46, 564n660; French, 359, 370, 467, 550n524; friendship with, credibility gained by, 70; heavens of, 387; as lovers, 44, 148; married men, views on, 74; monks as, 133; of Oxford, 330; Persian, 168; poverty, 132; pretend, 387, 390, 406, 442, 444–46; public speaking; 208; sorrow, 132, value of, 296
schools, 208, 215–16, 233, 242, 246, 286, 304, 312, 332, 359, 404, 439, 443, 568n693

Fāriyāq, 236–37, 281, 283, 287, 368, 531n347, 541n447; into French, 359, 550n521, 566n679, 568n693, 574n766; of *Leg over Leg*, 468–78, 527n317, 528n329, 529n334, 530n343, 532n359, 538n418, 538n420, 540n439, 540n440, 543n471, 544–45n488, 545n490, 545n493, 545n494, 546n497, 546n498, 547n504, 548–49n513, 550n528, 550–51n529, 555n572, 557–58n599, 558n603, 558n604, 561n636, 563n656, 570n731, 574n766, 575n775, 576n776
travel, ardors, 166; of Atanāsiyūs al-Tutūnjī, 174; in a dream, 103, 105–6, 108–9; of the Fāriyāq, to England, 203; of the Fāriyāq, to Italy, 130; of the Fāriyāq, to Syria, 125, 161; of the Fāriyāq, to Tunis, 176; infidelity, 130; by mule, 162; Orientals, 30; the wife of the Fāriyāq, 77–79, 92, 204; women, 77–79, 92
Tripoli, 197, 521n271
Tunis, Tunisian, 176, 178, 249, 265–66, 269, 273, 306, 366, 383, 444, 537n409, 537n410, 551n534, 555n574
Turk, Turks, Turkish, 73, 165, 211, 566n676
turnips, 212, 299, 524n296, 541n449
turtle dove, 468
al-Tutūnjī, 367–68, 544n483, 551n537. See Atanāsiyūs al-Tutūnjī
Ṭuways, 139, 505n137
'Udhrī, 41, 86, 585
Vauxhall, 356, 549n517
veil, 120, 131
verse, verses, amatory, 37, 41, 99, 119, 135, 503n117; by the Fāriyāq, 132, 137, 159–60, 171, 178; funeral lament, 68; hunger, adverse effects on, 155; on mendacious transmitters, 171–1972 paucity of, by monks, 133; by unhappy husbands, 148
village, villages, 79, 133, 157, 159; life in, 210, 236, 288, 313, 317, 324, 325, 531n347, 542n464, 543n469; people of, 223, 246, 288, 298–99, 366, 524n293; sanctity of, 294; travel to, 235, 287, 528n324, 539n267
Virgil, 267
virginity, 41, 48, 72, 74, 78
visualize, 222, 226–27, 239, 252, 276, 528–29n329, 529n331, 529n333
vizier, 310
voyage, of the Fāriyāq, to the Island of the Foul of Breath, 77, 80, 82; of the Fāriyāq, to Syria, 134, 157; of the Fāriyāq, to Tunis, 176; separation of spouses, 125
wealth, 215, 247, 300, 303–5, 309, 323, 350, 367, 389–90, 398, 527–28n323
wedding, consummation, 74, 131; in Damascus, book describing, 67–70; of the Fāriyāq, 46, 77, honeymoon, 37; jewelry, 35; between an old man and a young girl, 121
white, ashes, 338; dull white, 254; of the face, 541n454; of the eye 270, 318, 333, 342; hair, 403, 545n492, 560n617; not everything, is a truffle, 445, 568n690; semen, 535n390; sepulcher, 290; wash, 403, 559n614; women, 219, 222, 253, 269, 325, 332, 336, 338, 342

whore, 290, 301, 311, 337, 346
wife, wives, 147–49; abandonment, 24; age disparity, 34, 121; being away from, 217–18, 244, 260, 524n298, 562n645, 563n652; childbirth, 67; and children, 226, 281, 303, 315; companionship, 24, 32, 138; conniving, 76, 146–47; desirability, 77, 126; disagreements with, 218, 225, 244, 250, 256, 261–62, 264, 270, 280, 285, 289, 325, 432, 539n431; disliked by husband, 146–49; of the Fāriyāq, 77–78, 80, 82, 93, 94–97, 117–20, 124, 159, 163, 169, 180, 199; fertility, 9; Frankish, 139; as hosts, 226, 295; jealousy, 255, 273–74, 303, 338, 346, 548n509; loved by husband, 207–8, 211, 218, 222, 225, 249, 255, 260–63, 270, 276, 278, 315, 346, 348, 359, 361, 365, 372, 377, 536n398, 542n459, 552n542; loving her husband, 226, 277, 295, 310, 389, 533n364, 523n365, 533n366, 540n445; ill treatment, 119–23, 181; infidelity, 113, 122, 135, 148, 181, 186; jealousy, 35, 45, 148; kissing, 94; marital rights, 36, 113, 181; marital strife, 34; marriage arrangements, 47; money spent on, 117; multiple, 211, 223, 228, 269–70, 309; not having, 309, 415; position, 121–22; regarded as chattel, 34; rejection of husband, 34, 43; relationship with husband, 34, 138–40, 143; reuniting with, 249; rights and obligations of, 215; separation of spouses, 187; sexual appetite, 113–15, teaching, 210; travel, 77–79; travelling with, 281–82, 324, 331; words for, 434, 436. See also Woman, women, womenfolk
William the Conqueror, 302
woman, women, womenfolk; affairs of, 114, 164; anger, 182–83; attacking, 151, 155, 376; attraction to men, 44, 45, 95–100, 125–26; attraction to monks, 157; avoidance of, 137; barrenness, 78–79; beauty, 133; bodies, 33, 35, 45–47, 82–92, 138, 140, 164–65, 177; books for, 208, 211; burdens, 151, 153–54; childbirth, 154; and children, 140, 153, 171, 186–87, 226, 232, 260, 263, 346, 537n407; compassion, 183; complaining of, 291, 297, 308, 325; conceitedness, 196; controlling men, 331, 341, 250–52, 255, 278, 294–95, 535n393; cunningness, 145, 150; of Damascus, 164; dancing, 119; desiring, 207, 219–20, 231–32, 237–41, 244–45, 249, 254–59, 262, 268–73, 280, 283–85, 289–90, 310–11, 327, 341–43, 357–58, 360, 371, 441, 468, 471, 525n308, 525n309, 528n324, 529n333, 533n371, 534n382, 537n407, 537n414, 541n448, 547n506, 574n766; discourse concerning, 197; diseases, 16, 20; dislike of, by husbands, 146–50; in a dream, 105–6; dreams of, 113; and dress, 72, 90, 93, 164, 257–58, 264, 273–77, 325, 327–29, 340, 344, 357, 534n376, 533n371, 555n572; education, 101; effects on men, adverse, 66; of Egypt, 274; Egyptian Christian views on, 120; falling in love with, 42–43;

English, 236–40; 242, 244–46, 249, 327, 343, 347, 349–50, 365; the Fāriyāq's esteem for, 123; flirtation, 35; Frankish, 67, 138; of the Franks, 246, 267, 275, 327, 340; French, 343, 344, 343, 349, 360, 366; funeral lament for, 68–72; at gatherings, 214, 218, 262, 338, 356; generally, 212, 222–25, 237, 244, 245, 268–71, 277–78, 364, 539n430; gladness, 162; hair, 66; honesty, 131; honor, 126; impatience, 125; importance, 143; infidelity, 134, 181–83, 185–86; intelligence, 81; jealousy and treachery, 135, 218–22, 224–27, 260–61, 277–78, 327, 345–47, 357, 525n307, 526n310, 526n315, 226n316, 529n331, 529n332, 534n378, 541n447, 548n507; Jewish, 177; kissing, 94; left behind by husband, 125; of London, 252–54, 283, 337–38, 347, 350, 355, 357, 365; in love with another, 41; marital rights, 186–88; and marriage, 47–48, 135, 228, 251, 278–80, 302–3, 325, 348, 548n510; marriage, turning into men upon, 78; men's desire for, 9–10, 25, 38, 48–51, 54, 126–27, 128, 160, 164, 166, 170; of the Mountain, 136–37; Muslim and Christian, 164–65; mysteries surrounding, 95; nature, 122; need for social interaction, 123, 143; obedience to, 121; old, 76, 89, 164; outnumber men, 252; outnumbered by men, 253, 287; of Paris, 339–41, 344–50, 357, 360, 364–66, 381–82, 547n505, 548n511, 565n669; patience, 180; poetry on, 135; position below men, 181; preferring summer, 227; procuring, 95; provision for, 149; respectability, 40, 101, 125, 131; rights of, 280; running businesses, 339, 344–46; seclusion, 152; secrets, 199; seduction of, 92, 128, 181; selling, 305; sexual appetite, 189, 200; sin, 169; singers, 139; suspicions concerning, 171; temptresses of men, 51, 131; travel, 77–79, 92; as treatment for madmen, 170; of Tunis, 273–74; turning her back on her husband in bed, 83–92; types of, 43–46; virtues of, 230, 254–55, 287, 308, 527–28n323; ways of, 250, 260–64, 284–86, 291–93, 295, 313, 325, 337, 344, 346–47; weeping, 32; wiles, 35; words for, 219, 237, 268, 276–78, 327, 333–37, 357, 364, 433, 435–38, 468, 473–74, 476, 526n313, 527n319, 527n322, 532n362, 533n372, 534n383, 536n399, 536n400, 539n401, 540n442, 540n444, 549n518, 550n526, 555n569, 562n648, 564n661, 543n475, 545n491; wonderful, 213. worries, 119; worthiness, 42. See also females, girl, girls, wife, wives

worker, 299

youth, female, 191; male, corrupted by women, 148; male, educated, 82; male, folly of, 155; male, in love, 39, 54–55

Ya'qūb, 225, 529n330, 537n411

Zalzal, 139, 505n137

al-Zunnām, 139, 505n137

About the NYU Abu Dhabi Institute

The Library of Arabic Literature is supported by a grant from the NYU Abu Dhabi Institute, a major hub of intellectual and creative activity and advanced research. The Institute hosts academic conferences, workshops, lectures, film series, performances, and other public programs directed both to audiences within the UAE and to the worldwide academic and research community. It is a center of the scholarly community for Abu Dhabi, bringing together faculty and researchers from institutions of higher learning throughout the region.

NYU Abu Dhabi, through the NYU Abu Dhabi Institute, is a world-class center of cutting-edge research, scholarship, and cultural activity. The Institute creates singular opportunities for leading researchers from across the arts, humanities, social sciences, sciences, engineering, and the professions to carry out creative scholarship and conduct research on issues of major disciplinary, multidisciplinary, and global significance.

About the Translator

Humphrey Davies is an award-winning translator of some twenty works of modern Arabic literature, among them Alaa Al-Aswany's *The Yacoubian Building* and Elias Khoury's *The Gate of the Sun*. He has also made a critical edition, translation, and lexicon of the Ottoman-period *Hazz al-quḥūf bi-sharḥ qaṣīd Abī Shādūf* (*Brains Confounded by the Ode of Abū Shādūf Expounded*) by Yūsuf al-Shirbīnī and compiled with a colleague an anthology entitled *Al-ʿāmmiyyah al-miṣriyyah al-maktūbah: mukhtārāt min 1400 ilā 2009* (*Egyptian Colloquial Writing: selections from 1400 to 2009*). He read Arabic at the University of Cambridge, received his Ph.D. from the University of California at Berkeley, and, previous to undertaking his first translation in 2003, worked for social development and research organizations in Egypt, Tunisia, Palestine, and Sudan. He is affiliated with the American University in Cairo, where he lives.

The Library of Arabic Literature

Classical Arabic Literature
Selected and translated by Geert Jan Van Gelder

A Treasury of Virtues, by al-Qāḍī al-Quḍāʿī
Edited and translated by Tahera Qutbuddin

The Epistle on Legal Theory, by al-Shāfiʿī
Edited and translated by Joseph E. Lowry

Leg over Leg, by Aḥmad Fāris al-Shidyāq
Edited and translated by Humphrey Davies

Virtues of the Imām Aḥmad ibn Ḥanbal, by Ibn al-Jawzī
Edited and translated by Michael Cooperson

The Epistle of Forgiveness, by Abū l-ʿAlāʾ al-Maʿarrī
Edited and translated by Geert Jan Van Gelder and Gregor Schoeler

The Principles of Sufism, by ʿĀʾishah al-Bāʿūnīyah
Edited and translated by Th. Emil Homerin

The Expeditions, by Maʿmar ibn Rāshid
Edited and translated by Sean W. Anthony

Two Arabic Travel Books
Accounts of China and India, by Abū Zayd al-Sīrāfī
Edited and translated by Tim Mackintosh-Smith
Mission to the Volga, by Ahmad Ibn Faḍlān
Edited and translated by James Montgomery

Disagreements of the Jurists, by al-Qāḍī al-Nuʿmān
Edited and translated by Devin Stewart

Consorts of the Caliphs, by Ibn al-Sāʿī
Edited by Shawkat M. Toorawa and translated by the Editors of the Library of Arabic Literature

What ʿĪsā ibn Hishām Told Us, by Muḥammad al-Muwayliḥī
Edited and translated by Roger Allen

The Life and Times of Abū Tammām, by Abū Bakr al-Ṣūlī
Edited and translated by Beatrice Gruendler